COMPUTER GRAPHICS

Volume 22 • Number 4 • August 1988
A publication of ACM SIGGRAPH
Production Editor Richard J. Beach

SIGGRAPH '88 Conference Proceedings
August 1-5, 1988, Atlanta, Georgia
Program Chair John Dill

Sponsored by the Association for Computing Machinery's
Special Interest Group on Computer Graphics

The Association for Computing Machinery, Inc.
11 West 42nd Street
New York, New York 10036

SIGGRAPH '88 is sponsored by the Association for Computing Machinery's Special Interest Group on Computer Graphics in cooperation with the IEEE Technical Committee on Computer Graphics.

Sample Citation Information:
...Proceedings of SIGGRAPH '88 (Atlanta, Georgia, August 1-5, 1988). In *Computer Graphics 22,* 4 (August 1988), ACM SIGGRAPH, New York, pp. xx-yy.

ORDERS:
Mail non-member orders to:

Addison-Wesley Publishing Company
Route 128
Reading, MA 01867

Other offices: Menlo Park, California; Don Mills, Ontario; Wokingham, England; Amsterdam; Sydney; Singapore, Tokyo; Madrid, Bogota; Santiago; San Juan.

Addison-Wesley ISBN 0-201-09196-8

A limited number of copies are available to ACM members. Copies may be ordered from:

ACM Order Department
P.O. Box 64145
Baltimore, MD 21264

ACM Order Number: 428880
ACM ISBN 0-89791-275-6
ACM ISSN 0097-8930

Credit card payments: (800) 342-6626
All other orders: (301) 528-4261

Manufactured By Promotion Graphics, NY

Printed in the U.S.A.

Contents

Technical Program, Thursday, 4 August 1988

Technical Program, Friday, 5 August 1988

Invited Papers, Wednesday, 3 August 1988

Panel Sessions, Wednesday, 3 August 1988

Panel Sessions, Thursday, 4 August 1988

Panel Sessions, Friday, 5 August 1988

Preface

Welcome to SIGGRAPH '88, the 15th annual ACM Conference on Computer Graphics and Interactive Techniques. The conference is being held August 1-5, 1988 in Atlanta, Georgia. These proceedings contain the papers presented during the three days of the Technical Program and are published as a special issue of *Computer Graphics*. Out of 161 papers submitted for review, 34 were selected to represent the state-of-the-art in computer graphics research. An additional three invited papers representing advanced innovative applications of computer graphics were also presented and are a part of these proceedings.

The paper selection process began with the call for participation, published and distributed at the previous year's SIGGRAPH conference. Paper arrival times were distributed approximately according to a delta function around the submission deadline, this year January 12th.

The papers were then sent to members of the Technical Program Committee, who acted as senior reviewers for the papers. As has been done in previous years, I asked two committee members to assist me with this task to help ensure a good match between papers and reviewers. I thank Hank Christiansen and Turner Whitted for their invaluable assistance in this important step.

Each committee member was responsible for reviewing each paper they received, and for obtaining at least two other reviews from different institutions. Each committee member also received a complete list of all papers submitted. Thus, each member could request a copy of any paper of particular interest and provide additional input on it. Interestingly, several members did so, which proved helpful during subsequent discussions.

After assembling the resulting reviews and ranking the papers, the Technical Program Committee met for two days to discuss, review, sort, argue about and finally select those papers representing a "snapshot" of the best results in this rapidly developing field. The quality of this process is a direct reflection of the quality of the committee and the 1988 committee was excellent. Thank you all very much for your time and energy, without which this whole process would not work. I also thank all those who reviewed papers; their names are listed in the next section.

This year's committee had an advantage over earlier committees which made our job even more arduous: no preset limit on the number of papers we could accept. Previous conference guidelines required a single set of technical sessions, which meant a maximum of 34 or 35 papers. To encourage a more flexible technical program, the SIGGRAPH executive committee recently removed the restriction on parallel sessions. However, at least for SIGGRAPH '88, the restriction appears not to have been a significant one, as the number of accepted papers indicates. Perhaps a larger effect will be noticeable next year when there has been more opportunity for the graphics community to adapt to the change; only time will tell (good luck, Jeff!).

A second significant change for '88 is the special session of invited papers on applications of computer graphics. The three papers chosen for the resulting inaugural session all represent areas where high quality and high performance graphics are critical to the success of their applications. I am very fortunate to have had Hank Christiansen organize this session and I express my appreciation to him for a first class result.

I also express my thanks to Rick Beach, SIGGRAPH Editor-in-Chief, whose efforts in working with the authors and the printer resulted in the superb appearance of these proceedings. Last year's Technical Chair, Maureen Stone, and her assistant, Subhana Menis, provided much good information and advice, and patiently answered many questions--thank you both!

Finally, I want to give special thanks to my secretary, executive assistant and senior management, Ann Merchant, who expertly handled the organizational and administrative tasks associated with the Technical Program.

John Dill
SIGGRAPH '88 Technical Program Chair

Conference Committee

CONFERENCE CO-CHAIRS

Andrew C. Goodrich
(University of Michigan)
Adele Newton
(University of Waterloo)

CONFERENCE COMMITTEE CHAIRS

John C. Dill, *Technical Program*
(Simon Fraser University)
Richard L. Phillips, *Panels*
(Los Alamos National Laboratory)
Michael J. Bailey, *Courses*
(Megatek Corporation)
Carol Byram, *Exhibits*
(Cubicomp Corporation)
Amie Slate, *Film and Video Show*
(Cubicomp Corporation)
Lucy Petrovich, *Art Show*
(University of Wisconsin)
John E. French, Jr., *Special Interest Groups*
(GeoQuest Systems, Inc.)
Michelle Amato, *Audio/Visual*
(Northeastern University)
Maira Palazzi, *Audio/Visual*
(Rutgers State University-Camden)
Steven M. Van Frank, *Treasurer*
(Lynxys, Inc.)
B. J. Anderson, *Public Relations*
(The Anderson Report)
Ines Hardtke, *Registration*
(National Film Board of Canada)
Brian Herzog, *Merchandise*
(AT&T Conversant Systems)
E. Jan Hurst, *Local Arrangements*
(History of Computer Graphics Project)
Eric G. Bosch, *Student Volunteers*
(McMaster University Medical Centre)
James A. Banister, *Speaker Slides*
(TRW)
Bruce Eric Brown, *Slide Sets*
(Wang Laboratories, Inc.)

CONFERENCE PLANNING COMMITTEE

James J. Thomas, *Chair* (Battelle Pacific Northwest Laboratories)
Raymond L. Elliott (Los Alamos National Laboratory)
Branko J. Gerovac (Digital Equipment Corporation)
Andrew C. Goodrich (University of Michigan)
Ellyn Gore (Concept Productions)
Christopher F. Herot (Bitstream, Inc.)
Adele Newton (University of Waterloo)
Robert J. Young (CAD/CAM Management Consultants)

TECHNICAL PROGRAM COMMITTEE

Alan H. Barr (California Institute of Technology)
Richard H. Bartels (University of Waterloo)
Richard J. Beach (Xerox PARC)
Edwin E. Catmull (Pixar)
Bernard Chazelle (Princeton University)
Hank Christiansen (Brigham Young University)
Robert L. Cook (Pixar)
Tony D. DeRose (University of Washington)
John C. Dill (Simon Fraser University)
David P. Dobkin (Princeton University)
Nick England (Sun Microystems, Inc.)
A. Robin Forrest (University of East Anglia)
Alain Fournier (University of Toronto)
Donald P. Greenberg (Cornell University)
Doris Kochanek (National Film Board of Canada)
Jeffrey Lane (Digital Equipment Corporation)
Dan R. Olsen, Jr. (Brigham Young University)
Rob Pike (AT&T Bell Laboratories)
Tom Sederberg (Brigham Young University)
Turner Whitted (Numerical Design, Ltd.)

PANELS COMMITTEE

Christine A. Barton (Morgan Guaranty Trust Company)
Sara Bly (Xerox PARC)
James George (Mesa Graphics)
Robert Judd (Los Alamos National Laboratory)
Micheal Keeler (Ardent Computer)
David D. Loendorf (Los Alamos National Laboratory)
Dick Phillips, *Chair* (Los Alamos National Laboratory)
Theodore Reed (Los Alamos National Laboratory)
Diana Tuggle (Los Alamos National Laboratory)
Manuel Vigil (Los Alamos National Laboratory)

COURSES COMMITTEE

Sheldon Applegate (Interactive Computer Modelling)
Michael J. Bailey, *Chair* (Megatek Corporation)
Frank Bliss (Electronic Data Systems)
Rich Ehlers (Evans and Sutherland)
Dave Nadeau, *Notes Coordinator* (Megatek Corporation)

TECHNICAL PROGRAM REVIEWERS

John Abel	Ricki Blau
Debra Adams	Jim Blinn
George Allen	Jules Bloomenthal
John Amanatides	Ian C. Braid
Tony Apodaca	Rikk Carey
Jim Arvo	Loren Carpenter
Peter Atherton	David Caughey
Norman I. Badler	Indranil Chakravarty
Ron Baecker	Rosemary Chang
Ezekiel Bahar	Ken Chase
Alan Barr	Fuhua Cheng
Ronen Barzel	Henry N. Christiansen
John C. Beatty	Richard Chuang
Ron Beck	Jim Clark
Steven A. Benzler	Elaine Cohen
Larry Bergman	Ephraim Cohen
Eric Bier	Michael Cohen
Chuck Bigelow	Rob Cook
Gary Bishop	Bill Cook

(TECHNICAL PROGRAM REVIEWERS, continued)

William B. Cowan
Frank Crow
Carl de Boor
Peter Dew
Mark Dippé
Scot Drysdale
Tom Duff
Rich Eaton
H. Edelsbrunner
Tim Everett
Gerald Farin
Rida T. Farouki
Dan Filip
Ken Fishkin
Eugene Fiume
Jim Foley
Tom Foley
David R. Forsey
Alain Fournier
Jean Francon
Richard Franke
Harold Frisch
Henry Fuchs
Don Fussell
Steve Gabriel
Michael Gangnet
Geoffrey Gardner
Andrew Glassner
Ronald N. Goldman
Cindy Goral
James Gosling
A. Grayer
Mark Green
John Gross
Leo J. Guibas
Robert Haber
Paul Haeberli
Eric Haines
Roy Hall
Pat Hanrahan
Ines Hardtke
Paul Heckbert
William L. Hibbard
Terry Higgins
McShaun Ho
Eric Hoffert
Christopher Hoffman
James Houston
Scott Hudson
Dave Immel
Robert J. K. Jacob
Thomas W. Jensen
Kenneth Joy
Mark Kahrs
James T. Kajiya
Michael Kaplan
David Kasik
Mike Keeler
David Kirk
R. Victor Klassen
Michael Kleyn
Gary Knott
Kevin Koestner
Bill Kovacs
Sid Kraus
Robert Lackman
Mark Leather

D. T. Lee
Marc Levoy
John Lewis
Richard Littlefield
Martin Livesey
Bart N. Locanthi
Charles Loop
William Lorensen
A. E. MacDonald
Jock MacKinlay
Mark Manasse
David Martindale
Nelson Max
Larry McCleary
Gary Meyer
Victor Milenkovic
Gene Miller
Don Mitchell
Ken Musgrave
Brad Myers
Bruce Naylor
Shawn Neely
Greg Nelson
Martin Newell
Gregory M. Nielson
Tomoyuki Nishita
Daniel O'Donnell
Joe O'Rourke
Eben Ostby
Fred Parke
Darwyn Peachey
Ken Perlin
Rob Pike
John Platt
Michael Potmesil
Vaughan Pratt
Przemyslaw Prusinkiewicz
Lyle Ramshaw
Bill Reeves
Aristides Requicha
Craig Reynolds
Jim Rhyne
Henry Rich
Alyn Rockwood
Holly Rushmeir
David Salesin
Hanan Samet
Ray Sarraga
Dan Schlusselberg
Robert Schumaker
Michael Shantz
Linda Shapiro
Ken Shoemake
John Sibert
Baldev Singh
Kenneth Sloan, Jr.
Wade Smith
John Snyder
Robert F. Sproull
Vijay Srinivasen
Darlene Stewart
Maureen C. Stone
David Sturman
Peter Tanner
Bruno Tezenas
Spencer Thomas
Wayne Tiller

(TECHNICAL PROGRAM REVIEWERS, continued)

Jay Torborg
Kenneth Torrance
Martin Tuori
Ken Turkowski
Craig Upson
Steve Upstill
Samuel Uselton
Arthur V. Valliliadis
Tim Van Hook
Christopher van Wyk
Michael W. Vannier
Jane Veeder
Chan Verbeck
Herb Voelcker
Brian Von Herzen

Colin Ware
G. S. Watkins
Paul Wawrzynek
David Weimer
Marceli Wein
Joel Welling
Lee Westover
David White
Jane Wilhelms
Allan R. Wilks
Lance Williams
Andy Witkin
John Woodwark
Tom Wright
Polle T. Zellweger

PROFESSIONAL SUPPORT

ACM SIGGRAPH '88 Conference Coordinator
Linda Norton

ACM SIGGRAPH Conference Coordinator
Betsy Johnsmiller

Administrative Assistants
Cheri Bailey, *Courses*
Lisa Fremont, *Art Show*
Ann Merchant, *Technical Program*
Betty Phillips, *Panels*

Audio/Visual Management
Audio Visual Headquarters Corporation
(An Eagle Trust PLC Company)
Jim Bartolomucci
David Elliott
Rich Farnham
Doug Hunt
George Miller

Conference Management / National Public Relations
Smith Bucklin and Associates, Inc.
Susan Argenti
Leona Caffey
Ellen Frisbie
Sheila Hoffmeyer
Joy Lee
Deidre Ross
Cynthia Stark

Conference Travel Agency
Association Travel, Inc.
Becky Shapleigh

Decorator/Drayage
Andrews-Bartlett and Associates, Inc.
Bob Borsz
Betty Fuller
Ken Gallagher
Barby Patronski
John Patronski

Exhibition Management
Robert T. Kenworthy, Inc.
Hank Cronan
Barbara Voss

Graphic Design
The Watt Group
Teruya Harada
Jennifer Sirek

Brochure Production
George Wong

Exhibitors

Abekas Video Systems, Inc.
Academic Press, Inc.
Addison-Wesley Publishing Company
ADEX Corporation
Advanced Electronics design
Advanced Micro Devices
Advanced Technology Center
Alias Research Inc.
Alliant Computer Systems
Ampex Corporation
Apollo Computer, Inc.
Apple Computer, Inc.
Ardent Computer
AT&T Graphic Software Labs
AT&T Pixel Machines
AT&T Truevision
ATC Graphic Systems
AV Video Magazine
Aviation Week and Space Technology
AZTEK
Barco Electronics, Inc.
Barco Industries, Inc.
benchMark Technologies
Brooktree
Bruning Computer Graphics
BTS
BYTE
CADKEY
CELCO, Inc.
CFME
Chromatics Inc.
Chugai International Corp./Cadcision
CMP Publications, Inc.
Commodore Business Machines, Inc.
Compugraphic Corporation
Computer Aided Engineering
Computer Design
Computer Friends Inc.
Computer Graphics & Applications
Computer Graphics Today
Computer Graphics World
Computer Society of the IEEE
Computerworld
Conrac Corporation, Display Products Group
Control Data
Convex Computer Corporation
Cubicomp Corporation
Cyberware Laboratory
Data Translation, Inc.
DEC Professional
Diaquest Inc.
DICOMED Corporation
Digital Arts
Digital Equipment Corporation
Digital News
Digital Review
Display TEK, Inc.
DOTRONIX, Inc.
Dubner Computer Systems

Dunn Instruments
DYNAIR Electronics, Inc.
Eastman Kodak Company
EIKONIX Corporation
Electrohome Limited, Display Systems
Electrohome Limited, Projection Products
Electronic Systems Products
ESD Software
Evans & Sutherland
Flamingo Graphics
Flying Moose Systems & Graphics Ltd.
Folsom Research Inc.
French Expositions in U.S.
Gammadata Computer GmbH
Gems of Cambridge Ltd.
General Electric, Projection Display Products Operation
General Electric, Silicon Systems Technology Dept.
General Parametrics
Genigraphics Corporation
Government Computer News
Grafpoint
Graftel
Graphic Controls Corporation
GraphOn Corporation
GTCO Corporation
Helios Systems
Hewlett-Packard Company
hi-tech Marketing Corporation
Hitachi America, Ltd.
Houston Instrument Div. of Ametek
Howtek Inc.
HP Professional
Human Designed Systems
Ikegami Electronics
Image Innovation Ltd.
Imagraph Corporation
Intel Corporation
Intelligent Light, Inc.
Interactive Machines Inc.
Intergraph Corporation
Intergrated Arts
International Software Corporation
Ioline Corporation
Iris Graphics, Inc.
Island Graphics Corporation
Ithaca Software
Jack Ward Color Service Inc.
James Grunder & Associates, Inc.
Joinap Inc.
Karl Gutmann Inc.
KMS Advanced Products
KMW Systems Corporation
Kurta Corporation
Lasergraphics, Inc.
Lazerus
Leader Instruments Corporation
LSI Logic Sciences
Lundy Electronics & Systems, Inc.
Lyon Lamb Video Animation Systems, Inc.

Machine Design
Management Graphics, Inc.
Maxtrox Electronic Systems Ltd.
McGraw-Hill Publishing
Measurement Systems, Inc.
Media Cybernetics, Inc.
Megascan Technology Inc.
Megatek Corporation
Meiko, Inc.
Mercury Computer Systems
Metheus Corporation
Microfield Graphics
Millimeter
Minolta Corporation
Mitsubishi Electronics America, Inc.
Mitsubishi International Corporation
Moniterm Corporation
Monitronix Corporation
Montage Publishing/Media Horizons
Morgan Kaufmann Publishers
Multiwire Division
National Computer Graphics Association
National Semiconductor Corporation
National Technical Information Services
    U.S. Department of Commerce
NEC Home Electronics, Computer Prod. Div.
NEC Home Electronics, Professional Sys. Div.
NEC Information Systems
Neo-Visuals, Inc.
Networked Picture Systems, Inc.
Nichimen America, Inc.
Nissei Sangyo America, Ltd.
Nova Graphics International
Nth Graphics
Number Nine Computer Corporation
Numonics Corporation
Omnicomp Graphics Corporation
Ontario Canada Trade Office
Optotech, Inc.
Oxberry
Panasonic Industrial Company
Panasonic Industrial Company, Computer Products Division
Pansophic Systems, Inc.
Parallax Graphics
PC Week
PennWell Publishing Company
Penton Publishing
Photron Limited
Pictureware, Inc.
PIXAR
Polaroid Corporation
Polhemus Navigation Sciences
Primagraphics Ltd.
Prime Computer
PRIOR Data Sciences Ltd.
Productivity Products International, Inc.
QMS, Inc.

Quantum Data Inc.
Rainbow Technologies
Ramtek Corporation
Raster Technologies
Renaissance GRX, Inc.
Ron Scott, Inc.
S. Klein Computer Graphics Review
Sampo Corporation of America
Seiko Instruments USA
Sentry Publishing
Shima Seiki USA Inc.
Silicon Graphics
Slide Tek Inc.
Softimage Inc.
Software News
Solid Ideas Inc.
Sony Coporation
Sony Corporation, Computer Peripheral Products Division
Spaceward Microsystems
Spring-Verlag New York, Inc.
Steadi-Film Corporation
Stellar Computer, Inc.
StereoGraphics Corporation
Summagraphics Corporation
Sun Microsystems, Inc.
Symbolics Inc., Graphics Division
Tech Valley Publishing
Techexport Inc.
Technology & Business Communications
Tektronix, Inc.
Template Graphics Software, Inc.
Texas Instruments
Texas Memory Systems, Inc.
Texnai Inc.
Text & Measurement Systems, Inc.
The Winsted Corporation
Three3D Systems, Inc.
Time Arts
Toshiba America Inc.
University of Lowell
UNIX World Magazine
Versatec, A Xerox Company
Verticom, Inc.
Videography
Visual Information, Inc.
Wacom Company, Ltd.
Waldmann Lighting Company
Wasatch Computer Technology, Inc.
Wavefront Technologies, Inc.
Wyse Technology
XTAR Corporation
Zenith Electronics Corporation
Zenographics
Ziff-Davis Publishing

1988 ACM SIGGRAPH Awards

Computer Graphics Achievement Award

Alan H. Barr

Prof. Alan H. Barr is being recognized for his contribution to graphics, primarily for extending computer graphics shape modeling to include physically based and "teleological" modeling. He is a leader in the recent push toward integrating dynamic constraints and physics into the animation of computer-synthesized scenes -- an important advance in computer graphics.

The ultimate goal in simulation is to be able to model the actual behavior of objects whether based on physical or "cartoon" principles. Dr. Barr's research brings us closer to achieving that goal. Using a "teleological" modeling element (from the Greek word *teleos*, meaning end or goal) allows representation of abstract, physically realistic, time-dependent objects and systems of objects in mathematically consistent schema. Potential applications include mechanical CAD, robotics, goal-oriented motion, self-assembling mechanical systems and computer vision.

Dr. Barr was educated at Renssalaer Polytechnic Institute, receiving BS, MS and PhD degrees in Mathematics in 1973, 1976, and 1983. His interest in computer graphics was stimulated at Renssalaer Polytechnic Institute's Center for Interactive Computer Graphics. There he created a collection of new solid modeling primitives, called superquadrics. From 1982 through 1983 while finishing his PhD at Renssalaer, Barr was a senior research scientist at Raster Technologies Inc. In 1984 he became an assistant professor of Computer Science at the California Institute of Technology where he conducts his research and is a superb mentor of graduate students.

Dr. Barr has lectured in and chaired several SIGGRAPH tutorials. He and his colleagues are regular contributors of stunning images for the SIGGRAPH film shows. It has been said he has the distinction of having the most images reproduced without credit!

Selected references

[1] A.H. Barr, "Ray Tracing Deformed Surfaces," Proceedings of SIGGRAPH'86 (Dallas, Texas, August 18-22, 1986). In *Computer Graphics 20*, 4 (August 1986), 287-296.

[2] A.H. Barr, "Global and Local Deformations of Solid Primitives," Proceedings of SIGGRAPH'84 (Minneapolis, Minn., July 23-27, 1984). In *Computer Graphics 18*, 3 (July 1984), 21-30.

[3] A.H. Barr, "Superquadrics and Angle Preserving Transformations," *IEEE Computer Graphics and Applications, 1*, 1 (January 1981), 11-23

[4] A.H. Barr, B. Von Herzen, R. Barzel, and J. Snyder, (1987) "Computational Techniques for the Self Assembly of Large Space Structures," *Proceedings of the 8th Princeton/Space Studies Institute Conference on Space Manufacturing* (Princeton New Jersey, May 6-9 1987), to be published by the American Institute of Aeronautics and Astronautics.

[5] R. Barzel, A. Barr, "A Modeling System Based on Dynamic Constraints," Proceedings of SIGGRAPH'88 (Altanta, Ga., August 1-5, 1988). In *Computer Graphics 22*, 4 (August 1988), 179-188, this issue.

[6] "Caltech studies in modeling and motion" [videotape], in "Visualization in Scientific Computing," *SIGGRAPH Video Review*, 28, a

supplement to *Computer Graphics 21*, 6 (November 1987).

|7| J. Platt, A.H. Barr, "Constraint methods for Flexible Models," Proceedings of SIGGRAPH'88 (Altanta, Ga., August 1-5, 1988). In *Computer Graphics 22*, 4 (August 1988), 279-288, this issue.

|8| Terzopoulos, Demetri, John Platt, Alan Barr and Kurt Fleischer "Elastically Deformable Models," Proceedings of SIGGRAPH'87 (Anaheim, Calif., July 27-Aug 1, 1987). In *Computer Graphics 21*, 4 (July 1987), 205-214.

|9| A. Witkin, K. Fleischer and A.H. Barr, "Energy Constraints on Parametrized Models," Proceedings of SIGGRAPH'87 (Anaheim, Calif., July 27-Aug 1, 1987). In *Computer Graphics 21*, 4 (July 1987), 225-232.

Previous award winners
1987: Robert Cook
1986: Turner Whitted
1985: Loren Carpenter
1984: James H. Clark
1983: James F. Blinn

A Parallel Algorithm for Polygon Rasterization

Juan Pineda
Apollo Computer Inc.
Chelmsford, MA 01824
juan@apollo.uucp

Abstract

A parallel algorithm for the rasterization of polygons is presented that is particularly well suited for 3D Z–buffered graphics implementations. The algorithm represents each edge of a polygon by a linear **edge function** that has a value greater than zero on one side of the edge and less than zero on the opposite side. The value of the function can be interpolated with hardware similar to hardware required to interpolate color and Z pixel values. In addition, the edge function of adjacent pixels may be easily computed in parallel. The coefficients of the "Edge function" can be computed from floating point endpoints in such a way that sub–pixel precision of the endpoints can be retained in an elegant way.

CR catagories and subject descriptors: I.3.1 [Computer Graphics]: Hardware Architecture – *Raster display devices*; I.3.3 [Computer Graphics]: Picture/Image Generation – *Display algorithms*.

General terms: Algorithms.

Additional keywords and phrases: Polygon rasterization, sub–pixel vertices, linear edge function, parallel processing.

1. Introduction

The fast rendering of 3D Z–buffered linearly interpolated polygons is a problem that is fundamental to state of the art workstations. In general, the problem consists of two parts: 1) the 3D transformation, projection and light calculation of the vertices, and 2) the rasterization of the polygon into a frame buffer. This paper deals with one aspect of the latter problem: the computation of the boundaries of the polygon.

Traditionally, the edges of a polygon are computed by a line interpolation algorithm, and each scan line is filled with linearly interpolated color and Z values [2]. This method is generally scan line serial, and is consequently not so convenient for frame buffers with more desirable rectangular word organizations [5].

The "PIXEL–PLANES" [3] system uses a parallel multiplier tree to simultaenously compute, for all pixels in the frame buffer, a linear function which is used to define edges. This method has the nice property that it is highly parallel, but it has the disadvantage that it requires dedicated logic for each pixel, and consequently requires custom memory chips.

The algorithm presented in this paper also uses a linear function to define polygon edges, but it allows for painting algorithms that are

©1988   ACM-0-89791-275-6/88/008/0017 $00.75

better suited to frame buffers using conventional DRAM and VRAM technology. The algorithm is inherently parallel, so that the rendering performance is memory bandwidth limited, rather than computation limited.

The **edge function** is a linear function which can be used to classify points on a 2D plane that is subdivided by a line, into three regions: the points to the "left" of the line, the points to the "right" of the line, and the points on the line. The function has the property that points to the "left" of the line have a value greater than zero, points to the "right" have a value less than zero, and points exactly on the line have a value of zero. Since the function is linear, it can be computed incrementally in the same way as color and Z values.

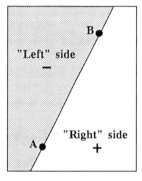 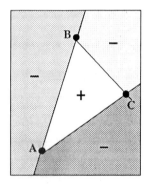

Subdivision of plane by line through points A and B   *Triangle formed by union of right sides of AB, BC and CA*

Figure 1. A Triangle Can be Formed by Combination of Edges

Figure 1 shows how it is possible to define a triangle by the union of three edges which are specified by edge functions. It is possible to define more complex polygons by using boolean combinations of more than three edges. Note that a tie breaker rule must be applied to the points that lie exactly on any of the edges to determine whether the points are to be considered interior or exterior to the polygon.

With this formalism, it is possible to compute at each pixel center on the plane an n–tupple: (R, G, B, Z, E1...En), where R, G, B and Z components form the fill value, and E1...En are the values of the edge functions which are used to determine whether the pixel is interior or exterior to the polygon. Given the value of this n–tupple at a single pixel position, the n–tupple of adjacent pixels can be computed by simple linear interpolators that require one addition per component per iteration.

E1..En can then be used as a "stencil" that allows a pixel to be modified only if it is interior to the polygon. The process of painting the polygon can then be reduced to an algorithm that traverses an area that includes the interior of the triangle, but that does not have to be particularly careful about the edges because the "stencil" forms the actual edge. The particular order of traversal is not important, only that each interior pixel is covered once and only once.

Any traversal algorithm that touches all interior points once and only once will produce the correct result, but some may be more efficent than others, depending on how many pixels are covered by the traversal that are not actually drawn.

The elegance of this approach is in the way that it orthogonalizes and unifies the traversal of a polygon and the filling of interior pixels. The orthogonality is convenient for the formulation of efficient strategies for painting a polygon with the least number of memory cycles and is especially useful with parallel rectangular memory organizations.

2. The Edge Function

Consider, as shown in figure 2, a vector defined by two points: (X,Y) and (X+dX,Y+dY), and the line that passes through both points. This vector and line can be used to divide the two dimensional space into three regions: all points to the "left" of, to the "right" of, and exactly on the line.

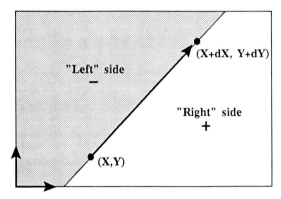

Figure 2. An Edge is Defined by a Vector

We define the **edge function** E(x,y) as:

$$E(x,y) = (x-X)\ dY - (y-Y)\ dX$$

This function has the useful property that its value is related to the position of the point (x,y) relative to the edge defined by the points (X,Y) and (X+dX, Y+dY):

$$E(x,y) > 0 \text{ if } (x,y) \text{ is to the "right" side}$$
$$E(x,y) = 0 \text{ if } (x,y) \text{ is exactly on the line}$$
$$E(x,y) < 0 \text{ if } (x,y) \text{ is to the "left " side}$$

To convince oneself that this is true, recognize that the formula given for E(x,y) is the same as the formula for the magnatude of the cross product between the vector from (X,Y) to (X+dX, Y+dy), and the vector from (X,Y) to (x,y). By the well know property of cross products, the magnatude is zero if the vectors are colinear, and changes sign as the vectors cross from one side to the other.

This function is convenient for rasterization algorithms, since it can be computed incrementally by simple addition:

$$E(x+1,y) = E(x,y) + dY$$
$$E(x,y+1) = E(x,y) - dX$$

The edge function is related to the error value or "draw control variable" (DCV) in Bresenham line drawing algorithms [1,2]. The difference is that Bresenham line drawing algorithms maintain the DCV value only for pixels within 1/2 pixel of the line, while E(x,y) is defined for all pixels on the plane. In addition, the value of the DCV at a given point differs from E(x,y) by a constant offset. In any case, the reason that both algorithms work is fundamentally the same.

As mentioned earlier, this same property of E(x,y) is used by the "PIXEL-PLANES" [3] graphics system, where this function is computed in parallel for all pixels in the frame buffer by a multiplier tree.

3. Incremental Classification of Points around a Convex Polygon

Consider a convex polygon defined by the vertices (Xi, Yi) 0< i <=N. For the convenience of notation, take (X0, Y0) = (XN, YN), and consider the i'th edge as the edge between the i'th and the [i-1] vertex. The initial values of the edge function interpolators at a starting point (Xs, Ys) would then be:

$$dXi = Xi - X[i-1]$$
$$dYi = Yi - Y[i-1]$$
$$Ei(Xs, Ys) = (Xs - Xi)\ dYi - (Ys - Yi)\ dXi$$

$$\text{for } 0< i <=N$$

The edge functions may then be computed incrementally for a unit step in the X or Y direction:

$$Ei(x+1, y) = Ei(x, y) + dYi,$$
$$Ei(x-1, y) = Ei(x, y) - dYi,$$
$$Ei(x, y+1) = Ei(x, y) - dXi,$$
$$Ei(x, y-1) = Ei(x, y) + dXi.$$

If we use a tie breaker rule that considers a point on an edge as interior to the edge, then a point is interior to the convex polygon if:

$$Ei >= 0 \text{ for all } i : 0<i<=N .$$

4. Traversing the Polygon

Given the initialized edge interpolators, the interpolation coefficients, the tie breaker rule, and the Boolean function for combining the edges, we still need to traverse the area of the triangle in order to paint it.

The polygon can be traversed by any algorithm that is guaranteed to cover all of the pixels. Figure 3 shows two simple algorithms. Simply traversing the bounding box is perhaps the simplest strategy, but generally not the most efficient. A smarter algorithm would advance to the next line when it walked off the edge of a triangle.

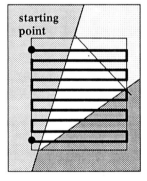 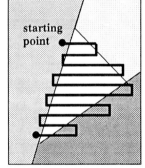

Traversing the Bounding Box   *A More Efficient Traversal Algorithm*

Figure 3. Simple Traversal Algorithms

One complicaton of the smart algorithm is that when it advances to the next line, it may advance to a point inside the triangle. In that case, the algorithm must search for the outside of the edge before it begins the next scan line. An example of this problem is shown on the top right hand edge of the triangle in figure 4.

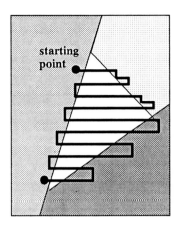

Figure 4. Traversal Algorithms May Have to Search for Edge

A smarter algorithm is shown in figure 5. It proceeds down from the starting point, working its way outward from a center line. The advantage of this algorithm over the simpler algorithm is that it never has to search for an edge, then double back. The tradeoff is that the interpolator state for the center line must be saved while traversing the outer points, since the interpolators must be restarted back at the center line. Notice that at the bottom, the "center" line shifts over if it ends up exterior to the triangle.

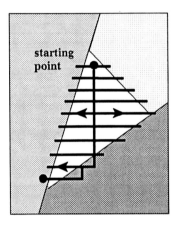

Figure 5. Smarter Algorithm Proceeds Outward From Center Line

There are many traversal algorithms possible. The best algorithm will depend on the cost/performance tradeoffs in the implementation.

5. Clipping

Left and right clipping can be viewed as additional polygon edges that are part of the pixel's value: (R, G, B, Z, E1..En, El, Er), where El and Er represent the left and right clip "edge functions". If the traversal algorithm views them as edges, then a smart traversal algorithm will turn back when it crosses a clip boundary and it will not spend time rendering clipped areas of a polygon.

The top clip boundary can be used to control the starting point, while the bottom clip boundary can be used to control the last scan line rendered.

Figure 6 shows clipping.

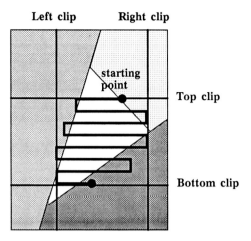

Figure 6. Clipping a Triangle

6. Sub-pixel Accuracy of Vertices

Typically in 3D graphics rendering, polygon vertices are in floating point format after 3D transformation and projection. Some implementations round the X and Y floating point ordinates to integer values, so that simple integer line algorithms can be used compute the triangle edges. This rounding can leave gaps on the order of 1/2 pixel wide between adjacent polygons that do not share common vertices. Gaps also occur as a result of the finite precision used in specifying the endpoints, but these gaps are much narrower. Some implementations attempt to eliminate these gaps by growing the edges of triangles to insure overlap, but these solutions cause other artifacts.

In order to minimize these artifacts, it is desirable to render triangle edges as close as possible to the real line between two vertices. This is conveniently done with this algorithm by performing the interpolator setup computations in floating point, and converting to fixed point at the end:

$$dXi = Xi - X[i-1]$$
$$dYi = Yi - Y[i-1]$$
$$Ei(Xs, Ys) = (Xs - Xi) \, dYi - (Ys - Yi) \, dXi$$

$$dXi' = FIX(dXi)$$
$$dYi' = FIX(dYi)$$
$$Ei' = FIX(Ei)$$

Note that as in any digital interpolator, the fractional precision used in the iteration must be chosen to give an acceptable error across the interpolation.

While this computation does require five floating point additions and two floating point multiplies per edge, the cost is small when compared with the other computations required to transform and set up a 3D triangle.

Notice that the computation only modifies the setup values of the Ei's, but does not require any special treatment of the endpoints, except to insure that the traversal algorithm covers the entire area including the endpoints.

7. Parallel Implementation

Since the edge function is linear, it is possible to compute the value of the edge function for a pixel an arbitrary distance L away from a given point (x,y):

$$E(x+L, y) = E(x) + L \, dy$$

This property allows a group of interpolators, each responsible for a pixel within a block of contiguous pixels, to simultaneously compute the edge function of an adjacent block in a single cycle. If the blocks were L pixels wide, then there would be L interpolators. In order to compute the edge function of the block L pixels away in the +x direction, each interpolator would increment by (L dx).

Since color and Z components are linear as well, they may also be computed in parallel.

Graphics frame buffers are usually organized to provide simultaneous access to a block of adjacent pixels [5]. The block is usually called a word, and the pixels within the block are called interleaves. If a group of interpolators are dedicated to each interleave, then the RGBZ value and whether the pixel should be drawn can be computed in parallel for an entire word. If the interpolator cycle time is at least as fast as the memory cycle time (which is the case with current gate array and DRAM technology), then shaded triangles can be rendered at the memory cycle time.

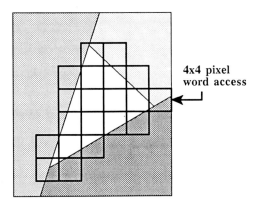

Figure 7. Covering a Triangle by Rectangular Accesses

8. Future Work and Extensions

The edge functions described in this paper have been linear. It is possible to compute higher order edge functions. A second order edge function would yield conic edges such as circles or elipses. Combined with more interesting Boolean functions, it would be possible to efficiently compute complex shapes, such as wide lines with rounded endpoints.

By proper normalization of the partial derivatives and intial value of $E(x,y)$, it is possible to perform the interpolation of the edge functions in a floating point like manner, thus maximizing the precision obtained from a finite width interpolator. This method has the desirable property that it gradually looses precision as triangles get larger, rather than abruptly breaking.

Because triangle edges are specified by the coefficients in the edge function, rather than end points, it is actually possible to transform the coefficients directly, rather than forming a triangle from the transformed and projected vertices. While this does not directly save computation, it may reduce some of the computational difficulties encountered in perspective projection. Specifically, since the objects being transformed are edges rather than points, the precision and dynamic range problems encountered with perspective projection of points near the eye point or behind the hither plane can be eliminated. This means that it may be possible to transform polygons without the need for exception cases for vertices behind the hither plane. This property could be useful in pipeline implementations where the exception case would limit performance.

Since the value of the edge function is proportional to the distance of a point from the edge, it is possible to use this value to anti-alias edges. This could be performed using a method proposed by Fujimoto and Iwata [4]. In this method, the Bresenham DCV value and increments for a polygon edge are put through a lookup table that performs a divide and computes a low precision estimate of the distance of the pixel center from the edge center line. This distance is then used to adjust the contribution of the fill value to the background value.

Going one step further with anti-aliasing, it is possible to have the lookup table produce a crude sub-pixel resolution bitmap for each edge. The bitmaps of all edges would then be anded together, and the number of set sub-pixels would be counted to determine the contribution for that pixel. Since the method aproximates the actual sub-pixel bitmap for the triangle, it has excellent behavior at verticies, and at places where edges are less than 1 pixel apart.

9. Conclusion

An algorithm for rasterization of polygon edges has been presented. The algorithm has several useful properties: 1) it can be conveniently computed in parallel and used with common refresh buffer word organizations, 2) it can be computed with hardware similar to hardware required to interpolate color and Z values for 3D solids, and 3) it elegantly maintains the subpixel accuracy of vertices. These properties make the algorithm particularly attractive for use in 3D solid graphics implementations.

10. Acknowledgements

I would like to give special thanks to Bill Brandt for time spent on numerous discussions during the intial formulation of the ideas presented here. I would also like to thank Casey Dowdell, Bill Brandt, John Beck, Jane Critchlow and the conference reviewers for their time spent reviewing this text and for their helpful suggestions. Finally, I would like to thank Kathy Ford for help in the preparation of the final copy for publication.

References

1. Bresenham, J. Algorithm for Computer Control of Digital Plotter. *IBM Systems Journal 4,1* (1965), 25-30.

2. Foley, J. and A. Van Dam, "Fundamentals of Interactive Computer Graphics."

3. Fuchs, H. and Poulton J. PIXEL-PLANES: A VLSI-Oriented Design for a Raster Graphics Engine. *VLSI DESIGN (Third Quarter 1981)*, 20-28.

4. Fujimoto, A. and Iwata, K. Jag-Free Images on Raster Displays. *IEEE Computer Graphics and Applications 3,9* (December 1983), 26-34.

5. Whitton, M. Memory Design for Raster Graphics Displays. *IEEE Computer Graphics and Applications 4,3* (March 1984), 48-65.

The Triangle Processor and Normal Vector Shader: A VLSI System for High Performance Graphics

Michael Deering* *Stephanie Winner*†
Bic Schediwy‡ *Chris Duffy* *Neil Hunt*

Schlumberger Palo Alto Research, 3340 Hillview Avenue, Palo Alto, CA 94304

Abstract

Current affordable architectures for high-speed display of shaded 3D objects operate orders of magnitude too slowly. Recent advances in floating point chip technology have outpaced polygon fill time, making the memory access bottleneck between the drawing processor and the frame buffer the most significant factor to be accelerated. Massively parallel VLSI systems have the potential to bypass this bottleneck, but to date only at very high cost. We describe a new more affordable VLSI solution. A pipeline of *triangle processors* rasterizes the geometry, then a further pipeline of *shading processors* applies Phong shading with multiple light sources. The triangle processor pipeline performs 100 billion additions per second, and the shading pipeline performs two billion multiplies per second. This allows 3D graphics systems to be built capable of displaying more than one million triangles per second. We show the results of an anti-aliasing technique, and discuss extensions to texture mapping, shadows, and environment maps.

CR Categories and Subject Descriptors: B.2.1 [Arithmetic and Logic Structures]: Design Styles - pipeline. C.1.1 [Computer Systems Organization]: Single Data Stream Architectures - pipeline processors. I.3.1 [Computer Graphics]: Hardware Architecture - raster display devices. I.3.3 [Computer Graphics]: Picture/Image Generation - display algorithms. I.3.7 [Computer Graphics]: 3D Graphics and Realism - color, shading, shadowing and texture, visible lines / surface algorithms.

Additional Keywords: real-time image display, triangle processor, interpolation, hardware lighting models, shading, graphics VLSI.

---

* Current address: Sun Microsystems Inc., 2550 Garcia Avenue, Mountain View, CA 94043.

† Current address: Apple Computer Inc., 20525 Mariani Avenue, Cupertino, CA 95014.

‡ Current address: Hewlett Packard Labs (3-U), 1501 Page Mill Road, Palo Alto, CA 94304.

Permission to copy without fee all or part of this material is granted provided that the copies are not made or distributed for direct commercial advantage, the ACM copyright notice and the title of the publication and its date appear, and notice is given that copying is by permission of the Association for Computing Machinery. To copy otherwise, or to republish, requires a fee and/or specific permission.

©1988   ACM-0-89791-275-6/88/008/0021 $00.75

1 INTRODUCTION

Computer graphics has become an integral component of the modern concept of a general purpose computer. The graphical metaphor is more intuitive, flexible, and efficient than the old text-only man machine interface. Also, much of the usefulness of modern computing is the ability of the computer to simulate the real world to more and more exacting degrees. The graphics interface must support this, by portraying the three dimensional dynamic world more and more accurately.

Currently affordable architectures for realistic display of three dimensional objects have severe constraints on scene complexity and display rates. The improvements needed are far beyond the factor of two or three typical of incremental improvements on existing techniques. We re-examined the whole process of image generation, looking for an improvement of at least an order of magnitude over conventional state of the art systems.

After describing the prior art, we will introduce the concept of the *Triangle Processor* and *Normal Vector Shader* chips, and show how they can be configured into a high performance 3D display system. Certain important details of the architecture and chips are examined in more depth, followed by a discussion of extensions to support more sophisticated effects, including anti-aliasing and texture maps.

2 PRIOR WORK

Most commercial 3D graphics systems are based on DRAM Z-buffers. Until very recently, almost all reasonable cost systems (less than $100 000) rasterized polygons one pixel at a time, with read-modify-write cycle times of approximately one micro-second. Coupled with geometry transform systems capable of processing no more than 10 000 triangles a second, such systems take many seconds or even minutes to draw complex scenes containing large numbers of small triangles. This is so even though most modern systems include some form of VLSI support [2, 13]. Recently announced systems employ parallelism to rasterize polygons several pixels at a time [14]. But as detailed in Appendix A, the pixel write efficiency does not scale linearly, and overall performance is increased by less than an order of magnitude.

To get around the Z-buffer write limit, a number of massively parallel VLSI systems have been proposed. Most have an array of intelligent pixel processors, through which edges of polygons are broadcast; each pixel processor examines the polygon geometry, and sets its pixel color to the polygon's color if the polygon both contains this pixel *and* has a closer Z value than any other polygon previously containing this pixel.

One of the first such systems is Fuchs' Pixel-Planes system [5, 11]. Here a processor is dedicated to each pixel in the display screen. The advantage is that any n-sided polygon can be rendered in constant time, without regard to its area. The disadvantages include the relatively large amount of time taken to enter the geometry for each polygon (tens of microseconds), and the large amount of silicon required (several thousand chips for 1024 × 1024).

The SLAM architecture [4] combines a static RAM for 2D pixel storage with a 1D run-length pixel fill hardware unit on the same custom IC. This is like a Pixel-Planes chip with time multiplexed pixel fill hardware. While this results in better silicon density, the improvement is still not large enough to make 1024 × 1024 72-bit pixels practical, and is better suited to limited pixel depth 2D applications. Other disadvantages include the need to slice up geometry into 1D runs *outside* the SLAM chips, and rendering time complexity linearly proportional to the height of a polygon.

The Super-Buffer [6] dispenses with the 2D array concept, and uses a single scan line of pixel processors. This finally reduces the number of replicated custom chips to a reasonable count, but adds the requirement to pre-sort and buffer all polygons by their first active scan line in the displayed image. The rendering time is proportional to the height of the triangles, and (as in the SLAM system) the data for a given polygon must be externally sequenced and entered repeatedly into the chips until the polygon has been rendered. Nishizawa *et al.*[10] describe another VLSI implementation of this concept.

The lighting model is also an important issue. Most high speed hardware implementations rely upon simple linear interpolation of color between vertices. More comprehensive lighting model computations have not been integrated into the VLSI solution.

The systems discussed above all associate processors with pixels; an alternative is to associate processors with polygons. Many early flight simulator architectures had an architecture of the latter form, as well as an unpublished system of Cohen and Demetrescu. Our system fits into this category.

3 THE TRIANGLE PROCESSOR CONCEPT

The key concept is that of the *Triangle Processor*, a processor dedicated to the rasterization of a single triangle. A number of these processors are connected in series to form a *triangle pipe*, into which a raster ordered stream of "blank" pixels is fed. Each Triangle Processor is responsible for one triangle in the image. If a received pixel falls within the triangle, the processor may substitute triangle specific data; otherwise the pixel is passed along un-altered.

Each Triangle Processor contains the value of the normal to the surface and Z depth at each vertex of the local triangle, and also color data. It generates point samples of these values for each pixel position within the triangle by bi-linear interpolation between the vertex values.

Triangle Processors are designed only to overwrite received pixels that are further back in Z than the interpolated Z

value for their local triangle. Thus the triangle pipe implements triangle rasterization with depth sort.

Triangle parameters are loaded by sending data down the triangle pipe in specially marked packets between scan lines of "blank" pixels. They are loaded into the first available Triangle Processor encountered.

A Triangle Processor can only handle one triangle at a time, but since most triangles cover only a relatively small portion of the image, it is not necessary that a Triangle Processor remain allocated to a single triangle for the whole image. When the last pixel in a triangle has been rendered, its processor becomes available for re-use with another triangle, whose parameters may be loaded any time after the current scan line. Thus during the processing of an image, a single Triangle Processor may be used to render a number of triangles which do not overlap in the y direction.

Because of the extremely deep pipelining, the processors at the end of the pipeline are operating several thousand cycles behind those at the front. Thus at any point in time, the pipeline contains pixels from several different scan lines, as well as the packets of new triangle data sandwiched between them. Using the same pipeline for loading the new triangle data as well as rasterizing solves the problem of synchronizing the loads to the different processors in a very elegant manner.

4 THE NORMAL VECTOR SHADER

Figure 1: Nine rounded cubes with simple environment mapping.

To complete the rendering process, a shading pipeline applies a lighting model to the stream of normal vector values and other data from the triangle pipe. This second pipe is comprised of "Normal Vector Shader" (NVS) chips, which support a full multiple light source Phong illumination model, which is applied *independently* to each pixel. Since the majority of polygons are only a few pixels across, algorithms such as that of Bishop and Weimer [1], which take 10 pixels per scan line to break even, were deemed too slow. The realism of the image is further enhanced by also interpolating the viewpoint vector to each pixel within the NVS chips, as can be seen in the reflection of the environment in Figure 1 (rendered at 1280 × 1024). This technique host workstation → RAM → display list runner → XTC → Y buffer → [triangle processor pipe: ΔP → ΔP → ... ΔP] → [NVS pipe: NVS → NVS → ... NVS] → RGBZ buffer → CRT

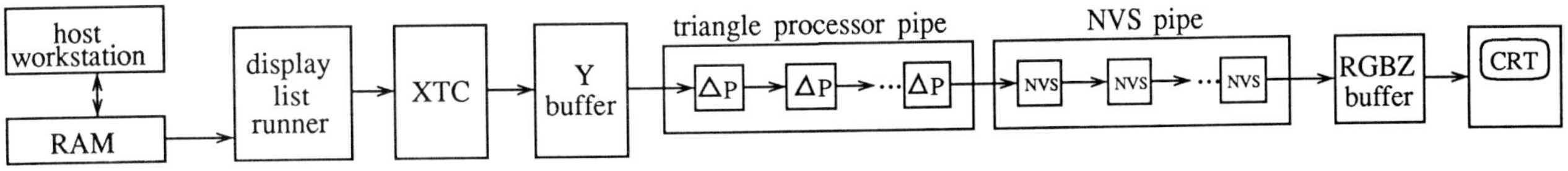

Figure 2: Block diagram of the GSP-NVS system.

avoids the "flat flash" problem associated with Phong shading of flat surfaces by planar light sources.

5 SYSTEM OVERVIEW

We now describe a complete graphics system based on "graphical signal processing" with "normal vector shading" (GSP-NVS), which achieves a processing rate of one million triangles per second. A block diagram of the overall system is shown in Figure 2. Up to the Y-buffer, the processing is fairly conventional, although the computations must be performed at a rate of several million triangles per second.

A display list runner (DLR) extracts geometry and display commands from the memory of the host workstation. The DLR handles viewing matrix manipulation, simple subroutine jumps, picks, bounding box tests, mode bit settings, and so on, but passes triangle and line stroke (vector) commands to the next stage without interpretation, keeping the overhead to a minimum.

The transform, clip, and set-up stage (XTC) performs the usual calculations on triangles and vectors. The resulting 448 bits of "pre-digested" triangle data are then passed to the Y-buffer. A much higher throughput (nearly a Gigaflop) than past systems is required here to support the rest of the architecture.

The Y-buffer is organized as 1024 (or more) linked lists, one for each scan line on the display. The Y-buffer input process accepts triangles from the XTC, sorts them into bins indexed by their first active scan line number, and holds them in DRAM storage until all of the triangles in a given frame have been buffered. Then the output process feeds these triangles into the triangle pipe for rasterization, but now in scan line order.

The Y-buffer also sequences the rasterizing within the triangle pipe. First, data representing all the triangles that become active on the current line are sent into the triangle pipe. Then the Y-buffer sends (1280) "blank" pixels for one scan line into the triangle pipe. This is repeated for all the scan lines in the frame (1024).

The triangle pipe accepts the triangle data, and converts the "blank" pixels into a stream of rasterized (and depth sorted) pixels in scan line order, as described above. Once the data for a triangle has been entered into the pipe, it will remain lodged in a Triangle Processor somewhere within, without need for any additional control, for as many scan lines as the triangle is tall.

The NVS pipe takes the rasterized output of the triangle pipe, and converts the surface normal vector pixels to RGB pixels. These are finally stored in an RGB frame buffer prior to display on a CRT.

6 SYSTEM PROPERTIES

The GSP-NVS system has several advantages. The amount of silicon required by the custom rendering pipelines is realistic, and indeed is less than needed elsewhere in a balanced system. This is partly due to the compact layout of the Triangle Processor cell, allowing as many as ten triangle processors per (inexpensive) chip. The hardware is not restricted to any fixed size image for output.

To a first approximation, the rasterization time for a complete image is the time taken to load all the triangle data, plus the time to send through a screen-full of pixels. Thus in many normal cases, the rasterization time is *independent* of the sizes of the triangles. The load time is short, because each triangle need only be entered into the pipe once, and special care has been taken to make this entry as fast as possible (8 cycles of 50ns). The time to send pixels into the pipe is also very small, at 50ns per pixel. Typical load time might be 20% of the rasterization time.

There are some disadvantages. As is the case with the Super-Buffer, a Y-buffer is required to pre-sort the geometry. Unlike the processor-per-pixel architectures, geometry overflow is possible if too many triangles are active on the same scan line. This is not a fundamental limit, as the pixels can be passed through the triangle pipe multiple times, effectively increasing the number of Triangle Processors available.

7 TRIANGLE PROCESSOR INTERNAL ARCHITECTURE

The feasibility of a machine with a processor per triangle is dependent on such processors being relatively inexpensive. We have designed a complete Triangle Processor in full custom CMOS VLSI, using less than 25 000 transistors; prototype chips containing one triangle processor have been fabricated, tested and shown to be fully operational at expected speed. Modern VLSI densities allow upwards of ten such processors to be instanced onto a single die; furthermore, as VLSI densities increase, additional Triangle Processors can be added to the chip with little effort and *without* modifying the chip pin-outs. Because these chips are made to be directly wired together in a linear pipe (with no support chips required), upwards of 1 000 Triangle Processors occupy less than a square foot of PC board space (assuming 8 processors per chip in 1.2μ technology).

Figure 3 shows the external data flow between individual Triangle Processor chips, and the internal data flow between Triangle Processors within the same chip. The x pixel location is locally generated within each chip by the G-unit; consequently, this value does not have to be passed between the chips, reducing the pin count. Another factor of two reduction in pin count is obtained by double clocking

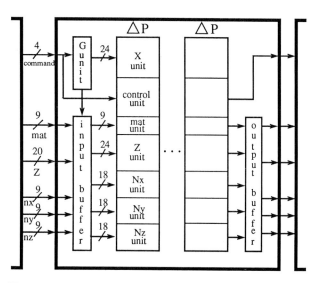

Figure 3: External data flow and internal organization of the Triangle Processors chip. (Note that only 30 data input pins are needed for the 60 signals shown, as the pins are double clocked.)

the I/O pins*, enabling the Triangle Processors and NVS chips to be housed in 68-pin leaded chip carrier packages.

Each Triangle Processor is broken down into a number of function units, also shown in Figure 3. Each unit operates on a different component of the pixel value flowing past. The X channel propagates the 24-bit fixed point number indicating the x location of the current pixel. The Z channel also propagates a 24-bit fixed point number, representing the z depth generated for the current pixel. The 18-bit N channels (N_x, N_y, and N_z) propagate the interpolated (denormalized) surface normal vector. The M channel propagates the associated "material index" (information about color and other triangle surface properties). The processor control unit interprets the command instructions, which sequence the loading of initial values and incremental parameters into the function units, and control the rasterization of the image.

7.1 The X-Unit.

Figure 4 shows the X-unit, which interpolates the points where the edges of the triangle cross each scan line in turn. Before the first scan line on which the triangle is active, x coordinates of the left and right edges of the triangle, and y-increment values are loaded. At the end of each scan line, the X-unit updates the left and right x coordinates by adding the y increment, thus obtaining the coordinates where the edges cross the *next* scan line.

Also, a counter is decremented; when the counter goes negative, either the current triangle has expired, or one of the edges has reached a vertex. In the former case, the triangle processor becomes passive, and awaits the next packet of new triangle data to arrive. If a vertex has been reached on one of the edges, new initial and incremental values are set for that edge, and also a new counter value, from *local*

---
* Data is transferred on both rising and falling phases of the clock, using each pin twice per clock cycle.

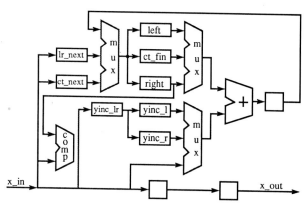

Figure 4: Schematic of the X-unit, used to track left and right edges of triangles, relative to the current scan line.

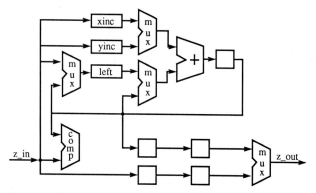

Figure 5: Schematic of the Z-unit, used to interpolate and compare Z depth values.

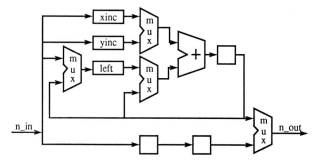

Figure 6: Schematic of the N-unit, used to interpolate surface normal vectors.

backup registers. Whether it is the left or right edge which changes direction is known at set-up time, and indicated by a triangle "type" bit in the data initially loaded for the triangle.

The X-unit continuously compares the pixel x coordinate (which increases on each incoming pixel) with the x positions of the left and right edges of the local triangle on the current scan line. (The values of x are generated by a single G unit on each chip, and are then pipelined through all the X-units on that chip.) Other units of the processor are signalled whenever the current pixel falls within the local triangle.

7.2 The Z-Unit. Figure 5 shows the Z-unit schematic, which interpolates the z depth in both x and y directions across the triangle. The data loaded for a triangle before the scan line on which the triangle first becomes active is the initial z value, and also x- and y-increments. At the start of each scan line, the z value is stored in the **left** register. On every pixel clock cycle, the x-increment is added to the current z value, interpolating triangle surface depth from left to right across the image. At the end of each scan line, the y-increment value is added to the stored z value from the **left** register, and this is used for subsequent x-interpolation on the next scan line. In this way, the z depth at each pixel in the triangle is computed.

Note that the interpolation is across the *entire* scan line, regardless of where the triangle is actually active. This saves having to activate the interpolation part way through a scan line, without affecting the interpolated value within the triangle in any way*.

Each Z-unit compares the z value input from the preceding Triangle Processor to that locally computed. When the current pixel falls within the local triangle (as determined by the X-unit), *and* when the z depth of the local triangle is less than that for triangles computed by preceding Triangle Processors for this pixel, the local triangle "wins", and will be visible in the image (unless some other triangle later in the pipeline subsequently wins over it). For a winning triangle, the interpolated z depth at this pixel is propagated to the next Triangle Processor in the pipeline; otherwise, the previous best z from the preceding Triangle Processors will be passed forward unchanged.

If a pixel is unclaimed by any triangle, the z value is undefined, and is usually set to the back clipping plane value.

7.3 The N-Unit. Figure 6 shows a schematic of an N-unit. Three such units N_x, N_y, and N_z are used to interpolate the surface normal vector **N** over the triangle. Before the triangle becomes active, an initial **N** vector is loaded, along with x- and y-increments. The x-increment updates the **N** vector across each scan line, while the y-increment updates the **N** vector at the end of each scan line, just as in the Z-unit. The output multiplexer selects the locally interpolated **N** normal vector if the local triangle pixel "wins", and is to be substituted; otherwise the input **N** normal value from the previous best triangle is propagated.

The value interpolated is the normal vector to the surface of the winning triangle at the point center of the current pixel. Implementing the interpolation in this fashion ensures that all triangles are uniformly sampled and avoids a number of aliasing artifacts and "holes" in the image.

7.4 The M-Unit. The M-unit latches the 9-bit material index of the local triangle during load time. At each pixel, the input material index is propagated, unless the local triangle wins, in which case the stored material index is substituted.

7.5 Commands. The Triangle Processor control unit sequences the N, Z, X, and M-units in response to commands received via the command data bus. Only nine commands are needed:

RESET Global reset. Force all Triangle Processors to state **free**.

ENABLE Global enable. Set the enable bit in all Triangle Processors.

IDLE No operation. Used to pad processing.

NEW Header of an eight word packet of new triangle data.

SOL Start of line. Used to mark an eight word header starting rasterization for each line.

EOL End of line. Used to terminate rasterization of each line.

RAZ Rasterization command. Represents a background pixel to be processed.

RAZD Rasterization command with data. Represents a pixel previously claimed by some triangle.

EXT External commands. Normal Vector Shader commands and other user defined non-Triangle Processor commands.

7.6 Additional Features.

- The Triangle Processor includes support for simple 2×2 "screen-door" translucency.

- Line strokes can be displayed efficiently by converting them to parallelograms (a special case of a triangle with parallel sides, with the point cut off prematurely).

- Because the fixed-point bit position is externally selectable, the 24-bits of accuracy in x and y values allow a large variety of screen address ranges. Note that the internal registers and data paths of the Triangle Processor chip have a few more bits than the width of the data paths off-chip, to maintain interpolation accuracy, while keeping the pin-count down.

- A number of features facilitate testing of the chips. These include the ability to map out defective processors, which can reduce the cost of building the chips, as those with some fabrication defects are still usable.

8 SIMPLIFIED LIGHTING MODEL

The GSP-NVS lighting model is similar to that used in most software based polygon display systems, but is more sophisticated than any other video rate hardware systems to date. Most high speed graphics systems only apply their lighting model at the vertices of polygons, obtaining an RGB value for each vertex. These color values are interpolated across the face of the polygon (Gouraud shading). We apply our full Phong lighting model to each pixel, for inherently superior shading. Our "Normal Vector Shader" (NVS) chips implement, in silicon, all interior shading methods, and full lighting and depth cueing equations, as specified by the PHIGS+ proposal [15], except point and cone light sources. Five planar, colored light sources are simultaneously supported at full speed.

---

* Small triangles having large curvatures have very large increment values; this is not a problem, as we simply subtract enough from the initial value, allowing for the overflow wrap-around which may occur, so that the value is correct within the area of the triangle.

Given as input the un-normalized surface normal vector $\mathbf{N}'$, and the internally interpolated un-normalized viewpoint vector $\mathbf{V}'$, we first compute re-normalised values $\mathbf{N}$ and $\mathbf{V}$, and also a reflection vector $\mathbf{R}$:

$$\mathbf{N} = \frac{\mathbf{N}'}{\sqrt{\mathbf{N}' \cdot \mathbf{N}'}}, \quad \mathbf{V} = \frac{\mathbf{V}'}{\sqrt{\mathbf{V}' \cdot \mathbf{V}'}}, \quad \mathbf{R} = 2(\mathbf{N} \cdot \mathbf{V})\mathbf{N} - \mathbf{V}.$$

From these values, the **RGB** color is computed:

$$\mathbf{RGB} = \sum_{i=1}^{i=5} [(\mathbf{N} \cdot \mathbf{L}_i + la_i)\mathbf{mc} + (\mathbf{R} \cdot \mathbf{L}_i)^{sp}]\,\mathbf{lc}_i.$$

Here $\mathbf{L}_i$, $\mathbf{lc}_i$, and la_i are the normal to, color of, and ambient component, respectively, of the ith light source, and $\mathbf{mc}$ and sp are the color of, and specular power of the material under illumination, looked-up with the material index of the pixel. The square root, power function, and specular reflection coefficient (not shown) are implemented via on-chip ROM tables. It is beyond the scope of this paper to describe all the details of the full lighting model, which include depth cueing, intensity of specular illumination, built-in simple environment map (including reflections – as seen in Figure 1), and hooks for texture maps, shadows, and local light sources.

9 LIGHTING MODEL CHIP

The illumination pipe of the GSP-NVS system consists of 16 identical NVS chips, with pin-outs *identical* to the Triangle Processors chip. Each is capable of applying the entire five light source lighting model to a single pixel (surface normal vector $\mathbf{N}'$ + depth z + material index M) in 16 clock cycles. Round robin scheduling enables the 16 chips in the pipe to shade a stream of pixels at the full clock rate.

Internally the NVS chips are heavily pipelined, and in fact take 64 clock cycles to shade each pixel. However, four pixels can be at various stages of shading at the same time, providing the 16 clock cycle throughput per chip. Figure 7 displays the specialized vector function units of the NVS chip, which are the key to the efficiency of the NVS pipeline (two billion multiplies per second with 16 chips). They allow for efficient area layout, as well as simplified scheduling. An alternative to building a custom lighting model engine would be to use a general purpose DSP chip. However, such chips typically contain only a single scalar function unit, and for a given area of silicon, will tend to be at least an order of magnitude slower than our custom chips. For example, the DSP32 chips employed in the Pixel Machine [9] individually run at 10 million multiply-adds per second, and it would take *at least* 200 of these chips (with several support chips each) to perform the equivalent computation.

10 TRIANGLE PIPE OVERFLOW

The previous discussion has assumed that there were a sufficient number of Triangle Processors to handle all the triangles active on a particular scan line; in other words, no overflow. Our strategy for dealing with overflow is to always detect it *before* it occurs. This allows us to split the problem into two tasks: overflow detection and overflow correction.

For detection, we must know the number of Triangle Processors in the **free** state at any time. To this end, the

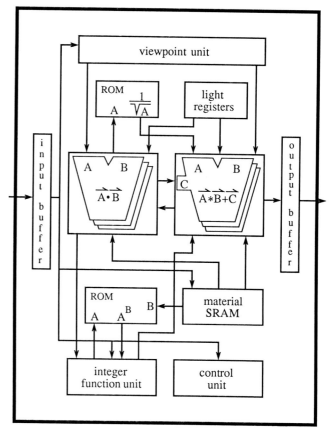

Figure 7: Block diagram of the Normal Vector Shader chip, displaying the internal function units and their (simplified) interconnection.

Y-buffer keeps a **free** counter and an **auxiliary** table. The **free** counter represents the number of Triangle Processors known to be **free** (initially all of them), and the **auxiliary** table records the number of Triangle Processors scheduled to become **free** on a particular scan line. Whenever a new triangle is to be entered into the pipe, the **free** counter is tested: if it is zero, the triangle is *not* entered, and overflow processing commences; otherwise, the counter is decremented, showing one less free Triangle Processor. When a triangle is successfully entered into the pipeline, the scan line on which that triangle ends is computed (by adding the height of the triangle to the current scan line number), and the entry in the **auxiliary** table corresponding to that line is incremented. After each scan line has been processed, the free counter is incremented by the **auxiliary** table entry for the current line, representing the number of Triangle Processors somewhere within the pipe that have just become **free**.

When an overflow condition is detected, the first action is to stop entering new triangles into the pipe, as there are no free Triangle Processors waiting for them. The overflowed triangles are left in the Y-buffer for a second rendering pass, while processing continues for triangles already in the pipe; the resulting pixels are stored in the RGBZ buffer, along with their associated z depth values, which will be used to merge later passes. Subsequent scan lines may or may not also overflow, depending upon the local triangle population growth. At the end of the frame some of the triangles have been rendered into the RGBZ buffer, while the remainder are still waiting in the Y-buffer. Another pass is made, rasterizing some or all of these overflowed triangles; the z values generated by the pipeline are compared with those stored in the RGBZ buffer from previous passes, the pixel with the nearer z value being stored in the buffer as a result. This is repeated as many times as necessary to rasterize all the triangles in the Y-buffer.

While it appears that the machine will take a factor of two hit if even one triangle overflows, and linearly more for each additional pass required, such is not the case. Overflows tend to be localized to a few areas. Hence, the second pass need not rasterize an entire frame of pixels, but only those scan lines touched by overflowed triangles. System simulations have statistically validated this, showing that small overflows tend to increase rasterization time by less than 20%. Large overflows imply large numbers of input triangles, and the extra rasterization passes are overlapped by extra XTC computation time.

One must have enough Triangle Processors in the system to match the throughput of the XTC section. For non-pathological display lists, there is a balance point where the time taken by the XTC to deliver the triangles will always exceed the time taken by the total rasterization process, including multiple overflow passes. This is because both times grow approximately linearly in the number of triangles to be processed. As a specific example, at one million renderable triangles per second, the balance point is on the order of one thousand triangle processors. The balance point also places an upper bound on the required size of the Y-buffer, limiting costs.

In support of multiple rendering passes, the Y-buffer uses a servoing control algorithm that balances overflows of the triangle pipe, the Y-buffer storage, and the XTC. For display lists small enough to be rendered at frame rates (in other words, no overflows), the Y-buffer double buffers frames of triangle data. For larger display lists, the Y-buffer switches into single buffer mode, and after a high water mark, sets the triangle pipe to rasterizing, even though the XTC is still delivering triangles for the current frame. The assumption here is that multiple passes will be required, so the Y-buffer becomes a quantized FIFO between the XTC process and the triangle pipe. Detailed systems simulations have shown this approach to be viable and capable of sustaining full performance.

11   ANTI-ALIASING

While everyone is for anti-aliasing, few wish to pay large amounts extra for it. Thus versions of the Triangle Processor with circuitry to generate pixel percent coverage data were rejected as too inaccurate when high quality was required, and too expensive when only speed was desired.

The single sample per pixel model used by the Triangle Processors avoids a number of smooth-surface aliasing artifacts in previous hardware implementations. This accuracy allows high quality anti-aliased images to be produced by a variety of oversampling techniques.

Within the system, there are two general anti-aliasing hardware support features. Where speed is essential, the system computes 960×1280 images, and then averages blocks of

2×2 pixels in real-time to NTSC video. When accuracy is required, a stochastic sampling is obtained by filtering together multiple renderings of the same display list, but from sub-pixel jitters in viewpoint position. By using a 24-bit per color component accumulator frame buffer, as many different pseudo-random samplings can be summed together as desired. Within each pass the pixel sample positions are coherent with each other, making the technique somewhat more restricted than software implementations of stochastic anti-aliasing [3].

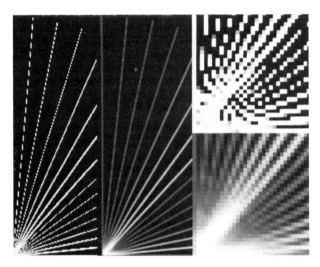

Figure 8: Demonstration of anti-aliasing technique. The image is of a fan of cylinders of random thickness, in the range of 0.6 to 1.6 pixels in width.

Figure 8 displays an example of this technique. The data base is a fan of cylinders of varying thickness, from 0.6 to 1.6 pixels in width. The leftmost image is a single sampling with no anti-aliasing, rendered at 256×96. The upper right insert is a blowup of a portion of this. The middle image is the result of 16 pseudo-stochastic samplings weighted by a Gaussian low-pass filter. To the right is the corresponding blowup of it. This technique was also employed in the making of Figure 1. Other techniques based on stochastic sampling may be implemented on a GSP-NVS system using variations of this approach.

12   SOPHISTICATED EFFECTS

Historically, hard-wired graphics has implied limited rendering models; general purpose machines have had to be used to get most of the recent improvements in graphics algorithms. While machines such as the Pixar [8] and the Pixel Machine [9] seem to cross this line, at heart they are built on top of general purpose processors. Without graphics specific VLSI, the speeds are only fast relative to full general purpose computers. The intent of this section is to show how simple enhancements of the GSP-NVS system can support some very sophisticated options, at speeds orders of magnitude faster than existing hardware. One way or another, such sophisticated options will emerge in hardware systems of the future.

Texture mapping, environment mapping, and shadowing can all be implemented in a related fashion. Each requires an additional frame store, and hardware for a number of transformation functions to generate addresses for this store from rendering information. The data output from the store forms additional lighting model input parameters. These processes must be combined with multiple anti-aliasing passes to sample the data properly.

Texture mapping requires an auxiliary texture map frame store, storing the desired texture(s) at multiple levels of resolution. Three intermediate values a, b, and c, derived from the values of the texture addresses at the corners of the triangles, must be interpolated across the faces of triangles. The final u, v texture map addresses are obtained by performing a perspective division: $u = a/c$, $v = b/c$. The texture map of the appropriate resolution is chosen as a function of the local scale, and can involve a filtered combination of two scales [7]. The three additional interpolations can be performed by a second triangle pipe in parallel with the first, interpolating a, b, and c in place of the surface normal vector. An alternative is to make two passes using a single triangle pipe, once for normals, and then once for a, b, and c, buffering the outputs until needed. The u, v image is sent as a stream of addresses for the texture frame store, resulting in an RGB pixel stream to be sent into the NVS pipe in place of the RGB color indexed by the material tag.

Environment mapping requires the vector computed as the reflectance of the viewpoint vector by the surface normal vector. This value is generated within the NVS chips as part of their normal processing, and a mapping function converts this vector into an environment map address. A simple mapping function is $u = \tan^{-1} R_y/R_x$, $v = R_z$. The RGB output from the environment map is then averaged into the results of the regular lighting model computation, with a mixing factor proportional to surface reflectivity. (Indeed, a simplified version of environment mapping is implemented within the NVS chips for simple color ramps, as seen in Figure 1.)

For shadows, the vector from each light source to the surface must be computed for each pixel. These vectors are used to generate addresses into precomputed depth buffer tables containing the maximum distance to which the light source reaches in each direction. A comparison of the length of the vector with the stored value is used to enable or disable each light source at each pixel in the regular lighting model computation. (Reeves *et al.* [12] discuss depth buffer shadowing with anti-aliasing.)

Since these look-up process for texture, environment mapping and shadowing involve random pixel addressing, the full pipeline rate of the machine will not be sustained. However, with complex images, the rendering stage normally requires multiple passes, balancing the time taken for the table accesses which are only performed once per output pixel.

13   SIMULATORS

The development of a set of simulator tools was tightly coupled with the evolution of the GSP-NVS architecture. The simulators span the range from a high level simulation fast enough to create short video test sequences, to a low level transistor by transistor simulation of the custom graphics chips. All of these simulators maintain the same numerical precision as the real hardware. We used the simulators to verify the algorithms, and also to generate the performance

numbers. All the color images in this paper were generated by the high level simulator, from very complex data bases.

Of course, the ultimate simulation is the real silicon. An incremental approach to the VLSI layout was taken, with individual function units fabricated as separate test chips. This allowed each unit to be fully verified in silicon as the design progressed. Test patterns for the design fragments, and for a complete Triangle Processor, were generated by the software simulators.

14   PERFORMANCE

The GSP-NVS concept and family of VLSI chips can be used to build a variety of high performance graphics systems. We have been designing such a system capable of sustained rendering of one million triangles per second. This system uses twenty 40-Megaflop floating point chips within the transform and clip subsystem to process 1.6 million triangles per second, ensuring adequate throughput at the triangle pipe after various overheads. The display region is split into left and right halves, each with its own 20MHz triangle and NVS pipes. This effectively halves the total time taken to load triangles and rasterize pixels. Thus triangles are loaded at 200ns each, and then the whole region is rendered at 25ns per pixel. The Y-buffer allows transformation and rasterization to be 100% overlapped most of the time.

Figure 9 shows a comparatively simple scene generated by a simulation of the GSP-NVS system. The data base used contained 24 784 triangles, of which 11 327 were visible. Rendered at a resolution of 1280 × 1024, the 1.25 million pixel image would be generated in less than one twentieth of a second. Note that the triangle load time was less than 5% of the total frame time, indicating that the system was running at only a quarter of its capacity. Simulations of larger display lists involving multiple triangle pipe overflows have shown rendering times to scale almost linearly. More aggressive uses of additional rendering pipes can lead to processing rates upwards of five million triangles per second.

15   CONCLUSIONS

We have described a highly parallel 3D graphics architecture based upon a pipeline of VLSI chips, which overcomes the frame-buffer DRAM access bottleneck present in all of today's general commercial systems. Our architecture achieves at least an order of magnitude increase in rendering rate over previous systems, so that much more complex scenes can be rendered in a reasonable time. A further pipeline of dedicated lighting model chips enhances the reality of the output with no loss in speed.

An additional improvement in speed over present systems is achieved by decoupling the transformation process from the rendering process using a large buffer; this keeps both processes running in parallel for the majority of the time. The architecture has been tuned to support the statistical mix of geometry encountered in *real* applications, rather than simplified benchmarks.

Our sampling model is built on a mathematically sound basis, similar to that used in ray-casting techniques. This avoids a number of aliasing artifacts and holes inherent in

Figure 9: Example of 1280 × 1024 20Hz frame rate performance.

Figure 10: Example of complex mechanical CAD object. Satellite database courtesy of NASA JPL.

many other polygon fill algorithms. It also allows the system to be extended to support a number of sophisticated rendering techniques; for example we have already simulated a form of stochastic anti-aliasing.

It is no longer sufficient to concentrate on only a single aspect of the 3D graphics problem; we believe that to obtain significant improvements for *real* applications, the entire rendering process must be balanced from display list to photon. GSP-NVS represents our attempt to advance the state of the art.

ACKNOWLEDGMENTS

The authors would like to thank the Applicon hardware crew: Brian Schroeder, Tony Barkans, Roger Day, Dorothy Gordon, Tom Durant, Jorge Lach, Mark Turner, Mark Hood, Gene Pinkston, Mike Garrity, Stan Sclaroff, and Peter Masters for their efforts in the development of the system. Glen Stone was responsible for the early layout of the Triangle Processor. We would also like to thank Dick Lyon for comments on the VLSI design, Steve Rubin for the Electric VLSI design system and the support thereof, and Shane Robison for his support of us.

A WHAT'S IN A TRIANGLE ?

The GSP-NVS system supports the RISC primitive of 3D graphics: the triangle. For our system to support non-uniform rational B-splines (NURBS) as a primitive, they would have to be tessellated into triangles at extremely high speed, in excess of one million triangles per second. The computational overhead of doing this to complex objects was considered too high. The major problem with building hardware to directly tessellate NURBS is dealing with the trimming curves.

As is the case with many other complex computational systems, there is great confusion in benchmarking the performance of 3D display systems. There are many assumptions: what percent backface rejection?, clipping enabled?, what lighting model?, area of polygon?, what is a polygon? Typically the benchmark represents a "never to be

exceeded" performance number. The benchmark for a particular system usually consists of identical polygons which are sized such that the transformation and clipping time exactly equals the polygon pixel fill time. This is reminiscent of similar "creative" benchmarks of identical length vectors that were used to benchmark vector stroke displays 20 years ago. They provide very little insight as to where and how much to improve the performance of 3D display systems. Thus, one of the first tasks of the GSP-NVS project was to create some more realistic benchmarks.

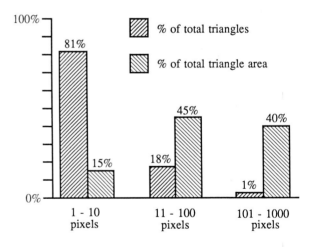

Figure 11: Percentage of triangles and triangle area for the cubes in Figure 1 sorted by the area of the triangle.

Figure 1 displays an image of nine rounded cubes, formed of 9 × 956 triangles, of which 3 986 were non back-facing and were rendered. The triangles in this figure (rendered at 480 × 484) were grouped by their displayed area into three categories, as shown in the chart in Figure 11. In each category, the left bar shows the relative *number* of triangles in the group, while the right bar shows the relative *area* contributed by triangles in that group. The three groups roughly correspond to three classes of polygons: a few large ones (the flat faces of the cubes), a number of long thin ones (the rounded edges), and a large number of very small ones (the rounded corners), of which many are sub-pixel in size. While this scene was somewhat artificial, experiments with a number of other objects from real mechanical CAD data bases bore out similar results. This chart gives part of the reason why real world applications typically run *at least* two to four times slower than the theoretical peak rate of the graphics system. The activity of the transform and clip section is proportional to the height of the left boxes in each group, while rasterization activity is proportional to the height of the right boxes. For any given triangle size, typically only one of the two processes is active. Thus most polygons are either transform bound *or* polygon fill bound, resulting in significant idle time for the other process. This is responsible for nearly a factor of two reduction is speed over the "perfect" case. Additional reductions arise from idle rasterization cycles due to long chains of triangles that are back-facing or outside the clipping window, as well as overhead for starting a new triangle, moving to the next scan line, et cetera.

An increase in graphics performance is more likely to cause users to display more complex objects, rather than the same objects faster. This is the so-called "four second" rule. Figure 10 (1280 × 1024) displays an extremely large CAD object (by present standards). It represents a 70 000 triangle simplification of a 1 000 000 triangle satellite. Two trends appear in this and other similar objects that we have examined: realistic background environments will almost always cover every pixel in the frame at least once; and more detailed, more complex objects will involve large numbers of small polygons. Furthermore, the mid-size polygons tend to be long and very thin, bordering on sub-pixel. From statistics of these objects we have concluded that pixel fill architectures using $n \times m$ block write schemes will be less effective than might be assumed. We simulated a number of different block sizes, applied to the data base of Figure 1 (without ground pattern), and the resulting write efficiencies are given in Table 1.

Total Write Efficiency	
Block Size	Pixels written/cycle
1 × 1	0.69
2 × 1	1.04
2 × 2	1.57
4 × 1	1.41
4 × 2	2.22
4 × 4	3.10
8 × 4	4.04
8 × 8	5.27

Table 1: Efficiency of various parallel write architectures.

The statistics are only for *rendered triangles*. The 1 × 1 number is less than unity because of triangles not containing valid sample points on every scan line. All these numbers would be even lower if back-facing and clipped triangles were to be counted.

References

[1] **Gary Bishop and David M. Weimer.** Fast Phong shading. Proceedings of SIGGRAPH'86 (Dallas, Texas, August 18-22, 1986). In *Computer Graphics*, pages 103–106, 1986.

[2] **James. H. Clark.** The geometry engine, a VLSI geometry system for graphics. Proceedings of SIGGRAPH'82 (Boston, Massachusetts, July 26-30, 1982). In *Computer Graphics*, pages 127–133, 1982.

[3] **Robert. L. Cook.** Stochastic sampling in computer graphics. *ACM Transactions on Computer Graphics*, 5(1):51–72, January 1986.

[4] **Stefan Demetrescu.** High speed image rasterization using scan line access memories. In *1985 Chapel Hill Conference on Very Large Scale Integration*, pages 221–243, Computer Science Press, 1985.

[5] **Henry Fuchs and John Poulton.** Pixel-planes: a VLSI-oriented design for a raster graphics engine. *VLSI Design*, 2(3):20–28, 1981.

[6] **Nader Gharachorloo and Christopher Pottle.** SUPER BUFFER: a systolic VLSI graphics engine for real time raster image generation. In *1985 Chapel Hill Conference on Very Large Scale Integration*, pages 285–305, Computer Science Press, 1985.

[7] **Paul S. Heckbert.** Survey of texture mapping. *IEEE Computer Graphics and Applications*, 6(11):56–67, November 1986.

[8] **Adam Levinthal and Thomas Porter.** Chap - a SIMD graphics processor. Proceedings of SIGGRAPH'84 (Minneapolis, Minnesota, July 23-27, 1984). In *Computer Graphics*, pages 77–82, 1984.

[9] **Leonard McMillan.** Graphics at 820 MFLOPS. *ESD: THE Electronic Systems Design Magazine*, 17(9):87–95, September 1987.

[10] **Teiji Nishizawa** *et al.* A hidden surface processor for 3-dimension graphics. In *Proceedings of ISSCC'88*, pages 166–167,351, 1988.

[11] **John Poulton** *et al.* PIXEL-PLANES: building a VLSI-based graphic system. In *1985 Chapel Hill Conference on Very Large Scale Integration*, pages 35–60, Computer Science Press, 1985.

[12] **William T. Reeves, David H. Salesin, and Robert L. Cook.** Rendering antialiased shadows with depth maps. Proceedings of SIGGRAPH'87 (Anaheim, California, July 27-31, 1987). In *Computer Graphics*, pages 283–291, 1987.

[13] **Roger W. Swanson and Larry J. Thayer.** A fast shaded-polygon renderer. Proceedings of SIGGRAPH'86 (Dallas, Texas, August 18-22, 1986). In *Computer Graphics*, pages 95–101, 1986.

[14] **John G. Torborg.** A parallel processor architecture for graphics arithmetic operations. Proceedings of SIGGRAPH'87 (Anaheim, California, July 27-31, 1987). In *Computer Graphics*, pages 197–204, 1987.

[15] **Andries van Dam** *et al.* PHIGS+ functional description rev. 2.0. July 20 1987. Jointly developed PHIGS+ specification.

An Efficient Algorithm for Finding
the CSG Representation of a Simple Polygon*

David Dobkin[1], Leonidas Guibas[2,3], John Hershberger[3], and Jack Snoeyink[2]

[1]Princeton University, [2]Stanford University, [3]DEC Systems Research Center

Abstract

We consider the problem of converting boundary representations
of polyhedral objects into constructive-solid-geometry (CSG)
representations. The CSG representations for a polyhedron P are
based on the half-spaces supporting the faces of P. For certain
kinds of polyhedra this problem is equivalent to the corresponding problem for simple polygons in the plane. We give a new
proof that the interior of each simple polygon can be represented
by a monotone boolean formula based on the half-planes supporting the sides of the polygon and using each such half-plane
only once. Our main contribution is an efficient and practical
$O(n \log n)$ algorithm for doing this boundary-to-CSG conversion
for a simple polygon of n sides. We also prove that such nice
formulæ do not always exist for general polyhedra in three dimensions.

CR Categories and Subject Descriptions: F.2.2 [**Analysis
of Algorithms and Problem Complexity**]: Nonnumerical
Algorithms and Problems–Geometrical problems and computations; Computations on discrete structures; I.3.5 [**Computer
Graphics**]: Computational Geometry and Object Modeling–
Curve, surface, solid, and object representations; Geometric algorithms, languages, and systems

General Terms: Algorithms, theory

Additional Key Words and Phrases: Solid modeling,
constructive solid geometry, boundary-to-CSG conversion algorithms, simple polygons

*The first author would like to acknowledge the support of the National
Science Foundation under Grant CCR87-00917. The fourth author was supported in part by a National Science Foundation Graduate Fellowship. This
work was begun while the first author was visiting the DEC Systems Research Center.

1 Preliminaries

One of the most important topics in solid modeling is the mathematical representation of solid objects. It is desirable that such
representations be compact and efficient in the simulation of the
real-world operations that we may wish to perform on the objects. Over the years two different styles of representation have
emerged; these are used by nearly all geometric modeling systems currently in existence. The first style of representation describes an object by the collection of surface elements forming its
boundary: this is a *boundary representation*. In effect, boundary representations reduce the solid modeling problem to that of
representing surface elements. This is a somewhat simpler problem, since we work in one dimension less. The second style of
representation describes a solid object as being constructed by
regularized boolean operations on some simple primitive solids,
such as boxes, spheres, cylinders, etc. Such a description is referred to as a constructive solid geometry representation, or *CSG
representation*, for short. Each style of representation has its
advantages and disadvantages, depending on the operations we
wish to perform on the objects. The reader is referred to one
of the standard texts in solid modeling [12, 15], or the review
article [21] for further details on these representations and their
relative merits.

If one looks at modelers in either camp, for example the ROMU-
LUS [15], GEOMOD [23], and MEDUSA [16] modelers of the boundary persuasion, or the PADL-1 [25], PADL-2 [2], and GMSOLID [1]
modelers of the CSG persuasion, one nearly always finds provi-
sions for converting to the other representation. This is an important and indispensable step that poses some challenging computational problems[1]. In this paper we will deal with certain cases
of the boundary-to-CSG conversion problem and present some
efficient computational techniques for doing the conversion.

Peterson [19] considered the problem of obtaining a CSG representation for simple polyhedral solids, such as prisms or pyramids (not necessarily convex), based on the half-spaces supporting the faces of the solid. Such solids are in effect two-dimensional
objects (think of the base of the prism or pyramid) in which
the third dimension has been added in a very simple manner.
Thus Peterson considered the problem of finding CSG representations for simple polygons in the plane; this problem is related
to the problem of finding convex decompositions of simple poly-

[1]To quote from [21]: "..the relative paucity of known conversion algorithms poses significant constraints on the geometric modeling systems that
we can build today."

gons [3, 17, 18, 24, 26]. By a complicated argument, Peterson proved that every simple polygon in the plane admits of a representation by a boolean formula based on the half-planes supporting its sides. This formula is especially nice in that it is monotone (no complementation is needed) and each of the supporting half-planes appears in the formula exactly once. We call such a formula a *Peterson-style formula*.

In this paper we first give a short and elegant new proof that every polygon has a Peterson-style formula (Section 3). Peterson did not explicitly consider algorithms for deriving this CSG representation from the polygon. A naïve implementation based on his proof would require $\Theta(n^2)$ time for the conversion, where n is the size (number of sides or vertices) of the polygon. We provide in this paper an efficient $\Theta(n \log n)$ algorithm for doing this boundary-to-CSG conversion (Section 4). We regard this algorithm as the major contribution of our paper; the algorithm uses many interesting techniques from the growing field of computational geometry [4, 20]. Nevertheless, it is very simple to code—its subtlety lies in the analysis of the performance and not in the implementation. Finally (Section 5), we show that Peterson-style formulæ are not always possible for general polyhedra in three dimensions and discuss a number of related issues.

We believe that the work presented in this paper illustrates how several of the concepts and techniques of computational geometry can be used to solve problems that are of clear importance in solid modeling and computer graphics. The solution that we obtain is both mathematically interesting and practical to implement. We expect to see more such applications of computational geometry to other areas in the future and hope that this paper will motivate some researchers in the graphics area to study computational geometry techniques more closely.

2 Formulation and history of the problem

Let P be a simple polygon in the plane; in this context, simple means non-self-intersecting. By the Jordan curve theorem, such a polygon subdivides the plane into two regions, its interior and its exterior. In general, we identify the polygon with its interior. Let us orient all the edges of P so that the interior of P lies locally to the right of each edge, and give each such oriented edge a name. We will call these names *literals*. To each literal we also give a second meaning. A literal m also represents the half-plane bounded by the infinite line supporting the edge m and extending to the right of that line. We will speak of such a half-plane as *supporting* the polygon (even though P might not all lie in the half-plane). See Figure 1 for an illustration of these concepts.

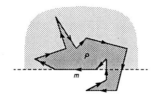

Figure 1: A simple polygon P and the half-plane supporting side m

Notice that, for each point x of the plane, if we know whether x lies inside or outside each of the half-planes supporting P, then we know in fact if x is inside P. This follows, because each of the regions into which the plane is subdivided by the infinite extensions of the sides of P lies either wholly inside P, or wholly outside it. As a result, there must exist a boolean formula whose atoms are the literals of P and which expresses the

interior of P. For example, if P is convex, then this formula is simply the "and" of all the literals.

Since "and"s and "or"s are somewhat cumbersome to write, we will switch at this point to algebraic notation and use multiplication conventions for "and" and addition conventions for "or". Consider the two simple polygons shown in Figure 2. Formulæ for the two polygons are $uv(w(x + y) + z)$ for polygon (a) and $uvw(x + y + z)$ for polygon (b). The associated boolean expression trees are also shown in Figure 2. Notice that these are Peterson-style formulæ: they are monotone and use each literal exactly once. The reader is invited at this point to make sure that these formulæ are indeed correct.

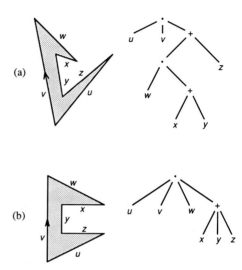

Figure 2: Formulæ for two polygons

A more complex formula for a simple polygon was given by Guibas, Ramshaw, and Stolfi [8] in their kinetic framework paper. That style of formula for the two polygons of Figure 2 is $\overline{u\overline{v} \oplus v\overline{w} \oplus w\overline{x} \oplus \overline{x}y \oplus \overline{y}z \oplus z\overline{u}}$. Here $\oplus$ denotes logical "xor" and the overbar denotes complementation. As explained in [8], that type of formula is purely local, in that it depends only on the convex vs. concave property of successive angles of the polygon. The rule should be obvious from the example: as we go around, we complement the second literal corresponding to a vertex if we are at a convex angle, and the first literal if we are at a concave angle. Thus the formula is the same for both of the example polygons.

Although a formula of this style is trivial to write down, it is not as desirable in solid modeling as a Peterson-style formula, because of the use of complementation and the "xor" operator. The Peterson formula is more involved to derive, because it captures in a sense how the polygon nests within itself and thus is more global in character. It can be viewed naïvely as an inclusion-exclusion style formula that reflects this global structure of the polygon. We caution the reader, however, that this view of the Peterson formula is too naïve and gave rise to a couple of flawed approaches to this problem.

In general there are many boolean formulæ that express a simple polygon in terms of its literals. Proving the equivalence of two boolean formulæ for the same polygon is a non-trivial exercise. The reason is that of the 2^n primitive "and" terms one can form on n literals (with complementation allowed), only $\Theta(n^2)$ are non-zero, in the sense that they denote non-empty regions of the plane. Thus numerous identities hold and must be used in proving formula equivalence.

The decomposition of a simple polygon into convex pieces [3, 17, 18, 24, 26] gives another kind of boolean formula for the polygon, one in which the literals are not half-planes, but convex polygons. Depending on the type of decomposition desired, the convex polygons may or may not overlap; in the overlapping case, the formula may or may not contain negations. If we expand the literals in a convex decomposition into "and"s of half-planes, the result need not be a Peterson style formula: negations, repeated literals, and half-planes that do not support the polygon are all possible.

If we leave the boolean domain and allow algebraic formulæ for describing the characteristic function of a simple polygon, then such formulæ that are purely local (in the same sense as the above "xor" formula) are given in a paper of Franklin [5]. Franklin gives algebraic local formulæ for polyhedra as well. We do not discuss this further here as it goes beyond the CSG representations we are concerned with.

3   The existence of monotone formulæ

In this section we will prove that the interior of every simple polygon P in the plane can be expressed by a Peterson-style formula, that is, a monotone boolean formula in which each literal corresponding to a side of P appears exactly once.

As it turns out, it is more natural to work with simple bi-infinite polygonal chains (or *chains*, for short) than with simple polygons. An example of a simple bi-infinite chain c is shown in Figure 3. Such a chain c is terminated by two semi-infinite rays and in between contains an arbitrary number of finite sides. Because it is simple and bi-infinite, it subdivides the plane into two regions. We will in general orient c in a consistent manner, so we can speak of the region of the plane lying to the left of c, or to the right of c, respectively. By abuse of language, we will refer to these regions as *half-spaces*.

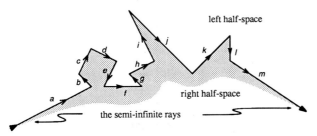

Figure 3: A simple bi-infinite chain

The interior of a simple polygon P can always be viewed as the intersection of two such chain half-spaces. Let ℓ and r denote respectively the leftmost and rightmost vertex of P. As in Figure 4, extend the sides of P incident to ℓ infinitely far to the left, and the sides incident to r infinitely far to the right. It is clear that we thus obtain two simple bi-infinite chains and that the interior of P is the intersection of the half-space below the upper chain with the half-space above the lower chain. Notice also that the literals used by the upper and lower chains for these two

half-spaces form a partition of the literals of P. Thus it suffices to prove that a chain half-space admits of a monotone formula using each of its literals exactly once.

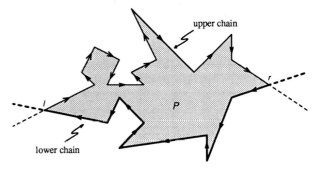

Figure 4: The interior of a simple polygon P

We will prove this fact by showing that, for any chain c, there always exists a vertex v of c such that if we extend the edges incident to v infinitely far to the other side of v, these extensions do not intersect c anywhere. In particular, the extensions create two new simple bi-infinite chains c_1 and c_2 that, as before, partition the literals used by c. See Figure 5 for an example. It is easy to see that the half-space to the right (say) of c is then either the intersection or the union of the half-spaces to the right of c_1 and c_2. It will be the intersection if the angle of c at v in the selected half-space is convex (as is the situation in Figure 5), and the union if this angle is concave.

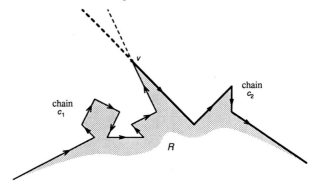

Figure 5: The splitting vertex v for a chain c

The existence of the desired vertex v is relatively easy to establish. Of the two half-spaces defined by c there is one that is bounded by the two semi-infinite rays in a "convex" fashion. What we mean by this is that when we look at this half-space from a great distance above the xy-plane (so we can only discern the semi-infinite rays bounding it) it appears as a convex angle ($\leq \pi$). For example, in Figure 5, the right half-space R of c is the convex one. If we now look at the convex hull $h(R)$, this hull will be a polygon whose vertices are vertices of c. Clearly at least one such vertex has to exist, and any vertex on this hull is a good vertex at which to break c, that is, it can serve as the vertex v of the previous argument. The reason is clear from Figure 6: at any such vertex the extensions of the sides incident upon it cannot intersect c again.

It is worth remarking here that the determination of the splitting vertex v in the above manner is not at all influenced by

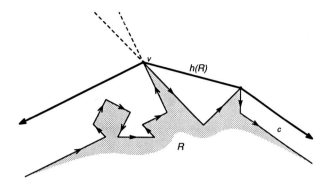

Figure 6: The convex hull $h(R)$

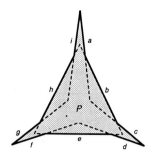

Figure 7: Our methods cannot obtain all valid formulæ for this polygon

whether we are are trying to obtain a boolean formula for the right half-space of c or the left half-space of c. The choice of which half-space to take the convex hull of is determined solely by the behavior of the semi-infinite rays of c. Indeed, if we were to choose the wrong ("concave") half-space, its convex hull would be the whole plane and would contain no vertices. We can summarize the situation by saying that we always split at a vertex of the convex hull of the polygonal chain c; this definition automatically selects the correct half-space.

By recursively applying this decomposition procedure until each subchain becomes a single bi-infinite straight line we can conclude the following theorem.

Theorem 3.1 *Every half-space bounded by a simple bi-infinite polygonal chain has a monotone boolean formula using each of the literals of the chain exactly once. The same holds for the interior of any finite simple polygon.*

If we are given a polygonal chain c, such as the one in Figure 3, then certain aspects of the boolean formula of (say) the right half-space R of c can be immediately deduced by inspection. For example, it follows from the above arguments that there exists a boolean formula for R that not only uses each literal exactly once, but in fact contains these literals in the order in which they appear along c: if we were to omit the boolean operators and parentheses in the formula, we would just get a string of all the literals in c in order. Furthermore, the boolean operators between these literals are easy to deduce. As the previous discussion makes clear, between two literals that define a convex angle in R the corresponding operator has to be an "and", and between two literals that define a concave angle the corresponding operator has to be an "or". Thus, with parentheses omitted, the boolean formula for the chain c in Figure 3 has to look like $a + bcde + f + gh + ij + kl + m$.

This shows that the crux of the difficulty in the boolean formula problem is to obtain the parenthesization, or equivalently, the sequence of the appropriate splitting vertices. We call this the *recursive chain-splitting problem* for a simple bi-infinite chain. The solution of this problem is the topic of the next section. For the chain of Figure 3 a valid solution is $((a + bc)(de + f) + g(h + i))(j + k(l + m))$.

We conclude by noticing that our procedure for solving this problem is non-deterministic, since in general we will have a choice of several splitting vertices. We can in fact simultaneously split at any subset of them. Still, not all valid Peterson-style formalæ for a simple polygon are obtained in this fashion. Our formulæ all have the property that the literals appear in the formula in the same order as in the polygon. Figure 7 shows an example of a Peterson-style formula where that is not true: a valid formula for the polygon shown is $(a + c)(d + f)(g + i) + beh$.

4   The conversion algorithm

We have seen in Section 3 that we can find a monotone boolean formula for a simple polygon if we can solve the following *recursive chain-splitting problem*:

> Given a simple bi-infinite polygonal chain with at least two edges, find a vertex z of its convex hull. Split the chain in two at z and extend to infinity the two edges incident to z, forming two new chains. Because z is on the convex hull, both chains are simple. Recursively solve the same problem for each chain that has at least two edges.

This section presents an $O(n \log n)$ algorithm to solve the chain-splitting problem, where n is the number of vertices of the polygon P. The algorithm uses only simple data structures and is straightforward to implement.

Before we describe our algorithm, let us consider a naïve alternative to it. Many algorithms have been published that find the convex hull of a simple polygon in linear time [6, 14, 10, 13, 22]. With slight modifications, any of these algorithms can be used to find a vertex on the hull of a simple bi-infinite polygonal chain. If we use such an algorithm to solve the recursive hull splitting problem, the running time is $O(n)$ plus the time needed to solve the two subproblems recursively. The worst-case running time $t(n)$ is given by the recurrence

$$t(n) = \max_{0 < k < n} (t(k) + t(n - k)) + O(n),$$

which has solution $t(n) = O(n^2)$.

This quadratic behavior occurs in the worst case, shown in Figure 8a, because each recursive step spends linear time splitting a single edge off the end of the path. In the best case, on the other hand, each split divides the current path roughly in half, and the algorithm runs in $O(n \log n)$ time. This asymptotic behavior can be obtained for the path shown in Figure 8b, if the splitting vertices are chosen wisely.

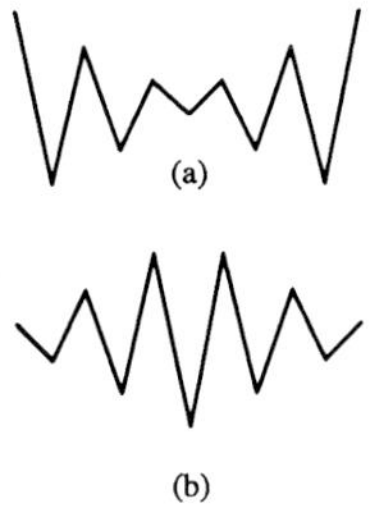

Figure 8: Paths with worst- and best-case splitting behavior

The best case of this naïve algorithm is like a standard divide-and-conquer approach: at each step the algorithm splits the current path roughly in half. In general, however, it is difficult to guarantee an even division, since all vertices on the convex hull might be extremely close to the two ends of the path. Thus, to avoid quadratic behavior, we must instead split each path using less than linear time. Other researchers have solved similar problems by making the splitting cost depend only on the size of the smaller fragment [7, 9]. If the running time $t(n)$ obeys the recurrence

$$t(n) = \max_{0 < k < n} (t(k) + t(n - k)) + O(\min(k, n - k)),$$

then $t(n) = O(n \log n)$. Our method uses a similar idea: the splitting cost is $O(\log n)$ plus a term that is linear in the size of one of the two fragments. The fragment is not necessarily the smaller of the two, but we can bound its size so as to ensure an $O(n \log n)$ running time overall. The details of this argument appear in Section 4.5.

We present our algorithm in several steps. We first make a few definitions, then give an overview of our approach. We follow the informal overview with a pseudo-code description of the algorithm. Section 4.3 gives more detail on one of the pseudo-code operations, and Section 4.4 describes the data structure used by the algorithm. Section 4.5 concludes the presentation of the algorithm by analyzing its running time.

4.1 Definitions

As shown in Section 3, we can find a boolean formula for P by splitting the polygon at its leftmost and rightmost vertices to get two paths, then working on the two paths separately. We denote by π the current path, either upper or lower. If u and v are vertices of π, we use the notation $\pi(u, v)$ to refer to the subpath of π between u and v, inclusive. The convex hull of a set of points A is denoted by $h(A)$; we use $h(u, v)$ as shorthand for $h(\pi(u, v))$. A path $\pi(u, v)$ has $|\pi(u, v)|$ edges; similarly, $|h(u, v)|$ is the number of edges on $h(u, v)$.

We can use the path $\pi(u, v)$ to specify a bi-infinite chain by extending its first and last edges. Let e_u be the edge of $\pi(u, v)$ incident to u, and let $\vec{e_u}$ be the ray obtained by extending e_u beyond u. Let e_v and $\vec{e_v}$ be defined similarly. Then $\pi(u, v)$ specifies the bi-infinite polygonal chain obtained by replacing e_u by $\vec{e_u}$ and e_v by $\vec{e_v}$. In general, for arbitrary u and v, this bi-infinite chain need not be simple. Our algorithm, however, will guarantee the simplicity of each bi-infinite chain it considers. We assume in what follows that $\vec{e_u}$ and $\vec{e_v}$ are not parallel, but only

slight modifications to the algorithm are needed if this is not true.

4.2 The algorithm

This section presents the algorithm that recursively splits a polygonal chain. We first outline the algorithm and then present it in a pseudo-code format. Subsequent sections give the details of the operations sketched in this section.

We now outline the algorithm. Given a polygonal path $\pi(u, v)$ with at least two edges, we partition it at a vertex x to get two pieces $\pi(u, x)$ and $\pi(x, v)$ with roughly the same number of edges. Note that x is not necessarily a vertex of $h(u, v)$; this partitioning is merely preparatory to splitting $\pi(u, v)$ at a hull vertex. In $O(|\pi(u, v)|)$ time we compute the convex hulls of $\pi(u, x)$ and $\pi(x, v)$ in such a way that for any vertex z of $\pi(u, v)$, we can easily find $h(x, z)$. Our data structure lets us account for the cost of finding $h(x, z)$ as part of the cost of building $h(u, x)$ and $h(x, v)$. The details of this accounting appear in Section 4.5.

The next step of the algorithm locates a vertex z of the convex hull of the bi-infinite chain $\pi(u, v) \cup \vec{e_u} \cup \vec{e_v}$. We will split $\pi(u, v)$ at z. The vertex z can be on the path $\pi(u, x)$ or on the path $\pi(x, v)$. Without loss of generality let us assume that z is a vertex of $\pi(u, x)$; note that z cannot be u. We recursively split $\pi(u, z)$, partitioning it at its midpoint, building convex hulls, and so on. However, and this is the key observation, we do not have to do as much work for $\pi(z, v)$ if $z \neq x$. We already have the hull $h(x, v)$, and we can easily find $h(z, x)$ from our data structure for $h(u, x)$. Thus we can recursively split $\pi(z, v)$ without recomputing convex hulls. Intuitively speaking, we do a full recursion (including convex hull computation) only on pieces whose length is less than half the length of the piece for which we last computed convex hulls.

The key to our algorithm's efficiency is avoiding the recomputation of convex hulls. The naïve algorithm builds $O(n)$ hulls whose average size can be as much as $n/2$; our algorithm also builds $O(n)$ hulls, but their average size is only $O(\log n)$. Our algorithm locates n splitting vertices in $O(\log n)$ time apiece, which contributes another $O(n \log n)$ term to the running time. These two terms dominate the time cost of the algorithm, as Section 4.5 shows.

We present the algorithm more formally in the pseudo-code below. The pseudo-code uses a data structure called the *path hull*, $PH(x, v)$, to represent the convex hull of the path $\pi(x, v)$. This structure stores the vertices of $h(x, v)$ in a linear array. The path hull $PH(x, v)$ is used to produce $PH(x, z)$ efficiently, for any splitting vertex z in $\pi(x, v)$. The algorithm consists of two mutually recursive subroutines, $f()$ and $p()$, whose names stand for *full* and *partial*. The routine $f(u, v)$ partitions $\pi(u, v)$ at x to get two equal parts, builds a path hull structure for each, and calls $p(u, x, v)$. The subroutine $p(u, x, v)$ uses $PH(x, u)$ and $PH(x, v)$ to find the splitting vertex z; Section 4.3 gives the details of this operation. The routine then splits $\pi(u, v)$ at z and recurses on each fragment; it ensures that the required path hulls have been built whenever $p()$ is called. We start the algorithm by invoking $f()$ on the entire path π.

```
    f(u, v)      /* Precondition: u ≠ v */
        begin
1.      if π(u, v) is a single edge then return;
        else
            begin
2.              Let x be the middle vertex of π(u, v);
3.              Build PH(x, u) and PH(x, v);
4.              p(u, x, v);
            end
        end



    p(u, x, v)      /* x is a vertex of π(u, v), not equal to u
                        or v. Path hulls PH(x, v) and PH(x, u)
                        have been computed. */
        begin
5.      Find a vertex z of h(π(u, v) ∪ e⃗_u ∪ e⃗_v), the convex
        hull of the bi-infinite chain specified by π(u, v);
6.      if x = z then begin f(u, x);   f(x, v); end
        else
            begin
7.              Build PH(x, z) from PH(x, u) or PH(x, v), as
                appropriate;
                if z is a vertex of π(u, x) then
8.                  begin f(u, z);   p(z, x, v); end
                else
9.                  begin p(u, x, z);   f(z, v); end
            end
        end


                The chain-splitting algorithm
```

4.3   Finding a splitting vertex

This section shows how to use the path hull data structure to find the splitting vertex z. Our method exploits the fact that $PH(x, v)$ represents $h(x, v)$ as a linear array of convex hull vertices: we perform binary search on the array to find the splitting vertex.

Given a path $\pi(u, v)$, we want to find a vertex of the convex hull of the bi-infinite chain that $\pi(u, v)$ specifies. Each such vertex belongs to the finite convex hull $h(u, v)$; we solve our problem by finding a vertex of $h(u, v)$ that is guaranteed to belong to the infinite hull. The edges of the infinite hull $h(\pi(u, v) \cup \overrightarrow{e_u} \cup \overrightarrow{e_v})$ have slopes in a range bounded by the slopes of $\overrightarrow{e_u}$ and $\overrightarrow{e_v}$. Vertices of the hull have tangent slopes in the same range. We simply find a vertex of $h(u, v)$ with a tangent slope in the range. Let d_u and d_v be the direction vectors of the rays $\overrightarrow{e_u}$ and $\overrightarrow{e_v}$. Because $\overrightarrow{e_u}$ and $\overrightarrow{e_v}$ are not parallel, d_u and d_v define an angular range of less than 180 degrees; define d to be the negative of the bisector of this angular range. An extreme vertex of $h(u, v)$ in direction d is guaranteed to be a vertex of the infinite hull.[2] See Figure 9

---

[2]To avoid computing square roots, in practice we do not compute the bisector of the angle defined by d_u and d_v. Instead, we find the normals to

for an example.

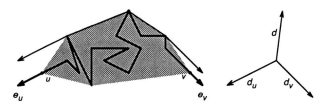

Figure 9: We find an extremal vertex in the direction d

We use binary search on each of the two path hulls $PH(u, x)$ and $PH(x, v)$ to find an extreme vertex in direction d. We compare the two vertices and pick the more extreme of the two. If we break ties consistently in the binary searches and in the comparison of the two extreme vertices (say, by preferring the left vertex of tied pairs), the vertex we find is guaranteed to be a vertex of the infinite hull.

4.4   Implementing path hulls

In this section we describe the path hull data structure used in the previous two sections. The path hull $PH(x, v)$ represents the convex hull of $\pi(x, v)$. It is not symmetric in its arguments: it implicitly represents $h(x, v')$ for all vertices v' in $\pi(x, v)$, but does not represent $h(v', v)$ for any v' not equal to x. The structure $PH(x, v)$ has three essential properties:

1. $PH(x, v)$ represents $h(x, v)$ by a linear array of vertices. Let $\hat{v}$ be the vertex of $h(x, v)$ closest to v on $\pi(x, v)$. Then the array lists the vertices of $h(x, v)$ in clockwise order, starting and ending with $\hat{v}$.

2. Given $PH(x, v)$, we can transform it into $PH(x, v')$ for any vertex v' in $\pi(x, v)$, destroying $PH(x, v)$ in the process. Let the vertices of $\pi(v, x)$ be numbered $v = v_1, v_2, \ldots, v_k = x$; we can successively transform $PH(x, v)$ into $PH(x, v_i)$ for each v_i in sequence from $v_1 = v$ to $v_k = x$ in total time proportional to $|\pi(x, v)|$.

3. $PH(x, v)$ can be built from $\pi(x, v)$ in $O(|\pi(x, v)|)$ time.

We get these properties by adapting Melkman's algorithm for finding the convex hull of a polygonal path [14]. We satisfy requirement 2 by "recording" the actions of Melkman's algorithm as it constructs $h(x, v)$, then "playing the tape backwards."

Many linear-time algorithms have been proposed to find the convex hull of a simple polygon [6, 14, 10, 13, 22]. Some of these algorithms need to find a vertex on the hull to get started; we use Melkman's algorithm because it does not have this requirement. It constructs the hull of a polygonal path incrementally: it processes path vertices in order, and at each step it builds the hull of the vertices seen so far.

The algorithm keeps the vertices of the current convex hull in a double-ended queue, or *deque*. The deque lists the hull vertices in clockwise order, with the most recently added hull vertex at both ends of the deque. Let the vertices in the deque be $v_b, v_{b+1}, \ldots, v_{t-1}, v_t$, where $v_b = v_t$. The algorithm operates on the deque with *push* and *pop* operations that specify the end of

---

d_u and d_v that point away from the infinite hull, then add the two to get a direction d strictly between these normals.

the queue, bottom or top, on which they operate. The algorithm appears below; it assumes that no three of the points it tests are collinear, though this restriction is easy to lift.

Get the first three vertices of the path with the function *NextVertex*() and put them into the deque in the correct order.

while $v \leftarrow NextVertex()$ returns a new vertex **do**

    if v is outside the angle $\angle v_{t-1}v_t v_{b+1}$ **then**

        begin

            while v is left of $\overrightarrow{v_b v_{b+1}}$ **do** $pop(v_b, \text{bottom})$;

            while v is left of $\overrightarrow{v_{t-1} v_t}$ **do** $pop(v_t, \text{top})$;

            $push(v, \text{bottom})$; $push(v, \text{top})$;

        end

Melkman's convex hull algorithm

We now sketch a proof of correctness; for a full proof see [14]. We first consider the case in which v is discarded. This happens when v is inside the angle $\angle v_{t-1}v_t v_{b+1}$. (See Figure 10.) We know that v_{b+1} is connected to v_{t-1} by a polygonal path, and that v is connected to v_b by a polygonal path. The two paths do not intersect, so v must lie inside the current hull. When v is not discarded, it lies outside the current hull, and the algorithm pops hull vertices until it gets to the endpoints of the tangents from v to the current hull. The algorithm is linear: if it operates on a path with n vertices, it does at most $2n$ pushes and $2n - 3$ pops.

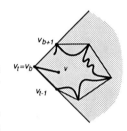

Figure 10: Discard v if it lies in the shaded sector

We can use the algorithm to build an array representation of the hull. The algorithm does at most n pushes at either end of the deque, so we can implement the deque as the middle part of an array of size $2n$. Pushes and pops increment and decrement the array indices of the ends of the queue; pushes write in a new element, pops read one out. The resulting deque contains the vertices of the convex hull in a contiguous chunk of an array.

The algorithm described so far satisfies requirements 1 and 3; how can we use it to satisfy requirement 2? When the algorithm builds $h(x, v)$ starting from x and working toward v, at intermediate steps it produces $h(x, v')$ for every vertex v' in $\pi(x, v)$. We need to be able to reconstruct these intermediate results. To do this, we add code to the algorithm to create a transcript of all the operations performed, recording what vertices are pushed and popped at each step. The structure $PH(x, v)$ stores not only the deque that represents $h(x, v)$, but also the transcript of the operations needed to create the deque from scratch. To reconstruct $PH(x, v')$ from $PH(x, v)$, we read the transcript in reverse order, performing the inverse of each recorded operation (pushing what was popped, and vice versa), until the deque represents $h(x, v')$. We throw away the part of the transcript we have just read, so that $PH(x, v')$ stores only the transcript of the operations needed to create $h(x, v')$. Because we discard every

step we have read over, we look at each step of the transcript at most once during the playback. Therefore, reconstructing the intermediate results takes time proportional to the original cost of finding $PH(x, v)$. This completes the proof that the path hull data structure satisfies all three of its requirements.

4.5 Analyzing the running time

In this section we analyze the running time of the chain-splitting algorithm. The analysis uses a "credit" scheme, in which each call to $f()$ or $p()$ is given some number of credits to pay for the time used in its body and its recursive calls. We give $O(n \log n)$ credits to the first call to $f()$, then show that all calls have enough credits to pay for their own work and that of their recursive calls.

We begin the analysis by proving that $f()$ and $p()$ are called $O(n)$ times: Every call to $p(u, x, v)$ splits $\pi(u, v)$ into two nontrivial subpaths, and every call to $f(u, v)$ for which $\pi(u, v)$ has more than one edge passes $\pi(u, v)$ on to $p()$. The initial path π can only be split $O(n)$ times, so the recursion must have $O(n)$ calls altogether.

How much work is done by a call to $f(u, v)$, exclusive of recursive calls? We assume that the vertices of π are stored in an array. Therefore line 2 of $f()$ takes only constant time. Line 3 is the only step of $f()$ that takes non-constant time; as shown in Section 4.4, line 3 takes $O(|\pi(u, v)|)$ time. We define the value of a credit by saying that a call $f(u, v)$ needs $|\pi(u, v)|$ credits—one credit per edge of $\pi(u, v)$—to pay for the work it does, exclusive of its call to $p()$. The constant-time steps in $f()$ take $O(n)$ time altogether and hence are dominated by the rest of the running time.

A call to $p(u, x, v)$ does accountable work in lines 5 and 7. The cost of line 5 is dominated by two binary searches, which take $O(\log n)$ time. Line 5 therefore takes $O(n \log n)$ time over the whole course of the algorithm. Section 4.4 shows that the cost of building $PH(x, z)$ at line 7 can be accounted as part of the construction cost of the path hull from which $PH(x, z)$ is derived. Thus we can ignore the work done at line 7 of $p()$; its cost is dominated by that of line 3 of $f()$.

To complete our analysis of the running time, we must bound the cost of all executions of line 3 of $f()$. In a single call to $f(u, v)$, line 3 uses $|\pi(u, v)|$ credits. The sum of all credits used by line 3 is proportional to the time spent executing that line. We give $n \lceil \log_2 n \rceil$ credits to the first call to $f()$, then show that this is enough to pay for all executions of line 3. We use the following two invariants in the proof:

1. A call to $f(u, v)$ is given at least $m \lceil \log_2 m \rceil$ credits, where $m = |\pi(u, v)|$, to pay for itself and its recursive calls.

2. A call to $p(u, x, v)$ is given at least $(l + r) \lceil \log_2 \max(l, r) \rceil$ credits, where $l = |\pi(u, x)|$ and $r = |\pi(x, v)|$, to pay for its recursive calls.

Lemma 4.1 *If a call to $f()$ or $p()$ is given credits in accordance with invariants 1 and 2, it can pay for all executions of line 3 it does explicitly or in its recursive calls.*

    Proof: Let m, l, and r be as defined above. The proof is by induction on m. A call to $f(u, v)$ with $m = 1$ gets no credits and needs none, since it does not reach line 3. There are no calls to $p()$ with $m = 1$.

A call to $f(u,v)$ with $m > 1$ gets at least $m\lceil\log_2 m\rceil$ credits and spends m of them executing line 3. It has $m\lceil\log_2(m/2)\rceil$ to pass on to its call to $p(u,x,v)$. The larger of l and r is $\lceil m/2\rceil$, and $\lceil\log_2(m/2)\rceil = \lceil\log_2\lceil m/2\rceil\rceil$, so the call to $p(u,x,v)$ gets at least $m\lceil\log_2(m/2)\rceil = (l+r)\lceil\log_2\max(l,r)\rceil$ credits, as required by invariant 2.

A call to $p(u,x,v)$ splits $\pi(u,v)$ into two paths $\pi(u,z)$ and $\pi(z,v)$ with a and b edges, respectively. The call to $p(u,x,v)$ divides its credits between its recursive calls evenly according to subpath size. If $z = x$, then the two calls to $f()$ get at least $l\lceil\log_2\max(l,r)\rceil \geq l\lceil\log_2 l\rceil$ and $r\lceil\log_2\max(l,r)\rceil \geq r\lceil\log_2 r\rceil$ credits, satisfying invariant 1. If $z \neq x$, then without loss of generality assume that z belongs to $\pi(u,x)$ and line 8 is executed; the other case is symmetric. The call to $f(u,z)$ gets at least $a\lceil\log_2\max(l,r)\rceil \geq a\lceil\log_2 a\rceil$, as required. The call to $p(z,x,v)$ gets at least $b\lceil\log_2\max(l,r)\rceil \geq b\lceil\log_2\max(b-r,r)\rceil$, as required by invariant 2. This completes the proof. ■

Altogether the calls to $f()$ and $p()$ take $O(n\log n)$ time, plus the time spent building path hulls at line 3. The preceding lemma shows that all the executions of line 3 take only $O(n\log n)$ time, and hence the entire algorithm runs in $O(n\log n)$ time.

4.6 Implementation

The algorithm described in this section has been implemented. The implementation is more general than the algorithm we have so far described: it correctly handles the cases of collinear vertices on convex hulls and parallel rays on bi-infinite chains. These improvements are not difficult. Handling collinear vertices requires two changes: the program detects and merges consecutive collinear polygon edges, reporting them to the user, and the **while** loop tests in Melkman's algorithm are changed from "v is left of" to "v is on or to the left of the line supporting." When a chain has parallel infinite rays, the direction d (see Section 4.3) is perpendicular to the rays, and the program needs a special case to avoid selecting u or v as the splitting vertex. As input the program takes a list of polygon vertices in order (either clockwise or counterclockwise), specified as x-y coordinate pairs. As output the program produces a list of the splitting vertices in the order they are computed, as well as a correctly parenthesized boolean formula for the input polygon.

When the program is applied to the polygon shown in Figure 11, it produces the following (slightly abbreviated) output:

```
main: Calling f() on 8..17
p: splitting at vertex 16, 15, 9, 10, 13, 11,
                12, 14
main: Calling f() on 17..25, 0..8
p: splitting at vertex 18, 19, 20, 0, 25, 24,
                21, 22, 23, 7, 1, 6, 5, 2, 3, 4


Boolean formula is:

(8 * 9 * (10 * (11 + 12) + 13 * 14) + 15) * 16 *
17 * 18 * 19 * (20 * (21 + 22 + 23) + 24 + 25 +
                (0 + (1 + 2 + 3 * 4) * 5 * 6) * 7)
```

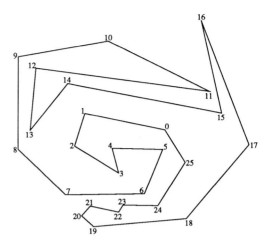

Figure 11: Sample program input, displayed as a polygon

In this formula, the number i refers to the edge joining vertex i to vertex $(i+1)$ mod n; here n is 26.

5 Formulæ for polyhedra

We have shown that the interior of a simple polygon can be represented by a Peterson-style formula: a monotone boolean formula that uses each literal once. We would like to find such a formula for a polyhedron P in space. Here, the literals are half-spaces bounded by the planes supporting the faces.

In this section we will prove that not all polyhedra have a Peterson-style formula. Figure 12 illustrates a simplicial polyhedron (each face is a triangle) with eight vertices and twelve faces. Six of the faces are labeled; the six unlabeled faces lie on the convex hull of P. The edge between C and C' is a convex angle. The half-spaces defined by faces A and B intersect the faces A' and B'. Similarly, the half-spaces A' and B' intersect faces A and B. After we establish a couple of lemmas, we will prove that P has no Peterson-style formula by assuming that it has one and deriving a contradiction.

We begin by observing that any collection of planes divides space into several convex regions. (In the mathematical literature, this division is usually called an *arrangement* [4].) If a polyhedron P has a CSG representation in terms of half-spaces, then we can specify a subset of the planes bounding these half-spaces and derive a representation for the portion of P inside any convex region determined by the subset.

More precisely, let f be a boolean formula on the half-spaces of P; we can think of f as an expression tree. If the tree for f has nodes a and b, then we will denote the least common ancestor of a and b in f by $\text{lca}_f(a,b)$. Let $H_1, H_2, \ldots, H_n$ be a subset of the half-spaces of P. Each point in space can be assigned a string $\alpha \in \{0,1\}^n$ such that the i-th character of α is 1 if and only if the point is in half-space H_i. All the points assigned the string α are said to be in the region R_α. We use $f|_\alpha$ to denote the formula obtained by setting each $H_i = \alpha_i$ in f and simplifying the result by using algebraic rules: $a1 = 1a = a$, $a0 = 0a = 0$, $a + 1 = 1 + a = 1$, and $a + 0 = 0 + a = a$. The expression tree for $f|_\alpha$ inherits several important properties from the expression tree for f:

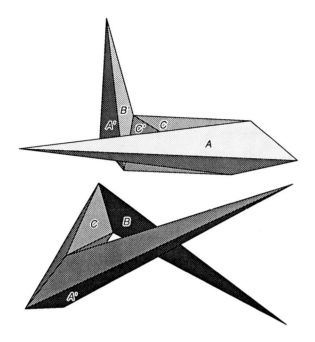

Figure 12: Two views of a simplicial polyhedron with no Peterson-style formula

Lemma 5.1 *Let f be a formula that uses the half-spaces $H_1, H_2, \ldots, H_n$ (and perhaps others) and let α be a string in $\{0,1\}^n$. Then the derived formula $f|_\alpha$ has the following three properties:*

1. *if f is monotone or Peterson-style, then so is $f|_\alpha$,*

2. *if the expression tree for $f|_\alpha$ has nodes a, b, and c, with $c = \mathrm{lca}_{f|_\alpha}(a,b)$, then $c = \mathrm{lca}_f(a,b)$ in the tree for f, and*

3. *if the expression tree for $f|_\alpha$ contains a node a at depth k, then the tree for f contains the node a at depth $\geq k$.*

> **Proof:** All three properties are maintained by the rules that form the expression tree for $f|_\alpha$ by simplifying the expression tree for f. ∎

The next lemma shows the interaction between the region R_α and boolean formulæ $f|_\alpha$.

Lemma 5.2 *If a polyhedron P has a formula f that uses half-spaces $H_1, H_2, \ldots, H_n$ (and others) then, for any string $\alpha \in \{0,1\}^n$, the portion of P inside the region R_α is described by the formula $f|_\alpha$.*

> **Proof:** The above statement simply says that formulæ f and $f|_\alpha$ agree inside the region R_α. This follows from the definition of $f|_\alpha$ and the fact that the simplification rules do not change the value of the formula. ∎

Two corollaries of Lemma 5.2 give us constraints on the formula of a polyhedron based on its edges and faces. In these corollaries and the discussion that follows, we will add an argument to a formula $f|_\alpha$ to emphasize which half-spaces are not fixed by the string α.

Corollary 5.3 *Let P be a polyhedron with Peterson-style formula f. If faces A and B of P meet at an edge, the operator in f that is the least common ancestor of A and B, $\mathrm{lca}_f(A,B)$, is an "and" if and only if A and B meet in a convex angle.*

> **Proof:** Let $H_1, H_2, \ldots, H_n$ be the half-spaces of P except for the two defined by A and B. Choose a point on the edge formed by faces A and B, and let α be its string. The two-variable formula $f|_\alpha(AB)$ must describe the edge, so by Lemma 5.1(2), $\mathrm{lca}_f(A,B)$ is an "and" if and only if A and B meet in a convex angle. ∎

Corollary 5.4 *Let P be a polyhedron with Peterson-style formula f using half-spaces $H_1, H_2, \ldots, H_n$ and A and B. If the half-space defined by face B intersects face A at some point with string α then $f|_\alpha(AB) = A$.*

> **Proof:** The two-variable formula $f|_\alpha(AB)$ must describe the face A both inside and outside the half-space of B, so B cannot appear in the formula. ∎

Now we are ready to look at the polyhedron P in Figure 12. Suppose P has a Peterson-style formula f. Then it has a formula $f|_{111111}(ABCA'B'C')$ that describes the region inside the unlabeled faces. We will look at the constraints on this formula and derive a contradiction.

Consider the three faces A, B, and C. By Corollary 5.3 we know that $\mathrm{lca}(B,C) = $ "or" and $\mathrm{lca}(A,B) = $ "and". Corollary 5.4 applied to faces A and C implies that the formula describing these three faces is

$$f|_{\alpha_1}(ABC) = A(B + C), \tag{1}$$

where the string α_1 appropriately fixes all the half-spaces except A, B, and C. Similarly, the formula describing A', B', and C' is

$$f|_{\alpha_2}(A'B'C') = A'(B' + C'). \tag{2}$$

Now consider the region inside all unlabeled half-spaces and outside C and C'. The portion of P within this region can be described by a Karnaugh map [11]:

		AB			
		00	01	11	10
	00	0	0	1	0
$A'B'$	01	0	0	1	0
	11	1	1	?	1
	10	0	0	1	0

The '?' appears because four planes cut space into only fifteen regions; since we want a monotone formula, Lemma 5.1(1) forces us to make it a '1'. Examining all Peterson-style formulæ on A, B, A', and B' reveals that the only formula with the above map is

$$f|_{\alpha_3}(ABA'B') = (AB) + (A'B'). \tag{3}$$

In order to combine the formulæ 1, 2, and 3 into a single formula on six variables, we must determine which operators are repeated in the three formulæ. We knew from formulæ 1 and 2 that the operators $\mathrm{lca}_f(A,B)$ and $\mathrm{lca}_f(A',B')$ were both "and"s—now we know that they are distinct "and"s because $\mathrm{lca}_f(\mathrm{lca}_f(A,B), \mathrm{lca}_f(A',B')) = $ "or" in formula 3. The "or"s of the first two formulæ are distinct because they are descendents of distinct "and"s. Finally, by Lemma 5.1(3), the "or" of formula 3 is different from the other "or"s because it is not nested as deeply as the "and"s.

Thus, all five operators of the formula on the six labeled half-spaces appear in the formulæ 1, 2, and 3. Using the nesting depth of the operators, we know that the formula looks like $(\Box(\Box + \Box)) + (\Box(\Box + \Box))$. Filling in the half-space names gives the formula for the portion of P inside the unlabeled faces:

$$f|_{111111}(ABCA'B'C') = (A(B+C)) + (A'(B'+C')).$$

Notice, however, that in this formula the lca of C and C' is an "or". Thus $\mathrm{lca}_f(C, C') = $ "or". But this contradicts Corollary 5.3, so the above formula cannot represent the portion of P inside the convex hull of P. This contradiction proves that P has no Peterson-style formula.

There are two natural questions that we will leave open. First, can the interior of a polyhedron with n faces be represented by a formula using $O(n)$ literals? The trivial upper bound on the size of a formula is $O(n^3)$. In fact, the interiors of any set of cells formed by a collection of n planes can be described by a formula that represents each convex cell as the "and" of its bounding planes and "or"s the cell representations together. The size of the formula is at worst the total number of sides of the cells formed by n planes, which is known to be $O(n^3)$ [4].

Second, can we characterize polyhedra that can be represented by Peterson-style formulæ? Peterson [19] showed that the representation of polygons gives such formulæ for extrusions and pyramids. We would like to extend this class.

References

[1] J. Boyse and J. Gilchrist. GMSolid: interactive modeling for design and analysis of solids. *IEEE Computer Graphics and Applications*, 2:86–97, 1982.

[2] C. Brown. PADL-2: a technical summary. *IEEE Computer Graphics and Applications*, 2:69–84, 1982.

[3] B. M. Chazelle. *Computational Geometry and Convexity*. Technical Report CMU-CS-80-150, Carnegie-Mellon University, Department of Computer Science, Pittsburgh, PA, 1980.

[4] H. Edelsbrunner. *Algorithms in Combinatorial Geometry*. Volume 10 of *EATCS Monographs on Theoretical Computer Science*, Springer-Verlag, 1987.

[5] W. Franklin. Polygon properties calculated from the vertex neighborhoods. In *Proceedings of the 3rd ACM Symposium on Computational Geometry*, pages 110–118, ACM, June 1987.

[6] R. L. Graham and F. F. Yao. Finding the convex hull of a simple polygon. *Journal of Algorithms*, 4:324–331, 1983.

[7] L. Guibas, J. Hershberger, D. Leven, M. Sharir, and R. Tarjan. Linear time algorithms for visibility and shortest path problems inside triangulated simple polygons. *Algorithmica*, 2:209–233, 1987.

[8] L. Guibas, L. Ramshaw, and J. Stolfi. A kinetic framework for computational geometry. In *Proceedings of the 24th Annual IEEE Symposium on Foundations of Computer Science*, pages 100–111, IEEE, 1983.

[9] K. Hoffmann, K. Mehlhorn, P. Rosenstiehl, and R. E. Tarjan. Sorting Jordan sequences in linear time. In *Proceedings of the ACM Symposium on Computational Geometry*, pages 196–203, ACM, 1985.

[10] D. T. Lee. On finding the convex hull of a simple polygon. *Internat. J. Comput. Inform. Sci.*, 12:87–98, 1983.

[11] M. M. Mano. *Digital Logic and Computer Design*. Prentice-Hall, 1979.

[12] M. Mäntylä. *An Introduction to Solid Modeling*. Computer Science Press, 1987.

[13] D. McCallum and D. Avis. A linear algorithm for finding the convex hull of a simple polygon. *Information Processing Letters*, 9:201–206, 1979.

[14] A. Melkman. On-line construction of the convex hull of a simple polyline. *Information Processing Letters*, 25:11–12, 1987.

[15] M. Mortenson. *Geometric Modeling*. John Wiley & Sons, 1985.

[16] R. Newell. Solid modelling and parametric design in the Medusa system. In *Computer Graphics '82, Proceedings of the Online Conference*, pages 223–235, 1982.

[17] J. O'Rourke. *Art Gallery Theorems and Algorithms*. Oxford University Press, 1987.

[18] T. Pavlidis. Analysis of set patterns. *Pattern Recognition*, 1:165–178, 1968.

[19] D. Peterson. *Halfspace Representation of Extrusions, Solids of Revolution, and Pyramids*. SANDIA Report SAND84-0572, Sandia National Laboratories, 1984.

[20] F. P. Preparata and M. I. Shamos. *Computational Geometry*. Springer Verlag, New York, 1985.

[21] A. Requicha. Representations for rigid solids: theory, methods, and systems. *ACM Computing Surveys*, 12:437–464, 1980.

[22] A. A. Schäffer and C. J. Van Wyk. Convex hulls of piecewise-smooth Jordan curves. *Journal of Algorithms*, 8:66–94, 1987.

[23] W. Tiller. Rational B-splines for curve and surface representation. *IEEE Computer Graphics and Applications*, 3, 1983.

[24] S. B. Tor and A. E. Middleditch. Convex decomposition of simple polygons. *ACM Transactions on Graphics*, 3(4):244–265, 1984.

[25] H. Voelcker, A. Requicha, E. Hartquist, W. Fisher, J. Metzger, R. Tilove, N. Birrell, W. Hunt, G. Armstrong, T. Check, R. Moote, and J. McSweeney. The PADL-1.0/2 system for defining and displaying solid objects. *ACM Comput. Gr.*, 12(3):257–263, 1978.

[26] J. R. Woodwark and A. F. Wallis. Graphical input to a Boolean solid modeller. In *CAD 82*, pages 681–688, Brighton, U.K., 1982.

Subnanosecond Pixel Rendering

with Million Transistor Chips

Nader Gharachorloo, Satish Gupta, Erdem Hokenek,
Peruvemba Balasubramanian, Bill Bogholtz,
Christian Mathieu, Christos Zoulas

IBM Research Division
Thomas J. Watson Research Center
Yorktown Heights, NY 10598
Phone: (914) 789-7100

Abstract

The desire for higher performance and higher resolution continuously increases the pixel update rates needed in high performance graphics systems. The increasing density of memory chips on the other hand reduces the pixel update rate that can be provided by the frame buffer. We present the design of of a VLSI chip and a graphics system that can sustain sub-nanosecond pixel rendering rates for three-dimensional polygons and can be used to render about a million Z-Buffered and Gourard shaded polygons per second. The chip has been designed at the IBM Research Division's Thomas J. Watson Research Center.

Introduction

Computer graphics users have an ever-increasing desire for higher performance, more functionality and better picture quality which is constantly fueled by rapid improvements in semiconductor technology. This has resulted in better and faster yet cheaper and smaller graphics systems. Today's graphics systems utilize a vast number of specialized chips such as graphics processors, fast floating point processors, customized video memories with separate serial ports (popularly called VRAMs), and fast video lookup tables with digital-to-analog converters. VRAM based frame buffers have become the basis for all high-performance graphics systems which then use dedicated graphics processors or specialized hardware for operations such as line drawing and polygon filling. An accompanying Z-buffer is often used to assist the system in removing hidden surfaces for three dimensional primitives.

The frame buffer is capable of displaying arbitrary images without imposing any limits to their complexity. However as users demand faster interactivity and migrate from line drawing graphics applications to shaded polygonal images, the frame buffer is becoming a bottleneck in its ability to change the picture rapidly. This bottleneck arises because area filling an object updates significantly more pixels than outlining the same object. If the average length of an edge is N pixels, then drawing the wireframe scene requires $O(N)$ operations, whereas area-filling the scene would require $O(N^2)$ operations. As a result of this fundamental difference between linear operations count for line drawing and quadratic operations count for polygon filling, rendering polygonal scenes is significantly slower than outlining wire frame pictures.

Figure 1 shows the pixel update rates required to update various scene complexities against various frame rates. The scene complexity is the total number of pixels that need to be updated to redraw the scene and it is a function of the number of polygons in the scene, average area of the polygons, and the screen resolution. For example, a 1024x1024 screen displaying a scene with 10,000 polygons of 1,000 pixels each would contain 10 million pixels in each frame. The same scene rendered on a 2048x2048 screen would contain 40 million pixels! It is not uncommon to render scenes at 4 or even 8 times the screen resolution and then filter the resulting image to produce a high quality anti-aliased picture. The pixel update time is a measure for both scene complexity and frame update time and is given by:

$$Tpixel = \frac{FrameTime}{PixelsInFrame}$$

Figure 1 illustrates the desire for pixel update times in the nanosecond to sub-nanosecond range to sustain dynamic pictures high resolution displays.

Pixels/ frame	1 sec.	1/10 sec.	1/30 sec.	1/60 sec.
1M	1,000	100	33	17
5M	200	20	6.7	3.3
10M	100	10	3.3	1.7
25M	40	4	1.3	0.7
50M	20	2	0.7	0.3

Figure 1. Required pixel update time in nanoseconds.

To compare the limitations imposed by the frame buffer memory bandwidth on pixel update time, we have to examine the underlying frame buffer implementations. Figure 2 shows the available frame buffer memory bandwidth using memory chips with different densities and organizations for a display with one million pixels. The memory chip organization determines the number of bits available in parallel in every memory access. The pixel update time is given by:

$$Tpixel = \frac{MemoryCycleTime \times MemoryChipSize}{PixelsOnScreen \times MemoryBitWidth}$$

We have assumed a memory cycle time of 256 nanoseconds, which is usually difficult to achieve because 3D rasterization involves a read-modify-write cycle to read, compare, and update the Z-buffer. Current systems which use 64Kx4 memory chips can achieve up to 16 nsec/pixel. As seen in Figure 2, with higher density memory chips, the frame buffer is unable to sustain the pixel rates needed, even in wide memory organizations. High performance graphics systems can either continue to use low density memory chips, or look for alternative VLSI architectures capable of utilizing the higher densities of technology and providing the required performance.

Density Width	256K	1M	4M	16M
X 16	-	16ns.	64ns.	256ns.
X 8	-	32ns.	128ns.	512ns.
X 4	16ns.	64ns.	256ns.	1μs.
X 1	64ns.	256ns.	1μs.	4μs.

Figure 2. Available Memory Pixel Update Time

The Rendering Primitive

Rendering pixels as the basic primitive into frame buffers leads to an enormously high pixel update rate which cannot be economically supported by the existing or future memory technologies. Changing the basic hardware rendering primitive from low level pixels to higher level primitives such as horizontal spans, trapezoids, or triangles has two advantages. First it reduces the interchip communication bandwidth in the system because of the smaller number of primitives transmitted. Second the chips can render the primitives in parallel by exploiting the wider and faster on-chip bussing structures.

Many other researchers and commercial graphics systems have chosen a higher level primitive instead of the pixel primitive. Some machines have chosen polygons and triangles as their primitive [2], some have provided rectangles [8, 14], others have tried trapezoids [13], and along with others [1, 7, 10] we have chosen the horizontal span as our lowest level hardware primitive. Different primitives lead to different system architectures, which are tuned to maximally exploit the parallelism in the primitive.

Filling three dimensional horizontal spans is the inner most loop of any polygon rendering algorithm. We have chosen the horizontal span as our rendering primitive for three reasons. First it is simple enough to be executed in hardware. Second it is powerful enough that if executed in parallel, it has the potential to achieve the nanosecond pixel rendering goal. And third, it is general enough to represent other non-polygonal shapes such as ellipsoids and curved surfaces, as well as allow for more sophisticated polygon edge interpolations.

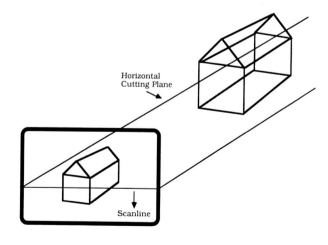

Figure 3. Projection of 3D polygons on a scanline.

PROCEDURE FILLSPAN (Xl,Xr,Z,ΔZ,RGB, ΔRGB)

static int ZBuf [0..1023], RGBBuf[0..1023]

```
FOR x := Xl to Xr DO BEGIN
   IF Z ≤ ZBuf [x] THEN   BEGIN
      ZBuf [x] := Z;
      RGBBuf [x] := RGBBuf;
      END;
   Z := Z + ΔZ;
   RGB := RGB + ΔRGB;
   END;
```

Figure 4. Span Command

Figure 3 shows a horizontal plane cutting through a three dimensional polygonal scene. The intersection of the plane with each polygon yields a three dimensional horizontal span. Rendering all the horizontal spans for a given cutting plane yields the final picture for the corresponding scanline on the screen. Figure 4 shows the procedure FillSpan with its input arguments which describe a three dimensional horizontal span. A span is described by the position of its two end points, its depth at the left end point, and change in depth with respect to unit pixel change along the scanline, and similarly a color triplet value at the left end point and rate of change for each color value.

Using the horizontal span as our primitive, the polygon rendering problem can be broken down into two pieces: a horizontal filling inner loop which transforms span primitives into pixels, and a vertical interpolation outer loop which breaks individual polygons into horizontal spans. The next section describes the process of mapping the horizontal span rendering loop into a parallel hardware algorithm which was then implemented on a million transistor custom CMOS chip called SAGE (Systolic Array Graphics Engine). The following section will then describe the Vertical Interpolation Processor (VIPs)

PROCEDURE FILLSPAN (Xl,Xr,Z,ΔZ,RGB, ΔRGB)

static int ZBuf [0..1023] , RGBBuf [0..1023]

```
FOR x := 0 to 1023 DO BEGIN

   IF xl ≤ x ≤ xr THEN BEGIN
      IF Z ≤ ZBuf [x]   THEN BEGIN
         ZBuf [x] := Z;
         RGBBuf [x] := RGBBuf;
         END;
      Z := Z + ΔZ;
      RGB := RGB + ΔRGB;
      END;
   END;
```

Figure 5. Span Command unrolled for systolic mapping.

which break polygons into spans, and combined with SAGE form a high performance polygon rendering graphics system.

SAGE: A Systolic Array Graphics Engine

SAGE maps the horizontal span rendering loop into a systolic array of pixel processors; one for every pixel on a scanline. Figure 5 shows the FillSpan loop modified to operate with fixed loop bounds. Execution of this modified loop always takes a fixed number of iterations (1024 iterations for 1Kx1K screen) where as the execution speed of the unmodified loop is proportional to the length of the span being rendered. This fixed execution speed which is independent of the length of the span, allows us to fully unroll the loop and assign a fixed length array of processors for executing the loop, as shown in Figure 6. Note that the first processor executes the first iteration of the loop, and passes the results to the second processor which executes the second iteration and so on. This continues in a pipelined manner, allowing the array to accept a new span command every clock cycle.

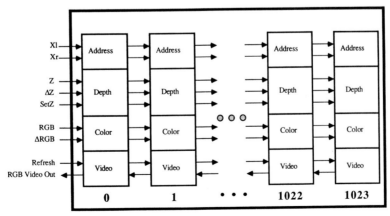

Figure 6. Systolic array of pixel processors in SAGE.

Figure 7 shows the input and outputs of a pixel processor for executing the body of the loop in the FillSpan procedure. If the state of the procedure is input at one end, then the output of the pixel processor corresponds to one iteration of the loop in FillSpan. The address block is composed of two comparators which compare the loop counter x (in this case processor number) against the left and right end points of the span xl and xr. The depth block contains a register for holding $ZBuf$, a comparator for comparing the input Z against $ZBuf$, connections for loading Z into $ZBuf$ if the comparison is successful, and an adder for adding Z with ΔZ. The color block contains three registers for storing the input RGB values into $RGBBuf$ if the depth comparison is successful, and three adders for adding RGB with ΔRGB. For initialization at the beginning of every scan line, the $SetZ$ control bit forces an unconditional loading of both $ZBuf$ and $RGBBuf$ independent of the result of the depth comparison.

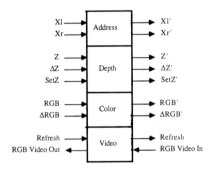

Figure 7. SAGE Pixel Processor Block Diagram.

The refresh block of the pixel processor allows the shifting out of the $RGBBuf$ from the SAGE chip. After all the spans for a given scan line have been clocked in, a one bit refresh token is sent which causes the contents of the scanline to be outputted on the video port at the rate of one pixel every clock cycle. All processors behind the refresh token have completed rendering of their pixel values and have already loaded the final pixel value into the video pipeline. The processor currently holding the refresh token is loading its pixel value into the pixel pipeline, and the processors ahead of the pixel token are still rendering the current scan line. Processors behind the refresh token that have completed rendering the current scan line, and may immediately start rendering spans for the next scan line. Figure 8 shows clock cycle snapshots of the SAGE pipeline and demonstrates how SAGE renders a number of horizontal spans, and then outputs the pixel values for that scan line.

Figure 9 shows a plot of the SAGE chip with 256 pixel processors. SAGE was implemented on 12.7 mm. by 12.7 mm. chip using 1.2μ CMOS technology and contains about one million transistors. The array of 256 processors is broken down into three rows which are connected at the break points. All inputs and outputs to the array are through the first pixel processor. Aside from power, ground, and two complementary clocks, there are no other global signals.

All the pixel processors are identical copies and were designed such that they could be replicated in an array without any external connections. After the chip was completed, a post-layout hard wired the pixel address of each processor into its address comparator block. The cells used to construct each processor are: shift register, address compare, adder, comparator, buffer cell, video cell, and a random logic control cell.

To achieve the fastest possible clock speed, pipelining is used both in the horizontal and vertical directions. In the horizontal direction, a 256 stage pipeline allows neighboring processors to communicate data in a systolic fashion. In the vertical direction, a three stage pipeline allows independent operation of the address block, the depth block, and the color and refresh blocks. A data skewer at the input of the array delays the depth parameters by one clock cycle, and the color parameters by two clock cycles in order to maintain proper operation of the pixel processors.

As a result of both horizontal and vertical pipelining as well as purely nearest neighbor data communication, the chip can operate at a 40 nanosecond clock cycle, which allows the processing of up to 25 million spans per second [5].

SAGE Configurations

Each SAGE chip only contains 256 pixel processors, and multiple chips need to be used to build a system with a higher horizontal resolution. For example, four chips would be needed to build a 1024x1024 system. This can be done by either connecting the chips in series or in parallel (Figure 10). When the chips are connected in series, the first chip contains processors 0 through 255, the second contains processors 256 through 511, and so on. Span commands are processed in the first chip and passed to the second, the video is similarly shifted out in the reverse direction. In this configuration spans are passed in at rate of 40 nsec/span, and video is output at the same rate. When the chips are connected in parallel, each chip contains pixel processors for every fourth pixel. The first chip contains processors 0,4,8,12 and so on, the second contains processors 1,5,9,13, and so on. Commands are passed in at rate of 40 nsec/span, but now video is output at 4 pixels every clock cycle or 10 nsec/pixel.

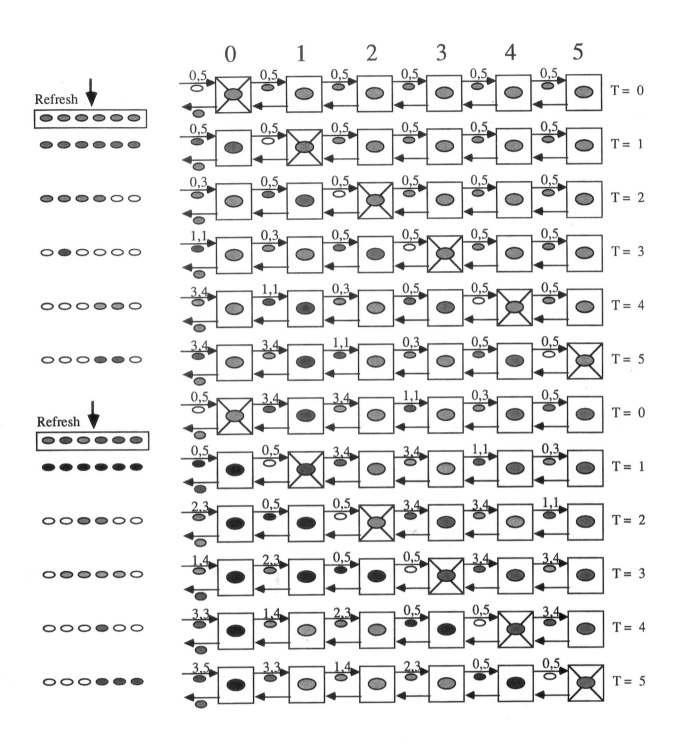

Figure 8. Clock cycle snapshots of SAGE operation.

One Million Transistors

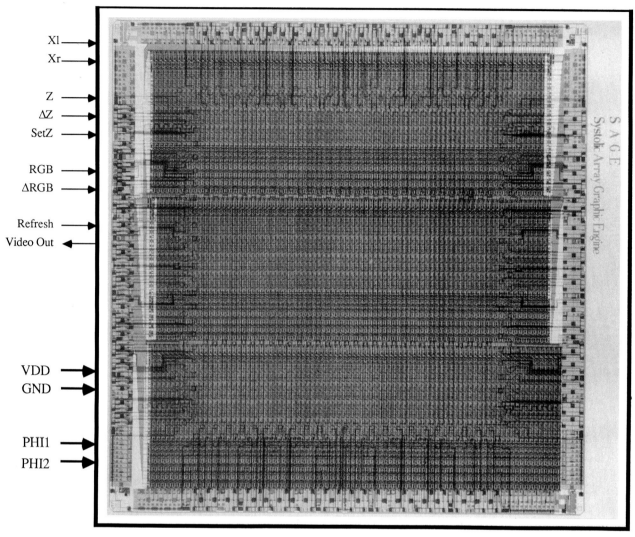

12.7x12.7mm   1.2μ CMOS

Figure 9. SAGE chip.

When the SAGE chips are connected in parallel, they all receive the same span command in parallel. Each chip internally modifies the span command based on its chip number and the value of Xl. For example if $Xl = 1$, then the first chip will modify its command from $FillSpan(Xl,Xr,Z, \Delta Z,RGB, \Delta RGB)$ to FillSpan ($Xl + 1,Xr,Z + 3\Delta Z,4\Delta Z, \quad RGB + 3\Delta RGB,4\Delta RGB \quad$). Since the video refresh rate for 1024x1024 CRT is 11 nsec/pixel, the four SAGE chips in parallel can drive the CRT directly. When operating synchronously with the CRT, the SAGE chips can process up to 256 spans for every scanline before refreshing the screen. Rendering more complex scenes requires an optional frame buffer for storing the output of the SAGE chips. The frame buffer has to be accessed through the input video port

serially which matches the SAGE refresh bandwidth of 10 nsec/pixel.

When the SAGE chips are connected in series, they can accept 1024 span commands before refresh. However the refresh is only 40 nsec/pixel, which is not fast enough to refresh a 1024x1024 CRT directly. A frame buffer is hence necessary to buffer the image.

A larger number of SAGE chips can be used to render images at sub-pixel resolutions. For example, 16 chips would be needed to compute 2 scan line which are 2048 pixels long. If connected in the parallel configuration, the refresh rate is now 16 pixels/cycle after both the scan lines have been rendered. These pixels can be filtered down to 4 screen pixels before driving the CRT or storing in a screen resolution frame buffer.

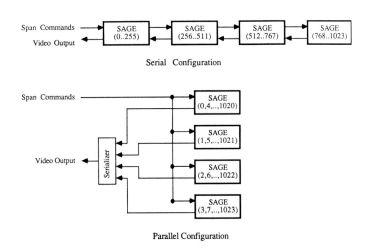

Figure 10. SAGE Configurations for 1024 processors.

SAGE Graphics System

A complete polygon rendering system also includes converting polygons into spans and managing the active polygon list for each scan line [4, 6, 9, 12]. Figure 11 shows the simplified PolySpan procedure for breaking a 3D trapezoids into a set of horizontal spans. Other primitives like triangles and polygons can be similarly broken into spans. The procedure receives the slopes for the polygon edges, sets up the parameters for the left and right polygon edges, and within the loop incrementally computes the change in the span parameters for the next scanline which correspond to a unit vertical change in screen coordinates.

$$PROCEDURE\ TrapezoidSpan$$
$$(Yt, Yb,$$
$$Xl, \nabla_y Xl, Xr, \nabla_y Xr,$$
$$Z, \nabla_y Z, RGB,$$
$$\nabla_y RGB, \Delta_x Z,$$
$$\Delta_x RGB)$$

$$FOR\ y := yt\ to\ yb\ DO\ BEGIN$$

$$SpanFill(Xl, Xr, Z, \Delta_x Z, RGB, \Delta_x RGB);$$

$$Xl := Xl + \nabla_y Xl;$$
$$Xr := Xr + \nabla_y Xr;$$
$$Z := Z + \nabla_y Z;$$
$$RGB := RGB + \nabla_y RGB;$$

$$END;$$

Figure 11. Polygon to Span Conversion.

A planar three dimensional polygon, i.e. xyZ, xyR, xyG, xyB planes, has a fixed slope with respect to the horizontal axis for all the horizontal spans in the polygon and does not change from scanline to scanline. Therefore out of the ten parameters of the SpanFill procedure, the four slopes are constants and don't change from scanline to scanline, and the other six parameters are incrementally computed for every scanline. This process is often called the six axis interpolation [11]

Figure 12 shows the internal configuration of the Vertical Interpolation Processor, and Figure 13 shows the system diagram with an array of 8 identical VIPs which execute the PolySpan procedure and provide SAGE with all its input parameters. The VIPs are responsible for supplying SAGE with all the horizontal span primitives on a given scanline by incrementally computing the intersection of a horizontal cutting plane with the three dimensional polygons in the scene. Since SAGE expects all the spans for a given scanline before it starts to compute the next scanline, the VIPs have internal storage to save the complete state of the interpolation loop. The internal memory of the VIPs can hold up to 512 active polygons. To generate all the spans for a given line, the VIPs go through a load state, interpolate span, and save new state sequence for all the active polygons in their internal memory. Six VIPs are used for performing the six axis interpolation and the other two are used are used as memories for storing the four constant slopes.

The polygon manager computes the slopes for the polygons and loads this information into the VIPs through the 32 bit bus. The polygon manager is responsible for setting up the state for newly activated polygons, updating the state information at polygon vertices, and

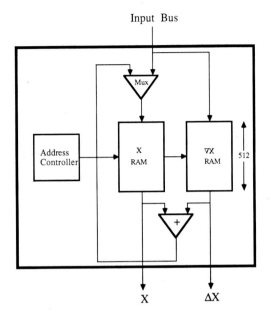

Figure 12. Vertical Interpolation Processor.

deactivating the polygons from the internal state memory of the VIPs. The polygon manager may wait for the VIPs to do the interpolation for the current scanline and then update the internal state of the VIPs. Alternatively by allowing the polygon manager to update the state information for any polygon which has been interpolated by the VIPs on the current scanline, one can achieve faster transparent loading of VIPs.

The VIPs are synchronized with the SAGE chips, span converting and rendering a span every 40 nanoseconds. For an average polygon height of 32 lines (1000 pixel polygons), the system is capable of rendering close to one million polygons per second. To supply this rendering system at this rate, we plan to use a floating point multiprocessor workstation, currently being prototyped For an average span width of 32 pixels, SAGE updates pixels at an average rate of 1.25 nanoseconds/pixel. For spans longer than 40 pixels, SAGE achieves subnanosecond pixel update times. [3].

Status

The SAGE chip is due back from fabrication in January 1988, and the rest of the rendering system is being designed. We hope to demonstrate a working system by the summer of 1988. The SAGE chip and system are IBM Research Division prototypes for research purposes, and are not planned to be part of IBM products.

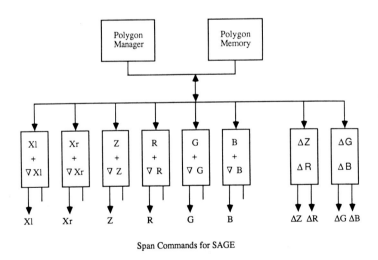

Figure 13. Polygon to Span Interpolation.

Bibliography

1. S. Demetrescu. High Speed Image Rasterization Using Scan Line Access Memories. *Proc. 1985 Chapel Hill Conference on VLSI*, pages 221-243, Computer Science Press, 1985.

2. H. Fuchs and J. Poulton. Pixel Planes: A VLSI-Oriented Design for a Raster Graphics Engine. *VLSI Design*, 2(3):20-28, 3rd. Quarter 1981.

3. A. Garcia. ACE: A High Performance Multiprocessor Workstation, IBM Internal Communication, IBM Thomas J. Watson Research Center, 1987.

4. N. Gharachorloo. Super Buffer: A systolic VLSI Graphics Engine for Real Time Raster Image Generation, Ph.D. Thesis, Electrical Engineering Department, Cornell Univ., Ithaca, NY. August 1985.

5. N. Gharachorloo, S. Gupta, E. Hokenek, P. Balasubramanian, W. Bogholtz, C. Mathieu, and C. Zoulas. A Million Transistor Systolic Array Graphics Engine. *Proceedings of International Conference on Systolic Arrays*, San Diego, May 1988.

6. N. Gharachorloo and C. Pottle. SUPER BUFFER: A Systolic VLSI Graphics Engine for Real Time Raster Image Generation. *Proc. 1985 Chapel Hill Conference on VLSI*, pages 285-305, Computer Science Press, 1985.

7. J.H. Jackson. Dynamic Scan-converted images with a Frame Buffer Display Device. *Computer Graphics*, 14(3):163-169, July 1980.

8. Bart Locanthi. Object Oriented Raster Displays. *Proceedings of Caltech Conference on VLSI*, pages 215-225, January 1979.

9. A.J. Myers. An Efficient Visible Surface Program, Ohio State University, Report to the NSF, July 1975.

10. H. Niimi, Y. Imai, M. Murakami, S. Tomita, and H. Hagiwara. A Parallel Processor System for Three Dimensional Color Graphics. *Computer Graphics*, 18(3):67-76, July 1984.

11. R.W. Swanson and L.J. Thayer. A Fast Shaded-Polygon Renderer. *Computer Graphics*, 20(4):95-101, August 1986.

12. G.S. Watkins. A Real Time Visible Surface Algorithm, University of Utah, Computer Science Department, June 1970.

13. Richard Weinberg. Parallel Processing Image Synthesis and Anti-Aliasing. *Computer Graphics*, 15(3):55-61, August 1981.

14. Daniel S. Whelan. A Rectangular Area Filling Display System Architecture. *Computer Graphics*, 16(3):147-153, July 1982.

A Rendering Algorithm for Visualizing 3D Scalar Fields

Paolo Sabella*
Schlumberger-Doll Research

Abstract

This paper presents a ray tracing algorithm for rendering 3D scalar fields. An illumination model is developed in which the field is characterized as a varying density emittter with a single level of scattering. This model is equivalent to a particle system in which the particles are sufficiently small. Along each ray cast from the eye, the field is expressed as a function of the ray parameter. The algorithm computes properties of the field along the ray such as the attenuated intensity, the peak density, and the center of gravity, etc.. These are mapped into HSV color space to produce an image for visualization.

Images produced in this manner are perceived as a varying density 'cloud' where color highlights the computed attributes. The application of this technique is demonstrated for visualizing a three dimensional seismic data set.

CR Categories: I.3.3 [**Computer Graphics**]: Picture/Image Generation; I.3.7 [**Computer Graphics**]: Three-Dimensional Graphics and Realism; I.4.0 [**Image Processing**]: General

General Terms: Algorithms

Additional Key Words and Phrases: 3D image, ray tracing, thresholding, light scattering.

*Author's curent affiliation: Visual Edge Software
 Author's current address: 37 Dragon St.
                                               Kirkland, PQ H9J-3B3 Canada

1. Introduction.

Computer graphics has made an irreplaceable contribution in the presentation of scientific data. The computer is indispensable as an aid in the visualization of certain kinds of functions. This paper focuses on the display of single valued functions of three variables, i.e. scalar fields. Such functions can be analytically defined but more commonly are computed numerically using finite difference or finite element techniques. Examples of such fields are the stress distribution over a mechanical part or the pressure distribution within a fluid reservoir.

Alternately, the field can be empirically measured. For example, sonic waveforms or tomography radiation measurements can be processed to obtain density samples of a solid over a three dimensional volume. A convenient representation for this is a three dimensional array of samples referred to as a **3D image**. The sample points are called voxels (volume elements). The cuberille [3] is a special case of the 3D image in which all the voxels are identical cubes. The retangular prism that is the spatial extent of the array is called the **image extent**.

The 3D image is not the only representation for sampled scalar fields. Octrees [14, 12] provide a more compact, structured means of encoding field samples in which both the spatial extent and the image are hierarchically organized. In finite element analysis, samples of a field are computed at the mesh nodes. Hence the mesh itself serves as a representation for the field.

In this paper we use the 3D image representation. Figure 7 shows a 3D image of sub-soil density obtained from surface seismic measurements. The density value is mapped into a gray scale. Notice that most of the cube, i.e. the interior, is not readily visible.

Although the objectives of manipulation 3D data is application dependent, the goal when visualizing the data is to understand the spatial distribution of the field values over the domain on which the function is defined. It is important to be able to see the location of the occurrence of any range of values, such as, for example, high values or 'hot spots' or changes in the field gradient. It is also important to perceive the manner in which the function varies from it's minimum to maximum values. This is especially true for geophysical imaging in which there is hardly any spatial correlation in the data and which does not lend itself to existing visualization techniques.

In this paper a new rendering model for visualizing scalar fields is proposed. In it, the field is rendered as a varying density emitter (**DE**) object. It is related, but not restricted, to the modeling of light occurring cloud-like objects. The goal here is the perception and understanding of the field, not the realistic rendering of natural phenomena. The visualization technique is unique in three ways:

  i)   A color map is utilized to visualize individual attributes.
  ii)   The use of a phase function to visualize the field gradient.
  iii)   The Kajiya and Von Herzen ray tracing algorithm is recast for computational efficiency, eliminating shadowing while retaining occlusion.

We first review the two existing rendering models of 3D images. Variations of these account for all attempts to date at rendering scalar fields. Next we look at scattering models and particle systems used to render realistic looking clouds and natural phenomena. We then propose the varying density emitter (**DE**) object which is actually a special case of a general scattering emitter and a generalization of the particle system. Finally, a ray tracing algorithm is described for rendering the DE object incorporating false coloring in order to present multidimensional information.

Although the data presented in the figures actually represent a sampled density field, the visualization model is intended to be used on any field. It can be adapted to render analytically defined fields or to incorporate bounding surfaces such as those of a solid over which the field is defined. It can also be extended to render octrees or finite element meshes.

2. Rendering Models for 3D images
There are two common techniques to date for rendering 3D images, cross-section rendering and threshold rendering. Each of these implicitly are models of the interaction of light on the 3D model. It is important to place the DE rendering model within the context of existing schemes.

2.1 Cross-section rendering
In cross-section rendering, the 3D image is considered to be an opaque array of voxels packed inside the image extent. A user can interactively remove portions of the image in order to see interior voxels. The rendering model is that of light illuminating the cross-sectional surfaces, or slices.

Good response time is valuable here in order to perceive the field in three dimensions. This perception is achieved by the user sequentially viewing multiple slices and mentally interconnecting the features of interest. For example, in order to search for a region of maximum value the user may scan through slices until one is found. Then many sections taken in possibly different orientations are viewed to see the extent of the peak region.

An important consideration is the coloring of the voxels. Color is used both to indicate the field value at a voxel as well as to provide surface orientation cues. The cross-section is therefore a texture mapped surface [1]. Usually the intensity is varied according to a shading model while the base color, either hue or gray scale is used to indicate field value.

2.2 Threshold rendering
Threshold rendering is common in medical applications when dealing with 3D images of densities measured by computer aided tomography (CAT) scanners . In this application there are different categories of materials each falling within a specific density range. In order to render a particular category, for example the bones, the rendering model considers voxels falling outside the range to be non-existent. Consequently, the resulting view is of the surface of a constant field value. Figure 8 shows a threshold rendering of the same 3D image shown in figure 7.

Thresholding is important since it is a three dimensional view of iso-value surfaces. There are three categories of rendering techniques for thresholding, back to front traversal of the 3D image [7], ray tracing [5], and surface reconstruction [11]. A variation of the threshold illumination model is to assume that the iso-value surface has a normal vector, computed from the field gradient. This allows the iso-valued surface to be shaded using Gouraud or Phong shading [8].

The threshold rendering model throws away much of the data held in the 3D image. Except for applications, like medical imaging, in which a small number of density ranges are of interest, it is like cross-section rendering in that it requires many views of the field which have to be mentally combined in order for a user to entirely perceive the field. In an application like geophysical imaging, a 3D seismic image does not portray as much coherence as a medical image. Hence a threshold rendering is not satisfactory because it generates fragmented pieces instead of cohesive surfaces.

3. Scattering Models
We wish to see more than just iso-value surfaces when rendering a 3D image. It is natural therefore to establish a model for viewing three dimensional translucent solids. We do not often encounter such solids with varying translucency in every day circumstances. However clouds, smoke, mist and other systems of suspended particles are common. Through these we do have experience in perceiving variations of density. A haze in the atmosphere has been modeled by Dugan [4] and opaque clouds, represented as elipsoidal height fields, was modeled by Fishman and Schacter [6]. However true cloud-like scenes are achieved by modeling the scattering of light.

Although the goal here is not the rendering of natural clouds, it is important to consider the interaction between light and a medium that occurs in clouds so that it may be used to exploit our ability to perceive density fields.

3.1 Background
Blinn's model [2] of the rings of Saturn was the first graphics model of the scattering through a thin uniform density cloud of low albedo. Max [13] modeled clouds bounded by quadric surfaces. The emphasis was in

modeling the enclosing volume within which the particles reside.

More recently, Kajiya and Von Herzen [9] introduced a ray tracing technique for rendering 'volume density' models, their term for a 3D image of a density field. They presented a solution for multiple radiative scattering.

Another amorphous class of model is the particle system introduced by Reeves [16,17]. While they have been used to model many natural phenomena, such as blades of grass, the use of particle systems to model fire is most striking. This is because the particles are point light sources that are additively combined when rendered.

There are three effects observed when illuminating translucent objects.
i) Occlusion of a portion of the model occurs when light is scattered by the portions of the cloud closer to the observer.
ii) Shadows are created depending on the position of the light source.
iii) Color variations are caused by separation due to differing amounts of scattering at different wavelengths.

All of these are highly desirable cues for the realistic rendering of clouds. Computationally however, they are expensive; especially when combined with secondary effects like multiple scattering.

3.2 Varying Density Emitters
For the purpose of viewing scientific data, shadowing and scattering color variations, while visually appealing, may actually detract from perception of the density variation. On the other hand, since occlusion is proportional to density, it enhances this perception. A system that solely exhibits occlusion would be a good one to use, at the same time keeping the computation cost low. Such a system is a field of varying density emitters.

A DE object is a system of particle light sources. Unlike Reeve's particle system in which particles are modeled individually the DE object models the density of particles, not the particles themselves. The size of the particle is sufficiently small compared to other dimensions so that the density of the particles can be regarded as a continuous function.

For convenience we define the density $\rho(x,y,z)$ non-dimensionally as the ratio of the volume occupied by particles, Vp to the total volume of the cloud V. Since the ratio is only valid locally we have

$$\rho(x,y,z) = \frac{dVp}{dV} \ .$$

This is actually the probability that a particle is present at the point (x,y,z). Each particle has a volume v_p. The expected number of particles within a region Ω is

$$N_\Omega = \frac{\int\limits_\Omega dVp}{v_p} = \frac{\int\limits_\Omega \rho \ dV}{v_p} \ .$$

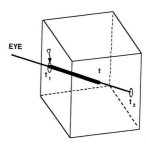

Figure 1 The volume encountered before the ray parameter t.

3.3 The Brightness Equation
Figure 1 sketches the path of a ray traversing the cube. We follow a derivation for the intensity of light, of a fixed wavelength, reaching the eye that is similar to Blinn [2] but allow for varying density and ignore self illumination. The density field $\rho(x,y,z)$ can be parameterized along the ray as $\rho(x(t),y(t),z(t))$, or simply $\rho(t)$. If each particle has an intensity κ, a cylindrical volume element of cross sectional area σ and length dt at a point t along the ray contributes

$$\kappa N_\sigma = \kappa \frac{\rho \ dV}{v_p} = \frac{\kappa\sigma}{v_p} \rho(t) \ dt$$

to the intensity of light emitted toward the eye.

This light emitted by the volume element is scattered backward when traveling on it's way toward the eye due to the particles lying within the volume between t and t_1. The expected number of particles N in this volume, V, is

$$N = \frac{\sigma}{v_p} \int_{t_1}^{t} \rho(\lambda) \, d\lambda \quad .$$

The intensity of light reaching the eye is equal to the light emitted, attenuated by the probability, P(0;V), that there exists zero particles in the volume V. Assuming ρ is small, this can be approximated by a Poisson distribution

$$P(0;V) = e^{-N} \quad .$$

The intensity of the light reaching the eye from the point t is thus

$$I(t) = P(0;V) \, \kappa N_\sigma - e^{-N} \frac{\kappa \sigma}{v_p} \rho(t) \, dt \quad . \tag{1}$$

The total intensity due to all contributions along the ray between t_1 and t_2 is the integral of (1)

$$B = \frac{\kappa \sigma}{v_p} \int_{t_1}^{t_2} e^{-\frac{\sigma}{v_p} \int_{t_1}^{t} \rho(\lambda) \, d\lambda} \rho(t) \, dt \quad . \tag{2}$$

The term $\frac{\sigma}{v_p}$ can be replaced by one constant τ. It has dimensions 1/length and is related to the optical length. We can normalize the entire equation by choosing

$$\frac{\kappa \sigma}{v_p} = 1$$

since we are not dealing with actual radiation measurements. Equation (2) simplifies to

$$B = \int_{t_1}^{t_2} e^{-\tau \int_{t_1}^{t} \rho(\lambda) \, d\lambda} \rho(t) \, dt \tag{3} .$$

This is a simplified version of Kajiya and Von Herzen's brightness equation, omitting the line integrals from the light source [9]. In order for this to hold we have assumed that $\rho(t)$ is small. We can adjust the value of τ to scale $\rho(t)$ in the exponent integral. Higher values of τ increases the attenuation producing a medium that darkens more rapidly.

Finally, taking advantage of the fact that ρ lies between 0 and 1, the transformation

$$\rho' = \rho^\gamma$$

is used to control the spread of density values. Higher γ intensifies the appearance of dense portions relative to the more diffuse regions while lower γ makes the entire cloud appear more diffuse. This transformation is order preserving, i.e. the ordering of two values $\rho'(\lambda_1)$ and $\rho'(\lambda_2)$ is the same as that of $\rho(\lambda_1)$ and $\rho(\lambda_2)$. It is useful to spread out the function ρ since not all density variations are perceptible.

The total brightness along a ray is:

$$B = \int_{t_1}^{t_2} e^{-\tau \int_{t_1}^{t} \rho^\gamma(\lambda) \, d\lambda} \rho^\gamma(t) \, dt \tag{4} .$$

In figure 5 the field in figure 7 is ray-traced using equation (4). The results of varying the two parameters γ and τ are show . Each image is normalized to use the full intensity range. The image lies within a unit cube. As expected, the images on the upper row, in which $\tau = 1$, are not sufficiently attenuated. This is corrected by making the value of τ larger than the distance $t_2 - t_1$ in the second and third rows $\tau = 2$ and $\tau = 3$.

The density spread, controlled by γ, is highest in the first column in which $\gamma = 1$. In the adjacent columns γ equals 5 and 10 respectively. We observe, as predicted in figure 2a, the spread narrows and the higher densities dominate.

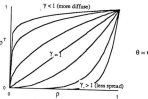
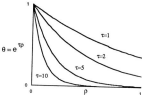

Figure 2a Transformations on ρ Figure 2b Transmittance functions

3.4 Equivalence to Discrete systems.

The model utilized in discrete systems for transmission of light through translucent surfaces or particles in a particle system is equivalent to equation (3). The total intensity remaining after traversing n translucent particles or surfaces, is

$$\sum_{i=1}^{n} b_i \prod_{j=1}^{i-1} \theta_j \, , \tag{5}$$

Where b_i is the amount of light emitted from the ith surface either by reflecting light received from light sources or due to the fact that the surface is itself a light source. The transmittance factor of the ith surface, i.e. the proportion of entering light allowed to go through the surface, is θ_i. It varies between 0 and 1. Since the ith surface is seen through the preceding i-1 surfaces, the total attenuation of b_i is the product of the preceding i-1 θ terms.

Equation (5) is actually equivalent to the discrete form of equation (3)

$$B = \sum_{i=1}^{n} e^{-\tau \sum_{j=1}^{i} \rho(t_j) \, \delta t_j} \rho(t_i) \, \delta t_i$$

$$= \sum_{i=1}^{n} \rho(t_i) \, \delta t_i \prod_{j=1}^{i} e^{-\tau \rho(t_j) \, \delta t_j} \tag{6},$$

in which the surface for i=1 is at $t=t_1$ and the surface for i=n is at $t=t_2$. The ith surface has a thickness δt_i over which the density can be assumed constant. The equivalent terms are

$$b_i = \rho(t_i) \, \delta t_i \, ,$$

and

$$\theta_j = e^{-\tau \rho(t_j) \, \delta t_j} \quad . \tag{7}$$

The threshold rendering model explicitly controls the relationship between θ and ρ. Figure 3a is an example of a threshold window on ρ and figure 3b shows the corresponding θ, ρ relationship.

The equivalent functions for the DE model are shown in figures 2a and 2b. The shapes of these graphs indicate that the DE model is a continuous version of the threshold model. In the limit, as γ goes to infinity, we obtain a threshold model with a range of zero width around $\rho = 1$.

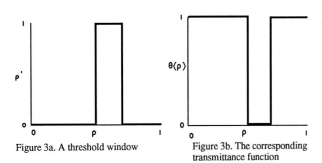

Figure 3a. A threshold window

Figure 3b. The corresponding transmittance function

4. Mapping into Color Space

Since we have ruled out the color variations caused by differential wavelength scattering we are left with the question of whether or not to incorporate the use of color at all. Color can be the result of a realistic model of light or it can be utilized symbolically. Even though models of color space are three dimensional, human perception of color is not.

Robertson and O'Callaghan in [18] give details of their scheme to simultaneously display multiple 2D image data sets. In it, one image is rendered realistically as the surface of a height field while another is used to determine the hue of the displayed surface. The rendering of a DE object is different from their application in that here we are interested in rendering one 3D image. However, we can adapt the idea that realism cues the human visual system thereby enhancing the perception of additional variables.

In ray tracing a surface model, a ray is fired from the eye through a pixel to determine the pixel color. The closest surface that is encountered is the one whose color is chosen as a base color for the pixel. Even though the final color is computed by taking into account light sources and the shading model, the surface color indicates **symbolically** which surface was encountered. The same is true recursively for reflected and refracted rays.

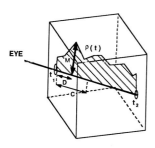

Figure 4. Properties along the ray

We have a more difficult problem when ray tracing a field. Instead of choosing a color that indicates which surface was hit, the ray encounters the density function $\rho(t)$. Since it is not possible to choose one color that will uniquely represent all the values of the function over the ray, we use color to indicate certain characteristic properties of the function. The properties chosen to compute along the ray are (see figure 4):

$$M = (Max(\rho(t)))_{t_2}^{t_1} \text{ Peak value encountered along the ray,}$$

$$D = \text{Distance at which the peak value is encountered,}$$

$$I = \text{The attenuated intensity, equation (4),}$$

$$C = \frac{\int_{t_1}^{t_2} \lambda \rho(\lambda)\, d\lambda}{\int_{t_1}^{t_2} \rho(\lambda)\, d\lambda} \text{ The centroid or center of gravity.}$$

In Robertson and O'Callaghan's scheme, the underlying model is that of rendering a surface whose height was determined by one data set and whose color was based on a model of paint pigmentation. The colors chosen were evenly spaced in the uniform color space proposed by Meyer and Greenburg [15].

We take a simpler view with regard to the choice of color scale. The goal in our scheme is the rough identification of extrema such as 'hot spots'. It is important to realize that such a scale is **symbolic** and are not intended for reading absolute values or distances.

Our scheme was implemented in HSV space. In it the Value component, corresponding to the light intensity, was obtained from the I variable and the Hue component from the peak encountered along the ray, M. The hue scale was reversed to be a scale in which 'hot' colors, reds, represent high values.

Saturation can be a strong depth cue because decreasing saturation gives the effect of seeing in a fog [10]. Hence a depth parameter such as D or C was chosen for the Saturation component.

To illustrate the scheme a charge field was computed for two point charges. Figure 6 shows the M, D and I properties computed as gray images as well as the (M->H, D->S, I->V) color image. Notice that the charge to the left which is further away appears more saturated.

Figure 9a shows in gray scale, the M property for the (τ=2, γ=5) image. Similarly, figures 9b and 9c show the D and I properties and figure 9d the (M->H, D->S, I->V) color image. In this image, if the appearance of a hue is unsaturated, i.e. appears gray, it indicates that it is further away. If it is darker, it is in a diffuse region.

Using the centroid, C property (figure 10a) for saturation is illustrated in figure 10b. This gives the effect of having a denser fog when the centroid is farther. Therefore a hue appears unsaturated due to the average densities, not just the peak, being farther.

In both cases, the existence of any 'hot spot' or high value can be detected by the appearance of a region colored with a hue representing the value, or higher. Unfortunately, this implies that regions of 'low values' are hidden and more difficult to observe; an obvious result of mapping peak values.

The existence of any 'hot spot' or high value is detected by the appearance of a region colored with a hue representing that value, or higher. Unfortunately, this implies that regions of 'low values' are hidden and more difficult to observe; an obvious result of mapping peak values.

4.1 Incorporating Phase functions

To this point, the fact that the DE object is itself a distribution of backward scattering light sources meant that we could ignore the effects of the phase function $\Phi(s,\bar{s})$, the function characterizing the amount of scattering from the direction s to direction $\bar{s}$. Actually, any backward scattering phase function would be adequate for such a model. In a system of a large number of particles, such as we have assumed for the DE object, the phase function is not dependent on local properties of the medium. This is the isotropic case. The anisotropic case occurs when there is a preference in orientation as occurs in the case of Lambertian surfaces.

We diverge from the model of a physical system and assume that the DE object is anisotropic and has a phase function equal to the dot product between a preferred direction, the field gradient, and the direction of lighting. This provides a further attenuation in the brightness equation (3) of $j^{(s)}$ giving

$$B = \int_{t_1}^{t_2} e^{-\tau \int_{t_1}^{t} \rho(\lambda)\, d\lambda} \rho(t)\, j^{(s)}(x,y,z)\, dt \qquad (8).$$

We assume that $j^{(s)}$ is given by

$$j^{(s)}(x,y,z) = \sum_{i=1}^{n} \nabla \rho \cdot \bar{L_i} ,$$

where there are n external light sources and L_i is the direction from the point (x,y,z) to the ith external light source.

Figure 11a is a gray scale rendering of the DE object shown in figure 9 using equation (8) with two light sources. The combined HSV image using the centroid image of figure 10a for Saturation is shown in figure 11b. The main difference between this figure and figure 9d is the darkening of the image in regions where the gradient points away from the light sources and there is a high density.

5. The ray tracer

The ray tracing algorithm is very straight forward. It consists of three steps, ray generation, computation, and display.

The ray generator fires rays from the eye through each screen pixel toward the scene.

When a ray intersects the extent of the 3D image it is stepped through the image extent and the four properties M, D, I and C are evaluated. The stepping algorithm is essentially identical to the one described by Snyder and Barr [19]. Since the centroid C requires the denominator line integral, this is also calculated and the final value for C is computed when the ray exits the image extent.

The four properties are stored as a temporary four dimensional image. When the entire image has been ray traced, an image may be created mapping functions of any three of the properties to the HSV components. As discussed in the previous section, the more intuitive combinations are the (M->H,D->S,I->V) and (M->H,C->S,I->V) mappings. The reason for storing the properties first is to establish a scale for the range of variation of each property. This allows the fullest usage of the HSV components.

Spatial coherence within the 3D image allows stepping the ray in the direction of increasing ray parameter. If there were a terminating criterion, such as minimum attenuation factor, the algorithm could stop the stepping before traversing the entire span of the extent. Unfortunately, with the exception of the intensity, all the properties have no such criterion. This is the price paid to be able to see the peak value behind even dim regions.

Even though there are no other types of rays fired, such as shadow or reflection rays, ray tracing was chosen as the rendering technique due to the simplicity in computing the attenuated integral in equation (3). Ray tracing matches well with the physical paradigm of light propagation and scattering in a non-homogeneous medium.

5.1 Results

The 3D images rendered in figures 5, 7, 8, 9, 10 and 11 have dimensions 64 x 64 x 400. The 256 x 256 images in figure 7 each took 450 seconds on a Sun 4 workstation to compute. The 512 x 512 images in the figures 9 and 10 took on the order of 2550 seconds to compute while figure 11 which took 4530 seconds. The 512 x 512 images in figures 2 and 3 took on the order of 76 seconds to compute, showing that thresholding, being a surface technique, is relatively fast.

The image generation phase takes on the order of 1 second on a Sun 3/160.

6. Conclusion

The technique presented for rendering a scalar field in color is by no means exhaustive. Color is added to the intensity computed in order to identify high valued regions, 'hot spots'. Even though the intensity calculation is a continuous generalization of the threshold rendering model, the full color image is superior since important hot spots cannot be occluded.

One obvious extension is the x-ray illumination model. In an x-ray, an attenuated line integral is computed similar to the brightness given in equation (3). This allows high density regions to be detected by the absence of light due to higher scattering.

Another extension is to go toward greater realism and perform shadowing and color scattering on non-density emitter models, i.e models that only scatter. This would allow the combination of backward and forward illumination. Discrete light sources could be placed within such a model to highlight regions of interest.

Another technique of visualization, which is important for three dimensional perception, is animation. As in particle systems, a fuzzy object 'comes alive' when animated.

7. Acknowledgements

The author thanks Schlumberger-Doll Research and in particular Stan Vestal, director of the systems science department, for providing the environment in which this work was possible. Indranil Chakravarty has always been there to discuss and help and has made suggestions in reviewing this paper.

8. References

[1] J. Blinn and M. Newell, "Texture and Reflection in Computer Generated Images," Comm. ACM, Oct. 1976, pp. 542-547.

[2] J. Blinn, "Light Reflection Functions for Simulation of Clouds and Dusty Surfaces",Computer Graphics 16(3), July 1982, pp. 21-29.

[3] L. Chen, G. Herman, R. Reynolds and J. Udupa, "Surface Shading in the Cuberille Environment", IEEE Computer Graphics and Applications 5(12), December 1985, pp.33-43.

[4] W. Dugan, "A terrain and cloud computer image generation model", Computer Graphics 13(2), 1979, pp.143-150.

[5] E. Farrell, "Color Display and Interactive Interpretation of Three-Dimensional Data", IBM J. Res. Develop 27(4), July 1983, pp.356-366.

[6] B. Fishman and B. Schacter, "Computer display of height fields", Computers and Graphics 5, 1980, pp.53-60.

[7] G. Frieder, D. Gordon, R. Reynolds, "Back-to-front Display of Voxel-based Objects", IEEE Computer Graphics and Applications, 5(1), Jan. 1985, pp.52-60.

[8] K. Hohne and R. Bernstein, "Shading 3D-Images from CT Using Gray-Level Gradients", IEEE Trans. on Medical Imaging MI-5, 1, March 1986, pp.45-47.

[9] J. Kajiya, B. Von Herzen, "Ray Tracing Volume Densities", Computer Graphics 18(3), July 1984, pp.165-174.

[10] R. Klassen, "Modeling the Effect of Atmosphere on Light", ACM Trans. on Graphics, 6(3), July 1987, pp.215-237.

[11] W. Lorensen and H. Cline, "Marching Cubes: A High Resolution 3D Surface Construction Algorithm", Computer Graphics 21(4), July 1987, pp. 163-169.

[12] X. Mao, T. Kunii, I. Fuhishiro and T. Noma, "Hierarchical Representations of 2D/3D Gray-Scale Images and Their 2D/3D Two-Way Conversion", IEEE Computer Graphics and Applications 7(12), December 1987 pp. 37-44.

[13] N. Max, "Light Diffuson through Clouds and Haze", Computer Vision, Graphics and Image Processing 33, 1986, pp.280-292.

[14] D. Meagher. "Geometric Modeling Using Octree Encoding" Computer Graphics and Image Processing 19(2), June 1982, pp 129-147.

[15] G. Meyer and D. Greenberg, "Perceptual Color Spaces for Computer Graphics", Computer Graphics 14, 1980, pp.247-261.

[16] W. Reeves, "Particle Systems- a technique for modeling a class of fuzzy objects", Computer Graphics 17(3), July 1983, pp.359-373.

[17] W. Reeves and R. Blan, "Approximate and Probabilistic Algorithms for Shading and Rendering Structured Particle Systems", Computer Graphics 19(3), July 1985, pp.313- 322 .

[18] P. Robertson and J. O'Callaghan, "The Application of Scene Synthesis Techniques to the Display of Multidimensional Image Data", ACM Trans. on Graphics , 4(4), Oct. 1985, pp.247-275.

[19] J. Snyder and A. Barr, "Ray Tracing Complex Models Containing Surface Tessellations", Computer Graphics 21(4), July 1987, pp.119-128.

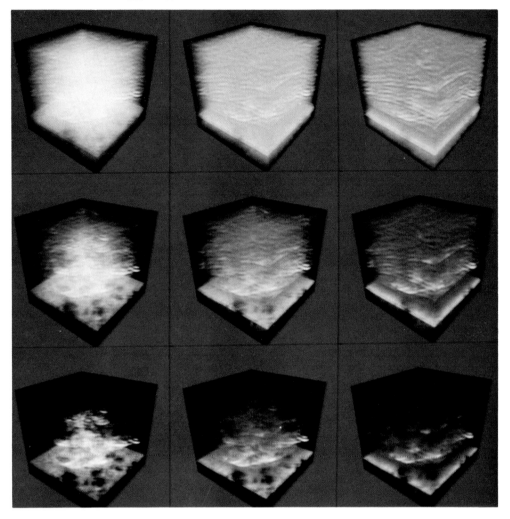

Figure 5, Intensity of the 3D image. $\tau = 1, 2, 3$ across the columns.
$\gamma = 1, 5, 10$ down the rows.

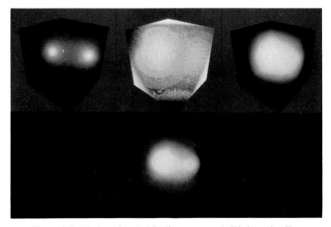

Figure 6, Rendering of peak (M), distance to peak (D), intensity (I)
and the HSV mapping (M->H, D->S, I->V) for a simple field.

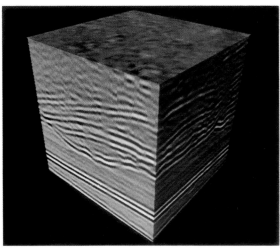

Figure 7. 3D image of sub-soil seismic data.

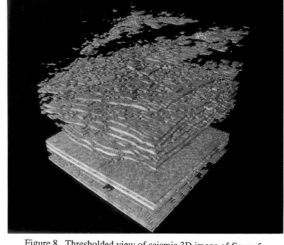

Figure 8. Thresholded view of seismic 3D image of figure 5.

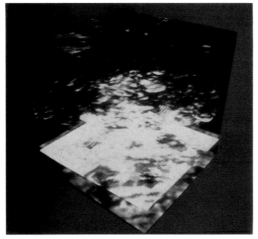

figure 9a. The peak values (M) for $\tau=2$, $\gamma=5$.

Figure 9b. Distance to the peak (D) for $\tau=2$, $\gamma=5$.

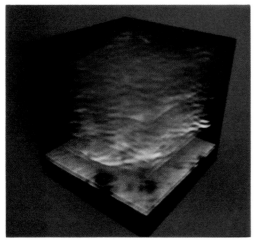

Figure 9c. The intensity (I) for $\tau=2$, $\gamma=5$.

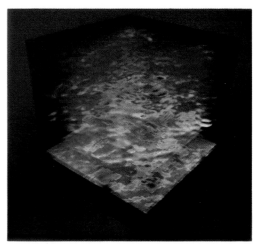

Figure 9d. The HSV mapping (M->H, D->S, I->V)
combining figures 9a, 9b and 9c.

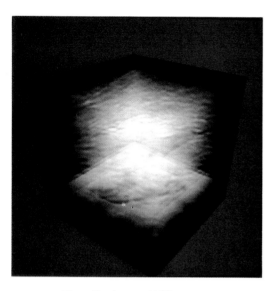

Figure 10a. the centroid (C).

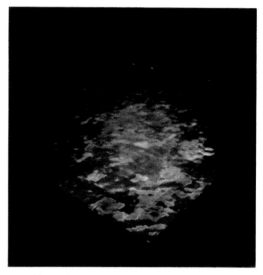

Figure 10b. The HSV mapping (M->H, C->S, I->V)
combining figures 9a, 10a, 9c.

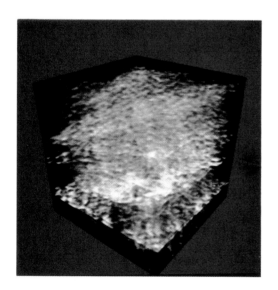

Figure 11a. the intensity (I)
using a phase function derived to highlight the gradient.

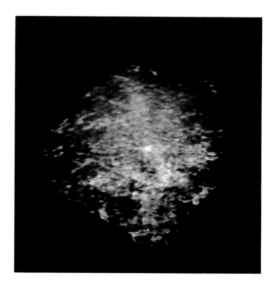

Figure 11b. The HSV mapping (M->H, C->S, I->V)
combining figures 9a, 10a, 11a.

V-BUFFER: Visible Volume Rendering

Craig Upson
Stellar Computer, Inc.
Milpitas, California

Michael Keeler
Ardent Computer Corp.
Sunnyvale, California

1. Abstract

This paper presents rendering techniques that use volumes as the basic geometric primitives. It defines data structures composed of numerous subvolumes, in excess of 100,000. Over each subvolume, a scalar field describes the variation of some physical quantity. The two rendering methods described herein assume a trilinear variation of this scalar field within each volume element, unlike voxel-based techniques that assume a constant value for each subvolume. The result is a higher order approximation of the structures within the volume. In addition, solid texture mapping, atmospheric attenuation, and transfer functions relating the dynamic range of the scalar field to color and opacity are used to isolate important data features. The result is a new method for the visualization of three-dimensional data resulting from numerical simulations and observations of natural phenomena. This method continuously covers the gap between surface-based and voxel-based techniques.

CR Categories: I.3.3, I.3.5, I.3.7

Keywords: Volume Rendering, Voxel, Isosurface, Natural Phenomena, Ray Tracing

2. Introduction

In ever increasing numbers, data sets are being generated that represent three-dimensional, volumetric information. These data are coming from complex computational simulations in many fields - from scientific experiments and sophisticated observations, particularly medical imaging. These volume datasets present a challenge to current imaging techniques to display clearly as much information contained throughout the domain as possible but not to restrict interpretation and analysis by simplifying the data for the sake of rendering ease. The fact that these datasets are very large and that numerical simulations can easily produce numerous data volumes as a time series in a single run compounds the problem.

Volumetric data are typically a set of scalar or vector values defined on a grid in three-space. In most cases the grid is rectilinear and the data are either point values at the nodes or voxels representing a constant value for that volume element. Computational cells differ from voxels in that they are defined as the volume contained within the rectangular box bounded by eight corner nodes and, importantly, that the scalar function varies throughout the cell. Traditional techniques for visualizing such 3D volumes have consisted of either constructing wireframes or surfaces at a threshold value of the scalar field within the volume or using a cuberille representation for the constant-valued voxel.

©1988   ACM-0-89791-275-6/88/008/0059 $00.75

One of the first methods of representing isosurfaces was to draw a mesh or net of vectors from sets of 2D line contours from each of two or three orthogonal planes (20). Because many datasets originate as a series of planar slices, especially in medical imaging, other algorithms were developed to generate polygonal surfaces from stacks of 2D contours. These processes work well enough on cases where the connectivity is fairly obvious (8,12), but they become complicated by ambiguous branching situations and must be resolved either by user interaction (4) or with a heuristic approach (6). A more general approach is to tile a surface using the cell information and to perform surface-volume intersection calculations at specific threshold levels (5,18,21). Recently, the Marching Cubes algorithm has been used to generate detailed surfaces and shading information from medical imaging data (14).

Surface representations are appropriate when the goal is to show a boundary layer or a specific threshold within the volume. They are less useful in attempts to understand the whole of the volume, especially of an amorphous dataset, because by their nature, they display a small sample of the overall data and ignore the rest. Furthermore, the polygonal geometry of the surface is derived data created by a binary classification of the data (either the cell contains the surface threshold value, or it doesn't), and this limitation introduces biases and aliasing that can interfere with correct interpretation. The polygonal representation frequently requires more disk space (by a factor of four to ten for the examples in this paper†) which presents an added burden on computational, and especially I/O, capabilities.

Medical imaging technologies, such as computed tomography and other scanners, generate three-dimensional data by assigning intensity values to small, contiguous regions in the domain of interest. A cuberille model represents such data by decomposing the spatial extent with three regularly spaced, mutually orthogonal sets of parallel planes (10). Boundary surfaces are detected (1) and rendered as planar faces on voxel boundaries. Improvements to the shading algorithms have resulted in much smoother surface appearances (3).

Recent hardware advances in computational power and especially in large and cheaper memories have spurred the development of other voxel-based rendering. PIXAR has developed a software package for its machine that enables a user to visualize volumetric data by classifying each voxel with a constant value for color, opacity, and/or refractive index. Structures in the domain's interior are displayed by deriving the optical depth from the opacity of the voxels along the viewing path and then summing their colors (16). In this method the resolution of the computed image is determined by the spatial resolution of the data, not by the sampling density of the pixels. Thus small data sets result in a very "blocky" image, and the only way to improve this is to resample the data at a higher frequency (in three space).

Voxel-based renderers work directly upon the volume data and are therefore better at presenting a holistic view of the dataset. However, visualizations of smaller datasets suffer from the discretization and inherent implication that the variation from voxel to voxel is a discontinuous step function.

A more sophisticated approach, using ray tracing to determine optical depth, is presented by Kayija and Von Herzen (11). Their work is oriented toward modeling the scattering of light and energy within the volume to create visually realistic scenes with less emphasis on the enhancements needed for scientific visualization.

---

† Volume data: 100 x 40 x 25 = 100K nodes, x 4 bytes/node = 400Kbytes. As a surface of 50K polygons: 3 vertices/poly x 24 bytes/vertex x 50K polygons = 3.6Mbytes.

We present a visualization method that displays datasets of computational cells, that is, a scalar function S on a rectilinear (although not necessarily uniformly spaced) net of nodes:

$$S(x_i, y_j, z_k) \quad i = 1, N_i \quad j = 1, N_j \quad k = 1, N_k \quad \Delta x_i = c_{x_i} \quad \Delta y_j = c_{y_j} \quad \Delta z_k = c_{z_k}$$

In numerical simulations, as in nature, there are few discontinuities and fewer step functions. Thus we can be assured that there is some smooth variation in this function between nodes of the domain mesh. However the actual form of this variation is not known. In fact the only statement that can be made concerning this variation is that it is not constant. In this work we assume that the variation between any two adjacent nodes is linear in space, and by assuming this simple functional form, we have minimized the amount of subjective interpretation of the data. By assuming that the variation is not constant, but rather a higher order interpolation, we can generate smoother representations of the underlying data - something that is essential for lower resolution datasets resulting from numerical simulations.

3. The Visible Volume Method

3.1 Overview

Two independent methods are employed for visibility detection. One method, ray-casting, processes all cells encountered by a view ray before moving onto the next ray (or pixel). The second method processes all pixels into which a cell projects before moving onto the next cell. A general summary of the method is as follows: First, a correlation is made between the screen coordinate system and the volume data. The cell/pixel combination that is to be processed is then determined by one of the two visibility detection methods. A traversal path within the cell is calculated and scalar values along the path are generated using a trilinear interpolation of the values at the cell's node points. At each evaluation point of the scalar field the object's properties are determined by mapping the scalar value to color and opacity via independent transfer functions, and additional data is added using three-dimensional texture mapping. Finally, these values are accumulated by integrating through the cell until either opacity reaches unity or the entire cell has been traversed. the algorithm then picks the next pixel or cell, depending on which algorithm is used.

Other traditional cues for three-dimensional shape recognition are also used, such as depth cueing and illumination from light sources. Currently only ambient and diffuse shading have been implemented but an extension to other illumination models is straightforward.

The traditional compromise between image quality and rendering time is handled by employing the two visible volume determination algorithms. In general, the faster method is a simplified ray casting technique while the higher-quality (and usually, but not always, slower) method is an object space-based cell-by-cell algorithm.

3.2 Interpolation Form

As mentioned previously, the variation within a cell is linear in each axis, or trilinear in 3-space. The equation for this C^1 function is:

$$S(x,y,z) = a_1 + a_2x + a_3y + a_4z + a_5xy + a_6xz + a_7yz + a_8xyz \quad (1)$$

where the coefficients, a_i, are determined by the matrix system:

$$X_{ij}A_j = S_i \quad (2)$$

where X_{ij} is an 8-by-8 matrix containing products of the coordinates of the corner nodes, A_j is the coefficient vector, and S_i is the scalar value at the nodes. This system can be solved with an L-U decomposition method or by direct substitution. The advantage of the decomposition is that it is also used with a different right-hand-side to determine the variation of the shading coefficients within the cell (as well as the texture map). It is more efficient simply to interpolate in 3-space to evaluate the scalar field within a cell, but this speed advantage rapidly disappears with repeated evaluations in the volume integration. When parameterized in distance from the viewpoint, the trilinear form becomes a cubic equation, and it is in this form that the interpolation takes place.

3.3 Object Properties and Transfer Functions

Transparency, color, shading, and texture mapping are essential to effectively visualize the scalar field using a volume-based renderer. Opacity, the inverse of transparency, is defined as a transfer function of the scalar field. Thus there is a mapping from the dynamic range of the variation in the scalar field into a range of opacities: $O(S(x,y,z))$. Similarly there is a mapping from the range of the scalar field into color space via additional transfer functions: $R(S(x,y,z))$, $G(S(x,y,z))$, $B(S(x,y,z))$. In this manner, relevant structures in the domain can be isolated via a variation in opacity and highlighted via color. The transfer functions can be specified to show a variation in the scalar field as a smooth gradation in color or opacity (Figure 1a), or object features occuring at particular scalar ranges may be highlighted by a mapping such as that in Figure 1b. Isosurfaces at a particular threshold are obtained by specifying the opacity transfer function as a step function with a large discontinuity on the opacity axis over a relatively narrow range of scalar values (Figure 1c). In addition, solid-texture mapping (15) is used to facilitate the correlation of multiple scalar fields at one time.

3.4 Visible Volume Detection

3.4.1 Method 1: Ray Casting

Two techniques are employed for the determination of visibility. The faster method is similar to a ray tracing method (11) but with higher order interpolation, subcell quadrature, and enhanced efficiency due to the simple data structure (and no interobject effects such as shadowing). In this method, rays emanate from the viewpoint, pass through pixels in the view plane, and intersect the data volume. At each pixel, a ray is tracked through the volume until either the accumulated opacity reaches unity or the volume is exhausted, at which time the accumulated colors and opacity are stored and the processing moves onto the next pixel. The scalar function is evaluated at the nearest face of each cell along its path and is stepped along until it traverses the entire cell with evaluations of the scalar field, shading function, opacity, texture map, and depth cueing at each stepping point. As the slope of the ray determines which three of six faces it can penetrate on any given cell, the probability of a ray intersecting a given face perpendicular to a coordinate axis is inversely proportional to the slope of the ray with respect to that axis. In this manner, the testing for penetration can be minimized. The intersections of the ray with respect to each set of parallel planes (aligned with the coordinate axis) can also be generated and the three lists merged after all have been calculated. Although this requires no testing during the intersection generation, it is slower in the merge stage. This technique also generates the entire traversal through the data volume when, in fact, the ray will probably terminate early due to its accumulated opacity. At the expense of vectorization, we have chosen to integrate the pixel color and opacity as the ray is tracked, rather than to generate the entire traversal list for several pixels and integrate them at once in vector loops. In this manner the reduced efficiency of scalar processing is more than compensated by the saved operations. The integration to determine opacity and color is

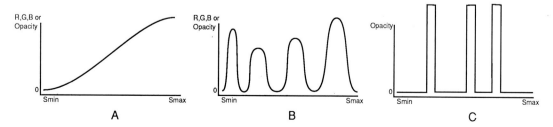

Figure 1. Examples of transfer functions mapping scalar value to color or opacity.

similar to the second method and will be presented in another section of this paper.

3.4.2 Method 2: Cell-by-Cell Processing

The alternative method of visibility determination is object-space oriented and is based on sweeping through the domain processing one cell at a time. Because the database is very simple in structure, it is possible to determine a cell processing order that completely determines which cells occlude, or partially occlude, others. Cells are processed starting with those on the plane closest to the the viewpoint and progress plane by plane until the farthest cells have been processed. The processing order of cells within each plane proceeds from the closest cell to those adjoining this cell according to their distance from the viewpoint. This results in a concentric sweep about the initial cell (Figure 2). After the first cell's contribution is computed several other cells can be processed concurrently because they will not overlap in screen space.

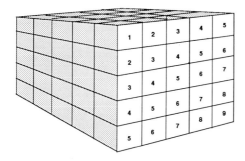

Figure 2. Cells numbered by processing priority. Cells with the same number do not affect each other and thus may be processed in parrallel.

In this technique the trilinear interpolation coefficients are computed for the scalar, shading, and texture mapping functions, and a bounding box for the cell is determined. The bounding box is clipped to each scanline creating pixel runs. Integration (in depth) occurs at the four corners of each pixel in the run into which the cell projects. These evaluations are then averaged resulting in the current pixel color and opacity. For each scanline in the bounding box, the cell is intersected with the scan plane and the resulting convex polygon is broken down into at most five spans (Figure 3). The pixels are then integrated from front to back similarly to the ray casting method. However, all spatial functions - opacity, shading, and texture mapping - vary as a cubic function within the cell making evaluations efficient and vectorizable. Because the functional form is known, an explicit variable-stepsize quadrature method can be used for depth integration, thus further reducing the computations.

Once a cell has been processed, the technique moves onto the next cell in its predetermined order. In this manner the visibility determination is the volumetric analog of a traditional Z-Buffer algorithm, and as such, it might be possible to implement in hardware. In addition, because this is a front to back algorithm, it lends itself to incremental display during the visibility determination. In this method a large fraction of the visible image is computed early in the process while refinements occur later and more slowly. This is different than other methods of adaptive refinement (2) in that the representation (volumetric) remains the same during the refinement process, and improvements later on add information farther from the viewpoint. Thus the user is able to terminate a rendering process early either if any of the viewing parameters are obviously wrong or if only qualitative behavior is required. The effect on the screen as each cell is processed and pixels are updated is visually akin to what one might experience watching a fog-shrouded hillside as the fog recedes and ever more detail of the landscape is revealed (19).

3.4.3 Comparison of the two Methods

Three criteria have been chosen to compare the two methods: memory requirements, antialiasing, and computational efficency.

Memory requirements: The ray casting method requires that the scalar, shading, and texture map function coefficients for all active cells projecting into the current pixel be in memory at once. For some images in

which the object occupies a small amount of screen space, these coefficients could consume a substantial amount of memory (up to 16MB for a 64*64*64 cell domain). The cell-by-cell method, on the other hand, needs only the current cells' interpolation coefficients in memory, but it may require the entire frame buffer if a single cell projects into the entire screen (1.3MB for video resolution).

Antialiasing: Because the ray casting technique is essentially a point sampling method, the only straight forward approach to antialias the image is by way of distributed ray casting (7,13) with several ray samplings per pixel. However the cell-by-cell method does lend itself to a nearly analytic solution in the integration. With this method one can choose a small number of sample points within a cell to analytically integrate the function exactly. Our current implementation does not go to this effort because the images produced by this volumetric renderer are generally without distinct boundaries. Thus we find the object-space non-analytic antialiasing currently implemented in the cell-by-cell method to be sufficient for our needs.

Computation efficiency: A comparison of computational efficiency between the two methods falls into two catagories: image-space and object-space issues. The image-space criteria are based on coherency, vectorization, and parallelism. The object-space issues are based on volume culling and optical depth issues.

Vectorization of the ray caster is difficult because there are few occasions when enough information has been collected to make vectorization pay off. In the cell-by-cell method, vectorization occurs along a span within a cell. This method most naturally parallelizes at the scan line level while the ray caster, like its ray tracing relatives, parallelizes at the pixel level. The cell-marching method could be implemented on a highly parallel machine in which each floating point processor has only a modest amount of local memory. The ray caster would require a global shared memory.

Both techniques examine each cell prior to processing to determine whether or not there is any visible material. The dynamic range of the scalar field within the cell is mapped into its corresponding opacity range. Both methods cull the volume if the summation of the opacity is zero while the cell method also tests on the scan plane and pixel levels to further reduce possible work. Another object space concern that affects the efficiency of the two methods is the average optical depth. This is the number of cells that an average pixel must traverse before it becomes opaque. In general the ray caster is much more efficient when the object is fairly opaque, and the cell-by-cell method can reach the same efficiency when the object is quite transparent. The latter technique also improves as the field of view decreases and thus the average span length does not decrease much with depth.

In conclusion, the ray caster is generally more efficient for conventional machine architectures and opaque data volumes while the cell by cell method holds the greatest potential for vector and highly parallel machines.

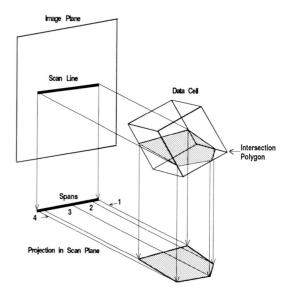

Figure 3. Determination of the spans for the cell-by-cell technique.

3.5 Nodal Shading Function

The shading coefficients are determined on a node-by-node basis prior to the visibility calculation. These coefficients are a function of the dot product of the surface normal at the node point and the light sources. Because the rendering technique is not surface oriented, a normal vector does not exist and is replaced by a normal space of dimensionality three. For illumination effects, however, we assume that the sample point lies on a level surface. The normal at a point on a level surface is the gradient, and this is used for the dot product with the light source. Because the interpolation function is continuous within the cell, the gradient (or normal) could be analytically calculated from this. However, the interpolation form is not differentiable at the cell boundaries, and thus any shading based on this analytical differentiation will show anomalies from cell to cell. To avoid this problem, finite differences are used to approximate the gradient of the field at the node points. The normal function, when interpolated similar to the scalar field, is then a continuous function over the cell and continuous but not differentiable between cells. The dot product of the normal vector at a node and the light source vector(s) is then stored as the nodal shading function. If the light sources and the object remain in the same orientation relative to each other, then this shading function is not recomputed from frame to frame.

3.6 Integration and the Illumination Model

The intent of this visualization technique is to represent abstract datasets of natural phenomena while minimizing the amount of subjective aesthetics during the image creation process. In this regard, this work differs from others whose goals are to simulate the visual aspects of the phenomena realistically. Our goal allows us to simplify the illumination model to the bare minimum needed to represent the data. On the other hand, we desire to have as much flexibility as possible with regard to feature isolation, and therefore we have additional transfer functions imbedded in the illumination model.

Hall (9) has categorized illumination models into three basic types: empirical (incremental), true geometric (ray tracing), and analytical (radiosity). The illumination model used here is empirical, employing true geometry for pixel calculations with some simplifications:

$$I(\lambda) = K_a(\lambda)I_a + K_d(\lambda)\Sigma(N^*L_j)I_j \qquad (3)$$

Here $I(\lambda)$ is the perceived intensity as a function of wavelength (λ), K_a is the ambient coefficient, I_a is the ambient intensity, K_d is the diffuse coefficient, N is the local gradient, L_j is the jth light source vector, and I_j is the diffuse intensity of the jth light source. We have chosen to leave out the specular term as it adds few visual cues in an object without distinct surfaces (although it is easy to add). In actuality the diffuse coefficient is a function of more than the wavelength:

$$K_d = K(\lambda)^*T_d(\lambda,S(x,y,z))^*M(\lambda,x,y,z) \qquad (4)$$

Where K is the actual diffuse coefficient, T_d is the object color transfer function, and M is the solid texture map color.

The determination of a pixel's color is the result of a three-dimensional integration from front to back. The cell-by-cell method sums contributions from all cells that project into the pixel, while the ray caster may miss some cells due to sampling errors. For some pixels the integration will terminate before all cells have been included because the amount of material already encountered has summed to the maximum opacity. The two visibility methods perform essentially the same integration with the exception that the ray caster is a point sampling-technique and the cell-by-cell is a volume-approximation method. We present the integration details for the cell method because the ray caster is a simplification of the former. The integral is as follows:

$$I(\lambda) = \int_x \int_y \int_z [f(d)O(S)[K_a(\lambda)I_a + K_d(\lambda,S,M)\Sigma(N^*L_j)I_j] + (1 - f(d))bg(\lambda)]dxdydz \qquad (5)$$

where $f(d)$ is the normalized atmospheric attenuation as a function of distance (depth cueing), O is the optical depth per unit density and is a transfer function of the scalar field $O(S(x,y,z))$, and $bg(\lambda)$ is the background intensity as a function of frequency. The limits of integration are determined by clipping the pixel to the span (Figure 4).

The integral is approximated as a discrete summation by evaluating the scalar, opacity, texture map, depth cuing, and shading functions at the corners of the clipped pixel on the nearest face and then by stepping through the sub-volume in depth accumulating intensity and opacity using trapezoid rule quadrature (17). This summation is continued until either the cell is exhausted or the accumulated opacity reaches unity. If the opacity exceeds the maximum in a step, then the correct termination point at which opacity reaches unity is determined and the functions are evaluated at that point. Once a pixel is opaque, it is flagged and not processed again. A voxel approximation is used if the entire cell projects into a pixel. In this case, the functions (scalar field, opacity, shading, and texture maps) evaluated at the corner points of the cell are averaged into a single contribution that is multiplied by the pixel coverage and stored. Traditional voxel rendering has also been implemented as an option of the cell-by-cell technique. In this case, a cell will be processed as a constant-valued voxel or as a continuous cell depending on criteria supplied by the user.

4. Examples

Two examples taken from the computational sciences have been chosen to illustrate this technique. All figures were rendered with the cell-by-cell technique for maximum image quality.

The first, from computational fluid dynamics, is the result of a three-dimensional, transient calculation of turbulent shear flow of two fluids on a 50 by 40 by 100 cell grid. The top fluid is traveling at mach 1.1 while the lower fluid is stationary. The result of their interaction is a turbulent interface along the shear plane. The scalar quantity depicted is a derivation of the mass fraction of one fluid with respect to the other. In this image (Figure 5), simple piece-wise linear variation is used for the nodal color and opacity transfer functions with shading effects. Cells containing only one fluid or the other are completely transparent, while those with a mixture are semi-opaque. This representation is contrasted with a surface technique (using a polygonal tiler (18)) in Figure 6 in which the stationary fluid is shown. Evident in the volumetric rendering is that the mixing is not confined to a narrow region in space and that the thickness of the mixing layer is far from uniform as seen in the color variation.

The second example, from computational meterology, is the result of a finite difference simulation on a grid of 109 by 109 by 31 cells. In this numerical experiment a severe storm resembling a tornado is simulated. The variable shown in Figure 7 is the rain water content as a function of three space during the storm's evolution. In this image three spikes are used in the color and opacity transfer functions to isolate a range of water content within the cloud with no shading effects. This is contrasted with Figure 8 in which shading from a light source is used to give a better three-dimensional perception. A step function in the opacity transfer function is used (in the red region) to show a distinct, opaque surface, thus demonstrating the surface rendering capabilities of the method.

In Figure 9 the rain water field is texture mapped with another field variable, the vertical vorticity. In this manner one can correlate the destructive wind effects (due to the intense circulation) with the most obvious visual representation of a cloud: the moisture content due to rain water. The red color indicates high values of vertical vorticity, especially apparent in the tornado's funnel region. The funnel image is nearly transparent at the ground level, implying low moisture content, a phenomenon commonly observed in tornados. At the top of the funnel the

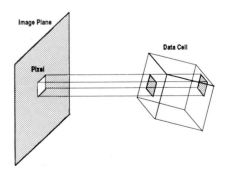

Figure 4. Integration volume for a single cell.

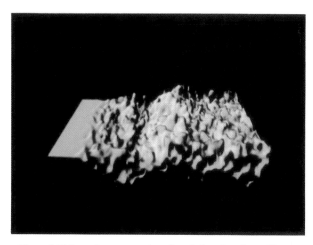

Figure 5. Volumetric representation of a turbulent shear layer. (Data courtesy of Michael Norman, National Center for Supercomputing Applications)

Figure 6. Shear layer represented by a polygonal surface composed of 107,434 polygons consolidated from 293,585 triangles.

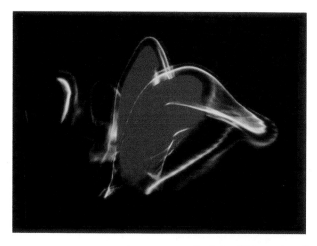

Figure 7. Rain water content of a severe storm simulation. (Data courtesy of Robert Wilhelmson, NCSA).

Figure 8. Rain water image with illumination from a single light source.

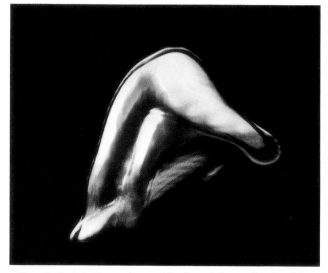

Figure 9. Shaded rain water image with color variation as a function of the vertical vorticity distribution. The opacity is a function of the rain water content.

color transitions to white denoting a drop to near zero vertical vorticity. At this point the image is opaque due to high rain water content. The conclusion is that atmospheric material entrained in the funnel is swept up vertically until it reaches the anvil of the cloud. Here the storm weakens and water precipitates, thus forming a squall-line behind the tornado.

5. Conclusion

The V-Buffer has several advantages over other methods of visualizing volumetric data sets. Of primary importance is that the data are considered point samples at nodes and that the scalar field is assumed to vary within each computational cell. This is a more accurate representation of the real world and allows for smooth, continuous representations of even small datasets. Analysis and exploration of the data is enhanced by easily modified transfer functions for color and opacity. Depth information is conveyed by both attenuation and shading. Three-dimensional texture mapping is available to correlate multiple scalar fields at once. The effects possible with this volumetric technique range continuously from a surface representation, by using a step function in the opacity transfer function and shading, to an amorphous transparent wisp of form, with the opacity nearly zero and no shading.

This method uniquely combines the capabilities of volumetric rendering with variable transparency and solid texture mapping to provide the visual cues required for insight into complex three-dimensional phonenomena, such as the tornado example above.

The V-Buffer is designed as an analytic tool, not as a technique to synthesize realistic images. The illumination model is sufficient to render a smooth image and minimizes other visual effects that may bias the interpretation. This algorithm, while inefficient for some very large volumetric datasets where projected voxels are sufficiently small relative to pixels, can be accurately used in such cases.

Obvious enhancements would be to provide boolean operations on volume datasets that will allow additional viewing options, such as cut-away sections and internal clipping. Although such operations may be performed as a preprocessing step, the size of the data calls for these abilities to be built into the renderer. Also, this volume technique could be integrated with traditional surface renderers so that various types of data can be displayed simultaneously.

6. Acknowledgement

This work was done at the National Center for Supercomputer Applications, Champaign, Illinois, and the San Diego Supercomputer Center, San Diego, California.

7. References

1. Artzy, E., Frieder, G., Herman, G., "The Theory, Design, Implementation and Evaluation of a Three-Dimensional Surface Detection Algorithm", Computer Graphics and Image Processing, Vol 15, No 1, Jan. 1981, p. 1-24.

2. Bergman, L., Fuchs, H., Grant, E., "Image Rendering by Adaptive Refinement", Computer Graphics, Vol 20, No 4, Aug. 1986, p. 29-37

3. Chen, L., Herman, G., Reynolds, R., Udupa, J., "Surface Shading in the Cuberille Environment", IEEE Computer Graphics and Applications, Vol 5, No 12, Dec. 1985, p. 33-43.

4. Christiansen, H., Sederberg. T., "Conversion of Complex Contour Line Definitions into Polygonal Element Mosaics", Computer Graphics, Vol 12, No 3, 1978, p. 187-192.

5. Christiansen, H., Stephenson, M., Nay, B., Grimsrud, A., "Movie.BYU Training Text", Graphics Utah Style, Provo, Utah, 1987.

6. Cook, L., Dwyer, S., Batnitzky, S., Lee, K., "A Three-Dimensional Display System for Diagnostic Imaging Applications", IEEE Computer Graphics & Applications, Vol 3, No 5, Aug. 1983. p. 13-19.

7. Cook, R., Porter, T., Carpenter, L., "Distributed Ray Tracing", Computer Graphics, Vol 18, No 3, 1984, p. 137-145.

8. Fuchs, H., Kedem, Z., Uselton, S., "Optimal Surface Reconstruction from Planar Contours", CACM, Vol 20, 1977, p.693-712.

9. Hall, R., "A Characterization of Illumination Models and Shading Techniques", Visual Computer, Vol 2, No 5,1986, p. 268-277.

10. Herman, G., Lui, H., "Three-Dimensional Display of Human Organs from Computed Tomograms", Computer Graphics and Image Processing, Vol 9, No 1, Jan.1979, p. 1-21.

11. Kajiya, J., Von Herzen, B., "Ray Tracing Volume Densities", Computer Graphics, Vol 18, No 3, 1984, p. 165-173.

12. Keppel, E., "Approximating Complex Surfaces by Triangulation of Contour Lines", IBM J. Res. Development, Vol. 19, 1975, p.1-21.

13. Lee, M., Redner, R., Uselton, S., "Statistically Optimized Sampling for Distributed Ray Tracing", Computer Graphics, Vol 19, No 3, 1985, p. 61-67.

14. Lorensen, W., Cline, H., "Marching Cubes: A High Resolution 3D Surface Construction Algorithm", Computer Graphics, Vol 21, No 4, 1987, p. 163-169.

15. Peachey, D., "Solid Texturing of Complex Surfaces", Computer Graphics, Vol 19, No 3, 1985, p. 279-286.

16. PIXAR, "ChapVolumes Volume Rendering Package, Technical Summary", July, 1987.

17. Press, W., Flannery, B., Teukolsky, S., Vettering, W., "Numerical Recipes: The Art of Scientific Computing", Cambridge Univ. Press, 1986.

18. Upson, C., "The Visual Simulation of Amorphous Phenomena", Visual Computer, Vol 2, No5, 1986, p.321-326.

19. Watts, A., "Cloud-Hidden, Whereabouts Unknown; A Mountain Journal", Pantheon, New York, 1973.

20. Wright, T., "A One-pass Hidden-line Remover for Computer Drawn Three-Space Objects", Proc. 1972 Summer Computer Simulation Conference, 1972, p.261-267.

21. Yost J., "Computational Fluid Dynamics for Realistic Image Synthesis", M.S. Thesis, University of Utah, Dept of Computer Science, August 1987

Volume Rendering

Robert A. Drebin, Loren Carpenter, Pat Hanrahan

Pixar
San Rafael, CA

Abstract

A technique for rendering images of volumes containing mixtures of materials is presented. The shading model allows both the interior of a material and the boundary between materials to be colored. Image projection is performed by simulating the absorption of light along the ray path to the eye. The algorithms used are designed to avoid artifacts caused by aliasing and quantization and can be efficiently implemented on an image computer. Images from a variety of applications are shown.

CR Categories: I.3.3 [Computer Graphics] Computational Geometry and Object Modeling - Curve, surface, solid, and object representations. I.3.5 [Computer Graphics] Three-Dimensional Graphics and Realism - Color, shading, shadowing and texture; Visible line/surface algorithms.

Additional Keywords and Phrases: Medical imaging, computed tomography (CT), magnetic resonance imaging (MRI), non-destructive evaluation (NDE), scientific visualization, image processing.

Introduction

Three-dimensional arrays of digital data representing spatial volumes arise in many scientific applications. Computed tomography (CT) and magnetic resonance (MR) scanners can be used to create a volume by imaging a series of cross sections. These techniques have found extensive use in medicine, and more recently, in non-destructive evaluation (NDE). Astrophysical, meteorological and geophysical measurements, and computer simulations using finite element models of stress, fluid flow, etc., also quite naturally generate a volume data set. Given the current advances in imaging devices and computer processing power, more and more applications will generate

volumetric data in the future. Unfortunately, it is difficult to see the three-dimensional structure of the interior of volumes by viewing individual slices. To effectively visualize volumes, it is important to be able to image them from different viewpoints, and to shade them in a manner which brings out surfaces and subtle variations in density or opacity.

Most previous approaches to visualizing volumes capitalize on computer graphics techniques that have been developed to display surfaces by reducing the volume array to only the boundaries between materials. Two-dimensional contours from individual slices can be manually traced (Mazziotta, 1976) or automatically extracted (Vannier, 1983) and connected to contours in adjacent slices to form triangle strips (Keppel, 1975, Fuchs, 1977, Christianson, 1978, Ganapathy, 1982) or higher order surface patches (Sunguruff, 1978). These techniques have problems with branching structures, particularly if the distance between serial sections is large relative to the size of the volume elements or *voxels*. Other surface techniques output polygons at every voxel. The *cuberille* technique first sets a threshold representing the transition between two materials and then creates a binary volume indicating where a particular material is present. Each solid voxel is then treated as a small cube and the faces of this cube are output as small square polygons (Herman, 1979). Adjacent cubes can be merged to form an oct-tree; this representation compresses the original voxel array and reduces the subsequent processing requirements (Meagher, 1982). The *marching cubes* technique places the sample values at the vertices of the cube and estimates where the surface cuts through the cube (Lorensen, 1987). A variation of this technique, called the *dividing cubes* algorithm, approximates the polygon with points (Cline, 1988). These techniques are analogous to algorithms used to extract surfaces from implicit functions (Norton, 1982, Bloomenthal, 1987, Wyvill, 1986), or to produce three-dimensional contour maps (Wright, 1979).

Several researchers have developed methods which directly image the volume of data. The *additive reprojection* technique computes an image by averaging the intensities of voxels along parallel rays from the rotated volume to the image plane (Harris, 1978, Hoehne, 1987). This has the effect of simulating an x-ray image. The *source-attenuation reprojection* technique assigns a source strength and attenuation coefficient to each voxel which allows for object obscuration (Jaffey, 1982, Schlusselberg, 1986). Attenuation coefficients are often referred to as *opacities*. Depth shading algorithms trace rays through the volume array until they hit a surface and

©1988   ACM-0-89791-275-6/88/008/0065 $00.75

then assign an intensity inversely proportional to the distance to the eye (Vannier, 1983). This is usually referred to as *depth cueing* in the computer graphics literature. Radiation transport equations have been used to simulate transmission of light through volumes (Kajiya, 1984). The *low-albedo* or *single scattering* approximation has also been applied to model reflectance functions from layered volumes (Blinn, 1982). Several of these algorithms require the ability to trace rays in any direction through a volume array. Various algorithms for ray tracing volumes are described in (Fujimoto, 1986, Tuy, 1984, Levoy, 1988, Schlusselberg, 1986)

An implicit assumption in surface rendering algorithms is that a model consisting of thin surfaces suspended in an environment of transparent air accurately represents the original volume. Often the data is from the interior of a fluid-like substance containing mixtures of several different materials. Subtle surfaces that occur at the interface between materials, and local variations in volumetric properties, such as light absorption or emission, are lost if the volume is reduced to just surfaces. Also, since a voxel represents a point sample, information about the exact position and orientation of microsurfaces may be lost in the sampling process, and it is not reasonable to expect to be able to recover that information.

The technique presented in this paper deals with volumes directly. The volume array is assumed to be sampled above the Nyquist frequency, or if this is not possible, it is assumed that the continuous signal is low-pass filtered to remove high frequencies that cause aliasing. If this criterion is met, the original continuous representation of the volume can be reconstructed from the samples. The sampled volume will look smooth and realistic, and artifacts such as jagged edges will not be present. Each stage in the volume rendering algorithm is designed to preserve the continuity of the data. Thresholding and other highly non-linear operations are avoided, and when geometric transformations are applied to the data, the result is resampled carefully. The goal is to avoid introducing computational artifacts such as aliasing and quantization, since these interfere with the viewer's ability to interpret the data.

Overview of the Algorithm

Figure 1 shows a process diagram of the volume rendering algorithm. Associated with each stage is a slice from a volume corresponding to the stage. The first step in using the volume rendering algorithm is to convert the *input data volume* to a set of *material percentage volumes*. The values in each voxel of the material percentage volumes are the percentage of that material present in that region of space. These material percentage volumes either can be input directly, or can be determined from the input data volumes using probabilistic classification techniques. Many different classification techniques are possible and the one of choice depends on the type of input data. The classification of a CT volume data set is shown in Figure 1.

Given any material property and the material percentage volumes, a composite volume corresponding to that property can be calculated by multiplying the percentage of each material times the property assigned to that material. For example, a composite *color volume* is formed by summing the product of the percentage of each material times its color. An *opacity volume* is computed by assigning each material an opacity value. In Figure 1, the color volume shown is actually the product of the color and the opacity volume.

Boundaries between materials are detected by applying a three-dimensional gradient to a *density* or ρ *volume*. The ρ volume is computed from the material percentage volumes by assigning a ρ value to each material. The gradient is largest where there are sharp transitions between materials with different ρ's. The magnitude of the gradient is stored in a *surface strength volume* and is used to estimate the amount of surface present. The direction of the gradient is stored in the *surface normal volume* and is used in shading computations.

The *shaded color volume* represents the sum of the light emitted by the volume and scattered by the surfaces. The relative contributions of volume emission and surface scattering can be varied depending on the application. The reflected component is computed using a surface reflectance function whose inputs are the position and color of the light sources, the position of the eye, the surface normal volume, the surface strength volume, and the color volume. The amount of emitted light is proportional to the percentage of luminous material in the voxel.

To form an image, the shaded volume is first transformed and resampled so that it lies in the viewing coordinate system. In many cases the transform is just a rotation. Figure 1 shows the result as the *transformed volume*. In this coordinate system the eye is at infinity, so all rays are parallel to an axis of the volume. An image of the rotated volume can be formed by projecting the volume onto the image plane taking into account the emission and attenuation of light through each voxel. This projection may be calculated using a simple compositing scheme modeled after an optical film printer (Porter, 1984).

Voxel Mixtures and Classification

The volume rendering algorithm presented in this paper operates on volumes which are modeled as a composition of one or more materials. Examples include: a set of physical substances, such as bone, soft tissue, and fat in the musculoskeletal system; a set of simulated measurements, such as stress and strain in a finite element model; or a set of signals, such as the individual spin echoes of magnetic resonance. A voxel's composition is described by the percentage of each material present in the voxel.

When the material composition at each voxel is not provided, classification is used to estimate the percentages of each material from the original data. It is very important when classifying the data not to make *all-or-none* decisions about which material is present, but rather to compute the best estimate of how much is present within each voxel. Making material decisions by thresholding introduces artifacts in the material percentages which are easily visible in the final images (Drebin, 1987). Probabilistic classifiers work particularly well, because the probability that a material is present can be used as an estimate of the percentage of the material present in the voxel.

The first probabilistic classifier developed for this volume rendering technique was a maximum-likelihood classifier for musculoskeletal CT volumes. In this case the intensities in the input volume represent x-ray radiation absorption. The classification yields volumes containing the percentages of air, bone, soft-tissue, and fat. A histogram of the x-ray absorption of the input volume is the sum of three overlapping distributions, corresponding, in increasing order of intensity, to fat, soft-tissue, and bone. In the general case, the probability that any voxel has value (intensity) I is given by

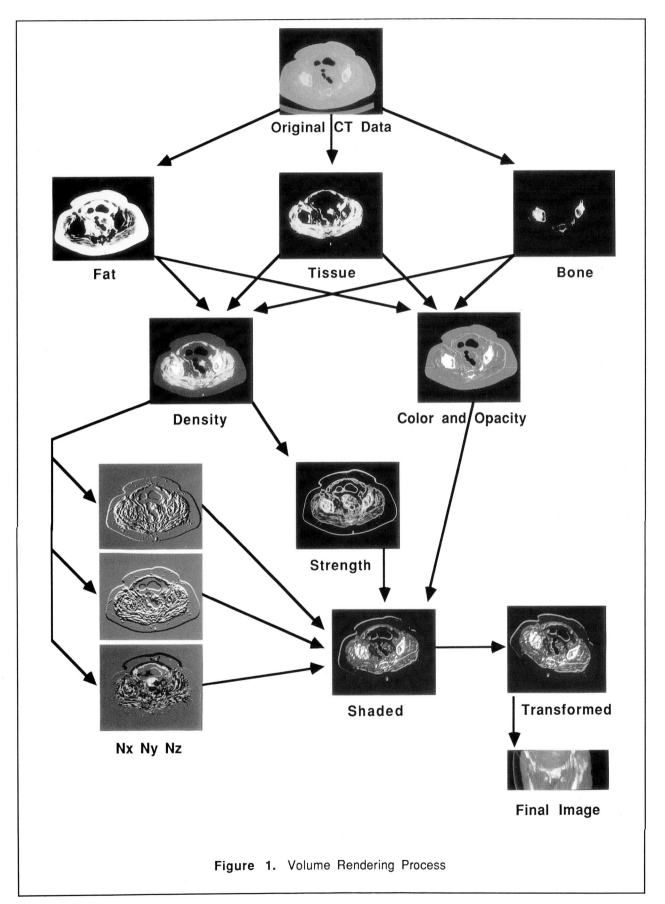

Figure 1. Volume Rendering Process

$$P(I) = \sum_{i=1}^{n} p_i P_i(I)$$

where n is the number of materials present in the volume, p_i is the percentage of material i in a given voxel, and $P_i(I)$ is the probability that material i has value I. In the case of musculoskeletal CT, the distribution functions $P_i(I)$ represent the x-ray absorption of each material, and are known *a-priori*. Once the individual distribution functions are known, the Bayesian estimate of the percentage of each material contained within a voxel of value I is given by:

$$p_i(I) = \frac{P_i(I)}{\sum_{j=1}^{n} P_j(I)}$$

Note that when the classification is a function of only a single intensity volume, as in this case, the classification can be performed by using table lookup on the input values. Furthermore, if no more then two material distributions overlap, the percentage of each material varies linearly between their peaks. This is roughly the case with musculoskeletal CT, because bone and fat intensity distributions rarely overlap, so voxels are either linear combinations of fat and soft-tissue or soft-tissue and bone. Figure 2 shows a hypothetical histogram, material distributions, and resulting classification functions. The first step in Figure 1 shows an actual classification of a CT data set.

Maximum likelihood classifiers can be built that handle more than one input data volume; these are like the multispectral classification algorithms commonly employed in remote sensing and statistical pattern recognition. However, maximum likelihood methods will not always work well. In performing the musculoskeletal classification described above, voxels are never classified as being a mixture of air and bone since the soft-tissue distribution lies between the air and bone distributions. However, within nasal passages mixtures of air and bone are common. Using knowledge about what combinations of materials may potentially mix will improve the classification and hence the estimates of the material percentages. Adaptive classification algorithms which take advantage of local neighborhood characteristics (Tom, 1985), multi-spectral mixture analysis (Adams, 1986), or probabilistic relaxation algorithms (Zucker, 1976) can all be used with the volume rendering algorithm. However, it should be stressed again, that only probabilistic classification algorithms should be used, since binary classification algorithms will introduce artifacts in the subsequent renderings.

Once material percentage volumes are available, volumes corresponding to other properties can be easily computed. As an example, consider creating a RGBα color-opacity volume. In this paper, a piece of colored material is modeled with four coordinates: R, G, B are the intensities of red, green and blue light, and α is the opacity. An α=1 implies that the material is completely opaque, and α=0 implies that it is completely transparent. (A more accurate model of transparency would use three color components because a real material will filter red, green and blue light differently.) The color of a mixture of materials is given by

$$C = \sum_{i=1}^{n} p_i C_i$$

where $C_i = (\alpha_i R_i, \alpha_i G_i, \alpha_i B_i, \alpha_i)$ is the color associated with material i. Note that in this representation, the colors are

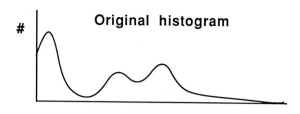

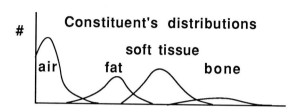

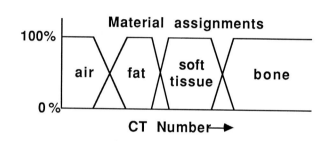

Figure 2. CT Classification

premultiplied by their opacities. This representation of colors and the advantages of premultiplying colors by opacity are is discussed in (Porter, 1984).

Matting

After the volume is classified, it is often helpful to remove sections or lessen the presence of certain regions or materials. *Matte volumes* are created for these operations. Each voxel of a matte is a scalar fraction, which defines the percentage of the voxel contained by the matte. Matte volumes can be simple geometric shapes, such as wedges or halfplanes, or regions computed from other volumes, such as an *air* matte volume which is the region not contained in any material percentage volumes.

Matting operations correspond roughly to fuzzy set operations. This allows *spatial set operations* to be performed on volumes. An example of this is merging multiple volumes into a single volume using union. Another example is to carve a shape out of a solid. One of the most common uses of matte volumes is to perform cut-aways; another is to remove regions where the data is unreliable or uninteresting. Finally, since matte values are fractional, they can be used to lower the percentage of material in a region, or to change the material properties in different regions. Depth cueing is done by matting a ramp in z with the final shaded color volume before projection. This has the effect of making near colors brighter than the far colors.

Each voxel of a matte volume M contains a value between 0 and 1 which indicates the presence or absence of the matte. A volume, V, is combined with a matte, M, with the following operations:

$$V \text{ in } M = MV$$

$$V \text{ out } M = (1-M)V$$

The **in** operator yields the portion of V inside of M. Set intersection is accomplished by multiplying the two volumes. The **out** operator returns the portion of V outside of M. This is done by complementing M and then forming the set intersection. Complementing M is performed by subtracting M from 1. By making mattes fractional instead of binary, the boundaries between inside and outside are smooth and continuous. This is important if the continuity of the data is to be preserved. Binary mattes will lead to artifacts in the final images.

Surface Extraction

The shading model described below requires information about surfaces within each voxel, including their normal and "strength." The strength of a surface is a combination of the percentage of surface within the voxel and the reflection coefficient of that surface. In this paper, the surface physics is approximated by assigning to each material a density characteristic ρ. A surface occurs when two or more materials of different ρ's meet. The strength of the surface is set equal to the magnitude of the difference in ρ.

A ρ volume is computed by summing the products of the percentage of each material in the voxel times the material's assigned ρ, such that:

$$D = \sum_{i=1}^{n} p_i \rho_i$$

where D is the total ρ of a voxel and ρ_i is the density assigned to material i. The material ρ assignments can be arbitrary; they do not have to be related to the actual mass of the materials or the imaged intensities. By assigning two materials the same ρ's they are effectively coalesced into a single material and the surface between them will not be detectable. The surface normal and strength volumes are derived from the ρ volume's gradient. The strength of a surface is proportional both to the magnitude of the difference in ρ and to the sharpness of the transition from one material to the other. The surface strength volume is used to indicate the presence of surfaces.

The surface normal, $\vec{N}$, is defined as:

$$N_x = \nabla_x D = D_{x+1} - D_x$$
$$N_y = \nabla_y D = D_{y+1} - D_y$$
$$N_z = \nabla_z D = D_{z+1} - D_z$$

This vector is normalized to have unit length and stored in a *surface normal volume*. The magnitude of the gradient is stored in a *surface strength volume*.

$$S = |\vec{N}|$$

Since a derivative is a high-pass filter, noisy volumes will have very noisy derivatives. When this is a problem, more accurate estimates of the derivatives can be computed by first blurring or running a low-pass filter over the material volume. This is directly analogous to the two-dimensional problem of

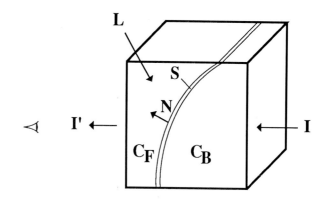

Figure 3. Voxel shading model

detecting edges in the presence of noise.

Figure 1 shows a ρ volume and the resulting surface normal and strength volumes. Note that surfaces are represented by a surface strength and not a binary value indicating whether surfaces are present or not. This allows diffuse transitions between material to be represented, and positions of surfaces in the final image often appear to lie between voxel boundaries.

Lighting Model

Figure 3 shows the lighting model used in each voxel. A light ray traveling towards the eye enters the voxel from behind with incoming intensity I, and exits from the front with outgoing intensity I'. The light intensity changes due to the following effects: i) materials may act as translucent filters, absorbing the incoming light, ii) they may be luminous and emit outgoing light, and iii) they may contain surfaces or particle scatterers which both attenuate the incoming light and also reflect light from light sources towards the eye. Light transmission through a volume can be modeled as a radiation transport problem (Kajiya, 1984). However, in this paper only a single scattering of radiation from a light source to the eye is assumed. Light rays from the light source are also not attenuated as they travel through the volume. These assumptions make the lighting model very easy to implement.

If a light ray travels through a colored translucent voxel, the resulting color is

$$I' = C \text{ over } I = C + (1-\alpha_C)I$$

where α_C is the alpha component of C. The first term models the emitted light and the second term the absorption of incoming light. In order to include surface shading, the voxel is subdivided into two regions: the region in front and behind a thin surface region. Each of these regions is assigned an RGBα color so that it can both emit and absorb light. The outgoing intensity is then

$$I' = (C_F \text{ over } (C_S \text{ over } (C_B \text{ over } I))) = C \text{ over } I$$

Since the **over** operator is associative, the three color volumes corresponding to front C_F, back C_B and surface C_S can be combined into a single volume $C = C_F \text{ over } C_S \text{ over } C_B$ before the integration is performed.

The reflected surface color, C_S, is a function of the surface normal, the strength of the surface, the diffuse color of the surface C_D, the direction $\vec{L}$ and color C_L of the light source, and the eye position $\vec{E}$. The color of the reflected light has two components, a diffuse component whose color is given by the

color of the surface, and a specular component whose color is given by the color of the light. The formula is

$$C_S = (f(\vec{N},\vec{L})C_D + g(\vec{E},\vec{N},\vec{L})C_L) \text{ in } S$$

where f and g are diffuse and specular shading functions, and C_D is the diffuse color of the surface. Appropriate functions for f and g are discussed in (Phong, 1975, Blinn, 1982, Cook, 1982). Note that the amount of surface shading is proportional to the strength of the surface. No reflected light will appear in the interior of a homogeneous material.

The simplest approach is to set the surface diffuse color equal to $C_D = C_F + C_B$; that is, treat the color of the surface as the color of the mixture, and to just add it into the mixture. C is then set equal to $C_S \text{ over} C_D$. The problem with this approach is that color from neighboring materials bleed into the surface. For example, if white bones are next to red muscle tissue, the bleeding will cause the surfaces of the bones to appear pink. The best choice for C_D is C_B, but this is technically difficult because it is not known which of the materials in the mixture is the back material and which is the front. One solution to this problem is to examine the sign of the density gradient in the direction of view. If it is positive, the front of the voxel has a lower ρ than the back; otherwise the front has a higher ρ. Once the materials are ordered from front to back, the colors can be assigned accordingly.

Viewing and Projection

An image is computed by projecting the volume onto the image plane. One common method used to perform this projection is to cast rays through the volume array. The problem with this approach is that sampling artifacts may occur and it is computationally expensive since it requires random access to the volume data. The approach used in this algorithm is to first transform the volume so that the final image lies along the front face of the viewing pyramid, and so that rays through the vantage point are all parallel and perpendicular to the image plane. The transformation of the volume can be done efficiently in scanline order which also allows it to be properly resampled. Modeling light transmission during projection is also particularly convenient in this coordinate system.

After the shading calculation, there exists a RGBα volume C. As the projection occurs, the intensity of light is modeled according to the equations described in the previous section. Each colored plane of the volume is overlaid on top of the planes behind it from back to front using the **over** operator. The orthographic projection through the $z'th$ plane of the volume can be expressed as:

$$I_z = C_z \text{ over } I_{z+1}$$

where I is the accumulated image, C_z is the color-opacity of plane z. The initial image I_n is set to black and the final image is I_0. This algorithm need not store the I volume, just the final image. This multi-plane merge could just as easily be done from front to back using the **under** operator (A **under** $B \equiv B$ **over** A).

It is important to be able to view the volume with an arbitrary viewing transformation, which includes translation, rotation, scaling, and perspective. In order to preserve the simplicity of the parallel merge projection, the viewing coordinate system is fixed, and the volume is geometrically transformed and resampled to lie in that coordinate system. This is done as a sequence of 4 transformations,

$$T = P_z(z_e)\, R_z(\psi) R_y(\phi) R_z(\theta)$$

where R_z and R_y are rotations about the z and y axes, respectively, and P_z is the perspective transformation. The transformations are parameterized by the Euler angles, (θ,ϕ,ψ), and z_e, the z coordinate of the eye point. In many applications, a sequence of orthographic views corresponding to a rotation about only single axis is required, so that only one of the rotates is required, and the viewing transformation can be done in 1/4 the time. Since each rotation is perpendicular to an axis of the volume, the volume rotation can be performed by extracting individual slices along the axis perpendicular to the rotation axis, rotating them individually as images, and then placing them into the result volume. Performing a three-dimensional rotation using a sequence of three rotates requires the ability to extract planes perpendicular to at least two axes (y and z). This requires either an intermediate transposition of the volume, or a storage scheme which allows fast access along two perpendicular directions. P_z is a perspective transformation with the eye point on the z-axis. This can be efficiently implemented by scanning sequentially through slices in z, and resizing the x-y images by $1/(z_e - z)$ — that is, magnifying images near the eye relative to images far from the eye. Rotations and scalings are both special cases of an affine transformation. Two-dimensional affine transformations can be performed using the two-pass scanline algorithms discussed in (Catmull, 1980). For the viewing transformation outlined above, this requires as many as 8 resampling operations. It should be possible to generalize the two-pass image transformation to a three-pass volume transformation and reduce the number of resampling operations. It is important when performing these geometric manipulations that the images be reconstructed and resampled using either triangular or bicubic filters to preserve the continuity of the data. Poor reconstruction and resampling will introduce artifacts in the final images.

Results

Figures 4-12 show images of various volumes rendered with the above techniques. Figures 4-6 are medical images based on CT data sets. Figure 4 shows four images rendered with different material properties and variations of the algorithms presented in this paper. Figure 5 illustrates an application of a matte volume to cut-away a wedge from the child's head. Figure 6 shows a whole body reconstruction of an adult male with different colors and opacities on the left and right halves. The volume rendering technique has been shown to be valuable in clinical applications (Fishman, 1987, Scott, 1987). A biological application of the volume rendering algorithm is shown in Figure 7: a whole body scan of a sea otter. This image lead to the discovery that adult sea otters have an extra wrist bone not present in young otters (Discover, 1988). Figure 8 shows a physical sciences application of volume rendering. Figure 8 is a rendered image of a smoke puff. The original input data set was acquired as a sequence of images from a CCD camera. Each image was a cross section of the smoke

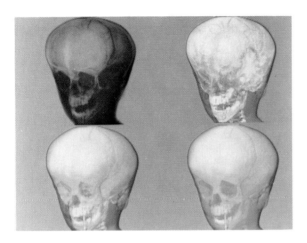

Figure 4(a-d). Rendered images from a 124 slice 256x256 CT study of a child. **4a** is a self-illuminated rendering with depth shading. **4b** and **4c** are surface-only renderings shaded with a directional light source. Cf+Cb is used as the surface color in **4b**, while a computed Cb is used to color the surface in **4c**. **4d** is rendered with both self-illumination and surface shading with a directional light source. The CT study is courtesy of Franz Zonnefeld, Ph.D., N.V. Philips.

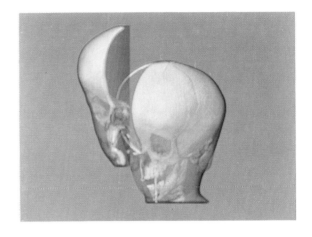

Figure 5. A matte volume is used to extract a section of the child's head.

puff illuminated by a plane of laser light. Figures 9-11 are images computed from the results of computer simulations. Figure 9 is an image of the results of the simulation of the containment of a plasma in a magnetic fusion reactor. Figure 10 is a simulation of the energy surrounding a "broom handle" moving at Mach 1.9. Figure 11 shows a comparison of volume rendering vs. standard surface rendering. In the image created by the volume rendering technique, the stress throughout the volume is visible. Regions of high stress are both more opaque and a "hotter" color. Showing the stress on just the surface doesn't convey nearly as much information. Finally, Figure 12 is an example of the NDE (non-destructive evaluation) of air flow through a turbine blade. An obstruction in the air flow inside the turbine blade is detected in the volume rendering. Since this obstruction is internal, it cannot be seen by direct visual inspection. The original input data set was a CT volume.

The volumetric qualities of these images are much more apparent when viewed in motion. The algorithm presented above can be efficiently adapted for this purpose, because only the stages of the calculation that change from frame to frame need to be recomputed.

Summary and Discussion

A method has been described for imaging volume arrays. This method produces significantly better images than conventional computer graphics renderings of extracted surfaces primarily because both volumetric color and opacity, and surface color and opacity are modeled and a great deal of attention was paid to maintaining a continuous representation of the image.

The distinguishing feature of volume rendering algorithms is that surface geometry is never explicitly represented as polygons or patches (even if a surface model alone would be

sufficient). For a volume which contains fine detail, this approach makes more sense because the size of the polygons would be on the order of the size of a pixel. Rendering millions of small polygons is inefficient because it takes more information to represent a voxel-sized polygon than just a voxel, and because it is very difficult to produce high-quality antialiased renderings of subpixel-sized polygons.

Each stage in the algorithm inputs a volume and outputs another volume. Care is taken at all stages to not introduce any digital artifacts. Each input volume is interpreted as a sampled continuous signal, and each operation preserves the continuity of the input. All quantities are stored as fixed point fractional values with 11 bits to the right of the decimal point. Intermediate calculations typically use 16 bits, although when computing normals 32 bits are used. This appears to be enough precision to avoid quantization artifacts and numerical problems.

All the volume operations described in this paper can be performed on slices or small sets of adjacent slices − thus reducing volume computation to image computation. This is desirable since there is a large body of information about image computing. Many of the two-dimensional algorithms mentioned in this paper − table lookup, affine transformation, compositing, etc. − are typically available in standard image computing libraries. Special purpose processors exist to quickly execute image computations, making these techniques practical. Almost all two-dimensional image processing algorithms have analogous three-dimensional versions. Developing three-dimensional volume processing algorithms is a good area of research.

The viewing transformation and projection stages of the volume rendering algorithm can also be done using ray tracing. The technique for computing the attenuation of light along parallel rays as done in this paper can be generalized to

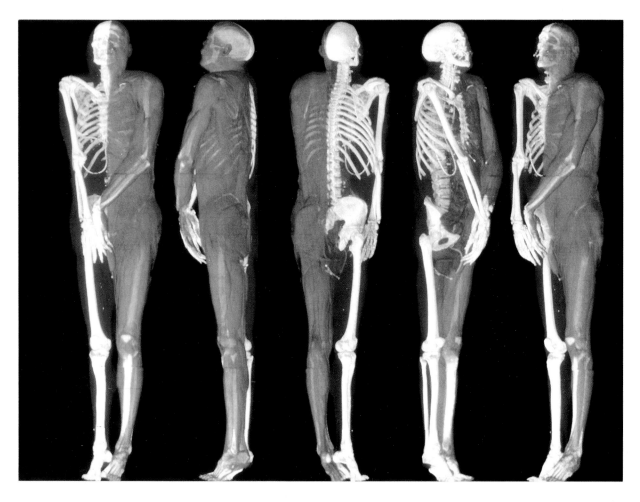

Figure 6. Rendered images from a 650 slice 256x256 CT study of a man. A matte volume was used to apply different levels of translucency to the tissue on the left and right halves. The CT study is courtesy of Elliot Fishman, M.D., and H.R. Hruban, M.D., Johns Hopkins Medical Institution.

attenuate light along a ray in any direction. One potential advantage of a ray tracer is that if a ray immediately intersects an opaque material, voxels behind that material need not be processed since they are hidden; however, in many situations a volume is easier to visualize if materials are not completely opaque. The major disadvantage of ray tracing is that it is very difficult to avoid artifacts due to point sampling. When rays diverge they may not sample adjacent pixels. Although rays can be jittered to avoid some of these problems, this requires a larger number of additional rays to be cast. Ray tracers also require random access (or access along an arbitrary line) to a voxel array. The algorithm described in this paper always accesses images by scanlines, and thus in many cases is much more efficient.

Future research should attempt to incorporate other visual effects into volume rendering. Examples of these include: complex lighting and shading, motion blur, depth-of-field, etc. Finding practical methods of solving the radiation transport equation to include multiple scattering would be useful. Tracing rays from light sources to form an illumination or shadow volume can already be done using the techniques described in the paper.

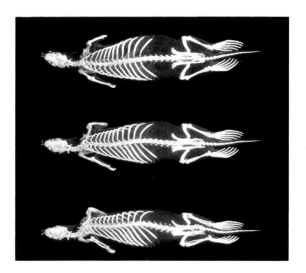

Figure 7. Rendered images from a 400 slice CT study of a sea otter. Data courtesy of Michael Stoskopf, M.D., and Elliot Fishman, M.D., The Johns Hopkins Hospital.

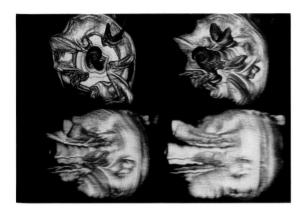

Figure 8. Rendered images of a smoke puff volume. Data courtesy of Juan Agui, Ph.D., and Lambertus Hesselink, Ph.D., Department of Aeronautics and Astronautics, Stanford University.

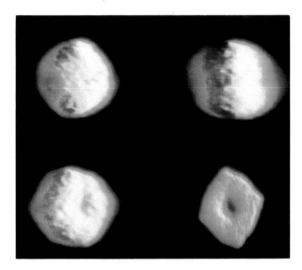

Figure 9. Magnetic fusion simulation. Data courtesy of Dan Shumaker, Ph.D., Lawrence Livermore National Laboratory.

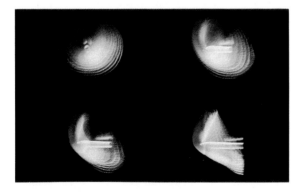

Figure 10. Rendered images showing the simulated energy near a cylinder moving at Mach 1.9. Data courtesy of University of Illinois, CSRD.

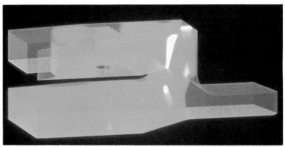

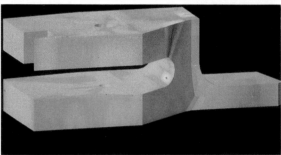

Figure 11. Comparison of volume and conventional surface rendering techniques depicting the stresses through the material of a simulated mechanical part. Figure 11a is volume rendered, and 11b is constructed from Gouraud-shaded polygons. Data courtesy of Mr. Harris Hunt, PDA Engineering.

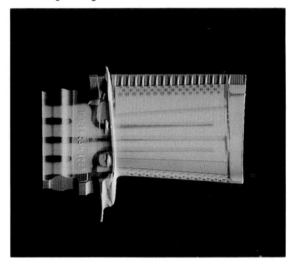

Figure 12. Turbine blade CT study. Air cooling passages are blue. Notice the obstruction in the lower left. Data courtesy of General Electric Aircraft Division Industrial CT.

Acknowledgements

Dana Batali and Malcolm Blanchard made many of the pictures shown in this paper; they also enthusiastically tried different techniques on different data sets. Dr. Elliot Fishman provided the original hip data set that motivated this work and later verified its clinical applications. Ed Catmull, Rob Cook, Tom Porter, and Alvy Ray Smith provided many ideas during frequent discussions which we have incorporated into the algorithm presented. Walter Karshat and Flip Phillips helped with the current implementation on the Pixar Image Computer.

References

"Why Abalones Don't Find Otters Cute," *Discover*, p. 10 (April 1988).

ADAMS, JOHN B., MILTON O. SMITH, AND PAUL E. JOHNSON, "Spectral Mixture Modeling: A New Analysis of Rock and Soil Types at the Viking 1 Lander Site," *Journal of Geophysical Research* 91(B8) pp. 8098-8112 (July 1986).

BLINN, JAMES F., "Light Reflection Functions for Simulation of Clouds and Dusty Surfaces," *Computer Graphics (SIGGRAPH '82 Proceedings)* 16(3) pp. 21-29 (July 1982).

BLOOMENTHAL, JULES, "Polygonization of Implicit Surfaces," Report CSL-87-2, Xerox PARC (May 1987).

CATMULL, EDWIN AND ALVY RAY SMITH, "3-D Transformations of Images in Scanline Order," *Computer Graphics (SIGGRAPH '80 Proceedings)* 14(3) pp. 279-285 (July 1980).

CHRISTIANSON, H. N. AND T. W. SEDERBERG, "Conversion of Complex Contour Line Definitions into Polygonal Element Mosaics," *Computer Graphics (SIGGRAPH '78 Proceedings)* 12 pp. 187-192 (1978).

CLINE, HARVEY E., WILLIAM E. LORENSEN, SIGWALT LUDKE, CARL R. CRAWFORD, AND BRUCE C. TEETER, "Two Algorithms for the Reconstruction of Surfaces from Tomograms," *Medical Physics*, (June, 1988).

COOK, ROBERT L. AND KENNETH E. TORRANCE, "A Reflection Model for Computer Graphics," *ACM Transactions on Graphics* 1(1) pp. 7-24 (1982).

DREBIN, ROBERT A., ELLIOT K. FISHMAN, AND DONNA MAGID, "Volumetric Three-dimensional Image Rendering: Thresholding vs. Non-thresholding Techniques," *Radiology* 165 p. 131 (1987).

FISHMAN, E. K., R. A. DREBIN, D. MAGID, AND ET. AL., "Volumetric Rendering Techniques: Applications for 3-Dimensional Imaging of the Hip," *Radiology* 163 pp. 737-738 (1987).

FUCHS, H., Z. M. KEDEM, AND S. P. USELTON, "Optimal Surface Reconstruction for Planar Contours," *CACM* 20(1977).

FUJIMOTO, AKIRA, TAKAYUKI TANAKA, AND KANSEI IWATA, "ARTS: Accelerated Ray-Tracing System," *IEEE Computer Graphics and Applications*, pp. 16-26 (Apr. 1986).

GANAPATHY, S. AND T. G. DENNEHY, "A New General Triangulation Method for Planar Contours," *Computer Graphics (SIGGRAPH '82 Proceedings)* 16 pp. 69-75 (1982).

HARRIS, LOWELL D., R. A. ROBB, T. S. YUEN, AND E. L. RITMAN, "Non-invasive numerical dissection and display of anatomic structure using computerized x-ray tomography," *Proceedings SPIE* 152 pp. 10-18 (1978).

HERMAN, GABOR T. AND H. K. LIU, "Three-Dimensional Display of Organs from Computed Tomograms," *Computer Graphics and Image Processing* 9(1) pp. 1-21 (January 1979).

HOEHNE, KARL HEINZ, ROBERT L. DELAPAZ, RALPH BERNSTEIN, AND ROBERT C. TAYLOR, "Combined Surface Display and Reformatting for the Three-Dimensional Analysis of Tomographic Data," *Investigative Radiology* 22(7) pp. 658-664 (July 1987).

JAFFEY, STEPHEN M. AND KALYAN DUTTA, "Digital Perspective Correction for Cylindrical Holographic Stereograms," *Proceedings of SPIE* 367(August 1982).

KAJIYA, JAMES T. AND BRIAN P. VON HERZEN, "Ray Tracing Volume Densities," *Computer Graphics (SIGGRAPH '84 Proceedings)* 18(3)(July 1984).

KEPPEL, E., "Approximation of Complex Surfaces by Triangulation of Contour Lines," *IBM Journal of Research and Development* 19 pp. 2-11 (1975).

LEVOY, MARC, "Display of Surfaces from Volume Data," *IEEE Computer Graphics and Applications*, (May, 1988).

LORENSEN, WILLIAM E. AND HARVEY E. CLINE, "Marching Cubes: A High Resolution 3D Surface Construction Algorithm," *Computer Graphics (SIGGRAPH '87 Proceedings)*, (July 1987).

MAZZIOTTA, J. C. AND K. H. HUANG, "THREAD (Three-Dimensional Reconstruction and Display) with Biomedical Applications in Neuron Ultrastructure and Display," *American Federation of Information Processing Society* 45 pp. 241-250 (1976).

MEAGHER, DONALD J., "Efficient Synthetic Image Generation of Arbitrary 3-D Objects," *Proceedings of the IEEE Computer Society Conference on Pattern Recognition and Image Processing*, pp. 473-478 (June 1982).

NORTON, ALAN, "Generation and Display of Geometric Fractals in 3-D," *Computer Graphics (SIGGRAPH '82 Proceedings)* 16(3) pp. 61-67 (July 1982).

PHONG, BUI-THONG, "Illumination for Computer Generated Images," *CACM* 18(6) pp. 311-317 (June 1975).

PORTER, THOMAS AND TOM DUFF, "Compositing Digital Images," *Computer Graphics (SIGGRAPH '84 Proceedings)* 18(3) pp. 253-260 (July 1984).

SCHLUSSELBERG, DANIEL S., WADE K. SMITH, AND DONALD J. WOODWARD, "Three-Dimensional Display of Medical Image Volumes," *Proceedings of NCGA*, (March 1986).

SCOTT, W. W. JR., E. K. FISHMAN, AND D. MAGID, "Acetabular Fractures: Optimal Imaging," *Radiology*, pp. 537-538 (1987).

SUNGURUFF, A AND D. GREENBERG, "Computer Generated Images for Medical Applications," *Computer Graphics (SIGGRAPH '78 Proceedings)* 12 pp. 196-202 (1978).

TOM, VICTOR T., "Adaptive Filter Techniques of Digital Image Enhancement," *SPIE Digital Image Processing: Critical Review of Technology* 528(1985).

TUY, HEANG K. AND LEE TAN TUY, "Direct 2-D Display of 3-D Objects," *IEEE Computer Graphics and Applications* 4(10) pp. 29-34 (October 1984).

VANNIER, MICHAEL W., JEFFREY L. MARSH, AND JAMES O. WARREN, "Three Dimensional Computer Graphics for Craniofacial Surgical Planning and Evaluation," *Computer Graphics (SIGGRAPH '83 Proceedings)* 17(3) pp. 263-273 (July 1983).

WRIGHT, THOMAS AND JOHN HUMBRECHT, "ISOSURF - An Algorithm for Plotting Iso-Valued Surfaces of a Function of Three Variables," *Computer Graphics (SIGGRAPH '79 Proceedings)* 13(2) pp. 182-189 (August 1979).

WYVILL, BRIAN, CRAIG MCPHEETERS, AND GEOFF WYVILL, "Data Structure for Soft Objects," *The Visual Computer* 2(4) pp. 227-234 (1986).

ZUCKER, STEVEN W., "Relaxation Labelling and the Reduction of Local Ambiguities," *Proceedings 3rd International Conference on Pattern Recognition*, pp. 852-861 (November 1976).

A Progressive Refinement Approach to Fast Radiosity Image Generation

Michael F. Cohen, Shenchang Eric Chen, John R. Wallace, Donald P. Greenberg

Program of Computer Graphics, Cornell University

Abstract

A reformulated radiosity algorithm is presented that produces initial images in time linear to the number of patches. The enormous memory costs of the radiosity algorithm are also eliminated by computing form-factors on-the-fly. The technique is based on the approach of rendering by progressive refinement. The algorithm provides a useful solution almost immediately which progresses gracefully and continuously to the complete radiosity solution. In this way the competing demands of realism and interactivity are accommodated. The technique brings the use of radiosity for interactive rendering within reach and has implications for the use and development of current and future graphics workstations.

CR Categories and Subject Descriptors: I.3.3 [Computer Graphics]: Picture/Image Generation - Display algorithms. I.3.7 [Computer Graphics]: Three-Dimensional Graphics and Realism

General Terms: Algorithms

Additional Key Words and Phrases: radiosity, progressive refinement, backward ray tracing, z-buffer, global illumination, adaptive subdivision.

©1988   ACM-0-89791-275-6/88/008/0075 $00.75

1 Introduction

Two goals have largely shaped the field of image synthesis since its inception: visual realism and interactivity. The desire for realism has motivated the development of global illumination algorithms such as ray tracing [19], [5], [12] and radiosity [7], [13], [3], with often impressive results. However, the need for interactive manipulation of objects for geometric modeling and other computer aided design areas has generated another path of evolution. This path, dominated by speed, led from the work of early researchers [18], [8], [14] and others, to the development of current engineering workstations capable of drawing thousands of shaded polygons a second [16], [6]. In order to achieve this performance, much of what is central to the goal of realism has had to be sacrificed, including the effects of shadows and global illumination. On the other hand, algorithms like ray-tracing and radiosity are too expensive on current machines to be used as the basis of interactive rendering.

One approach to accommodating the competing demands of interactivity and image quality is offered by the method of rendering by adaptive refinement [2]. In this approach rendering begins with a simple, quickly rendered version of the image, and progresses through a sequence of increasing realism, until a change in the scene or view requires that the process start again. The aim is to provide the highest quality image possible within the time constraints imposed by the user's manipulation of the scene. It is crucial to this approach that the early images be of usable quality at interactive speeds and that the progression to greater realism be *graceful*, that is, automatic, continuous, and not distracting to the user. In the words of Bergman, what is needed is a *golden thread*, a single rendering operation that, with repeated application, will continually refine the quality of an image.

This paper presents a reformulation of the radiosity algorithm that provides such a *thread*. The radiosity approach is a particularly attractive basis for a progressive approach for two reasons. First, the process correctly simulates the global illumination of diffuse environments. Second, it provides a view-independent solution of the diffuse component of reflection. Thus the refinement process may continue uninterrupted as the user views the scene from different directions. Unfortunately, the conventional radiosity algorithm provides no usable results until after the solution is complete, a computation of order n^2, (where n is the number of discrete surface patches). The original algorithm has the additional disadvantage of using $O(n^2)$ storage.

In the revised radiosity algorithm presented here, an initial approximation of the global diffuse illumination provides a starting point for refinement. A reorganization of the iterative solution of the radiosity equations allows the illumination of all surfaces in the environment to be updated at each step and ensures that the correct solution is approached early in the process. In addition to providing a basis for graceful image refinement, the new algorithm requires only $O(n)$ storage.

2   The Cost of Realism for the Conventional Radiosity Algorithm

The radiosity algorithm is a method for evaluating the intensity or radiosity at discrete points and surface areas in an environment. The relationship between the radiosity of a given discrete surface area, or patch, and the radiosity of all other patches in the environment is given by:

$$B_i A_i = E_i A_i + \rho_i \sum_{j=1}^{n} B_j F_{ji} A_j \qquad (1)$$

where
B_i = radiosity of patch i (energy/unit area/unit time),
E_i = emission of patch i (energy/unit area/unit time),
A_i = area of patch i, A_j = area of patch j,
F_{ji} = form-factor from j to i (fraction of energy leaving patch j which arrives at patch i),
ρ_i = reflectivity of patch i, and
n = number of discrete patches.

Using the reciprocity relationship for form-factors [15],

$$F_{ij} A_i = F_{ji} A_j \qquad (2)$$

and dividing through by Ai, the more familiar radiosity equation is obtained:

$$B_i = E_i + \rho_i \sum_{j=1}^{n} B_j F_{ij} \qquad (3)$$

or in matrix form:

$$\begin{bmatrix} 1 - \rho_1 F_{11} & -\rho_1 F_{12} & \cdots & -\rho_1 F_{1n} \\ -\rho_2 F_{21} & 1 - \rho_2 F_{22} & \cdots & -\rho_2 F_{2n} \\ \cdot & \cdot & \cdots & \cdot \\ \cdot & \cdot & \cdots & \cdot \\ -\rho_n F_{n1} & -\rho_n F_{n2} & \cdots & 1 - \rho_n F_{nn} \end{bmatrix} \begin{bmatrix} B_1 \\ B_2 \\ \cdot \\ \cdot \\ B_n \end{bmatrix} = \begin{bmatrix} E_1 \\ E_2 \\ \cdot \\ \cdot \\ E_n \end{bmatrix} \qquad (4)$$

The computation involved in the conventional hemi-cube radiosity algorithm is divided into three major sections as follows:

1. Computing the form-factors (F_{ij}). This requires determining the patches visible to each patch over the entire hemisphere of directions above the patch. For each patch, all the other patches of the environment are projected onto the five faces of a *hemi-cube* placed over the patch and a z-buffer hidden-surface operation is performed for each face [3]. Using standard scan conversion and hidden surface routines, the cost of each hemi-cube is proportional to the number of discrete patches as well as the resolution of the hemi-cube. This results in an $O(n^2)$ computation for the whole environment.

2. Solving the radiosity matrix equation (4) using the Gauss-Siedel method. Due to the strict diagonal dominance of the matrix, the solution converges in a few iterations and its cost is thus proportional to square of the number of patches [10]. The solution is performed for each color band. Since the form-factors are dependent on geometry only, this does not have a significant impact on the cost of the radiosity algorithm.

3. Displaying the results. This involves selecting viewing parameters, determining hidden surfaces, and interpolating the radiosity values. Current workstations are capable of rapidly displaying high resolution radiosity images from any vantage point through the use of Gouraud shading and z-buffer hardware.

The overwhelming cost of the radiosity method lies in the computation of the form-factors. To reduce this cost, the form-factors are calculated once and stored for repeated use during the iterative matrix solution. The total number of form-factors to be stored is potentially the number of patches squared, although the matrix of coefficients is normally quite sparse since many patches cannot *see* each other. Even so, the n by n matrix of coefficients will quickly exceed a reasonable storage size. For example, assuming a matrix that is 90 percent sparse and four bytes of memory per form-factor, an environment of 50,000 patches will require a gigabyte of storage.

For rendering by progressive refinement, an important criterion is the time required to achieve a useful as opposed to complete solution. In the conventional radiosity algorithm, all the form-factors for the entire environment are pre-calculated before the solution begins at a cost of $O(n^2)$. Furthermore, using the Gauss-Siedel solution for the system of radiosity equations, an estimate of the radiosity of all patches is not available until after the first complete iteration cycle. This clearly cannot be implemented at interactive speeds and is not the graceful first step required for progressive refinement.

3   Progressive Refinement Methods for the Radiosity Algorithm

The radiosity algorithm can be restructured to achieve the goals of progressive refinement. In the restructured algorithm, form-factors are calculated on-the-fly to eliminate the $O(n^2)$ storage and startup costs. Although the basic Gauss-Siedel approach still remains, the order of operations of the iteration cycle has been modified so that a good approximation of the final results can be displayed early in the solution process.

The restructured algorithm differs from the previous ones primarily in two aspects. First, the radiosity of all patches is updated simultaneously. Second, patches are processed in sorted order according to their energy contribution to the environment.

To further improve the quality of the images generated during the earliest stages of the algorithm, an estimate of global illumination is determined directly from the known geometric and reflective characteristics of the environment. This estimate is gradually replaced by more exact information as the solution progresses, providing a graceful and continuous convergence to a realistic image.

3.1 Simultaneous Update of Patch Radiosities: Shooting vs. Gathering Light

In the conventional radiosity algorithm, the Gauss-Siedel method is used to obtain the solution to the simultaneous equations(4). This iterative approach converges to the solution by solving the system of equations one row at a time. The evaluation of the $i'th$ row of the equations provides an estimate of the radiosity of patch i based on the current estimates of the radiosities of all other patch radiosities:

$$B_i = E_i + \rho_i \sum_{j=1}^{n} B_j F_{ij} \tag{5}$$

In a sense, the light leaving patch i is determined by *gathering* in the light from the rest of the environment (figure 1).

A single term from the summation in (5) determines the contribution to the radiosity of patch i from patch j:

$$B_i \text{ due to } B_j = \rho_i B_j F_{ij} \tag{6}$$

It is possible to reverse this process by determining the contribution made by patch i to the radiosity of all other patches. The reciprocity relationship (2) provides the basis for reversing

this relationship. The contribution of the radiosity from patch i to the radiosity of patch j is:

$$B_j \text{ due to } B_i = \rho_j B_i F_{ij} A_i / A_j \tag{7}$$

This is true for all patches j. Thus the total contribution to the environment from the radiosity of patch i is given by:

$$For\ all\ patches\ j: B_j\ due\ to\ Bi = \rho_j B_i F_{ij} A_i / A_j \tag{8}$$

It should be noted that while this equation adds radiosity to patches j, the form-factors used, F_{ij}, are still the form-factors calculated using the hemi-cube placed at patch i. Thus, each step of the solution now consists of performing a single hemi-cube over a patch and adding the contribution from the radiosity of that patch to the radiosities of all other patches, in effect, *shooting* light out from that patch into the environment.

During the course of the iterative solution this step may be repeated for patch i several times as the solution converges. Each time the estimate of the radiosity of patch i will be more accurate. However, the environment will already include the contribution of the previous estimate of B_i. Thus, only the difference, ΔB_i, between the previous and current estimates of B_i needs to be considered. ΔB_i represents the *unshot radiosity*.

The solution step may be restated as follows:

```
for each iteration, for each patch i:
    calculate the form-factors F_ij using a hemi-cube at
        patch i;
    for each patch j:
        ΔRad = ρ_j ΔB_i F_ij A_i / A_j;
        ΔB_j = ΔB_j + ΔRad; /* update change since last
            time patch j shot light */
        B_j = B_j + ΔRad; /* update total radiosity of
            patch j */
    ΔB_i = 0; /*reset unshot radiosity for patch i to zero*/
```

All radiosities, Bi and ΔB_i, are initialized to zero for all non-light sources and are set to the emission values for emitting patches.

The above step continues until the solution converges to within the desired tolerance. Each intermediate step simultaneously improves the solution for many patches, providing intermediate results which can be displayed as the algorithm proceeds.

This approach bears some relationship to backward ray-tracing solutions [1] which shot light out from light sources onto diffuse surfaces, but did not propagate the reflected light any further into the environment. A recursive extension of the Atherton-Weiler shadow algorithm was proposed and briefly described by Heckbert and Hanrahan [9] as a way of propagating light from light sources through the environment, but light reflected from diffuse surfaces was likewise not propagated further.

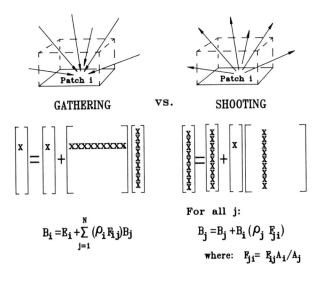

Figure 1: Gathering vs. Shooting

Gathering light through a hemi-cube allows one patch radiosity to be updated. In contrast, shooting light through a single hemi-cube allows the whole environment's radiosity values to be updated simultaneously.

3.2 Solving in Sorted Order

In addition to converging gracefully, it is desirable for the solution to improve in accuracy as quickly as possible.

The final radiosity B_j of a given patch j consists of the sum of the contributions from all other patches. The final value of this sum will be approached earliest in the process if the largest contributions are added first. These will tend to come from those patches which radiate the most energy, i.e. have the largest product B_iA_i. Stated intuitively, those patches radiating the most light energy typically have the greatest effect on the illumination of the environment and should be treated first.

The algorithm is implemented by always shooting from the patch for which the difference, ΔB_iA_i, between the previous and the current estimates of unshot radiant energy is greatest. Most light sources are automatically processed first by this rule, since initially all other patches will have a radiosity of zero. Since lights are typically the most significant source of illumination for many patches, following the initial processing of light sources much of the environment will already be well illuminated. The next set of patches processed according to this rule will be those patches that received the most light from the light sources, and so on.

When solving in sorted order, the solution tends to proceed in approximately the same order as light would propagate through the environment. A similar approach was taken by Immel [11] in order to increase the efficiency of the view-independent specular radiosity algorithm. The reordering of the patches generally provides an accurate solution in less than a single iteration, substantially reducing computation costs.

3.3 The Ambient Term

Using the procedures described above, intermediate images will progress from a dark environment, continuously brightening to a fully illuminated scene including all diffuse interreflection. The illumination of the scene during early stages of the solution process will be inadequate, particularly for regions which do not receive direct illumination, since global illumination is not yet accurately represented. In earlier lighting models, the effect of global illumination was approximated by adding an arbitrary ambient term. Similar use is made of an *ambient* term here, but its value at any given point during the solution is based on the current estimate of the radiosities of all patches and the reflectivity of the environment. The ambient term is added for display purposes only and is not taken into account by the solution itself. The contribution of the ambient term gracefully decreases as the solution continues, providing a useful image almost immediately which unobtrusively progresses to an accurate rendering.

3.3.1 Computation of the Ambient Term

A reasonable first approximation to the form-factors can be made without any knowledge of the visibility or the geometric relationships between patches. The form-factor from any patch i to patch j can be approximated as the fraction of the total area of the environment taken up by the area of patch j. As with the correct form-factors the total will sum to unity. Thus,

$$F_{*j} \approx \frac{A_j}{\sum_{j=1}^{n} A_j} \tag{9}$$

An average reflectivity for the environment can be computed as an area weighted average of the patch reflectivities:

$$\rho_{ave} = \frac{\sum_{i=1}^{n} \rho_i A_i}{\sum_{i=1}^{n} A_i} \tag{10}$$

For any unit energy sent into the environment, ρ_{ave} will on average be reflected, and some of that will be reflected, etc. Thus, an overall interreflection factor R is simply the geometric sum:

$$R = 1 + \rho_{ave} + \rho_{ave}^2 + \rho_{ave}^3 + \dots = \frac{1}{1 - \rho_{ave}} \tag{11}$$

From these assumptions an *Ambient* radiosity term is derived. It is simply the area average of the radiosity which has not yet been *shot* via form-factor computation times the reflection factor R.

$$Ambient = R \sum_{j=1}^{n} (\Delta B_j F_{*j}) \tag{12}$$

Thus at any point in the computation, the estimate of the radiosity of each patch can be improved by adding the contribution of the ambient radiosity. If B_i is the radiosity of patch i due to the radiosity received via shooting from other patches, an improved estimate is given by:

$$B_i' = B_i + \rho_i Ambient \tag{13}$$

This estimate of B_i' is used for display purposes only since the ambient contribution is not added to ΔB_i and thus is not shot during the solution. As the solution progresses the average unshot energy decreases and thus the ambient term decreases along with it. The values of B_i and B_i' converge and the initial ambient image yields gracefully to the more accurate estimate of global illumination provided by the radiosity equations.

3.4 Adaptive Subdivision: Achieving an Appropriate Surface Discretization

There are competing influences on how fine the subdivision of the surfaces of the environment should be. A finer subdivision means more computation but results in a more accurate representation of the sharp radiosity gradients that can occur at shadow boundaries. The original hemi-cube algorithm solved this problem by using a two level subdivision in which patches are further subdivided into elements [4].

In the revised algorithm as in the original algorithm, patch subdivision is kept coarse since the specific distribution of radiosity is less important for the patches, which act as the illuminators of the environment. The patches are subdivided into smaller elements. It is the elements which act as the receivers of light from the patches. The elements are projected onto a single hemi-cube for each patch to determine patch-to-element form-factors, F_{ie}. The light is thus shot from the patch to all elements. The radiosity of a patch is determined as the area weighted average of its element radiosities.

The number of patches, and thus the number of hemi-cubes, generally will grow very little during the radiosity analysis. Large patches need to be subdivided only if the radiosity varies greatly across the surface causing illumination inaccuracies or if the ratio of the areas in equation (7) causes the form-factor term $(F_{ij}A_i/A_j)$ to grow larger than unity.

The elements are free to be adaptively subdivided based on radiosity gradients without changing the patch geometry and thus no additional hemi-cube computation is required. The number of elements projected onto the hemi-cubes will grow as high gradients such as shadow boundaries are discovered. Images are generated by rendering the elements themselves as Gouraud shaded polygons with the radiosity at the vertices interpolated from adjacent elements.

4 Implementation

The complete algorithm is summarized in the following pseudo-code description:

```
/* initialization */
determine reflection factor, R;
/* determine initial ambient from given emission */
Ambient = R ∑_{i=1}^{n} (E_i A_i) / ∑_{i=1}^{n} A_i;
/* initialize unshot radiosity to given emission */
for each patch: ΔB_i = E_i;
/* element e is a sub-unit of patch i */
for each element: B_e = E_i + ρ_i Ambient;
/* initialize change in ambient radiosity */
ΔAmbient = 0;

/* radiosity solution */
Until convergence {
    select patch i with greatest unshot energy, ΔB_i A_i;
  † project elements onto hemi-cube located at patch i
        to compute patch i to element form-factors, F_ie;
    for each element e {
        /* determine increase in radiosity of element e due to
           ΔB_i */
        ΔRad = ρ_e ΔB_i F_ie A_i / A_e;
        /* add area weighted portion of increased radiosity of
           element e to radiosity of the patch j which contains
           element e */
        B_e = B_e + ΔRad + ρ_e ΔAmbient;
        ΔB_j = ΔB_j + ΔRad A_e / A_j;
    }
    interpolate vertex radiosities from neighboring elements;
    if( gradient from neighboring vertices is too high )
        subdivide elements and reshoot patch i;
    ΔB_i = 0;
    determine ΔAmbient from new unshot radiosities, ΔB_j;
  † display environment as Gouraud shaded elements;
}
```

†Processes which can take advantage of current graphics hardware for scan conversion and hidden surface calculation.

The algorithms described above were implemented initially on a VAX 8700 and then on an HP 825 with an SRX graphics accelerator. The hemi-cube algorithm was performed in software and alternatively with the use of graphics hardware for the hidden surface determination and scan conversion portions of the form-factor routines. The ability to perform transformations, clipping and scan conversion on the HP workstation can potentially accelerate the hemi-cube computation and allows the intermediate results to be interactively displayed as a fully rendered image.

5 Results

The methods described above were compared experimentally in several combinations to determine the effect on the solution process. Tests included comparing the use of Gathering vs. Shooting, Sorted vs. Unsorted Patches, and With and Without Ambient effects. All the methods converged to the same final radiosity results in different amounts of time and with different intermediate results. The final converged results were used as a control with which to measure the error at stages in the image refinement. Individual errors were determined as the absolute differences between the converged and estimated radiosities of each element. (The average radiosity values of the color bands was used for the purposes of error measurement.) The square root of the area weighted mean of the square of individual errors (RMS) is used as a quantitative measure of overall radiosity inaccuracy.

$$RMS\ Error = \sqrt{\frac{\sum_{e=1}^{m}((B_e^* - B_e)^2 A_e)}{\sum_{e=1}^{m} A_e}} \qquad (14)$$

where B_e^* is the converged radiosity and B_e is the intermediate radiosity of element e. m is the total number of elements.

The images themselves offer a qualitative basis for comparison.

5.1 A Test Environment

Test were performed on a model of two office cubicles subdivided into 500 patches and 7000 elements. Four iterative approaches to solving the radiosity equations were run. After each hemi-cube, images using the current radiosity estimates were displayed as hardware Gouraud shaded polygons on a Hewlett Packard 825SRX workstation.

The four approaches were:

1. Gathering Only: This is the *traditional* radiosity method using a Gauss-Siedel solution. One hemi-cube is placed at each element.

2. Shooting Only: This method consists of reversing the process by shooting light to each element through a hemi-cube placed at each patch.

3. Shooting with Sorting: The same as the second approach, but with the patch with the largest *unshot* energy being used at each step.

4. Shooting with Sorting and Ambient: This time the radiosity due to an estimated ambient term is included for display.

Figures 2 through 5 each contain eight images from methods 1 through 4 respectively. From top to bottom they show the results after 1, 2, 24, and 100 hemi-cubes. The right hand image is a pseudo-color version. Gray indicates an accurate solution when comparing each of these images to the converged result in figure 6. The blue intensity indicates under-estimated radiosity values and red indicates an over-estimate. The inclusion of the ambient term provides an immediately useful image as illustrated in figure 5, (repeated on the cover). Note that as the algorithm progresses, the over-estimates in the shadowed regions due to the ambient term are continuously redistributed

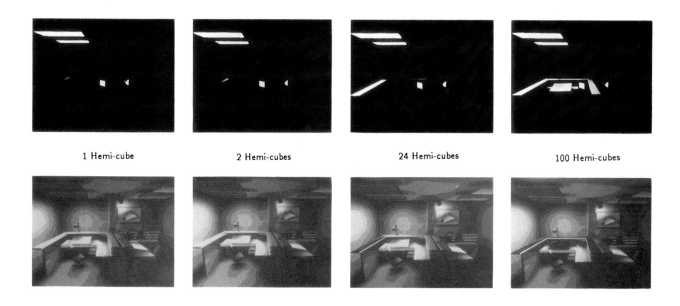

| 1 Hemi-cube | 2 Hemi-cubes | 24 Hemi-cubes | 100 Hemi-cubes |

Figure 2: Gathering Only

Since the radiosity of only one patch is estimated for each hemi-cube performed, the gathering approach converges very slowly. Thus even after 100 hemi-cubes, the radiosity of very few surfaces in the environment have been estimated. The pseudo-color images on the right indicate underestimates of radiosity in blue and overestimates in red. (The small amounts of red are due to numerical differences between the hemi-cubes used for gathering and shooting.)

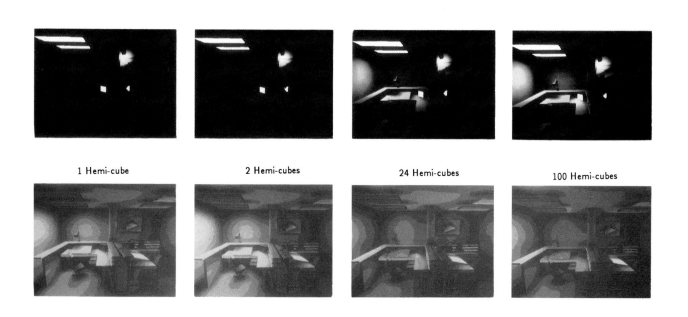

| 1 Hemi-cube | 2 Hemi-cubes | 24 Hemi-cubes | 100 Hemi-cubes |

Figure 3: Shooting Only

By shooting light, more of the environment is illuminated for each hemi-cube. However, the order in which the patches shoot light is arbitrary, thus loosing potential efficiency. Note in the graph of figure 3, the jumps which occur when original light sources are processed.

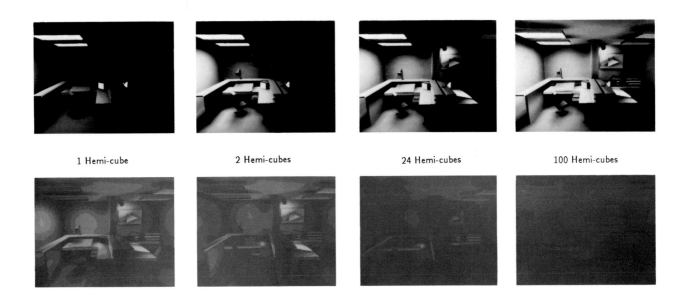

Figure 4: Shooting and Sorting

By sorting the patches according to "unshot" energy, a continuity and efficiency are achieved. Note the continual brightening of the environment as the interreflection between surfaces is accounted for. After only 100 hemi-cubes, a near complete radiosity solution has been found. Note that the under-illumination, indicated by the blueness of the pseudo-color images diminishes gradually after each step in the solution.

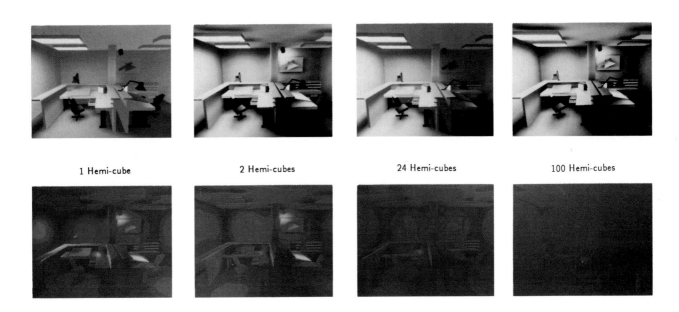

Figure 5: Shooting, Sorting and Ambient

The inclusion of the ambient radiosity provides an immediately useful image after only a single hemi-cube. Note that as the solution continues, the contrast is enhanced as the over-illumination in shadowed areas (indicated by the red pseudo-color) is transferred to the under-illuminated (blue) regions. The ambient term maintains a consistent overall illumination level allowing a more graceful transition to a final image.

to the brighter areas of the environment which were initially under-estimated.

Figure 6 contains an image produced after allowing the methods to run until convergence. The graph below, figure 7, follows the first 100 hemi-cubes and shows the RMS error of the radiosities of the elements. The graph clearly illustrates the improvements generated by the reformulation of the radiosity algorithm. In figure 8, all four methods are compared at the same point early in the solution process. At a cost of only two hemi-cubes, a radiosity image sufficient for many applications is rendered by the fourth method.

The computation of a single hemi-cube with resolution 150 by 150 for the test environment takes approximately ten seconds in the software implementation on the Hewlett Packard 825SRX workstation. The Hewlett Packard workstation was able to display each intermediate stage of the test environment in one to two seconds. Although these clearly cannot be termed interactive speeds at present, the next generation of workstation hardware should acheive near interactive speeds for an environment like the one shown. In addition, the ability to rotate or move through the environment does not depend on hemi-cube computation time. If the display of the environment and the hemi-cube calculations are performed in parallel on separate processors, walkthroughs can be performed during the iterative cycle without disturbing the radiosity computation.

Figure 6: Two Office Cubicles: The Converged Results

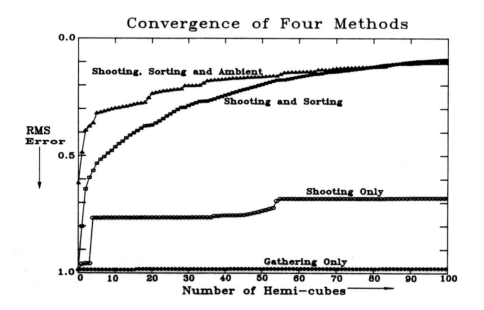

Figure 7: Plot of Normalized RMS Errors for the First 100 Hemi-Cubes

Note the initial improvement in accuracy of the fourth method due to the inclusion of the ambient term.

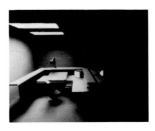

Gathering Only   Shooting Only   Shooting and Sorting   Shooting, Sorting, and Ambient

Figure 8: The Four Methods Compared After Two Hemi-cubes

These four images extracted from the same point in the previous four sequences illustrate the great advantage provided by the fourth method for displaying immediate results.

5.2   A Steel Mill

An early software version of the shooting and sorting algorithm described above was implemented on a VAX8700 and run on a highly complex scene to test its performance. A model of a steel mill was constructed containing 30,000 patches which were subdivided into 50,000 elements. The patch solution was run for only 2,000 of the patches in 5 hours providing a close approximation of the global diffuse illumination. This was followed by a view dependent post-process taking 190 hours in which the radiosity at the vertices of visible elements was computed by gathering light through a hemi-cube at each vertex. The results were then displayed by interpolating radiosity values across the elements. Figure 9 is the result of this process.

A traditional radiosity approach would have required the computation of 1.5×10^9 form-factors or 6 gigabytes worth of storage (sparcity would probably have reduced this by an order of magnitude). The iterative approach required the storage of only one row of form-factors or 0.12 Mbytes. In addition, the preprocess solution required only 2,000 hemi-cubes, or less than 5 percent of the 50,000 required for earlier implementations.

Figure 9: The Steel Mill

A radiosity solution for this complex environment containing 50000 elements would have been virtually impossible due to storage and computational requirements without the use of the reformulated radiosity approach described in this paper.

6   Conclusion and Future Directions

A reformulated version of the radiosity algorithm for image synthesis has been presented. Two major advantages over the traditional radiosity algorithm are evident: a useful image (although not the final image) is produced in time linear to the number of patches, and the $O(n^2)$ storage requirements for the form-factors have been eliminated. The reformulation allows the rapid generation of approximate solutions which gracefully, progressively refine themselves to accurate representation of global illumination in diffuse environments. This allows the method to be used in applications requiring interaction. It also provides a means to examine the progress of image development early in the rendering process thus providing a valuable previewing capability.

The results of the radiosity analysis make possible the display of high quality diffuse realistic images from any view point. This view independent solution provides a starting point for further adaptive refinement to add view dependent effects such as highlights and specular reflection. Such refinement might include pixel by pixel post processes as as the modified ray tracing algorithm as described in [17], or Monte Carlo methods which can take advantage of global illumination information for importance sampling.

A variety of issues arise when implementing the methods described above. How much and when should the patches and elements be subdivided? How high a hemi-cube resolution is necessary to eliminate form-factor aliasing? What is the inter-relationship between patch size, element size, hemi-cube resolution, radiosity gradients, and image resolution. The answers are environment dependent and also clearly depend on the uses to which the images will be applied. Further research should be directed towards providing a body of heuristics tuned to environments, computational resources, and user needs.

Taking advantage of all information about environmental illumination at each stage in the solution process is a concept central to the ideas described in this paper. Future research should be able to apply similar ideas to the problem of rendering dynamic environments needed for geometric modeling and other applications.

Future research should also examine the possible impact of this approach on the design of graphics workstations. Hardware design can provide specialized frame buffers dedicated to hemi-cube computation or for complex reflectance computation. The goal is clear; to provide the best image possible in interactive times and to provide a continuity to a realistic image synthesis.

7   Acknowledgements

The research in this paper was carried out under a grant from the National Science Foundation #DCR8203979 with equipment generously donated by Digital Equipment Corporation and Hewlett Packard. The office model was originally created by Keith Howie and modified by Shenchang Eric Chen. The Steel Mill was modeled through a great effort by Stuart I. Feldman. The photography was done by Emil Ghinger. Special thanks to Holly Rushmeier for technical discussions and to Julie O'Brien and Helen Tahn for helping assemble the paper.

References

[1] Arvo, James, "Backward Ray Tracing," *Developments in Ray Tracing(SIGGRAPH '86 Course Notes)*, Vol.12, August 1986.

[2] Bergman, Larry, Henry Fuchs, Eric Grant, Susan Spach, "Image Rendering by Adaptive Refinement," *Computer Graphics(SIGGRAPH '86 Proceedings)*, Vol.20, No.4, August 1986, pp.29-38.

[3] Cohen, Michael F., Donald P. Greenberg, "A Radiosity Solution for Complex Environment," *Computer Graphics(SIGGRAPH '85 Proceedings)*, Vol.19, No.3, July 1985, pp.31-40.

[4] Cohen, Michael F., Donald P. Greenberg, David S. Immel, Philip J. Brock, "An Efficient Radiosity Approach for Realistic Image Synthesis," *IEEE Computer Graphics and Applications*, Vol.6, No.2, March 1986, pp.26-35.

[5] Cook, Robert L., Thomas Porter, Loren Carpenter, "Distributed Ray Tracing," *Computer Graphics(SIGGRAPH '84 Proceedings)*, Vol.18, No.3, July 1984, pp.137-145.

[6] Fuchs, Henry, et. al., "Fast Spheres, Shadows, Textures, Transparencies, and Image Enhancements in Pixel-Planes," *Computer Graphics(SIGGRAPH '85 Proceedings)*, Vol.19, No.3, July 1985, pp.111-120.

[7] Goral, Cindy M., Kenneth E. Torrance, Donald P. Greenberg, "Modeling the Interaction of Light Between Diffuse Surfaces," *Computer Graphics(SIGGRAPH '84 Proceedings)*, Vol.18, No.3, July 1984, pp.213-222.

[8] Gouraud, H., "Continuous Shading of Curved Surfaces," *IEEE Transactions on Computers*, Vol.20, No.6, June 1971, pp.623-628.

[9] Heckbert, Paul S. and Pat Hanrahan, "Beam Tracing Polygonal Objects," *Computer Graphics(SIGGRAPH '84 Proceedings)*, Vol.18, No.3, July 1984, pp.119-128.

[10] Hornbeck, Robert W., *Numerical Methods*, Quantum Publishers, New York, NY, 1974, pp.101-106.

[11] Immel, David S., Michael F. Cohen, Donald P. Greenberg, "A Radiosity Method for Non-Diffuse Environments," *Computer Graphics(SIGGRAPH '86 Proceedings)*, Vol. 20, No.4, August 1986, pp.133-142.

[12] Kajiya, James T., "The Rendering Equation," *Computer Graphics(SIGGRAPH '86 Proceedings)*, Vol.20, No.4, August 1986, pp.143-150.

[13] Nishita, Tomoyuki, Eihachiro Nakamae, "Continuous Tone Representation of Three-Dimensional Objects Taking Account of Shadows and Interreflection," *Computer Graphics(SIGGRAPH '85 Proceedings)*, Vol. 19, No.3, July 1985, pp.22-30.

[14] Phong, Bui Tuong, "Illumination for Computer Generated Pictures," *Communications of the ACM*, Vol.18, No.6, June 1975, pp.311-317.

[15] Siegel, Robert, John R. Howell, *Thermal Radiation Heat Transfer*, Hemisphere Publishing Corp., Washington DC., 1981.

[16] Swanson, Roger W. and Larry J. Thayer, "A Fast Shaded-Polygon Render," *Computer Graphics(SIGGRAPH '86 Proceedings)*, Vol.20, No.4, August 1986, pp.95-102.

[17] Wallace, John R., Michael F. Cohen, Donald P. Greenberg, "A Two-pass Solution to the Rendering Equation: A Synthesis of Ray Tracing and Radiosity Methods," *Computer Graphics(SIGGRAPH '87 Proceedings)*, Vol. 21, No.4, July 1986, pp.311-320.

[18] Watkins, G. S., "A Real-Time Visible Surface Algorithm," *University of Utah, UTECH-CSC-70-101*, 1970.

[19] Whitted, Turner, "An Improved Illumination Model for Shaded Display," *Communication of the ACM*, Vol.23, No.6, June 1980, pp.343-349.

A Ray Tracing Solution
for
Diffuse Interreflection

Gregory J. Ward
Francis M. Rubinstein
Robert D. Clear

Lighting Systems Research
Lawrence Berkeley Laboratory
1 Cyclotron Rd., 90-3111
Berkeley, CA 94720
(415) 486-4757

Abstract

An efficient ray tracing method is presented for calculating interreflections between surfaces with both diffuse and specular components. A Monte Carlo technique computes the indirect contributions to illuminance at locations chosen by the rendering process. The indirect illuminance values are averaged over surfaces and used in place of a constant "ambient" term. Illuminance calculations are made only for those areas participating in the selected view, and the results are stored so that subsequent views can reuse common values. The density of the calculation is adjusted to maintain a constant accuracy, permitting less populated portions of the scene to be computed quickly. Successive reflections use proportionally fewer samples, which speeds the process and provides a natural limit to recursion. The technique can also model diffuse transmission and illumination from large area sources, such as the sky.

General Terms: Algorithm, complexity.

Additional Keywords and Phrases: Caching, diffuse, illuminance, interreflection, luminance, Monte Carlo technique, radiosity, ray tracing, rendering, specular.

1. Introduction

The realistic computer rendering of a geometric model requires the faithful simulation of light exchange between surfaces. Ray tracing is a simple and elegant approach that has produced some of the most realistic images to date. The standard ray tracing method follows light backwards from the viewpoint to model specular reflection and refraction from specular surfaces, as well as direct diffuse illumination and shadows [15]. Accuracy has been improved with better reflection models [4] and stochastic sampling techniques [6]. Unfortunately, the treatment of diffuse interreflection in conventional ray tracers has been limited to a constant "ambient" term. This approximation fails to produce detail in shadows, and precludes the use of ray tracing where indirect lighting is important.

We present a method for modeling indirect contributions to illumination using ray tracing. A diffuse interreflection calculation replaces the ambient term directly, without affecting the formulas or algorithms used for direct and specular components. Efficiency is obtained with an appropriate mix of view-dependent and view-independent techniques.

©1988   ACM-0-89791-275-6/88/008/0085 $00.75

2. Interreflection in Ray Tracing

Ray tracing computes multiple reflections by recursion (Figure 1). At each level, the calculation proceeds as follows:

1. Intersect the ray with scene geometry.
2. Compute direct contributions from light sources.
3. Compute specular contributions from reflecting surfaces.
4. Compute diffuse contributions from reflecting surfaces.

The complexity of the calculation is closely related to the difficulty of step 1, and the number of times it is executed as determined by the propagation (recursion) of steps 2 through 4. Step 2 requires as many new rays as there are light sources, but the rays do not propagate so there is no growth in the calculation. Step 3 can result in a few propagating rays that lead to geometric growth if unchecked. Methods for efficient specular component computation have been described by [8], [5] and [14]. The diffuse contributions in step 4, however, require many (>100) propagating rays that quickly overwhelm a conventional calculation. Most methods simply avoid this step by substituting a constant ambient term. Our goal is to find an efficient method for computing diffuse interreflection and thereby complete the ray tracing solution. We start with a summary of previous work in this area.

An advanced ray tracing method developed by Kajiya follows a fixed number of paths to approximate global illumination at each pixel [8]. Using hierarchical "importance" sampling to reduce variance, the illumination integral is computed with fewer rays than a naive calculation would require. This brings ray tracing closer to a full solution without compromising its basic properties: separate geometric and lighting models, view-dependence for efficient rendering of specular effects, and pixel-independence for parallel implementations. Unfortunately, the method is not well suited to calculating diffuse interreflection, which still requires hundreds of samples. A high-resolution image simply has too many pixels to compute global illumination separately at each one.

The radiosity method, based on radiative heat transfer, is well suited to calculating diffuse interreflection [12][10][2]. Surfaces are discretized into patches of roughly uniform size, and the energy exchange between patches is computed in a completely view-independent manner. The method makes efficient use of visibility information to compute multiple reflections, and sample points are spaced so that there is sufficient resolution without making the calculation intractable. In areas where illumination changes rapidly, the patches can be adaptively subdivided to maintain accuracy [3]. However, the standard radiosity method models only diffuse surfaces, which limits the realism of its renderings. Immel extended the approach to include non-diffuse environments, adding bidirectional reflectance to the energy equations [7]. Unfortunately, the view-independent solution of specular interreflection between surfaces requires sampling radiated directions over very small (approaching pixel-sized) surface patches. The resulting computation is intractable for all but the simplest scenes.

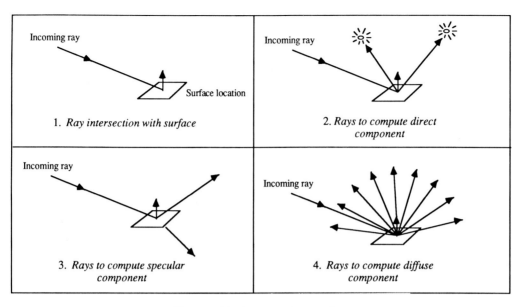

Figure 1: The four steps of ray tracing.

A combined ray tracing and radiosity approach was designed by Wallace to take advantage of the complementary properties of the two techniques [13]. Wallace divides energy transport into four "mechanisms:" diffuse-diffuse, specular-diffuse, diffuse-specular, and specular-specular. He then proceeds to account for most of these interactions with clever combinations of ray tracing and radiosity techniques. Unfortunately, there are really an infinite number of transport mechanisms, such as specular-specular-diffuse, which are neglected by his calculation. The generalization Wallace suggests for his approach is equivalent to *view-independent* ray tracing, which is even more expensive than general radiosity [7].

3. Diffuse Indirect Illumination

Our development of an efficient ray tracing solution to diffuse interreflection is based on the following observations:

* Because reflecting surfaces are widely distributed, the computation of diffuse indirect illumination requires many sample rays.

* The resulting "indirect illuminance" value† is view-independent by the Lambertian assumption [9].

* The indirect illuminance tends to change slowly over a surface because the direct component and its associated shadows have already been accounted for by step 2 of the ray tracing calculation.

For the sake of efficiency, indirect illuminance should not be recalculated at each pixel, but should instead be averaged over surfaces from a small set of computed values. Computing each value might require many samples, but the number of values would not depend on the number of pixels, so high resolution images could be produced efficiently. Also, since illuminance does not depend on view, the values could be reused for many images.

How can we benefit from a view-independent calculation in the inherently view-dependent world of ray tracing? We do not wish to limit or burden the geometric model with illuminance information, as required by the surface discretization of the radiosity method. By the same token, we do not wish to take view-independence too far, calculating illuminance on surfaces that play no part in the desired view. Instead we would like to take our large sample of rays only when and where it is necessary for the accurate computation of an image, storing the result in a separate data structure that puts no constraints on the surface geometry.

In our enhancement of the basic ray tracing technique, indirect illuminance values are cached in the following manner:

> If one or more values is stored near this point
> > Use stored value(s)
> Else
> > Compute and store new value at this point

The computation of a new value uses the "primary method." The technique for finding and using stored values is called the "secondary method." The primary method is invoked to calculate a new value the first time it is needed, which is when the secondary method fails to produce a usable estimate from previous calculations (Figure 2). Determining the appropriate range and presenting a surface-independent storage technique are the two main points of this paper. Before we explore these issues, we present a basic computation of indirect illuminance.

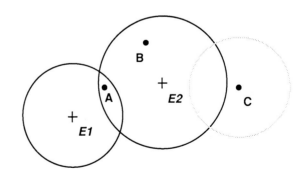

Figure 2: Illuminances *E1* and *E2* were calculated previously using the primary method. Test point **A** uses an average of *E1* and *E2*. Point **B** uses *E2*. Point **C** results in a new indirect illuminance value at that location.

---

†We define indirect illuminance as the light flux per unit area arriving at a surface location via non-self-luminous surfaces.

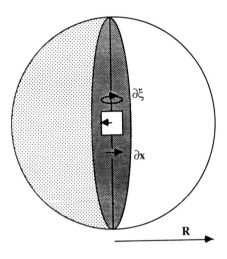

Figure 3: The split sphere model. A surface element is located at the center of a half-dark sphere.

3.1. The Illuminance Integral

Illuminance is defined on a surface as the integral of luminance over the projected hemisphere [9]:

$$E = \int_0^{2\pi} \int_0^{\frac{\pi}{2}} L(\theta, \phi) \cos\theta \sin\theta \, d\theta \, d\phi \tag{1}$$

where θ = polar angle

        ϕ = azimuthal angle

        $L(\theta, \phi)$ = luminance from direction (θ, ϕ)

In our primary method for calculating indirect illuminance, the integral is approximated with a discrete set of sample rays that do not intersect light sources. A uniform segmented Monte Carlo distribution is derived by standard transformation methods [11]:

$$E \approx \frac{\pi}{2n^2} \sum_{j=1}^{n} \sum_{k=1}^{2n} L(\theta_j, \phi_k) \tag{2}$$

where: $\theta_j = \sin^{-1}\left(\sqrt{\frac{j - X_j}{n}}\right)$

        $\phi_k = \pi \frac{(k - Y_k)}{n}$

        X_j, Y_k = uniform random numbers between 0 and 1

        $2n^2$ = total number of samples

In general, a better approximation to (1) may be obtained with fewer rays using hierarchical sampling techniques [8]. The particular method chosen does not affect the remainder of this discussion.

3.2. Illuminance Averaging

The secondary method performs two functions alternatively. It either approximates illuminance by averaging between primary values, or determines that a new primary value is needed. To maintain a constant accuracy with a minimum of primary evaluations, it is necessary to estimate the illuminance gradient on each surface. Where the illuminance changes slowly, as in flat open areas, fewer values are required. Where there is a large gradient, from high surface curvature or nearby objects, more frequent primary evaluations are necessary. Our method uses an estimate of the change in illuminance over a surface based on scene geometry. The inverse of this change serves as the weight for each primary value during averaging. If none of the values has a weight above a specified minimum, the primary method is invoked at that location.

We introduce a simple model to relate the illuminance gradient to scene geometry based on the assumption that narrow concentrations of luminance can be neglected. (Such localized sources should be included in the direct component calculation, since Monte Carlo sampling is a bad way to find them.) A surface element is located at the center of a sphere (Figure 3). Half of the sphere is bright, the other half is dark. The surface element faces the dividing line between the two halves. The "split sphere" has the largest gradient possible for an environment without concentrated sources.

An approximate bound to the change in illuminance in the split sphere, ϵ, is given by the first order Taylor expansion for a function of two variables:

$$\epsilon \leq \left| \frac{\partial E}{\partial x}(x - x_o) + \frac{\partial E}{\partial \xi}(\xi - \xi_o) \right| \tag{3a}$$

Because the illuminance at the center is proportional to the projected area of the bright half of the hemisphere, the partial differentials with respect to x and ξ are proportional to the partial changes in this projection. In terms of x, the differential change over the projected area is $\frac{2R \, \partial x}{\frac{1}{2}\pi R^2}$, which is $\frac{4\partial x}{\pi R}$. In terms of ξ, the ratio is $\frac{\frac{1}{2}\pi R^2 \partial \xi}{\frac{1}{2}\pi R^2}$, or simply $\partial \xi$. Combining these results with the triangle inequality, we get:

$$\epsilon \leq \frac{4}{\pi} \frac{E_o}{R} \left| x - x_o \right| + E_o \left| \xi - \xi_o \right| \tag{3b}$$

Note that the change in illuminance with respect to location is inversely proportional to the radius, R, while the change with respect to orientation does not depend on the sphere geometry. We can extend our approximation to more complicated geometries by replacing x and ξ with vector-derived values:

$$\epsilon(\vec{P}) \leq E_o \left[\frac{4}{\pi} \frac{\|\vec{P} - \vec{P}_o\|}{R_o} + \sqrt{2 - 2\vec{N}(\vec{P}) \cdot \vec{N}(\vec{P}_o)} \right] \tag{4}$$

where: $\vec{N}(\vec{P})$ = surface normal at position $\vec{P}$

        $\vec{P}_o$ = surface element location

        E_o = illuminance at $\vec{P}_o$

        R_0 = "average" distance to surfaces at $\vec{P}_0$

The change in x becomes the distance between two points, and the change in ξ becomes the angle between two surface normals. This equation is used to estimate the relative change in illuminance for any geometry. Both the points and the surface normals are determined by the ray intersection calculation. R_0 is the harmonic mean (reciprocal mean reciprocal) of distances to visible surfaces, which can be computed from ray lengths during primary evaluation.

The inverse of the estimated error is used in a weighted average approximation of illuminance:

$$E(\vec{P}) = \frac{\sum\limits_{i \in s} w_i(\vec{P}) E_i}{\sum\limits_{i \in s} w_i(\vec{P})} \qquad (5)$$

where: $\quad w_i(\vec{P}) = \dfrac{1}{\dfrac{\|\vec{P} - \vec{P}_i\|}{R_i} + \sqrt{1 - \vec{N}(\vec{P}) \cdot \vec{N}(\vec{P}_i)}}$

E_i = computed illuminance at $\vec{P}_i$

R_i = harmonic mean distance to objects visible from $\vec{P}_i$

S = $\{ i : w_i(\vec{P}) > 1/a \}$

a = user selected constant

The approximate illuminance, $E(\vec{P})$, is given by the weighted mean of all "adjacent" illuminance values. The weight of a value is equal to the inverse of its estimated error, without the constant terms that are valid only for the split sphere ($4/\pi$ and $\sqrt{2}$). An illuminance value with an error of zero ($\vec{P}_i$ equal to $\vec{P}$) will have infinite weight. All values with an estimated error less than a will be included in the set of adjacent illuminances, S. If S is empty, a new primary illuminance value must be calculated at $\vec{P}$. (An efficient method for determining the members of S is given in the next section.)

The constant a is directly related to the maximum approximation error. When the approximation is applied to the split sphere, the error is less than $1.4a\bar{E}$, where $\bar{E}$ is a straight average of E_i over S. In general, the illuminance gradient may be larger or smaller than the split sphere, but it will always be roughly proportional to a. It is interesting to note that for a less than or equal to 1, S will not contain any value farther than the average spacing or with a surface normal more than 90 degrees from the test location. Intuitively, such a value would be expected to have 100% error.

In practice, additional tests are required to restrict the values included in S. The ray recursion depth must be considered so that values computed after one or more bounces are not substituted for final illuminances. This is easily prevented by keeping separate value lists at each recursion level. A different problem arises from our generalization of the split sphere model. Equation (4) assumes that motion in any direction is equivalent to motion in x. As a result, the set S can include illuminance values that lie on objects shadowing the test point, $\vec{P}$ (Figure 4). We therefore introduce a test to reject illuminance values that are "in front" of $\vec{P}$:

$$d_i(\vec{P}) = \left(\vec{P} - \vec{P}_i\right) \cdot \left[\vec{N}(\vec{P}) + \vec{N}(\vec{P}_i)\right] / 2 \qquad (6)$$

If $d_i(\vec{P})$ is less than zero, then $\vec{P}_i$ is in front of $\vec{P}$ so the value is excluded.

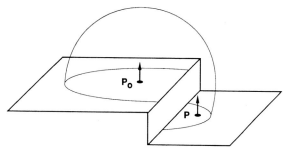

Figure 4: $\vec{P}_0$ sees few close-by surfaces, so its estimated error at $\vec{P}$ is small. But $\vec{P}$ is shadowed by the surface under $\vec{P}_0$, and the true illuminance is different.

Caching indirect illuminance is simple and efficient. The error estimate results in a minimum of primary evaluations and a nearly constant accuracy. Sections of the scene that do not contribute to the image, directly or indirectly, are not examined since no rays reach them. Areas where the indirect illuminance varies rapidly, from changing surface orientation or the influence of nearby objects, will have a higher concentration of values. Flat areas without nearby influences will have only a few values. Dynamic evaluation obviates surface discretization and presampling, so scene representation is not restricted.

Figure 5a shows three colored, textured blocks on a table illuminated by a low-angle light source. Figure 5b shows the placement of indirect illuminance values. Note that the values crowd around inside corners, where surfaces are in close visual contact, and outside corners, where the surface curvature is large. Also, the space between and immediately surrounding the blocks is more densely populated than the background, where only a few values are spread over a wide area. This distribution is different from the standard radiosity technique, which computes values at grid points on each surface. By selecting value locations based on the estimated illuminance gradient, a more accurate calculation is obtained with fewer samples.

Averaging illuminance values over surfaces results in lower pixel variance than produced by standard ray tracing techniques. Figure 5c was produced by a pure Monte Carlo computation that used as many rays as the calculation of Figure 5a. The speckling results from inadequate integration of the indirect contributions at each pixel. Since every pixel requires a separate calculation, only a few diffuse samples are possible over the hemisphere. If a sample happens to catch a bright reflection, the illuminance computed at that point will be disproportionately large. Caching permits a better integration to be performed less frequently, thereby obtaining a more realistic rendering than is feasible with pixel-independent ray tracing.

3.3. Illuminance Storage

For the secondary method to be significantly faster than the primary method, we need an efficient technique for finding the members of S (Equation 5). Without placing any restrictions on scene geometry, an octree permits efficient range searching in three dimensions [1]. A global cube is identified that encompasses all finite surfaces in the scene. When the primary method calculates a new indirect illuminance at a scene location, the global cube is subdivided as necessary to contain the value. Each illuminance, E_i, is stored in the octree node containing its position, $\vec{P}_i$, and having a size (side length) greater than twice but not more than four times the appropriate "valid domain," aR_i. This guarantees that the stored illuminance value will satisfy the condition for S in no more than eight cubes on its own octree level, and a value with a small valid domain will only be examined in close-range searches. Each node in the octree will contain a (possibly empty) list of illuminance values, and a (possibly nil) pointer to eight children. (A two-dimensional analogy is given in Figure 6.) To search the tree for values whose valid domain may contain the point $\vec{P}$, the following recursive procedure is used:

> For each illuminance value at this node
> > If $w_i(\vec{P}) > 1/a$ and $d_i(\vec{P}) \geq 0$
> > > Include value
>
> For each child
> > If $\vec{P}$ is within half the child's size of its cube boundary
> > > Search child node

This algorithm will not only pick up the nodes containing $\vec{P}$, but will also search nodes having boundaries within half the cube size of $\vec{P}$. In this way, all lists that might have an illuminance value whose valid domain contains $\vec{P}$ will be examined. The worst case performance of this algorithm is $O(N)$, where N is the number of values. Performance for a uniform distribution is $O(log(N))$.

The scale of the sorting algorithm can be changed so that the octree cubes are either larger or smaller than the domains of the values they contain. If the cubes are smaller, each examined list will be more likely to contain usable values. However, many of the cubes will be empty. If the cubes are larger, more of the values will have to be examined, but less searching through the tree will be necessary. In any case, changing the scale does not affect the functioning of the algorithm, only its performance in a given situation.

Figure 5a: Colored blocks with diffuse indirect calculation.

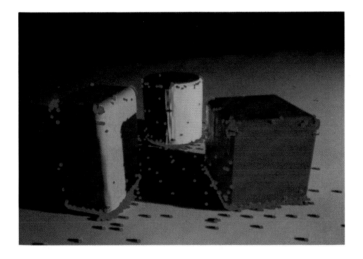

Figure 5b: Blocks with illuminance value locations in blue.

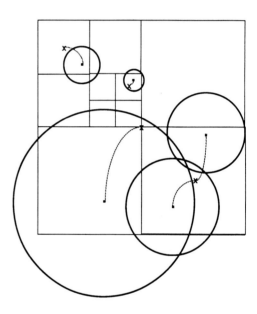

Figure 6: Five indirect illuminance values are shown with their respective domains (circles) linked by dotted lines to the appropriate nodes (squares).

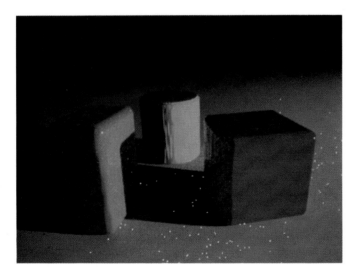

Figure 5c: Blocks using conventional ray tracing techniques.

Writing illuminance values to a file permits their reuse in subsequent renderings. By reusing old values, the indirect calculation will not only proceed more quickly, it will be more accurate since the illuminance is already calculated in some areas of the scene. Normally, the secondary method takes the estimated error right to its tolerance level before calculating a new value. Where the necessary values are precalculated, the tolerance is never reached because all points are within one or more valid domains.

3.4. Multiple Diffuse Reflections

It is often desirable to limit the calculation of diffuse reflections separately from the direct and specular components. A record is kept of how many diffuse bounces have occurred, and this is checked against a user-specified limit. When the limit is reached, a constant ambient value is substituted for the calculation. (This value can be zero.)

The first ray traced in a computation with multiple diffuse reflections begins a cascade of illuminance values (Figure 7). The initial primary evaluation uses many ray samples, and these rays in turn produce many more samples, with the last recursion level exhibiting the densest sampling. As the higher recursion levels become filled with primary illuminance values, fewer rays propagate in the calculation. The computation of multiple diffuse reflections therefore begins slowly, and speeds up as fewer recursion levels require primary evaluation. This process is similar to the "solution" stage of a radiosity technique, which calculates energy transfer between all surfaces before rendering is possible. Producing different views of the same scene is then relatively quick. The thrifty computation of multiple views is also present in our method, with an additional savings from ignoring surfaces that do not contribute to the desired images.

In the computation of multiple reflections, a simple optimization reduces the number of samples required for a given accuracy. If the mean surface reflectance is 50 percent, twice as much error can be tolerated in the calculation of each successive bounce. By increasing the value of a by 40 percent and decreasing the Monte Carlo sampling by 50 percent, each reflection uses one quarter as many rays as the last, with the same contribution to error. The total number of sample rays is then a bounded series, which can serve as a soft limit to recursion when accuracy is critical.

4. Results

The accuracy of the secondary method was tested with an analytical solution of a sphere resting on an infinite plane with seventy percent reflectance, and a parallel light source overhead (Figure 8). The illumination on the sphere due to direct light plus first bounce was determined. Since the scene is radially symmetric, the sphere illuminance is completely described by a one dimensional function of the angle below the horizontal (γ), as measured from the center of the sphere. A closed form for illuminance was found for the upper half of the sphere, and an analytical function was integrated numerically for the lower half. The illuminance caching calculation was then applied to the problem, and the mean and maximum errors of the secondary method were found for different values of a. In each case, the distribution of error was relatively uniform over the sphere, though the density of primary evaluations varied by several orders of magnitude. The mean error was about one fourth, and the maximum error was about twice the estimated error for the split sphere. The relationship between error and a had the expected linear correlation.

Figures 9a, 9b and 9c show a daylit office space with direct only, first bounce, and seven bounces, respectively. The blind-covered window was modeled as six area sources with precalculated distributions accounting for solar and sky components. The images took 25, 40, and 70 hours in separate calculations on a VAX 11/780.

Figure 10 shows an ice cream store illuminated by indirect cove lighting. The total computation took about 30 hours on a Sun 3/60. We estimate the image would have taken more than 500 hours using pixel-independent ray tracing, or 100,000 hours for an accurate radiosity solution. Although a combined radiosity and ray tracing approach would be comparable to our method in computation time, it would not model many of the interactions shown in this image, such as the illumination under the parfait glass.

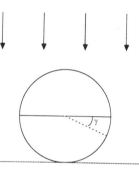

Figure 8: A sphere on an infinite plane, used to validate the secondary method.

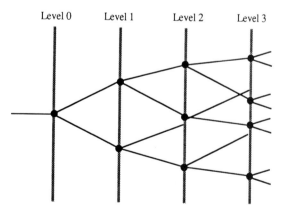

Figure 7: The lines represent rays, and the points represent primary evaluations. The rays that reuse computed values do not propagate.

Figure 10: Ice cream store with indirect cove lighting.

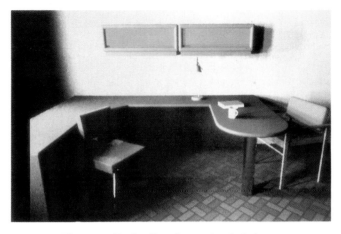

Figure 9a: Daylit office, direct only calculation.

Figure 9b: Daylit office, first bounce calculation.

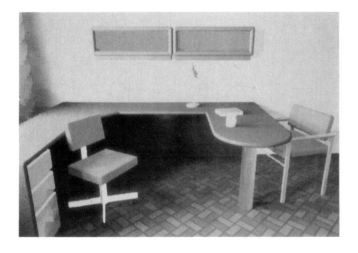

Figure 9c: Daylit office, seven bounce calculation.

5. Discussion

Because our averaging technique was derived from a simplified model (the split sphere), it is important to study its performance in situations where the model is not predictive. Two such cases are illustrated in Figure 11. They are both related to bright, localized reflections, such as those that might result from a spotlight or mirror. If a bright spot is partially hidden by an occluding surface, or on the horizon, then small changes in element location and orientation can result in large changes in illuminance. The averaging technique we have developed will not respond appropriately, and the error related to a will be much larger than the original split sphere model. However, bright spots also make trouble for the Monte Carlo calculation, which requires a higher sample density to find and integrate such luminance spikes. There is no known lighting calculation that can track these small "secondary sources" efficiently. Our technique uses a smaller value for a together with a higher Monte Carlo sample density to model these effects, with a corresponding increase in complexity.

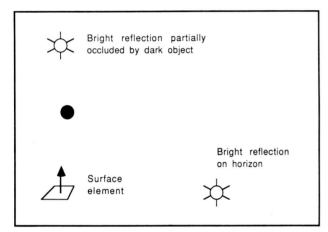

Figure 11: Two cases of indirect illumination that are difficult to model.

Besides diffuse interreflection, the caching technique can also be applied to illumination from large sources, such as a window or the sky. Wide area sources present a problem for conventional ray tracing calculations because they are difficult to sample adequately. Normally, when a ray participating in the diffuse interreflection calculation hits a light source, it is ignored. This prevents counting light sources twice, since they participate in a separate direct component calculation. By moving a large source from the direct to the indirect step of the computation, it is possible to obtain a more accurate sampling of its area. We have found this approach effective for sources with a solid angle greater than 1 steradian.

The calculation of diffuse transmission can also be accelerated by caching. Translucent surfaces become more difficult to model with conventional point sampling techniques as they become more nearly diffuse. The indirect calculation can be used to obtain a more accurate integral of light striking a translucent surface on either side. If the transmission function is not purely diffuse, scattered specular rays can be used to supplement the Monte Carlo calculation, just as they are for reflection.

6. Conclusion

We have developed an efficient ray tracing method for calculating diffuse interreflection, which when combined with standard computations of direct and specular contributions results in a complete simulation of global illumination. Only those illuminance computations required for accurate rendering are performed, and the values can be reused in other images. Thus the method provides an good mix of view-dependent and view-independent qualities. The criterion for evaluation of diffuse interreflection is an estimate of the illuminance gradient from convenient measures of scene geometry. The separation of lighting and geometric models is a basic strength of ray tracing, and it is preserved in this technique. The method can also model diffuse transmission and illumination from large area sources.

7. Acknowledgements

Our thanks go to the reviewers for their comments, and to Sam Berman for his continuing support. We would also like to thank the LBL Computer Science Research Department and the UCB Center for Environmental Design for the use of their equipment. Our special thanks go to Bill Johnston and Paul Heckbert. This work was supported by the Assistant Secretary for Conservation and Renewable Energy, Office of Building Energy Research and Development, Buildings Equipment Division of the U.S. Department of Energy under Contract No. DE-AC03-76SF00098.

8. References

1. Bentley, Jon Louis and Jerome Friedman, "Data Structures for Range Searching," *ACM Computing Surveys*, Vol. 11, No. 4, 1979, pp. 397-409.

2. Cohen, Michael and Donald Greenberg, "A Radiosity Solution for Complex Environments," *Computer Graphics*, Vol. 19, No. 3, July 1985, pp. 31-40.

3. Cohen, Michael, Donald Greenberg, David Immel, Phillip Brock, "An Efficient Radiosity Approach for Realistic Image Synthesis," *IEEE Computer Graphics and Applications*, Vol. 6, No. 2, March 1986, pp. 26-35.

4. Cook, Robert L. and Kenneth E. Torrance, "A Reflection Model for Computer Graphics," *ACM Transactions on Graphics*, Vol. 1, No. 1, January 1982, pp. 7-24.

5. Cook, Robert, Thomas Porter, Loren Carpenter, "Distributed Ray Tracing," *Computer Graphics*, Vol. 18, No. 3, July 1984, pp. 137-147.

6. Cook, Robert L., "Stochastic Sampling in Computer Graphics," *ACM Transactions on Graphics*, Vol. 5, No. 1, January 1986, pp. 51-72.

7. Immel, David S., Donald P. Greenburg, Michael F. Cohen, "A Radiosity Method for Non-Diffuse Environments," *Computer Graphics*, Vol. 20, No. 4, August 1986, pp. 133-142.

8. Kajiya, James T., "The Rendering Equation," *Computer Graphics*, Vol. 20, No. 4, August 1986, pp. 143-150.

9. Kaufman, John, *IES Lighting Handbook*, Reference Volume, IESNA, New York, NY, 1981.

10. Nishita, Tomoyuki and Eihachiro Nakamae, "Continuous Tone Representation of Three-Dimensional Objects Taking Account of Shadows and Interreflection," *Computer Graphics*, Vol. 19, No. 3, July 1985, pp. 23-30.

11. Rubenstein, R.Y., *Simulation and the Monte Carlo Method*, J. Wiley, New York, 1981.

12. Siegel, R. and J. R. Howell, *Thermal Radiation Heat Transfer*, Hemisphere Publishing Corp., Washington DC., 1981.

13. Wallace, John R., Michael F. Cohen, Donald P. Greenburg, "A Two-Pass Solution to the Rendering Equation: A Synthesis of Ray Tracing and Radiosity Methods," *Computer Graphics*, Vol. 21, No. 4, July 1987, pp. 311-320.

14. Weghorst, Hank, Gary Hooper, Donald P. Greenburg. "Improved computational methods for ray tracing" *ACM Transactions on Graphics*, Vol. 3, No. 1, January 1984, pp. 52-69.

15. Whitted, Turner, "An Improved Illumination Model for Shaded Display," *Communications of the ACM*, Vol. 23, No. 6, June 1980, pp. 343-349.

A NEW RADIOSITY APPROACH BY PROCEDURAL REFINEMENTS
FOR REALISTIC IMAGE SYNTHESIS

Min-Zhi Shao, Qun-Sheng Peng, You-Dong Liang

CAD/CAM Research Center
Zhejiang University
P. R. OF CHINA

ABSTRACT

According to the rendering equation, the diffuse and the specular components of the outgoing intensity of each surface patch should be solved simultaneously. Rather than establishing a huge set of linear equations defining the unknown directional intensities for all directions and all surface patches, we expand the concept of the delta form-factor which concerns the light energy transfer of a surface patch along a respective direction. As the delta form-factor for non-diffuse surface patches are dependent on the spatial and spectral distributions of light energy, they could not be calculated geometrically. In this paper, we present a new radiosity approach which progressively approximates the delta form-factors and the light energy distributions within a general environment to the correct solution. The nucleus of our approach is procedural iteration. Statistics indicate the potentials of this method for complex non-diffuse environments.

CR Categories and Subject Descriptors: I.3.3 [Computer Graphics]: Picture/Image Generation; I.3.7 [Computer Graphics]: Three-Dimensional Graphics and Realism

General Terms: Algorithms

Additional Key Words and Phrases: Distributed ray tracing, form-factors, global illumination, hemi-cube, procedural iteration, progressive refinement, radiosity

INTRODUCTION

In recent years, along with the vigorous developments of computer graphics, ray tracing and radiosity methods have gradually become the two main techniques for realistic image synthesis.

Ray tracing is used as a method of determining the global illumination information that is relevant to the image plane. It correctly simulates the light outgoing a smooth surface by mirror reflection and regular transmission. Since the methodology was introduced by Whitted [14] in 1980, it has been widely used and has generated some of the most realistic images to date. However, there are many scenes that cannot be adequately modeled by ray tracing. The illumination model posed by ray tracing method ignores the interaction of light between diffusely reflecting surfaces. Furthermore, the ray tracing methodology, which just provides limited point-sampled information, is not sufficient for the application of energy equilibrium models to light behavior. Only the intra-environment specular effects are considered. [6]

In 1984, Goral et al. [5] introduced a so called radiosity method from thermal engineering [10] [11] to computer graphics. This method models the interaction of light between diffusely reflecting surfaces and accurately presents the global illumination effects. Since then, Cohen et al. successively proposed two famous algorithms to make the radiosity method a practical rendering technique. One is the hemi-cube algorithm which extends the radiosity solution to environments with occluded surfaces so as to render complex scenes [1]; the other is the substructuring algorithm which provides means for local discretization of critical portions of the environment without affecting the remainder of the global solution [2]. However, the ideal diffuse reflection is assumed in all those algorithms and specular reflections from non-diffuse surfaces are not considered. This unfortunately limited the extensive use of the radiosity method.

Since the form-factors in non-diffuse environments are dependent on the spatial and spectral distributions of light energy and should be evaluated conforming to the specific illumination attributes of each surface, a modified hemi-cube algorithm which successively approximates the correct form-factors of general complex environments is introduced in this paper. The nucleus of our method is procedural iteration. First, we obtain a sketchy light distribution of the environment by applying a standard radiosity method. Then, the new form-factors of non-diffuse patches are calculated according to this distribution. They in turn propose a more accurate light distribution within the environment. After several repetitions of the iteration, we arrive at the correct solution.

Note that a constant radiosity is assumed for each surface patch and an accurate light radiation distribution at the sample point of each patch is retained. This may suggest a direct scan line conversion to generate the desired image. However, since the specular component of the outgoing intensity typically changes very quickly over the patch, a view-independent solution may require that the specular surfaces be subdivided into fine details, invoking enormous amount of computations. Rather, we adopt a two-pass approach and employ distributed ray tracing to evaluate the specular components of the outgoing intensities of the concerned surface patches which contribute to the final view-dependent image. Statistics indicate the potentials of this procedure for complex non-diffuse realistic image synthesis.

GLOBAL ILLUMINATION MODELS FOR GENERAL ENVIRONMENTS

Although both ray tracing and radiosity are recognized as global illumination solutions, they describe only the two extreme situations of light energy distributions within ideal environments. Much efforts were made to remedy the deficiencies of the two methods to cover a more general situation.

From the angle of ray tracing: In 1984, Cook et al. [3] [4] presented the algorithm of distributed ray tracing. This algorithm provides a correct and easy solution to some previously unsolved or partially solved difficult problems in ray tracing, including fuzzy reflections. In 1986, Kajiya [8] made some further advances on the idea of Cook's method. He described an algorithm that solves a so called rendering equation using Monte Carlo and variance reduction techniques for stochastic ray tracing. Although, theoretically, this approach could eventually converge to the accurate solution, the computation time would preclude the substantial increase of the sample points. Then, the inefficiency of point-sampling becomes the main problem. It has not been well solved for general complex environments, especially concerning the diffuse reflection.

From the angle of radiosity: In 1986, Immel et al. [7] firstly introduced a general radiosity method accounting for all interreflections of light between diffuse and non-diffuse surfaces in complex environments. The relationship between a patch and all other patches in the environment becomes, in this method, a relationship between a given outgoing direction for a patch and all outgoing directions for all other patches. Unfortunately, the computational resources to be expended are too huge to make this method a practical approach.

In 1987, Wallace et al. [13] presented a two-pass approach that integrates ray tracing and radiosity into a whole. It is thus capable of dealing with complex environments (including mirror surfaces). The first pass is based on the hemi-cube radiosity algorithm with extension to include the light energy transfer via diffuse to specular, specular to specular and specular to diffuse mechanism, the second pass is based on an alternative to distributed ray tracing. The two-pass approach which combines ray tracing and radiosity organically, takes advantages of both the classic methods and avoids their shortcomings. This is a successful scheme indeed.

By careful analysis of the two-pass approach, we can easily see that the crux step is the first pass which calculates the view-independent illumination effects for a non-diffuse environment. According to the rendering equation, the outgoing intensity of a surface is composed of three components, namely an emission term, a diffuse term and a specular term:

$$I_{out}(\theta_{out}) = E(\theta_{out}) + I_{d,out} + I_{s,out}(\theta_{out}) \tag{1}$$

where

$$I_{d,out} = \kappa_d \rho_d \int I_{in}(\theta_{in})\cos(\theta)d\omega \tag{2}$$

$$I_{s,out}(\theta_{out}) = \kappa_s \int \rho_s(\theta_{out},\theta_{in})I_{in}(\theta_{in})\cos(\theta)d\omega \tag{3}$$

with κ_d , κ_s indicating respectively the diffuse and the specular reflection coefficients of the surface, $\kappa_d + \kappa_s = 1$. Obviously, the outgoing diffuse and specular terms each depend on all incoming intensities of the surface. As these incoming intensities are just the outgoing intensities from other surfaces, they in turn contain both diffuse and specular components.[13] Thus it is impossible to derive an accurate diffuse energy distribution of the environment without precisely determining the specular reflection component of each surface. In other words, both diffuse and specular terms of the outgoing intensity of each patch should be solved simultaneously by one integrated process. Wallace et al. simplified the situation by assuming all non-diffuse surfaces to be planar mirror surfaces. To incorporate the effects of these mirror surfaces, Wallace adopted a so called image method [11] from thermal engineering. The principle is simple and straightforward, namely that the light reflected from a plane mirror appears to come from an image located behind the mirror (Figure 1). Apparently, each mirror introduces an additional virtual world into the environment.

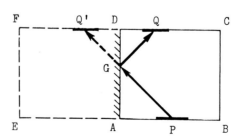

Figure 1. Enclosure with one specular surface (AD).

Now let us make a brief analysis on the image method (Figure 2). If AD is a mirror, then one projection of all patches in front of AD turns the entire environment into EBCF, in which the number of the patches almost increases by one time. If DC is also a mirror, the further mirror reflections turns the environment into EBHI, and the number of the patches within EBHI increases nearly three times. Note that the total computation time of form-factors is of $O(N^2)$ (N is the number of patches in the environment, representing the complexity of the environment). As the calculation of form-factors will cost about 90% of computation time in the implementation of the radiosity method, the image method may turn to be a very expensive solution when the mirror surfaces introduced into the environment are increased. In general, with multiple interreflections between mirror surfaces, the computation time may go up in exponential order. This is because the images have their images too. Consequently, a simple environment may get very complicated after several mirror reflections.

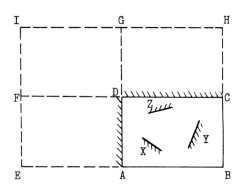

Figure 2. Enclosure with two adjacent (AD,DC) and three arbitrarily positioned (X,Y,Z) specular surfaces.

This paper presents a new radiosity approach and solves the problem effectively. The concept of delta form-factors is developed to simulate both the diffuse and specular reflections of each surface patch. The correct light energy distribution of the environment is determined by a single pass. Non-diffuse surfaces in such an environment may possess arbitrary illumination attributes and need no longer be limited to perfect planar mirrors.

PROCEDURAL REFINEMENT

Firstly, we define the form-factor between any two patches in a general complex environment. The form-factor of patch i to patch j can be defined as follows:

$$F_{ij} = \frac{B_{ij}}{B_i} \qquad (4)$$

where B_{ij} represents the light energy that is transfered directly to patch j from patch i, and B_i represents the total radiant light energy of patch i.

Generally, in an ordinary non-diffuse environment, we have:

$$F_{ij} = \kappa_{id} F_{ij}^d + \kappa_{is} F_{ij}^s \qquad (5)$$

where F_{ij}^d represents the fraction of light energy transfer to patch j via diffuse reflections of patch i and can be calculated using the standard hemi-cube algorithm, F_{ij}^s represents the other portion of light energy transfer to patch j via specular reflections of patch i ($\sum_{j=1}^{N} F_{ij}^d = 1$, $\sum_{j=1}^{N} F_{ij}^s = 1$, so $\sum_{j=1}^{N} F_{ij} = 1$). κ_{id} , κ_{is} are coefficients regarding the diffuse and the specular reflection of patch i respectively ($\kappa_{id} + \kappa_{is} = 1$).

Note that the definition of form-factor in our approach is different from that in the previous two-pass method. This leads to a series of differences between the two algorithms. The following points are then listed:

1. B_{ij} is not limited to the radiant light energy transfered from patch i to patch j by diffuse reflection. It also includes the light energy which is transfered from patch i via self specular reflection to patch j (if patch i is a specular patch). Thus, B_{ij} represents the total energy that is directly transfered from patch i to patch j.

2. B_{ij} concerns the direct radiant light energy transfer only. The light energy being transfered from patch i to patch j via any other intermediate patches is not included. For instance, the light energy radiated from patch i then reflected by mirror k and landed on patch j is not included in B_{ij}. This part of energy, according to our definition of the form-factor, is determined by B_k and F_{kj}. (Figure 3)

3. For an ideal diffuse patch i, the form-factor F_{ij} (j may be any other patch in the environment) depends only on the relative locations of patch i and patch j and accounts for nothing with the distribution of light energy in the environment. Though B_i may vary (which happens during a disturbance of the enclosure), the fraction of its energy which is transfered to any other patch in the environment remains the same. In other words, its form-factor is purely geometrical. (Figure 4)

4. If patch i is a specular patch, however, the form-factor F_{ij} will depend on the spatial and

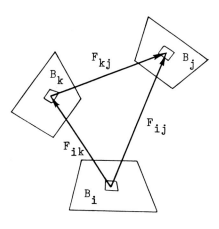

Figure 3. The light energy from patch i which is reflected by mirror k and then transfered to patch j is not included in B_{ij}.

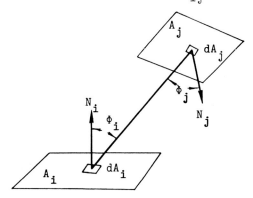

Figure 4. Form-factor geometry.

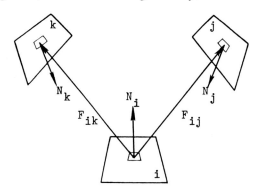

Figure 5. Light energy distribution and form-factor.

spectral distributions of light energy in the environment. For example, in Figure 5, patch j and patch k are reflection symmetrical about patch i. If i is an ideal diffuse patch, then $F_{ij} = F_{ik}$. But

if i is a mirror patch, the matter will not be so simple. If k is a light source, F_{ij} turns greater.

On the other hand, if k is a blackbody, F_{ij} will

turn smaller. Since the total distribution of light energy in the environment is unknown (in fact, this is exactly what we want to resolve), it is difficult to evaluate the specular form-factors of non-diffuse patches in a immediate way. Therefore the nucleus of our work is to approximate these form-factors first, then successively refining them by procedural iterations. Finally, we obtain the correct distribution of light energy within a general complex environment.

Analogous to the traditional radiosity method, we have:

$$B_i = E_i + \rho_i \sum_{j=1}^{N} B_j F_{ji} A_j / A_i \,, \qquad i = \overline{1, N} \qquad (6)$$

where

B_i = radiosity of patch i which is the total rate of radiant energy leaving the patch per unit time per unit area (watts/meter**2)

E_i = rate of direct energy emission from patch i per unit time per unit area (watts/meter**2)

ρ_i = reflectivity of patch i and represents the fraction of incident light which is reflected back into the hemispherical space (unitless)

F_{ji} = form factor which represents the fraction of radiant energy leaving patch j and impinging on patch i (unitless)

A_i = area of patch i (meter**2)

Note that in general non-diffuse environments, the following identical equation:

$$F_{ij} A_i = F_{ji} A_j \qquad (7)$$

is not tenable, hence expression (6). In this equation, $B_j F_{ji} A_j$ represents the radiant light

energy leaving patch j and impinging on patch i. After being divided by A_i and then multiplied by ρ_i, it

represents a portion of the radiosity of patch i which is contributed by patch j.

Denote $A_{ji} = A_j / A_i$ and $D_{ij} = F_{ij} A_{ij}$, we obtain the following set of linear equations:

$$\begin{bmatrix} 1-\rho_1 D_{11} & -\rho_1 D_{21} \cdots & -\rho_1 D_{N1} \\ -\rho_2 D_{12} & 1-\rho_2 D_{22} \cdots & -\rho_2 D_{N2} \\ \cdot & \cdot & \cdot \\ \cdot & \cdot & \cdot \\ -\rho_N D_{1N} & -\rho_N D_{2N} \cdots & 1-\rho_N D_{NN} \end{bmatrix} \begin{bmatrix} B_1 \\ B_2 \\ \cdot \\ \cdot \\ B_N \end{bmatrix} = \begin{bmatrix} E_1 \\ E_2 \\ \cdot \\ \cdot \\ E_N \end{bmatrix} \qquad (8)$$

Note: The matrix is formed and solved for the radiosities regarding each color band of interest. It is usually solved for three channels (R, G, B) but could be done on a wavelength basis if desired. Not only ρ_i but also F_{ij} may have different values for

each channel.

Next, we discuss the calculation of form-factors of specular patches. An imaginary hemi-cube is created around the center (sample point) of each specular patch, all other patches in the environment are then projected onto the cube. (Figure 6) Each pixel on the hemi-cube relates to a specific patch index, and each patch index refers to a certain radiosity. So a hemi-cube retains not only the geometrical, but also the physical characteristics of the related patches in the environment. In fact, it has the global light energy distribution of the environment projected onto its faces. Therefore, the form-factor of patch k to every other patch in the environment can be easily obtained as soon as the delta form-factor is calculated which concerns the light energy transfer along a direction from the sample point to every pixel on the hemi-cube within a solid angle.

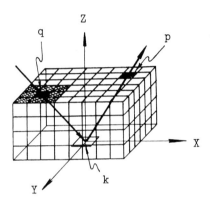

Figure 6. The distribution of light energy in the environment is projected on the hemi-cube.

Now let us consider the delta form-factor associated with any pixel p on the imaginary hemi-cube of a specular patch k (Δf_{kp}). Firstly, we find out the pixel q which is reflection symmetrical with p on the hemi-cube. Apparently, the radiant energy which is transfered towards pixel p by specular reflection of patch k is released by surface patches recorded in pixel q and pixels around q. If k is a perfect mirror patch, we have the following expression:

$$\Delta f_{kp} = \frac{\rho_k B_q \Delta A}{\rho_k \sum_s (B_s \Delta A)} = \frac{B_q}{\sum_s B_s} \qquad (9)$$

where B_s is the partial radiosity of a surface patch recorded in pixel s reaching patch k from a corresponding direction, thus $\sum_s (B_s \Delta A)$ represents the total energy landed on patch k. As ρ_k is the reflectivity of patch k, Δf_{kp} represents the fraction of energy leaving patch k in a specified direction. Obviously, $\sum_p \Delta f_{kp} = 1$. If k is not a perfect mirror patch (e.g. it satisfies the Phong distribution, see Figure 7), we sample pixel q and pixels around q, and calculate the weighted average (weights are determined by the specified bidirectional reflectance of patch k).

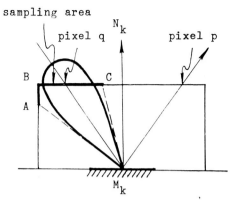

sampling area

Figure 7. Weighted sampling according to the related bidirectional reflectance.

In general, for each patch k in the environment, we have:

$$\Delta f_{kp} = \kappa_d \Delta f_{kp}^d + \kappa_s \Delta f_{kp}^s \qquad (10)$$

in which, Δf_{kp}^d is the diffuse delta form-factor, Δf_{kp}^s is the specular delta form-factor. Since $\sum_p \Delta f_{kp}^d = 1$, $\sum_p \Delta f_{kp}^s = 1$, then $\sum_p \Delta f_{kp} = 1$. It satisfies the normal condition for form-factors. Particularly, if $\kappa_d = 0$, k is a perfect mirror patch; if $\kappa_s = 0$, patch k is ideal diffuse.

Finally, we give the basic program structure of our procedural iterative and progressive refined radiosity method.

STEP 1. Assume the whole environment to be an ideal diffuse environment first. The form-factors between all pairs of patches within the environment are calculated using the standard hemi-cube algorithm, and the radiosity of each patch is then obtained. Meanwhile, the hemi-cube of every non-diffuse patch is preserved as an item buffer with each item retaining the information of patches visible from the corresponding pixel on the cube.

All form-factors are then calculated. The results are correct for the ideal diffuse patches but just rough estimations for the non-diffuse patches. Since specular reflections account for only a small proportion of the total radiant light energy within the environment, we have obtained a relatively correct radiosity solution for the whole environment, although in some directions (e.g. the mirror reflecting direction of light source) the error might be very large.

STEP 2. Now we take the radiosity of each patch obtained in the first step as the initial value (the distribution of light energy on the hemi-cube), recalculate the form-factors (R, G, B) of the non-diffuse patches. We firstly find out the pixel q which is reflection symmetrical with each pixel p on the hemi-cube (Figure 6). If the index of visible patch preserved in pixel q is i, then $B_i F_{ik}$ is the radiosity of pixel q to patch k. Calculate the weighted average of delta form-factors at pixels around q according to the distribution function of bidirectional reflectance of patch k and evaluate the delta form-factor Δf_{kp} (R, G, B) using formular (9) and (10). Since the hemi-cube of every non-diffuse patch has been preserved in a data file, this step involves only reading from the data file and sampling pixels on the hemi-cube, avoiding the more expensive process of patch clipping, projecting and hidden surface removal. [9]

SEPT 3. Solve the global systems of linear equations again with the more accurate form-factors of the non-diffuse patches and obtain a new solution of light energy distribution of the environment. Comparing the radiosity of each patch with its previous value. If the difference is smaller than a given tolerance, then the iteration process is accomplished, otherwise, go to step 2 and repeat the above processes.

It should be mentioned that every environment in the radiosity method is assumed to be an enclosure. No energy could be transfered in, and no energy might be scattered out. The enclosure always maintains its light energy balance. Furthermore, it is a stable equilibrium, namely once the balance is disturbed, it will reach the next equilibrium simultaneously. A simple example serves to illustrate this phenomenon. Let us construct two equivalent processes regarding the light energy transfer in an environment. (see Figure 8) Without losing generality, the situations of three patches A, B and C among the surfaces in the enclosure will be illustrated. In case 1, patch A, B, and C are always treated as mirrors and the environment keeps in a certain equilibrium. In case 2, patch A, B, and C are treated as ideal diffuse reflectors first, but are gradually transformed into mirrors (the reflectivities remain the same). Therefore, the original balance is broken. As a fraction of light energy emitted by the light source will gradually transfer to these patches via their specular reflection, the form-factors F_{AB}, F_{BC} and the radiosities B_A, B_B, B_C in Figure 8 will

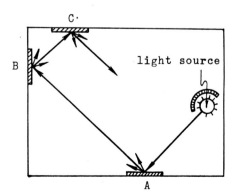

Figure 8. The conservation of light energy in an enclosure.

successively increase. Nevertheless, the scale of increments are gradually decreased as little of the light energy which is emitted by the source will transfer back to it again. And this happens to all patches in the enclosure. So case 2 is convergent. Clearly, our progressive refinement procedure is exactly the same with the energy conservation process mentioned above and will successively converge to the correct distribution.

Implementations have demonstrated that the convergent speed of our algorithm is very fast. For general complex environments, the accurate light energy distribution may be obtained after four to six iterations. The time required by these iterations is less than 20% of that by STEP 1 which invokes a standard radiosity procedure. Compared with the image method, our approach is regular and fast. It is a breakthrough to the traditional method in radiative heat transfer.

RESULTS

Figure 9 (A) and (B) show a test environment. The left object is a volume light source. All of its surfaces emit light energy except the top one (in green). In the right side, the blue object is a light-shelter. It shields off the direct illumination by the volume light source to the right wall. Overall illumination of the room is provided by two dim area light sources on the ceiling.

In Figure 9(A), all patches in the environment are ideal diffuse. The image is generated using the standard radiosity method.

In Figure 9(B), the floor is treated as a non-diffuse surface ($\kappa_d = 0.4$, $\kappa_s = 0.6$). The image is generated using our progressive refined radiosity method. The effect of specular to diffuse reflection is accounted for. Please pay attention to the difference of the light energy distribution on the right wall and the subtle variation of the intensity of the blue light-shelter between image (A) and image (B). The number of iterations accomplished is five. The implementation data are listed in Table 1, in which, MAXIMUM (AVERAGE) ERROR represents the maximum (average) errors of radiosities within all patches between two successive iterations. The fuzzy images on the floor are generated using a distributed ray tracing technique in the post-process.

Figure 10 (A), (B) and (C) show a simple and crude room. In the middle of the front wall, there is a nearly perfect mirror ($\kappa_d = 0.02$, $\kappa_s = 0.98$). A very bright light source (in blue) whose backface scatters light to the front wall is located at the left-top corner of the room. Figure 10(A) is the top view.

Figure 10(B) shows the environment in which all patches are treated as ideal diffuse reflectors. In Figure 10(C), the specular reflection of the mirror has been accounted for. Please pay attention to the differences of light spot on the floor, the right wall and the top of the table between these two images. Also note the changes of light intensity on the legs and the backface of the table appeared in the mirror. The implementation data about Figure 10 are listed in Table 2.

For each mirror surface in Figure 10 (A), (B) and (C), the distributed ray tracing is used in the post-process.

Since the main storage of our microcomputer is 1 Mb, we have no choice but to simplify the complexity of our test environments as far as possible. All lanterns are carefully made light enough to be suspended in midair.

The program was written in C under an UNOS operating system and ran on an UNIVERSE 68000. All images were displayed on a 640X480 resolution E&S PS340 color screen.

CONCLUSIONS

The outgoing intensity of a surface patch in a general environment may consist of three components, namely an emission term, a diffuse term and a specular term. With the inclusion of the emission term and the specular term, the outgoing intensity of a surface becomes direction dependent. According to the rendering equation, the radiative intensity along an outgoing direction is the function of all incoming intensities arrived at the surface patch from the other directions and these incoming intensities, radiated by other surfaces in the environment, can also be decomposed into the above three terms. Thus, the diffuse and the specular components of light energy transfer between surface patches should be solved by one integrated process. Rather than establishing a huge set of linear equations defining the unknown directional intensities for all directions and all surface patches and solving them simultaneously, we expand the concept of the delta form-factor which concerns light energy transfer of a surface patch along a respective direction. While the delta form-factors for ideal diffuse surface patches are evaluated using the standard hemi-cube algorithm, the delta form-factors for non-diffuse surface patches are calculated by distributedly sampling the incoming incident rays within a solid angle. Apparently, these delta form-factors for non-diffuse surface patches are dependent on the spatial and spectral distributions of light energy and cannot be determined geometrically. An iterative solution is then developed. We first calculate the form-factors of all surface patches, ignoring specular reflections between them, and solve for the radiosity for each surface patch. The more accurate form-factors for non-diffuse surface patches are obtained based on the light energy distribution of the environment just derived. Thus, both the delta form-factors for non-diffuse surface patches and hence the light energy distribution of the environment can be successively approximated to the correct solution by procedural iterations. Statistics indicate the potentials of this approach for solving complex non-diffuse environments.

Although we have obtained the average radiosity of each surface patch, the spatial and spectral distributions of the outgoing intensity is accurate at the sample point of each non-diffuse surface patch only. Thus, instead of conducting a further discretization, we adopt distributed ray tracing as a post-process to evaluate the emission and the specular components of the outgoing intensities of the concerned surface patches which contribute to the final view-dependent image. Our approach is thus a two-pass solution.

There are two main methods in solving systems of linear equations. One is the direct method (e.g. Gaussian elimination scheme); the other is the iterative method (e.g. Gauss-Siedel iteration scheme). The time required by Gaussian eliminative approach is of $O(N^3)$ (N represents the order of linear equations). Therefore, for solving large systems of linear equations, the direct method is too awkward to be invoked and the iterative method is commonly used. It can greatly reduce the computation time in general cases. [12] This should give us some enlightenment. When the specular surfaces are included in the environment and the computation time increases hopelessly, why don't we try to use a seemingly unassured but actually smart progressive refined radiosity method? In fact, our approach is fast and effective for rendering non-diffuse environments (see Table 1 and Table 2).

By the way, as a procedural iterative radiosity method proposed for computer graphics, we believe, it can also be effectively applied to thermal engineering for calculating the radiative heat transfer. Computer graphics is a new interdiscipline. Pursuing some well-painted non-existent pictures is not the whole purpose. Computer graphics ought to make greater contributions to the developments of other disciplines. This problem should, at least partially, be paid attention to in the future research.

ACKNOWLEDGEMENTS

We thank all those who helped in the preparation of this article. In particular, we are grateful to Prof. Tong-Guang Jin for helpful suggestions and encouragement during this study. Thanks also go to Guo-Zhao Wang, Yi-Ning Zhu, Hao Xu and Ping-Ping Shao for many valuable discussions. Finally, we would like to thank the reviewers for their helpful comments. This research was performed in the CAD/CAM Research Center at Zhejiang University.

ITERATION NUMBER	FORM FACTOR	MATRIX SOLUTION	MAXIMUM ERROR			AVERAGE ERROR		
			R	G	B	R	G	B
STANDARD RADIOSITY	207.6 Min	3.6 Min						
1st	4.6 Min	3.9 Min	178	161	167	29.307	23.071	26.941
2nd	4.6 Min	3.9 Min	9	4	4	1.054	0.602	0.741
3rd	4.6 Min	3.9 Min	1	1	1	0.036	0.030	0.030
4th	4.6 Min	3.9 Min	1	1	1	0.012	0.012	0.012
5th	4.6 Min	3.9 Min	0	0	0	0.000	0.000	0.000
TOTAL	23.0 Min	19.5 Min						

Table 1

ITERATION NUMBER	FORM FACTOR	MATRIX SOLUTION	MAXIMUM ERROR			AVERAGE ERROR		
			R	G	B	R	G	B
STANDARD RADIOSITY	326.8 Min	3.9 Min						
1st	2.5 Min	4.1 Min	338	339	342	64.430	68.774	62.439
2nd	2.5 Min	4.1 Min	11	16	5	0.529	0.783	0.362
3rd	2.5 Min	4.1 Min	2	3	1	0.015	0.021	0.010
4th	2.5 Min	4.1 Min	0	1	1	0.000	0.005	0.005
5th	2.5 Min	4.1 Min	0	0	0	0.000	0.000	0.000
TOTAL	14.5 Min	20.5 Min						

Table 2

REFERENCES

[1] Cohen, M. F., and Greenberg, D. P., The Hemi-Cube: A Radiosity Solution for Complex Environments, Computer Graphics (Proceedings SIGGRAPH 85), Vol.19, No.3, July 1985, pp.31-40.

[2] Cohen, M. F., Greenberg, D. P., Immel, D. S., and Brock, P. J., An Efficient Radiosity Approach for Realistic Image Synthesis, IEEE CG&A, Vol.6, No.3, March 1986, pp.26-35.

[3] Cook, R. L., Stochastic Sampling in Computer Graphics, ACM Transactions on Graphics, Vol.5, No.1, January 1986, pp.51-72.

[4] Cook, R. L., Porter, T., and Carpenter, L., Distributed Ray Tracing, Computer Graphics (Proceedings SIGGRAPH 84), Vol.18, No.3, July 1984, pp.137-145.

[5] Goral, C. M., Torrance, K. E., Greenberg, D. P., and Battaile, B., Modeling the Interaction of Light Between Diffuse Surfaces, Computer Graphics (Proceedings SIGGRAPH 84), Vol.18, No.3, July 1984, pp.213-222.

[6] Hall, R. A., and Greenberg, D. P., A Testbed for Realistic Image Synthesis, IEEE CG&A, Vol.3, No.8, November 1983, pp.10-20.

[7] Immel, D. S., Cohen, M. F., and Greenberg, D. P., A Radiosity Method for Non-Diffuse Environments, Computer Graphics (Proceedings SIGGRAPH 86), Vol.20, No.4, August 1986, pp.133-142.

[8] Kajiya, J. T., The Rendering Equation, Computer Graphics (Proceedings SIGGRAPH 86), Vol.20, No.4, August 1986, pp.143-150.

[9] Rogers, D. F., Procedural Elements for Computer Graphics, McGraw-Hill, New York, 1985.

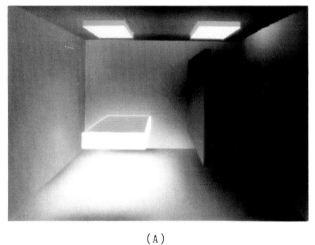

(A)

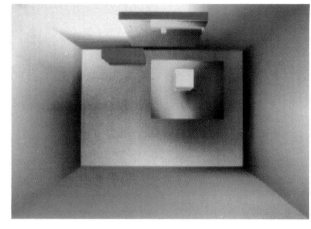

(A)

(B)

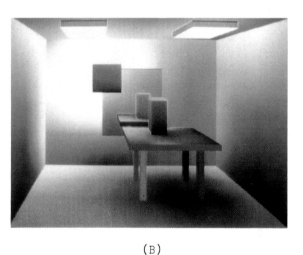

(B)

Figure 9

[10] Siegel, R., and Howell, J. R., Thermal Radiation Heat Transfer, Hemisphere Publishing Corporation, Washington DC., 1981.

[11] Sparrow, E. M., and Cess, R. D., Radiation Heat Transfer, Hemisphere Publishing Corporation, Washington DC., 1978.

[12] Varga, R. S., Matrix Iterative Analysis, Prentice-Hall, New Jersey, 1962.

[13] Wallace, J. R., Cohen, M. F., and Greenberg, D. P., A Two-Pass Solution to the Rendering Equation: A Synthesis of Ray Tracing and Radiosity Methods, Computer Graphics (Proceedings SIGGRAPH 87), Vol.21, No.4, July 1987, pp.311-320.

[14] Whitted, T., An Improved Illumination Model for Shaded Display, Comm. ACM, Vol.23, No.6, June 1980, pp.343-349.

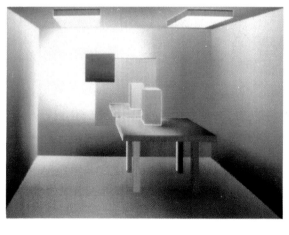

(C)

Figure 10

ConMan: A Visual Programming Language for Interactive Graphics

Paul E. Haeberli

Silicon Graphics, Inc.
Mountain View, CA 94043

ABSTRACT

Traditionally, interactive applications have been difficult to build, modify and extend. These integrated applications provide bounded functionality, have a single thread of control and a fixed user interface that must anticipate everything the user will need.

Current workstations allow several processes to share the screen. With proper communication between processes, it is possible to escape previous models for application development and evolution.

ConMan is a high-level visual language we use on an IRIS workstation that lets users dynamically build and modify graphics applications. To do this, a system designer disintegrates complex applications into modular components. By interactively connecting simple components, the user constructs a complete graphics application that matches the needs of a task. A connection manager controls the flow of data between individual components. As a result, we replace the usual user-machine dialog with a dynamic live performance that is orchestrated by the user.

CR Categories and Subject Descriptors: D.2.2 [**Software Engineering**]: Tools and Techniques - User interfaces, D.3.2 [**Programming Languages**]: Language Classifications - Data-flow languages, Nonprocedural languages; I.3.6 [**Computer Graphics**]: Methodology and Techniques - Interaction techniques, Languages;

Additional Key Words and Phrases: Visual Programming Languages.

©1988   ACM-0-89791-275-6/88/008/0103 $00.75

Introduction

Often we think of a user interface toolkit as a set of facilities that a *developer* can use to shape the feel of an application. For example, to make a choice available a developer can use a pop-up menu or a screen button. But after the developer compiles an application, the user is left with a static user-interface that reflects the developer's vision. If the user's task doesn't fit into the developer's model, then the user must use a different approach or try to find another application that does a better job.

An alternative is to present *users* with a toolkit and let them match it to a given task. In the UNIX* world, there are lots of simple tools a user can combine to solve different problems. The mechanism that joins these tools is a pipe, a simple one-directional interprocess communication (IPC) facility. This is an approach where the power of the sum is much greater than the power of the individual parts. ConMan (Connection Manager) provides a conceptually similar graphical facility for connecting visually-oriented tools. With ConMan, developers can concentrate on the purity of simple components. With good components that perform individual tasks well, a user can find a combination to solve problems that the designers didn't envision.

To escape the mechanical world of tools and toolkits, we'll use the culinary metaphor of a sandwich. Conventional systems present you with a ready made sandwich. You can add mustard and relish, but most choices have been made by the sandwich maker and your job is to find a sandwich that is closest to your needs. ConMan gives you the ingredients for the sandwich and leaves it to you to design a good one. This glosses over an important point: if you aren't a good cook, then the sandwich won't be very tasty. This isn't entirely facetious - the tradeoff between an expressive system and a ready-made system will always benefit some users and leave others unsatisfied.

Background

Although there have been amazing advances in graphics display hardware in the last ten years, applications have been slow in using the new capabilities pro-

---

* UNIX is a trademark of Bell Laboratories.

vided by the current generation of interactive graphics workstations. The structure of interactive applications has changed very little.

A typical application is integrated and self-contained with a single process and address space. The user interface is compiled into the program, or read in from an external description as in [Schulert 85]. The behavior of the application is described by a textual language that is compiled into an executable program. Functional binding happens at compile time and is static.

Users are prevented from expanding the design space interactively because the scope of an application is often limited by the vision of its designer. Also, traditional graphics applications are anti-social because they don't play nicely with other applications.

These characteristics often result in the user being dominated by applications. Instead of the user driving an application, the user is often driven and constrained by the application.

We want to use the facilities of the modern interactive medium more effectively to give the user more expressive power and freedom to construct and modify applications in a flexible way. Why isn't application development more like making a bacon, lettuce, and tomato, cucumber, salami, avocado, Jell-O®† [Heckbert 87] and sushi sandwich? Can't we use the interactive medium itself to help us?

Visual Programming

Visual programming describes any system that lets the user specify a program using a two dimensional notation. Instead of editing a one dimensional stream of characters, the user interacts with a two dimensional representation. A good discussion of various visual programming languages is given in [Myers 86].

Smith's Alternate Reality Kit [Smith 86] is a dynamic simulation environment with a visual interface. Objects have mass, velocity and a visual representation. The user can interact with the objects and change how one object influences another.

Other interesting visual programming systems are described in [Kimura 86a], [Kimura 86b], [Cardelli 86], [Blythe 86], and [Galloway 87]. These use two dimensional data-flow constructs to describe program behavior. Kimura's system, *Show and Tell*, runs on the Macintosh computer. It's a general purpose system that handles pictorial and textual data. It has some interesting graphical constructs for conditionals and iteration.

Cardelli has developed a conceptual framework for a system he calls *Fragments of Behavior*. In his system, each fragment has an interface for communicating with other fragments and possibly a dialog for communicating with users. The behavior of each fragment is described in the *Squeak* language [Cardelli 85], which resembles Hoare's language for communicating sequential processes [Hoare 78].

The systems by Blythe and Galloway use data-flow constructs to control music synthesis and design digital filters interactively.

Tanner's Switchboard [Tanner 86] supports flexible communication between a population of processes running under the Harmony operating system.

The World of ConMan

In ConMan, we also use a data flow metaphor. The user constructs and modifies applications by creating components that are interconnected on the screen. The window manager supports creation and deletion of individual components, while the user changes the interconnection by interacting with ConMan, the connection manager.

Figure 1 shows how this interconnection can be described by a directed graph with components as nodes, and connections as edges. Connections establish dependencies between one component and another. Each component can have up to eight input ports and up to eight output ports. By interacting with the connection manager, the user may alter this dependency graph at any time, without the knowledge of the components.

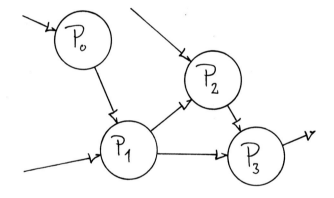

Figure 1. A directed graph representation.

Any dynamic interaction is easier to demonstrate than to describe. To show how ConMan works, we'll discuss a composite application that lets the user interactively design swept surfaces. This example will use six simple components:

- *view-ed with sliders*. This component controls the view of a surface with a set of sliders.

- *view-ed with hemispherical control*. This component allows the user to control the view of a surface with hemispherical control.

- *curv-ed*. A simple curve editor lets the user interactively enter or modify two dimensional shapes.

- *sweep*. The sweep component takes a shape, for example a curve from curv-ed, and sweeps it through space to create a surface.

† Jell-O® is a trademark of General Foods.

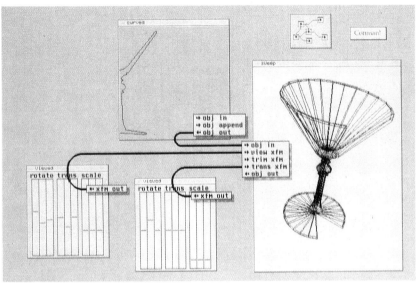

Figure 2. A simple ConMan application.

- *tape*. The tape recorder has one input port and one output port. By interacting with a menu we can erase the recording, start recording, or play back what has been recorded. While the recorder is in record mode, new objects are saved in a linked list as they arrive.

- *render*. The rendering component supports different rendering qualities from wire-frame to ray tracing. As input, it takes a description of a geometric object and a set of viewing transformations.

Now we will show how to combine these tools to interactively design swept surfaces. First, the user starts the components and connects them together as shown in Figure 2. The curve editor is connected to a sweep component. Two view editors are connected to the sweep component. One of these controls the view of the surface. The other provides a transformation that is iterated to create a swept surface. We can make a wide variety of surfaces in this way. For instance, a surface of extrusion is created by setting this to just translate in z, while a surface of rotation is made by setting the sliders to rotate in x or y.

There are two types of data that are being communicated between components in this application: short lists of transformations from the view editors, and descriptions of geometry from the curve editor and the sweep component. A typical output from one of the view editors is shown in Figure 3, while Figure 4 shows the output of the curve editor.

The user constructs this composite application by interacting with the connection manager. To do this, the components were created by making selections on a menu.

Next, the components were interconnected by displaying the terminals on each component, and drawing wires between them. This complete network was built in less than a minute.

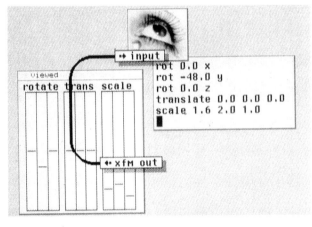

Figure 3. Output from a view editor.

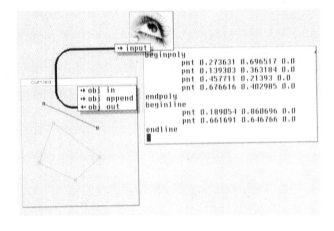

Figure 4. Output from a curve editor.

Interacting with the Application

Every component provides a separate context for interaction: an interaction frame. The interaction frame of each component supports a visual representation and lets the user interact with this representation using the mouse. The window system allows the user to direct input events to a particular interaction frame.

The composite application consists of a population of interactive components. Each component reacts to messages that are received from the user or from other components. This reaction normally involves updating the visual representation and possibly sending a message out one of its output ports. Since components are dependent on each other, changes made while interacting with one component can propagate to other components.

In this example, interactive changes to the shape in two dimensions can propagate to the sweep component. This lets the user edit the shape in two dimensions and see the result in three dimensions. Interacting with the top view editor causes the sweep component to display the surface from different view points. In the same way, interaction with the lower view editor modifies the incremental transformation that is applied by the sweep component as it generates the surface.

Extending the Application

This composite application (sandwich) can easily be modified or extended. Suppose we want to create an animated set of views of the swept surface. This can be done by adding a component that acts as a tape recorder, as shown in Figure 5.

The tape recorder has one input port and one output port. By interacting with a menu we can erase the recording, start recording, or play back what has been recorded.

While the recorder is in record mode, new objects are saved in a linked list as they arrive. Notice that the view editor output is connected to the recorder *and* the sweep component. Any output port can deliver data to any number of input ports. This lets us monitor the effect of the view editor as we record its output. After a series of objects has been recorded, the recording can be played back once or continuously in a loop. While the recorder is playing and the view of the surface is changing, we can interact with the shape of the surface or the sweep transformation and see the result in real time.

The recorder is a general purpose component that can be used to save and replay a sequence of objects whether they are viewing transformations or geometrical shapes. So we could also use a recorder to play a sequence of different shapes created by the curve editor.

If we decide we don't like using sliders to control our view of the swept surface, we can use different kind of view controller. Figure 6 shows how a hemispherical viewer can be added to the application. Notice that the output of *both* view editors are connected to the view input of the sweep component. The view of the swept surface will follow the sliders or the hemispherical view editor, depending on which component we interact with.

This demonstrates how different user interfaces may be bound to an application. It's equally easy to support multiple simultaneous user interfaces.

As a final example, let's create a shaded rendering of the swept surface. To do this, a general purpose rendering component is used with its own view editor. Figure 7 shows how the renderer has been connected.

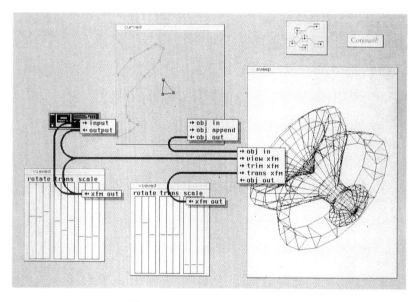

Figure 5. Adding a tape recorder.

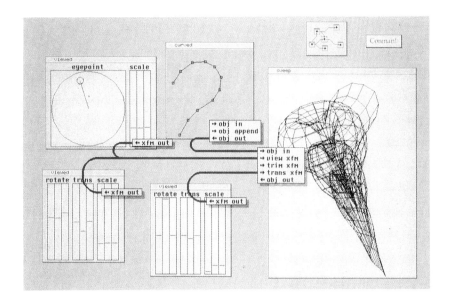

Figure 6. Using a Hemispherical view editor.

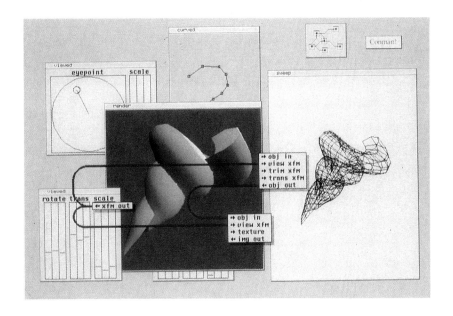

Figure 7. Connecting in a renderer.

Other Useful Data-Flow Components

Many other components have been developed for this data-flow environment. A watch component lets the user inspect data that is flowing across the screen, and a simple interface to the file system has also been developed. A mixer has two input ports and one output port. This component can be used to interpolate between two views, two shapes or two rgb colors. The mixer can also be used to concatenate the two inputs or randomly interpolate between individual components of the inputs.

A component called *tolines* converts an image into outline geometry. Figure 8 shows this component being used with sweep and render to make an extruded logo. A low-pass filter component can be placed between a view editor and another component to filter view transformations over time (See Figure 9). With this component in place, a sudden step translation will result in the geometric model moving along an exponential curve towards the new position in time. This kind of pseudo-dynamics gives the model a feeling of mass. The low-pass filter component is also competely generic - it can be applied to changing geometry as well.

A graftal plant [Smith 84] component accepts a gene description on one of its input ports, a leaf shape and view transform on other input ports. Figure 10 shows this composite application.

As a final illustration, figure 11 shows a paint component that gets the current drawing color from a simple color editor, and the brush shape from a curve editor. The curve editor output is connected to a component that transforms a geometric shape. This gives the user control over the scale and rotation of the brush.

Implementation

ConMan runs on the Silicon Graphics IRIS Workstation under the Mex window manager [Rhodes 85]. Each component process is programmed in the C programming language using the IRIS graphics library [Silicon 84] for graphic display. A detailed description of how this system is implemented can be found in [Haeberli 86].

The connection manager ConMan is a user process running under the window manager. Client components need to describe text labels for input and output ports. The user needs to be able to alter the interconnection of components.

When a client component starts up, it sends messages to ConMan indicating the input and output ports it uses, with a text string to label each port. The user can interact with the connection manager to add or delete connections between different ports on different components. The structure of the interconnection is maintained by the connection manager.

The graphics system supports an input queue to deliver events to each component. User, system and interprocess communication (IPC) events appear in this input queue. User events indicate changes in the mouse

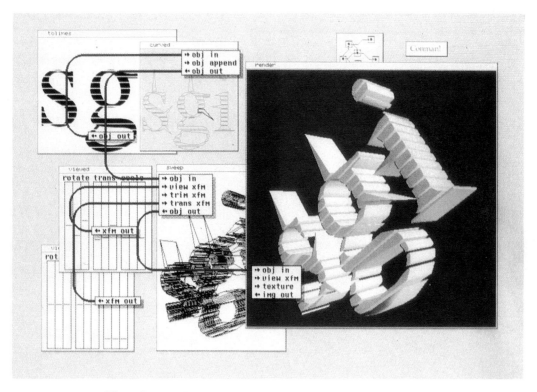

Figure 8. Extracting geometry from an image to make an extruded logo.

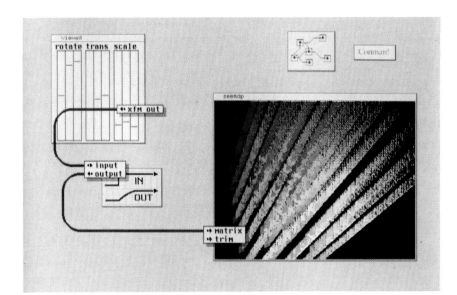

Figure 9. Using a low-pass filter for pseudo-dynamics.

Figure 10. An application for graftal plant design.

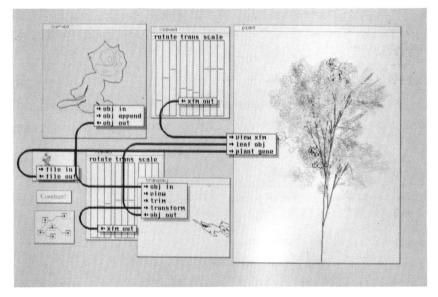

Figure 11. A paint application.

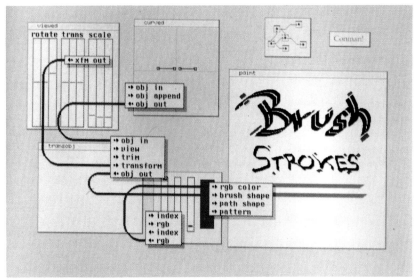

buttons, or position. System events notify a component that it should redraw because its window has received additional exposure. IPC events indicate that a message is available from another component.

Communication between components is accomplished by typed, variable sized, synchronous messages. To send a message, data is written into a file that is associated with the output port. Then the component notifies the system that there is new data available from this particular output port. This blocks the sender and places notification tokens in the input queues of all the components that are dependent on this output port. When a component receives an IPC event, it reads the message from the appropriate file, and explicitly replies.

In the current implementation, all data is transferred using a textual interchange format. System performance could be improved by using binary messages. The IPC mechanism described briefly above, using files and special system calls has recently been reimplemented to use standard UNIX sockets.

Conclusions

By providing graphical support for communicating sequential processes we create a primitive visual language that lets users interactively construct and modify applications on the fly. The connection manager lets the user create dynamic visual expressions out of interactive components.

Currently, the only data types (nouns) being transmitted between components are transformations, geometric shapes, RGB colors and bitmap images. We plan to extend the vocabulary by adding data types to describe text, fonts, and streams of input events. We also expect the vocabulary of data-flow components (verbs) to grow to support key frame animation, solid deformations and image processing.

ConMan has many implications for application developers and users of interactive workstations. Applications are really programmed at two distinct levels. A developer uses a conventional programming language at the component level. Both the user and the developer use a visual language at the level of the application.

Developers are encouraged to break monolithic applications into functional components that communicate with each other using high level data structures. Careful design of components makes them usable in many different contexts, and communication between applications is easy. ConMan promotes software modularity and healthy competition between components. For example, if a better view editor becomes available, it can easily be used by everyone. In this system, sharing of functionality happens at the component level.

Instead of supporting a single interaction frame with a single process, we use multiple processes in a windowed environment to provide multiple interaction frames, each with their own user interface state. An application is an orchestrated collection of interaction frames.

Components and the data passed between them form a vocabulary that is used to express the behavior of an application. This allows the user to explore the design space instead of being limited by the vision of the system implementors. The functionality of applications is open-ended.

Control over the application is returned to the user. Components of the user interface can be easily exchanged with each other. In this system, multiple simultaneous interaction techniques may be dynamically bound to an application. The functional binding of an application is completely dynamic.

That applications must be monolithic and self-contained is an illusion. We use the interactive medium itself to let the user design and extend applications.

Acknowledgement

I would like to thank Rob Myers for his continued enthusiasm for this project. Eric Brechner now at RPI implemented a version of ConMan that uses UNIX sockets for interprocess communication. Thanks to John Danskin at Digital Equipment Corporation in Palo Alto for allowing me to use their digital film recorder for the illustrations. Special thanks also to Dan Sears and Amy Smith for help with the manuscript.

References

[Blythe 86] David Blythe, John Kitamura, David Galloway and Martin Snelgrove, "Virtual Patch-Cords for the Katosizer", Computer Systems Research Institute, University of Toronto, Toronto, Ontario, Canada, 1986.

[Cardelli 85] Luca Cardelli, "Fragments of Behavior", Personal Communication. DEC Systems Research Center, Palo Alto, CA, 1985.

[Cardelli 85] Luca Cardelli, and Pike, R., "Squeak: a language for communicating with mice", Computer Graphics, 1985.

[Galloway 87] David Galloway, David Blythe and Martin Snelgrove, "Graphical CAD of Digital Filters", Proceedings of IEEE Conference on Computers, Communications, and Signal Processing, June 1987.

[Haeberli 86] Paul Haeberli, "A Data-Flow Manager for an Interactive Programming Environment", Proceedings of Usenix Summer Conference, 1986.

[Heckbert 87] Paul S. Heckbert, "Ray Tracing Jell-O® Brand Gelatin", Computer Graphics, 1987. [Hoare 78] C.A.R. Hoare, "Communicating Sequential Processes", Communications of the ACM 21(8), August 1978.

[Kimura 86a] Takayuki Dan Kimura, "Determinancy of Hierarchical Dataflow Model", Technical Report WUSC-86-5, Department of Computer Science, Washington University, March 1986.

[Kimura 86b] Takayuki Dan Kimura, Julie W. Choi, and Jane M. Mack, "A Visual Programming Language for Keyboardless Programming", Technical Report WUSC-86-6, Department of Computer Science, Washington University, June 1986.

[Myers 86] Brad A. Myers, "What are Visual Programming, Programming by Example, and Program Visualization?", Proceedings of Graphics Interface 1986.

[Rhodes 85] Rocky Rhodes, Paul Haeberli, and Kipp Hickman, "Mex - A Window Manager for the IRIS", Proceedings of Usenix Winter Conference, 1985.

[Schulert 85] Andrew J. Schulert, George T. Rogers and James A. Hamilton, "ADM - A Dialog Manager", Proceedings of SIGCHI 1985.

[Silicon 84] Silicon Graphics Inc., IRIS User's Guide, 1984.

[Smith 84] Alvy Ray Smith, "Plants, Graftals, and Formal Languages", Computer Graphics, 1984.

[Smith 86] Randal. B. Smith, "The Alternate Reality Kit: An Environment for Creating Interactive Simulations." Proceedings of the IEEE Computer Society Workshop on Visual Languages, 1986.

[Tanner 86] Peter B. Tanner, Stephen A. MacKay, Darlene A. Stewart, and Marceli Wein, "A Multitasking Switchboard Approach to User Interface Management", Computer Graphics, 1986.

Graphical Search and Replace

David Kurlander
Computer Science Department
Columbia University
New York, NY 10027

Eric A. Bier
Xerox PARC
3333 Coyote Hill Rd.
Palo Alto, CA 94304

Abstract

Graphical search is a technique for finding all instances of a graphical pattern in a synthetic picture in which objects are regions bounded by lines and curves. The pattern may describe shape, color and other properties. Matched objects may be allowed to differ from the pattern in rotation and scale or may differ in shape by a specified tolerance. *Graphical replace* is a technique for replacing the shape, color, or other properties of matched objects with new properties described in a replacement pattern. Combined, the two techniques are similar to textual search and replace in text editors. Graphical search and replace can be used to make global changes to illustrations with repetitive patterns, independent of the means used to make those patterns. It can also be used to create a class of iterative or recursive shapes that can be specified by replacement rules.

CR Categories: I.3.6 [Computer Graphics]: Methodology and Techniques – interaction techniques; I.5.4 [Pattern Recognition]: Applications – graphical editing

Additional Keywords and Phrases: Search and replace, graphical editing, curve matching, graphical grammars, graphical macros

1. Introduction

Most graphic arts quality illustrations contain some degree of coherence. For example, the same font, color or stroke width is used throughout a set of shapes, or a particular shape is used repeatedly at different translations, rotations, or sizes. Changing one of the coherent properties of an illustration (e.g., changing all red circles into orange ellipses), requires making the change throughout the illustration. Pictures can be structured to make such changes easy. For example, some editors allow objects to be grouped into a cluster that can be selected as a unit, making it easy to change properties of the clustered objects all at once. Other editors allow the user to declare that an object is an instance of a library object; changes to the library object are reflected in all of its instances at once. However, both of these techniques require the user to decide at an early stage what properties will need to be edited coherently, and to structure the illustration accordingly. We propose an alternative technique,

graphical search and replace, that allows graphical scenes to be edited coherently without special structuring of the illustration.

Graphical search and replace works much like text substitution in a word processor. The user first describes a search pattern composed of a set of synthetic shapes (regions bounded by lines, conics, and splines), a set of style properties such as stroke width, stroke color, and fill color, and a set of search parameters including an error tolerance and an indication of whether or not a match may be a rotation of the pattern. Next, the user describes a replacement pattern made up of synthetic shapes and style properties. The graphics editor then searches in the illustration for an object that matches the pattern. If the user requests a replacement, the editor replaces the shape, changes its style properties, or both. This can be done one shape at a time, in a top to bottom, left to right order, or can be performed on all matching shapes at once.

Graphical search and replace has a number of applications. It can be used to make changes to many objects at once. If the replacement pattern is more elaborate than the search pattern, these multiple changes can turn a simple repetitive picture, used as a template, into an elaborate composition. Furthermore, if the replacement pattern contains parts that match the search pattern, graphical search and replace can be used repeatedly to build up a recursive shape. If an editing macro is performed on each set of matched objects instead of a replacement, graphical search leads to an even more general way to modify illustrations. Finally, if performed on multiple files, graphical search can be used to find those picture files containing specified graphical features.

Graphical search and replace is related to a wide variety of other topics. It can be viewed as an interface to a graphical database, where typical transactions include queries for objects with a particular set of graphical properties and modifications of these properties. The representation of graphical information in databases has been studied [7, 15]. Graphical search and replace can also be viewed as a method for specifying graphical grammars that generate recursive shapes. Shape grammars, a subset of graphical grammars, have been analyzed extensively [5, 12], and grammars have been used in graphics to make realistic imagery [11]. Pattern recognition algorithms have been used to search for occurrences of a particular shape [6, 8]. Some of these algorithms are appropriate for use in graphical search and replace. Instancing was used in the earliest of drawing systems, Sketchpad [13], and continues to be used in many current systems. Graphical search and replace is proposed as an alternative to instancing for producing coherent changes in graphical documents.

Graphical search and replace has been implemented in the MatchTool, a companion to the Gargoyle two-dimensional illustrator [1, 10] running in the Cedar programming environment [14] on the Xerox Dorado high-performance personal workstation [9]. The MatchTool is similar in user interface to the EditTool, a textual search and replace tool that works with Tioga, the Cedar text editor, to edit multi-font tree-structured documents. All figures in this paper were created with the MatchTool and Gargoyle.

In section 2, we describe the MatchTool from the user's point of view, showing graphical search and replace in action. In section 3, we describe the implementation of the MatchTool, including the control structures needed to search the scene in top to bottom, left to right order and the algorithm that determines whether or not two objects match. In section 4, we discuss some of the applications of graphical search and replace. In section 5, we present our conclusions and future research directions.

2. User Interface

2.1 Search and Replace for Shapes

In this section, we describe how graphical search and replace can be used to make changes to an illustration. We need two windows on our workstation display. In the Gargoyle editing window is the illustration that we are editing. In the MatchTool window, we specify search and replace requests. At the top of the MatchTool are two panes (sub-windows), each of which is a small Gargoyle editing window. In the first of these, the Search Pane, we construct the pattern that we wish to search for in our illustration. In the second of these, the Replace Pane, we construct the replacement pattern.

Figure 1 shows an illustration of a map that is being edited in a Gargoyle window. This is a synthetic picture; the highway sign borders are represented as arcs, line segments and parametric curves, and the roadways are parametric curves. The text is represented as an ASCII string, a font name and an affine transformation. Recently, sections of Highway 17 have been renamed Interstate 880. We can use the MatchTool to make the substitutions.

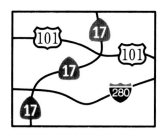

Figure 1. An illustration of the freeways near San Jose, California.

Figure 2 shows the two panes of the MatchTool. In the Search Pane, we put a Highway 17 sign, copying it from the illustration. In the Replace Pane, we put an Interstate 880 sign, drawing it in place or copying it from a different illustration. We make sure that the centers of both signs are at the same coordinates, so that no offset will be introduced when replacements are performed. The centers can be aligned, for instance, by positioning both signs in the Search Pane, and then moving the Interstate 880 sign into the Replace Pane with a "move" operation that preserves coordinates.

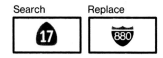

Figure 2. Search and replacement patterns in the MatchTool.

The MatchTool user interface has four buttons that initiate search actions: Search, Yes, No, and ChangeAll. If we press the Search button at this point, the MatchTool will search the illustration in top to bottom, left to right order, looking for Highway 17 signs. When it finds the topmost one, it selects it. If we then press the Yes button, the MatchTool will delete the Highway 17 sign, add an

Interstate 880 sign, and initiate another search. This search finds the second sign. Pressing Yes again, we replace the second Highway 17 sign and select the third. Since Highway 17 has only been renamed north of Interstate 280, we are done. If we press the No button at this point, the MatchTool will leave the third Highway 17 sign as it is and report that there are no further matches. The resulting picture is shown in Figure 3. Had we wished to replace all of the Highway 17 signs at once, we could have used the ChangeAll button.

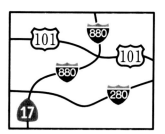

Figure 3. The San Jose freeways after the northern sections of Highway 17 have been relabeled.

In the example above, we searched for a collection of shapes of known size, shape and orientation. Less restrictive searches can be achieved by varying one or more of six search parameters – Granularity, Rotation Invariance, Scale Invariance, Polarity, Context Sensitivity, and Tolerance. The user interface for these features is shown in Figure 4. The first four search parameters will be discussed in this section, the last two in section 2.3.

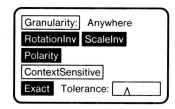

Figure 4. The six search parameters. Options that are white on black are active. All of the regions bordered with a black rectangle are mouse-sensitive.

Granularity may take on the values "cluster", "object", or "anywhere". It tells the MatchTool how much of the structure of the illustration may be ignored when performing matches. If Granularity is set to "cluster", then a group of objects that have been clustered in Gargoyle will only match a similar complete cluster in the MatchTool; the individual objects in the cluster cannot match separately. At the "object" granularity, a Gargoyle object A will match a similar object B in the pattern, even if A is part of a cluster. At this granularity, A must be matched in entirety; a pattern containing only a subset of A's parts will not match. At the "anywhere" granularity, parts of an object A may be matched by a pattern object B if all of B's parts match corresponding parts in A. At this granularity, an entire object in the MatchTool search pane can match a portion of a single object in the editor scene.

In an "anywhere" match, the lowest-level scene elements, segments, are treated as atomic; it is impossible to match on parts of them. This certainly has performance benefits, but also avoids other problems inherent in replacing portions of particular object classes. For example, it is impossible to replace portions of some segment types, such as non-local splines, without potentially causing changes to the entire segment.

When Rotation Invariance is turned on, the pattern matches a configuration of scene objects if some combination of translation and rotation will bring the pattern and configuration into correspondence. If more than one rotation is possible, the MatchTool will choose the smallest rotation that works. When Scale Invariance is turned on, the pattern matches a configuration of scene objects if some combination of translation and scaling will bring the pattern and configuration into correspondence. Likewise, when both Rotation Invariance and Scale Invariance are on, the MatchTool will try to use combinations of translation, rotation, and scaling to bring the pattern into correspondence with the scene objects.

When Polarity is on, two curves will only match if they were drawn in the same direction. For instance, if a rotation-invariant match is performed where the pattern is a straight line segment, the pattern will match any straight line segment that has the same length as the pattern. With Polarity off, each match can be made with two rotations, differing by 180 degrees. With Polarity on, the MatchTool will take into account the direction in which each line segment was drawn, and will choose the rotation that aligns those directions.

We can use these search parameters to construct a triadic Koch snowflake. We draw an equilateral triangle, constructing the line segments in clockwise order, giving us Figure 5. Next, we select one edge of the triangle and copy it into the Search Pane. In the Replace Pane, we draw four line segments each 1/3 the length of the original. These line segments are drawn in the same direction (lower left to upper right) as the original segment. We must also be careful that the replacement shape begins and ends at the same coordinates as the original segment, so that when scene objects are replaced, no offset will be introduced. The resulting Search and Replace Panes are shown in Figure 6.

Figure 5. An equilateral triangle. Grey arrows show the directions in which the edges were drawn.

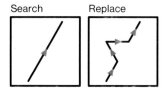

Figure 6. Preparing to replace a line segment with four line segments. Grey arrows show the directions in which the edges were drawn.

We set Granularity at "anywhere" so that the search can find individual segments of the original triangle. We turn on Rotation Invariance. We turn on Polarity. We press ChangeAll. All of the line segments in the original triangle are replaced by four-segment paths as shown in Figure 7(a). If we hit ChangeAll again, nothing happens, because the picture no longer contains any segments that are the same length as the pattern segment. If we turn on Scale Invariance and try ChangeAll again, all of the segments of Figure 7(a) are replaced by four-segment paths to produce Figure 7(b).

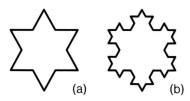

Figure 7. Triadic Koch snowflakes. (a) After one ChangeAll operation using the search and replacement patterns of Figure 6. (b) After a second ChangeAll, with Scale Invariance turned on.

2.2 Search and Replace for Graphical Style

Often, we will want to search for properties of graphical objects other than shape, such as object class — Box, Circle, or Polygon; curve type — line, Bézier, B-spline, natural spline, conic, or arc; area color; line properties — line color, stroke width, dash pattern, joint blending, or stroke end shape; or text properties — ASCII string, font family, or font transformation. Likewise, we may be interested in replacing properties of the matched objects other than shape. Figure 8 shows a portion of the MatchTool control panel called the Search Column and the Replace Column. The black squares in the Search Column indicate those properties of the objects in the Search Pane that must agree with the scene objects for a match to succeed; other properties can be ignored. The black squares in the Replace Column indicate those graphical properties of the objects in the Replace Pane that will be applied to the matched objects when a replacement is performed; other properties are left alone unless they are determined by the specified properties. The user can toggle each square between white and black by clicking on it with the mouse.

	Search	Replace
Shape	■	■
Object Class	■	■
Curve Type	■	■
Area Color	□	■
Line Color	□	□
Line Width	□	□
Line Dashes	□	□
Line Joints	□	□
Line Ends	□	□
Text String	□	■
Text Font	□	■
Text Font Transform	□	■

Figure 8. The Search Column and Replace Column.

When the search and replacement properties are specified appropriately, the MatchTool can be used to change the shape of an object while leaving its color unchanged. For example, to make a multi-colored snowflake, we might start with a triangle as before but give its three edges different colors, as shown in Figure 9(a). If we turn off Line Color in the Search Column, then all three edges will still match the pattern we used above. If we turn off Line Color in the Replace Column, then as each edge is replaced, its color is applied to the replacement shape. If we use the same Search Pane and Replace Pane as before, then after two ChangeAlls, we get the picture in Figure 9(b). The MatchTool can also change the color of an object while leaving its shape unchanged.

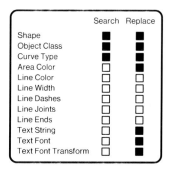

Figure 9. Replacing the shape of the edges of a triangle while leaving the colors as they were.

2.3 Advanced Search and Replace

In this section, we discuss the last two search parameters — context-sensitive search, and variable error tolerance.

Context-sensitive search allows the user to search for the occurrence of a set of shapes, A, in the presence of another set of shapes, B. Only the shapes that match A are selected and eligible to be replaced. To perform a context-sensitive search, the user places all of the pattern shapes, A and B, in the Search Pane and indicates which shapes are in set A by selecting them. The user then turns Context Sensitivity on and initiates a search.

Context-sensitive search, by reducing the set of shapes that are eligible to be replaced, can remove ambiguities present in certain pattern specifications. For instance, if the Shapes property in the Replace Column is on but the Line Color property is off, the MatchTool must replace the matched shapes with the replacement shapes, copying the line color of the matched shapes to the replacement shapes. A problem occurs if the search pattern matches a set of shapes that have several different line colors; we don't know which objects in the replacement pattern should receive which line colors from the match. To solve this problem, we can break up the search into several context-sensitive searches, each of which will only select objects of a single line color.

Figures 10 and 11 give an example of this use of context-sensitive search. The user starts with a picture of a gumball machine containing softballs and replaces the softballs by footballs. Each football will take its orientation from the stitching direction of the softball it replaces and will take its area color and the line color of its stitching from this softball as well. Because the line color of the stitching and the line color of the outer circle are different in a single softball, we cannot perform this replacement all at once. Instead, we perform one context-sensitive search and one regular search, both shown in Figure 10, to get the desired result, shown in Figure 11. The first search replaces circles (in the presence of stitching) by footballs with the proper orientation, area color and line color. The second search replaces the stitching by football stitching with the proper line color.

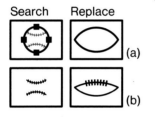

Search   Replace

(a)

(b)

Figure 10. (a) Search for a circle in the context of stitches and replace with a football outline. The black boxes on the circle indicate that it is selected. (b) Search for softball stitches and replace by football stitches.

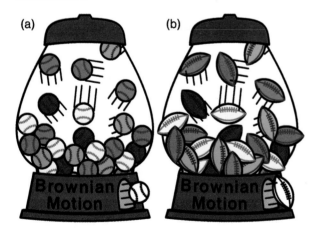

(a)   (b)

Figure 11. (a) A gumball machine filled with softballs, used as a T-shirt design for a softball team. (created by Polle Zellweger and Jock Mackinlay) (b) The softballs are replaced by footballs.

Variable error tolerance allows the user to find shapes that match the search pattern approximately, but not exactly. By adjust-

ing a slider, the user can increase or decrease the amount of error that the matching algorithms will permit when identifying matches. For example, an appropriate tolerance and search pattern would enable matches of all shapes that approximate circles or all shapes that approximate straight lines. To successfully use this feature, the user must understand some of the details of the shape matching mechanism and must determine an appropriate tolerance by trial and error. One use of inexact matches is described in section 4.4 on graphical grep.

3. Implementation

3.1 Control Structures

Since the data in text documents is ordered in a linear fashion, and graphical data tends to be distributed over at least two dimensions, the control structures for a graphical search and replace program must be more elaborate than those of its textual analog. In textual search and replace, very little state information needs to be kept. A current location specifies the point from which the search will proceed, and when a replacement is made, there is no ambiguity over where the replacement text will be placed. In addition, there is a clear choice for the order in which items will be searched provided by the linear order of the character stream. The mechanism for graphical search and replace is more complex.

We search graphical objects in a top to bottom, left to right order. This search order is familiar to users of textual search and reduces screen updates because matches located close to one another in the scene tend to be found together. Reverse searches proceed in exactly the opposite order from forward searches. The Gargoyle software cursor, the *caret*, represents the current location of the search. In a forward search, only objects below the caret are considered, and in a backward search, only objects above the caret are considered. The user can move the caret in the Gargoyle scene in order to direct the search.

Before searching begins, a snapshot is taken of all scene objects that may participate in the search. This prevents the search from finding objects that are added to the scene by a replace operation in progress. As a result, replacement operations are predictable and will always terminate. The snapshot is a singly-linked list, called the *search list*. Each list element is either a cluster of scene objects, if Granularity is set to "cluster", or an individual object, if Granularity is set to "object" or "anywhere". The list is ordered by the upper left corner of the bounding box (a tight-fitting rectangle aligned with the coordinate axes) of each element. For a forward search, the elements are in top to bottom, left to right order. For a backward search, the order is reversed. Updated snapshots of the scene are taken whenever an entirely new search is initiated. A search is considered "entirely new" if, since the last search operation, the caret has been manually repositioned, the scene has been edited, a new Gargoyle window is being searched, the pattern has been modified, or the search direction has changed.

The current search pattern is represented by a list of lists, called the *pattern list*. Each element of the pattern list is a list of property-value pairs representing the relevant properties of one of the graphical objects in the Search Pane. The possible properties appear in Figure 8. All of the property-value lists will include the same set of properties, namely the set that is active in the Search Column. The pattern list is recomputed at the beginning of a search if the Search Pane or Search Column have been modified since the last search.

Searching involves trying to find a correspondence between elements of the pattern list and elements of the search list. To begin, we choose one element of the pattern list, called the *leading object*, and compare it against the members of the search list in order, starting with the member nearest the current search position. The algorithm that we use to compare two curves for shape equality will be discussed in section 3.2. Once we have found a match for the leading object, we attempt to find matches for all of the other elements in the pattern list. If we succeed, we are done. Otherwise, we try to match the leading object differently. If Rotation Invariance is on, we try matching the leading object against the same object in the search list at a different orientation. When all possible orientations are exhausted, we move on to the next object on the search list.

If we are matching on shape, we use two techniques to improve performance. First, when we have found a match for the leading object, we know where in the scene to look for the remaining shapes in the pattern list. We use bounding boxes to quickly rule out many of the objects on the search list. For instance, we compute where one point of a given pattern object would have to match in the scene and rule out all objects on the search list whose bounding boxes do not contain that point. If the search is not exact, we enlarge the bounding boxes by an amount proportional to the tolerance before testing the point for inclusion. Furthermore, the search list is ordered by the upper left hand corner of the bounding boxes, so we can quickly rule out entire sections of the search list. Second, we choose a good leading object. If possible, we choose an open curve to be the leading object because open curves can match other curves at no more than two different orientations. If all of the pattern objects are closed curves, we choose the curve with the least number of potential matching orientations (see section 3.2).

When Granularity is set to "anywhere", the search mechanism is more elaborate. Objects in the pattern list are matched against both entire objects and portions of objects in the search list. When a match is found, information is saved indicating precisely where the search terminated, so the next search can continue with another part of the same search list object if any unexamined parts remain. Note that it is possible to invoke a search on an object, part of which has already been changed by a prior search and replace.

Let there be m objects in the editor scene and n objects in the search pattern. The worst case complexity of the search algorithm to find all matches of the pattern in the scene is $O(m^2n)$ object to object comparisons, assuming that the search is being made at either the "cluster" or "object" granularity, and the leading object matches no scene object at more than a constant number of orientations. If the granularity of the search is set to "anywhere", then we are effectively matching against a greater number of scene objects, since each object and its eligible subsets (continuous runs of segments) must be considered in the match process. In this case, we redefine m to be the sum over all objects in the scene of the number of eligible subsets in each object, and the complexity expression remains valid.

The expected number of object to object comparisons required to find all matches of a pattern in the scene is no worse than $O(m^2)$. It is rare for the first few elements of the pattern list to match objects in the scene without a complete match occurring. When a complete match does occur, the scene objects participating in the match are removed from further consideration, so no more than m/n matches can be found. Together, these observations lead to the tighter bound. In addition, the use of bounding boxes to narrow down the matching process for shape searches does much to speed up the search. In practice, we have found the speed of this algorithm to be acceptable for our applications.

After a match is found, the search list is updated to disallow future matches on the same objects. The objects in the Gargoyle window that were found by the search are selected, and all other objects are deselected. Selection performs a dual function. First, the selection feedback indicates to the user which set of objects has been matched. Second, it prepares the matched objects to be modified by any of the Gargoyle operations that act on selected objects, including deletion, color changes, and transformations. The caret is relocated to the position of the match. If a Yes or ChangeAll is in progress, a replacement or macro operation will be performed at this point. Macro operations are described in section 4.3.

If a replacement is to be performed, we examine the Replace Column. If we are replacing only non-shape properties, the values of these properties are extracted from the shapes in the Replace Pane and applied to the matched objects. If we are replacing shape, the matched objects are deleted and the objects in the Replace Pane are copied into the scene. The new scene objects inherit from the matched shapes the properties not specified in the Replace Column. The new scene objects are positioned in the scene as follows: If we are matching on shape, we have found a transformation that maps the pattern objects onto the matching scene objects; we apply this same transformation to the Replace Pane shapes. Otherwise, we position the replacement so that the center of its bounding box coincides with the bounding box center of the match.

3.2 Curve Matching

At the core of our searching algorithm is a set of routines for comparing two curves for equality. We wish to be able discover that two curves are the same even if the two curves are at different sizes and orientations and even if the curves have different representations. For example, one curve might be a B-spline and the other a collection of Bézier cubic pieces, or one curve might be made of two small arcs and the other a single large arc. Our method is simple and general at the expense of performance. We discuss a technique for improving performance in section 5.2.

To compare two curves, we begin by approximating each curve by a piecewise linear path—a *polyline*. We construct polyline approximations adaptively, so that areas of high curvature are represented by more line segments than flatter areas. To keep polylines from having too many segments, we enforce a minimum length on the polyline segments. Many graphics systems already perform this vectorization, a common step in rendering curves. As shown in Figure 12, the polylines for copies of a curve at different scales may not be scales of one another. The test for equality must tolerate this error (see below).

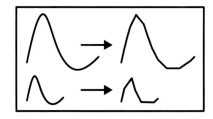

Figure 12. A curve and a scaled down copy of the curve, approximated as polylines. The roughness of the polylines is exaggerated for clarity.

Polylines are transformed to a canonical form so that they can be quickly compared. The nature of the canonical form depends upon whether the match is to be rotation-invariant, scale-invariant, neither, or both, as shown in Figure 13. One point of the polyline is chosen as the *starting point*. For open curves, the first endpoint is used. For closed curves, we use the point of greatest distance from the center of mass of a wire of uniform density lying along the curve (Figure 13(a)). A closed curve may have several points farthest from the center of mass; in this case the curve will have several canonical positions. The polyline is transformed so that its starting point lies at the origin (Figure 13(b)). If a rotation-invariant match is chosen, the polyline is rotated so that the center of mass lies along the positive x axis (Figure 13(c)). If a scale-invariant match is desired, then the polyline of the curve is normalized to have a particular arc length (Figure 13(d)).

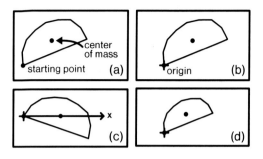

Figure 13. Polyline canonical forms. (a) The original polyline. (b) For all matches, the starting point is translated to the origin. (c) For rotation-invariant matches, the center of mass is rotated onto the positive *x* axis. (d) For scale-invariant matches, the curve is scaled to have a known total arc length.

A set of quick-reject tests can now be applied to the polylines to avoid further computation on pairs of curves that obviously do not match. Several quantities, including arc length, the maximum distance from a curve to its center of mass, and the position of the center of mass relative to the starting point, can now be compared. If these values for two polylines differ by more than a minimal quantity (accounting for floating point error or differences in quantization), then we conclude, without further computation, that the curves do not match.

If these quantities are similar enough, then it is still possible for the two polylines to represent equivalent shapes and a more comprehensive comparison is made. For each vertex of both polylines, we examine the Manhattan (1-norm) distance to the point of parametrically equivalent distance along the other polyline, found by interpolating between vertices if necessary. If this distance ever exceeds a certain threshold the match fails. This threshold, and the quantities used in the quick-reject tests can be adjusted to reflect a user-specified match tolerance.

We use a 1-norm metric because it can be computed quickly, and always produces correct responses with respect to exact shape matches. Other metrics may provide better measures of inexact shape matches, as evaluated by the human eye; however, inexact shape matches are selected relatively infrequently. It may be desirable to have several shape metrics: one for exact matches, and one or more for inexact matches. In the conclusion we mention an inexact shape metric that we are currently investigating. It is important to note that the 1-norm metric together with the quick-reject tests form our shape-matching criteria. In the case of inexact matches, it is possible for curves that would have passed the 1-norm test for equality to fail at least one of the initial tests, and thus be considered unequal.

When comparing two closed curves with the 1-norm metric, we must examine every canonical orientation of one of the curves with a single canonical orientation of the other before declaring a mismatch, unless the arc length or maximum distance to center of mass tests indicate this is not necessary. Although this algorithm for comparing curves is linear with respect to the number, n, of samples in the polylines for all open and some closed curves, there are certain closed shapes that will slow it down to $O(n^2)$. Other representations such as sampling the distance of a curve from its centroid [4] or sampling the curve's curvature [16] can be used to improve this bound.

4. Applications

In addition to coherent changes in illustrations with repeated components, graphical search and replace can be used to make recursive and iterative shapes, to create pictures that have a standard form by modifying graphical templates, to apply graphical editing macros, and to search for picture files based on graphical content. We discuss these applications in this section.

4.1 Graphical Grammars

Graphical search and replace can interactively generate complex shapes described by *graphical grammars*, an extension of shape grammars that allows graphical properties other than shape, such as color and line width, to participate in production rules. The Search Pane and Column specify the left side of a production rule, and the Replace Pane and Column specify the right side. Each replacement operation amounts to a single expansion of the production.

For example, Figure 14 shows the Search and Replace panes for a replacement rule that builds a spiral. We activate area color (in addition to shape and object class) in the Search Column and in the Replace Column. We turn on Rotation Invariance and Scale Invariance. If the initial scene is the same as the picture in the Search Pane, then by clicking the ChangeAll button 27 times, we produce the picture in Figure 15. The innermost copy of the word "MATCHTOOL" is grey.

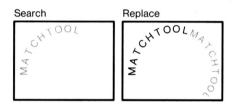

Figure 14. The Search and Replace patterns for a graphical grammar that makes a word spiral.

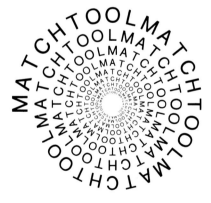

Figure 15. A spiral made of the word "MATCHTOOL" repeated 28 times.

As another example, Figure 16(a) describes a rule that replaces a grey line segment by a brown line segment of the same size, with two grey branches attached. Line Color and Shape are selected in both the Search Column and in the Replace Column. Rotation Invariance and Scale Invariance are turned on. Beginning with a single vertical grey line, we apply the rule five times to produce a leafless brown tree with grey outermost branches. Figure 16(b) describes a second rule that replaces all grey branches by brown branches attached to green leaves. Applying this rule produces the simple graftal tree shown in Figure 16(c). For grammars with more than one rule, it is useful to have multiple pairs of Search and Replace Panes.

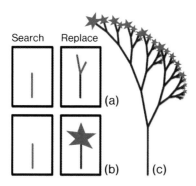

Figure 16. Drawing a binary tree. (a) Replace a grey line with a brown line and two grey lines. Apply this rule five times. (b) Replace a grey line with a brown line and a leaf. (c) The resulting tree.

Figure 17 shows a third example. A triangle is replaced with three triangles, each having half the linear dimensions of the original (Figure 17(a)). If we begin with a single triangle and apply the replacement four times, we get Figure 17(b).

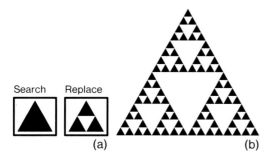

Figure 17. Nested triangles. (a) Replace one large triangle with three smaller triangles. Apply this rule four times. (b) The result.

4.2 Graphical Templates

Graphical search and replace can be used to produce scenes containing complex shapes from scenes containing simple shapes. For example, Figure 18(a) shows three test-tubes containing line segments of different sizes and orientations. The MatchTool is used to replace each segment with an amoeba, using the rule in Figure 18(b). After the large amoeba is colored orange, Figure 19 results. Because drawing line segments is easier than scaling and rotating shapes into place, this picture can be made very rapidly. In this example, Figure 18(a) serves as a graphical template. Many other illustrations could be made from this template by varying the shape in the Replace Pane. Regular polygons make good templates for patterns with cyclic symmetry. Other templates can be made for frieze symmetries and crystallographic symmetries.

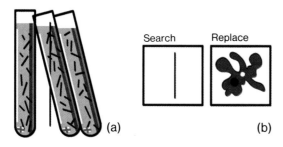

Figure 18. (a) A set of line segments is drawn on a picture of test-tubes. (b) Each line segment is replaced by an amoeba.

Figure 19. "The Day of the Amoebas."

4.3 Mouse-click Macros

As mentioned above, when a graphical search succeeds in finding a match, the matched objects are selected in preparation for either replacing them or for manually editing them using Gargoyle. The MatchTool provides an alternative to manual editing called *mouse-click macros*. Before invoking a search operation, the user employs the MatchTool to record a macro by performing a set of Gargoyle operations in the Replace Pane. All of the mouse coordinates and button presses are recorded. The user then tells the MatchTool to perform the macro instead of doing replacements and invokes one of the replacement operations (e.g., ChangeAll).

After each match is found, the MatchTool plays back the recorded actions, transforming the mouse coordinates by the same transformation that would have been applied to replacement objects if a replacement were being performed. To prevent unexpected results, the macro commands are restricted to operate only on matched objects.

Mouse-click macros can be used to perform coherent changes that would be difficult with simple replacement. For instance, we can give a set of objects drop shadows by recording a macro that copies an object, colors the copy grey, offsets the copy from the original, and moves the copy underneath.

4.4 Graphical Grep

Grep is a utility in the UNIX[TM] environment for locating files that contain a particular text pattern. An analogous function for graphical scene files can be implemented on top of graphical search. The user specifies a pattern in the Search Pane and Column and a list of one or more file names, optionally containing wildcards. Graphical grep searches the named files for the specified graphical pattern. The user can choose to list the names of files that contain the graphical pattern or to invoke the editor on the first match, edit the file, and resume the search. The ability to specify a shape tolerance is useful in conjunction with graphical grep. If an exact copy of the graphical pattern cannot be copied from a document, the user can draw an approximate pattern shape by hand.

5. Conclusion

5.1 Summary

We have described a technique for making coherent changes to a graphical scene. The technique requires that the user specify, via a graphical pattern, those objects that are to change, and, via a second graphical pattern, what change is to take place. The two patterns are very similar. Both consist of a pane containing graphical shapes and of a column of buttons describing the properties of interest in the pane. In addition, there are six parameters that are used only for the search operation. This user interface is relatively easy to understand and provides a great deal of power. Furthermore, graphical search and replace can be added to an existing graphical editor with little modification to the editor or its data structures.

Graphical search and replace can accomplish any coherent change that can be accomplished using instancing, and it can be applied more widely. Because it requires no special structuring of the illustration, our technique can be used in editors that do not support instancing and in situations where only a "flat" description of a picture is available. Furthermore, it can be used to modify a collection of objects with identical shapes but different style properties, while instancing schemes tend to require that the instances of a library object be identical in all respects expect for an affine transformation. Graphical search and replace can consider replacements on a case by case basis, allowing changes to some objects but not others.

In addition to making coherent changes, graphical search and replace can be used to make recursive shapes and to copy shapes to positions specified in a graphical template. It extends shape grammars by allowing style properties to appear on each side of the production as well as shapes.

Finally, graphical search can be combined with operations other than replacement. More general coherent modifications can be achieved by playing back a macro on each match. Searching in multiple files provides graphical grep, a means for retrieving graphical documents by content instead of name.

5.2 Future Work

Graphical search could be improved by allowing for more general patterns. We would like to be able to search for all angles of a certain value, or junctions with a certain number of lines radiating from them. We would also like to be able to capture positional relationships such as finding all circles above squares. Such relational metrics have appeared in the literature [3]. We would also like a better way to search for objects that "look like" the search pattern. We may be able to apply string matching techniques [2] to this problem.

Exact pattern matches on curves of known type are an important special case for graphical search. By comparing the curve control points directly instead of comparing polyline representations, we could significantly speed up the majority of searches.

It appears that graphical search and replace can be used as a user interface paradigm for systems that use instancing internally. In fact, for scenes that have an instancing hierarchy it should be possible to speed up graphical search by using pointer comparisons, where possible, in place of geometric comparisons. Likewise, graphical replace can take advantage of instancing by replacing matched objects with library object instances, where possible, instead of allocating new data structures.

Finally, graphical search could serve as the basis for a tool that compares two graphical scene files and reports their differences. Such a tool would be useful for regression testing of graphical editors and for understanding how one picture was changed to make another.

Acknowledgments

We are grateful to Xerox PARC for providing the environment that made this research possible. We would like to thank Ken Pier, Maureen Stone, Subhana Menis, and Jock Mackinlay for comments that lead to an improved paper. We give special thanks to Maureen Stone and Ken Pier for their encouragement during the project.

References

1. Bier, Eric A., and Stone, Maureen C. Snap-Dragging. Proceedings of SIGGRAPH '86 (Dallas, Texas, August 18-22, 1986). In *Computer Graphics 20*, 4 (August 1986), 233-240.

2. Burr, D. J. A Technique for Comparing Curves. In *IEEE Conference on Pattern Recognition and Image Processing* (Chicago, Illinois, August 6-8, 1979), 271-277.

3. Chang, Shi-Kuo, Shi, Qing-Yun, and Yan, Cheng-Wen. Iconic Indexing by 2D Strings. In *IEEE Computer Society Workshop on Visual Languages* (Dallas, Texas, June 25-27, 1986), 12-21.

4. Freeman, Herbert. Shape Description Via The Use of Critical Points. *Pattern Recognition 10*, 3 (1978), 159-166.

5. Gips, James. *Shape Grammars and Their Uses: Artificial Perception, Shape Generation, and Computer Aesthetics.* Birkhauser, Verlag, Basel, Switzerland, 1975.

6. Levine, Martin D. *Vision in Man and Machine*, chapter 10. McGraw Hill, New York, New York, 1983.

7. Palermo, Frank and Weller, Dan. Some Database Requirements for Pictorial Applications. Data Base Techniques for Pictorial Applications (Florence, Italy, June 1979). Edited by A. Blaser. In *Lecture Notes in Computer Science, 81*. Springer-Verlag, Berlin, West Germany, 1980.

8. Pavlidis, Theo. A Review of Algorithms for Shape Analysis. *Computer Graphics and Image Processing 7*, 2 (April 1978), 243-258.

9. Pier, Kenneth A. A Retrospective on the Dorado, a High-Performance Personal Computer. In *Proceedings of the 10th Symposium on Computer Architecture.* SIGARCH/IEEE, (Stockholm, Sweden, June 1983), 252-269.

10. Pier, Kenneth A., Bier, Eric A., and Stone, Maureen C. An Introduction to Gargoyle: An Interactive Illustration Tool. In van Vliet, J.C. (editor), *Proceedings of the International Conference on Electronic Publishing, Document Manipulation and Typography* (EP88), (Nice, France, April 1988), Cambridge University Press, 223-238.

11. Smith, Alvy Ray. Plants, Fractals, and Formal Languages. Proceedings of SIGGRAPH '84 (Minneapolis, Minnesota, July 23-27, 1984). In *Computer Graphics 18*, 3 (July 1984), 1-10.

12. Stiny, George. *Pictorial and Formal Aspects of Shape and Shape Grammars.* Birkhauser, Verlag, Basel, Switzerland, 1975.

13. Sutherland, Ivan E. Sketchpad: A Man-Machine Graphical Communication System. In *AFIPS Conference Proceedings, Spring Joint Computer Conference, 23.* Spartan Books, Washington, 1963, 329-346.

14. Swinehart, Daniel, Zellweger, Polle, Beach, Richard, and Hagmann, Robert. A Structural View of the Cedar Programming Environment. *ACM Transactions on Programming Languages and Systems 8*, 4 (October 1986), 419-490.

15. Weller, Dan, and Williams, Robin. Graphic and Relational Data Base Support for Problem Solving. Proceedings of SIGGRAPH '76 (Philadelphia, Pennsylvania, July 14-16, 1976). In *Computer Graphics 10*, 2 (Summer 1976), 183-189.

16. Wolfson, Haim. On Curve Matching. Technical Report #256, Courant Institute of Mathematical Sciences, New York, New York, November 1986.

A Study in Interactive 3-D Rotation Using 2–D Control Devices

Michael Chen
Department of Electrical Engineering/
Dynamic Graphics Project
University of Toronto[†]

S. Joy Mountford
Human Interface Group
Apple® Computer Inc.[‡]

Abigail Sellen
Institute for Cognitive Science
University of California, San Diego[#]

ABSTRACT

This paper describes and evaluates the design of four virtual controllers for use in rotating three-dimensional objects using the mouse. Three of four of these controllers are "new" in that they extend traditional direct manipulation techniques to a 3-D environment. User performance is compared during simple and complex rotation tasks. The results indicate faster performance for complex rotations using the new continuous axes controllers compared to more traditional slider approaches. No significant differences in accuracy for complex rotations were found across the virtual controllers.

A second study compared the best of these four virtual controllers (the Virtual Sphere) to a control device by Evans, Tanner and Wein. No significant differences either in time to complete rotation task or accuracy of performance were found. All but one subject indicated they preferred the Virtual Sphere because it seemed more "natural".

CR Categories and Subject Descriptors: I.3.6 [Computer Graphics]: Methodology and Techniques – interaction techniques; D.2.2 [Software Engineering]: Tools and Techniques – User interfaces; H.1.2 [Models and Principles]: User/Machine Systems – Human factors; B.4.2 [Input/Output devices]; J.6 [Computer-Aided Engineering]: Computer-aided manufacturing.

General Terms: Algorithms, Experimentation, Performance, Human Factors.

Additional Key Words and Phrases: input devices, virtual controllers, I/O devices, virtual sphere, mouse, interactive graphics, 3-D graphics, real-time graphics, rotation control, user performance.

[†] Department of Electrical Engineering, University of Toronto, Toronto, Ontario, Canada, M5S 1A4. Tel # (416) 978-6619.

[‡] Apple Computer Inc., 20525 Mariani Ave MS 27A0, Cupertino, CA, 95014. Tel # (408) 973-4801.

[#] Institute for Cognitive Science, C-015, University of California, San Diego, La Jolla, CA, 92093. Tel # (619) 534-2541.

©1988   ACM-0-89791-275-6/88/008/0121 $00.75

1. INTRODUCTION

The recent increase in the available power of special purpose computer graphics machines has extended the operational range of capabilities for users. Objects can now be more easily generated in 3-D (in wireframe, solid and shaded forms), and manipulated in real-time. Despite advances in the ability to display 3-D objects, there is a lack of methods by which the user can easily manipulate and control the position of an object on the screen. Currently, simple direct manipulation controllers do not exist for 3-D object positioning. The design of such controllers could be important interface contributions for application environments such as manufacturing, architecture, and engineering design, which rely heavily on the display and control of three dimensions. The mouse is a successful interface tool, performing well for direct manipulation control of two-axis problems, either through manipulation of x and y separately, or the coupled control of x and y axes together. However, the issue of how best to extend the use of the mouse to accommodate the additional capabilities afforded by three-dimensional graphics is still relatively unexplored.

The ultimate goal is to provide users with an easy way of performing translation, rotation and sizing operations for complete manipulation of 3-D objects. This current performance study focuses on the use of virtual controllers in conjunction with a mouse to perform tasks involving rotation. In performing rotations users can manipulate all three axes simultaneously, whereas in performing translations and sizing operations users more often use fewer axes.

Most 3-D graphics machines use a mouse with one to three discrete buttons as the main input control device. Currently, there are four popular display techniques used to control object rotations:

1) Sliders: Typically the user adjusts the x, y and z sliders graphically displayed on the screen to indicate the amount of rotation in each axis independently. (Alternatively, physical sliders can be used).

2) Menu selection: The user first selects the axis from a text menu and then holds down the mouse button while moving the mouse in one dimension to indicate the amount of rotation.

3) Button press: The user holds down one of three buttons on the mouse or keyboard, and moves the mouse in one dimension to indicate the amount of rotation.

4) Two-axes valuator: The user moves the mouse in two dimensions to control rotation in two of the three axes.

The first three conventional approaches do allow access to rotation on all three axes but use the mouse as a one-dimensional input device. For example, the same left-and-right motion is used to control different rotation directions. However, there is little stimulus-response (S-R) compatibility or kinesthetic correspondence between the direction of mouse movement and direction of object rotation [7] Pique, 1986. The fourth conventional technique, (the two-axis valuator), does provide better S-R correspondence.

The amount of left-and-right and up-and-down movement of the mouse can proportionally rotate the object left-and-right and up-and-down on screen. Rotation about an arbitrary axis on a plane can also be done by moving the mouse diagonally. However, this technique does not allow the user to rotate the object clockwise or counter-clockwise. Therefore systems that use this technique often require the user to work with 3 independent orthogonal views to execute complete 3-D manipulations.

One possible solution to permit full object manipulation is to use input devices with additional degrees of freedom. However, few people seem able to construct reliable mental models about the relative contributions and effects of all the coupled axes which are associated with these extra degrees of freedom. An earlier study described by [5] Mountford, Spires and Korner, 1986, showed how much time subjects spent using all the different axes involved in 3-D control (i.e. the single axes x, y, z; the coupled axes xy, yz, xz; and all axes, xyz attached/coupled together). In this study, subjects performed translation, rotation and sizing operations during an object construction task. The results indicated that during rotation operations subjects used mostly the single independent axis, x, y or z; during translation mostly the coupled xy axis; and during sizing, all three axes together, xyz. Very few subjects in this study used (or had use for) coupled axes of control, except for the familiar xy coupled axis. Subjects did not use either of the other pairs of axes (xz, yz) to move, rotate or size objects.

This performance evaluation study suggests that users did not have enough familiarity or experience with coupled axes (ie xz, yz, or xyz) to successfully perform fully integrated 3-D control manipulations using all the different combinations of axes. Users are particularly unfamiliar with the visual appearance and movement associated with rotating an object around xz or yz. If this is indeed the case, then it is unlikely that users will want to have new devices that make simultaneous use of **all** of the additional degrees of freedom that can be provided for 3-D object manipulation. It is possible that for more complex manipulation tasks such as docking, a device with some extra degrees of freedom may be appropriate. A full six degrees-of-freedom controller called the IIISPACE™ Digitizer (Polhemus) is available, but such input devices are not yet affordable for most users. Traditional 2-D input devices will continue to be the most available and dominant devices. Thus it is important to design 3-D manipulation techniques assuming such a 2-D device.

The current paper describes the conventional slider approach as well as three alternate "virtual rotational controllers" that allow users to directly manipulate 3-D objects using a one-button mouse. These controllers were designed not to have any knobs, drag boxes or menus that could distract the user from the task of rotating the object. Furthermore, each controller was designed to be overlaid on top of the object to be rotated, helping the user focus attention on the object being manipulated. This suggested another constraint, that the controllers be as transparent as possible for a clear view of the object. Finally, the intention was that the controllers be easily understood by novices and be as natural to use as possible. That is, the goal was to make them "transparent" and easy to use. We designed the controller operations to perform as analogously to real object manipulations as possible. This was achieved by extending the use of successful 2-D direct manipulation techniques to a 3-D environment.

This paper also describes two studies which were carried out to evaluate the controllers by comparing subjects' performance in rotating object in 3-D. The first study compares relative performance of all four controllers, the traditional slider and the 'new' three virtual controllers developed by Chen. The second study compares the best of these controllers to a controller developed by [4] Evans, Tanner and Wein, 1981.

2. DESCRIPTION OF VIRTUAL ROTATIONAL CONTROLLERS

Figure 1 shows a representation of the displayed house used in all rotation tasks. Rotations in x, y and z correspond to rotating the object up-and-down, left-and-right and clockwise-counter-clockwise, respectively. Thus, in this study, rotation is with respect to the user's (camera's) frame of reference.

Even though there are systems that perform rotations about the object's frame, (e.g. [1] Bier, 1986, [6] Nielson and Olsen, 1986], it has been suggested that inexperienced users can perform rotations more easily in the user's reference frame [5] Mountford et al, 1986.

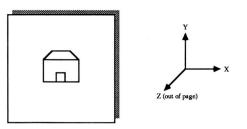

Figure 1. Definition of the coordinate axes.

The four controller displays used in the evaluation test are shown in Figure 2. Note that the Continuous XY with additional Z and the Virtual Sphere controllers have the same displays. They differ in the rotation axes available inside the circular region (described later).

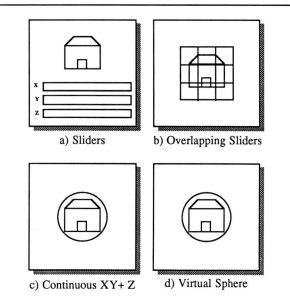

a) Sliders   b) Overlapping Sliders

c) Continuous XY+ Z   d) Virtual Sphere

Figure 2. Screen displays of the four virtual controllers with object in centre.

2.1. Graphical Sliders Controller

The Graphical Sliders controller uses a traditional approach to allow users to perform 3-D rotations and serves as a control for performance comparisons. In this study, we chose horizontal sliders and placed them below the object to be rotated (see Figure 2a), similar to other graphical control interfaces. The sliders simulate "treadmills" and therefore provide relative control over the amount of rotation. A full sweep across a slider provides 180 degrees of rotation about an independent axis. As long as the mouse button is initially depressed inside one slider, the user can rotate about the corresponding axis even if accidentally crossing into another slider.

2.2. Overlapping Sliders Controller

The Overlapping Sliders controller [3] Chen, 1987, is a modification of the conventional slider approach in three respects:

1) The x, y, and z axes are represented by a vertical, horizontal and circular slider, respectively.

2) All three sliders are overlapped (as shown in Figure-3a) and then simplified to look like a nine-square grid (Figure 3b).

3) The grid is superimposed over the object to be rotated (Figure 2b)

In this implementation, a full sweep of the vertical or horizontal slider rotates the object 180 degrees about the x or y axis respectively. A full circle around the outside squares rotates the object 360 degrees about z (see Figure 3b). Note that only near vertical, horizontal and circular movement of the mouse inside the middle column, middle row and outside squares (respectively) are recognized by this controller. A diagonal movement in the middle square, for example, is ignored since this is a coupled rotation in x and y (i.e. the rotation axis lying somewhere on the x-y plane). Thus, this controller still operates on the basis of single axis control. The difference between this controller and conventional sliders, though, is increased controller-display compatibility. The direction of movement of the mouse more closely corresponds with the direction of rotation. In addition, superimposing the controller on the object is intended to give the user more of a sense of directly manipulating the object.

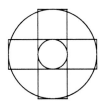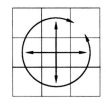

Figure 3. a) Three overlapped sliders, b) idealized version

2.3. Continuous XY with Additional Z Controller

The Continuous XY with added Z controller (Figure 2c) operates in two modes. If the mouse button is depressed while the mouse cursor is inside the circle, left-and-right and up-and-down movement of the mouse will rotate the object left-and right and up-and-down on the screen. Diagonal movement will rotate the object the proportional amount about the x-axis and y-axis (i.e. the axis of rotation is on the x-y plane and is perpendicular to the direction of mouse movement). If the mouse button is depressed while the mouse cursor is outside the circle, the user can rotate the whole object clockwise by going around the outside of the circle. Thus, this controller provides either 1) continuous rotation on the x-y plane, or 2) exact rotation about the z-axis. In this implementation, a full sweep of the mouse across the circle rotates the object 180 degrees about the corresponding axis in the x-y plane. A full circle around the outside rotates the object 360 degrees about z.

2.4. Virtual Sphere Controller

The virtual sphere controller simulates the mechanics of a physical 3-D trackball that can freely rotate about any arbitrary axis in 3-space. On the display screen (see Figure 2d), the user can imagine viewing an object encased in a glass sphere. Rotation is then a matter of rolling the sphere and therefore the object with the mouse cursor. Up-and-down and left-and-right movement at the centre of the circle is equivalent to "rolling" the imaginary sphere at its apex and produces rotation about the x-axis and y-axis respectively. Movement along (or completely outside) the edge of the circle is equivalent to rolling the sphere at the edge and produces rotation about z. The amount of rotation is adjusted so that a full sweep of the mouse across the circle rotates the object 180 degrees about the corresponding axis in the x-y plane; a full circle around the outside rotates the object 360 degrees

about z. The implementation of the Virtual Sphere is outlined in Appendix A.

The difference between this and the Continuous XY with additional Z, is that the Virtual Sphere allows continuous rotation about all three axes inside the circle[1] while the latter only allows continuous control of two axes inside. To rotate in z, the user must go outside the circle.

3. EXPERIMENT 1

This first experiment was designed to compare the subject performance using the four controllers described above. The main performance measures recorded were time to complete rotation task and accuracy in performing that task. The experimentor gave minimal instruction in the use of each controller, so that no explicit conceptual model was imparted to the subjects. For example, the subjects were not told that the Virtual Sphere controller simulated a physical 3-D trackball.

The previously described four controllers were presented to subjects in order of increasing computational and cognitive complexity. It may be reasonable to assume that users would have more difficulty in grasping the idea behind the latter controllers. We were especially interested in how novices would perform without first being told the conceptual models of the controllers. We wanted to find out how easy the controllers were to learn by allowing subjects to just start trying to use them.

3.1. Method

3.1.1. Subjects

Twelve right-handed, male subjects were tested, consisting of both undergraduate and graduate students at the University of Toronto. All were familiar with using a mouse while none had any experience with any of the four controllers. Only three of the twelve had any experience with 3-D graphics systems.

3.1.2. Apparatus

The experiment was run entirely on an Silicon Graphics IRIS 3020 workstation. The IRIS (Integrated Raster Imaging System) is a high-performance, high-resolution (1024 by 768) colour computing system for 2-D and 3-D graphics. The heart of the IRIS is a custom VLSI chip called the Geometry Engine. A pipeline of ten or twelve Geometry Engines accepts points, vectors, polygons, characters and curves in user-defined coordinate systems and transforms them to screen coordinates, with rotations, translation, scaling and clipping. The four virtual controllers, the solid rendered house and the testing programs were written in C.

In addition to the Geometry Pipeline, an IRIS system consists of a general-purpose microprocessor, a raster sub-system, a high-resolution colour monitor, a keyboard and a three-button optical mouse. Only the left button of the mouse was used for these controllers and the mouse worked best using stroke-lift-stroke tactics. The mouse acceleration algorithm was disabled so that the amount of cursor movement was not affected by the speed of the mouse movement. An IRIS was used because it is a very fast machine and runs in real-time and can provide full colour rendering of solid objects.

---

[1]The Virtual Sphere controller may actually be better than a real physical 3-D trackball in at least one respect. With a physical trackball, it is impossible to have the entire top hemisphere of the ball exposed. This is because one of the rotation sensors must be placed at the "equator" of the sphere. Thus it is nearly impossible for the user to physically twist the trackball while rolling it. Accordingly, a 3-D trackball is better described as a 2+1D device (Buxton, 1986).

3.1.3. Task

In order to compare user performance on all four virtual controllers, subjects were asked to perform a series of matching tasks. Subjects were shown a solid-rendered, upright house in colour on the right-hand side of the screen and were asked to match its orientation to a tilted house on the left-hand side of the screen. The house was coloured differently on all of its faces so as to aid the subject in identifying its various surfaces. The centre of rotation was fixed at the centre of gravity of the house. Subjects were told to press the space bar when satisfied with the match, and were instructed that both speed and accuracy were important. Both task completion time and accuracy were recorded on-line.

After pressing the spacebar to indicate a match, subjects were given feedback on the accuracy of the match for each trial. This feedback was provided to subjects to illustrate the desired quality of exactness in house positioning to help subjects achieve optimal performance. Accuracy was obtained by comparing the 3x3 rotation matrices of the two houses. The accuracy measure was calculated as the sum of the differences between the corresponding elements in the rotation matrices squared. From the subject's perspective, accuracy was rated as "Excellent****" (squared error from 0 to 0.02), "Good Match***" (squared error of 0.02 to 0.035), or "Not good enough, try harder next time**" (squared error greater than 0.035). The squared error of 0.02 and 0.035 corresponds to a rotation mismatch of 5.7 and 7.6 degrees respectively.

3.1.4. Design

Each subject performed using all four controllers, using a within subject design. Order of controllers was counterbalanced according to a Latin-square design. For each controller, there were nine different non-upright house positions to be matched. Three of the nine orientations required only simple rotations about the x-, y- or z-axis. The other six orientations were more complex, requiring coupled axes of rotation using the full range of axes manipulation. Each orientation was presented three times for a total of 27 trials per controller. Orientations were presented randomly and sampled without replacement, with the constraint that simple orientations were presented first, followed by complex ones.

3.1.5. Procedure

All instructions for the experiment were provided on-line. At the start of the session, subjects were given a general description of the experimental procedure. Specific instructions for using the first controller were then presented, followed by three minutes of practice. During these three minutes, subjects could attempt to match as many orientations as possible, and performance feedback was provided. Figure 4 shows a photograph of the actual experimental screen with instructions on the left, the house orientation to be matched in the middle and the house to be rotated in the right window. Each subject was then given two practice trials (not timed) and then 27 timed trials consisting of 9 different orientations each repeated three times. At the end of each of the block of 27 trials, the subject was given a break. The same procedure was then repeated for the remaining three controllers. The entire experimental session lasted approximately 1 1/2 hours.

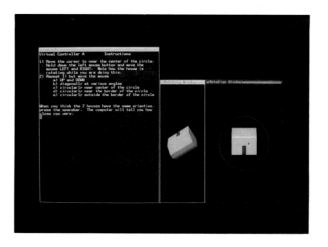

Figure 4. Photo of actual experimental screen of the IRIS. Instructions for each controller are presented on the left, the house orientation to be matched in the middle window, and the house to be rotated in the right window.

3.2. Results and Discussion

Figure 5 shows the average time and standard deviations in seconds to complete rotations for simple versus complex orientations collapsed across all subjects. The results show an interesting interaction between type of controller and complexity of the matching task. In performing simple, single-axis tasks, the conventional slider and the overlapping sliders produced significantly faster performance (p<0.001). However for complex rotations, the Continuous XY with additional Z, and Virtual Sphere controllers were clearly faster (p<0.001). The variance in speed of performance remained relatively constant across controllers for both simple and complex tasks, larger for complex rotations and smaller for simple rotations.

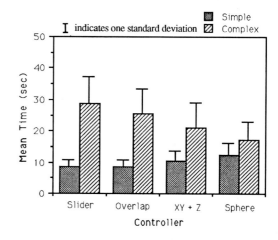

Figure 5. Mean time to complete simple and complex rotations.

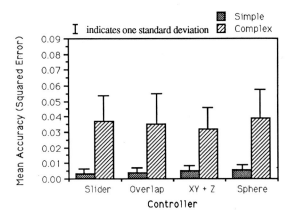

Figure 6. Mean accuracy for simple and complex rotations.

As a result of observing subjects performing single-axis rotation with the slider controllers, it was clear that when subjects selected the correct slider, the time to complete the match was short. However, subjects would often begin by selecting the wrong slider and then spend their time correcting the error. However, for the continuous controllers (XY + Z and the Virtual Sphere), initial movement was almost always in the correct direction, but the extra degrees of freedom made single axis rotation more difficult, so more time was needed to compensate for small deviations from rotation about that axis. This suggests that allowing the user to work with independent axes of control may be best when precise rotation is required around one axis. The real word situations in which such rotations may be required, however, seem limited.

When subjects performed complex rotations, the Virtual Sphere was clearly superior in terms of speed. On the basis of these data, we can expect an average savings of almost twelve seconds for a single, complex rotation task by using the Virtual Sphere as compared to conventional slider controllers. Furthermore, most subjects commented that they preferred the Virtual Sphere of the four controllers that they used, while two subjects preferred the Continuous XY with Additional Z controller. Subjects remarked that the Virtual Sphere seemed "more natural" and that they felt like they were actually rotating the object directly, rather than manipulating a controller which in turn rotated the object. It seems that the use of continuous control is one important aspect in the design of virtual controllers for this kind of task.

A further point of interest is that the overlapping sliders, while not producing performance as fast as the continuous controllers, did give a shorter mean task completion time than the traditional slider approach. This performance difference is probably due to the increased S-R compatibility of this controller versus the traditional slider controller.

Subjects performing simple rotations were significantly less accurate using the continuous controllers compared to the two slider controllers ($p<0.05$). These results are shown in Figure 6. However, the actual magnitude of these differences was small (at most a squared deviation of 0.003) . There were no significant differences in accuracy for the complex rotations. Again, variances across controllers were fairly constant, both simple and complex rotations indicated the same trends.

The data suggest that if the task to be performed is extremely simple, and if it is important that the rotation be accurate, then sliders may be most suitable. However, given any increase in the complexity of the task, controllers designed based on the principles of direct manipulation produce faster and just as accurate performance.

4. EXPERIMENT 2

In experiment 1 the Virtual Sphere produced the best user performance of the four controllers in complex rotations. It seemed of interest to know how the Virtual Controllers would perform relative to a similar controller developed by Evans et al. [4]. This further experiment was prompted by some experts in the area claiming that the two controllers were very similar. However, it was our opinion that several differences existed between these two controllers, both in terms of technical implementation and in visual presentation style.

Technically, the Evans et al. technique is a combination of the "two-axis trackball" and the "stirrer" techniques described in their paper. Their implementation recognizes straight line (continuous rotation in x and y) and circular (rotation in z) gestures. To detect the different motions, a "stirring angle" is calculated based on the change in movement of the last three positions of the input device. This value is then compared to a threshold to decide whether the movement is in a "relatively" straight-line or not. Unfortunately, the threshold is dependent on two interrelated variables: the speed with which each individual user likes to draw the circle and the frequency of taking a reading from the input device. If the sampling rate is too fast or the user prefers to draw the circle slowly, the three readings would tend to indicate that a straight line is drawn. Thus, threshold adjustments may be needed for different systems and different users with this technique[1]. The Virtual Sphere, on the other hand, allows rotation about an arbitrary axis in 3-space. The direction and amount of rotation is based only on the last two locations of the input device, and no user dependent adjustment is necessary.

The two techniques also have different visual presentations. With the Evans et al. technique, the location of the cursor which is controlled by the input device is not important; the user can ignore the cursor and just concentrate on the object being rotated. With the Virtual Sphere, the cursor must stay inside the "circle" to control rotation about all three axes. This technique works best when the circle is surrounding the object being rotated, so as to take advantage of the direct manipulation quality that the controller affords. With respect to the cursor, the Evans et al device is a relative controller whereas the Virtual Sphere is an absolute controller. Our Virtual Controller provides the user with some additional visual guidance as to where to concentrate their manipulation movements.

To implement the Evans et al. technique, we invited one of the co-authors, Peter Tanner, to help us reproduce the "feel" of their original implementation. The following adjustments were made to deal with the sampling problem mentioned above:

- Cursor movement is only recognized if the change is greater than a 3 pixels radius.
- The largest stirring angle (rotation in z) is limited to approximately 33 degrees per screen update.
- The stirring angle is scaled proportional to the amount of cursor movement.

The stirring threshold was set to approximately 13 degrees so that an angular change in movement of less than 13 degrees is considered movement along a straight line.

Quantitatively, a 360 degrees of rotation of an object requires about 3200 degrees of quick small circular motion or 1100 degrees of quick large circular motion. For the same rotation in x-y, the implementation required about 2.5 times the movement distance as the Virtual Sphere controller.

---

[1]The Evans et al paper suggested that it is possible to perform rotations in x, y and z together, by reducing the x and y rotations when the stirring motion is large, and reducing z rotation when stirring motion is small. However, Tanner informed us [personal communication] that their implementation *did* use an angular threshold to decide whether to perform rotation in x-y or in z.

4.1. Method

The method for this experiment was identical to that used in the previous experiment 1, with the following exceptions:

- Six different, right-handed, male subjects were used instead of twelve. Again, all were familiar with the mouse while only two of the six had used any 3-D computer graphics systems.
- Only two controllers were used in this experiment. Half the subject used the Virtual Sphere first, while the other half used the Evans et al. controller first.
- The entire session lasted about 45 minutes.
- An IRIS 2400 Turbo with a mechanical mouse was used in this experiment. The mechanical mouse provided about the same controller-display ratio as the optical mouse used in experiment 1.

4.2. Results and Discussion

Figure 7 shows the average time in seconds to complete rotations for simple versus complex orientations collapsed across subjects. Figure 8 shows the mean accuracy scores for both simple and complex rotations. The results under all conditions show the Virtual Sphere and the Evans et al. technique to be similar. Statistical tests showed there were no significant differences between the two controllers at the 0.05 level.

Note that Figure 7 and 8 also show the result for the Virtual Sphere from experiment 1. Some performance variations between the experiments using the same controller are to be expected, see Figure 7, and these differences are relatively small. However, Figure 8 shows noticeably different standard deviations for the Virtual Sphere between the two experiments, larger in the second than the first. This may be a result of using different subjects who used only two controllers in experiment 2, compared with four in experiment 1, or because of using two different Iris machines with two different types of mice.

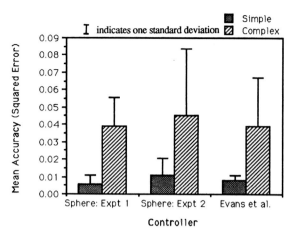

Figure 8. Mean accuracy for simple and complex rotations.

Comments from the subjects indicated that the majority (5 out of 6) preferred the Virtual Sphere over the Evans et al. controller. They commented that the Virtual Sphere felt more "natural", even though only two subjects were explicit about comparing the controller to manipulating a sphere. The one subject that preferred the Evans et al. controller indicated he liked it because he did not have to watch the cursor, only the object being manipulated. However, all the subjects said that they had difficulty in making fine rotation in z, since this required quick but short circular motions. Also a large rotation in z requires a lot of circular motion since the controller has a built-in maximum rotation speed. Large circles were also said to be less effective because often the stirring threshold was not reached, and resulted in x-y rotations.

5. CONCLUSIONS

The data reported in the first study support the use of continuous-axes controllers for complex multi-axis object manipulations. Observation of the subjects confirmed that moving between axes is cumbersome with the sliders, since there is no inherent direct manipulation capability. However, the slider controllers are just as good for simple single axis rotation, where the axes are already constrained to only one axis movement at a time, a situation which simplifies the user's control options. This would indicate that some constraint mechanism should be provided to limit the axis of rotation for more continuous-type controllers, if they are to be used in a real system.

In both of our experiments, the new controllers have a "one-to-one" controller to display (C-D) ratio. This created the impression that when using the Virtual Sphere controller, subjects thought they could actually grab the corners of the house and move it. A smaller C-D ratio might have made fine adjustments easier. However, subjects had more difficulty in judging orientation accurately than in performing fine mouse movements. Nevertheless, it would be useful to test the effects of different C-D ratios or dynamic ratios which would vary with the speed of motion. It might also be worthwhile to re-test our subjects to examine any performance changes now they know the conceptual model behind the controllers.

The fact that the results in experiment 2 showed no significant difference between Evans et al.'s technique and the Virtual Sphere in itself *is* significant. It would be tempting to regard these controllers as competitors, where one controller could be chosen and then used by all users. However as we mentioned before, these two techniques differ both in implementation and more importantly, in their visual presentation. Note also that both techniques deal with only one aspect of rotation manipulation. We have ignored the processes involved with the user having to actually select the object as well as selecting it's centre of rotation. Designing these additional performance features and integrating them successfully into the entire interface design is an important and critical next step. The results indicate that either of the techniques would perform better relative to other existing

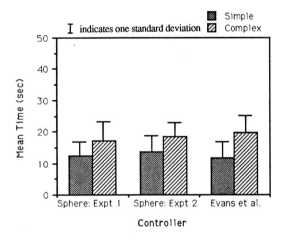

Figure 7. Mean time to complete simple and complex rotations.

techniques for 3-D interface rotations. The ultimate decision should be based on user's preference, and on which technique fits in better with the entire interface design for the broadest range of different user tasks.

The Evans et al. paper presented a catalogue of interesting techniques, but gave no supporting behavioural data comparing these techniques, or to other existing techniques that were common at the time. While some of the techniques described were novel and appeared to be fairly powerful, they are not in common usage. For example, we are not aware of any commercial system that makes use of their technique that we replicated in this experiment. One of the driving forces in the current work was not just to introduce another interaction technique, but to provide objective comparative user data which allows the reader to quantatively access the relative strengths and weaknesses of the different controllers.

We plan to further develop these techniques and to explore their use in a range of more complex tasks. More complex and diverse tasks may further indicate where the advantages for different controllers exist. Furthermore, the "complex" rotations subjects performed in these studies may be viewed as relatively simple when compared to the kinds of tasks that may be required in real-world settings. Users need to rotate objects in the context of other objects as well as to perform translation and sizing operations in the 3-D graphics environment.

Our virtual, alternative continuous-axes controllers did not require the use of special purpose 3-D control devices, nor did they require the use of a multi-button mouse. The performance value of the continuous controllers, (Continuous XY with additional Z and the Virtual Sphere), lies both in their intuitive easy-to-learn features and their direct manipulation capabilities. These controllers are worthy of further experimental validation and refinement for use in designing interfaces by extending the user interface principle of *WYSIWYG*, What You See is What You Get, to *WYDIWYS*, What You Do Is What You See!

Acknowledgements

This research was supported in part by the Natural Sciences and Engineering Research Council of Canada and with a grant and internship program from Apple Computer Inc. It was undertaken at Apple Computer Inc., Cupertino, and at the Dynamic Graphics Project and the Department of Landscape Architecture, both at the University of Toronto. We are especially indebted to Prof. John Danahy and his students at the Department of Landscape Architecture, as well as Jim Batson in the Advance Technology Group (Apple Computer Inc.) for the use of their IRIS' on short notice.

We would like to thank Peter Tanner for helping us reproduce their interaction technique for the experiment. We also thank Bill Buxton, Eric Hulteen, and Bill Gaver for suggestions and comments on this paper.

APPENDIX A: The Implementation of the Virtual Sphere Controller

A.1. Rotation of a 3-D Trackball

On a 3-D trackball (see Figure 9), if one touches the ball at point **P**, and rotates it in a tangential direction $\vec{d}$, the axis of positive rotation $\vec{a}$, can be computed by the cross product:

$$\vec{a} = \overrightarrow{OP} \times \vec{d}$$

where **O** is the centre of the trackball, and $\overrightarrow{OP}$ is a vector from the point **O** to **P**.

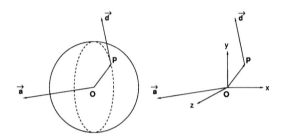

Figure 9. Rotation of a 3-D trackball.

A.2. Emulation of a 3-D Trackball Using a 2-D Control Device

The computation of the corresponding axis of rotation using a 2-D control device is done in three steps as shown in Figures 10, 11 and 12.

Step 1:

Figure 10 shows the top hemisphere of the 3-D trackball conceptually being flattened into a disk. Let **O'** be the centre of the disk. Let **P'** be the starting point where the 2-D control device is first moved, and $\vec{d'}$ be the direction of movement. If **P' = O'** and $\vec{d'}$ makes angle τ' with the x-axis, the axis of rotation is on the x-y plane perpendicular to $\vec{d'}$ and can be obtained from equation (1):

$$\vec{a}\,(x,y,z) = [-\sin(\tau')\ \cos(\tau')\ 0] \qquad (1)$$

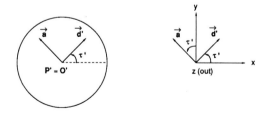

Figure 10. Movement of a 2–D device where **P' = O'**.

Step 2:

If **P'** is on the positive x-axis along the line $\overline{\text{O'R'}}$ as show in Figure 11, the axis of rotation is that obtained from equation (1) but rotated by $\omega = f\left(\dfrac{|\overrightarrow{\text{O'P'}}|}{|\overline{\text{O'R'}}|}\right)$ degrees about the y-axis. Namely,

$$\overrightarrow{a}(x,y,z) = \begin{bmatrix} -\sin(\tau') & \cos(\tau') & 0 \end{bmatrix} \cdot \begin{bmatrix} \cos f(\omega) & 0 & -\sin f(\omega) \\ 0 & 1 & 0 \\ \sin f(\omega) & 0 & \cos f(\omega) \end{bmatrix} \qquad (2)$$

where $|\overrightarrow{\text{O'P'}}|$ and $|\overline{\text{O'R'}}|$ are the length of the (2-D) vector $\overrightarrow{\text{O'P'}}$ and the line $\overline{\text{O'R'}}$ respectively, and $f(x)$ can be any monotonically-increasing function with conditions:

$$f(x) = \begin{cases} 0° & \text{if } x \leq 0 \\ 90° & \text{if } x \geq 1 \end{cases}$$

The function $f(x)$ describes how the hemisphere is distorted into the flat disk. The Virtual Sphere controller in the experiments used $f(x) = x$, with the above constraints. Note that if $|\overrightarrow{\text{O'P'}}| = 0$, equation (2) is the same as equation (1). If $|\overrightarrow{\text{O'P'}}| = |\overline{\text{O'R'}}|$, then the axis of rotation is on the y-z plane.

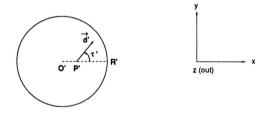

Figure 11. Movement of the 2-D device where **P'** is on $\overline{\text{O'R'}}$.

Step 3:

In the general case (see Figure 12),

$\overrightarrow{\text{O'P'}}$ makes angle θ' with the x-axis, and
$\overrightarrow{d}$ " " $\theta'+\tau'$ " ".

Since Figure 12 is just Figure 11 rotated by θ' degrees about the z-axis, the axis of rotation is that obtained from equation (2) excepted rotated by θ' degrees about z. Namely,

$$\overrightarrow{a}(x,y,z) = \begin{bmatrix} -\sin(\tau') & \cos(\tau') & 0 \end{bmatrix} \cdot \begin{bmatrix} \cos f(\omega) & 0 & -\sin f(\omega) \\ 0 & 1 & 0 \\ \sin f(\omega) & 0 & \cos f(\omega) \end{bmatrix}$$
$$\cdot \begin{bmatrix} \cos \theta' & \sin \theta' & 0 \\ -\sin \theta' & \cos \theta' & 0 \\ 0 & 0 & 1 \end{bmatrix} \qquad (3)$$

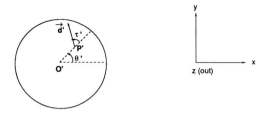

Figure 12. Movement of the 2-D device where **P'** is arbitrarily located.

Once the axis of rotation is obtained from equation (3), the rotation matrix **R** can be computed by:

$$\mathbf{R}_{\overrightarrow{a}}(\varphi) = \begin{bmatrix} ta_x^2+c & ta_xa_y+sa_z & ta_xa_z-sa_y \\ ta_xa_y-sa_z & ta_y^2+c & ta_ya_z+sa_x \\ ta_xa_z+sa_y & ta_ya_z-sa_x & ta_z^2+c \end{bmatrix} \qquad (4)$$

where a_x, a_y and a_z are the components of $\overrightarrow{a}$, $s = \sin\varphi$, $c = \cos\varphi$, and $t = 1-\cos\varphi$, and φ is the amount of rotation about $\overrightarrow{a}$ [7].

The angle of rotation φ can simply be the distance of cursor movement times a suitable scaling factor. However, we decided to model the rolling of the sphere more precisely. We scaled the amount of rotation such that:

1) a full sweep of the mouse across the circle (passing through **O'**) produces 180 degrees of rotation;
2) a full circle around the edge (or outside) the circle produces 360 degrees of rotation.

The following formula for φ in degrees (obtained empirically) was used in the experiment, and provides a good approximation to the two desirable properties described above:

$$\varphi = 90° * \frac{|\overrightarrow{d}|}{|\overline{\text{O'R'}}|}\left\{1 - (1 - \frac{0.2}{\pi})\frac{\omega}{90°}(1 - |\cos \tau'|)\right\} \qquad (5)$$

References

1. Bier, Eric A. Skitters and Jacks: Interactive 3-D Positioning Tools. In *Proceedings 1986 Workshop on Interactive 3-D Graphics* (Chapel Hill, North Carolina, October 1986), 183-196.

2. Buxton, William. There's More to Interaction than Meets the Eye: Some Issues in Manual Input. In *User Centred System Design: New Perspectives on Human-computer Interaction,* D. A. Norman, & S. W. Draper Eds. Lawrence Erlbaum Associates, Hillsdale, N.J, 1986. pp. 319-337.

3. Chen, Michael. A Technique for Specifying Rotations in Three Dimensions Using a 2D Input Device. In *Proceedings IEEE Montech'87 – Compint'87* (Montréal, Québec, November 1987), 118-120.

4. Evans, Kenneth B, Tanner, Peter P. & Wein, Marceli. Tablet Based Valuators that Provides One, Two or Three Degrees of Freedom. Proceedings of SIGGRAPH'81 (Dallas, Texas, August 1981). In *Computer Graphics* 15, 3 (August 1981), 91-97.

5. Mountford, S. Joy, Spires, Shannon & Korner, Kim. Visage: A Three-Dimensional Graphics Editor – Evaluation and Review. MCC Technical Report #HI-105-86-P, Microelectronics and Computer Technology Corporation, Austin, Texas, 1986. Data presented at 31st Annual Meeting of *Human Factors Society* in New York, October 19-22, 1987.

6. Nielson, Gregory M, Olsen, Dan R. Jr. Direct Manipulation Techniques for 3-D Objects Using 2D Locator Devices. In *Proceedings 1986 Workshop on Interactive 3-D Graphics* (Chapel Hill, North Carolina, October 1986), 175-182.

7. Pique, Michael E. Semantics of Interactive Rotations. In *Proceedings 1986 Workshop on Interactive 3-D Graphics* (Chapel Hill, North Carolina, October 1986), 259-269.

Harnessing Chaos for Image Synthesis[1]

Michael F. Barnsley[2],

Arnaud Jacquin, Francois Malassenet,

Laurie Reuter[3], Alan D. Sloan[2]

School of Mathematics,

Georgia Institute of Technology,

Atlanta, Ga 30332

Abstract

Chaotic dynamics can be used to model shapes and render textures in digital images. This paper addresses the problem of how to model geometrically shapes and textures of two dimensional images using iterated function systems. The successful solution to this problem is demonstrated by the production and processing of synthetic images encoded from color photographs. The solution is achieved using two algorithms: (1) an interactive geometric modeling algorithm for finding iterated function system codes; and (2) a random iteration algorithm for computing the geometry and texture of images defined by iterated function system codes. Also, the underlying mathematical framework, where these two algorithms have their roots, is outlined. The algorithms are illustrated by showing how they can be used to produce images of clouds, mist and surf, seascapes and landscapes and even faces, all modeled from original photographs. The reasons for developing iterated function systems algorithms include their ability to produce complicated images and textures from small databases, and their potential for highly parallel implementation.

Key Words and Phrases: Iterated Function Systems; Fractals; Textures; Geometric Modeling.

---

1 Research supported in part by DARPA, Applied and Computational Mathematics Program, through grant #N00014-86-C-0446.
2 Barnsley and Sloan are also affiliated with *Iterated Systems Inc.*
3 Dept. of Electrical Engineering and Computer Science, George Washington University, Washington D.C. 20052.

1. Introduction

The mathematical theory of Iterated Function Systems (IFS) has unique advantages for addressing a broad class of modeling problems including the modeling of natural objects and scenes. The feasibility of using IFS theory in computer graphics was reviewed previously at SIGGRAPH [Demk 85, Barns 87]. The present work concerns the development of IFS as a practical tool for the production of images including clouds and smoke, seascapes and landscapes, and even faces. Specifically, it addresses the problem of how IFS may be used to geometrically model the shapes and textures of two-dimensional objects.

The approach presented here has its roots in fractal geometry, whose applications in computer graphics have been investigated by a number of authors including Mandelbrot [Mand 82], Kawaguchi [Kawa 82], Oppenheimer [Oppe 86], Fournier et al. [Four 82], Smith [Smit 84], Miller [Mill 86], and Amburn et al. [Ambu 86]. In all cases the focus has been on the modeling of natural objects and scenes. Both deterministic and random geometries have been used. The present work is based on the use of iterated function systems. This provides a single framework which can reach a seemingly unlimited range of images. It is distinct from earlier work in that it concentrates on measure theory rather than geometry. The mathematical basis of the theory can be found in a rapidly growing literature [Hutc 81], [Hata 85], [Diac 86], [Barn 86], [Barn 88].

We introduce two new IFS-based algorithms. The first one, the Collage algorithm, is a geometric modeling tool for interactively finding iterated function system codes. The second one is called the Measure Rendering algorithm. It applies chaotic dynamics to the computation of the geometry and texture of IFS encoded images.

The Collage algorithm is based on Collage Theorem [Barn 85], [Barn 88]. It provides a means for interactive geometric modeling using IFS. In the two-dimensional case, the input to the algorithm is a target image; for example, a polygonal approximation to the boundary of a leaf, a digitized image of a leaf, or a representation of leaves on a branch. The output from the algorithm is an IFS code which, when input to the Measure Rendering algorithm, produces a textured version of the original target. The closeness of this rendition to the desired image depends on the accuracy with which the user is able to solve interactively a certain geometric problem.

The Measure Rendering algorithm starts from an input IFS code, explained in §2, and with the aid of random iteration produces a deterministic geometric object together with rendering values. Despite the use of random iteration, a unique final image is obtained once the viewing window, resolution and a color assignment function, have been specified.

The usage of our two algorithms in the geometric modeling and rendering of two-dimensional images is demonstrated in § 4, 5. In these two sections we show how to produce images of clouds, a field of sunflowers, a forest scene, and the face of a girl.

2. Textured Objects from IFS Codes

§2.1 <u>What an IFS Code Is</u>

An affine transformation $w : \mathbf{R}^2 \to \mathbf{R}^2$ from two dimensional space $\mathbf{R}^2$ into itself is defined by

$$w \begin{bmatrix} x_1 \\ x_2 \end{bmatrix} = \begin{bmatrix} a_{11} x_1 + a_{21} x_2 + b_1 \\ a_{21} x_1 + a_{22} y_2 + b_2 \end{bmatrix}$$

where the a_{ij}'s and b_i's are real constants. Let A denote the matrix (a_{ij}), $\underline{b}$ denote the vector $(b_1 , b_2)^t$, where t denotes the transposition operator, and $\underline{x}$ denotes the vector $(x_1 , x_2)^t$. We write

$$w (\underline{x}) = A \underline{x} + \underline{b}.$$

An affine transformation is thus completely specified by six real numbers.

Given an affine transformation, one can always find a nonnegative number s so that

$$\| w (\underline{x}) - w (\underline{y}) \| \le s \cdot \| \underline{x} - \underline{y} \| \text{ for all } \underline{x} \text{ and } \underline{y} \text{ in } \mathbf{R}^2.$$

The smallest number s for which this is true is called the *Lipshitz constant* for w. In this paper we use the usual Euclidean norm

$$\| (x_1 , x_2)^t \| = \sqrt{ x_1^2 + x_2^2 } .$$

Such an affine transformation is called *contractive* if $s < 1$, and it is called a *symmetry* if

$$\| w (\underline{x}) - w (\underline{y}) \| = \| \underline{x} - \underline{y} \| \text{ for all } \underline{x} \text{ and } \underline{y} \text{ in } \mathbf{R}^2.$$

It is *expansive* if its Lipshitz constant is greater than one.

A two-dimensional IFS consists of a set of N affine transformations, where N is an integer. The set is denoted by

$$\{w_1, w_2, w_3, \dots , w_N\},$$

where each w_n takes $\mathbf{R}^2$ into $\mathbf{R}^2$. Also required is a set of probabilities

$$\{p_1, p_2, p_3, \dots , p_N\},$$

where each $p_n > 0$ and

$$\sum_{n=1}^{N} p_n = 1.$$

Let s_n denote the Lipshitz constant for w_n for each $n = 1, 2, \dots , N$. Then we say that the IFS obeys the *average contractivity condition* if

$$s_1^{p_1} \cdot s_2^{p_2} \cdot s_3^{p_3} \cdot \dots \cdot s_N^{p_N} < 1.$$

An *IFS code* is a set $\{w_n, p_n : n = 1, 2, \dots, N \}$ such that the average contractivity condition is obeyed.

§ 2.2 <u>The Underlying Model Associated with an IFS Code</u>

Let $\{w_n, p_n : n = 1, 2, \dots, N \}$ be an IFS code. Then by a theorem of Barnsley and Elton [Barn 86b] there is a unique associated geometric object, subset of $\mathbf{R}^2$, that is called the *attractor* of the IFS and is denoted by A. A has the property of being invariant under application of the N affine transformations $\{w_1, w_2, w_3, \dots , w_N\}$. In set-theoretic notation,

$$A = \bigcup_{n=1}^{N} w_n (A).$$

There is also an unique associated *invariant measure*, supported by A and denoted by μ. This measure assigns a non-negative number to each subset of $\mathbf{R}^2$. It may be thought of as a distribution of infinitely fine sand, of fixed total mass, lying upon A. The measure of a subset β of A is the weight of sand which lies upon β . It is denoted by $\mu(\beta)$. The *underlying model* associated with an IFS code consists of the attractor A together with the measure μ, and is symbolized by (A, μ).

The structure of A is controlled by the affine maps $\{w_1, w_2, \ldots, w_N\}$ in the IFS code. That is, the $6 \times N$ numbers in the affine maps specify the geometry of the underlying model that in turn determine the geometry of associated images. The measure μ is governed by the probabilities $\{p_1, p_2, \ldots, p_N\}$ in the IFS code. It is this measure which provides the rendering information for images.

The underlying model (A, μ) may be thought of as a subset of the two-dimensional space, whose geometry and texture (fixed by the measure) are defined at the finest imaginable resolution. The way in which it defines images, via projection through viewing windows onto pixels, is described in the next section. The algorithm for the computation of these images is given in § 2.4.

§2.3 How Images are Defined from the Underlying Model

Let (A, μ) be the underlying model associated with an IFS code. Let a viewing window, V, be defined by

$$V = \{ (X, Y) : a \leq X \leq b , c \leq Y \leq d \}.$$

It is assumed that $V \cap A$ is not empty and has positive measure, namely $\mu(V) > 0$. Let a viewing resolution be specified by partitioning V into a grid of $L \times M$ rectangles as follows. The interval $[a, b)$ is divided into L subintervals $[X_{l-1}, X_l)$ for $l = 1, 2, \ldots, L$ where

$$X_l = a + (b-a) \cdot l / L.$$

Similarly $[c, d)$ is divided into M subintervals $[Y_{m-1}, Y_m)$ for $m = 1, 2, \ldots, M$ where

$$Y_m = c + (d-c) \cdot m / M.$$

Let $V_{l,m}$ denote the rectangle

$$V_{l,m} = \{(X, Y) : X_{l-1} \leq X < X_l , \quad Y_{m-1} \leq Y < Y_m \}.$$

Then the *discretized model* associated with V at resolution $L \times M$ is denoted by $I (A, \mu, V, L, M)$. It consists of all those rectangles $V_{l,m}$ such that $\mu (V_{l,m}) \neq 0$, (that is, all those rectangles upon which there resides a positive mass of sand).

The discretized model $I (A, \mu, V, L, M)$ is rendered by assigning an RGB index to each of its rectangles $V_{l,m}$. To achieve this color assignment, one specifies a color map f which associates integer color indices with real numbers in $[0,1]$. Let *num-cols* be the number of different colors which are to be used. One might choose for example eight greytones on an RGB system; then $num\text{-}cols = 8$ and color index i is associated with $12.5 \cdot i$ % Red, $12.5 \cdot i$ % Green, and $12.5 \cdot i$ % Blue, for $i = 0, 1, 2, \ldots, 7$. The interval $[0,1]$ is broken up into subintervals defined by real numbers C_i that satisfy

$$0 = C_0 < C_1 < C_2 < \ldots < C_{num\text{-}cols} = 1.$$

The color map is defined by

$$f(x) = \begin{cases} i, \text{ if } C_{i-1} \leq x < C_i, \text{ for } i = 0, 1, 2, \ldots, num\text{-}cols-1; \\ \\ num\text{-}cols-1, \text{ if } x = 1. \end{cases}$$

$I (A, \mu, V, L, M)$ is rendered by assigning color index $f(\mu(V_{l,m})/\mu(V))$ to the rectangle $V_{l,m}$.

In summary, the underlying model is converted to an image, corresponding to a viewing window V and resolution $L \times M$, by discretizing at resolution $L \times M$ the part of the attractor which lies within the viewing window. The rendering values for this discretization are determined by the relative measure $\mu(V_{l,m})/\mu(V)$, (which corresponds to the proportion of sand which lies upon the pixel).

§ 2.4 The Measure Rendering Algorithm

The Measure Rendering Algorithm starts from an IFS code $\{ w_n, p_n : n = 1, 2, \ldots, N \}$ together with a specified viewing window V and resolution $L \times M$. It computes the associated IFS image, as defined in the previous section. In effect a random walk in $\mathbb{R}^2$ is generated from the IFS code, and the measures $\mu(V_{l,m})$ for the pixels are obtained from the frequencies with which the different rectangles $V_{l,m}$ are visited. A theorem by Elton [Elto 86] guarantees that the algorithm always produces the correct result.

An initial point $(x_0, y_0) \in \mathbb{R}^2$ needs to be fixed. For simplicity assume that the affine transformation $w_1 (\underline{x}) = A_1 \underline{x} + \underline{b}_1$ is a contraction. Then, (x_0, y_0) is obtained by solving the following linear system for the fixed point of w_1:

$$\begin{bmatrix} x_0 \\ y_0 \end{bmatrix} - A_1 \begin{bmatrix} x_0 \\ y_0 \end{bmatrix} = \begin{bmatrix} b_{11} \\ b_{12} \end{bmatrix}$$

An $L \times M$ array I of integers is associated with the discretized window. A total number of iterations, *num-its*, large compared to $L \times M$, also needs to be specified. The $L \times M$ array I is initialized to zero.

The random walk part of the algorithm now proceeds as follows

```
for n = 0 to num_its
    begin
        rand = a random number in [0,1];
        total = p₁;  k = 1;
        while ( total < rand )
            begin
                k = k + 1 ;
                total = total + p_k;
            end;
```

$$\begin{bmatrix} x_{n+1} \\ y_{n+1} \end{bmatrix} = w_k \begin{bmatrix} x_n \\ y_n \end{bmatrix} ;$$

```
        n1 = int ( x_{n+1} ) ;
        n2 = int ( y_{n+1} ) ;
        I [n1][n2] = I [n1][n2] + 1;
    end.
```

Finally the elements of the array I are normalized by dividing by the maximum entry in the array, J. Colors are then assigned to the array according to

$$I[n1][n2] = f (I[n1][n2] / J) .$$

Provided that *num-its* is sufficiently large (see examples in § 5), the ergodic theorem of Elton ensures that the rendering values $I[n1][n2]$, assigned to the pixels, stabilize to the unique values defined in §2.3. It is this algorithm which is used to calculate all of the images given with this paper.

3. Determination of IFS Codes

In an IFS code $\{w_n, p_n : n = 1, 2, ..., N \}$, the w_n's determine the geometry of the underlying model, i.e. the structure of the attractor A, while the p_n's provide rendering information through the intermediary of the measure μ. Here we describe an interactive two-dimensional geometric modeling algorithm for determining the w_n's that correspond to a desired model. The algorithm has its mathematical basis in the Collage Theorem [Barn 85b].

The algorithm starts from a target image T which lies within a viewing window V, here taken to be $[0,1] \times [0,1]$. T may be either a digitized image (for example a white leaf on a black background) or a polygonal approximation (for example a polygonized leaf boundary). T is rendered on the graphics

workstation monitor. An affine transformation $w_1(\underline{x}) = A^1\underline{x} + b^1$ is introduced, with coefficients initialized at $a_{11}^1 = a_{22}^1 = 0.25$, $a_{12}^1 = a_{21}^1 = b_2^1 = 0$ (the superscripts correspond to the indexes of the transformations). The image $w_1(T)$ is displayed on the monitor in a different color from T. $w_1(T)$ is a quarter-sized copy of T, centered closer to the point $(0, 0)$. The user now interactively adjusts the $a_{i,j}^1$'s by specifying changes with a mouse or some other interaction technique, so that the image $w_1(T)$ is variously translated, rotated, and sheared on the screen. The goal of the user is to transform $w_1(T)$ so that it lies over part of T. It is important that the dimensions of $w_1(T)$ are smaller than those of T, to ensure that w_1 is a contraction. Once $w_1(T)$ is suitably positioned, it is fixed, and a new subcopy of the target, $w_2(T)$, is introduced. w_2 is interactively adjusted until $w_2(T)$ covers a subset of those pixels in T which are not in $w_1(T)$. Overlap between $w_1(T)$ and $w_2(T)$ is allowed, but in general it should be made as small as possible.

In this way the user determines a set of contractive affine transformations $\{w_1, w_2, ..., w_N\}$ with this property: the original target T and the set

$$\tilde{T} = \bigcup_{n=1}^{N} w_n (T)$$

are visually close, while N is as small as possible. $w_n(T)$ is called the nth *tile* of the collage. The mathematical indicator of the closeness of T and $\tilde{T}$ is the Hausdorff distance $h(T, \tilde{T})$ defined below; and by "visually close" we really mean "$h(T, \tilde{T})$ is small". The maps $\{w_1, w_2, ..., w_N\}$ thus determined are stored. The Collage Theorem, stated below, then assures us that the attractor A of any IFS code $\{w_n, p_n : n = 1, 2, ..., N \}$, which uses these maps, will also be "visually close" to T. Moreover if $T = \tilde{T}$, that is, if $h(T, \tilde{T}) = 0$, then $A = T$. The algorithm produces IFS codes such that the geometry of the underlying model resembles that of the target.

The algorithm is illustrated in Figure 1 which shows a polygonal leaf target T at the upper and lower left. In each case T has been approximately covered by four affine transformations of itself. The task has been poorly carried out in the lower image and well done in the upper image. The corresponding attractors are shown on the right hand side : the upper one is much closer to the geometry of the target because the collage is better. The process is also illustrated in Figure 2 which shows a collage of a square. The resulting coefficients are displayed in Table 1.

The precise statements which govern the above algorithm are as follows. The *Hausdorff distance* $h(A, B)$ between two closed bounded subsets A and B of $\mathbf{R}^2$ is defined as:

$$h\,(\,A\,,\,B\,)\,=\,\mathrm{Max}\,\left\{\,\underset{\underline{x}\,\varepsilon\,A}{\mathrm{Max}}\ \underset{\underline{y}\,\varepsilon\,B}{\mathrm{Min}}\,\|\underline{x}-\underline{y}\|\,;\ \underset{\underline{y}\,\varepsilon\,B}{\mathrm{Max}}\ \underset{\underline{x}\,\varepsilon\,A}{\mathrm{Min}}\,\|\underline{x}-\underline{y}\|\,\right\}$$

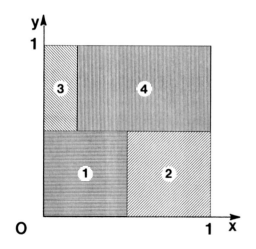

Figure 1 Illustrations of the Collage Algorithm. The upper collage is good, so the corresponding attractor, shown upper right resembles the leaf target.

Figure 2 Application of the Collage Algorithm applied to a classical square. The resulting IFS code is shown in Table 1.

W	a	b	c	d	e	f	p
1	0.5	0	0	0.5	0	0	0.25
2	0.5	0	0	0.5	0.5	0	0.25
3	0.2	0	0	0.5	0	0.5	0.10
4	0.8	0	0	0.5	0.2	0.5	0.40

Table 1 IFS code for a Square.

Figure 3 shows a portion of $[0,1]\times[0,1]$ painted by the Hausdorff distance between different points and a fern-like image F. The point $\underline{x}$ is colored according to the value of $\underset{\underline{y}\,\varepsilon\,F}{\mathrm{Min}}\,\|\,\underline{x}\,-\,\underline{y}\,\|$.

__Collage Theorem__ [Barn 85b] *Let* $\{w_n,\,p_n:n=1,\,2,\,...,\,N\,\}$ *be an IFS code of contractive affine maps. Let* $s<1$ *denote the largest Lipshitz constant for the maps. Let* $\epsilon>0$ *be any positive number. Let* T *be a given closed bounded subset of* $\mathbb{R}^2$*, and suppose the* w_n*'s have been chosen so that*

$$h\,(T,\,\underset{n=1}{\overset{N}{\cup}}\,w_n(T))\,<\,\epsilon,$$

then

$$h\,(T,\,A)\,<\,\frac{\epsilon}{(1-s)}.$$

where A *denotes the attractor of the IFS.*

4. From Forests to Faces

At this point, we know how to obtain ifs codes for simple two-dimensional objects and how to recreate them as textured sets from the codes. We will now see how this encoding/decoding scheme is an extremely powerful tool for the modeling of any two-dimensional color image.

§ 4.1 Clouds and Mist

Figure 5 shows the image of a cloud which is the attractor of a two-dimensional IFS code made of five affine transformations obtained by the Collage algorithm. The probabilities p_n were chosen proportional to the areas of the corresponding tiles $w_n(T)$. A color map $f\,(x)$ which assigns a linear grey-scale, from black to white, to the interval $0\leq x\leq1$ was used.

An IFS model can provide visually meaningful images on several different scales. This is illustrated in Figures 12 and 13 where we show a zoom on an IFS encoded image. These images are discussed in § 5.2. The number of iterations *num_its* must be increased with magnification to keep the number of points landing within the viewing window constant. This requirement ensures the consistency of the textures in an image throughout the magnification process. An efficient texture-preserving magnification algorithm has been developed [Reut 87].

There are three classes of free parameters that can be adjusted to modify a texture. The first class consists of the set of probabilities, $\{p_n:\text{for }n{=}1,\,2,\,...,\,N\,\}$. Typically, each probability p_n is initially assigned a value that is proportional to the relative area of the *tile* $w_n(T)$. The result is a uniform distribution of the measure μ. If a probability p_j is increased then $\mu(w_j(T))$

increases as well.

Another class of free parameters is obtained by introducing redundant maps into the collage of the target set. For example, an extra map may be added to an already satisfactory collage of a cloud. The coefficients and probability associated with this map provide a control which does not effect the geometry of the image. This control is convenient for animation where the position of the extra tile in the collage can be moved in time. If the movement of the tile is smooth, then the resulting attractors show smooth changes in the measure rendering.

The third class of free parameters is provided by the color assignment function. This may be specified by a piecewise linear function, whose coefficients are adjusted to change the rendering of the image. Smooth interpolations from one color to another are often used in the specification of the color look-up table. By mapping interpolated colors to incremental changes in the measure, images appear smoothly shaded.

Figures 6 and 7 are examples of simple scenes representing clouds and mist over a lake. The IFS codes for Figure 7 were obtained by slightly altering those in Figure 6. However the process is very different from keyframe animation. One moves smoothly from Figure 6 to Figure 7, by combining changes to the free parameters described above. This process is also illustrated in Figure 8.

§ 4.2 Basics of image modeling

An IFS code can be viewed as a *dynamical entity* that can be interactively modified to give rise to a whole class of related images. Suppose that $\{w_n, p_n : n = 1, 2, ..., N\}$ is an IFS code with associated attractor A, and invariant measure μ, and that t is an invertible transformation from $\mathbf{R}^2$ to $\mathbf{R}^2$. For example, t might be a translation, a rotation, a contraction, or a shear. The IFS code for the mapping of A under t is simply $\{t \circ w_n \circ f^1, p_n : n = 1, 2, ..., N\}$. In particular, this means that if an IFS code for a leaf is available in a library of codes, images of the same leaf from any viewpoint or any distorted copy of that leaf, can be readily encoded, decoded and displayed.

Figures 9, 11, 12, 13, and 14 were encoded from color photographs taken from *National Geographic*. Segmentation according to color was performed on the originals to define textured pieces. IFS codes for these components were obtained via the Collage algorithm. The Measure Rendering algorithm was then applied to those codes to synthesize the images. The IFS data base contained less than 180 maps for the Monterey seascape, and less than 160 maps for the Andes Indian girl.

5. Hierarchical structures

§5.1 Patterns in Nature

The modeling of natural scenes is a difficult issue in computer graphics. Photographs of natural scenes contain redundant information in the form of subtle patterns and variations. The analysis of these patterns is the focus of ongoing research in computer graphics.

Two characteristic features of natural scenes have already become clear from this research. They are (i) the presence of complex geometrical structure at all scales of observation, and (ii) the hierarchical layout of primitive objects. (i) Natural boundaries and textures are not smoothed out under magnification; they preserve some degree of ruggedness. (ii) Natural scenes are organized in hierarchical structures: A forest is made of trees, that consist of branches along trunks. On these branches, pine needles or leaves cluster into bundles. Each bundle is a group of individual entities. These two important intuitive aspects can be integrated into IFS modeling.

§5.2 Condensation Sets and Hierarchical IFS

Here we describe some aspects of IFS with condensation which can be used for hierarchical structure rendering. A detailed treatment can be found in [Barn 88].

As in the previous sections, the underlying metric space is the Euclidean plane $\mathbf{R}^2$. An *IFS with condensation* is denoted by $\{w_0, w_1, w_2, ..., w_N\}$. It consists of an IFS $\{w_1, w_2, w_3, ..., w_N\}$, together a set-valued map w_0. This set-valued map is defined by a closed bounded subset C in $\mathbf{R}^2$ according to

$$w_0(x) = C \text{ for all } x \in \mathbf{R}^2.$$

C is called the *condensation set C* of the IFS. It can be shown that its attractor A_C is uniquely defined by the equation :

$$A_C = \bigcup_{n=0}^{N} w_n(A_C)$$

If C is the empty set this reduces to the usual situation. If C is nonempty then it can be shown that

$$A_C = \text{closure of } \{C \cup \bigcup_{n=1}^{\infty} \mathbf{W}^{\circ n}(C)\}$$

where $\mathbf{W}(C)$ denotes the union of the images of the set C under the N affine transformations $w_1, w_2, w_3, ..., w_N$. That is

$$\mathbf{W}(C) = \bigcup_{n=1}^{N} w_n(C).$$

Note that w_0 is not an affine transformation, but, as a set map, it is a contraction.

An IFS with condensation may be used to provide a global model of a *structured set* of geometric objects such as a field of flowers, a tree, an orchard or a forest. This is feasible because the Collage Theorem can be extended to the case of an IFS with condensation. When implemented in software this provides the user with a means for finding a collection of contractive affine transformations $\{w_1, w_2, w_3, \ldots, w_N\}$ along with a condensation set C such that so that the attractor of the associated IFS with condensation is visually "close to" a given target set T. A formal statement of the theorem is given below:

Collage with Condensation [Barn 88] *Let $\{w_n: n = 1, 2, \ldots, N\}$ be an IFS code of contractive affine maps. Let C be a closed bounded subset of $\mathbb{R}^2$. Let w_0 denote the set transformation associated with C, defined by $w_0(B) = C$ for all nonempty closed bounded subsets $B \subset \mathbb{R}^2$. Let $s < 1$ be the largest Lipshitz constant for the maps. Let $\epsilon > 0$ be any positive number. Let T be a given nonempty closed bounded subset of $\mathbb{R}^2$, and suppose the w_n's have been chosen so that*

$$h\left(T, \bigcup_{n=0}^{N} w_n(T)\right) < \epsilon.$$

Then

$$h(T, A_C) < \frac{\epsilon}{(1-s)}$$

where A_C denotes the attractor of $\{w_n: n = 0, 1, 2, \ldots, N\}$.

In Figure 4, we illustrate the application of the Condensation Collage Theorem. On the left-hand side top and bottom we show a shaded target image on which we have overlayed in white a condensation collage consisting in each case of a "trunk" condensation set and two affine transforms of the target. In each case the collage determines a different IFS with condensation. On the right-hand side of each image we show the attractor of this associated IFS. The theorem tells us that the closer the "white image" (i.e. the union of the condensation set together with the affine transformed copies of the target) is to the shaded image (i.e. the target), the closer the attractor of the associated IFS "with condensation" will be to the shaded image. Closeness is measured objectively with the Hausdorff distance. The top collage is better than the bottom collage, and this is echoed in the improved subjective match of the top right attractor to the original tree image.

To obtain a *hierarchical* IFS we choose C to be the attractor of an IFS, say $\{v_m: m = 1, 2, \ldots, M\}$. In this way the ordered pair of IFS $(\{v_m\}, \{w_n\})$ defines a unique subset of $\mathbb{R}^2$. Here again we can choose $\{v_n\}$ to be an IFS with condensation and the process can be repeated to obtain an ordered triple of IFS, and so on. This allows us to build up more and more complicated models, while maintaining the smooth dependence of images on the parameters in the IFS.

Two primitives, a leaf and a flower, in Figure 10 were used as condensation sets in the picture *Sunflower Field*, Figure 11. Here we see the hierarchical structure: the leaf is itself the attractor of an IFS; and the flower is an overlay of four IFS attractors. In the pictures *Sunflower Field* and *Black Forest*, shown in Figures 11 and 12, the primitives were displayed from back to front. The data bases for the *Sunflower Field* and *Black Forest* contain less than 100 and 120 maps respectively. A zoom on the *Black Forest* is shown in Figure 13.

6. Conclusion

In this paper we have presented some theorems that are the basis of methods for encoding images using IFS theorem. The methods described apply to all types of images, and are not restricted to those which display typical "fractal" features.

The IFS approach is very different from the random fractal geometry approach. The latter consists of random recursive refinement algorithms to produce terrain models, stochastic procedures used to produce clouds and textures, and random branching and growth models for plants. In all these cases the final product depends upon the precise random number sequence generated during computation. The Measure Rendering algorithm presented in this paper has the feature that small visual changes in the parameter values of the input IFS code yield only small changes in the resultant image. This is important for system independence, interactive usage and animation. Furthermore, images vary consistently with respect to changes of viewing window and resolution. Images can be generated from the same data base to a very high resolution or equivalently viewed within a small window, without reducing to blocks of solid color.

The are several reasons for the continuing development of IFS algorithms in computer graphics. First, IFS codes are powerful data amplification primitives: very small data bases are used to generate complex images. Second, IFS algorithms are such that they can be implemented in a highly parallel manner. This means that images could be generated and manipulated in real time.

References

[Ambu 86] Amburn, P., Grant, E., Whitted, T., "Managing Geometric Complexity with Enhanced Procedural Methods," *Computer Graphics*, 20 (4) (August 1986).

[Barn 85a] Barnsley, M. F. and Demko, S., "Iterated Function Systems and the Global Construction of Fractals," *The Proceedings of the Royal Society of London* A399, pp. 243-275 (1985).

[Barn 85b] Barnsley, M. F., Ervin, V., Hardin, D. and Lancaster, J., "Solution of an Inverse Problem for Fractals and Other Sets," *Proceedings of the National Academy of Science*, Vol. 83 (April 1985).

[Barn 86a] Barnsley, M. F., "Fractal Functions and Interpolation," *Constructive Approximation*, 2, pp. 303-329 (1986).

[Barn 86b] Barnsley, M. F., Elton, J., "A New Class of Markov Processes for Image Encoding, " to appear in the *Journal of Applied Probability* (1986).

[Barn 87] Barnsley, M. F., (SIGGRAPH tutorial) "Fractal Modelling of Real World Images," to appear in *The Science of Fractals*, Springer-Verlag, Berlin (1988).

[Barn 88] Barnsley, M. F., *Fractals Everywhere*, to appear, Academic Press (1988).

[Bedf 86] Bedford, T. J., "Dimension and Dynamics for Fractal Recurrent Sets," *Journal of the London Mathematical Society* 2 (33), pp. 89-100 (1986).

[Demk 85] Demko, S., Hodges, L., and Naylor, B., "Construction of Fractal Objects with Iterated Function Systems," *Computer Graphics* 19 (3), pp. 271-278 (July 1985). SIGGRAPH '85 Proceedings.

[Diac 86] Diaconis, P., Shahshahani, M., "Products of Random Matrices and Computer Image Generation," *Contemporary Mathamatics*, 50, pp. 173-182 (1986).

[Elto 86] Elton, J., "An Ergodic Theorem for Iterated Maps," To appear in the *Journal of Ergodic Theory and Dynamical Systems* (1986).

[Four 82] Fournier, A., Fussell, D., Carpenter, L., "Computer Rendering of Stochastic Models," *Communications of the ACM* 25 (6) (June 1982).

[Hata 85] Hata, M. "On the Structure of Self-Similar Sets," *Japan Journal of Applied Mathematics*, 2 (2), pp. 381-414 (Dec. 1985).

[Hutc 81] Hutchinson, J., "Fractals and Self-similarity," *Indiana University Journal of Mathematics*, 30, pp. 713-747 (1981).

[Kawa 82] Kawaguchi, Y., "A Morphological Study of the Form of Nature," *Computer Graphics*, 16 (3), (July 1982). SIGGRAPH '82 Proceedings.

[Mand 82] Mandelbrot, B., *The Fractal Geometry of Nature*, W. H. Freeman and Co., San Francisco (1982).

[Mill 86] Miller, G. S. P., "The Definition and Rendering of Terrain Maps," *Computer Graphics*, 20 (4), (August 1986). SIGGRAPH '86 Proceedings.

[Oppe 86] Oppenheimer, P. E., "Real Time Design and Animation of Fractal Plants and Trees," *Computer Graphics*, 20 (4), (August 1986).

[Reut 87] Reuter, L., "Rendering and Magnification of Fractals using Iterated Function Systems", Ph. D. Thesis, Georgia Institute of Technology, Dec 1987.

[Smit 84] Smith, A. R., "Plants, Fractals, and Formal Languages," *Computer Graphics* 18 (3), pp. 1-10 (July 1984). SIGGRAPH '84 Proceedings.

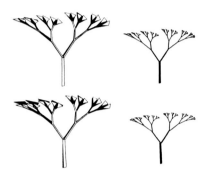

Figure 4   Illustration of the Condensation Collage Theorem.

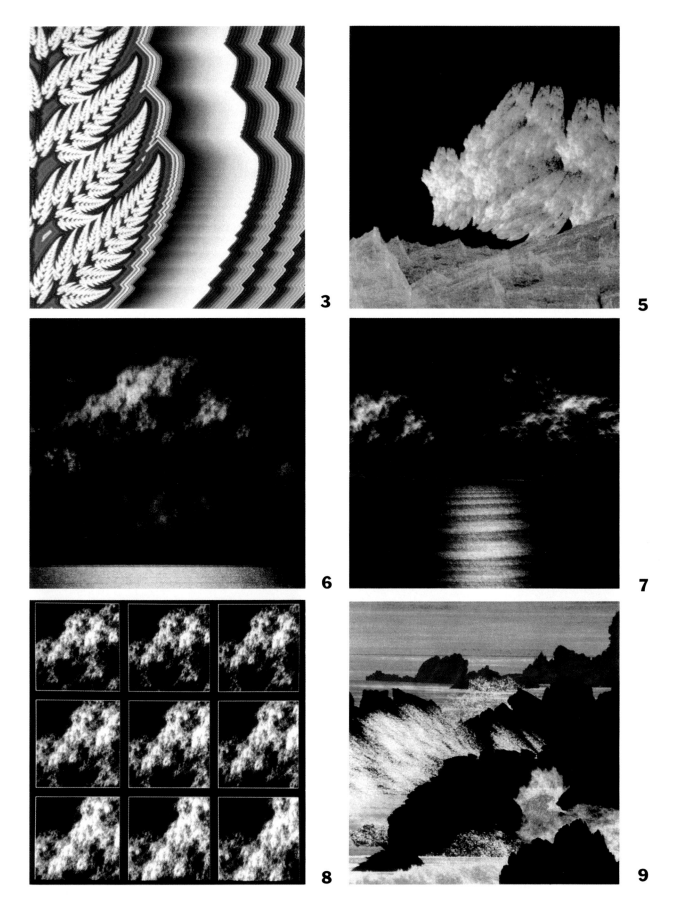

10

11

12

13

14

Figure 3 Fern with the space painted by Hausdorff distance.

Figure 5 Image of a cloud.

Figure 6 Simple scene representing clouds and mist over a lake.

Figure 7 IFS codes for Figure 5 have been modified.

Figure 8 Linear interpolation from one cloud to another.

Figure 9 *Monterey Coast.*

Figure 10 Primitives used in *Sunflower Field.*

Figure 11 *Sunflower Field.*

Figure 12 *Black Forest.*

Figure 13 Zoom on *Black Forest* .

Figure 14 *Bolivian Girl.*

Developmental Models of Herbaceous Plants
for Computer Imagery Purposes

Przemyslaw Prusinkiewicz[†], *Aristid Lindenmayer* [‡] and *James Hanan*[†]

† Department of Computer Science
University of Regina
Regina, Saskatchewan, Canada S4S 0A2

‡ Theoretical Biology Group
University of Utrecht
Padualaan 8, 3584 CH Utrecht, The Netherlands

ABSTRACT

In this paper we present a method for modeling herbaceous plants, suitable for generating realistic plant images and animating developmental processes. The idea is to achieve realism by simulating mechanisms which control plant growth in nature. The developmental approach to the modeling of plant architecture is extended to the modeling of leaves and flowers. The method is expressed using the formalism of L-systems.

CR Categories and Subject Descriptors: F.4.2 [**Mathematical Logic and Formal Languages**]: Grammars and Other Rewriting Systems: *Parallel rewriting systems.* I.3.5 [**Computer Graphics**]: Computational Geometry and Object Modeling: *Curve, surface, solid and object representation.* I.3.7 [**Computer Graphics**]: Three-Dimensional Graphics and Realism. J.3 [**Life and Medical Sciences**]: *Biology.*

Keywords: realistic image synthesis, L-system, parallel graph grammar, turtle geometry, developmental morphology and physiology of plants, scientific visualization.

1. INTRODUCTION.

In recent years, the modeling of plants has received considerable attention. The problem was approached from two directions. Kawaguchi [21], Aono and Kunii [2], Reeves and Blau [36], Bloomenthal [7] and Oppenheimer [31] defined branching structures primarily in geometrical terms, such as the lengths of branches and branching angles. Smith [39, 40], Prusinkiewicz [33, 34], Beyer and Friedel [6] and Eyrolles [10] concentrated on the specification of plant topology. In all cases, plants were defined by a small number of rules applied repetitively to produce complex structures. Some approaches made it possible to create forms which looked "younger" or "older", and even produce an impression of plant growth, as witnessed in the films of Aono and Kunii [3] and Smith [41]. However, the simulation of development was not a focal point of any of these methods.

We present a plant modeling method in which the simulation of development is the key to realism. Thus, in order to model a particular form, we attempt to capture the essence of the *developmental process* which leads to this form. The view that growth and form are interrelated has a long tradition in biology. D'Arcy Thompson [44] traces its origins to the late seventeenth century, and comments:

> The rate of growth deserves to be studied as a necessary preliminary to the theoretical study of form, and organic form itself is found, mathematically speaking, to be a function of time... We might call the form of an organism an *event in space-time*, and not merely a *configuration in space*.

This concept is echoed by Hallé, Oldeman and Tomlinson [16]:

> The idea of the form implicitly contains also the history of such a form.

The developmental approach to plant modeling has two distinctive features:

- **Emphasis on the space-time relation between plant parts.** In many plants, various developmental stages can be observed at the same time. For example, some flowers may still be in the bud stage, others may be fully developed, and still others may have been transformed into fruits. If the developmental technique is consistently used down to the level of individual organs, such *phase effects* are reproduced in a natural way.

- **Inherent capability of growth simulation.** The mathematical model can be used to generate biologically correct images of plants of different ages and to provide animated growth sequences.

We reenact plant development by simulating natural control mechanisms. Emphasis is put on the modeling and generation of growth sequences of *herbaceous* or non-woody plants, since the internal control mechanisms play a predominant role in their development. In contrast, the form of woody plants is determined to a large extent by the environment, competition between trees and tree branches, and accidents [47], which are unrelated to the mechanisms considered in this paper.

We express control mechanisms and simulate developmental processes using the formalism of L-systems [24]. In this sense, our approach to the modeling of plants has its origin in biological studies expressed in terms of L-systems [11-14, 20, 28]. Other approaches using L-systems for modeling purposes are also possible. For example, Hogeweg and Hesper [19] and Smith [40] searched a particular class of context-sensitive L-systems and selected those which generated interesting shapes.

2. BRANCHING STRUCTURES AND L-SYSTEMS.

2.1. Graph-theoretical and botanical trees.

In the context of plant modeling, the term "tree" must be carefully defined to avoid ambiguity. To this end, we introduce the notion of an axial tree (Fig. 1) which complements the graph-theoretic notion of a rooted tree [32] with the botanically motivated notion of branch axis.

A *rooted tree* has edges which are labeled and directed, and form paths from a distinguished node called the *root* or the *base* to the *terminal nodes*. In the biological context, these edges are referred to as *branch segments*. A segment followed by at least one more segment in some path is called an *internode*. A terminal segment (with no following edges) is called an *apex*.

An *axial tree* is a special type of rooted tree. At each of its nodes we distinguish at most one outgoing *straight* segment. All remaining edges are called *lateral* or *side* segments. Within an axial tree, a sequence of segments is called an *axis* if: (a) the first segment in the sequence originates at the root of the tree or as a lateral segment at some node, (b) each subsequent segment is a straight segment, and (c) the last segment is not followed by any straight segment in the tree. Together with all its descendants, an axis constitutes a *branch*. A branch is itself an axial tree.

Axes and branches are ordered. The axis originating at the root of the entire plant has order zero. An axis originating as a lateral segment of an *n*-order parent axis has order *n*+1. The order of a branch is equal to the order of its lowest-order or *main* axis. The terminal node of this axis is called the branch *top*.

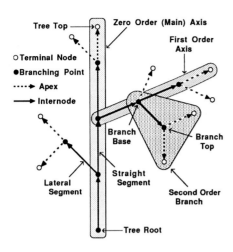

Figure 1. An axial tree.

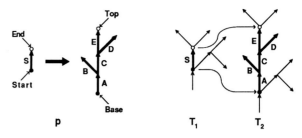

Figure 2. A tree production p and its application to the edge S in a tree T_1.

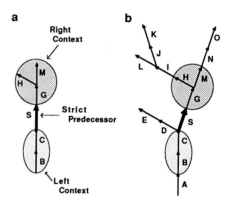

Figure 3. The predecessor of a context-sensitive production (a) matches the edge S in a tree T (b).

Axial trees are purely topological objects. The geometric connotation of such terms as straight segment, lateral segment and axis should be viewed at this point as an intuitive link between the graph-theoretic formalism and real plant structures.

2.2. Definition of tree L-systems.

An essential aspect of plant development is the process in which some segments (usually the apices) are transformed into more complex structures. We model this process by a graph-rewriting mechanism which operates on axial trees. From the viewpoint of graph grammar theory, this is a special case of edge rewriting [15]. A rewriting rule, or *tree production*, replaces an edge, specified as the production *predecessor*, by an axial tree called the *successor*, in such a way that the starting node of the predecessor is identified with the successor's base and the ending node is identified with the successor's top (Fig. 2).

In the case of *context-free* rewriting the label of the replaced edge determines the production to be applied. In contrast, a *context-sensitive* production requires context, or the neighbour edges of the replaced edge, to be tested as well. Thus, a predecessor of a context-sensitive production p consists of three components: a path l called the *left context*, an edge S called the *strict predecessor*, and an axial tree r called the *right context* (Fig. 3). The asymmetry between the left context and the right context reflects the fact that there is only one path from the root of a tree to a given edge, while there can be many paths from this edge to various terminal nodes. Production p matches a given occurrence of the edge S in a tree T if l is a path in T terminating at the starting node of S, and r is a subtree of T originating at the ending node of S. The production can then be applied by replacing S with the axial tree specified as the production successor.

A rewriting system can operate either in a sequential or in a parallel manner. The former type of rewriting is found in Chomsky grammars. However, parallel rewriting is more appropriate for the modeling of biological development, since development takes place concurrently in all parts of the organism.

Parallel rewriting systems are commonly referred to as L-systems. Specifically, a *tree L-system G* is specified by three components: a set of edge labels called the *alphabet* and denoted by V, an axial tree ω with labels from V called the *axiom*, and a set of *tree productions P*. If for any edge label A and any context (l, r) there exists exactly one applicable production in P, the L-system is *deterministic*; otherwise it is *nondeterministic*. Nondeterministic L-systems provide a convenient tool for representing general features of a developmental process without considering mechanisms which control production selection (Section 4.3).

Given an L-system G, an axial tree T_2 is *directly derived* from (or *generated* by) a tree T_1, $T_1 \Rightarrow T_2$, if T_2 is obtained from T_1 by **simultaneously** replacing each edge in T_1 by its successor according to the production set P. A tree T is generated by an L-system G in a *derivation of length n* if there exists a *developmental sequence* of trees $T_0, T_1, \ldots, T_n$ such that $T_0 = \omega$, $T_n = T$ and $T_0 \Rightarrow T_1 \Rightarrow \cdots \Rightarrow T_n$ (see Section 2.4 for examples).

2.3. Representation of tree L-systems.

The definition of a tree L-system does not specify the data structure for representing axial trees. One possibility is to use a list representation with a tree topology. A different representation makes use of *bracketed strings* as introduced by Lindenmayer [24]. In this case, a tree with edge labels from alphabet V is represented by a string over alphabet $V \cup \{[,]\}$, where the bracket symbols [and] enclose branches. For example, the tree shown in Fig. 3b is represented by the bracketed string: .

$$ABC[DE][SG[HI[JK]L]MNO] \qquad (*)$$

A context-free production is denoted $A \rightarrow w$, where A belongs to V and w is a (possibly empty) bracketed string over V. A derivation step from string $x = a_1 a_2 \cdots a_n$ to string $y = w_1 w_2 \cdots w_n$ is performed by concatenating terms $w_1, w_2, \ldots, w_n$ obtained from productions with predecessors $a_1, a_2, \ldots, a_n$. The brackets are rewritten into themselves. In the case of a context-sensitive production, symbols < and > separate the strict predecessor from the left and right context, respectively. Since the string representation of axial trees does not preserve segment neighbourhood, the context matching procedure must skip over branches or branch portions when necessary. For example, a production with the predecessor $BC < S > G[H]M$ can be applied to symbol S in the string (*) (compare with Fig. 3).

2.4. L-systems and control mechanisms in plants.

The mechanisms which control plant development in nature can be divided into two classes, called *lineage* and *interactive* mechanisms. The term *lineage* refers to the transfer of genetic information from an ancestor cell to its descendants. *Interaction* is a mechanism in which information is exchanged between neighbouring cells (for example, in the form of nutrients or hormones). Within the formalism of L-systems, lineage mechanisms are represented by context-free productions, while interactive mechanisms correspond to context-sensitive productions. Two simple L-systems which simulate development controlled by lineage mechanisms are given below.

	L-system (a)		**L-system (b)**
ω:	S	ω:	A
p:	$S \rightarrow S[S]S[S]S$	p_1:	$A \rightarrow S[A]S[A]A$
		p_2:	$S \rightarrow SS$

Figure 4. Structures which branch everywhere (left)
and branching structures with a subapical growth pattern (right).

In case (**a**) all segments S branch. Only primitive organisms (for example, some bacteria and algae) develop this way. Herbaceous plants employ *subapical* growth mechanisms, in which new branches are created exclusively by apices. L-system (**b**) provides a simple example of such development. Production p_1 simulates the creation of new branches by apices A. Production p_2 simulates the gradual elongation of internodes, represented by sequences of symbols S. The resulting structures are shown in Fig. 4.

In the simulation of interaction between cells, the left context represents control signals which propagate *acropetally*, i.e. from the root or the basal leaves towards the apices of the modeled plant, while the right context represents signals which propagate *basipetally*, i.e. from the apices towards the root. The following L-systems simulate signal propagation in non-growing branching structures as illustrated in Fig. 5.

L-system (c)	L-system (d)
ω: $J[I]I[I]I[I]I$	ω: $I[I]I[I]I[I]J$
p: $J < I \rightarrow J$	p: $I > J \rightarrow J$

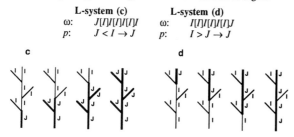

Figure 5. Acropetal (c) and basipetal (d) signal propagation.

The symbol J represents an internode already reached by the signal, while I represents an internode which has not yet been reached. In order to keep the specification of these (and subsequent) L-systems short, the following two conventions are observed: (1) if no production applies to a given symbol, this symbol is replaced by itself, and (2) if a context-free production and a context-sensitive production both apply to a given symbol, the context-sensitive production is chosen.

3. GEOMETRICAL INTERPRETATION OF AXIAL TREES.

The L-systems (**a**)-(**d**) considered above specify branching structures on a topological level. For the purpose of image synthesis, it is also necessary to specify geometric and graphical aspects of the modeled objects. Some previous approaches to the geometrical interpretation of L-systems are presented in [5, 17, 19]. Our approach was originally introduced to generate geometric patterns and fractals [43, 33] and was extended to describe three-dimensional plant structures in [34]. The method is as follows. After a string has been generated by an L-system, it is scanned from left to right and the consecutive symbols are interpreted as commands which maneuver a LOGO-like turtle in three dimensions [1]. The turtle is represented by its *state* which consists of turtle *position* and *orientation* in the Cartesian coordinate system, as

well as other attribute values, such as current color and line width. The orientation is defined by three vectors $\vec{H}, \vec{L}, \vec{U}$, indicating the turtle's *heading* and the directions to the *left* and *up*. These vectors have unit length, are perpendicular to each other, and satisfy the equation $\vec{H} \times \vec{L} = \vec{U}$. Rotations of the turtle can then be expressed by the equation $[\ \vec{H}'\ \vec{L}'\ \vec{U}'\ ] = [\ \vec{H}\ \vec{L}\ \vec{U}\ ]\ \mathbf{R}$, where $\mathbf{R}$ is a 3×3 rotation matrix.

Segment symbols such as S, A, I and J in L-systems (**a**)-(**d**) move the turtle forward by a distance d and cause a line to be drawn between the previous and the new position. Seven attribute symbols are used to control turtle orientation given an angle increment δ.

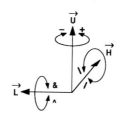

Symbols + and − *turn* the turtle left and right around the vector $\vec{U}$, ^ and & *pitch* the turtle up and down around the vector $\vec{L}$, and / and \ *roll* the turtle left and right around its own axis, the vector $\vec{H}$ (Fig. 6). The symbol | is used to turn the turtle 180° around the vector $\vec{U}$ regardless of the value of δ. Branches are created using a stack; [pushes the current state on the stack, while] pops a state from the stack and makes it the current state of the turtle. No line is drawn in this case, although the position of the turtle usually changes.

Figure 6. Turtle interpretation of geometric attribute symbols.

Figure 7. A bush.

Figure 8. A comparison of branching structures modeled without tropism (left) and with tropism (right).

The list of attribute symbols can be augmented to control color, diameter and length of segments, incorporate predefined surfaces and objects in the model, and perform other functions as required. The extensions related to organ definition are discussed further in Section 6. Symbols without a specified interpretation are ignored by the turtle, which means that they can be used in the derivation process without affecting the interpretation of the resulting string.

Geometric extensions of L-systems (a) and (c) actually used to generate the left-hand structures in Figs. 4 and 5 are given below.

	L-system (a')		L-system (c')
ω:	S	ω:	$J[+I]I[-I]I[+I]I$
p:	$S \to S[-'S]S[+'S]S$	p:	$J < I \to J$

In case (a'), the edge length d is constant, the angle increment $\delta = 27.5°$, and the derivation lengths n are equal to 4 and 5. The attribute symbol ' increments the index to the color table. In case (c'), d is constant, $\delta = 45°$ and $n = 0{-}3$. The symbols + and − are ignored while context matching.

A more complex L-system generating the three-dimensional bush taken from [34] and shown in Fig. 7 is given below.

ω:	$!!a$
p_1:	$a \to [[\&sl!a]/\!/\!/\!/'[\&sl!a]/\!/\!/\!/\!/\!/'[\&sl!a]]$
p_2:	$s \to Sl$
p_3:	$S \to S/\!/\!/\!/\!/s$
p_4:	$l \to ['''\,^\wedge\{-S+S+S-|-S+S+S\}]$

The attribute symbol ! decreases the diameter of segments S. The symbols a, s and l are not interpreted geometrically. The system operates as follows. Production p_1 creates three branches from an apex a. A branch consists of a stem s, a leaf l and an apex a which will subsequently create three new branches. Productions p_2 and p_3 specify the growth process of a stem; in subsequent derivation steps it gets longer by acquiring new segments S and produces new leaves l (in violation of the subapical growth rule, but with an acceptable visual effect in a still picture). Production p_4 describes the leaf as a filled polygon with six edges (see Section 6). More examples of completely specified L-systems which generate two-dimensional figures and three-dimensional objects are given in [33, 34, 35].

A characteristic feature of turtle interpretation is that directions are relative to the current orientation. However, absolute directions play an important role in the development of plants. For example, the axes may bend up towards the source of light, or down due to gravity. We simulate these effects by rotating the turtle slightly in the direction of a predefined *tropism vector* $\vec{T}$ after drawing each segment (Fig. 8). The angle α is calculated using the formula $\alpha = e\,\vec{H} \times \vec{T}$, where e is a parameter capturing axis susceptibility to bending. This heuristic formula has a physical motivation; if $\vec{T}$ is interpreted as a force applied to the endpoint of segment $\vec{H}$ and $\vec{H}$ can rotate around its starting point, the torque is equal to $\vec{H} \times \vec{T}$. A detailed analysis of tree dynamics for simulation purposes is presented in [4].

4. DEVELOPMENTAL MODELS OF PLANT ARCHITECTURE.

In this section we use the formalism of L-systems to present developmental models of herbaceous plants on the topological level. The geometric aspects are discussed in sections 5 and 6. We put particular emphasis on the modeling of compound flowering structures or *inflorescences*. As there is no commonly accepted terminology referring to inflorescence types, we chose to follow the terminology of Müller-Doblies [29], which in turn is based on extensive work by Troll [45]. Our presentation is organized by the control mechanisms which govern inflorescence development.

4.1. Racemes, or the phase beauty of sequential growth.

The simplest possible flowering structures with multiple flowers are those with a single stem on which an indefinite number of flowers are produced sequentially. Inflorescences of this type are called *racemes*. Their development can be described by the following L-system:

ω:	A	
p_1:	$A \to I_0[I_0F_0]A$	
p_2:	$I_i \to I_{i+1}$	$i \geq 0$
p_3:	$F_i \to F_{i+1}$	$i \geq 0$

The symbol A denotes the apex of the main (zero-order) axis, I_i denotes the i-th stage of internode elongation, and F_i is the i-th stage of flower development. The indexed notation, such as $F_i \to F_{i+1}$, stands for a set

of productions $F_0 \to F_1, F_1 \to F_2, F_2 \to F_3, \cdots$. The developmental sequence begins as follows:

$$A$$
$$I_0[I_0F_0]A$$
$$I_1[I_1F_1]I_0[I_0F_0]A$$
$$I_2[I_2F_2]I_1[I_1F_1]I_0[I_0F_0]A$$
$$I_3[I_3F_3]I_2[I_2F_2]I_1[I_1F_1]I_0[I_0F_0]A$$
$$\cdots$$

At each developmental stage, the inflorescence contains a sequence of flowers of different ages. The flowers newly created by the apex are delayed in their development with respect to the older ones situated at the stem base. This effect is illustrated in Fig. 9, to which the following quotation from d'Arcy Thompson [44] applies:

> A flowering spray of lily-of-the-valley exemplifies a growth-gradient, after a simple fashion of its own. Along the stalk the growth-rate falls away; the florets are of descending age, from flower to bud; their graded differences of age lead to an exquisite gradation of size and form; the time-interval between one and another, or the "space-time relation" between them all, gives a peculiar quality - we may call it phase-beauty - to the whole.

A similar phase effect can be observed in other plants. For example, consider the fern-like structure shown in Fig. 10. In this case, nine zero-order branches grow subapically and produce new first-order branches, which also grow subapically and produce leaves. These processes are described by the following L-system:

ω:	$[A][A][A][A][A][A][A][A][A]$	
p_1:	$A \to I_0[B]A$	
p_2:	$B \to I_0[L_0][L_0]B$	
p_3:	$I_i \to I_{i+1}$	$i \geq 0$
p_4:	$L_i \to L_{i+1}$	$i \geq 0$

A and B denote apices of zero-order and first-order axes, $I_0, I_1, I_2, \cdots$ denote the internodes, and $L_0, L_1, L_2, \cdots$ denote the subsequent stages of leaf development.

4.2. Cymose inflorescences, or the use of delays.

In racemes the apex of the main axis produces lateral branches and continues to grow. In contrast, the apex of the main axis in *cymes* turns to a flower shortly after a few lateral branches have been initiated. Their apices turn into flowers as well and second-order branches take over. In time, branches of higher and higher order are produced. Thus, the basic structure of a cymose inflorescence is captured in the production

$$A \to I[A][A]IF$$

According to this description, the two branches are identical and grow in concert. In reality, this need not be the case, and one lateral branch may start growing before the other. This effect can be modeled by assuming that apices undergo a sequence of state changes which delay their further growth until a particular state is reached. For example, the development of the rose campion (*Lychnis coronaria*) shown in Fig. 11 is described by the following L-system:

ω:	A_7	
p_1:	$A_7 \to I_0[L_0][L_0][A_0][A_4]I_0F_0$	
p_2:	$A_i \to A_{i+1}$	$0 \leq i < 7$
p_3:	$X_i \to X_{i+1}$	$i \geq 0,\ X \in \{I, L, F\}$

Production p_1 specifies that, at their creation time, the lateral apices have different states A_0 and A_4. Production p_2 advances the apex states. Thus, the first apex requires eight derivation steps to produce a flower and new branches, while the second requires only four steps. Concurrently internodes elongate, leaves grow and each flower undergoes a sequence of changes, progressing from the bud stage to an open flower to a fruit. These processes are captured in production p_3. For a further analysis of the above model see [37].

4.3. Modeling qualitative changes of developmental processes.

The developmental sequences considered so far are homogeneous in the sense that the same structure is produced repeatedly at fixed time intervals. However, in many cases a qualitative change in the nature of development can be observed at some point in time. For example, consider the shepherd's purse (*Capsella bursa-pastoris*) shown in Fig. 12.

Figure 9. Lily-of-the-valley.

Figure 12. Development of a shepherd's purse.

Figure 10. A fern.

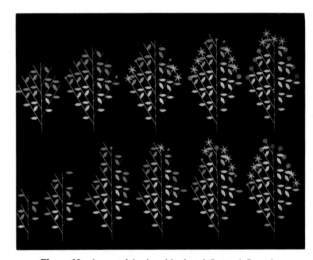

Figure 13. Acropetal (top) and basipetal (bottom) flowering sequences generated by the model with a single acropetal signal (shown as yellow-colored segments).

Figure 11. Development of a rose campion.

Figure 14. Two developmental stages of an aster.

In principle, its development can be described as follows:

$$
\begin{aligned}
\omega: &\quad A \\
p_1: &\quad A \to I_0[L_0]A \\
p_2: &\quad A \to I_0[L_0]B \\
p_3: &\quad B \to I_0[I_0F_0]B \\
p_4: &\quad X_i \to X_{i+1} \qquad i \geq 0,\ X \in \{I, L, F\}
\end{aligned}
$$

The initial vegetative growth is represented by production p_1 which describes creation of successive internodes and leaves by apex A. At some point in time, production p_2 changes the apex from the vegetative state A to the flowering state B. From then on, flowers are produced instead of leaves (production p_3), forming a raceme as discussed in Section 4.1. However, the moment in which this change occurs is not specified; the L-system is a nondeterministic one. Thus, for modeling purposes it must be complemented with an additional control mechanism which will determine the developmental switch time. Three applicable mechanisms are outlined below. Each of them is biologically motivated, and corresponds to a different class of L-systems.

4.3.1. A delay mechanism. The apex undergoes a series of state changes which delay the switch until a particular state is reached:

$$
\begin{aligned}
\omega: &\quad A_0 \\
p_1: &\quad A_i \to I_0[L_0]A_{i+1} \qquad 0 \leq i < n \\
p_2: &\quad A_n \to I_0[L_0]B \\
p_3, p_4: &\quad \text{as before}
\end{aligned}
$$

According to this model, the apex *counts* the leaves it produces. While it may seem strange that a plant counts, it is known that some plant species produce a fixed number of leaves before they start flowering.

4.3.2. A stochastic mechanism. The vegetative apex has a probability π_1 of staying in the vegetative state, and π_2 of transforming itself into a flowering apex:

$$
\begin{aligned}
\omega: &\quad A \\
p_1: &\quad A \xrightarrow{\pi_1} I_0[L_0]A \\
p_2: &\quad A \xrightarrow{\pi_2} I_0[L_0]B \\
p_3, p_4: &\quad \text{as before}
\end{aligned}
$$

For a formal definition of stochastic L-systems see [8, 46].

4.3.3. Environmental change. Many plants change from a vegetative to a flowering state in response to an environmental factor (such as the number of daylight hours or temperature). We can model this effect by using one set of productions (called a *table*) for some number of derivation steps before replacing it by another table.

Table 1

$$
\begin{aligned}
\omega: &\quad A \\
p_1: &\quad A \to I_0[L_0]A \\
p_2: &\quad X_i \to X_{i+1} \qquad i \geq 0,\ X \in \{I, L\}
\end{aligned}
$$

Table 2

$$
\begin{aligned}
p_1: &\quad A \to I_0[L_0]B \\
p_2: &\quad B \to I_0[I_0F_0]B \\
p_3: &\quad X_i \to X_{i+1} \qquad i \geq 0,\ X \in \{I, L\}
\end{aligned}
$$

The concept of table L-systems is formalized in [18, 38].

The developmental switch mechanism can also be applied to transform an apex from producing lateral flowers to producing a terminal flower which stops axis development. A raceme with a terminal flower is called a *closed* raceme, in contrast to the *open* racemes considered so far.

4.4. Inflorescence development with interactions.

Even in the presence of delays, the phase effects discussed so far reflect the sequential creation of branches, flowers and leaves by the subapical growth process. Consequently, organs near the plant roots develop earlier and more extensively than those situated near the axis ends. Such development results in *basitonic* plant structures (heavily developed near the base) with *acropetal* flowering sequences (the zone of blooming flowers progresses upwards along each branch). However, nature also creates *acrotonic* structures (heavily developed near the apex) and *basipetal* flowering sequences (progressing downwards). These structures and developmental patterns cannot be viewed as a simple consequence of subapical growth; for example, basipetal flowering sequences progress in the direction which is precisely opposite to that of plant growth. An intuitively straightforward and biologically well founded explanation can be given in terms of signals (Section 2.4)

which propagate through the plant and control the timing of developmental switches. Below we consider two developmental models with signals. The first model employs a single acropetal signal, while the second one uses both acropetal and basipetal signals.

4.4.1. Developmental model with a single acropetal signal.

Let us assume that a flower-inducing signal (which represents the hormone *florigen*) stops axis development and causes production of a terminal flower upon reaching the apex. In this case, the overall phase effect results from an interplay between growth and control signal propagation [25, 20]. Assuming that only the first-order lateral branches are present, the development can be described by the following L-system:

$$
\begin{aligned}
\omega: &\quad D_0A_0 \\
p_1: &\quad A_i \to A_{i+1} & 0 \leq i < m-1 \\
p_2: &\quad A_{m-1} \to I[L_0][B_0]A_0 \\
p_3: &\quad B_i \to B_{i+1} & 0 \leq i < n-1 \\
p_4: &\quad B_{n-1} \to J[L_0]B_0 \\
p_5: &\quad D_i \to D_{i+1} & 0 \leq i < d-1 \\
p_6: &\quad D_d \to S_0 \\
p_7: &\quad S_i \to S_{i+1} & 0 \leq i < \max\{u, v\} - 1 \\
p_8: &\quad S_z \to \varepsilon & z = \max\{u, v\} - 1 \\
p_9: &\quad S_{u-1} < I \to IS_0 \\
p_{10}: &\quad S_{v-1} < J \to JS_0 \\
p_{11}: &\quad S_0 < A_i \to F_0 & 0 \leq i < m-1 \\
p_{12}: &\quad S_0 < B_i \to F_0 & 0 \leq i < n-1 \\
p_{13}: &\quad X_i \to X_{i+1} & i \geq 0,\ X \in \{L, F\}
\end{aligned}
$$

This L-system operates as follows (Fig. 13). The apex A produces segments of the main axis I, (optional) leaves L and the lateral apices B (p_1, p_2). The time between the production of two consecutive segments of the main axis, called its *plastochron*, is equal to m units (derivation steps). In a similar way, the first-order apices B produce segments J of the lateral axes and leaves L with plastochron n (p_3, p_4). After a delay of d time units a signal S is sent from the tree base towards the apices (p_6). The signal is transported along the main axis with a delay of u time units per internode I (p_7, p_9), and along the first-order axes with a delay of v units per internode J (p_7, p_{10}). Production p_8 removes the signal from a node after it has been transported further along the structure (ε stands for the empty string). When the signal reaches an apex (either A or B), the apex is transformed into a terminal flower F (p_{11}, p_{12}). Leaves and flowers undergo the usual developmental sequence (p_{13}).

In order to analyze the plant structure and flowering sequence resulting from the above development, let us denote by t_k the time at which the apex of the k-th first-order axis is transformed into a flower, and by l_k the length of this axis (expressed as the number of internodes) at the transformation time. Since it takes km time units to produce k internodes along the main axis and $l_k n$ time units to produce l_k internodes on the first-order axis, we obtain $t_k = km + l_k n$. On the other hand, the transformation occurs when the signal S reaches the apex. The signal is sent d time units after the development starts, uses ku time units to travel through k zero-order internodes and $l_k v$ time units to travel through l_k first-order internodes, resulting in $t_k = d + ku + l_k v$. Solving the above system of equations for l_k and t_k (and ignoring for simplicity some inaccuracy due to the fact that this system does not guarantee integer solutions), we obtain:

$$
t_k = k\frac{un - vm}{n - v} + d\frac{n}{n - v}, \qquad l_k = -\frac{k}{n}\frac{m - u}{n - v} + \frac{d}{n - v}.
$$

In order to analyze these solutions, let us first notice that the signal transportation delay v must be less than the plastochron of the first-order axes n (if this were not the case, the signal would never reach the apices). Under this assumption, the sign of the expression $\Delta = un - vm$ determines the flowering sequence, which is acropetal for $\Delta > 0$ and basipetal for $\Delta < 0$ (Fig. 13). If $\Delta = 0$, all flowers occur simultaneously. The sign of the expression $m - u$ determines whether the plant has a basitonic ($m - u < 0$) or acrotonic ($m - u > 0$) structure. Two stages of the development of an aster, modeled using the above L-system with $\Delta < 0$, are shown in Fig. 14.

4.4.3. Developmental model with several signals.

The development of some inflorescences is controlled by several signals, which may propagate with different delays and trigger each other. The use of more than one signal is instrumental in the modeling of a large class of inflorescences (found, for instance, in the family Compositae) characterized by terminal flowers on all apices, indefinite order of branching and basipetal flowering sequence. Figure 15 illustrates this type of development with an example of wall lettuce (*Mycelis muralis*). The underlying L-system operates as follows. First, the main axis is formed in a process of subapical growth which produces subsequent internodes and lateral apices. At this stage further development of lateral branches is suppressed (in botany, this effect is known as *apical dominance*). At some moment a flowering signal S_1 is sent from the bottom of the inflorescence up along the main axis. When this signal reaches its apex, the terminal flower is initiated and a basipetal signal S_2 enabling the growth of lateral axes is sent down the main axis. After a delay, a secondary basipetal signal S_3 is sent from the apex of the main axis. Its effect is to send the flowering signal S_1 along subsequent first-order axes as they are encountered on the way down. This entire process repeats recursively for each axis: its apex is transformed into a flower, the growth of lateral axes of the next order is successively enabled, and the secondary basipetal signal is sent to induce the flowering signal S_1 in these lateral axes. The resulting structure depends heavily on the values of plastochrons, delays, and signal propagation times. In the example under consideration, signal S_2 travels faster than S_3. Consequently, the time interval between the arrival of signals S_2 and S_3 increases while moving down the plant, potentially allowing the lower axes to grow longer then the upper ones. On the other hand, the lower branches start developing later, so in younger plants (in the middle of Fig. 15) they have not yet reached their full length. A detailed biological analysis of the above developmental pattern is given by Janssen and Lindenmayer [20].

4.5. Adding variation to models.

All plants generated by a deterministic L-system are identical. An attempt to include them in the same picture would produce a striking, artificial regularity. In order to prevent this effect it is necessary to introduce specimen-to-specimen variation which preserves the general aspects of a plant while modifying its details. We employ stochastic L-systems [8, 46] for this purpose. For example, Fig. 16 presents a field consisting of sixteen flowers generated by an L-system in which internode elongation is described by three stochastic rules:

$$
\begin{aligned}
\omega: &\quad A \\
p_1: &\quad I \xrightarrow{\pi_1} I \\
p_2: &\quad I \xrightarrow{\pi_2} II \\
p_3: &\quad I \xrightarrow{\pi_3} I[L][L]I
\end{aligned}
$$

where the probabilities π_1, π_2 and π_3 are equal to 1/3. The resulting field appears to consist of various specimens of the same (albeit fictitious) plant species. For more details on the use of stochastic L-systems for plant modeling purposes see [30, 34].

5. A NOTE ON PHYLLOTAXIS.

The longitudinal and angular displacement of consecutive branches or appendages with respect to each other is an important attribute of plant form, known as *phyllotaxis* [9, 42, 44]. In terms of the turtle interpretation of axial trees, these parameters represent the segment length and the *divergence angle* corresponding to the turtle's rotation about the heading vector $\vec{H}$. Abstracting from the mechanisms which govern the formation of phyllotactic patterns, two situations can be distinguished. In *alternating* patterns and *whorls* the angular positions of branches are repeated after a few nodes. In these cases, the divergence angle is equal to $360°/n$, where n is a small integer. This type of arrangement occurs in lilac (Fig. 17), where consecutive pairs of $(n+1)$-order axes lie in the planes passing through the n-order axis and perpendicular to each other (Fig. 18). The divergence angle of 90° is also found in the rose campion (Fig. 11). On the other hand, in *spiral* patterns repetition occurs after a long period or cannot be detected at all. In these cases, the divergence angle is often close to the Fibonacci angle (approximately 137.5°). For examples, see shepherd's purse (Fig. 12), aster (Fig. 14) and wall lettuce (Fig. 15).

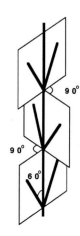

Figure 18. Branch arrangement in lilac inflorescences.

6. MODELING OF ORGANS.

So far we have discussed the modeling of "skeletal" trees with branches consisting of mathematical lines. In this section we extend the model to include surfaces and volumes.

Conceptually, the simplest approach is to incorporate predefined surfaces in the tree, with positions and orientations specified by the turtle. For example, leaves of the lily-of-the-valley (Fig. 9), buds, flowers and fruits of the rose campion (Fig. 11), buds, petals and fruits of the aster (Fig. 14) as well as leaves and flowers of the lilac (Fig. 17) were modeled using bicubic patches. Bicubic surfaces were also applied to model cylindrical stem segments in all these structures. Patches make it easy to manipulate and modify surface shapes interactively, but are incompatible with the developmental approach to modeling since they do not "grow". Consequently, each developmental stage of an organ must be modeled separately.

In order to fully simulate plant development and model phase effects present in plant structures, it is necessary to provide a mechanism for changing the size and shape of surfaces in time. A simple approach is to fill a polygon made of lines defined by an L-system. For example, leaves of the fern (Fig. 10) the shepherd's purse (Fig. 12) and the aster (Fig. 14) were modeled using the following L-system:

$$
\begin{aligned}
\omega: &\quad L \\
p_1: &\quad L \rightarrow \{-SX+X+SX-\vdash-SX+X+SX\} \\
p_2: &\quad X \rightarrow SX
\end{aligned}
$$

Production p_1 defines a leaf as a closed planar polygon. The parentheses { and } indicate that the polygon should be filled. Production p_2 linearly increases the lengths of the polygon edges.

The tracing of polygon boundaries leads to acceptable effects in the case of small, flat surfaces. In other cases it is more convenient to define surfaces using an underlying tree structure as the frame. The entire surface consists of polygons bounded by tree segments and extra edges inserted between appropriate terminal nodes of the tree to form closed contours. The three leaf shapes shown in Fig. 19 were obtained by modifying branching angles and growth rates of axes. Specifically, the blade of the *cordate* leaf (the leftmost one) was generated by the following L-system:

$$
\begin{aligned}
\omega: &\quad [A][B] \\
p_1: &\quad A \rightarrow [+A?]C\# \\
p_2: &\quad B \rightarrow [-B?]C\# \\
p_3: &\quad C \rightarrow IC
\end{aligned}
$$

The axiom contains symbols A and B which generate the left-hand side and the right-hand side of the blade. Each of the productions p_1 and p_2 creates a sequence of axes starting at the leaf base and gradually diverging from the midrib. Production p_3 increases the axis lengths. The axes close to the midrib are the longest since they were created first (thus, the leaf shape is yet another manifestation of the phase effect). The symbols ? and # indicate the endpoints of edges to be inserted while forming closed polygons. The following string represents the left-hand side of the leaf after four derivation steps:

$$[+[+[+[+A?]C\#?]IC\#?]IIC\#?]IIIC\#$$

The arrows indicate the inserted edges (the first one has zero length, the second is collinear with an axis, and the subsequent ones bound triangles). The developmental sequence is shown in Fig. 20. Leaves generated in a similar way were incorporated in the model of the rose campion (Fig. 11).

The frame-based approach can be extended to three-dimensional organs. The right-hand images in Fig. 19 illustrate construction of the flowers for the lily-of-the-valley in Fig. 9. The L-system generates a supporting framework composed of five curved lines which spread radially from the flower base and are connected by a web of inserted edges. In this case each polygon is a trapezoid bounded by two "regular" and two inserted edges.

Another developmental approach to leaf modeling was recently proposed by Lienhardt and Françon [23] and Lienhardt [22].

7. IMPLEMENTATION.

The concepts described in this paper were implemented using a modeling program called *pfg* designed for an IRIS 3130 workstation. The input to the program consists of an L-system specified in the bracketed string notation and approximately 30 parameters, most of which control rendering and viewing. Additionally, an arbitrary number of

Figure 15. Development of a wall lettuce.

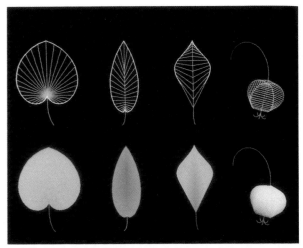

Figure 19. Developmental models of leaves and a flower. The top row shows the underlying tree structures (yellow lines) and the edges inserted to form closed polygons (white lines). The bottom row shows the same structures with filled polygons.

Figure 16. A flower field.

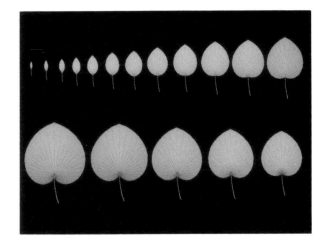

Figure 20. Developmental sequence of a cordate leaf.

Figure 17. A lilac twig.

files containing patch descriptions can be read in (patches are edited outside of *pfg*). The animation of developmental processes is controlled interactively. The total simulation and rendering time for plants images shown in this paper ranges from one to five minutes. The consecutive frames of schematic developmental sequences (such as shown in Fig. 13) are generated a few seconds apart, which is sufficient for analysis of development using animation.

8. CONCLUSIONS.

In this paper we presented guidelines for modeling herbaceous plants and simulating their development. Plant structures have been described in terms of developmental processes controlled by lineage and interactive mechanisms. The developmental approach was extended to model plant organs.

In computer imagery applications, construction of a developmental model is an intermediate step leading to the final goal, a realistic image of a synthetic plant. To a biologist the model itself can be of primary interest as a formal description of a developmental process. The notion of L-systems makes it easy to specify a model in terms consistent with those used in developmental morphology and physiology, and to experiment with a wide range of processes and structures. Thus, the modeling methods presented in this paper can be used as a research tool for visualizing scientific hypotheses related to development in nature.

A number of problems are open for further research.

- **Addition of texture.** The surfaces shown in this paper lack texture. Specifically, a major component of leaf texture is its venation. For consistency with the developmental approach to modeling, the venation itself should be generated by a developmental algorithm. The problem is that veins may form closed cycles and therefore cannot be described in terms of axial trees. An extension of tree L-systems to graphs with cycles (map L-systems) was proposed by Lindenmayer [26, 27] but has not been applied yet to model venation.

- **Improved surface models.** The described model of surface development is difficult to apply to complex three-dimensional surfaces, such as snap-dragon flowers or wrinkled petals of petunias. A difficult situation also occurs when organs composing a larger structure are crowded, for example cabbage leaves, or the petals in rose and peonia flowers. More flexible developmental surface models would be very useful in these cases.

- **Time step control.** The formalism of L-systems is discrete in nature. A developmental model can be constructed assuming longer or shorter time intervals, but once the choice has been made, the time step is a part of the model and cannot be changed easily. From the viewpoint of computer animation it would be preferable if the time step were controlled by a single parameter, decoupled from the underlying L-system.

- **Analysis of simulation complexity.** Various data structures can be used to represent axial trees and carry out the derivation process (Section 2.3). Although bracketed strings appear to be more memory-efficient than list representations, no formal analysis of time and space trade-offs related to the choice of data structure has been made. Such analysis could lead to optimal algorithms.

- **Addition of a graphical interface.** In the present implementation of the *pfg* program, input L-systems are specified in the bracketed string notation. In some applications, such as computer-assisted instruction of developmental morphology, it may be preferable to avoid the textual interface and define productions graphically, as shown in Fig. 2a. The formalism of tree L-systems, which dissociates the graph-theoretic concept from the string implementation, could lend itself to such an interface.

ACKNOWLEDGMENTS

The aster flowers were modeled by Debbie Fowler. The generous support from the Department of Computer Science, University of Regina, and the Natural Sciences and Engineering Research Council of Canada is gratefully acknowledged.

REFERENCES

1. Abelson, H., and diSessa, A. A. *Turtle geometry.* M.I.T. Press, Cambridge (1982).

2. Aono, M., and Kunii, T. L. Botanical tree image generation. *IEEE Computer Graphics and Applications* **4**, 5 (1984), 10-34.

3. Aono, M., and Kunii, T. L. *Botanical tree image generation.* [Video tape], IBM, Tokyo (1985).

4. Armstrong, W. W. The dynamics of tree linkages with a fixed root link and limited range of rotation. *Actes du Colloque Internationale l'Imaginaire Numérique '86* (1986), 16-21.

5. Baker, R., and Herman, G. T. Simulation of organisms using a developmental model, Parts I and II. *Int. J. of Bio-Medical Computing* **3** (1972), 201-215 and 251-267.

6. Beyer, T., and Friedell, M. Generative scene modelling. *Proceedings of EUROGRAPHICS '87* (1987), 151-158 and 571.

7. Bloomenthal, J. Modeling the Mighty Maple. Proceedings of SIGGRAPH '85 (San Francisco, CA, July 22-26, 1985). In *Computer Graphics* **19**, 3 (1985), 305-311.

8. Eichhorst, P., and Savitch, W. J. Growth functions of stochastic Lindenmayer systems. *Inf. and Control* **45** (1980), 217-228.

9. Erickson, R. O. The geometry of phyllotaxis. In J. E. Dale and F. L. Milthrope (Eds.): *The growth and functioning of leaves*, Cambridge University Press (1983), 53-88.

10. Eyrolles, G. *Synthèse d'images figuratives d'arbres par des méthodes combinatoires.* Ph.D. Thesis, Université de Bordeaux I (1986).

11. Frijters, D., and Lindenmayer, A. A model for the growth and flowering of *Aster novae-angliae* on the basis of table (1, 0) L-systems. In G. Rozenberg and A. Salomaa (Eds.): *L Systems*, Lecture Notes in Computer Science **15**, Springer-Verlag, Berlin (1974), 24-52.

12. Frijters, D., and Lindenmayer, A. Developmental descriptions of branching patterns with paracladial relationships. In A. Lindenmayer and G. Rozenberg (Eds.): *Automata, languages, development*, North-Holland, Amsterdam (1976), 57-73.

13. Frijters, D. Principles of simulation of inflorescence development. *Annals of Botany* **42** (1978), 549-560.

14. Frijters, D. Mechanisms of developmental integration of *Aster novae-angliae* L., and *Hieracium murorum* L. *Annals of Botany* **42** (1978), 561-575.

15. Habel, A., and Kreowski, H.-J. On context-free graph languages generated by edge replacement. In H. Ehrig, *et al.* (Eds.): *Graph grammars and their application to computer science; Second Int. Workshop*, Lecture Notes in Computer Science **153**, Springer-Verlag, Berlin (1983), 143-158.

16. Hallé, F., Oldeman, R., and Tomlinson, P. *Tropical trees and forests: an architectural analysis.* Springer-Verlag, Berlin (1978).

17. Herman, G. T., and Liu, W. H. The daughter of CELIA, the French flag, and the firing squad. *Simulation* **21** (1973), 33-41.

18. Herman, G. T., and Rozenberg, G. *Developmental systems and languages.* North-Holland, Amsterdam (1975).

19. Hogeweg, P., and Hesper, B. A model study on biomorphological description. *Pattern Recognition* **6** (1974), 165-179.

20. Janssen, J. M., and Lindenmayer, A. Models for the control of branch positions and flowering sequences of capitula in *Mycelis muralis* (L.) Dumont (Compositae). *New Phytologist* **105** (1987), 191-220.

21. Kawaguchi, Y. A morphological study of the form of nature. Proceedings of SIGGRAPH '82 (July 1982). In *Computer Graphics* **16**, 3 (1982), 223-232.

22. Lienhardt, P. *Modélisation et évolution de surfaces libres.* Ph.D. Thesis, Université Louis Pasteur, Strasbourg (1987).

23. Lienhardt, P., and Françon, J. *Synthèse d'images de feuilles végétales.* Technical Report R-87-1, Département d'informatique, Université Louis Pasteur, Strasbourg (1987).

24. Lindenmayer, A. Mathematical models for cellular interaction in development, Parts I and II. *J. Theor. Biol.* **18** (1968), 280-315.

25. Lindenmayer, A. Positional and temporal control mechanisms in inflorescence development. In P. W. Barlow and D. J. Carr (Eds.): *Positional controls in plant development*, Cambridge University Press (1984).

26. Lindenmayer, A. Models for multicellular development: characterization, inference and complexity of L-systems. In A. Kelmenová and J. Kelmen (Eds.): *Trends, techniques and problems in theoretical computer science.* Lecture Notes in Computer Science **281**, Springer-Verlag, Berlin (1987), 138-168.

27. Lindenmayer, A. An introduction to parallel map generating systems. In H. Ehrig, *et al.* (Eds.): *Graph grammars and their application to computer science; Third Int. Workshop*, Lecture Notes in Computer Science **291**, Springer-Verlag, Berlin (1987), 27-40.

28. Lindenmayer, A., and Prusinkiewicz, P. Developmental models of multi-cellular organisms: A computer graphics perspective. Paper submitted to the *Proceedings of the Artificial Life Workshop* held in Los Alamos, NM, September 1987.

29. Müller-Doblies D., and U. Cautious improvement of a descriptive terminology of inflorescences. *Monocot newsletter* **4**, Institut für Biologie, Technical University of Berlin (West), 13 (1987).

30. Nishida, T. KOL-systems simulating almost but not exactly the same development - the case of Japanese cypress. *Memoirs Fac. Sci., Kyoto University, Ser. Bio.* **8** (1980), 97-122.

31. Oppenheimer, P. Real time design and animation of fractal plants and trees. Proceedings of SIGGRAPH '86 (Dallas, Texas, August 18-22, 1985). In *Computer Graphics* **20**, 4 (1986), 55-64.

32. Preparata F. P., and Yeh, R. T. *Introduction to discrete structures.* Addison-Wesley, Reading (1973).

33. Prusinkiewicz, P. Graphical applications of L-systems. *Proc. of Graphics Interface '86 - Vision Interface '86* (1986), 247-253.

34. Prusinkiewicz, P. Applications of L-systems to computer imagery. In H. Ehrig, *et al.* (Eds.): *Graph grammars and their application to computer science; Third Int. Workshop*, Lecture Notes in Computer Science **291**, Springer-Verlag, Berlin (1987), 534-548.

35. Prusinkiewicz, P., and Hanan, J. Lindenmayer systems, fractals, and plants. In D. Saupe (Ed.): *Fractals: Introduction, basics and applications.* [Course notes] SIGGRAPH '88 (Atlanta, Georgia, August 1-5, 1988).

36. Reeves, W. T., and Blau, R. Approximate and probabilistic algorithms for shading and rendering structured particle systems. Proceedings of SIGGRAPH '85 (San Francisco, CA, July 22-26, 1985). In *Computer Graphics* **19**, 3 (1985), 313-322.

37. Robinson, D. F. A symbolic notation for the growth of inflorescences. *New Phytologist* **103** (1986), 587-596.

38. Rozenberg, G., and Salomaa, A. *The mathematical theory of L-systems.* Academic Press, New York (1980).

39. Smith, A. R. About the cover: "Reconfigurable machines". *Computer* **11**, 7 (1978), 3-4.

40. Smith, A. R. Plants, fractals, and formal languages. Proceedings of SIGGRAPH '84 (Minneapolis, Minnesota, July 23-27, 1984). *Computer Graphics* **18**, 3 (1984), 1-10.

41. Smith, A. R. *Grammars for generating the complexity of reality.* [Video tape], Lucasfilm/PIXAR, San Rafael (1985).

42. Stevens, P. S. *Patterns in nature.* Little, Brown and Co., Boston (1974).

43. Szilard, A. L., and Quinton, R. E. An interpretation for DOL systems by computer graphics. *The Science Terrapin* **4** (1979), 8-13.

44. Thompson, d'Arcy. *On growth and form.* University Press, Cambridge (1952).

45. Troll, W. *Die Infloreszenzen*, Vol. I. Gustav Fischer Verlag, Stuttgart (1964).

46. Yokomori, T. Stochastic characterizations of E0L languages. *Information and Control* **45** (1980), 26-33.

47. Zimmerman, M. H., and Brown, C. L. *Trees - structure and function.* Springer-Verlag, Berlin (1971).

Plant Models Faithful
to Botanical Structure and Development

Philippe de Reffye[1], Claude Edelin[2], Jean Françon[3], Marc Jaeger[1,3], Claude Puech[4]

1. CIRAD, Montpellier, FRANCE.
2. Institut de Botanique, USTL, Montpellier, FRANCE.
3. Département d'Informatique, Université Louis Pasteur, Strasbourg, FRANCE.
4. Laboratoire d'Informatique, Ecole Normale Supérieure, Paris, FRANCE.

Abstract:

Some very impressive results have been obtained in the past few years in plants and trees image synthesis. Some algorithms are largely based on the irregularity and fuzziness of the objects, and use fractals, graftals or particle systems. Others focus on the branching pattern of the trees with emphasis on morphology. Our concern here is the faithfulness of the models to the botanical nature of trees and plants. We present a model which integrates botanical knowledge of the architecture of the trees: how they grow, how they occupy space, where and how leaves, flowers or fruits are located, etc. The very first interest of the model we propose is its great richness: the same procedural methods can produce "plants" as different as weeping willows, fir trees, cedar trees, frangipani trees, poplars, pine trees, wild cherry trees, herbs, etc. Another very important benefit one can derive from the model is the integration of time which enables viewing the aging of a tree (possibility to get different pictures of the same tree at different ages, accurate simulation of the death of leaves and branches for example). The ease to integrate physical parameters such as wind, the incidence of factors such as insects attacks, use of fertilizers, plantation density, and so on makes it a useful tool for agronomy or botany.

CR Categories and Subject Descriptors: I.3.5 [**Computer Graphics**]: Computational Gemetry and Object Modeling; I.3.7 [**Computer Graphics**]: Three-Dimensional Graphics and Realism; I.6.3 [**Simulation and Modeling**]: Applications; J.3 [**Life and Medical Sciences**] Biology.

General Terms: Trees, Models, Algorithms.

Additional Keywords and Phrases: plant, tree, botany, growth simulation, database amplification.

---

1. Centre de Coopération Internationale en Recherche Agronomique pour le Développement, BP 5035, 34032 Montpellier Cédex, FRANCE - Tel.: (33) 67 61 58 00

2. Institut de Botanique, Université des Sciences et Techniques du Langudoc, 163, Rue Auguste Broussonnet, 34000 Montpellier, FRANCE - Tel.: (33) 67 63 17 93

3. Département d'Informatique, Université Louis Pasteur, 7 Rue René Descartes, 67084 Strasbourg Cédex, FRANCE - Tel.: (33) 88 41 63 00

4. Laboratoire d'Informatique, Ecole Normale Supérieure, 45 Rue d'Ulm, 75230 Paris Cédex 05, FRANCE - Tel.: (33) (1) 43 29 12 25 - e-mail: puech@frulm63 (bitnet), puech@ens.ens.fr (uucp)

©1988   ACM-0-89791-275-6/88/008/0151 $00.75

1. Introduction.

The past few years have seen much effort devoted to image generation of natural phenomena by procedural methods. In this context, our interest lies in the generation of trees and plants images. Some very impressive results have already been obtained, using particular branching patterns (Kawaguchi [11], Aono and Kunii [1]), graftals (Smith [23]), particle systems (Reeves and Blau [18]), fractals (Oppenheimer [16]), extensions of graftals (Prusinkiewicz [17]) or combinatorics of trees (Eyrolles, Françon and Viennot [5]).

Our concern here is to produce images of plants and trees which should be faithful to their botanical nature and so to build a model which should include the known botanical laws which explain plants' growth and architecture. Such a concern is shared by Aono and Kunii in [1] but their study is limited to the cases of monopodial, dichotomic or ternary branching patterns which prove to be insufficient for the representation of a rich variety of plants and trees. In [7], Fournier proposed a taxonomy for the modelling of natural phenomena, categorizing the different models as empirical, purely physical, morphological, structural, impressionistic or self-models. As he noted in his course notes, our approach can be seen as a structural model; it can also be seen as a kind of physical model with botanical laws instead of physical ones as our approach integrates as much "knowledge" about the plant and its environment as possible: age of the plant, growing conditions, physics of the branches (for example, in our approach branches are bent by gravity or wind strength as opposed to their simulation by inhibitors and attractors by Aono and Kunii [1]).

From a botanical standpoint, the growth of plants has been studied by several authors. An extensive bibliography can be found in [24] and [17]. A "macroscopic" study of plant shapes more directly related to their "architecture" can be found in Fischer and Honda's paper ([6]) in the case of Terminalia; their work has been taken into account for image synthesis by Aono and Kunii [1].

A macroscopic approach can also be found in one of the authors' thesis (De Reffye [19]) where the mathematical model is applied to the simulation of the growth of the coffee-tree. The model has been enriched since and its domain of relevance widely enlarged; the aim of the present paper is to present its potential consequences in image synthesis of trees and plants.

As we want to emphasize here the topologic, not geometric model, its functioning and relation to the botanical and physical reality, we will not deal in this paper with important but somewhat different problems related to the graphical aspect of the image such as the smoothing of the limbs, the precise shape of the trunk, the rendering of the bark's texture, etc. These problems have been studied in the case of the maple tree by Bloomenthal ([3]).

The general idea of the method is to model the activity of buds at dicretized times: a bud, at a given clock signal can
- either become a flower and die (and disappear),
- or go into sleep (pause, break),
- or become a so called internode at the extremity of which one or several leaves appear with new so called lateral buds at their axil and a new so called apical bud at the end of the internode,
- or die (and disappear).

These events occur according to specific stochastic laws characteristic for each variety and each species. The geometric parameters, such as the length and diameter of an internode or the branching angles are also calculated according to specific stochastic characteristic laws.

These simulations rely on recent work on plant architecture.

The plan of the paper is as follows. In section 2, we give several simplified notions from botany on which the stochastic growth model explained in section 3 is founded. In section 4, we deal with the method used to simulate the growth of plants, and in section 5 we show how the model can be used to simulate other phenomena. The next section explains how the visualization is done and the last section gives results and conclusions.

2. A few simplified notions from Botany.

The growth of a plant is the result of the evolution of some specific cellular tissues (internal part of the bud), the so called *meristems*. A bud can, at a given time, die (abort), and it will not produce anything any longer, or it can give birth to a flower, or an inflorescence (and then the bud dies) or to an internode.

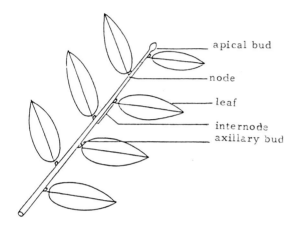

Figure 1: The leaves'axis.

The *leaves' axis* is the fundamental element of the architectural approach. It is the result of the activity of the bud situated at its tip, which is called the *apical bud*. It is made of a series of internodes; an *internode* is a (part of a) stem made of a ligneous material at the tip of which one can find one or several leaves. An internode's length can be very short (around 1 mm) in the case of some plants such as the fir tree, but can also measure up to several tenth of cms in the case of bamboo. Between two internodes there is a *node* which bears leaves and buds; each node bears at least one leaf (it is the symptom of the existence of a node); at each leaf's axil, one finds a so-called *axillary bud*. These notions are illustrated on Figure 1.

An axillary stem can either grow immediately (*sylleptic ramification*) or with some delay (*proleptic ramification*).

The growth of the leaves' axes of a plant is the result of the evolution of their apical buds. A central notion for the model is the notion of *growth*

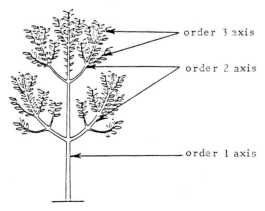

Figure 2: The notion of order of an axis.

unit which is a sequence of internodes and nodes produced (usually in a very short period of time) by the apical bud of the previous node. We will distinguish between two cases: short growth units with few internodes (one sometimes) and long growth units which are made of numerous internodes (each of which is usually short).

Another important notion is the notion of the *order* of an axis (see Figure 2). The *order 1 axis* of a plant is the sequence of growth units such that each of these growth units is born of the apical bud of the previous one, and such that the first one of the axis is grown out of the seed of the plant. An *order i axis*, for $i>1$, is a sequence of growth units such that the first internode of the sequence is born of an axillary bud on an order $i-1$ axis, called the *bearing axis*.

In the absence of traumatisms, the relative position of the lateral buds (and, as a consequence of the leaves) of a node with respect to the lateral buds of the previous node follow regular laws known for each variety of each species and each order; this phenomenon is called *phyllotaxy* . The *spiraled* and *distic* cases are illustrated on Figure 3.

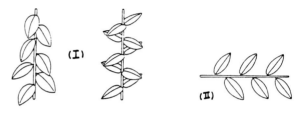

Figure 3: Phyllotaxy: (I) spiraled, (II) distic.

As regards the ramification process, in a growth unit, one can encounter (see Figure 4):

- *continuous ramification*: every node of an axis is the root of an axis of greater order,

- *rhythmic ramification*: some nodes (but not all of them) are the root of an axis of greater order, or

- *diffuse ramification*: the nodes forming roots of an axis of greater order are located at random.

These kinds of ramifications are functions of the order of the axis for a given variety and species. A *monopod* is a ramified system which includes a unique number *1* axis and a finite number of axes of higher order; if the orders go up to *k* (included), the monopod is said an *order k monopod*.

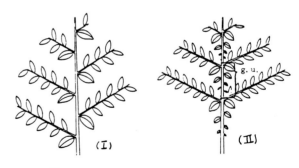

Figure 4: Ramification (I) continuous, (II) rhythmic

The geometric trend of an axis with respect to its bearing axis is also an important parameter; it is characterized usually by a general trend. If the latter is horizontal the development is said *plagiotropic*, if it is vertical it is said *orthotropic* (see Figure 15). An order 1 axis is usually orthotropic. The trend frequently effects the phyllotaxy: orthotropy is usually associated with a spiraled phyllotaxy whereas plagiotropy is associated with distic phyllotaxy.

Some plants do not grow as monopods: when the apical bud of an order *i* axis dies, some axillary buds of the previous node produce an axis whose behaviour is of an order *i* instead of *i+1* axis. Such a behaviour is called *sympodial growth*. A similar phenomenon can be observed after the pruning of a tree (see figure 5 and Photo 2). The observed phenomenon is called *traumatic reiteration*.

Another phenomenon alters the shape of "old" trees; it is called *reiteration* (see [4], [15]). It accounts for the following behaviour: an axillary bud can produce an axis which behaves as an order *1* axis (a new "young" tree) or, in a few cases as an axis of greater order. These are "natural" occurences of recursion! Reiteration is still very badly understood from a botanical point of view and will be ignored here except in the case of traumatic reiteration.

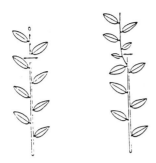

Figure 5: Traumatic reiteration.

Tree architecture has been studied rather recently from a scientific point of view, in a systematic way. Botanists Hallé, Oldeman and Tomlinson ([9]) studied the growth of tropical trees and sifted out the notion of *architectural model*, which can be seen as a growth strategy to occupy space. A surprisingly large variety of plants and trees grow and build their shape in the same kind of way, although the results seem very different from one to another. Altogether, there are only 23 different architectural types, called architectural models. The classification relies mainly on the presence/absence of sympodial growth, on ramification, continuous growth or not, and development trend (plagiotropy/orthotropy). Let us describe briefly four of these, among the most frequently encountered:

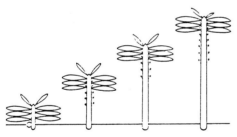

Figure 6: Corner model.

- in *Corner's model* (see Figure 6), there is one order *1* axis and no ramification at all. These plants are monopods; examples include coconut trees (see Photo 8) and date palm trees (see Figure 16).

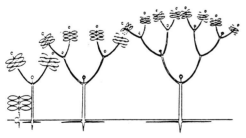

Figure 7: Leeuwenberg model.

- in *Leeuwenberg's model* (see Figure 7), the apical buds systematically die after one growth unit so that the growth is sympodial; examples include the frangipani tree (see Photo 13) and the mistletoe.
- in *Massart's model* (see Figure 8), the order *1* axis is orthotropic, the other ones are plagiotropic. These plants are monopods with a rhythmic ramification growth; examples include fir trees (Photo 1), spruce trees and cedar trees (Photo 10).
- in *Rauh's model* (see Figure 9), every axis is orthotropic. These plants

are monopods with a rhythmic ramification growth; examples include poplar trees (Photo 4), aspen trees (Photo 3), pine trees (Photo 5) and fruit trees of temperate regions (Photos 6, 7 and 9).

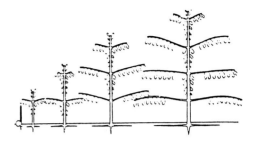

Figure 8: Massart model.

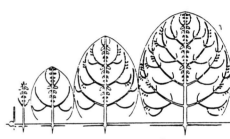

Figure 9: Rauh model.

To end this botany section, let us mention that the same architectural concepts are relevant to other botanical phenomena: the rhizome of some herbs can be considered as an underground monopod; an inflorescence can be viewed as a monopod whose apical buds are replaced by flowers. This will be used in section 4 for simulation purposes.

3. The growth model.

Our approach is based on a mathematical simulation of botanical architectural models which originated in Philippe de Reffye's thesis [19]. It is based on a botanically accurate simulation of the functioning of meristems. Although related botanical studies are of a qualitative nature, the proposed model is quantitative.

In this section, we will ignore the sexual organs of the plants (flowers and inflorescences).

As shown by botanical studies, three important phenomena characterize the functioning of meristems:
- growth,
- ramification,
- mortality.

They heavily depend on time so that models of plant architectures have to integrate time in growth, ramification and mortality processes.

In de Reffye's mathematical macroscopic model of plants' growth, the unit of discretized time is the time taken by the growth of a growth unit, this length of time being supposed constant for the axes a given order of a given plant. As a consequence, axes of different order of the same plant can grow with different speeds (see Figure 14).

Moreover, each bud is given two probabilities (stochastic parameters of the model): its probability to abort, and its probability to make a break, i.e. to wait during a unit of time without growing (if it is not dead). The "non-abort" probability of an axillary bud is, in fact, a ramification probability, that is the probability of birth of an axillary stem which is the start of a new axis.

Let us call the age of a node or a bud its date of birth according to the clock of the model, with time *0* being the time when the seed begins to grow; the dimension of a node or a bud is its age relative to the birthday of its axis.

We will give now several examples of the functioning of the model, starting with a very trivial one.

Example 0: Let us draw a growth unit as a straight segment and suppose that the seed has produced a growth unit at time *1*. Then, at time *2*, if the break and death probabilities are different from *0*, the 3 cases depicted on

Figure 10 can occur.

Figure 10: Growth model. Example 0.

To explain the branching process, let us recall that at each node two types of axillary buds can appear. Those which correspond to "standard" branching can give birth to an new axis of greater (by one) order; reiteration buds give birth to a reiteration. Moreover, these axillary buds become visible only if the apical bud is not dead or in a break phase. The number of buds of each type can be calculated by using a probability law called the branching law, but is usually constant for axes of a given order of a given plant (in our simulations).

With very straightforward hypotheses on the probabilities involved, a few simulations can be easily done. Let us suppose, for example, that the maximum order is 3 (this can be obtained when the ramification probability of axillary buds on order 3 axes is equal to 0, or when the buds on order 4 axes die systematically). With one axillary bud on the last node of each growth unit, with no axillary bud elsewhere, with the standard ramification probability equal to 1 and with growth speed identical on every axis, one can obtain the results of examples 1 to 4 (the geometry is very straightforward) below.

Example 1 (see Figure 11): break and death probabilities equal to 0.

Example 2 (see Figure 12): break probability equal to 0, death probabilities different from 0.

Example 3 (see Figure 13): death probability equal to 0, break probability equal to 0 on order 1 axis, different from 0 and large on the other axes.

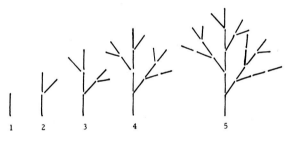

Figure 11: Growth model. Example 1 (age 1, 2, 3, 4, 5).

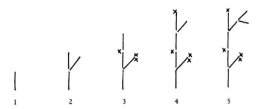

Figure 12: Growth model. Example 2 (age 1, 2, 3, 4, 5).

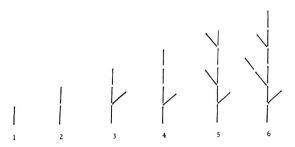

Figure 13: Growth model. Example 3 (age 1, 2, 3, 4, 5, 6).

Example 4: order 1 and 2 axes only, one internode per growth unit, 2 axillary buds per node on axis 1, distic phyllotaxy, death probability equal to 0, break probability equal to 0 on order 1 axis, different from 0 on order 2 axes, growth speed ratio (order 1 axis over order 2 axis) equal to r. For ages around 20 units of time on the order 1 axis, with a geometry similar to that of the robusta coffee tree, and fall of the leaves simulated, the architectures shown on Figure 14 can be obtained.

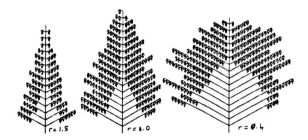

Figure 14: Growth of order 1 and order 2 axes, with growth ratio r (with break).

In the growth model, it is supposed that the probabilities are only functions of the age, dimension and order of the bud, for a given variety and species. It has been proved experimentally, for example, that the mortality of an apical bud is a monotonic increasing function of its dimension for a given order. As another example, the probability for a bud to make a break can be chosen as a monotonic increasing function of age, for a given order. For image synthesis purposes these hypotheses prove to be sufficient (even 0 and 1 probabilities produce a wide variety of forms). For a greater fidelity to botany, one has to take into account the dependence on other parameters such as the number of nodes in a growth unit.

All the probability laws involved can be measured experimentally; this has been done in several cases (for example the coffee-tree) for agronomic purposes, and the measures validate the model (cf. [20]). Moreover, with different choices of the probability laws, one can obtain the architectural types of Hallé, Oldeman and Tomlinson's classification.

4. Growth simulation.

Computer simulation of the growth of plants according to our model is possible as the model is a numerical one. Results of the first experiments appear in [20] and [21].

In order to simulate the growth of a plant, the following parameters have to be given:

- the age,
- the clocks or growth speeds of the axes,
- the number of possible buds at each node, as a function of order,
- the probabilities of death, pause, ramification and reiteration given as functions of age, dimension and order (see section 3). These probabilities are sufficient to generate images of great realism; a rather wide variety of forms can even be obtained with probabilities restricted to 0 and 1. The probability laws chosen for the simulation can either be the result of experimental measures or calculated from mathematical laws taken as hypotheses, or completely arbitrary, according to the objective of the simulation (although, up to now, the model has been used to give more faithful images of plants, it would be of interest, and very easy, to simulate the effect of "strange" growth laws). Most of the time, the probabilities are the same for all the buds of axes of a given order of a given plant; usually, the laws are uniform or exponential laws.

- the type of the growth unit and the number of nodes per growth unit, given as functions of the same parameters as the previous probabilities (if one seeks still greater fidelity to botany, one has to define these parameters as random variables which depend on various other parameters (see [10]));

- the geometric parameters of an internode: length and diameter as a function of the same parameters and of the age of the plant for the diameter (for cylindrical internodes) or diameters (for cone-shaped internodes);

- for every axis order, the development trend (orthotropy or plagiotropy), the insertion angle with the bearing axis (with the ground for order 1 axis), the phyllotaxy, which is also characterized by an angle. For a greater fidelity to botany, one has, as has been indicated above for the growth unit parameters, to define the insertion angle and the phyllotaxy as random variables, functions of various parameters and to consider the development trend as composite (see [10]).

The insertion angle and the development trend are used to smooth out the shape of an axis according to its trend. For example, in the case of a vertical order *1* axis bearing an order *2* axis, the orthotropic and plagiotropic case are dealt with as shown in Figure 15.

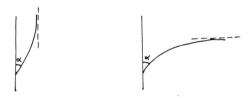

Figure 15: Development trend of a tree
(left:orthotropy, right: plagiotropy).

In order to obtain images with great fidelity to nature, the choice of the important parameters and their experimental measurement has to be done with particular care. This usually requires a good knowledge of botany and of the model.

The simulation consists in going through each instant of discretized time from the birth of the plant to the given age, and, for each of these instants, to consider all the buds which are alive at that moment. Each bud undergoes a mortality test; if necessary, a break test; and lastly, if necessary, a ramification test. According to the results of these tests, the bud can be suppressed from the set of living buds or a new internode can (if there is no break of the growth at that point) be created (with a new apical bud and new axillary buds with a given order and geometric position).

The simulation can be expressed in pseudo-code as follows:

```
for each clock signal do
  for each bud which is still alive do
  {order, age, dimension, position, etc. are known attributes of the bud}
    if bud doesn't die then
      if bud doesn't make a pause then
        create internode
          {with position in space}
        create apical bud
        for each possible bud do
          if ramification then create axillary buds
                              {with age, order and dimension}
        endfor
      endif
    endif
  endfor
endfor
```

Up to now, such a simulation of time has not been used in the actual implementation of the algorithm because of its requirements in memory space. A prefix traversal of the tree has been preferred: the axillary buds of a node are numbered *1, 2, ..., k* in any order, the apical bud is numbered *k+1*; a prefix traversal is the chain of prefix traversals of the "trees" stemmed from bud *i*, for *i=1,..., k*. This kind of traversal can be used for simulation purposes since, because of the hypotheses, when the traversal visits a bud, by previous processing its age, dimension, order (and, possibly others structural parameters if needed) and position are known. Since, in nature, the order of an axis is very rarely bigger than five, the size of the stack used for the simulation of the traversal is moderate.

The prefix traversal we used up to now is not suited to an animation of growth as it imposes that the whole plant is calculated again at each age used in the animation. Moreover, with such a traversal, one cannot take into account some significant botanical phenomena such as growth obstruction (growing of mortality or break, for example) due to fixed obstacles or to part of the plant against another part, or the effect of the shade cast by the tree on its own buds. A more accurate simulation of growth and its application to obstruction is in progress.

The growth simulation program manages the tests of death, break or ramification by calling a random number generator and the laws procedures for the probabilities. It also manages the geometric parameters. Its output is a file whose records' fields include a tag characteristic of the component (short or long internode, leaf,...), a position in space, and two 3D directions for the component.

The described generator is an architecture generator; for ease of exposition we have not mentioned, up to now, how to deal with the simulation of other phenomena. This will be done in the next section.

5. Other simulations.

Autumn's fall of leaves can be very easily simulated; one has only to define a life length for leaves, which is usually taken as constant for a given plant.

In a similar way, botanists know the laws that rule the birth of flowers and inflorescences, their life length and the fruits' life-time. The accordance with the botanical model insures that the leaves and fruits are inserted in the right places on the branches (according to the age of the tree). This implies that the model is also accurate when one looks at a precise part of the tree, instead of looking at its overall shape.

As for the pruning of trees, it is simulated by saying that when all the buds of the same branch are dead the branch itself is dead and falls after some time.

Lastly, the calculation of the bending of a branch under the action of forces like gravity or wind can be done according to the theory of material strength (see [20], [25]); it is done using the geometrical shape of internodes and the elasticity parameter (Young's modulus) which characterizes the wood of the branch. As regards wind effects no images are included here but an animation is in progress.

Although in a few cases other models exist ([8], [2]), the same plant generator can also be diverted to output parts of a plant instead of its overall architecture (according to [7] our modeling for image synthesis purposes is, in this case, structural but not physical). For example, an inflorescence is considered by the plant generator as a small tree bearing axes of order at most *2* or *3*, very regular, the last node on every axis bearing a flower. In a similar way, the sepals, petals, stamens and stigmas of a flower can be generated as specific internodes or growth units (for another approach, see [12]). A palm tree's palm can also be generated as

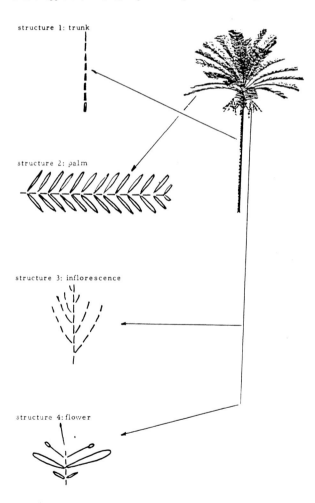

Figure 16: Four structures used for a date palm tree.

Photos

Previous page, from left to right:
- first row
  Photo 1: Fir tree.
  Photo 2: Pruned tree (with traumatic reiterations).
  Photo 3: Top of a poplar (aspen).
- second row
  Photo 4: Italy poplar.
  Photo 5: Pine tree.
  Photo 6: Approximate wild cherry tree with flowers.
- third row
  Photo 7: Another approximate wild cherry tree with fruits.
  Photo 8: Coconut tree.
  Photo 9: Fruit tree in spring.

This page:
- top left
  Photo 10: Young cedar tree.
- right column, from top to bottom:
  Photo 11: Weeping willow without leaves.
  Photo 12: Weeping willow with leaves.
  Photo 13: Frangipani tree.
  Photo 14: Herbs and trees.
  Photo 15: Herbs and poplars in autumn.

a growth unit with specific internodes (see figure 16). As a last example, let us mention that an underground rhizome can be calculated as a monopod with a rather simple architecture; at its nodes, herbs, which are monopods with another architecture, grow.

6. Visualization.

The plant generator's output is a file of records whose fields are the following ones: a tag which characterizes a botanical component (short or long internode, leaf, flower, fruit, and, if one enlarges the simulation, cf. sect. 5, rhizome internode, palm internode, petal internode, sepal internode, etc.) and geometric information needed to position the component in space.

A form taken from a library of forms is associated with every tag: for example, straight cylinders, hexagonal cylinders or straight truncated cones for internodes, polygons for leaves or flower petals,.... Moreover, the library of forms can be parametrized by age. For the photos we generated, we only used cones with hexagonal bases or even segments for internodes; for leaves, petals or sepals, we used an assembly of at most 4 convex plane polygons (in a few cases a vector is sufficient) with an associated normal if needed. Small fruits are made with a few vectors. To each form a color is associated.

The visualization is then the visualization of a set of vectors and faces. Basic rudimentary methods have then been used for the rendering: perspective, no antialiasing, uniform color for faces,... In a few cases a light source was used to change the polygons' luminosity according to the angle between the source direction and the normal to the polygon. Hidden surface removal is done by the use of a Z-buffer.

The use of such primitive rendering techniques proved to be sufficient for obtaining images with great realism: the richness of forms is such that antialiasing or texture is usually not necessary; the only exception is for close-ups of a part of a tree, of its trunk or of one of its branches. Usually using a rough Z-buffer (with a unique depth for all the pixels of a leaf for example) is enough.

Let us mention that the complexity of the structure grows rapidly with the age of the plant. A few tens of components are enough to describe a small plant, but several hundreds of thousands are needed to describe tall trees. In such cases, the computer time needed to generate the model and visualize can be important (a few tens of minutes instead of a few minutes for a small tree).

7. Conclusion.

We have presented a model for the growth of plants and trees which incorporates botanical knowledge of their architecture.

The very first interest of the model is its great richness: the same procedural methods can produce "plants" as different as weeping willows, fir trees, cedar trees, frangipani trees, poplars, pine trees, wild cherry trees, herbs, etc.

Another very important benefit from the model is the integration of time which enables to view the aging of a tree (accurate simulation of the death of leaves and branches for example). Using the model, a short movie showing the evolution of a tree from birth to death has been produced.

Let us also stress that part of the study has been developed for agronomic purposes: mathematical models of the architecture of plants and trees turn out to be very useful for studying land crops; the production is very often dependent on plant growth and architecture. The incidence of factors such as insect attacks, use of fertilizers, planting density, etc. can be studied using the architectural models combined with other mathematical models. This ability to put together different models should also be investigated for image synthesis purposes.

Another very promising study would be to simulate the growth with "arbitrary" non botanic parameters in order to obtain non existing architectures, strange shapes, etc. In doing so, one could benefit from the richness of the model for animation purposes.

Acknowledgements.
The authors would like to thank C. Schmitt, H. Brisse, and M. Hoff from Strasbourg University, who introduced the computer scientists (authors) to the work of botanists, CNRS Computer Center at Cronenbourg and its graphics group, CIRAD's Computer Center and its staff in Montpellier, the "Institut de Botanique" in Montpellier who provided several figures and the anonymous referees who suggested several improvements in the presentation of the paper.

References.

1. Aono M., Kunii T. L., "Botanical Tree Image Generation" IEEE Computer Graphics and Applications, vol. 4, No 5, 1984, pp. 10-33.
2. Bell A., "Computerized Vegetative Mobility in rhizomatous plants", in *Automata, Languages, Development,* Lindenmayer A. & Rozenberg G. (Eds.), North-Holland, 1976.
3. Bloomenthal J., "Modeling the Mighty Maple", Computer Graphics, vol. 19, No. 3, 1985, pp. 305-311.
4. Edelin C., *L'architecture Monopodiale: l'Exemple de Quelques Arbres d'Asie Tropicale,* Thèse de Doctorat ès Sciences, Université des Sciences et des Techniques du Languedoc, Montpellier, France, 1984.
5. Eyrolles G., Françon J., Viennot G., "Combinatoire pour la Synthèse d'Images Réalistes de Plantes", Actes du Deuxième Colloque Image, CESTA, 1986, pp. 648-652.
6. Fischer J. B., Honda H., "Computer Simulation of Branching Pattern and Geometry in Terminalia (Combretaceae) , a Tropical Tree", 1977.
7. Fournier A., "Prolegomenon", Unpublished course notes, Fournier A. ed., *The Modeling of Natural Phenomena* (SIGGRAPH'87 course notes #16, Anaheim, CA, July 1987) pp. 3-37.
8. Frijters D., Lindenmayer A., "A Model for the Growth and Flowering of *Aster Novae-Anglia* on the Basis of Table (0,1)-Systems", in *L-Systems,* Rozenberg G., Salomaa A. (Eds.), LNCS, 15, Springer-Verlag, Berlin, 1974, pp. 24-52.
9. Hallé, Oldeman, Tomlinson, *Tropical Trees and Forest: an Architectural Analysis,* Springer-Verlag, Berlin/Heidelberg/New-York, 1978.
10. Jaeger M., *Représentation et Simulation de Croissance de Végétaux,* Thèse de Doctorat, Université Louis Pasteur, Strasbourg, France, Déc. 1987.
11. Kawaguchi Y., "A Morphological Study of the Form of Nature", Computer Graphics, vol. 16, No. 3, 1982, pp. 223-232.
12. Lienhardt P., "Free-form Surfaces Modeling by Evolution Simulation", to appear, Proceedings Eurographics'88.
13. Lindenmayer A., "Paracladial Systems", in *Automata, Languages, Development* (Lindenmayer A., Rozenberg G. Editors), North-Holland Publishing Company, Amsterdam/New-York/Oxford, 1976.
14. Lück, "Elementary Behavioural Rules as Foundation for Morphogenesis", J. Theor. Biol., 54, 1975, pp. 23-24.
15. Oldemann R.A.A., "L'architecture de la Forêt Guyanaise", Mémoire 73, ORSTOM, 1974.
16. Oppenheimer P. E., "Real Time Design and Animation of Fractal Plants and Trees", Computer Graphics, vol 20, No. 4, 1986, pp. 55-64.
17. Prusinkiewicz P., "Applications of L-systems to Computer Imagery", in Proceedings of the Third Workshop on Graph Grammars and their Applications to Computer Science, Warrenton, Dec. 1986, pp. 534-548.
18. Reeves W. T., Blau R., "Approximate and Probabilistic Algorithms for Shading and Rendering Structured Particle Systems", Computer Graphics, vol. 19, No. 3, 1985, pp. 313-322.
19. Reffye (de) P., Modélisation de l'Architecture des Arbres Tropicaux par des Processus Stochastiques, Thèse de Doctorat ès Sciences, Université de Paris-Sud, Orsay, France, 1979.
20. Reffye (de) P., "Modéle Mathématique Aléatoire et Simulation de la Croissance et de l'Architecture du Caféier Robusta", Première partie, Café-Cacao-Thé, vol. 25, No. 2,1981, pp. 83-104. Deuxième partie, Café-Cacao-Thé, vol. 25, No. 4, 1981, pp. 219-230. Troisième partie, Café-Cacao-Thé, vol. 26, No. 2, 1982, pp. 77-96. Quatrième partie, Café-Cacao-Thé, vol. 27, No.1, 1983, pp. 3-20.
21. Reffye (de) P., Edelin C., Jaeger M., Cabart C., "Modélisation de l'Architecture des Arbres", in Proc. Int. Conf. "The tree", Montpellier, Sept. 85.
22. Rouane, "Un Modèle de la Ramification de la Croissance Végétale en tant qu'Image de la Différentiation Cellulaire", Comptes-Rendus de l'Académie des Sciences, Paris, T. 285, 26, Sept. 1977.
23. Smith A. R., "Plants, Fractals and Formal Languages", Computer Graphics, vol. 18, No. 3, 1984, pp. 1-10.
24. Smith A. R., Unpublished course notes, Fournier A. ed., *The Modeling of Natural Phenomena* (SIGGRAPH'87 course notes #16, Anaheim, CA, July 1987).
25. Stoker J.J., *Nonlinear Elasticity,* Gordon et Breach, New York, NY, 1968.

Spacetime Constraints

Andrew Witkin
Michael Kass

Schlumberger Palo Alto Research
3340 Hillview Avenue, Palo Alto, CA 94304

Abstract

Spacetime constraints are a new method for creating character animation. The animator specifies *what* the character has to do, for instance, "jump from here to there, clearing a hurdle in between;" *how* the motion should be performed, for instance "don't waste energy," or "come down hard enough to splatter whatever you land on;" the character's *physical structure*—the geometry, mass, connectivity, etc. of the parts; and the physical *resources* available to the character to accomplish the motion, for instance the character's muscles, a floor to push off from, etc. The requirements contained in this description, together with Newton's laws, comprise a problem of constrained optimization. The solution to this problem is a *physically valid* motion satisfying the "what" constraints and optimizing the "how" criteria. We present as examples a Luxo lamp performing a variety of coordinated motions. These realistic motions conform to such principles of traditional animation as anticipation, squash-and-stretch, follow-through, and timing.

Keywords — Animation, Constraints

I. Introduction

Computer animation has made enormous strides in the past several years. In particular, Pixar's *Luxo, Jr.* [13] marked a turning point as perhaps the first computer-generated work to compete seriously with works of traditional animation on every front. Key among the reasons for *Luxo, Jr.'s* success is that it was made by a talented animator who adapted the principles of traditional animation to the computer medium. *Luxo, Jr.*, in large measure, *is* a work of traditional animation that happens to use a computer to render and to interpolate between keyframes. John Lasseter spelled this out clearly in his presentation to

Siggraph '87 [12]. Although *Luxo, Jr.* showed us that the team of animator, keyframe system, and renderer can be a powerful one, the responsibility for defining the motion remains almost entirely with the animator.

Some aspects of animation—personality and appeal, for example—will surely be left to the animator's artistry and skill for a long time to come. However, many of the principles of animation are concerned with making the character's motion look *real* at a basic mechanical level that ought to admit to formal physical treatment. Consider for example a jump exhibiting anticipation, squash-and-stretch, and follow-through. Any creature—human or lamp—can only accelerate its own center of mass by pushing on something else. In jumping, the opportunity to control acceleration only exists during contact with the floor, because while airborne there is nothing to push on. Anticipation prior to takeoff is the phase in which the needed momentum is acquired by squashing then stretching to push off against the floor. Follow-through is the phase in which the momentum on landing is absorbed.

Such physical arguments make nice *post hoc* explanations, but can physics be brought to bear in *creating* the complex active motions of characters like Luxo? If so, how much of what we regard as "nice" motion follows directly from first principles, and how much is really a matter of style and convention?

This paper presents a physically-based approach to character animation in which coordinated, active motion is created automatically by specifying:

- *What* the character has to do, for instance "jump from here to there."

- *How* the motion should be performed, for instance "don't waste energy," or "come down hard enough to splatter whatever you land on."

- What the character's *physical structure* is—what the pieces are shaped like, what they weigh, how they're connected, etc.

- What physical *resources* are available to the character to accomplish the desired motion, for instance the character's muscles (or whatever an animate lamp has in place of muscles,) a floor to push off from, etc.

"Luxo" is a trademark of Jac Jacobsen Industries AS.

Our initial experiments with this approach have aimed at making a Luxo lamp execute a convincing jump just by telling it where to start and where to end. The results we present in this paper show that such properties as anticipation, follow-through, squash-and-stretch, and timing indeed emerge from a bare description of the motion's purpose and the physical context in which it occurs. Moreover, simple changes to the goals of the motion or to the physical model give rise to interesting variations on the basic motion. For example, doubling (or quadrupling) the mass of Luxo's base creates amusingly exaggerated motion in which the base *looks* heavy.

Our method entails the numerical solution of large constrained optimization problems, for which a variety of standard algorithms exist. These algorithms, while relatively expensive, spend most of their time solving sparse linear systems, and are therefore amenable to acceleration by array processors and other commonly available hardware. The greatest difficulty arises not in computing the numerical solution, but in setting up the intricate sparse matrix equations that drive the solution process. To address this problem we implemented an object-oriented symbolic algebra system that automates this difficult task almost entirely. We therefore believe the method described here can become a practical animation tool requiring no more mathematical sophistication of the end user than do current keyframing systems.

The remainder of the paper is organized as follows: the following section discusses the previous use of physical methods in animation. The spacetime method is then introduced using a moving particle as a toy example. Next, our extension of the method to complex problems is discussed. Finally, the Luxo model and the results obtained with it are described.

II.   Background and Motivation

Recently, there has been considerable interest in incorporating physics into animation using simulation methods. [10, 17, 18, 2, 16, 7, 9] The appeal of physical simulation as an animation technique lies in its promise to produce realistic motion automatically by applying the same physical laws that govern real objects' behavior.

Unfortunately, the realism of simulation comes at the expense of control. Simulation methods solve *initial value problems:* the course of a simulation is completely determined by the objects' initial positions and velocities, and by the forces applied to the objects along the way. An animator, however, is usually concerned as much with where the objects end up and how they get there as where they begin. Problems cast in this form are not initial value problems. For instance, while simulating a bouncing ball is easy enough, making the ball bounce *to* a particular place requires choosing just the right starting values for position, velocity, and spin. Making these choices manually is a painful matter of trial and error. Problems such as this one, in which both initial and final conditions are partially

or completely constrained, are called *two-point boundary problems,* requiring more elaborate solution methods than forward simulation.[6]

Character animation poses a still more difficult problem. Animals move by using their muscles to exert forces that vary as a function of time. Calculating the motion by simulation is straightforward once these time-dependent force functions are known, but the difficult problem is to calculate force functions that achieve the goals of the motion. Specifying these functions by hand would be hopeless, equivalent to making a robot move gracefully by manually varying its motor torques.

In an effort to reconcile the advantages of simulation with the need for control, several researchers [2, 10] have proposed methods for blending positional constraints with dynamic simulations. The idea behind these methods is to treat kinematic constraints as the consequences of unknown "constraint forces," solve for the forces, then add them into the simulation, exactly canceling that component of the applied forces that fights against the constraints.

Constraint force methods permit parts, such as a character's hands or feet, to be moved along predefined keyframed trajectories, but provide no help in defining the trajectories, which is the central problem in creating character animation. While allowing a character to be dragged around manually like a marionette, constraint forces sidestep the central issue of deciding how the character should move.

These shortcomings led us to adopt a new formulation of the constraint problem, whose central characteristic is that we solve for the character's motion and time-varying muscle forces over the entire time interval of interest, rather than progressing sequentially through time. Because we extend the model through time as well as space, we call the formulation *spacetime constraints*.

The spacetime formulation permits the imposition of constraints throughout the time course of the motion, with the effects of constraints propagating freely backward as well as forward in time. Constraints on initial, final, or intermediate positions and velocities directly encode the *goals* of the motion, while constraints limiting muscle forces or preventing interpenetration define properties of the physical situation. Additionally, Newtonian physics provides a constraint relating the force and position functions that must hold at every instant in time. Subject to these constraints we optimize functions that specify *how* the motion should be performed, in terms of efficiency, smoothness, etc. Solving this constrained optimization problem yields optimal, physically valid motion that achieves the goals specified by the animator.

III.   A spacetime particle

As a gentle but concrete introduction to the spacetime method, this section describes a minimal example involving a moving particle, influenced by gravity, and equipped with a "jet engine" as a means of locomotion. With no restrictions on the forces exerted by its engine, the particle can move any way it likes. The problem we formulate here is that of making the particle fly from a given starting point to a given destination in a fixed period of time, with minimal fuel consumption. This toy problem is too simple to produce any really interesting motion, but it exhibits all the key elements of the method, and will aid in understanding what follows.

A. Problem formulation

Let the particle's position as a function of time be $\mathbf{x}(t)$, and the time-varying jet force be $\mathbf{f}(t)$. Suppose for simplicity that the mass of the fuel is negligible compared to that of the particle, so the total mass may be treated as a constant, m, with a constant gravitational force $m\mathbf{g}$. Then the particle's equation of motion is

$$m\ddot{\mathbf{x}} - \mathbf{f} - m\mathbf{g} = 0, \qquad (1)$$

where $\ddot{\mathbf{x}}$ is the second time derivative of position. Given the function $\mathbf{f}(t)$, and initial values for $\mathbf{x}$ and $\dot{\mathbf{x}}$ at some time t_0, the motion $\mathbf{x}(t)$ from t_0 could be obtained by integrating equation 1 to solve the initial value problem.

Instead we wish to make the particle fly from a known point $\mathbf{a}$ to a known point $\mathbf{b}$ in a fixed period of time. Suppose for simplicity that the rate of fuel consumption is $|\mathbf{f}|^2$. In that case, we have constraints $\mathbf{x}(t_0) = \mathbf{a}$ and $\mathbf{x}(t_1) = \mathbf{b}$ subject to which

$$R = \int_{t_0}^{t_1} |\mathbf{f}(t)|^2 \, dt$$

must be minimized. The problem then is to find a force function $\mathbf{f}(t)$, defined on the interval (t_0, t_1), such that the position function $\mathbf{x}(t)$ obtained by solving equation 1 satisfies the boundary constraints, and such that the objective function R is a constrained minimum.

There exist a variety of standard approaches to solving problems of this form. Prevalent in the optimal control literature are iterative methods that solve the initial value problem within each iteration, using the equations of motion to obtain the position function from the force function (see [15] for a good survey.) We choose instead to represent the functions $\mathbf{x}(t)$ and $\mathbf{f}(t)$ independently. The equation of motion then enters as a constraint that relates the two functions, to be satisfied along with the other constraints during the solution process. Each function is discretized, that is, represented as a sequence of values, with time derivatives approximated by finite differences. This approach leads to a classical problem in constrained optimization, for which a variety of standard solution algorithms are available.

Let the discretized functions $\mathbf{x}(t)$ and $\mathbf{f}(t)$ be represented by sequences of values $\mathbf{x}_i$ and $\mathbf{f}_i$, $0 \le i \le n$, with h the time interval between samples. To approximate the time derivatives of $\mathbf{x}(t)$ we use the finite difference formulas

$$\dot{\mathbf{x}}_i = \frac{\mathbf{x}_i - \mathbf{x}_{i-1}}{h} \qquad (2)$$

$$\ddot{\mathbf{x}}_i = \frac{\mathbf{x}_{i+1} - 2\mathbf{x}_i + \mathbf{x}_{i-1}}{h^2} \qquad (3)$$

Substituting these relations into equation 1 gives n "physics constraints" relating the x_i's to the f_i's,

$$\mathbf{p}_i = m\frac{\mathbf{x}_{i+1} - 2\mathbf{x}_i + \mathbf{x}_{i-1}}{h^2} - \mathbf{f}_i - m\mathbf{g} = 0, \quad 1 < i < n. \quad (4)$$

In addition we have the two boundary constraints

$$\mathbf{c}_a = \mathbf{x}_1 - \mathbf{a} = 0$$

and

$$\mathbf{c}_b = \mathbf{x}_n - \mathbf{b} = 0.$$

Assuming that $\mathbf{f}(t)$ is constant between samples, the objective function R becomes a sum

$$R = h \sum_i |\mathbf{f}_i|^2 \qquad (5)$$

which is to be minimized subject to the constraints. The discretized objective and constraint functions are now expressed in terms of the $\mathbf{x}_i$'s and the $\mathbf{f}_i$'s, which are the independent variables to be solved for.

B. Numerical Solution

From the standpoint of the numerical solution process it is useful to suppress the structure of the particular problem, reducing it to a canonical form consisting of a collection of scalar independent variables S_j, $1 \le j \le n$, an objective function $R(S_j)$ to be minimized, and a collection of scalar constraint functions $C_i(S_j)$, $1 < i < m$, which must be driven to zero. In the current problem, the S_j's are the x, y, and z components of the $\mathbf{x}_i$'s and the $\mathbf{f}_i$'s, while the C_i's are the components of the $\mathbf{p}_i$'s, $\mathbf{c}_a$, and $\mathbf{c}_b$. Typically, setting up the linearized indices is the responsibility of a program that keeps track of the independent variables and the constraint functions.

In these terms, the standard constrained optimization problem is "Find S_j that minimizes $R(S_j)$ subject to $C_i(S_j) = 0$. For the sake of modularity, the numerical method that solves the problem is best regarded as an object that requests answers to certain standard questions about the system, and iteratively provides updated values for the solution vector S_j. Any method must be permitted to request the *values* of R and C_i at a given S_j. In addition, most effective methods require access to *derivatives* of R and C_i with respect to S_j, in order to move toward a solution.

The solution method we use is a variant of Sequential Quadratic Programming (SQP), described in detail in [6]. Essentially, the method computes a second-order Newton-Raphson step in R, and a first-order Newton-Raphson step in the C_i's, and combines the two steps by projecting the first onto the null space of the second (that is, onto the hyperplane for which all the C_i's are constant to first order.) Because it is first-order in the constraint functions and second-order in the objective function, the method requires that we be able to compute two derivative matrices: the *Jacobian* of the constraint functions, given by

$$J_{ij} = \frac{\partial C_i}{\partial S_j},$$

and the *Hessian* of the objective function,

$$H_{ij} = \frac{\partial^2 R}{\partial S_i \partial S_j}.$$

In addition, the first derivative vector $\partial R / \partial S_j$ must be available. The SQP step is obtained by solving two linear systems in sequence. The first,

$$-\frac{\partial R}{\partial S_i} = \sum_j H_{ij} \hat{S}_j$$

yields a step $\hat{S}_j$ that minimizes a second-order approximation to R, without regard to the constraints. The second,

$$-C_i = \sum_j J_{ij} (\bar{S}_j + \hat{S}_j)$$

yields a step $\bar{S}_j$ that drives linear approximations to the C_i's simultaneously to zero, and at the same time projects the optimization step $\hat{S}_j$ onto the null space of the constraint Jacobian. The final update is $\Delta S_j = \bar{S}_j + \hat{S}_j$. The algorithm reaches a fixed point when $C_i = 0$ and when any further decrease in R requires violating the constraints.

C.   Linear system solving

The choice of a method for solving these linear systems is critically important, because the matrices can be large. Although inverting a general $n \times n$ matrix is $O(n^3)$, the matrices arising in spacetime problems are nearly always extremely sparse. Exploiting the sparsity is essential to make the problem tractable. Moreover, over- and under-constrained systems, whose matrices are non-square and/or rank-deficient, can easily arise, in which case the inverse is undefined and the system cannot be solved. The latter problem is well treated by the pseudo-inverse [11, 7], which provides least-squares solutions to overconstrained problems, and minimal solutions to underconstrained ones. To compute the pseudo-inverse while exploiting random sparsity, we adapted a sparse conjugate gradient (CG) algorithm described in [14], which is $O(n^2)$ for typical problems. The CG algorithm solves the matrix equation $\mathbf{a} = \mathbf{Mb}$ by iteratively minimizing $|\mathbf{a} - \mathbf{Mb}|^2$, giving a least-squares solution to overconstrained problems. Provided that a zero starting-point is given for $\mathbf{b}$, the solution vector is restricted to the null-space complement of $\mathbf{M}$.

D.   Matrix evaluation.

Applying the SQP algorithm to the moving particle example requires evaluation of the sparse derivative matrices,

as well as the objective and constraint functions themselves. Apart from the bookkeeping required for indexing, these evaluations are straightforward. The Jacobian of the physics constraint is given by

$$
\begin{aligned}
\frac{\partial \mathbf{p}_i}{\partial \mathbf{x}_j} &= 2m/h^2, \quad i = j \\
&= -m/h^2, \quad i = j \pm 1 \\
&= 0, \quad \text{otherwise} \\
\frac{\partial \mathbf{p}_i}{\partial \mathbf{f}_j} &= 1, \quad i = j \\
&= 0, \quad \text{otherwise.}
\end{aligned}
$$

The Jacobians of the boundary constraints are trivial. The gradient of R is

$$\frac{\partial R}{\partial \mathbf{f}_i} = 2\mathbf{f}_i,$$

and the Hessian is

$$
\begin{aligned}
\frac{\partial^2 R}{\partial \mathbf{f}_i \partial \mathbf{f}_j} &= 2, \quad i = j \\
&= 0, \quad \text{otherwise.}
\end{aligned}
$$

Although it happens that the toy problem we chose constrains initial and final positions, nothing in the solution approach depends on this configuration: initial and final conditions could be left free, and constraints at arbitrary internal points could be added. Moreover, arbitrary constraints of the form $F(S_i) = 0$, not just position constraints, may be added provided that the constraint functions and their derivatives can be evaluated.

IV.   Extension to complex models

In principle, the procedure described in the last section extends to complex models, constraints, and objective functions. In practice, as the model grows more complex, the problem becomes prohibitively difficult. The difficulty lies not so much in calculating the numerical solution as in creating code to evaluate the constraint and objective functions and their sparse derivatives, and in coercing the evaluations into the form of a canonical constrained optimization. In particular, the required differentiations can lead to enormous algebraic expressions that are all but impossible to derive and code by hand.

To make the method practical, we developed a lisp-based system that performs these difficult tasks automatically. The system consists of three principle elements: a specialized math compiler that performs symbolic differentiation and simplification of tensor forms, and generates optimized code to perform the evaluations; a runtime system that allows the generated functions to be composed dynamically, automatically building the vectors and sparse matrices that drive the numerical solution; and an SQP solver.

Because the mathematical operations required to define a new primitive object or constraint are highly stylized, it is possible to reduce the programmer's job to a simple cookbook procedure. Once the primitives are defined, a user with little or no knowledge of the underlying mathematics can wire them together dynamically to create animation. Although a full description is beyond the scope of this paper, this section briefly outlines the system and the operations it performs.

A. Function Boxes

A *function box,* the lowest level construct in the system, consists of a set of input quantities, which may be scalars, vectors, matrices, or higher-order tensors, and a collection of output quantities each defined as a mathematical function of the inputs. To define a function box, the programmer specifies the inputs, the outputs, and the functions that relate them. The function definitions are mathematical expressions that may include differentiations as well as algebraic operations. Non-scalar quantities are expressed and manipulated using index notation with the summation convention. For each output, the system performs symbolic differentiation as called for, simplifies the resulting expression, extracts common sub-expressions, and generates an optimized lisp function that evaluates the output given the inputs. In addition, the system symbolically differentiates each output with respect to each input on which it depends, creates a lisp function to evaluate the derivative, and analyzes its sparsity. These functions form the Jacobians of the outputs. The generated functions, input-output dependencies, sparsities, etc., are recorded in a data structure accessible to the runtime system.

B. User Interface

Once defined, function boxes are manipulated using a graphical interface in which they appear as literal boxes on the screen, with ports representing the input and output quantities.[5] The user may instantiate boxes, connecting the ports to form a graph whose arcs represent function composition. In this way, complex systems are built dynamically by composing pre-compiled primitives. By default, input ports to which nothing has been connected are treated as internal constants whose values may be inspected and modified interactively, and unconnected output ports are ignored. However, inputs may also be flagged by the user as state variables to be solved for, and outputs may be flagged either as constraints or as terms to be summed into the objective function.

C. Runtime System

Once the graph representing the model has been constructed, and the state-variables, constraints, and objective terms declared, a pre-runtime computation is performed to set up the constrained optimization. The user-declared state variables, constraints, and objective terms are collected and indexed to form the quantities S_j, C_i, and R required by the solver. The sparse derivatives are formed by propagation through the graph using the chain rule, with the individual Jacobian functions associated with function boxes combined by a hierarchy of sparse

matrix multiplications and additions. An optimal sequence of adds and multiplies is pre-computed for each sparse matrix operation, and the sparsity patterns of the resulting global matrices are also precomputed. Evaluation of C_i, R, and their derivatives, then proceeds by recursing through the graph, calling the individual value and Jacobian functions, and performing the sparse matrix operations. The solver communicates with the model by requesting these evaluations and updating the state vector.

D. Defining Objects

Built on top of the basic system is a layer handling the specifics of physical object models, whose main job is to construct the object's equations of motion. In the case of the moving particle this just involved direct application of $f = ma$. However, deriving the equations of motion for more complicated objects can be difficult.

We derive the equations automatically using Lagrangian Dynamics [8], a classical cookbook procedure in which an expression for a body's kinetic energy is subjected to a series of symbolic differentiations. Lagrange's equations of motion are given by

$$\frac{d}{dt}\left(\frac{\partial T}{\partial \dot{\mathbf{q}}}\right) - \frac{\partial T}{\partial \mathbf{q}} - \mathbf{Q} = 0, \qquad (6)$$

where T is kinetic energy, $\mathbf{q}$ is a vector of *generalized coordinates,* and $\mathbf{Q}$ is a *generalized force.* The components of the generalized coordinates are whatever variables control the positions and orientations of parts of the body (e.g. translations, rotations, joint angles, etc.) The generalized force is just the sum of ordinary forces applied to body, transformed into generalized coordinates. For point forces, this transformation is accomplished by multiplying the force vector by the Jacobian of the point at which the force is applied with respect to $\mathbf{q}$.

To define an object, the user is required to supply expressions for T, and for the coordinates of points on the body to which forces or constraints may be applied. Although T must be derived manually, this is a manageable job and need only be done once when a primitive object is defined. Given these expressions, automatic construction of a function box representing the objects is straightforward: the kinetic energy expression is subjected to the rote symbolic differentiations called for in equation 6, with an additional derivative with respect to $\mathbf{q}$ used to define the Jacobian of the physics constraint. The expressions for material points are also differentiated with respect to $\mathbf{q}$ to create "force converter" functions, small Jacobian matrices that map applied forces into generalized coordinates. The function box takes as inputs values for $\mathbf{q}$, $\dot{\mathbf{q}}$, and $\ddot{\mathbf{q}}$, for applied forces, and for constants such as masses and dimensions. It produces outputs for the "physics constraint" defined by the equations of motion, and for the positions and velocities of the material points defined by the user.

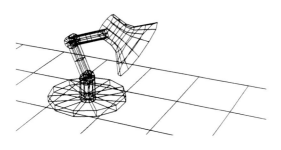

Figure 1: Luxo

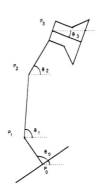

Figure 2: Luxo's parameters: P_0 is a translation, and θ_i is the orientation of the i-th link. Points P_1–P_3 are computed from these parameters.

E. Discretized functions of time

In developing the particle example of the last section, discretized functions representing forces and positions over time were incorporated into the equations of motion by direct substitution. Given the ability to compose functions and their sparse Jacobians automatically, we adopted the alternative of constructing specialized function boxes to represent discretized functions. These boxes contain the sequence of values representing the function, and output the values and the time-derivatives obtained using finite-difference formulas. The Jacobians of these output functions are trivial constant diagonal or banded matrices. The values and derivatives are connected to the corresponding inputs on the object model, causing the discretization to be effected automatically at runtime.

V. Spacetime Luxo

We are now equipped to proceed to a spacetime model of an animate Luxo Lamp. The model is composed of rigid bodies of uniform mass connected by frictionless joints. Each joint is equipped with a "muscle" modeled as an angular spring whose stiffness and rest angle are free to vary with time. The lamp is subject to the forces of its own muscles, in addition to the external force of gravity and the contact forces arising from its interaction with objects such as floors and skijumps. A picture of the model appears in Figure 1. In our initial examples, Luxo's motion is restricted to a plane. This expedient simplifies the mathematics, while still allowing the creation of complex, subtle, and interesting motion. Extension of the model to three dimensions involves no fundamental difficulties, although it leads to systems that are somewhat larger, somewhat slower, and more difficult to debug. The definition of the model consists of less than a page of tensor expressions, which expand into roughly 4000 lines of automatically generated lisp code.

A. Kinetic Energy

As discussed in the last section, our principle task in defining the model was to formulate an expression for the kinetic energy, T. In general, T is the volume integral over the body of the kinetic energy of each particle, $\frac{1}{2}\rho\,|\dot{\mathbf{x}}|^2$, where ρ is the mass density at point x. The kinetic energy of an articulated object is the sum of the kinetic energies of the parts. Each of Luxo's links is modeled as a rigid body rotating about an axis of fixed direction that passes through the origin in body coordinates (see Figure 2.) Because the axis is fixed, the orientation of the i-th link may be denoted by a single angle θ_i, with angular velocity $\omega_i = \dot{\theta}_i\mathbf{a}$, where $\mathbf{a}$ is a unit vector in the direction of the axis. In addition to rotation, the body origin undergoes a translation $\mathbf{p}_i$, with translational velocity $\mathbf{v}_i = d\mathbf{p}_i/dt$. Each link has mass m_i, a constant moment of inertia I_i about the rotation axis, and a center of mass $\mathbf{c}_i$ expressed as a displacement from the body origin. In these terms, the kinetic energy of the i-th link is

$$T_i = \frac{1}{2}m_i\,|\mathbf{v}_i|^2 + m_i\omega_i \cdot \mathbf{v}_i \times \mathbf{c}_i + \frac{1}{2}\,|\omega_i|^2\,I_i. \qquad (7)$$

To connect the links, each link inherits as its translation the position of the previous link's endpoint, with the base's translation, $\mathbf{P}$, serving as a translation parameter for the whole model. The translational velocity $\mathbf{v}_i$ of the i-th link is thus

$$\begin{aligned}
\mathbf{v}_i &= \frac{d\mathbf{P}}{dt}, \quad i = 0 \\
&= \mathbf{v}_{i-1} + \mathbf{r}_{i-1} \times \omega_{i-1}, \quad \text{otherwise}
\end{aligned}$$

where $\mathbf{r}_{i-1}$ is a vector from the $(i-1)$-th link's center of rotation to its point of attachment with the i-th link. The total kinetic energy T is obtained by recursively substituting this expression into equation 7 to obtain the T_i's, and summing over i.

B. Muscles

Luxo's muscles are three angular springs, one situated at each joint. The spring force on the joint connecting the i-th and $(i+1)$-th links is defined by

$$F_i = k_i(\phi_i - \rho_i),$$

where k_i is the stiffness constant, ϕ_i is the joint angle, and ρ_i is the rest angle. Our model is parameterized by link orientations rather than joint angles. The joint angle is $\phi_i = \theta_{i+1} - \theta_i$, the difference between the orientations of the surrounding links. The generalized force on θ_i, the orientation of the i-th link, due to the j-th muscle is

$$
\begin{aligned}
Q_i &= \sum_j F_j \frac{d\phi_i}{d\theta_j}, \\
&= k_j(\phi_j - \rho_j), \quad j = i+1 \\
&= -k_j(\phi_j - \rho_j), \quad j = i \\
&= 0, \quad \text{otherwise}
\end{aligned}
$$

Unlike passive springs whose stiffness and rest state are constants, k_i and ρ_i vary freely over time, allowing arbitrary time-dependent joint forces to be exerted.

VI. Results

A. Jumping Luxo

Jumping motion was created using kinematic constraints to specify initial and final poses, with linear interpolation between the poses to create a trivial initial condition for the spacetime iteration. Another constraint was used to put Luxo on the floor during the initial and final phases of the motion. Subject to these and the physics constraint, we minimized the power due to the muscles, $F_\theta \dot\theta$. In one variation, we adjusted the mass of Luxo's base, leaving the situation otherwise unchanged. In another, we additionally constrained the force of contact with the floor on landing, to produce a relatively soft landing. In a final variation, we added a hurdle, together with a constraint that the jump clear the hurdle.

The pose constraints consisted of values for the three joint angles, and were applied to the first two and last two frames of motion. Because we measure velocity using a finite difference, this incorporates the additional constraint that Luxo be at rest at the beginning and end of motion. Initial values for the orientations were obtained by linear interpolation between the two poses.

The floor enters both as a kinematic constraint and as a force. In general, collision constraints appear as inequalities, but to simplify matters, we chose to specify explicitly the time intervals during which Luxo was on the floor, imposing during those times the equality constraints

$$\theta_0 - \frac{\pi}{2} = 0, \mathbf{P} - \mathbf{P}_f = 0$$

where θ_0 is the orientation of the base, $\mathbf{P}$ is the position of the center of the base, and $\mathbf{P}_f$ is a constant point on the floor. In other words, the position and orientation of the base are nailed. The limitation of this formulation, compared to an inequality, is that the times at which contact occurs must be pre-specified, rather than allowing things to bounce freely. The floor constraint was enabled for the first and last five frames, allowing time for anticipation and follow-through. Of course, two different values were used for P_f at the start and finish, defining the start end points of the jump.

The floor constraint represents a mechanical interaction involving the transmission of force between the base and the floor. This contact force must be taken into account to satisfy the physics constraint. The simple contact model used for the jump has the base colliding with the floor inelastically with infinite friction, which means that the base comes to rest, losing its kinetic energy, at the moment of contact. The contact force is therefore whatever arbitrary force on the base—specifically, on $\mathbf{P}$ and θ_0—is required to satisfy physics in light of the floor constraint. No special provision need be made to solve for the contact forces beyond introducing additional state variables to represent them. Their values are then determined during the constraint-solving process. This method of solving for constraint forces applies to other mechanical constraints, such as joint attachments, and is closely related to the method of Lagrange multipliers.

The choice of optimization criteria is an area we have just begun to explore. In the examples shown, we sought to optimize a measure of the motion's mechanical efficiency by minimizing the *power* consumed by the muscles at each time step, which for each joint is the product of the muscle force and the joint's angular velocity. Our preliminary observation is that this criterion produces relatively fluid and natural motion, compared to kinematic smoothness criteria in terms of velocity and acceleration, which tend to come out looking somewhat arthritic.

Figure 3 shows a series of iterations leading from an initial motion in which Luxo translates, floating well above the floor, to a finished jump in which all the constraints are met and the objective function is minimized. Note that the elements of realistic motion already appear after the first iteration. The final motion shows marked anticipation, squash-and-stretch, and follow-through. From its pre-defined initial pose, Luxo assumes a crouch providing a pose from which to build momentum. The crouch is followed by a momentum-building forward-and-upward extension to a stretched launching position. While in flight, the center of mass moves ballistically along a parabolic arc determined by the launch velocity and by the force of gravity. Toward the end of the flight, Luxo once again assumes a crouched position in anticipation of landing, extending slightly while moving toward impact. This "stomp" maneuver has the effect of transferring kinetic energy into the base, where it vanishes in the inelastic collision with the floor. Following impact, luxo extends forward while compressing slightly, dissipating the remaining momentum of flight, then rises smoothly to its pre-specified final pose.

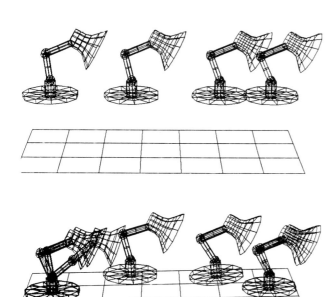

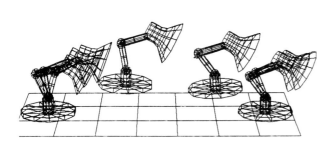

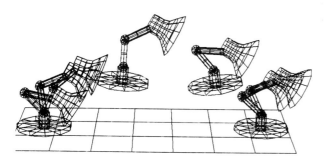

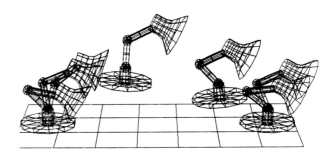

Figure 4: A variation on the basic jump in which the contact force on landing is constrained to be small. The force of impact is reduced by squashing just before landing, reducing the velocity and hence the kinetic energy of the base. In contrast, the jump in Figure 3 exhibits a slight *stretch* before impact, producing an energy-absorbing stomp.

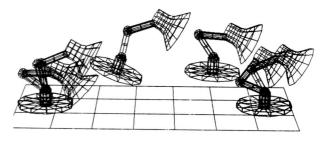

Figure 5: The mass of Luxo's base has been doubled. In other respects, the conditions are the same as those producing the basic jump.

Figure 3: From top to bottom, a series of iterations leading from an initial motion in which Luxo translates, floating above the floor, to a finished jump in which all the constraints are met and the optimization function is minimized. The final motion shows marked anticipation, squash-and-stretch, and follow-through.

In the first variation on the basic jump, we add an additional constraint fixing the contact force on landing. The value we choose provides control over a hard-to-soft landing dimension—a large landing force leads to an exaggerated stomp, as if trying to squash a bug, while a small value leads to a soft landing, as if trying to avoid breaking something fragile. Figure 4 shows a relatively soft landing, generated under the same conditions as the basic jump except for the contact force constraint. Comparing the motion to the basic jump, we see that Luxo softened the blow of impact by squashing while moving toward impact, reducing the velocity, and hence the kinetic energy of the base. In contrast, the basic jump has a small *stretch* before impact, producing an energy-absorbing stomp.

The next variation has the same conditions as the basic jump, but the mass of the base has been doubled. The final motion is shown in Figure 5. As expected, both the anticipation and follow-through are exaggerated in compensation for the greater mass.

A final variation, shown in Figure 6, has the conditions of the soft-landing jump, but with a hurdle interposed between start and finish, and an additional constraint that Luxo clear the hurdle. As one would expect, the extra height required is gained by squashing vigorously on approaching the wall.

The jumping examples each took under 10 minutes to compute on a Symbolics 3640. While this is hardly interactive speed, it constitutes a tiny fraction of the cost of high-quality rendering.

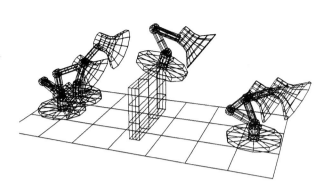

Figure 6: Hurdle Jump

Figure 7: Ski Jump

B. Ski Jumping

Figure 7 shows Luxo descending a ski jump. As in the previous case, Luxo is constrained to be on the ski jump and the landing at particular time samples. The biggest difference between the ski-jump and the infinite-friction floor of the previous example is that Luxo is free to slide, with the exact positions on the ski jump and the landing left unspecified except at the top and bottom of the ski jump. In addition, there is a constraint that the orientation of the base must be tangent to the surface it is resting on.

Both the ski jump and landing exert forces on Luxo. There is a normal force which keeps him from falling through and a frictional force which is tangent to the surface and proportional to the tangential velocity. The coefficients of friction were state variables in the optimization.

At one time instant while Luxo is in the air, the height of his base is constrained. In addition, there is a term in the objective function which gives him a preference for a particular pose while in the air. This is a "style" optimization without which Luxo is content to go through the air in a bent position.

Luxo is also given pose constraints at the beginning and end of the motion. Unlike the previous jumps, however, his initial velocity is unconstrained.

Figure 8: Spacetime constraints: a cartoonist's view. (c) 1988 by Laura Green, used by permission.

The initial condition for the optimization was a uniform translation in the air above both the ski jump and the landing. In the first iteration, Luxo puts his feet on the ski jump and landing. By iteration 4, there is significant anticipation and follow through. Figure 7 is the result after 16 iterations.

Both the ski jump and landing are built from two B-spline segments. The entire jump was computed with 28 time samples in the optimization. There were 223 constraints and 394 state variables. The Jacobian contained 3587 non-zero entries, about 4% of the total number of entries. The entire motion was computed in 45 minutes on a Symbolics 3600.

VII. Discussion

Our results show that spacetime methods are capable of producing realistic, complex and coordinated motion given only minimal kinematic constraints. Such basic attributes as anticipation, squash-and-stretch, follow-through, and timing emerge on their own from the requirement that the kinematic constraints be met in a physically valid way subject to simple optimization criteria.

The principle advantage of spacetime methods over simple keyframing is that they do much of the work that the animator would otherwise be required to do, and that only a skilled animator *can* do. Motions that would require highly detailed keyframe information may be sketched out at the level of "start here" and "stop there." This is a profoundly different and more economical means of control than conventional keyframing affords, an advantage that easily outweighs the greater mathematical complexity and computational cost of the method.

Beyond sparser keyframing, spacetime methods offer really new forms of motion control. For example, we saw in the previous section that constraints on forces, such as the force of a collision, can be used in a direct and simple way to say "hit hard" or "hit softly," producing subtle but very effective changes in the motion.

Of the new opportunities for motion control, perhaps the most exciting is the selection of optimization criteria to affect the motion globally, an area we have only begun to explore. With a little thought, it is clear that a magic "right" criterion, whether based on smoothness, efficiency or some other principle, is unlikely to emerge and would in any case be undesirable. This is because the "optimal" way to perform a motion, as with any optimization, depends on what you're trying to do. Consider for example several versions of a character crossing a room: in one case, walking on hot coals; in another, walking on eggs; in another, carrying a full bowl of hot soup; and in still another, pursued by a bear. Plainly the character's goals—and attendant criteria of optimality—are very different in each case. We would hope to see these differing goals reflected in the motion. The possibility of controlling motion directly in terms of its goals, not just where it goes but how, is one we intend to explore.

References

[1] William W. Armstrong and Mark W. Green, *The dynamics of articulated rigid bodies for purposes of animation,* in *Visual Computer,* Springer-Verlag, 1985, pp. 231-240.

[2] Ronen Barzel and Alan H. Barr, *Dynamic Constraints,* Topics in Physically Based Modeling, Course Notes, Vol. 16, Siggraph 1987

[3] Michael Brady et. al., eds, *Robot Motion: Planning and Control,* MIT Press, Cambridge, MA, 1982

[4] Charles E. Buckley, *The Application of Continuum Methods to Path Planning,* Doctoral Dissertation, Dept. of Mechanical Engineering, Stanford University, Stanford, CA, 1985

[5] Kurt Fleischer and Andrew Witkin, *A modeling testbed,* Proc. Graphics Interface, 1988.

[6] Phillip Gill, Walter Murray, and Margret Wright, *Practical Optimization,* Academic Press, New York, NY, 1981

[7] Michael Girard and Anthony a Maciejewski, *Computataional Modeling for the Computer Animation of Legged Figures,* Proc. SIGGRAPH, 1985, pp. 263-270

[8] Herbert Goldstein, *Classical Mechanics,* Addison Wesley, Reading, MA, 1950

[9] David Haumann, *Modeling the Physical Behavior of Flexible Objects,* Topics in Physically Based Modeling, Course Notes, Vol. 16, Siggraph 1987

[10] Paul Isaacs and Michael Cohen, *Controlling Dynamic Simulation with Kinematic Constraints, Behavior Functions and Inverse Dynamics,* Proc. Siggraph 1987, pp. 215-224

[11] Charles Klein and Ching-Hsiang Huang, *Review of Pseudoinverse Control for Use with Kinematically Redundant Manipulators,* IEEE Trans. SMC, Vol. 13, No. 3, 1983

[12] John Lasseter, *Principles of Traditional Animation Applied to 3D Computer Animation,* Proc. Siggraph 1987, pp. 35-44

[13] Pixar, *Luxo, Jr.,* (film,) 1986

[14] William Press et. al., *Numerical Recipes,* Cambridge University Press, Cambridge, England, 1986

[15] Robert S. Stengel, *Stochastic Optimal Control,* John Wiley and Sons, New York, 1986.

[16] Demetri Terzopoulos, John Platt, Alan Barr, and Kurt Fleischer, *Elastically Deformable Models,* Proc. SIGGRAPH, 1987.

[17] Jane Wilhelms and Brian Barsky, *Using Dynamic Analysis To Animate Articulated Bodies Such As Humans and Robots,* Graphics Interface, 1985.

[18] Andrew Witkin, Kurt Fleischer, and Alan Barr, *Energy constraints on parameterized models,* Computer Graphics, **21** (4) July 1987, pp. 225-232 (Proc. SIGGRAPH '87).

The Motion Dynamics of Snakes and Worms

Gavin S. P. Miller

Alias Research Inc.

110 Richmond St. East,

Toronto, Canada. M5C 1P1.

Abstract

Legless figures such as snakes and worms are modelled as mass-spring systems. Muscle contractions are simulated by animating the spring tensions. Directional friction due to the surface structure is included in the dynamic model and legless figure locomotion results. Various modes of locomotion are described.

Keywords: Modeling, Deformation, Elasticity, Dynamics, Animation, Simulation, Locomotion, Rendering, Texture.
CR categories: I.3.5 - Computational Geometry and Object Modeling (Surface and object representations); I.3.7 - Three-Dimensional Graphics and Realism (Color, shading, texture and animation).

1. Introduction

Modelling biological forms using computer graphics poses several difficult problems. The models must look convincing both in their static appearance and in the way they move. Legged figures, based on hierarchies of transformations, have received considerable attention in recent years. Both kinematic and dynamic models have been presented in the literature [5]. Whilst they are successful at animating skeletal structures, the problems of modelling skin and muscle remain . Waters presented a facial animation technique which modelled the effects of muscle tensions over a region of skin [13]. Whilst successful in that application, the model was purely geometrical rather than dynamic. It did not respond in a physically realistic fashion to external forces. For animations to be flexible and realistic, biological forms should not only work in isolation but they should be able to interact with each other and with their environment.

Elastically deformable models simulate the interaction of objects with external constraints by modelling the physical properties of the materials [12]. By modelling biological structures in this way, it should be possible to create life-like animations. The models will be made to look "alive" by animating the elastic properties of the muscles as a function of time.

Unfortunately, of course, real plants and animals have highly complex structures, leading to complicated and extremely expensive models. However, certain classes of creature are elegant in their simplicity, namely snakes, caterpillars and worms.

2. Motivation

Animals have been a favourite topic of animation from its earliest days. Being either loveable or frightening, they have a strong emotive effect on an audience. At the same time, the real-life counterparts are notoriously difficult to train as well as being potentially dangerous. Puppets have been used to good effect although they either require direct physical controls or tedious alteration for every frame [3]. Exceptions to this include models which have one actuator for each degree of freedom of the creature. Computer animation holds the promise of creating subtle motions automatically and synthesising large numbers of creatures without additional work on the part of the animator. Reynolds modelled the interaction of schools of fish and flocks of birds [11]. The individual creatures were comparatively simple, but collision avoidance strategies led to complex and beautiful motions.

Individual snakes and worms, on the other hand, change shape with every frame. They slither over the ground in a way which depends on how well they grip it. They deform elastically when external forces are applied. A simple model with these characteristics is described in the next section.

3. Modelling Elastically Deformable Strands

Snakes and worms have complex internal structures. For the purposes of this paper, a greatly simplified model was used. Each segment of the creature was modelled as a cube of masses with springs along each edge and across the diagonal of each face. For each time interval, the spring lengths and spring length velocities were used to compute the forces exerted on the masses at the end of each spring.

$$f = k\,(L - l) - D\,\frac{dl}{dt}$$

where f is the force along the spring direction, k is the spring constant, D is the damping, l is the current length of the spring and L is the minimum energy spring length. (L is animated as a function of time to simulate muscle contractions.) In addition, external forces such as gravity were computed, and the total force was divided by the mass to give the acceleration. The new position was then computed by integrating the acceleration twice with respect to time.

$$\vec{x}_p = \frac{1}{m_p} \iint \vec{f}_t \, dt \, dt$$

where $\vec{x}_p$ is the position of point p, m_p is the mass of the point and $\vec{f}_t$ is the total force acting on the point. This simple mass spring model is adequate to describe many physical objects such as pieces of rope and strands of hair. (Unfortunately a head of such hair would be extremely expensive to compute). The edge and diagonal springs together control the Young's modulus of the strand, whilst the diagonal springs affect the shear and twisting moduli.

The method of integration appropriate to compute the position of each point mass depends in part on how external constraints are implemented. Impulse-based collisions detect whether the motion of a point intersects a surface. If it does, the new position and velocity are computed analytically (see Figure 1).

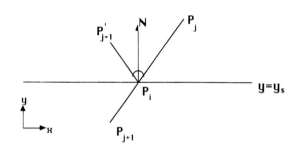

Figure 1. Point-plane constraint intersection.

For a point mass travelling from P_j to P_{j+1}, the intersection position (x_i, y_i) will be given by:

$$y_i = y_s$$

$$x_i = x_{j+1} + (y_s - y_{j+1}) \frac{(x_j - x_{j+1})}{(y_j - y_{j+1})}$$

For an inelastic collision, the new position (x'_{j+1}, y'_{j+1}) is given by:

$$y'_{j+1} = y_i + r_n (y_i - y_{j+1})$$

$$x'_{j+1} = x_i + r_t (x_i - x_{j+1})$$

where r_n is the coefficient of normal reflection, and r_t is the coefficient of tangent reflection.

The advantage of such a scheme is that the collision detection calculation is simple to compute. It is equivalent to intersecting a ray with a surface. Note that the collision calculation is done in the static coordinate frame of the constraint, so that P_j and P_{j+1} take account of the motion of the constraint relative to the world coordinate system between successive time steps. Another advantage is that the points are guaranteed not to penetrate the constraint. Impulse based constraints are most easily implemented when used in combination with Euler integration.

$$v_{j+1} = v_j + a_j \, \Delta t$$

$$x_{j+1} = x_j + v_j \, \Delta t + \frac{1}{2} a_j \, \Delta t^2$$

This is slower to converge than higher order methods such as the Runge-Kutta [14] or predictor-corrector methods [6], which assume that the forces vary smoothly as a function of time. These higher order methods have to be restarted when impulse based techniques are used. For such methods the constraints are usually expressed as a force of repulsion as the particle approaches the surface. The more localised the force, the smaller the time-step needed for correct integration. As explained later, forces such as directional friction can occur very suddenly, so this paper was illustrated using Euler integration, although the physical principles would apply equally well to other techniques.

Unfortunately, applying constraints to the point masses is not a general solution to collision detection. Sharp discontinuities in the constraints, such as at a cliff edge, should be tested against the edges of the cubes as well as the vertices. So there should really be both particle-surface and edge-surface collision detection. This will be especially important when creatures interact with each other and with themselves.

However, for this paper the actual locomotion of snakes and worms was of primary interest, so the constraints were kept simple: a horizontal floor and a rounded cliff edge.

4. Muscle Contractions and Directional Friction

In order to make the mass-spring systems move it is necessary to exert forces on the masses. This may be done globally using gravity and viscous drag [12] and directly, using force vectors applied to individual masses. This is equivalent to having a rubber puppet with strings and rods pulling and pushing it. However, to make the model look really alive it is necessary to generate the motive power internally. The mass-spring system must use frictional forces with constraints and changes of shape to achieve locomotion. Walking is one example of using friction to move the centre of mass. One foot stays in place on the ground as the other is moved through the air. In this way the frictional force with the ground is exploited whilst the geometry is reconfigured. Lifting feet is necessary because the frictional forces are isotropic i.e. they are independent of the direction in which the foot is slid. Sliding one foot forward causes the other foot to slide back equally far if the pressure on each foot is the same, hence the need to change pressure from one foot to the other. Snakes and worms, on the other hand, remain in contact with the ground at all times (sidewinding is an exception to this). So, in order to get along, they must have frictional forces which vary with the direction of sliding. This is achieved by the scales which cover the skin. Just as the microstructure of a surface affects its macroscopic optical properties, the small scale features of an object determine the frictional forces generated when it interacts with its environment.

If the body segment moves forwards, the scales slide relatively easily over the ground exerting little friction. When the body segment slides backwards, however, the scales dig in and the frictional force suddenly becomes very great. Worm locomotion is a simple application of this idea. Figure 2 illustrates a two mass, one spring worm.

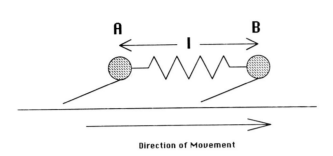

Direction of Movement

Figure 2. A two mass, one spring worm.

If the spring is expanded (l increased) scale B will slide over the ground and scale A will grip. If the spring is contracted (l decreased) scale B will dig in and scale A will slide. Both these motions lead to the system travelling in the same direction, so oscillating the spring length as a function of time will lead to forward motion.

A real worm, of course, consists of a number of such sections. If all of the spring lengths were varied in phase, only the front and back most scales would ever grip the floor. All of the intermediate scales would be constantly sliding. So, to prevent undue stresses at either end, a worm sends waves of compression from its head to its tail. The familiar worm-like motion results. In a real worm the travelling compression wave seems to be approximately a square-wave. Unfortunately, because of the coarse nature of the mass-spring approximation, square-waves lead to peculiar distortions of the shape of the worm. However, a travelling sine-wave gives well-behaved and acceptably realistic results for the worm.

In the computer simulation, the directional friction was implemented as follows. The local forward spine unit vector $\vec{s}$ was computed from the centre of the next and last segments.

$$\vec{s} = \frac{\vec{x}_{p+1} - \vec{x}_{p-1}}{|\vec{x}_{p+1} - \vec{x}_{p-1}|}$$

The velocity was then modified as follows :

$$\text{if } (\vec{s} . \vec{v} < 0.0) \ \vec{v} = \vec{v} - \vec{s}(\vec{s} . \vec{v})$$

This stops any backwards sliding of the worm. The frictional effect was only applied if the point mass was less than a certain distance from the floor so that is could be said to be in contact. Because the model is a dynamic one, it was possible to apply gravity as well. Image 1a shows a worm in free-fall colliding with the constraint, in this case a book. The nose slides forwards on impact. Image 1b shows the body mostly in contact, the tail exhibits a little "bounce". Image 1c shows the worm wriggling towards a vertical edge. The front begins to bend downwards under the weight. Image 1d shows the worm sliding off the edge. The tail flops over with the momentum from the sliding.

In a real worm, as the muscles contract they bulge out. This may be included in the model by making the circumferential spring lengths increase as a function of the axial compression. The model used for this animation was to keep the total volume of the worm constant. $1/\sqrt{l}$ along the worm was used to scale the value of L for the springs around the circumference of the worm. This then helps to conserve volume.

The anatomy of a snake is very different from a worm, both in its internal structure and in the formation of its scales (squamation). Snakes have a skeleton with a flexible spine and ribs. The scales on a snake are diamond shaped on the upper part, but on the bottom they are a linear array of slanted blades. Snakes come in a wide variety of shapes and sizes [8] but move in only four basic ways, just as there are various "gaits" for four-legged figures [4].

The worm motion described above is called "rectilinear progression" and is achieved by the snake sliding its skin over its ribs [7]. The more familiar sinusoidal motion is called "horizontal undulatory progression".

To model this, compression waves are again sent down the mass-spring system, but the springs on the left hand side of the snake are 180 degrees out of phase with those on the right hand side. This has the effect of bending the snake into the familiar waves. The directional friction with the floor leads to the snake being propelled along. When a snake has a good grip on the ground and has highly curved coils and is moving slowly, the body segments all follow along the same curve. It is as if the cross-sections of the snake follow along the same spline curve at constant distances. Indeed this technique has been used to model and animate snakes [2] and [10]. However, if the snake only has a poor grip on the surface, or if it is acted on by external forces, or if it is changing the amplitude of its coiling, then the segments will slide sideways as well.

Image 2a shows the mass spring system "at rest" with no muscle tensions. Image 2b shows the effects of undulations deforming the snake. The head-end has stayed virtually fixed while the tail is dragged forwards as the coils form. Image 2c shows the snake with the coils fully formed. Little forward motion of the head-end has been achieved. Image 2d shows the snake at a later stage. The segments are now all very nearly following each other along the same path.

The dynamic snake model is interesting in the way that it deviates from the spline following paradigm. The tail, because it is not laterally constrained, swishes slightly from side to side. (It looks like a happy snake). In addition, the mass spring system has secondary reactions to the spring contractions and the friction. This leads to a slightly irregular motion of the snake which looks both convincing and realistic. Finally, of course, the snake can fall under gravity and collide with constraints in the same way that the worm did.

A third form of snake locomotion is called "sidewinding". When grip on the ground is poor such as in open areas of sand, some snakes adopt a method of reducing their contact area with the sand so that the effective pressure increases. This also prevents undue heat exchange with the hot sand. This motion may be achieved using a vertical sinusoidal flexing of the snake which is 90 degrees out of phase with respect to the horizontal undulations. The vertical flexing has the effect of lifting all but a small portion of the snake off the ground. The wavelength used for the simulation in this paper was the length of the snake divided by 1.4.

Image 3a shows the sidewinder as the coils are forming. The back arches and the contact with the ground is localised. Image 3b shows the snake reaching its fully coiled state. Image 3c shows the snake as progression begins to take effect properly and Image 3d shows the snake at a later time. The diagonal nature of the locomotion is apparent.

The fourth form of snake locomotion is called "concertina progression" and involves successive flexing and straightening of the snake. It is only very rarely used and has not been simulated by the author.

Whilst most snakes are not adept at flexing their backs vertically in a sinusoidal fashion through large amplitudes, creatures such as caterpillars are. Since the underside of the caterpillar is lifted and thrust forward and then placed down again, there is no need for directional friction. Instead it is better to eliminate all tangential movement for any segments in contact with the surface. This gives the caterpillar the ability to scale steep gradients both up the slope and down. Image 4a shows the caterpillar at rest. The fanciful creature shown, called the Arctic caterpillar, is covered in fur to highlight the changes in orientation of the surface. Image 4b shows the caterpillar arching its back.

5. Timings for the Dynamics

The dynamics calculations for the snake animations took 30 seconds per frame on a Silicon Graphics 4D/70 workstation. In part this was due to the implementation in a convenient but interpreted procedural modelling language (Alias SDL) and in part it was due to the comparatively unstable nature of Euler integration. 25 subintervals per frame were used to ensure accuracy in the animation of the snakes. For the less rigid worms this was reduced to 10 subintervals.

The different creatures were animated using different values for the spring constants and the damping. The worm had a k spring strength of 1.5 and a damping D value of 0.9. The worm tends to bounce on contact with the floor and as it dangles over the edge of the book it takes on interesting chain-like oscillations. The snake, on the other hand, used a k of 0.5 and a D of 3.5. The difference is that the snake swishes its tail as it moves. Too little damping leads to standing waves in its body which interfere with locomotion and mean that the snake is in danger of shaking itself to pieces. The caterpillar had a k of 0.3 and a D of 0.6.

6. Rendering Worms, Snakes and Caterpillars

In order to render the snakes and worms, the lattice of masses was used to create control points for cardinal bicubic parametric patches. They were generated so that the cross-sections of the snakes and worms just touched the edges of the lattice. This prevented any possible intersections with the ground plane.

The worms for this paper were rendered using a colour map and a bump map [1]. The colour map gave the pink underside and the grey top. The bump map gave the wrinkles in the skin. The snake in Image 5 was rendered using a bump map and a colour map for the scales. The depth value for the scales was also used to blend between the texture mapped "markings" and the underlying skin colour. The hairs on the caterpillar were modelled as separate pieces of geometry. The roots of the hairs were generated as a dithered lattice in parameter space for each patch. The other end of the hairs were computed using linear combinations of the tangent vectors and the surface normal at the root to offset from the root position. This technique is discussed in more detail in [9]. The individual hairs in Images 4a to 4d also had collision detection with the floor. In the event of penetration of the ground plane, the hairs were individually rotated upwards about their roots until the ends were just in contact with the ground. This approach is trivial for an extended planar surface but would be more difficult for arbitrary obstructions. The hairs for these images were composed of three forward-facing triangles arranged in the form of a cone. The results were raycast with supersampling everywhere to avoid aliasing. Each hair was colour mapped along it length. The tips of each hair were black whilst the roots were white. The caterpillar images at 500 lines resolution each took 0.5 hours to render on a Silicon Graphics 4D/70 workstation.

7. Areas for Future Work

Now that the basic principles of legless figure locomotion have been implemented it is necessary to improve the collision detection computations. This will allow several snakes or worms to interact with each other and will enable the snakes to coil up without penetrating themselves. The task of directing the snakes to specific action needs to be investigated, giving the creatures goals and path planning skills. On a different tack, the dynamic models for legless creatures may be combined with legs to extend the models to such creatures as crocodiles and Chinese dragons which use their tails for locomotion extensively.

8. Acknowledgements

This research took place at Alias Research Inc. in Toronto as part of the Natural Phenomena Project. Thanks to Alias for encouraging this work. A big thank you to Patricia Anderson at Alias for modelling the snake head, to Freddi Gitelman for modelling the background to the worm sequence, and to Jim Craighead and Bob Leblanc for additional help with the snake rendering, and to Andrew Pearce, Steve Williams and Gary Mundell for help with the background to Image 6. A special thank you to David Ross for revealing to me the joys and complexities of procedural motion. Finally, thanks to Eileen O'Neill for introducing me to the beauty of snakes, and for leading the worm hunt without which the images in this paper would have been much less realistic.

9. References

1. Blinn, James F. "Simulation of Wrinkled Surfaces." Computer Graphics, Vol. 12, No. 3, August 1978.

2. Coquillart, Sabine, "A Control-Point-Based Sweeping Technique", IEEE Computer Graphics and Applications, November 1987 pp 36-45.

3. Culhane, John, "Special Effects in the Movies", Hilltown Press, Inc., ISBN 0-345-34536-3, November 1981.

4. Girard, Michael and Anthony A. Maciejewski, "Computational Modelling for the Computer Animation of Legged Figures", Computer Graphics, Vol. 19, No.3, July 1985 pp 263-270.

5. Isaacs, Paul M. and Michael F. Cohen, "Controlling Dynamic Simulation with Kinematic Constraints, Behavior Functions and Inverse Dynamics", Computer Graphics, Vol. 21, No. 4, July 1987 pp 215-224.

6. Johnson, Lee W., R. Dean Riess, "Numerical Analysis", Addison-Welsey Publishing Company Inc. 1982. ISBN 0-201-10392-3.

7. Klauber, Lawrence M., "Rattlesnakes", University of California Press, 1982. ISBN 0-520-04039-2.

8. Mehrtens, John M., "Living Snakes of the World", Sterling Publishing Co. Inc., New York. Blandford Press Dorset, England. 1987. ISBN 0-8069-6460-X.

9. Miller, Gavin S. P., "Computer Display and Manufacture of 3-D Models", Ph.D. thesis, June 1987, Cambridge University Engineering Department, Cambridge, England.

10. O'Neill, Eileen, personal communication Nov. 1987.

11. Reynolds, Craig W., "Flocks, Herds and Schools : A Distributed Behavioral Model", Computer Graphics, Vol. 21, No. 4, July 1987 pp 25-34.

12. Terzopoulos, D., J. Platt, A. Barr, K. Fleischer, "Elastically Deformable Models", Computer Graphics, Vol. 21, No. 4, July 1987 pp 205-214.

13. Waters, Keith, "A Muscle Model for Animating Three-Dimensional Facial Expression", Computer Graphics, Vol. 21, No. 4, July 1987 pp 17-24.

14. Willhelms, Jane and Matthew Moore, "Dynamics for Everyone", Appendix 1, SIGGRAPH '87 Course 10, Computer Animation : 3-D Motion Specification and Control pp 145-146.

Images 1a to 1d (top left to bottom right): Eric the Dynamic Worm

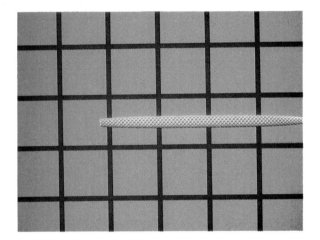
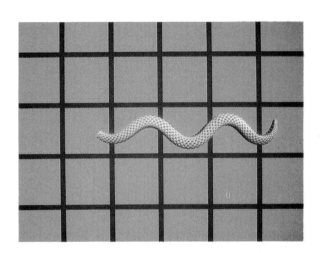

Images 2a to 2d (top left to bottom right): Horizontal Undulatory Progression

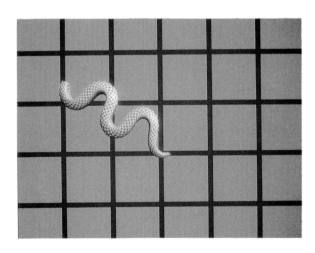

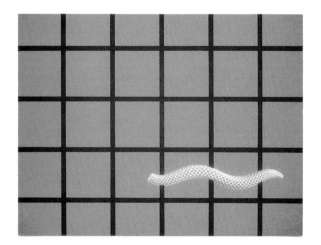 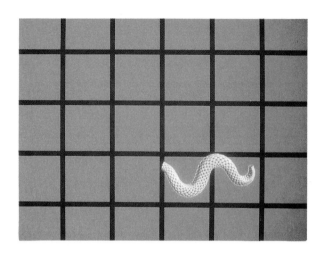

Images 3a to 3d (top left to bottom right): A Sidewinder

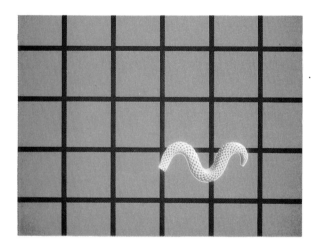 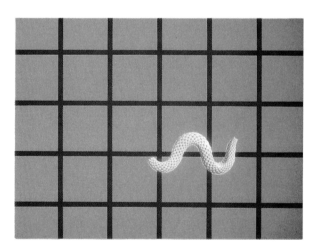

Images 4a and 4b: An Artic Caterpillar

Image 5: A Missisauga Rattler.

Image 6: Curling Up by the Fire

A Modeling System Based On Dynamic Constraints

Ronen Barzel
Alan H. Barr
California Institute of Technology
Pasadena, CA 91125

Abstract

We present "dynamic constraints," a physically-based technique for constraint-based control of computer graphics models. Using dynamic constraints, we build objects by specifying geometric constraints; the models assemble themselves as the elements move to satisfy the constraints. The individual elements are rigid bodies which act in accordance with the rules of physics, and can thus exhibit physically realistic behavior. To implement the constraints, a set of "constraint forces" is found, which causes the bodies to act in accordance with the constraints; finding these "constraint forces" is an *inverse dynamics* problem.

KEYWORDS: Modeling, Dynamics, Constraints, Simulation
CR categories: I.3.5—Computational Geometry and Object Modeling; I.3.7—Three-Dimensional Graphics and Realism

1 Introduction

Some of the most natural and graceful motion in computer animation has been achieved recently by simulating the physical behavior of objects. But physical simulation has not yet become the standard technique for modeling and animation, because of several limitations:

- *Simulations are hard to implement:* Typically, a special-purpose program is written to simulate the behavior of a given computer graphics model; the overhead for making new models is large.
- *Simulations are hard to control:* If "innate" behavior is programmed into models, it becomes hard to make the models do exactly what we want; the behavior is often determined indirectly by non-intuitive or non-orthogonal parameters.
- *Simulations are slow:* Physical simulation can be computationally intensive.

The goal of this work is to develop a modeling system in which it is easy to build and animate physically-based computer graphics models. To this end, our modeling approach is based on four features:

- *Generality:* A model is built from a collection of primitive physically-based elements.
- *Geometric Constraints:* A model is constructed by applying constraints to the objects, starting from an initial configuration of the primitive elements. A model is also positioned and animated through constraints.
- *Newtonian Mechanics:* Each primitive element is a rigid body whose motion is due to the effects of inertia and forces and torques acting on the body. Many of the forces and torques are externally applied; other forces and torques, however, are derived from the geometric constraints.
- *Equivalence of Modeling and Animation:* The temporal behavior of physically based objects is bound up in the model itself.

To implement the constraints, we solve an *inverse dynamics* problem: given constraints on the behavior of the model, the problem is to determine the forces which result in an example of the constrained

---

©1988   ACM-0-89791-275-6/88/008/0179 $00.75

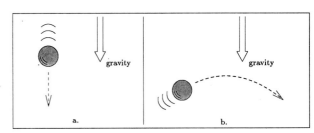

Figure 1: All primitive bodies obey Newton's laws. e.g. (a) A ball released in gravity falls; (b) A ball thrown in gravity moves in an arc.

behavior we desire. Thus, we convert each constraint into a "constraint force"; as the model animates, the constraint forces are continuously computed, to continuously maintain the constraints.

Sec. 2 of this paper presents the modeling system, and provides implementation notes. Sec. 3 discusses the inverse dynamics problem. Sec. 4 presents the technique for setting up and solving a "constraint-force" equation. The simulation of Newtonian mechanics, derivations for various examples of constraints, and miscellaneous mathematical details are found in the Appendices.

Related Work

[Witkin, Fleischer, and Barr 87] uses "energy" constraints to assemble 3D models, for changing the shape of parametrically-defined primitive objects. This work is not concerned with dynamic mechanical simulation of models. [Platt and Barr 88] uses augmented lagrangian constraints in the physical simulation of flexible objects. [Isaacs and Cohen 87] does physical simulation of rigid bodies, for the special case of linked systems without closed kinematic loops. They share our emphasis on ease of modeling, and also use an inverse-dynamics formulation to control the models' behavior. [Wilhelms and Barsky 85] utilizes physically based modeling, but has a reduced emphasis on control.

2 The Modeling System

Modeling with the "Dynamic Constraints" system consists of instantiating primitive bodies, connecting and controlling them with constraints, and influencing their behavior by explicitly applying external forces. The modeling system thus has three libraries:

- *Primitive bodies:* A collection of rigid bodies, such as spheres, rods, torii, and more complex shapes, that are the component elements of models. The modeler specifies the body density, as well as specific parameters such as the length and radius of a rod. Each body type defines the quantities needed for physical simulation, such as the rotational inertia tensor for that body type.
- *External applied forces:* Forces that the modeler can introduce into the model, including gravity, springs, and damping forces. Each force has parameters specific to the force, such as damping coefficients or spring constants.
- *Constraints:* Various types of geometric constraints, such as "point-to-nail" or "orientation" are described below.

To build a model, we make instances of objects, calculate the forces, and run the simulation. We also specify "timelines" of events to take place, such as creating or removing instances, turning constraints or explicit forces on or off, or otherwise adjusting parameters.

2.1 Newtonian Mechanics

Fig. 1 illustrates one of the simplest examples of a body obeying Newton's laws. This behavior is easy to simulate; Appendix A describes the general newtonian simulation procedure.

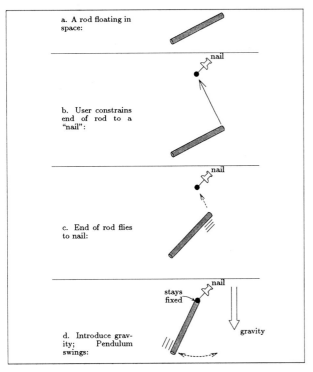

Figure 2: "Point-to-nail" constraint. A user creates a pendulum by fixing an endpoint of a rod at some location in space. The constraint causes the rod to "fly" into place, assembling the pendulum. See videotape [Caltech '87 Demo Reel].

All primitive bodies in our system exhibit physically realistic behavior, in the sense that they respond correctly to forces and torques.

2.2 Constraints

We show some examples of constraints supported by our modeling system.

- "Point-to-Nail" constraint (see Fig. 2): This fixes a point on a body to a user-specified location in space. The body may swivel and swing about the constrained point, but the constrained point may not move.
- "Point-to-Point" constraint (see Fig. 3): This forms a joint between two bodies. The bodies may move about freely, as long as the two constrained points stay in contact.
- "Point-to-Path" constraint (see Fig. 4a): We can require a point on an object to follow an arbitrary user-specified path; this allows us to animate models by using standard kinematic keyframe techniques.
- "Orientation" constraint (see Fig. 4b): A constraint to align objects by rotating them.
- Other constraints (not illustrated): Other constraints include "point-on-line," which restricts a point to lie on a given line, and "sphere-to-sphere," which requires two spheres to touch, but lets them slide along each other.

We can easily add new types of geometric constraints to our constraint library, by defining the constraint "deviation" function and deriving various required quantities, as described in Appendix C. The only restriction is that the "deviation" function be twice-differentiable (as is discussed in the appendix).

2.3 Constraint Forces

When we have built a model using dynamic constraints, the model is held together by constraint forces, as illustrated in Fig. 5. Thus the constraint forces are analogs of the internal forces which hold the parts of compound objects together.

Constraint forces also assemble the models, pulling the components into the proper configurations. Thus constraint forces represent forces which could be used to assemble real-world objects. For example, figures in the appendices show frames from animations demonstrating the self-assembly of space structures [Barr, Von Herzen, Barzel, and Snyder 87].

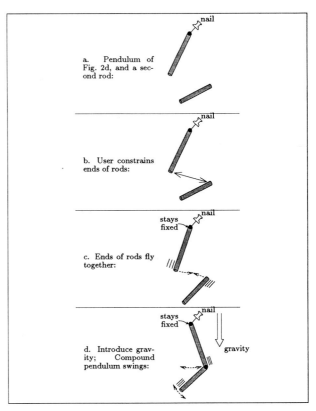

Figure 3: A "point-to-point" constraint. A users adds a second rod to the pendulum of Fig. 2, to create a compound pendulum. See videotape [Caltech '87 Demo Reel].

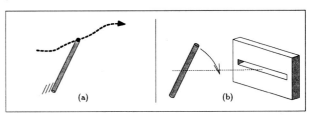

Figure 4: Other constraint examples. (a) "Point-to-path" constraint. This constraint pulls objects along user-specified paths. (b) "Orientation" constraint. We rotate the rod to make its axis parallel to the slot axis.

2.4 Implementation

We describe here the high-level program structure; details of simulating Newtonian mechanics are given in Appendix A, the procedure to calculate the constraint forces is given in Sec. 4.4.

Our modeling system is implemented in Common Lisp on Symbolics Lisp Machines, using Symbolics' object-oriented "Flavors" mechanism. The fundamental object classes we have defined are:

- *rigid-body:* a primitive body in the model. This class defines the functions and state variables needed for the dynamics calculation (see Appendix A), including a list of forces and torques acting on the body. There are subclasses for each type of body in our library; each subclass provides type-specific information, such as the rotational inertia tensor.
- *control-point:* a point on a body, or in space. A point on a body contains a reference to the body, as well as the position of the point in body-coordinates. A point in space defines its position, which can be constant, or a function of time. Forces and constraints are typically created by specifying the control-points at which they act.
- *force:* a force being applied to a body. Each force contains a reference to a control point at which it is applied. There are subclasses for each type of force in our library; each subclass provides a function that computes the force.
- *constraint:* any type of dynamic constraint. There are subclasses for each type of constraint in our library. Each subclass provides

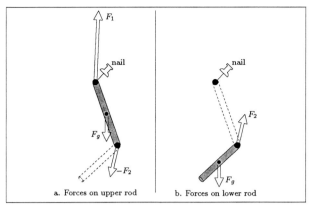

Figure 5: Constraint forces holding together compound pendulum of Fig. 3d. The constraint forces model the internal forces of a real-world pendulum. (a) shows forces on the upper rod, (b) shows forces on the lower rod: F_g is gravity pulling down on rods. F_1 is the "point-to-nail" constraint force on the upper rod, holding it at the nail. F_2 is the "point-to-point" constraint force on the lower rod, holding it to the upper rod; $-F_2$ is the reaction force on the upper rod.

the quantities needed to determine the constraint force (described in Appendix C). Each constraint also keeps references to the bodies being constrained, and associates the appropriate forces with the bodies.

All objects handle a "draw" message, which displays the object in its current state. For debugging a model, we send the "draw" message to all objects, including forces, control points, and constraints; for producing an animation, we send the "draw" message only to bodies. Some examples of subclasses are:

- *rod:* a subclass of *rigid-body.* This class provides the values specific to rods, e.g. the rotational inertia tensor (see Appendix A). The class also associates two control points with each rod, named "end1" and "end2", at the ends of the rod, and provides functions to access them.
- *nail:* a control point fixed at a location in space.
- *point-to-nail:* a subclass of *constraint.* Provides the functions which calculate the terms needed for a "point-to-nail" constraint (see Sec. 4, Example 1).

The addition of new types of bodies, forces, or constraints to the system merely requires the creation of an appropriate new subclass.

Currently, the user-interface is via the lisp environment; for example, the pendulum of Fig. 3 could be built via the series of commands:

```
; create bodies and control points
(make rod "upper-rod")
(make rod "lower-rod")
(make nail "nail" 0 0 100)
; specify constraints
(connect (end1 "upper-rod") "nail")
(connect (end2 "upper-rod") (end1 "lower-rod"))
; add external forces
(gravity-on)  ; apply gravity to each body
```

To animate a model once the instances are made, we simply iterate these steps:

- Simulate until end of frame (Appendix A).
- Send "draw" message to objects.

The implementation makes heavy use of a home-grown package of numerical routines, which include linear-system solvers, differential equation solvers, and the like; some useful references are [Press et. al. 88,Golub and Van Loan 83,Ralston and Rabinowitz 78, Boyce and Deprima 77]. We also have embedded into lisp an extension to "Einstein Summation Notation" for mathematical expressions [Barr 83,Misner, Thorne and Wheeler 73]; this makes it quite simple to create lisp functions by merely typing in the mathematical formulae using the same notation with which we derive them.

3 Inverse Dynamics

If we are given the forces which act on a collection of objects, we can easily solve the *forward dynamics* problem—that of determining the objects' behavior—as described in Appendix A. However, to meet constraints, we must solve the reverse problem: Given a partial description of the desired behavior, we must determine forces which will yield an appropriate behavior. This *inverse dynamics* problem, summarized in Fig. 6, consists of two parts: (a) finding forces to meet a constraint, and (b) finding forces to maintain a constraint.

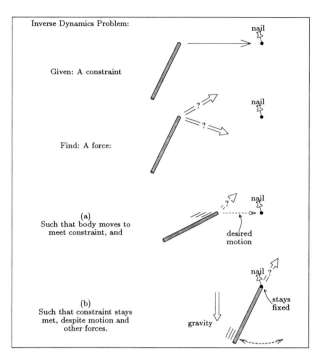

Figure 6: The inverse dynamics problem for dynamic constraints.

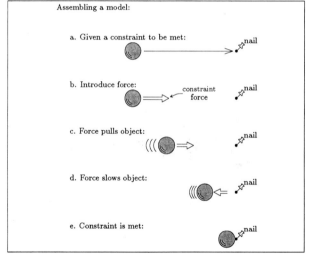

Figure 7: Meeting a Constraint. The constraint force pulls the ball towards the nail, then brings the ball to rest at the nail.

Meeting A Constraint

Fig. 7 shows a constraint force being used satisfy to part (a) of the inverse dynamics problem, that of moving the objects to meet an initially unmet constraint. Notice that this part of the problem is actually very loosely specified: How quickly should the constraint be met? Along what path should the object move? For our solution, as we shall see in Sec. 4.2, the "deviation" of the constrained point decays exponentially, with a user-specified time constant.

Maintaining A Dynamic Constraint

Fig. 8 shows a dynamic constraint force adapting to satisfy part (b) of the inverse dynamics problem, that of keeping a constraint met despite motion and other forces. There is typically a unique solution, in which the dynamic constraint forces provide the internal forces that hold together an object.

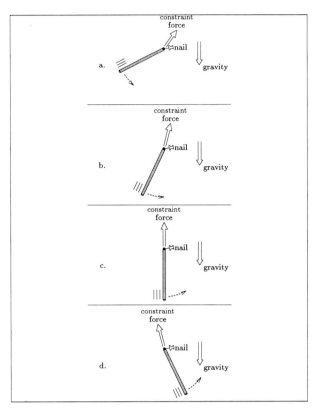

Figure 8: Maintaining a Constraint. (a-d) The constraint force adapts to hold constraint even as object moves and other forces act on it. The constraint force pulls up, to counteract gravity, and sideways, to keep the pendulum's inertia from flinging it sideways off the nail.

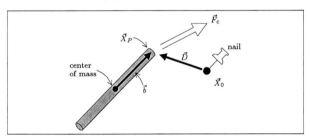

Figure 9: "Point-to-nail" constraint. The "deviation" measure is $\vec{D}(\mathcal{Y}) = \vec{X}_P(\mathcal{Y}) - \vec{X}_0$, the constraint force is $\vec{F}_c$, and the constraint torque is $\vec{b} \times \vec{F}_c$.

4 Calculating Constraint Forces

Note: We suggest skimming Appendix A, to become familiar with our notation and formulation of rigid-body mechanics, before reading this section.

In this section, we present the technique for computing the constraint forces. The presentation is in several sections:

1. Definition of several mathematical quantities associated with each constraint.
2. Construction of a "constraint-force" equation for a dynamic constraint; if the constraint force is chosen such that this equation holds, the constrained objects will behave in accordance with the dynamic constraint.
3. Grouping the constraint-force equations for multiple constraints into a single multidimensional constraint-force equation for all the dynamic constraints.
4. Setting up and solving the dynamic constraint-force equation.

4.1 Definitions

Fig. 11 gives the definition of the quantities which must be supplied for each constraint. The derivations of these quantities for various types of constraints are given in Appendix C.

$\vec{D}$	A measure of "deviation" for the constraint: $$\vec{D}(\mathcal{Y}, t) = 0 \Longleftrightarrow \text{constraint is met}$$ $\vec{D}$ is a d-dimensional vector.
d	The number of dimensions of $\vec{D}$.
$\vec{D}^{(1)}$	The rate of change of $\vec{D}$: $$\vec{D}^{(1)}(\mathcal{Y}(t), t) \equiv \frac{d}{dt}\vec{D}(\mathcal{Y}(t))$$ $\vec{D}^{(1)}$ is a d-dimensional vector.
$\vec{D}^{(2)}$	The acceleration of $\vec{D}$: $$D^{(2)}(\mathcal{Y}(t), \mathcal{F}(t), \mathcal{T}(t), t) \equiv \frac{d^2}{dt^2}\vec{D}(Y(t), t)$$ $D^{(2)}$ will depend linearly on $\mathcal{F}$ and $\mathcal{T}$; thus: $$D^{(2)} = \sum_{\text{bodies } i} (\mathbf{\Gamma}^i(\mathcal{Y})\vec{F}^i + \mathbf{\Lambda}^i(\mathcal{Y})\vec{T}^i) + \vec{\beta}(\mathcal{Y})$$ where we define:
$\mathbf{\Gamma}^i$	A $d \times 3$ matrix corresponding to the net force on body i; we have one such for each body in the constraint.
$\mathbf{\Lambda}^i$	A $d \times 3$ matrix corresponding to the net torque on body i; we have one such for each body in the constraint.
β	The part of $\vec{D}^{(2)}$ independent of $\mathcal{F}$ and $\mathcal{T}$; a d-dimensional vector.
f	The number of degrees of freedom in the constraint force.
$\mathbf{G}^i$	A $3 \times f$ matrix. The constraint force on body i is given by $\mathbf{G}^i\vec{F}_c$. We have one such matrix for each body in the constraint.
$\mathbf{H}^i$	A $3 \times f$ matrix. The constraint torque on body i is given by $\mathbf{H}^i\vec{F}_c$. We have one such matrix for each body in the constraint.

Figure 11: Quantities associated with a dynamic constraint. $\vec{F}_c$ is the unknown "constraint force" for the constraint. $\mathcal{Y}$, $\mathcal{F}$, and $\mathcal{T}$ are the state, net force, and net torque in the model, as defined in Eqn. 9 (Appendix A). See discussion in Sec. 4.1. Derivations of these quantities for various constraints are given in Appendix C

We also define

$$
\begin{aligned}
\vec{F}_c &\quad - \quad \text{The unknown "constraint force,"} \\
&\qquad\quad \text{an } f\text{-dimensional vector.} \\
\vec{F}_E^i &\quad - \quad \text{The net external applied force on the } i\text{-th body} \\
\vec{T}_E^i &\quad - \quad \text{The net external applied torque on the } i\text{-th body}
\end{aligned}
\tag{1}
$$

Note that strictly speaking, $\vec{F}_c$ is not necessarily a force, but rather is a quantity that determines the constraint force ($= \mathbf{G}^i\vec{F}_c$) and constraint torque ($= \mathbf{H}^i\vec{F}_c$) on the constrained bodies; colloquially, however, we refer to $\vec{F}_c$ as the "constraint force." The vectors $\vec{F}_E^i$ and $\vec{T}_E^i$ are due to the external forces, such as gravity, that act on the i-th body body.

The net force (torque) on a body is the sum of the net external force (torque) and the constraint forces (torques):

$$
\begin{aligned}
\vec{F}^i &= \left(\sum_{\text{constraints } j} \mathbf{G}_j^i\vec{F}_{c_j} \right) + \vec{F}_E^i \\
\vec{T}^i &= \left(\sum_{\text{constraints } j} \mathbf{H}_j^i\vec{F}_{c_j} \right) + \vec{T}_E^i
\end{aligned}
\tag{2}
$$

In the above equations, we label terms for the ith body with superscript i's, and the jth constraint with subscript j's.

See Example 1 for a description of terms needed for a "point to nail" constraint.

4.2 Constraint-force Equation

For each constraint, we describe the desired behavior of the constraint "deviation" by linearly combining $\vec{D}$, $\vec{D}^{(1)}$, and $\vec{D}^{(2)}$:

$$
\vec{D}^{(2)}(\mathcal{Y}, \mathcal{F}, \mathcal{T}, t) + \frac{2}{\tau}\vec{D}^{(1)}(\mathcal{Y}, t) + \frac{1}{\tau^2}\vec{D}(\mathcal{Y}, t) = 0, \ t \geq t_0
\tag{3}
$$

This equation is equivalent to the differential equation in Fig. 12; its solution brings $\vec{D}$ down to 0, then holds it at 0.[1] We will substitute for $D^{(2)}$, $D^{(1)}$ and D in Eqn. 3 to produce a linear system of equations in which we solve for $\vec{F}_c$. If we continually adjust the force so that Eqn. 3 is met, we will be solving the inverse dynamics problem.

Thus, we expand $\vec{D}^{(2)}$ in Eqn. 3, using the definitions in Fig. 11, yielding:

$$
\sum_{\text{bodies } i} (\mathbf{\Gamma}^i\vec{F}^i + \mathbf{\Lambda}^i\vec{T}^i) + \vec{\beta} + \frac{2}{\tau}\vec{D}^{(1)} + \frac{1}{\tau^2}\vec{D} = 0
\tag{4}
$$

---

[1] Analytically, if $\vec{D}_0 \neq 0$ the solution to the equation in Fig. 12 asymptotically approaches 0, but doesn't ever reach $\vec{D} = 0$. Numerically, however, we soon reach $\vec{D} = 0$ within error tolerances.

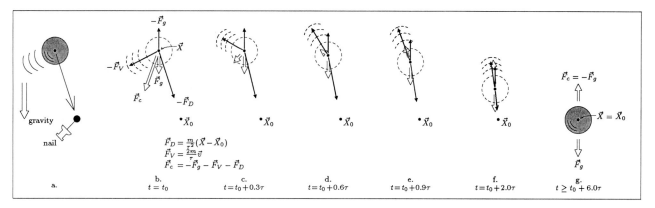

Figure 10: Constraint-force calculation for a "point-to-nail" constraint (details in Sec. 4.2): Constraint force has components opposing gravity ($-\vec{F}_g$), opposing motion ($-\vec{F}_v$), and pulling towards nail ($-\vec{F}_D$). (a) User specifies constraint at center of mass. (b) Constraint force initially pulls towards nail. (c-e) Once ball is moving towards nail, constraint force turns around. (f) Constraint force slows ball. (g) Steady-state: $\vec{F}_D = \vec{F}_V = 0$, $\vec{F}_c = -\vec{F}_g$. Net force on ball is 0; by Newton's first law, the ball remains at rest.

Example 1: "Point-to-Nail" Constraint. We choose $\vec{D}$ to be the vector from the constrained point, at $\vec{X}_P$, to the "nail", at $\vec{X}_0$ (see Fig. 9). We thus have:
$$
\begin{aligned}
d &= 3 \\
\vec{D}(\mathcal{Y}) &= \vec{X}_P - \vec{X}_0
\end{aligned}
$$
The differentiation in Appendix B.2 immediately gives us the quantities:
$$
\begin{aligned}
\vec{D}^{(1)}(\mathcal{Y}) &= \vec{v}_P(\mathcal{Y}) \\
\vec{D}^{(2)}(\mathcal{Y}, \vec{F}, \vec{T}) &= \vec{a}_P(\mathcal{Y}, \vec{F}, \vec{T}) \\
\Gamma &= \frac{1}{m} \\
\Lambda &= \mathbf{b}^{\bullet\mathsf{T}} \mathbf{I}^{-1} \\
\vec{\beta} &= \mathbf{b}^{\bullet\mathsf{T}} \mathbf{I}^{-1}(\vec{L} \times \vec{\omega}) + \vec{\omega} \times (\vec{\omega} \times \vec{b})
\end{aligned}
$$

We apply an arbitrary force to the constrained point. The "constraint force" $\vec{F}_c$ is used directly as a force on the body, and it contributes $\vec{b} \times \vec{F}_c = \mathbf{b}^{\bullet}\vec{F}_c$ to the torque. Thus we define:
$$
\begin{aligned}
f &= 3 \\
\mathbf{G} &= 1 \quad \textit{See Appendix C for other examples.} \\
\mathbf{H} &= \mathbf{b}^{\bullet}
\end{aligned}
$$

Example 2: "Point-to-Nail" Constraint. In Fig. 10, we illustrate a simple case: A single body, with a "point-to-nail" constraint acting at its center-of-mass, and with gravity. Since both the constraint force and gravity act on the ball's center-of-mass, there are no rotational terms. Thus the quantities in Example 1 reduce to:
$$
\begin{aligned}
\vec{b} = \mathbf{b}^{\bullet} = \Lambda = \vec{\beta} = \mathbf{H} &= \vec{T}_E = 0 \\
\vec{D} &= \vec{X} - \vec{X}_0 \\
\vec{D}^{(1)} &= \vec{v} \\
\vec{D}^{(2)} &= \frac{1}{\tau} \vec{F} \\
\Gamma &= \frac{1}{m} \\
\mathbf{G} &= 1 \\
\vec{F}_E &= \vec{F}_g
\end{aligned}
$$

Substituting into Eqn. 5 gives:
$$
\frac{1}{m} \vec{F}_c + \frac{1}{m} \vec{F}_g + \frac{2}{\tau} \vec{v} + \frac{1}{\tau^2}(\vec{X} - \vec{X}_0) = 0
$$

We easily solve for the constraint force:
$$
\vec{F}_c = -\vec{F}_g - \frac{2}{\tau} m\vec{v} - \frac{1}{\tau^2} m(\vec{X} - \vec{X}_0)
$$

Thus we see the constraint force has three components: One opposing the force of gravity, one opposing the ball's velocity, and one pulling the ball towards the nail. Fig. 10 illustrates the constraint force adapting to pull the ball to the nail, and bring it to rest. Once the ball is at rest at the nail, we have $\vec{X} - \vec{X}_0 = 0$ and $\vec{v} = 0$; so the constraint force becomes $\vec{F}_c = -\vec{F}_g$, yielding a net force on the ball of $\vec{F} = \vec{F}_c + \vec{F}_g = 0$

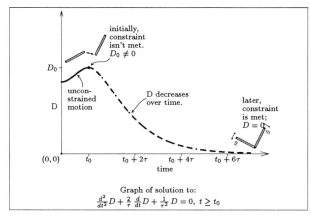

Figure 12: D evolving over time. We have picked a second-order differential equation to describe D as a function of time. The solution yields the behavior required by the inverse dynamics problem—the constraint "deviation" decays down to 0, assembling the model, then remains at 0, maintaining the constraint. The rate of assembly is controlled by the time constant τ. See [Boyce and Deprima 77] for a discussion of second-order differential equations.

Graph of solution to:
$$
\frac{d^2}{dt^2} D + \frac{2}{\tau} \frac{d}{dt} D + \frac{1}{\tau^2} D = 0, \quad t \geq t_0
$$

$$
\sum_{\text{constraints } j} \left(\sum_{\text{bodies } i} (\boldsymbol{\Gamma}^i \mathbf{G}_j^i + \boldsymbol{\Lambda}^i \mathbf{H}_j^i) \right) \vec{F}_{c_j}
$$
$$
+ \sum_{\text{bodies } i} (\boldsymbol{\Gamma}^i \vec{F}_E^i + \boldsymbol{\Lambda}^i \vec{T}_E^i) \qquad = 0 \qquad (5)
$$
$$
+ \vec{\beta} + \frac{2}{\tau} \vec{D}^{(1)} + \frac{1}{\tau^2} \vec{D}
$$

Notice that, to meet this one constraint, we must take into account the effect of all the constraint forces.

See Example 2 for a sample derivation of the constraint forces.

4.3 Multiple Constraints

Each constraint results in a version of Eqn. 5; with several constraints, we have a set of simultaneous equations which must be solved.

We duplicate Eqn. 5, for each constraint in the model:
$$
\sum_{\text{constraints } j} \left(\sum_{\text{bodies } i} (\boldsymbol{\Gamma}_k^i \mathbf{G}_j^i + \boldsymbol{\Lambda}_k^i \mathbf{H}_j^i) \right) \vec{F}_{c_j}
$$
$$
+ \sum_{\text{bodies } i} (\boldsymbol{\Gamma}_k^i \vec{F}_E^i + \boldsymbol{\Lambda}_k^i \vec{T}_E^i) \qquad = 0, \left\{ \begin{array}{l} \text{for all} \\ \text{constraints } k \end{array} \right. \qquad (6)
$$
$$
+ \vec{\beta}_k + \frac{2}{\tau_k} \vec{D}_k^{(1)} + \frac{1}{\tau_k^2} \vec{D}_k
$$

where we label terms for the kth constraint with subscript k's. Writing this system of equations more compactly, as a multidimensional vector equation, we have the constraint force equation for the model:

Substituting Eqn. 2 into Eqn. 4, we get the constraint-force equation for a single constraint:

$$\boxed{\mathcal{M}\mathcal{F}_c + \mathcal{B} = 0}$$

where

$$\mathcal{M}_{kj} = \sum_{\text{bodies } i} (\mathbf{\Gamma}_k^i \mathbf{G}_j^i + \mathbf{\Lambda}_k^i \mathbf{H}_j^i)$$

$$\mathcal{F}_{cj} = \vec{F}_{c_j} \tag{7}$$

$$\mathcal{B}_k = \sum_{\text{bodies } i} (\mathbf{\Gamma}_k^i \vec{F}_E^i + \mathbf{\Lambda}_k^i \vec{T}_E^i)$$

$$+ \vec{\beta}_k + \tfrac{2}{\tau_k} \vec{D}_k^{(1)} + \tfrac{1}{\tau_k^2} \vec{D}_k$$

Fig. 13 illustrates collecting individual constraint equations into the multidimensional vector equation. Notice that each element of $\mathcal{M}$ is a matrix, and each element of $\mathcal{F}_c$ and of $\mathcal{B}$ is a vector.

4.4 Solving the Constraint-Force Equation

Fig. 15 outlines the procedure to set up Eqn. 7, as well as solve it and compute the net force and torque on each body.

In step 3 of Fig. 15, we call a standard linear-system solver to solve Eqn. 7. There are many well-known methods for solving linear systems (see [Press et. al. 88,Ralston and Rabinowitz 78]). We note some characteristics of $\mathcal{M}$ that should be taken into account when choosing a solution method:

- $\mathcal{M}$ is typically sparse. The $[k,j]$th entry in $\mathcal{M}$ is non-0 only if some body is influenced by both constraint k and constraint j. Typically, most of the elements are zero.
- $\mathcal{M}$ is not necessarily square. A constraint may have $d \neq f$; for example, the "orientation" constraint (Appendix C.3) has $d = 1$ and $f = 3$, yielding a matrix which is "wider" than it is "tall."
- $\mathcal{M}$ may be singular, implying that Eqn. 7 is overconstrained or underconstrained.[2]

We most often use singular-value decomposition (SVD) to solve Eqn. 7, because it robustly handles singularity and near-singularity, as well as non-square systems. However, SVD does not take advantage of sparseness, and is a relatively slow technique.

Underconstrained Equations

Constraint-force equation Eqn. 7 will sometimes be underconstrained, thus having many solutions. This can occur, for example, when there are several constraints acting on a single body; it may be possible to vary some of the individual constraint forces without affecting the net torque or force on the object. An example is shown in Fig. 14a, in which the pair of forces labeled "V" yield the same net force ($= 2\vec{F}_V$) and torque ($= 0$) as the pair labeled "W".

There is no difficulty caused by having many solutions to Eqn. 7; we could use any solution, since they will all yield satisfactory behavior. We might wish to use the solution which is smallest in magnitude, to avoid numerical difficulties; SVD yields this solution.

Overconstrained Equations

eats In Fig. 14b, the user has specified constraints which can not be met; there is no "correct" constraint force to be applied. In Fig. 14c, the specified constraints can be met, but not by moving the constrained point in a straight line; however, Eqn. 3 requires that the point move in straight line if the constrained point is initially at rest.[3]

For overconstrained systems, using the least-squares solution for the constraint forces typically yields "reasonable" behavior – the object typically assumes some intermediate configuration, for the case of Fig. 14b, or moves along the feasible path, for the case of Fig. 14c. SVD computes the least-squares solution for overconstrained systems.

5 Summary

We have developed a modeling system featuring constraint-based control of rigid bodies. The bodies' behavior is determined by simulation of Newtonian mechanics. We compute dynamic "constraint forces" to apply to the bodies such that they behave in accordance with user-specified geometric constraints; the computation of these forces is an *inverse dynamics* problem.

The modeling system supports various types of geometric constraints, such as "point-to-nail" and "point-to-point." The modeler builds objects by using constraints to connect primitive components; the constraint forces cause the components to assemble themselves into the model, and ensure that the model stays assembled as it animates.

---

[2]Unfortunately, we have some overloading of the word "constrain": "overconstrained" and "underconstrained" refer to the linear system of equations Eqn. 7, rather than to the constraints themselves.

[3]A solution to the problem of unrealizable paths is to use scalar constraint measures ($d = 1$). For example, the "point-to-nail" constraint could be redefined so that D is the distance from the point to the nail, rather than the vector separating the point and the nail.

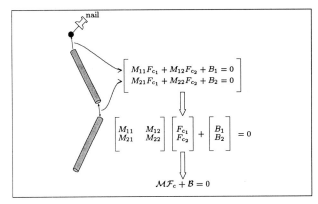

Figure 13: Multiple constraints: Each constraint contributes one line to the equation. The collection of constraints together yields a set of simultaneous linear equations, expressible as a linear matrix equation.

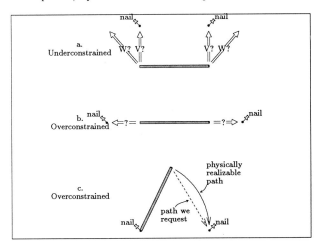

Figure 14: Under- and Overconstrained systems. (a) Underconstrained: Forces "V" and "W" yield the same net force. (b) Overconstrained: There is no way to meet both constraints. (c) Overconstrained: Both constraints could be met, but not via the path we have chosen.

We have developed a technique to compute the constraint forces by setting up and solving a "constraint-force equation." The constraint-force equation is a multidimensional linear equation of the form $\mathcal{M}\mathcal{F}_c + \mathcal{B} = 0$, where $\mathcal{F}_c$ is the collection of unknown constraint forces.

Each constraint is described by a "deviation" measure $\vec{D}$, such that $\vec{D} = 0$ when the constraint is met. $\vec{D}$ must be a twice differentiable function of the positions and orientations of the constrained bodies. Appendix C derives $\vec{D}$ for several types of constraints.

6 Future Work

Further work we are interested in pursuing includes:

- *Expanding the constraint library.* Deriving new constraint "deviation" functions, as described in Appendix C.
- *Interactive graphical modeler.*
- *Object Intersection.* Development of non-interpenetration constraints
- *Flexible bodies.* Incorporation of flexible-body simulation with dynamic constraint control [Platt and Barr 88, Terzopoulos, Platt, Fleischer, and Barr 87].
- *Special-case models* Direct implementation of the equations of motion for common objects, such as the linked systems of [Isaacs and Cohen 87,Armstrong and Green 85]. Decreasing the number of constraints in the model speeds up the constraint-force calculation.
- *Constraints on velocity or acceleration.*

We are also looking forward to using the dynamic constraints modeling system as a tool in other research areas, such as molecular biology [Lengyel 87] and robotics.

```
PROCEDURE TO COMPUTE FORCE AND TORQUE ON EACH BODY:


; 1. Compute net explicit forces and torques
for each body i
      F_E^i = T_E^i = 0
      for each explicit force j on body i
            compute force F_Ej
            F_E^i += F_Ej
            T_E^i += b_j × F_Ej
      end
      for each explicit torque j on body i
            compute torque T_Ej
            T_E^i += T_Ej
      end
end
; 2. Set up constraint-force equation
initialize M to 0
for each constraint k
      compute β_k, D_k^(1), and D_k
      B[k] = β_k + (2/τ_k) D_k^(1) + (1/τ_k²) D_k
      for each body i in constraint k
            compute Γ_k^i and Λ_k^i
            B[k] += Γ_k^i F_E^i + Λ_k^i T_E^i
            for each constraint j acting on i
                  M[k,j] += Γ_k^i G_j^i + Λ_k^i H_j^i
            end
      end
end
; 3. Solve constraint-force equation (Eqn. 7)
F_c = solve(M,B) ;linear-system solver
; 4. Compute net forces and torques.
for each body i
      F^i = F_E^i
      T^i = T_E^i
      for each constraint j acting on i
            F^i += G_j^i F_c[j]
            T^i += H_j^i F_c[j]
      end
end
```

Figure 15: The procedure to compute the constraint forces and the net force and torque on each body. See discussion in Sec. 4.4. Note that the [k,j]th element of $\mathcal{M}$ is a $d_k \times f_j$ matrix, and the [k]th element of $\mathcal{B}$ is a d_k-dimensional vector. Rather than implementing $\mathcal{M}$ as a "nested" array, it can be flattened into a $(\sum d) \times (\sum f)$ array; similarly, $\mathcal{B}$ is formed by concatenating the individual vectors into one $(\sum d)$-dimensional vector.

References

[Armstrong and Green 85] Armstrong, William W., and Mark W. Green, *The dynamics of articulated rigid bodies for purposes of animation,* in **Visual Computer,** Springer-Verlag, 1985, pp. 231-240.

[Barr 83] Barr, Alan H., *Geometric Modeling and Fluid Dynamic Analysis of Swimming Spermatozoa,* Ph.D. Dissertation, Rensselaer Polytechnic Institute, 1983

[Barr 88] Barr, Alan H., *Topics in Physically Based Modeling, to appear,* Addison Wesley

[Barr, Von Herzen, Barzel, and Snyder 87] Barr, Alan H., Brian Von Herzen, Ronen Barzel, and John Snyder, *Computational Techniques for the Self Assembly of Large Space Structures* Proceedings of the 8th Princeton/SSI Conference on Space Manufacturing, Princeton New Jersey, May 6-9 1987, to be published by the American Institute of Aeronautics and Astronautics.

[Boyce and Deprima 77] Boyce, William E., and DiPrima, Richard C., **Elementary Differential Equations and Boundary Value Problems,** John Wiley & Sons, New York, 1977.

[Caltech '87 Demo Reel] Caltech studies in modeling and motion (videotape), in SIGGRAPH video Review #28, *Visualization in Scientific Computing Computer Graphics,* volume 21 number 6. ACM SIGGRAPH, 1987

[Fox 67] Fox, E.A., **Mechanics,** Harper and Row, New York, 1967

[Gear 71] Gear, C. William, **Numerical Initial Value Problems in Ordinary Differential Equations,** Prentice-Hall, Englewood Cliffs, NJ, 1971

[Goldstein 83] Goldstein, Herbert, **Classical Mechanics,** 2nd edition, Addison-Wesley, Reading, Massachusetts, 1983.

[Golub and Van Loan 83] Golub, G., and Van Loan, C., **Matrix Computations,** Johns Hopkins University Press, Baltimore, 1983.

```
State variables of a body:
   m   - Mass of the body
   I   - Rotational inertia tensor of the body
   x   - Position of the body
   R   - Orientation of the body
   p   - Momentum of the body
   L   - Angular Momentum of the body,

auxiliary variables:
   v = (1/m) p    - Velocity of the body
   ω = I⁻¹ L      - Angular velocity of the body,

THE EQUATIONS OF MOTION:
   (d/dt) x = v
   (d/dt) p = F
   (d/dt) R = ω*R
   (d/dt) L = T,

where:
   F = net force on the body, and
   T = net torque of the body.

Note: ω* is the dual of ω (see Appendix B.1).
```

Figure 16: Summary of the equations of motion of a rigid body.

[Isaacs and Cohen 87] Isaacs, Paul M. and Michael F. Cohen, *Controlling Dynamic Simulation with Kinematic Constraints, Behavior Functions, and Inverse Dynamics,* Proc. SIGGRAPH 1987, pp. 215-224

[Lengyel 87] Lengyel, Jed, *Dynamic Assembly and Behavioral Simulation of the Flagellar Axoneme,* in **Caltech SURF Reports,** 1987

[Lien and Kajiya 84] Lien, Sheue-ling, and James T. Kajiya, *A symbolic method for calculating the integral properties of arbitrary nonconvex polyhedra,* IEEE Computer Graphics and Applications, Vol. 4 No. 10, Oct. 1984, pp. 35–41.

[Misner, Thorne and Wheeler 73] Misner, Charles W., Kip S. Thorne, and John Archibald Wheeler, **Gravitation,** W.H. Freeman and Co., San Francisco, 1973.

[Press et. al. 88] Press, William H., Brian P. Flannery, Saul A. Teukolsky, and William T. Vetterling, **Numerical Recipes in C/The Art of Scientific Computing,** Cambridge University Press, Cambridge, 1988.

[Platt and Barr 88] Platt, John, and Alan Barr, *Constraints on Flexible Objects,* Submitted to SIGGRAPH 1988.

[Ralston and Rabinowitz 78] Ralston, Anthony, and Philip Rabinowitz, *A First Course in Numerical Analysis,* McGraw-Hill, New York, 1978.

[Shoemake 85] Shoemake, Ken, *Animating Rotation with Quaternion Curves,* Computer Graphics, Vol. 19 No. 3, July 1985. pp. 245-254.

[Terzopoulos, Platt, Fleischer, and Barr 87] Terzopoulos, Demetri, John Platt, Alan Barr, and Kurt Fleischer *Elastically Deformable Models,* Proc. SIGGRAPH, 1987, pp. 205-214.

[Witkin, Fleischer, and Barr 87] Witkin, Andrew, Kurt Fleischer, and Alan Barr, *Energy Constraints on Parametrized Models,* Proc. SIGGRAPH 1987, pp. 225-232

[Wilhelms and Barsky 85] Wilhelms, Jane, and Brian Barsky *Using Dynamic Analysis To Animate Articulated Bodies Such As Humans and Robots,* Graphics Interface, 1985.

Appendices:

A   Simulating Newtonian Mechanics

Fig. 16 summarizes the equations of motion of a rigid body. A full discussion of rigid-body dynamics can be found in [Fox 67,Goldstein 83].

A.1   Notes On The Equations Of Motion

- *The Orientation Matrix* $\mathbf{R}$: $\mathbf{R}$ transforms tensors from body-coordinates to world coordinates (see Fig. 17). As we numerically integrate $\mathbf{R}$, numerical noise tends to cause $\mathbf{R}$ to drift away from a pure rotation, yielding noticeable skewing. This can be alleviated by using a feedback technique, as in [Barr 83]. Alternatively, we can represent the orientation as a quaternion $\mathbf{Q}$ (see [Shoemake 85] for an introduction to quaternions). The equation of motion for $\mathbf{Q}$ is (see [Misner, Thorne and Wheeler 73]):

$$\frac{d}{dt}\mathbf{Q} = \frac{1}{2}\vec{\omega}\mathbf{Q}$$

We then define $\mathbf{R}$ to be an auxiliary variable, which is computed from $\mathbf{Q}$ as discussed in [Shoemake 85].

- *Rotational Inertia Tensor* $\mathbf{I}$: $\mathbf{I}$ determines the rotational behavior of a body.[4] For a rigid body, $\mathbf{I}_{body}$ is constant. Note also that in Fig. 16

---

[4]A discussion of the characterstics of $\mathbf{I}$ is beyond the scope of this paper; see [Fox 67,Goldstein 83]. [Lien and Kajiya 84] gives an algorithm to compute $\mathbf{I}$ for arbitrary nonconvex polyhedra.

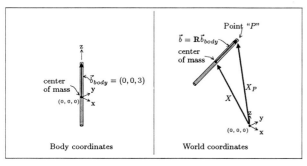

Figure 17: A rigid body. Orientation matrix $\mathbf{R}$ transforms vectors from body coordinates to world coordinates.

we use $\mathbf{I}^{-1}$ rather than $\mathbf{I}$. $\mathbf{I}_{body}^{-1}$ can be precomputed for each body; we convert to world coordinates using $\mathbf{R}$:

$$\mathbf{I}^{-1} = \mathbf{R}\mathbf{I}_{body}^{-1}\mathbf{R}^{\mathsf{T}}$$

- *The Net Force $\vec{F}$ and Torque $\vec{T}$*: Euler's principle of superposition allows us to combine the forces applied to a body into an equivalent net force applied at the center of mass. Each force applied at a radius $\vec{b}$ from the center of mass contributes $\vec{b} \times \vec{F}$ to the net torque on the body; we can also have "pure torques" acting on the body. The net force and torque are thus:

$$\vec{F} = \sum_{\text{forces } i} \vec{F_i}$$
$$\vec{T} = \sum_{\text{forces } i} (\vec{b_i} \times \vec{F_i}) + \sum_{\text{torques } j} \vec{T_j}$$

A.2 Canonical O.D.E. Notation

For brevity, we express the collection of equations in Fig. 16 as an ordinary differential equation (O.D.E.), in canonical form. For a single body, which we label A, we have:
$$\frac{d}{dt}Y^A = f(Y^A, \vec{F}^A, \vec{T}^A) \tag{8}$$

where we define

$$
\begin{aligned}
Y^A &= \{\vec{x}^A, \mathbf{R}^A, \vec{p}^A, \vec{L}^A\} &&\text{—State of body A} \\
\vec{F}^A &&&\text{—Net force on A} \\
\vec{T}^A &&&\text{—Net torque on A}
\end{aligned}
$$

For a model consisting of a collection of bodies, we have:
$$\frac{d}{dt}\mathcal{Y} = f(\mathcal{Y}, \mathcal{F}, \mathcal{T}) \tag{9}$$

where we define

$$
\begin{aligned}
\mathcal{Y} &= \{Y^A, Y^B, \dots\} &&\text{—State of the model} \\
\mathcal{F} &= \{\vec{F}^A, \vec{F}^B, \dots\} &&\text{—Forces in the model} \\
\mathcal{T} &= \{\vec{T}^A, \vec{T}^B, \dots\} &&\text{—Torques in the model}
\end{aligned}
$$

Numerical methods for solving first-order O.D.E.'s are well known (see [Press et. al. 88,Boyce and Deprima 77,Ralston and Rabinowitz 78]). When the equations are not stiff (stiff differential equations occur when there are multiple widely varying time constants for the solutions), an adaptive Adams predictor corrector is suitable; otherwise we recommend a method such as Gear's Method ([Gear 71]).

B Mathematical Details

B.1 Dual of a vector

The *dual* of a vector $\vec{b}$ is the antisymmetric matrix $\mathbf{b}^\bullet$:

$$\text{With } \vec{b} = \begin{bmatrix} b_1 \\ b_2 \\ b_3 \end{bmatrix}, \text{ define } \mathbf{b}^\bullet = \begin{bmatrix} 0 & b_3 & -b_2 \\ -b_3 & 0 & b_1 \\ b_2 & -b_1 & 0 \end{bmatrix}$$

For any vectors $\vec{b}$ and $\vec{a}$, we have the following identities:

$$
\begin{aligned}
\mathbf{b}^\bullet \vec{a} &\equiv \vec{b} \times \vec{a} \\
\mathbf{b}^{\bullet\mathsf{T}} \vec{a} &\equiv \vec{a} \times \vec{b} \\
\mathbf{b}^{\bullet\mathsf{T}} \vec{b} &\equiv 0
\end{aligned}
$$

B.2 Behavior of a Point

Consider a point "P" which is fixed relative to a rigid body (Fig. 17). We define $\vec{b}_{body}$ to be the vector from the center-of-mass of the body to P, expressed in the body's home coordinates; since the point is fixed, $\vec{b}_{body}$ is constant. We would like to derive expressions for the position, velocity, and acceleration of P.

We will need to know the derivative of $\mathbf{I}^{-1}$. Remember that since the body is rigid, $\mathbf{I}_{body}^{-1}$ is constant:

$$
\begin{aligned}
\mathbf{I}^{-1} &= \mathbf{R}\mathbf{I}_{body}^{-1}\mathbf{R}^{\mathsf{T}} \\
\frac{d}{dt}\mathbf{I}^{-1} &= (\frac{d}{dt}\mathbf{R})\mathbf{I}_{body}^{-1}\mathbf{R}^{\mathsf{T}} + \mathbf{R}\mathbf{I}_{body}^{-1}(\frac{d}{dt}\mathbf{R}^{\mathsf{T}}) \\
&= \omega^\bullet\mathbf{R}\mathbf{I}_{body}^{-1}\mathbf{R}^{\mathsf{T}} + \mathbf{R}\mathbf{I}_{body}^{-1}\mathbf{R}^{\mathsf{T}}\omega^{\bullet\mathsf{T}} \\
&= \omega^\bullet\mathbf{I}^{-1} + \mathbf{I}^{-1}\omega^{\bullet\mathsf{T}}
\end{aligned}
\tag{10}
$$

We have substituted $\omega^\bullet\mathbf{R}$ for $\frac{d}{dt}\mathbf{R}$, according to the equations of motion (Appendix A).

We will also need the derivative of $\vec{\omega}$:

$$
\begin{aligned}
\vec{\omega} &= \mathbf{I}^{-1}\vec{L} \\
\frac{d}{dt}\vec{\omega} &= (\frac{d}{dt}\mathbf{I}^{-1})\vec{L} + \mathbf{I}^{-1}(\frac{d}{dt}\vec{L}) \\
&= (\frac{d}{dt}\mathbf{I}^{-1})\vec{L} + \mathbf{I}^{-1}\vec{T} \\
&= \omega^\bullet\mathbf{I}^{-1}\vec{L} + \mathbf{I}^{-1}\omega^{\bullet\mathsf{T}}\vec{L} + \mathbf{I}^{-1}\vec{T} \\
&= \omega^\bullet\vec{\omega} + \mathbf{I}^{-1}(\omega^{\bullet\mathsf{T}}\vec{L} + \vec{T}) \\
&= \mathbf{I}^{-1}(\vec{L} \times \vec{\omega} + \vec{T})
\end{aligned}
\tag{11}
$$

We have substituted $\vec{T}$ for $\frac{d}{dt}\vec{L}$ according to the equations of motion. We can now differentiate $\vec{b}$:

$$
\begin{aligned}
\vec{b} &= \mathbf{R}\vec{b}_{body}, \text{ and} \\
\frac{d}{dt}\vec{b} &= \frac{d}{dt}(\mathbf{R}\vec{b}_{body}) \\
&= (\frac{d}{dt}\mathbf{R})\vec{b}_{body} \\
&= \omega^\bullet\mathbf{R}\vec{b}_{body} \\
&= \omega^\bullet\vec{b} \\
&= \vec{\omega} \times \vec{b} \\
\frac{d^2}{dt^2}\vec{b} &= (\frac{d}{dt}\vec{\omega}) \times \vec{b} + \vec{\omega} \times (\frac{d}{dt}\vec{b}) \\
&= (\frac{d}{dt}\vec{\omega}) \times \vec{b} + \vec{\omega} \times (\vec{\omega} \times \vec{b}) \\
&= (\mathbf{I}^{-1}(\vec{L} \times \vec{\omega} + \vec{T})) \times \vec{b} + \vec{\omega} \times (\vec{\omega} \times \vec{b}) \\
&= (\mathbf{b}^{\bullet\mathsf{T}}\mathbf{I}^{-1})\vec{T} + (\mathbf{b}^{\bullet\mathsf{T}}\mathbf{I}^{-1}(\vec{L} \times \vec{\omega}) + \vec{\omega} \times (\vec{\omega} \times \vec{b})) \\
&= \mathbf{H}\vec{T} + \vec{\beta}
\end{aligned}
\tag{12}
$$

where we define

$$
\begin{aligned}
\mathbf{H} &= \mathbf{b}^{\bullet\mathsf{T}}\mathbf{I}^{-1} \\
\vec{\beta} &= \mathbf{b}^{\bullet\mathsf{T}}\mathbf{I}^{-1}(\vec{L} \times \vec{\omega}) + \vec{\omega} \times (\vec{\omega} \times \vec{b})
\end{aligned}
$$

We have again substituted $\omega^\bullet\mathbf{R}$ for $\frac{d}{dt}\mathbf{R}$.

Finally, we can express the position, velocity, and acceleration of point P in terms of the state of the body and the net force and torque on the body:

$$
\begin{aligned}
\vec{X}_P &= \vec{X} + \vec{b} \\
\vec{v}_P &= \frac{d}{dt}\vec{X}_P \\
&= \frac{d}{dt}\vec{X} + \frac{d}{dt}\vec{b} \\
&= \vec{v} + \vec{\omega} \times \vec{b} \\
\vec{a}_P &= \frac{d^2}{dt^2}\vec{X}_P \\
&= \frac{d^2}{dt^2}\vec{X} + \frac{d^2}{dt^2}\vec{b} \\
&= \frac{1}{m}\vec{F} + \mathbf{H}\vec{T} + \vec{\beta} \\
&= \mathbf{G}\vec{F} + \mathbf{H}\vec{T} + \vec{\beta}
\end{aligned}
\tag{13}
$$

where we define

$$\mathbf{G} = \frac{1}{m}$$

C Constraint Derivations

For each type of constraint, we must derive expressions for the various quantities defined in Fig. 11. The steps we follow are:

1. Choose a simple "deviation" measure $\vec{D}$. $\vec{D}$ is a function of the positions ($\vec{X}$) and orientations ($\mathbf{R}$) of the constrained bodies, and may optionally depend on t.
2. Differentiate $\vec{D}$, to derive $\vec{D}^{(1)}(\mathcal{Y}, t)$, Substitute $\vec{v}$ and $\omega^\bullet R$ for the $\frac{d}{dt}\vec{X}$ and $\frac{d}{dt}R$ terms which will arise (see Fig. 11).
3. Differentiate again, to derive $\vec{D}^{(2)}(\mathcal{Y}, \vec{F}, \vec{T}, t)$. Replace $\frac{d}{dt}\vec{p}$ and $\frac{d}{dt}\vec{L}$ terms with $\vec{F}$ and $\vec{T}$, thus giving rise to the linear dependence of $\vec{D}^{(2)}$ on the forces and torques. Define the $d \times 3$ matrices $\mathbf{\Gamma}$, $\mathbf{\Lambda}$, and the d-vector $\vec{\beta}$.
4. Choose where to apply the constraint forces needed to meet the constraint. Most often, we apply a vector force to a fixed location of the constrained body; in this case, we have $f = 3$ degrees of freedom.
5. Use steps 2 and 3 to derive $\mathbf{G}$ and $\mathbf{H}$ for each body. These convert the f values in the "constraint force" $\vec{F}_c$ into the actual forces and torques on the bodies.

Often, some of the quantities $\mathbf{\Gamma}$, $\mathbf{\Lambda}$, $\mathbf{G}$, and $\mathbf{H}$, which are nominally matrices, turn out to be scalar. Scalars can be handled as a special case in the implementation, or scaled identity matrices can be used.

We give examples of the constraint derivations for the constraints illustrated in Sec. 2.2.

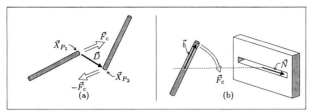

Figure 18: (a) "Point-to-point" constraint. We apply equal-and-opposites to the two constrained points, to cause the deviation function $\vec{D}(\mathcal{Y}) = \vec{X}_{P_2}(\mathcal{Y}) - \vec{X}_{P_1}(\mathcal{Y})$ to go to 0. (b) "Orientation" constraint. We rotate the body to cause the deviation function $\vec{D}(\mathcal{Y}) = \vec{b} \cdot \vec{N} - 1$ to go to 0. The constraint torque is given directly by $\vec{F}_c$; there is no force due to the constraint.

C.1 "Point-To-Path" Constraint

This constraint is met at a time t if the constrained point "P" is on the path, at $\vec{X}^{\text{path}}(t)$; it is the same as the "point-to-nail" constraint (Example 1 in Sec. 4) but with a nail that moves. Thus several terms have a dependency on $\vec{X}^{\text{path}}$:

$$
\begin{aligned}
\vec{D}(\mathcal{Y}, t) &= \vec{X}_P(\mathcal{Y}) - \vec{X}^{\text{path}}(t) \\
\vec{D}^{(1)}(\mathcal{Y}, t) &= \vec{v}_P(\mathcal{Y}) - \tfrac{d}{dt}\vec{X}^{\text{path}}(t) \\
\vec{D}^{(2)}(\mathcal{Y}, \vec{F}, \vec{T}, t) &= \vec{a}_P(\mathcal{Y}, \vec{F}, \vec{T}) - \tfrac{d^2}{dt^2}\vec{X}^{\text{path}}(t) \\
\vec{\beta} &= \mathbf{b}^{\bullet \mathsf{T}} \mathbf{I}^{-1}(\vec{L} \times \vec{\omega}) + \vec{\omega} \times (\vec{\omega} \times \vec{b}) \\
&\quad - \tfrac{d^2}{dt^2}\vec{X}^{\text{path}}(t)
\end{aligned}
$$

C.2 "Point-To-Point" Constraint

This constraint is met if the two constrained points "P_1" and "P_2" are at the same location (Fig. 18a). We thus define $\vec{D}$ to be the vector separating the two points. The derivation proceeds analogously to that of the "point-to-nail" constraint:

$$
\begin{aligned}
\vec{D}(\mathcal{Y}) &= \vec{X}_{P_2}(\mathcal{Y}) - \vec{X}_{P_1}(\mathcal{Y}) \\
\vec{D}^{(1)}(\mathcal{Y}) &= \vec{v}_{P_2}(\mathcal{Y}) - \vec{v}_{P_1}(\mathcal{Y}) \\
\vec{D}^{(2)}(\mathcal{Y}, \vec{F}, \vec{T}) &= \vec{a}_{P_2}(\mathcal{Y}) - \vec{a}_{P_1}(\mathcal{Y}) \\
\Gamma^1 &= \tfrac{1}{m_1}\mathbf{1} \\
\Lambda^1 &= \mathbf{b}_1^{\bullet \mathsf{T}} \mathbf{I}_1^{-1} \\
\Gamma^2 &= -\tfrac{1}{m_2}\mathbf{1} \\
\Lambda^2 &= -\mathbf{b}_2^{\bullet \mathsf{T}} \mathbf{I}_2^{-1}
\end{aligned}
$$

To be in keeping with Newton's third law, the two bodies must exert equal and opposite forces on each other. We apply an arbitrary force, $\vec{F}_c$, to one of the constrained points, and the negation of that force, $-\vec{F}_c$, to the other. We thus have $f = 3$, and define

$$
\begin{aligned}
\mathbf{G}^1 &= 1; & \mathbf{H}^1 &= \mathbf{b}_1^{\bullet} \\
\mathbf{G}^2 &= -1; & \mathbf{H}^2 &= -\mathbf{b}_2^{\bullet}
\end{aligned}
$$

C.3 "Orientation" Constraint

This constraint is met if a specified unit vector $\vec{b}$ fixed in the body lines up with a unit vector $\vec{N}$ fixed in the world (see Fig. 18b). We could define D to be the angle between the vectors; it easier, however, if we define D to be 0 when the cosine of the angle (i.e. the dot-product of the vectors) is 1. Thus we have $d = 1$, and:

$$
\begin{aligned}
D(\mathcal{Y}) &= \vec{b}(Y) \cdot \vec{N} - 1 \\
D^{(1)}(\mathcal{Y}) &= (\tfrac{d}{dt}\vec{b}(\mathcal{Y})) \cdot \vec{N} \\
D^{(2)}(\mathcal{Y}, \vec{T}) &= (\tfrac{d^2}{dt^2}\vec{b}(\mathcal{Y})) \cdot \vec{N} \\
&= ((\mathbf{b}^{\bullet \mathsf{T}} \mathbf{I}^{-1})\vec{T}) \cdot \vec{N} \\
&\quad + (\mathbf{b}^{\bullet \mathsf{T}} \mathbf{I}^{-1}(\vec{L} \times \vec{\omega}) + \vec{\omega} \times (\vec{\omega} \times \vec{b})) \cdot \vec{N} \\
\Gamma &= 0 \\
\Lambda &= \vec{N}^{\mathsf{T}} \mathbf{b}^{\bullet \mathsf{T}} \mathbf{I}^{-1} \\
\vec{\beta} &= (\mathbf{b}^{\bullet \mathsf{T}} \mathbf{I}^{-1}(\vec{L} \times \vec{\omega}) + \vec{\omega} \times (\vec{\omega} \times \vec{b})) \cdot \vec{N}
\end{aligned}
$$

Notice that Λ is a 1×3 matrix, and $\vec{\beta}$ is a scalar.

We apply an arbitrary pure torque, $\vec{F}_c$, to the body, and no force. We therefore have $f = 3$, and

$$
\mathbf{G} = 0; \quad \mathbf{H} = 1
$$

Notice that this constraint is "non-square" – we are applying 3 degrees of freedom to affect a scalar constraint "deviation."

Figure 19: Linking Chain between Two Towers. The chain swings naturally after assembly.

Figure 20: Linking Chain between Two Towers, continued

D Acknowledgements

Thanks to: Jed Lengyel, for being a "guinea pig" user of the modeling system, and for putting together the video system that was used in making animations; John Snyder, for the rendering of the animations; John Platt, for discussions and for numerical software; and Brian Von Herzen, for the motivation and modeling for the Harwood space-station self-assembly animations and for the polygonal playing card models.

Figure 21: Linking Chain between Two Towers, continued

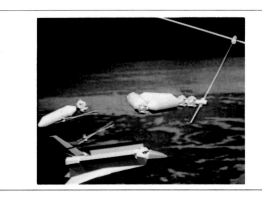

Figure 22: Space Station Assembly. The modules are assembled via "orientation", "point-to-point", and "point-to-nail" constraints. The constraint forces determine the strengths of the rocket thrusts.

Figure 23: Space Station Assembly, continued.

Figure 24: Cardhouse Assembly. We use "point-to-point," and "pt-to-plane" constraints to assemble a cardhouse.

Figure 25: Cardhouse Assembly, completed.

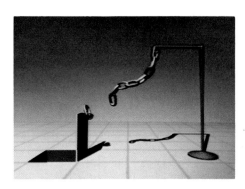

Figure 26: Pandora's Chain. The chain links are instructed to connect togetherand hook to a trap door. Torsion springs keep the links roughly perpendicular to each other. Gravity and viscous damping are applied to all bodies. The chains and trap door swing naturally once they are assembled.

Rendering Trimmed NURBS with Adaptive Forward Differencing

Michael Shantz and Sheue-Ling Chang

Sun Microsystems, Inc.
2500 Garcia Avenue
Mountain View, CA 94043

Abstract

Trimmed non-uniform rational B-splines have become a very useful surface representation form in the mechanical CAD industry. Previous rendering methods use the de Boor algorithm to evaluate the surface at equal increments in parameter space. This yields polygons which are then rendered. Alternatively the Oslo algorithm and Boehm's knot insertion algorithms are used in a subdivision approach. In this paper a new method is presented for rendering trimmed NURB surfaces of arbitrary order using the adaptive forward differencing (AFD) technique. This method extends the AFD technique to higher order, efficiently computes the basis matrix for each span, calculates the shading approximation functions for rational surfaces, and trims and image maps NURB surfaces. Trimming is accomplished by using AFD to scan convert the trimming curves in parameter space, thus producing the intersection points between the trim curves and an isoparametric curve across the surface. A winding rule is used to determine the regions bounded by the curve which are then rendered with AFD. The method is suitable for both hardware and software implementations, however, higher order surfaces require very high precision due to the forward difference nature of the algorithm.

CR Categories and Subject Descriptors: I.3.3 [**Computer Graphics**]: Picture/Image Generation - Display algorithms; I.3.7 [**Computer Graphics**]: Three-dimensional Graphics and Realism - Color, shading, shadowing, and texture.

Additional Key Words and Phrases: image synthesis, shading, adaptive forward differencing, graphics VLSI, parametric surfaces, B-splines, NURBS.

Introduction

Several methods have been used previously for rendering trimmed NURB surfaces. The de Boor Cox algorithm [4] is frequently used for evaluating a B-spline curve or surface at a particular point in parameter space. Also, subdivision techniques using knot insertion have been described by Boehm [2] and Cohen and others (the Oslo algorithm)[6]. The Oslo algorithm is capable of simultaneously inserting multiple knots in an efficient manner. A simple proof of the Oslo Algorithm is given by Prautzsch[13], and a more efficient way of using the Oslo algorithm is given by Lyche and Morken[12]. Lee [10] gives an algorithm for evaluating the derivatives of a NURB at a point in parameter space by using knot insertion. Boehm [3] later derived a more efficient scheme for the simultaneous evaluation of all surface derivatives at a point in parameter space.

Nonuniform B-spline curves and surfaces can be rendered by tesselation to piecewise linear vectors or planar polygons by evaluating at intervals in parameter space. They may also be subdivided to produce vector or polygon vertices or subdivided to individual pixels. Each of these methods has certain drawbacks. Subdividing using knot insertion down to the pixel level is very expensive. Piecewise planar methods, while fast, yield lower quality renderings if done coarsely and make image mapping and trimming more difficult.

The approach presented in this paper involves obtaining the functional description of each span by computing the basis function of the span, then rendering the span using the adaptive forward difference technique together with a Hermite shading function approximation.

In this paper the AFD technique is extended to higher orders and used to evaluate the NURB surfaces and their associated trimming curves incrementally. A recursive relation is derived for obtaining the coefficients of the basis functions for a given knot vector, and a method is given for computing shading function approximations for a rational surface. AFD is also used to evaluate the NURB trimming curves in parameter space "scanline" order to provide the parameter bounds for rendering curves across the surface. Figure 3 shows a result produced with these techniques, an image of trimmed NURB surfaces with image mapping and shading.

Summary of the AFD Technique

A previous paper[3] describes an adaptive forward differencing technique for rendering trimmed, image mapped, parametric surfaces. A similar technique for rendering parametric surfaces was also proposed by Rockwood[4], which computes the minimum possible steps for each surface and then renders the surface with ordinary forward differencing. A brief comparison between the two techniques and the error accumulation problem were mentioned in the discussion section.

The AFD method unifies the processes of recursive subdivision [1] and forward differencing [2] for curves and surfaces in the R^4 space (homogeneous coordinates x,y,z,w). A *linear substitution* transforms a parametric function $f(t)$ into $f(at+b)$ or $f(s,t)$ into $f(as+b,ct+d)$. The geometric effect of linear substitution is to translate and scale a segment or patch within the curve or surface containing it. Any segment of a curve can be mapped to any other segment of the same curve by some linear substitution, and likewise for patches. Let L be a linear substitution $t/2$ and R be $(t+1)/2$. L and R are the operators associated with recursive subdivision; they act on a segment C to yield the "left" and "right" halves LC and RC of C, see Figure 1. E is a linear substitution $t+1$, which acts on a segment C to yield its "right neighbor" EC. The process of applying a sequence of E operators to render a curve segment is known as forward differencing.

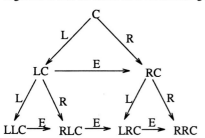

Figure 1. Relationship of linear substitutions L, R and E.

A disadvantage of forward differencing is that it may not traverse C with uniform velocity. Recursive subdivision avoids this difficulty by stopping at different depths in different parts of the recursion tree. The adaptive forward differencing technique transfers this advantage of recursive subdivision to forward differencing by inserting an occasional L or L^{-1} (the substitution $2t$) into the stream of E's whenever the velocity is too great or too small respectively. This has the effect of changing the level in the recursion tree while forward-differencing across it. While any basis will do for the AFD technique, the forward difference basis

$$B_0 = 1, \ B_1 = t, \ B_2 = \frac{t(t-1)}{2} \ .. \ B_n = \frac{t(t-1)(t-2) \cdots (t-n+1)}{n!}$$

is best suited. The forward step E, the adjust-down L, and the adjust-up L^{-1} operators of this basis of order 4 are:

$$E = \begin{bmatrix} 1 & 1 & 0 & 0 \\ 0 & 1 & 1 & 0 \\ 0 & 0 & 1 & 1 \\ 0 & 0 & 0 & 1 \end{bmatrix} \quad L = \begin{bmatrix} 1 & 0 & 0 & 0 \\ 0 & 1/2 & -1/8 & 1/16 \\ 0 & 0 & 1/4 & -1/8 \\ 0 & 0 & 0 & 1/8 \end{bmatrix} \quad L^{-1} = \begin{bmatrix} 1 & 0 & 0 & 0 \\ 0 & 2 & 1 & 0 \\ 0 & 0 & 4 & 4 \\ 0 & 0 & 0 & 8 \end{bmatrix}$$

The above linear operators can be applied to a cubic function

$$f(t) = aB_3(t) + bB_2(t) + cB_1(t) + dB_0(t)$$

to transform $f(t)$ into $f'(t) = a'B_3 + b'B_2 + c'B_1 + d'B_0$.

The E transformation performs a forward step operation $f'(t) = f(t+1)$:

$$\begin{bmatrix} d' \\ c' \\ b' \\ a' \end{bmatrix} = \begin{bmatrix} 1 & 1 & 0 & 0 \\ 0 & 1 & 1 & 0 \\ 0 & 0 & 1 & 1 \\ 0 & 0 & 0 & 1 \end{bmatrix} \begin{bmatrix} d \\ c \\ b \\ a \end{bmatrix}$$

The L operator can reduce the step size by $f'(t) = f(t/2)$:

$$\begin{bmatrix} d' \\ c' \\ b' \\ a' \end{bmatrix} = \begin{bmatrix} 1 & 0 & 0 & 0 \\ 0 & 1/2 & -1/8 & 1/16 \\ 0 & 0 & 1/4 & -1/8 \\ 0 & 0 & 0 & 1/8 \end{bmatrix} \begin{bmatrix} d \\ c \\ b \\ a \end{bmatrix}$$

and the L^{-1} operator can double the step size by

$$\begin{bmatrix} d' \\ c' \\ b' \\ a' \end{bmatrix} = \begin{bmatrix} 1 & 0 & 0 & 0 \\ 0 & 2 & 1 & 0 \\ 0 & 0 & 4 & 4 \\ 0 & 0 & 0 & 8 \end{bmatrix} \begin{bmatrix} d \\ c \\ b \\ a \end{bmatrix}$$

Extending AFD to Higher Order

The AFD technique can be generalized to arbitrary order by extending these matrices.

The forward difference matrix for one span of a NURB surface of arbitrary order is given by

$$A = [FD][DU][CU][P][CV]^T[DV]^T[FD]^T$$

where P is the matrix of control points for the given span of the NURB, CU and CV are the basis matrices in the u, v directions defined by the u and v knot vectors, DU and DV are the initial scaling matrices, FD is a matrix which converts polynomial basis (i.e. polynomial power series) into forward difference basis, and A is the resulting forward difference matrix. The matrix A has v columns and u rows when the NURB surface has order u and v in the u and v directions.

1. Computing NURB polynomial basis coefficients

The next major section will discuss a recursive method for obtaining the polynomial basis matrices CU and CV.

2. Initial scaling matrix

The DU and DV matrices are used to scale polynomial coefficients in the u and v direction to the appropriate initial forward step size. For nth order this matrix is simply

$$DU = \begin{bmatrix} 1 & 0 & 0 & 0 \\ 0 & du & 0 & 0 \\ 0 & 0 & du^2 & 0 \\ 0 & 0 & 0 & du^3 \end{bmatrix} \cdots$$

The scaling matrix can be trivially extended to higher order by filling in the jth diagonal elements with du^j, where du is the amount of scaling.

3. Converting polynomial to forward difference

The *FD* matrix converts from polynomial to forward difference basis. For a cubic this is the well known matrix

$$FD = \begin{bmatrix} 1 & 0 & 0 & 0 \\ 0 & 1 & 1 & 1 \\ 0 & 0 & 2 & 6 \\ 0 & 0 & 0 & 6 \end{bmatrix}$$

We note here that the FD matrix for higher order can be computed from an expression

$$a_0 + a_1 u + a_2 u^2 + \cdots + a_d u^d =$$

$$b_0 + b_1 u + b_2 \frac{u(u-1)}{2} + \cdots + b_d \frac{u...(u-d+1)}{d!}$$

which relates a set of forward difference basis coefficients $<b_i>$ to the corresponding polynomial basis coefficients $<a_j>$:

$$b_0 = a_0$$

$$b_i = \sum_{j=1}^{d} \left[\sum_{k=0}^{i} (-1)^{i-k} C_k^i k^j \right] a_j$$

$$\text{where } C_k^i = \frac{i!}{k!(i-k)!} \text{ and } d = degree$$

Thus the elements in matrix *FD* can be defined as

$$FD_{i,j} = \sum_{k=0}^{i} (-1)^{i-k} C_k^i k^j$$

For example the FD matrix for order 5 is

$$FD = \begin{bmatrix} 1 & 0 & 0 & 0 & 0 \\ 0 & 1 & 1 & 1 & 1 \\ 0 & 0 & 2 & 6 & 14 \\ 0 & 0 & 0 & 6 & 36 \\ 0 & 0 & 0 & 0 & 24 \end{bmatrix}$$

The resulting forward difference matrix *A* can then be calculated by concatenating all the matrices appropriately.

$$A = [FD][DU][CU][P][CV]^T[DV]^T[FD]^T$$

4. The forward step operation

The forward step operation $[E]$ is mathematically a linear substitution of v+1 for the parameter v. Practically it is used to advance from the current curve to the next or from the current pixel to the next. This operation can be extended trivially to higher order. In the forward difference basis a forward step is performed for all coefficients by adding the i+1 coefficient to the ith coefficient. Thus the $[E]$ matrix can be generalized as

$$E_{i,j} = 1 \text{ if } i=j \text{ or } j=i+1, otherwise \ 0$$

The forward step matrix for nth order is

$$E = \begin{bmatrix} 1 & 1 & 0 & & & . \\ 0 & 1 & 1 & & & . \\ 0 & 0 & 1 & & & . \\ & & & .. & & 0 \\ & & & & 1 & 1 \\ . & . & . & . & 0 & 1 \end{bmatrix}$$

5. The adjust down operation

To decrease the distance between two consecutive curves, an adjust down operation is performed on $[A]$. Let W be the matrix which adjusts down the polynomial basis coefficients by half, i.e. W is a scaling matrix with a scaling factor of 0.5.

$$W = \begin{bmatrix} 1 & 0 & 0 & 0 & 0 \\ 0 & 1/2 & 0 & 0 & .. \\ 0 & 0 & 1/4 & 0 & .. \\ 0 & 0 & 0 & 1/8 & .. \\ 0 & .. & .. & .. & .. \end{bmatrix}$$

The adjust-down operation is extended to higher order by

$$L = [FD][W][FD^{-1}].$$

where the $[FD^{-1}]$ matrix converts the forward difference coefficients into polynomial basis, the $[W]$ matrix scales the polynomial coefficients by 0.5, and $[FD]$ converts the scaled result back into forward difference basis again. For order 5 the adjust down matrix is

$$L = \begin{bmatrix} 1 & 0 & 0 & 0 & 0 \\ 0 & 1/2 & -1/8 & 1/16 & -5/128 \\ 0 & 0 & 1/4 & -1/8 & 5/64 \\ 0 & 0 & 0 & 1/8 & -3/32 \\ 0 & 0 & 0 & 0 & 1/16 \end{bmatrix}$$

6. The adjust up operation

The adjust-up matrix can be similarly extended by

$$L^{-1} = [FD][U][FD^{-1}], \text{ where } U = \begin{bmatrix} 1 & 0 & 0 & 0 & 0 \\ 0 & 2 & 0 & 0 & .. \\ 0 & 0 & 4 & 0 & .. \\ 0 & 0 & 0 & 8 & .. \\ 0 & .. & .. & .. & .. \end{bmatrix}$$

To increase the distance between two curves the matrix *A* is transformed by L^{-1}. For order 5 the adjust up matrix is

$$L^{-1} = \begin{bmatrix} 1 & 0 & 0 & 0 & 0 \\ 0 & 2 & 1 & 0 & 0 \\ 0 & 0 & 4 & 4 & 1 \\ 0 & 0 & 0 & 8 & 12 \\ 0 & 0 & 0 & 0 & 16 \end{bmatrix}$$

Notice that above order 4 the adjust down matrix contains values which are not powers of two. Up to order nine, the elements can all be represented as the sum of two powers of two.

Obtaining NURB basis functions

Trimmed NURBS have become a useful surface representation form in the MCAD industry[1]. Uniform splines have constant basis functions throughout the spans, i.e. the basis matrix is the same for all spans. Non-uniform splines instead have a different basis function for each span defined recursively by a knot vector. A B-spline curve is a piecewise polynomial curve

$$f(u) = \sum_i \mathbf{p}_i N_i^k(u)$$

where the coefficients $\mathbf{p}_i$ of the B-spline functions $N_i^k(u)$ are called control points or de Boor points. The functions $N_i^k(u)$

are piecewise polynomial of order k defined over a knot vector $\cdots < u_0 < u_1 < u_2 < \cdots$ by a recursive relation

$$N_i^1(u) = 0 \text{ if } u \notin [u_i, u_{i+1}]$$

$$N_i^1(u) = 1 \text{ if } u \in [u_i, u_{i+1}]$$

$$N_i^k(u) = \frac{u - u_i}{u_{i+k-1} - u_i} N_i^{k-1}(u) + \frac{u_{i+k} - u}{u_{i+k} - u_{i+1}} N_{i+1}^{k-1}(u)$$

Boehm's triangular scheme operates on the knot vectors and control points to give the values and the derivatives of the coordinate functions xyzw. This scheme can then be used to obtain the polynomial coefficients for each span of the surface and to calculate the normal vectors and the bicubic Hermite approximations of the shading function for a surface.

An alternative method is presented here which operates on the knot vectors to give the basis matrices of each span which then convert the control points for the span to polynomial or forward difference basis.

To render the surface with the AFD technique, the parameter u for a current span (u_l, u_{l+1}) is redefined to range between 0.0 and 1.0 by a linear substitution $u' = u_{l+1}u + (1-u)u_l$ so that

$$N_i^k(u) = \frac{(u_l - u_i) + (u_{l+1} - u_l)u}{u_{i+k-1} - u_i} N_i^{k-1}(u)$$

$$+ \frac{(u_{i+k} - u_l) - (u_{l+1} - u_l)u}{u_{i+k} - u_{i+1}} N_{i+1}^{k-1}(u) \quad (1)$$

Given the basis functions represented in polynomial power series, let $C_{i,j}^k$ denote the jth coefficient of the ith basis function $N_i^k(u)$ of order k:

$$N_i^k(u) = \sum_{j=0}^{k-1} C_{i,j}^k u^j \quad (2)$$

The coefficients $C_{i,j}^k$ can be defined recursively in terms of the lower order ones as

$$C_{i,j}^k = a\, C_{i,j-1}^{k-1} + b\, C_{i,j}^{k-1} + c\, C_{i+1,j-1}^{k-1} + d\, C_{i+1,j}^{k-1} \quad (3)$$

$$where \quad a = \frac{u_{l+1} - u_l}{u_{i+k-1} - u_i} \qquad b = \frac{u_l - u_i}{u_{i+k-1} - u_i}$$

$$c = -\frac{u_{l+1} - u_l}{u_{i+k} - u_{i+1}} \qquad d = \frac{u_{i+k} - u_l}{u_{i+k} - u_{i+1}}$$

This equation is used to obtain the NURB basis matrix CU and CV in the u, v directions from the u, v knot vectors. The derivation in (3) can be proved by observing that $N_i^k(u)$ is a product of a linear function times a polynomial. Substituting equation (2) into equation (1) gives the following equation

$$N_i^k(u) = \frac{(u_l - u_i) + (u_{l+1} - u_l)u}{u_{i+k-1} - u_i} \sum_{j=0}^{k-2} C_{i,j}^{k-1} u^j$$

$$+ \frac{(u_{i+k} - u_l) - (u_{l+1} - u_l)u}{u_{i+k} - u_{i+1}} \sum_{j=0}^{k-2} C_{i+1,j}^{k-1} u^j \quad (4)$$

from which the derivation follows trivially.

In Appendix A a recurrence formula is given for efficiently computing the *forward difference basis* matrix for a NURB span. This recursive equation is similar to the previous one. The above two methods allow the basis matrices CU and CV to be derived independently of the control point mesh. These matrices are concatenated with the control point arrays to give the forward difference matrices of the coordinate functions and the shading functions for the span.

Rational Shading Approximation

A shading function approximation method for non-rational surfaces was presented in a previous paper by the authors [15]. This method uses Hermite approximation to approximate the normalized shading functions $N \cdot L$ and $N \cdot H$ with two bicubic functions.

The shading approximation algorithm for rational surfaces is very similar to that described previously. The derivation of the shading function approximation for rational surfaces is included in Appendix B.

The calculation of derivatives of rational functions are generally more complex. The implementations of the two algorithms are the same except at the low level routines where the derivatives are computed. Here only the differences between the two are outlined.

For a non-rational surface

$$x(u,v) = UXV, y(u,v) = UYV, z(u,v) = UZV$$

the low level derivatives are

$$\frac{\partial x}{\partial u} = U'XV, \quad \frac{\partial x}{\partial v} = UXV', \quad \frac{\partial^2 x}{\partial u^2} = U''XV,$$

$$\frac{\partial^2 x}{\partial v^2} = UXV'', \quad \frac{\partial^3 x}{\partial u^2 \partial v} = U''XV', \quad \frac{\partial^3 x}{\partial u \partial v^2} = U'XV''$$

For a rational patch,

$$x(u,v) = \frac{UXV}{UWV}, y(u,v) = \frac{UYV}{UWV}, z(u,v) = \frac{UZV}{UWV}$$

the derivatives are more complicated as follows:

$$\frac{\partial X}{\partial u} = \frac{x_u w - x w_u}{w^2}$$

$$\frac{\partial^2 X}{\partial u^2} = \frac{1}{w^3}(w^2 x_{uu} - wx w_{uu} - 2ww_u x_u + 2x w_u w_u)$$

$$\frac{\partial^2 X}{\partial v^2} = \frac{1}{w^3}(w^2 x_{vv} - wx w_{vv} - 2ww_v x_v + 2x w_v w_v)$$

$$\frac{\partial^2 X}{\partial u \partial v} = \frac{1}{w^3}(w^2 x_{uv} - wx_u w_v - wx_v w_u - wx w_{uv} + 2x w_u w_v)$$

$$\frac{\partial^3 X}{\partial u^2 \partial v} = \frac{H1(u,v)}{w^3} - 3X_{uu}(u,v)\frac{w_v}{w}$$

$$\frac{\partial^3 X}{\partial u \partial v^2} = \frac{H2(u,v)}{w^3} - 3X_{vv}(u,v)\frac{w_u}{w}$$

where

$$H1(u,v) = \frac{\partial}{\partial v}(w^2 x_{uu} - wx w_{uu} - 2ww_u x_u + 2x w_u w_u)$$

$$H2(u,v) = \frac{\partial}{\partial u}(w^2 x_{vv} - wx w_{vv} - 2ww_v x_v + 2x w_v w_v)$$

The two spherical surfaces shown in figure 4 are rational biquadratic surfaces. The shading functions are computed using the method described in this section.

Trimming NURB Surfaces

Once the forward difference coefficients of the current span are obtained, the trimming curves are scan converted in u,v space using AFD to increment the curves to find their intersections with the curve $S(u_0,v)$. This curve is then rendered between intersections v_{min} and v_{max} using AFD in the v direction. Then we step to the next curve with a forward step in the u direction.

The AFD method allows polynomial parametric surfaces to be rendered in parameter space order rather than in scanline order. This greatly reduces the difficulty of trimming since the trim curves can be scan converted in parameter space order using the same techniques that are well known for scan converting polygons. The trimming curves are nth order, closed, NURB curves. Our trimming algorithm operates in 4 steps.

1) The NURB trim curves are converted to piecewise Bezier by knot insertion.

2) The Bezier sections are subdivided so they are all monotonically decreasing in the u parameter direction.

3) The Bezier sections are converted to forward difference basis.

4) They are sorted in u parameter order by their minimum u value.

5) For each AFD forward step in the u direction (from curve to curve) the active trim curve sections are forward-stepped down to find intersections with the new curve (vmin, vmax). The appropriate portions of the surface curve are drawn based on the trim curve winding rule.

Figure 5 shows a nut composed of NURB surfaces trimmed using the above technique. The rim portion of the nut is formed by a cone trimmed with two sets of trimming curves Figure 2 uses the rim example to illustrate the trimming algorithm.

NURB surface s(u, v)

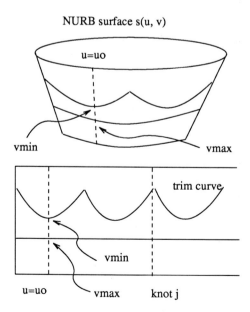

Figure 2. A NURB surface trimmed by a NURB curve.

Discussion

1. Reducing Adjustment Overhead

While rendering a surface, the decision to adjust up, adjust down, or forward step from the current curve to the next curve is made based on an estimate of the maximum distance between the two curves, $d(v)=f(u+\delta u,v)-f(u,v)$. This distance is an isoparametric function of v. By converting the distance function into Bezier basis and using the convex hull property, the maximum distance between two curves can be calculated. Cook catalogs the conversion matrices between several different basis in[7]. The overhead per curve for converting between the two bases can be reduced by keeping a dual matrix B of the forward difference matrix A :

$$A = [FD][DU][CU][P][CV]^T[DV]^T[FD]^T$$

$$B = [FD][DU][CU][P][CV]^T[DV]^T[BZ]^T$$

where $[BZ]$ converts from polynomial basis into Bezier basis. Matrix A is converted to forward difference basis in both u and v directions and B is in forward difference basis in u and Bezier basis in v. The first row of A contains the coordinates of the current curve in *forward difference basis* for used in AFD to render the curve. The second row of B contains the difference function $d(v)$ in *Bezier basis* for used in the adjustment decision making. A and B matrices are synchronized in the u direction, i.e. adjusted up or down or forward stepped at the same time, so that AFD can step from one curve to the next while keeping the distance function available in Bezier basis.

2. Degenerate Surfaces

Shown in Figure 4 are two spherical surfaces both defined as non-uniform rational B-spline surfaces. The shading approximation method discussed in this paper was applied directly to the non-degenerate surface on the left. The one on the right contains a degenerate edge with three coincident control points. A degenerate surface may have vanishing derivatives, which complicates the computation of the Hermite approximation to the normalized normal vector function. In this case, the vanishing derivatives were replaced using special case approximation before the shading method was applied.

3. Computation Complexity

The de Boor algorithm is popular for evaluating points on a NURB surface, or inserting knots in a subdivision technique for surface rendering. A full version of the de Boor algorithm for evaluating a point on a surface of order k requires $(k-1)k(k+1)/2$ multiplies and twice as many adds. This makes it expensive to evaluate many points on a surface or to subdivide the surface down to pixel size in order to render a high quality image. Boehm's triangular scheme gives the values and derivatives of a B-spline function. This scheme can be used to obtain the polynomial coefficients for each span of the surface. Each triangular operation requires $k(k-1)/2$ multiplies and $k(k-1)/2$ adds for an order k function, assuming the knot differences have been precomputed. A full version of Boehm's triangular scheme requires two triangle operations to compute all the derivatives of a single variable B-spline function, which is $k(k-1)$ multiplies and adds. For a bi-variate function, it would require $4k$ triangle operations to compute all the derivatives, which is $4k^2(k-1)$ multiplies and adds. Given the derivatives, k^2 multiplies are required to compute the polynomial coefficient matrix. The method presented here takes approximately $4k + 4(k-1)(k-2) + (k-1)(k-2)(2k-3)/6$ multiplies and adds to compute a basis function of order k, assuming the knot differences have been precomputed. This method requires the computation of all the basis functions in the u, v direction. Given the basis functions, it takes two kxk matrix multiplies to produce a polynomial coefficient matrix, which is $2k^3$ multiplies and $2k^2(k-1)$ adds per span. The computational complexity of the two methods is similar. Boehm's method operates on the control points directly instead of computing the basis functions for each span, and thus has more memory requirement.

4. Error Analysis

Although forward differencing is the fastest possible way to sample a large numbers of points on a surface, it tends to be more vulnerable to errors than other evaluation methods. After performing k forward step operations on a cubic function $f(t) = aB_3(t) + bB_2(t) + cB_1(t) + dB_0(t)$, the four coefficients become $d' = a\frac{k(k-1)(k-2)}{6} + b\frac{k(k-1)}{2} + ck + d$, $c' = a\frac{k(k-1)}{2} + bk + c$, $b' = ak + b$, and $a' = a$. The error accumulation in each coefficient is formulated as

$$E_d' = e_a\frac{k(k-1)(k-2)}{6} + e_b\frac{k(k-1)}{2} + e_ck + e_d$$

$$E_c' = e_a\frac{k(k-1)}{2} + e_bk + e_c$$

$$E_b' = e_ak + e_b$$

$$E_a' = e_a$$

where e_a, e_b, e_c and e_d are the initial errors in the coefficients and E_a, E_b, E_c and E_d are the errors accumulated after k steps. In fixed point arithmetic with all the coefficients having equal number of fractional bits, the term $e_ak(k-1)(k-2)/6$ contributes the most to the error, which can be as much as 30 bits for $k=2^{10}$. For higher order functions the error can accumulate even more rapidly. Both OFD and AFD techniques suffer error propagation problems, however, the AFD error is always bounded by the OFD error. The number of steps required by OFD to forward across a curve is always greater than or equal to that of AFD, because OFD uses the minimum step size while AFD can adjust up step size whenever needed and thus reducing the number of steps. An adjust-up operation cuts the number of forward steps in half, and at the same time requires an n-bit left-shift in the case of a degree-n function. It is clear from the dominating error term in the following relation that the AFD error with k forward steps following an adjust-up is always smaller than the OFD error with $2k$ forward steps.

$$e_a\frac{2k(2k-1)(2k-2)}{6} > 2^3e_a\frac{k(k-1)(k-2)}{6}$$

A section of error analysis on the OFD technique can also be found in Rockwood's paper.

5. Transparency and Anti-aliasing

Redundant pixel painting in AFD constitutes the major obstacle in rendering transparent objects. Quick solutions to get around the redundant pixel problem would be either to tesselate a transparent object into polygons or to keep a buffer for object identification at each pixel to eliminate redundancy. However, the object-id buffer still can not handle a folded surface. A new twin-curve buffer algorithm is under development by the author to tackle this problem. Still more work and testing are required.

One very successful anti-aliasing technique is based on *dicing* to produce *micropolygons* [1] followed by skittered sub-sampling and averaging. Previous methods for dicing used screen space derivatives to determine how finely to dice, and ordinary forward differencing to do the actual dicing. The AFD technique may have potential as a method for dicing since screen space step size is the condition which controls adjust up, adjust down, or forward step. Further investigation in this area is needed.

Conclusion

In this paper a technique for rendering nonuniform rational B-spline surfaces is described. The AFD technique is generalized to higher order, and a recursive relation is derived for efficiently computing the basis function coefficients of a NURB surface. An approximation method for computing the shading functions of a rational surface is developed and AFD is applied to the problem of trimming NURB surfaces with NURB trim curves using a method similar to polygon scanline algorithms. AFD based rendering methods for NURBS give the quality of subdivision methods with the efficiency of forward difference techniques. Image mapping and NURB trimming are also facilitated. Figure 6 shows a clevice rendered using these techniques.

The shading approximations and the recursive relation for computing basis functions are equally applicable to other rendering techniques such as polygon tesselation, ordinary forward differencing, or recursive subdivision.

Further work should be done on evaluating the accuracy of the Hermite approximation functions for shading and possibly extending these methods to higher order.

Acknowledgement

The authors would like to thank Lewis Knapp and David Elrod for aquiring the NURBS data bases and writing the database reader software. Thanks to Tony Wyant for providing the digitized images for mapping, and to Sue Carrie for helpful discussions on error analysis. We are grateful to Lewis Knapp for reviewing early drafts of this paper and for many helpful discussions. Special thanks to Automation Technology Products for providing trimmed NURB data.

Appendix A

This appendix derives the NURB forward difference basis function for a single span from the knot vectors.

We can redefine the B-spline function N_i^k in forward difference basis as

$$N_i^k(u) = B_{i,0}^k + B_{i,1}^k u + B_{i,2}^k \frac{u(u-1)}{2}$$
$$+ \cdots + B_{i,k-1}^k \frac{u(u-1)(u-2)...(u-(k-2))}{(k-1)!}$$

and

$$B_{i,j}^1 = \begin{cases} 1 & u_i \le u < u_{i+1} \text{ and } j=0 \\ 0 & otherwise \end{cases}$$

The jth coefficient $B_{i,j}^k$ of the NURB basis function N_i^k in the forward difference basis for the ith span of a curve of order k is given by

$$B_{i,j}^k = \frac{j B_{i,j-1}^{k-1} + (j-u_i)B_{i,j}^{k-1}}{u_{i+k-1}-u_i} - \frac{j B_{i+1,j-1}^{k-1} + (j-u_{i+k})B_{i+1,j}^{k-1}}{u_{i+k}-u_{i+1}}$$

Derivation:

From the B-spline basis definition we notice that $N_i^k(u)$ is the sum of two products of a linear equation times a polynomial.

$$N_i^k(u) = (au+b)N_i^{k-1} + (a'u+b')N_{i+1}^{k-1}$$

We proceed by first obtaining a recurrence relation for one product and then combine the relations for the two products. Taking $au+b$ times each term of N_i^{k-1} gives

$$B_0(au+b) = aB_0 u + bB_0$$

$$B_1 u \left[\frac{2a(u-1)}{2} + \frac{2(b+a)}{2} \right] = 2aB_1 \frac{u(u-1)}{2!} + (b+a)B_1 u$$

$$B_2 \frac{u(u-1)}{2!} \left[\frac{3a(u-2)}{3} + \frac{3(b+2a)}{3} \right] =$$

$$3aB_2 \frac{u(u-1)(u-2)}{3!} + (b+2a)B_2 \frac{u(u-1)}{2!}$$

$$B_j \frac{u(u-1)...(u-(j-1))}{j!}(au+b) =$$

$$(j+1)aB_j \frac{u(u-1)...(u-j)}{(j+1)!} + (b+ja)B_j \frac{u(u-1)...(u-(j-1))}{j!}$$

Grouping common terms and repeating similarly for the second product gives

$$B_{i,j}^k = jaB_{i,j-1}^{k-1} + (b+ja)B_{i,j}^{k-1} + ja'B_{i+1,j-1}^{k-1} + (b'+ja')B_{i+1,j}^{k-1}$$

Substituting for a and b gives the equation of the recursive relation.

Appendix B:

This appendix describes how to compute the derivitaves for the Hermite shading function approximations for the *rational* case. A rational bicubic patch is defined by

$$X(u,v) = \frac{UXV}{UWV} = \frac{x(u,v)}{w(u,v)}$$

$$Y(u,v) = \frac{UYV}{UWV} = \frac{y(u,v)}{w(u,v)}$$

$$Z(u,v) = \frac{UZV}{UWV} = \frac{z(u,v)}{w(u,v)}$$

where x(u,v), y(u,v), z(u,v) and w(u,v) are the nonrational polynomial functions describing the coordinates of a patch.

The normal vector $N = <n_x,n_y,n_z>$ is given by

$$n_x = Y_u Z_v - Y_v Z_u, \quad n_y = Z_u X_v - Z_v X_u, \quad n_z = X_u Y_v - X_v Y_u$$

The derivatives of the unnormalized normal vector function are given by

$$\frac{\partial n_x}{\partial u} = Y_{uu}Z_v + Y_u Z_{uv} - Y_{uv}Z_u - Y_v Z_{uu}$$

$$\frac{\partial n_x}{\partial v} = Y_{uv}Z_v + Y_u Z_{vv} - Y_{vv}Z_u - Y_v Z_{uv}$$

$$\frac{\partial^2 n_x}{\partial u \partial v} = Y_{uuv}Z_v + Y_{uu}Z_{vv} + Y_u Z_{uvv}$$

$$- Y_{uvv}Z_u - Y_{vv}Z_{uu} - Y_v Z_{uuv}$$

where the low level rational terms $X_u, X_{uu}, X_{uv}, X_{uuv}, X_{uvv}$, etc. can be derived separately in terms of the derivatives of the nonrational functions $x(u,v), y(u,v), z(u,v)$ and $w(u,v)$.

$$X_u = \frac{x_u w - x w_u}{w^2}$$

$$X_{uu} = \frac{1}{w^3}(w^2 x_{uu} - wx w_{uu} - 2ww_u x_u + 2xw_u w_u)$$

$$X_{vv} = \frac{1}{w^3}(w^2 x_{vv} - wx w_{vv} - 2ww_v x_v + 2xw_v w_v)$$

$$X_{uv} = \frac{1}{w^3}(w^2 x_{uv} - wx_u w_v - wx_v w_u - wx w_{uv} + 2xw_u w_v)$$

$$X_{uuv} = \frac{H1(u,v)}{w^3} - 3X_{uu}(u,v)\frac{w_v}{w}$$

$$X_{uvv} = \frac{H2(u,v)}{w^3} - 3X_{vv}(u,v)\frac{w_u}{w}$$

where

$$H1(u,v) = \frac{\partial}{\partial v}(w^2 x_{uu} - wx w_{uu} - 2ww_u x_u + 2xw_u w_u)$$

$$H2(u,v) = \frac{\partial}{\partial u}(w^2 x_{vv} - wx w_{vv} - 2ww_v x_v + 2xw_v w_v)$$

The normalized normal vector function, its derivatives and the cross derivatives in the u and v directions are derived exactly the same as for a nonrational patch. The normalized normal vector function is

$$\hat{n}_x(u,v) = n_x G, \quad \hat{n}_y(u,v) = n_y G, \quad \hat{n}_z(u,v) = n_z G,$$

$$where \quad G(u,v) = (n_x^2 + n_y^2 + n_z^2)^{-1/2}$$

The derivatives and the cross derivatives in the u and v directions are given by

$$\frac{\partial \hat{n}_x(u,v)}{\partial u} = \frac{\partial n_x}{\partial u} G + \frac{\partial G}{\partial u} n_x$$

$$\frac{\partial \hat{n}_x(u,v)}{\partial v} = \frac{\partial n_x}{\partial v} G + \frac{\partial G}{\partial v} n_x$$

$$\frac{\partial^2 \hat{n}_x}{\partial u \partial v} = \frac{\partial^2 n_x}{\partial u \partial v} G + \frac{\partial n_x}{\partial u}\frac{\partial G}{\partial v} + \frac{\partial^2 G}{\partial u \partial v} n_x + \frac{\partial G}{\partial u}\frac{\partial n_x}{\partial v}$$

$$\frac{\partial G}{\partial u} = -G^3 (n_x \frac{\partial n_x}{\partial u} + n_y \frac{\partial n_y}{\partial u} + n_z \frac{\partial n_z}{\partial u})$$

$$\frac{\partial G}{\partial v} = -G^3 (n_x \frac{\partial n_x}{\partial v} + n_y \frac{\partial n_y}{\partial v} + n_z \frac{\partial n_z}{\partial v})$$

$$\frac{\partial^2 G}{\partial u \partial v} = \frac{3}{G} \left[\frac{\partial G}{\partial v} \right] \left[\frac{\partial G}{\partial u} \right]$$

$$- G^3 \left[n_x \frac{\partial^2 n_x}{\partial u \partial v} + n_y \frac{\partial^2 n_y}{\partial u \partial v} + n_z \frac{\partial^2 n_z}{\partial u \partial v} \right]$$

$$- G^3 \left[\frac{\partial n_x}{\partial v}\frac{\partial n_x}{\partial u} + \frac{\partial n_y}{\partial v}\frac{\partial n_y}{\partial u} + \frac{\partial n_z}{\partial v}\frac{\partial n_z}{\partial u} \right]$$

To approximate the unit normal vector function we need

$$\hat{P}_x = \begin{bmatrix} \hat{n}_x(0,0) & \hat{n}_x(0,1) & \frac{\partial \hat{n}_x}{\partial v}(0,0) & \frac{\partial \hat{n}_x}{\partial v}(0,1) \\ \hat{n}_x(1,0) & \hat{n}_x(1,1) & \frac{\partial \hat{n}_x}{\partial v}(1,0) & \frac{\partial \hat{n}_x}{\partial v}(1,1) \\ \frac{\partial \hat{n}_x}{\partial u}(0,0) & \frac{\partial \hat{n}_x}{\partial u}(0,1) & \frac{\partial^2 \hat{n}_x}{\partial u \partial v}(0,0) & \frac{\partial^2 \hat{n}_x}{\partial u \partial v}(0,1) \\ \frac{\partial \hat{n}_x}{\partial u}(1,0) & \frac{\partial \hat{n}_x}{\partial u}(1,1) & \frac{\partial^2 \hat{n}_x}{\partial u \partial v}(1,0) & \frac{\partial^2 \hat{n}_x}{\partial u \partial v}(1,1) \end{bmatrix}$$

References

1. Richard Bartels, John Beatty, and Brian Barsky, *An Introduction to Splines for use in Computer Graphics and Geometric Modeling*, Morgan Kaufmann Publishers, 1987.

2. Wolfgang Boehm, *Inserting New Knots into B-Spline Curves*, 12, pp. 199-201, Computer Aided Design, 1980.

3. Wolfgang Boehm, *Efficient Evaluation of Splines*, 33, pp. 171-177, Computing, 1984.

4. Carl de Boor, *On calculating with B-splines*, 6, pp. 50-62, Journal of Approximation Theory, 1972.

5. Edwin Catmull, *A Subdivision Algorithm for Computer Display of Curved Surfaces*, UTEC-CSc-74-133, University of Utah, Computer Science, 1974.

6. Elaine Cohen, Tom Lyche, and Richard Riesenfeld, *Discrete B-Splines and Subdivision Techniques in Computer-Aided Geometric Design and Computer Graphics*, 14, Computer Graphics and Image Processing, October 1980.

7. Robert Cook, *Patch Work*, Tech. Memo 118, Computer Div., Lucasfilm Ltd., June 1985.

8. Robert Cook, Loren Carpenter, and Edwin Catmull, *The Reyes Image Rendering Architecture*, SIGGRAPH'87 Proceedings, July 1987.

9. James Foley and Andries Van Dam, *Fundamentals of Interactive Computer Graphics*, p. 533, Addison-Wesley Publishers, 1982.

10. E.T.Y. Lee, *Efficient Evaluation of Splines*, 329, pp. 365-371, Computing, 1982.

11. Sheue-Ling Lien, Michael Shantz, and Vaughan Pratt, *Adaptive Forward Differencing for Rendering Curves and Surfaces*, SIGGRAPH'87 Proceedings, July 1987.

12. Tom Lyche and Knut Morken, *Making the Oslo Algorithm More Efficient*, 23, pp. 663-675, SIAM J. Numer. Anal, 1986.

13. Hartmut Prautzsch, *A Short Proof of the Oslo Algorithm*, 1, Computer Aided Geometric Design, 1984.

14. Alyn Rockwood, *A Generalized Scanning Technique for Display of Parametrically Defined Surfaces*, 7, IEEE CG&A, August 1987.

15. Michael Shantz and Sheue-Ling Lien, *Shading Bicubic Patches*, SIGGRAPH'87 proceedings, July 1987.

Figure 3. A sphere subtracted by a cylinder tangent to the sphere surface. The image is shaded with two light sources.

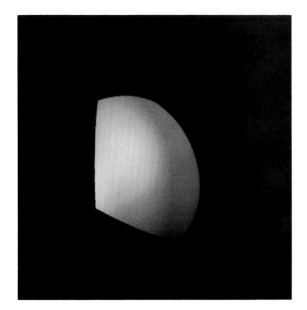
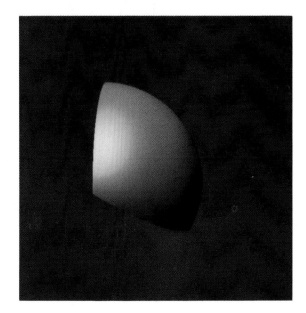

Figure 4. Two rational biquadratic surfaces shaded with a 4th order non-rational shading approximation function. Left) Non-degenerate surface. Right) Degenerate surface with one degenerate edge. Two light sources were used.

 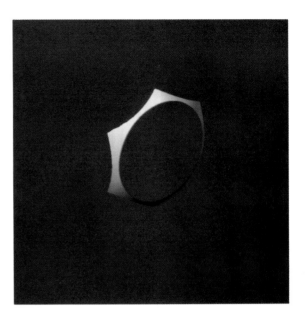

Figure 5. Nut composed of trimmed planes cylinders and cones. The beveled rim portion is a trimmed cone.

Figure 6. Trimmed, image mapped, NURB clevice.

A Recursive Evaluation Algorithm for a Class of Catmull-Rom Splines

Phillip J. Barry and Ronald N. Goldman
Computer Graphics Laboratory
Computer Science Dept., Univ. of Waterloo
Waterloo, Ontario, Canada N2L 3G1

Abstract: It is known that certain Catmull-Rom splines [7] interpolate their control vertices and share many properties such as affine invariance, global smoothness, and local control with B-spline curves; they are therefore of possible interest to computer aided design. It is shown here that another property a class of Catmull-Rom splines shares with B-spline curves is that both schemes possess a simple recursive evaluation algorithm. The Catmull-Rom evaluation algorithm is constructed by combining the de Boor algorithm for evaluating B-spline curves with Neville's algorithm for evaluating Lagrange polynomials. The recursive evaluation algorithm for Catmull-Rom curves allows rapid evaluation of these curves by pipelining with specially designed hardware. Furthermore it facilitates the development of new, related curve schemes which may have useful shape parameters for altering the shape of the curve without moving the control vertices. It may also be used for constructing transformations to Bézier and B-spline form.

Categories and Subject Descriptors: G.1.1 [**Numerical Analysis**]: Interpolation — *Spline and piecewise polynomial interpolation*; G.1.2 [**Numerical Analysis**]: Approximation — *Spline and piecewise polynomial approximation*; I.3.5 [**Computer Graphics**]: Computational Geometry and Object Modeling — *Curve and surface representation*

Additional Key Words and Phrases: B-spline, Catmull-Rom spline, de Boor algorithm, Lagrange polynomial, Neville's algorithm, recursive evaluation algorithm

1 Introduction

In computer aided design designers often use B-spline curves:

$$S(t) = \sum_i N_i^n(t) V_i \qquad (1)$$

where the V_i are points called *control vertices* and the $N_i^n(t)$ are degree n (order $n+1$) piecewise polynomial blending functions called *B-splines* or *B-spline basis functions*. These blending functions depend on a set of knots $\{t_i\}$. By altering the control vertices, and perhaps the knots, the designer is able to manipulate the shape of the curve [13].

B-spline curves are useful for many reasons, among them

— piecewise polynomials: B-spline curves are piecewise polynomial. They are therefore easy to store and manipulate, while often being faster to compute and analyze than single polynomials because usually one can use lower degree piecewise polynomials.

— differentiability: B-spline curves have a high degree of smoothness. Usually the curve will be $n-1$ times continuously differentiable, although by introducing multiple knots it can be designed to be less smooth.

— local control: altering a single control vertex affects only a limited portion of the curve rather than the entire curve. This is because the blending function $N_i^n(t)$ is 0 outside of the interval $[t_i, t_{i+n+1})$.

— affine invariance: the B-spline basis functions are normalized to sum to 1. This implies that B-spline curves are invariant under affine transformations. Thus these curves depend only on the relative geometry of their control vertices, and not on any absolute coordinate system.

— recursive evaluation algorithm: There is a simple, numerically stable, recursive evaluation algorithm for B-spline curves called the de Boor algorithm [4], which computes points along $S(t)$ without explicitly evaluating $N_i^n(t)$.

While B-spline curves do have many desirable properties, there are some desirable features they lack. For example, B-spline curves are approximating curves; that is, they approximate the shape and position of the control polygon (the polygon obtained by connecting the control vertices in order with line segments), but in general they do not interpolate the control vertices. For some applications in computer aided geometric design it is desirable for the control vertices to actually lie *on* the curve. Many known curve schemes interpolate their control vertices, however these curve schemes usually have other drawbacks. Natural cubic splines (see, e.g., [5] or [6]), for example, do not have local control or a known recursive evaluation algorithm.

Certain curve schemes have been developed which retain many B-spline curve properties while incorporating additional features. Catmull-Rom splines are one such scheme. Catmull and Rom noted that, in any curve scheme, one can replace control vertices with functions, and thus get a more general scheme [7]. Various choices of these functions impart different desirable properties to the curve. In particular, they observed that certain choices led to interpolatory curves. Although Catmull and Rom discussed a more general case, we will restrict our attention to an important class of Catmull-Rom splines obtained by combining B-spline basis functions and Lagrange interpolating polynomials. These Catmull-Rom splines, which we shall define more precisely below, have many nice features. They are piecewise polynomial, have local support, are invariant under affine transformations, and have certain differentiability and interpolatory properties. The purpose of this paper is to show that they also have a recursive evaluation algorithm similar to the de Boor algorithm for B-splines.

This new result is interesting for many reasons. First, by employing this algorithm and specially designed hardware one can evaluate and render such curves very rapidly [10]. Second, the fact that Catmull-Rom splines possess such an evaluation algorithm places them in a class of curves called "piecewise recursive curve schemes" [2]. These schemes generate new curves which may not only retain certain properties of Catmull-Rom splines but also possess shape parameters, scalars which affect the shape of a curve without moving the control vertices. Third, general results for recursive curve schemes provide ways of transforming Catmull-Rom splines to Bézier or B-spline form. Finally, the fact that Catmull-Rom splines have a recursive evaluation algorithm of this sort makes them noteworthy because very few well-known piecewise polynomial schemes have such an evaluation algorithm.

This paper is structured as follows: in Section 2 we will give more details concerning Catmull-Rom splines and then introduce the recursive evaluation algorithm and make some observations about it. In Section 3 we give some concrete examples by looking at a few cubic Catmull-Rom splines. Section 4 contains concluding remarks.

2 Catmull-Rom splines and their recursive evaluation algorithm

This section is divided into three parts. In Subsection 2.1 we define the class of Catmull-Rom splines with which we are concerned and discuss the properties of the splines in this class. In Subsection 2.2 we introduce the recursive evaluation algorithm for this class of curves. Subsection 2.3 contains a discussion of some aspects of the algorithm.

2.1 Catmull-Rom splines

Catmull and Rom noted that if one began with a curve scheme

$$D(t) = \sum_i F_i(t) V_i \qquad (2)$$

one could replace the control vertices V_i by functions $V_i(t)$ which may depend on new control vertices. The resulting curve scheme will be more general than the original scheme, since $V_i(t)$ can be thought of as a generalization of V_i. This generality can be exploited to endow the new curve with special properties; in particular Catmull and Rom observed that special choices of $V_i(t)$ will result in $D(t)$ interpolating certain points.

We will now center our attention on an important subclass of this class of curves. We will employ a notation more suitable for our needs than that used in [7].

Suppose one wishes to generalize B-spline curves. Let the blending functions $F_i(t)$ in (2) be the B-spline basis functions $N_i^n(t)$ with knot set $\{t_i\}$. One can choose the $V_i(t)$ to be the Lagrange interpolating polynomials of degree m which interpolate the control vertices $P_{i-m}, \ldots, P_i$ at any distinct nodes $s_{i-m}, \ldots, s_i$, respectively. Unlike the knots, we do not require the nodes to be increasing. Although Catmull and Rom equated the nodes s_j with the knots t_i, we will allow the nodes to be arbitrary, as long as they are distinct. Analogous to the interpolation result in [7], if $s_j \in [t_{j+n}, t_{j+m+1})$, then $D(s_j) = P_j$ (the spline is interpolatory). Note this requires $m \geq n$. (If t_{j+m+1} is not a knot of multiplicity $n+1$, then $D(s_j) = P_j$ if $s_j \in [t_{j+n}, t_{j+m+1}]$.) Regardless of whether or not the spline is interpolatory, it will always be a degree $n+m$ piecewise polynomial, $n-1$ times continuously differentiable, affine invariant, and have local control. All these properties are inherited from properties of the B-spline basis functions $N_i^n(t)$ and the Lagrange interpolating polynomials $V_i(t)$.

The Catmull-Rom splines in this class can be written either as

$$D(t) = \sum_i N_i^n(t) V_i(t) \qquad (3)$$

or, collecting coefficients of P_i, as

$$D(t) = \sum_i G_i(t) P_i \qquad (4)$$

for some functions $G_i(t)$. The $G_i(t)$ are called the Catmull-Rom blending functions and are sums of products of certain B-spline and Lagrange basis functions. More specifically if we let $L_{j,i}^m(t)$ denote the Lagrange cardinal function which has nodes $s_{j-m}, \ldots, s_j$ and which is 1 at s_i, $j-m \leq i \leq j$, then

$$V_i(t) = \sum_{w=i-m}^{i} L_{i,w}^m(t) P_w \qquad (5)$$

and it is then not difficult to see that

$$G_i(t) = \sum_{w=i}^{i+m} N_w^n(t) L_{w,i}^m(t). \qquad (6)$$

When $s_j \in [t_{j+n}, t_{j+m+1})$ for all j, then these blending functions satisfy the cardinal conditions $G_i(s_j) = \delta_{ij}$ since if $j \neq i$ then either $L_{w,i}^m(s_j) = 0$ or $N_w^n(s_j) = 0$ while if $j = i$ then $L_{w,i}^m(s_j) = 1$ for

$w = i, \ldots, i+m$ and $\sum_{w=i}^{i+m} N_w^n(s_j) = 1$.

For Catmull-Rom splines we have a set of knots $\{t_i\}$ and a set of nodes $\{s_j\}$. To simplify the number of parameters, we can express the s's in terms of the t's. For example, we can equate the nodes with the knots. If for all j we set $s_j = t_{j+k}$ for any integer k such that $n \leq k \leq m$ ($n \leq k \leq m+1$ if all the knots have multiplicity 1), we will not destroy any interpolation present. Another possibility is to equate the Lagrange nodes to the B-spline nodes (cf. [5, p.214]).

If the B-spline has multiple knots, equating knots and nodes will create a singularity in the Lagrange curve. The usual method of overcoming this difficulty is to use a scheme which also interpolates certain derivative values; however, such a scheme will not have a recursive evaluation algorithm of the type developed below. Thus, when the B-spline has multiple knots, one cannot totally equate the Lagrange nodes to the B-spline knots. One can do so partially as long as no assignments are made resulting in singularities.

Some examples of Catmull-Rom splines and their blending functions will be shown in Section 3.

2.2 The recursive evaluation algorithm

We now introduce a recursive evaluation algorithm for this class of Catmull-Rom curves. To do this, we call to mind two other recursive evaluation algorithms — the above mentioned de Boor algorithm [4] for B-spline curves, and Neville's algorithm (cf. [6]) for Lagrange polynomials.

To evaluate a B-spline curve $S(t)$ for $t \in [t_q, t_{q+1})$, set

$$P_i^0(t) = V_i \qquad i = q-n, \ldots, q$$

$$P_i^r(t) = \frac{t_{n+1+i-r} - t}{t_{n+1+i-r} - t_i} P_{i-1}^{r-1}(t) + \frac{t - t_i}{t_{n+1+i-r} - t_i} P_i^{r-1}(t)$$

$$r = 1, \ldots, n; \quad i = q-n+r, \ldots, q. \qquad (7)$$

Then $S(t) = P_q^n(t)$. The de Boor algorithm can be represented in a triangular array as shown in Figure 1. An example using this algorithm to evaluate a B-spline curve is given in Section 3.

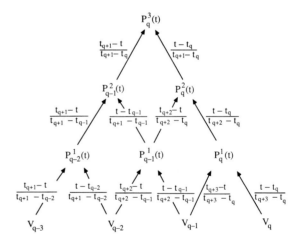

Figure 1: A diagram of the de Boor algorithm for evaluating a B-spline curve $S(t)$. The cubic case ($n = 3$) is shown where $t \in [t_q, t_{q+1})$. The control vertices V_i are placed at the bottom of the triangle and blended together until the point $P_q^n(t) = S(t)$ is obtained.

Neville's algorithm is a recursive algorithm for evaluating the Lagrange polynomial $L(t)$ which interpolates points $P_0, \ldots, P_m$ at nodes $s_0, \ldots, s_m$. It can be written as

$$P_i^0(t) = P_i \quad i = 0, \ldots, m$$

$$P_i^r(t) = \frac{s_i - t}{s_i - s_{i-r}} P_{i-1}^{r-1}(t) + \frac{t - s_{i-r}}{s_i - s_{i-r}} P_i^{r-1}(t)$$

$$r = 1, \ldots, m; \quad i = r, \ldots, m. \qquad (8)$$

Then $L(t) = P_m^m(t)$. Figure 2 shows a diagram of Neville's algorithm as a triangular array. An example using Neville's algorithm to evaluate a Lagrange polynomial is given in Section 3.

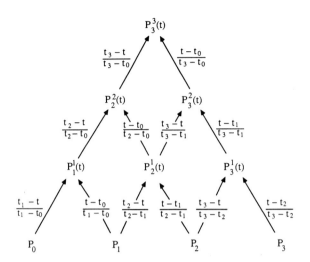

Figure 2: A diagram of Neville's algorithm for evaluating a Lagrange polynomial $L(t)$. The cubic case ($m = 3$) is shown. The control points P_i are placed at the bottom of the triangle and blended together until the point $P_m^m(t) = L(t)$ is obtained.

To evaluate a Catmull-Rom spline we could naively first use Neville's algorithm to calculate the functions $V_i(t)$ and then apply the de Boor algorithm to obtain a point on the curve $D(t)$. See Figure 3 for a diagram of this procedure. Note that although Figure 3 does present a recursive evaluation algorithm for Catmull-Rom curves, this algorithm is neither as efficient nor as elegant as, e.g., the de Boor algorithm for B-spline curves since the de Boor algorithm can be represented in a more compact triangular form (Figure 1).

What is remarkable about Catmull-Rom splines is that this naive recursive evaluation algorithm can be simplified extensively because there is substantial overlap in evaluating succesive $V_i(t)$'s. Let $P_{ji}^r(t)$ be the point $P_j^r(t)$ computed in evaluating $V_i(t)$ by Neville's algorithm. Then, since $V_i(t)$ and $V_{i+1}(t)$ share the nodes $s_{i-m+1}, \dots, s_i$ and the control vertices $P_{i-m+1}, \dots, P_i$, the parameters used in calculating $P_{j+1,i}^r(t)$ are identical to the corresponding parameters used in computing $P_{j,i+1}^r(t)$ when $j < m$. Therefore $P_{j+1,i}^r(t) = P_{j,i+1}^r(t)$ for $j < m$. In particular the points $P_{m-1,i+1}^r(t)$ are found in evaluating $V_i(t)$ and therefore do not need to be recomputed in evaluating $V_{i+1}(t)$. If we store these points, then (see Figure 2) we need only compute the m new values $P_{m,i+1}^r(t)$ $r = 1, \dots, m$ to evaluate $V_{i+1}(t)$.

This redundancy leads to a simpler and less costly evaluation algorithm for Catmull-Rom splines. This algorithm can be represented by a triangular diagram, an example of which is shown in Figure 4, similar to the diagrams in Figures 1 and 2.

We now write down explicitly the recursive evaluation algorithm for Catmull-Rom splines. To evaluate the Catmull-Rom curve $D(t)$ for $t \in [t_q, t_{q+1}]$, set

$$P_i^0(t) = P_i \quad i = q - n - m, \dots, q$$

$$P_i^r(t) = \frac{s_i - t}{s_i - s_{i-r}} P_{i-1}^{r-1}(t) + \frac{t - s_{i-r}}{s_i - s_{i-r}} P_i^{r-1}(t)$$

$$r = 1, \dots, m; \quad i = q - n - m + r, \dots, q.$$

$$P_i^r(t) = \frac{t_{n+1+i-r} - t}{t_{n+1+i-r} - t_i} P_{i-1}^{r-1}(t) + \frac{t - t_i}{t_{n+1+i-r} - t_i} P_i^{r-1}(t)$$

$$r = m+1, \dots, m+n; \quad i = q - n - m + r, \dots, q. \quad (9)$$

Then $D(t) = P_q^{m+n}(t)$.

To verify that $P_q^{m+n}(t)$ does indeed equal $D(t)$, merely note that the first stage of the algorithm produces the Lagrange curves $P_i^m(t) = V_i(t)$ $i = q - n, \dots, q$ and the second stage applies the de Boor algorithm to these curves.

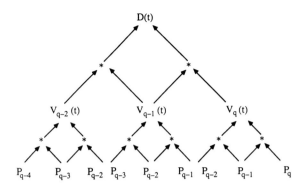

Figure 3: One possible means of evaluating Catmull-Rom splines is to evaluate each of the $V_i(t)$ separately by Neville's algorithm, and then blend these curves together by the de Boor algorithm to get $D(t)$. Such a technique can be represented as shown (for the case $n = m = 2$).

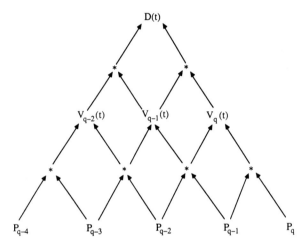

Figure 4: A diagram of the recursive evaluation algorithm for Catmull-Rom curves. The case shown is $n = m = 2$. The lower levels in Figure 3 can be combined to yield the algorithm shown here. This algorithm is theoretically less complicated and computationally less expensive than the one in Figure 3.

2.3 A discussion of the algorithm

In this subsection we will discuss a few important aspects of the recursive evaluation algorithm for Catmull-Rom splines.

As with B-splines, it is possible to use the standard tensor product construction to obtain rectangular tensor product Catmull-Rom surfaces. Such surfaces will possess geometric properties similar to those possessed by Catmull-Rom curves, and will also possess an analogous recursive evaluation algorithm. Whether one can construct similar surfaces for triangular domains is still an open question.

We mentioned above that one of the reasons the recursive evaluation algorithm for Catmull-Rom curves is important is that it allows fast evaluation of the curve. If one used a processor to compute each new point $P_i^r(t)$ and ran the processors in parallel, one could calculate points on the curve extremely rapidly [10]. A slightly more complicated multiprocessor architecture would allow rapid evaluation of Catmull-Rom tensor product surfaces. Such architectures would permit real-time interactive design using Catmull-Rom tensor product surfaces and/or large numbers of Catmull-Rom splines.

Shape parameters are scalars which affect the shape of the curve without moving the control vertices (cf. [3]). They are useful for introducing features such as tension into a curve. By altering a single shape parameter one can often obtain a curve which would otherwise have required simultaneously changing the positions of many control vertices. Catmull-Rom splines do not have shape parameters as such, although it may be possible to develop useful shape parameters based on the knots and/or the nodes. (Another possibility — *visually continuous* Catmull-Rom splines — has been studied in [9].) We can, however, use the recursive evaluation algorithm to construct curve schemes which have shape parameters and which are related to Catmull-Rom splines. One can modify the recursive evaluation algorithm so that for some choices of r, i and shape parameters $a_{r,i}, b_{r,i}$,

$$P_i^r(t) = \frac{a_{r,i} - t}{a_{r,i} - b_{r,i}} P_{i-1}^{r-1}(t) + \frac{t - b_{r,i}}{a_{r,i} - b_{r,i}} P_i^{r-1}(t) \qquad (10)$$

while the remainder of the algorithm stays the same. The resulting curves will still have a recursive evaluation algorithm, be piecewise polynomial, have local support, and be affine invariant. Depending on how the shape parameters are introduced, the curves may retain differentiability and interpolatory properties. Again, the effects of such shape parameters need further study.

Another reason that a recursive evaluation algorithm is important is that it can be applied to develop transformation formulas. By using the recursive evaluation algorithm and techniques such as degree raising and duality [1] or a method called "blossoming" [12], it is possible to transform Catmull-Rom curves to B-spline or Bézier form. Further research is needed to investigate the efficiency of these transformation techniques and to determine whether these methods can be generalized to yield other transformations algorithms.

As with B-splines (cf. [12]), the triangular arrays representing the recursive evaluation algorithm for contiguous segments of a Catmull-Rom spline mesh together. If we overlay the triangular arrays for two adjacent segments of the spline so that the shared control points lie directly on top of one another, then the functions on overlapping edges of the diagram will be identical [2]. This makes Catmull-Rom splines especially noteworthy since very few piecewise polynomial schemes have a simple evaluation algorithm, let alone one of this special form.

There are certain properties possessed by the de Boor algorithm which are not possessed by the Catmull-Rom evaluation algorithm. Since the de Boor algorithm calculates new points by taking convex combinations of old points, it is numerically stable. However, any reasonably smooth interpolatory curve will not lie in the convex hull of its control vertices; therefore the evaluation algorithm for Catmull-Rom splines may be unstable. In particular instability can occur when there is a large variation in the spacing between the knots or the nodes. This instability is a consequence of a similar problem in Neville's algorithm.

Another difference is that there is a closer connection between the de Boor algorithm and the B-spline basis functions than between the evaluation algorithm for Catmull-Rom splines and the Catmull-Rom basis functions.

For example, one can derive the Cox-Mansfield-de Boor recurrence relationship [4,8] for the B-spline basis functions from the de Boor algorithm. Similarly one can derive a recursion formula for the Catmull-Rom blending functions from the recursive evaluation algorithm for Catmull-Rom curves. However, in the recursion formula for B-splines, B-splines are computed directly from lower degree B-splines, while the Catmull-Rom blending functions are not computed directly from lower degree Catmull-Rom blending functions. Again this happens because Neville's algorithm does not compute the Lagrange basis functions from a Lagrange basis of lower degree.

3 Examples

In this section we will examine a few cubic Catmull-Rom splines and their recursive evaluation algorithms. We take the B-spline knots to be uniformly spaced with $t_i = i$, define the Lagrange nodes by $s_j = t_{j+m}$, and consider the evaluation algorithm for the interval $[0,1]$. For each example we will provide a set of four graphs: a diagram of the recursive evaluation algorithm, a spline curve, an example using the recursive evaluation algorithm to evaluate a point on the curve, and a graph of one of the blending functions. In the graphs showing evaluation, the only point $P_i^r(t)$ which lies on the curve is $P_0^3(t)$. That some of the other points appear to lie on the curve is merely coincidental. Also, since the knot spacing in the examples is uniform, all other blending functions are translates of the one shown in the blending function graphs.

For cubics we have four possibilities for n and m. If we choose $n = 3$, $m = 0$ we will obtain the usual cubic B-spline which is twice

continuously differentiable. The graphs for this case are shown in Figure 5. The case $n = 2, m = 1$ produces a spline which is C^1. Figure 6 shows the illustrations for this case.

The case $n = 1, m = 2$ illustrates some elegant properties of Catmull-Rom splines. The figures for this case are presented in Figure 7. The resulting spline is guaranteed to be C^0 and interpolating. It is, however, actually C^1. Indeed, for any Catmull-Rom spline if for all j we let $s_j = t_{j+k}$ for any integer k such that $n < k \le m$,

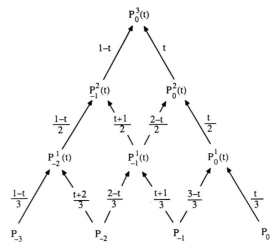

Figure 5a

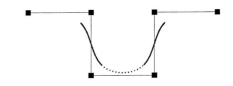

Figure 5b

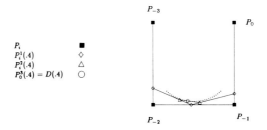

Figure 5c

Figure 5d

Figure 5: Various figures for cubic Catmull-Rom splines with $n = 3$, $m = 0$, $t_i = i$. Since $m = 0$ this is a C^2 B-spline curve. Figure 5a shows a diagram of the evaluation algorithm for $t \in [0, 1]$, Figure 5b shows an example of such a spline along with its control polygon, Figure 5c shows evaluation of the spline at $t = .4$, and Figure 5d shows a blending function $G_i(t)$.

then the curve is C^n [2]. Note too from Figure 7 that the case $n = 1$, $m = 2$, $s_j = t_{j+2}$ is identical to the case $n = 2$, $m = 1$ with $s_j = t_{j+2}$. In general, if $n+m = 2d+1$ for any nonnegative integer d, then by comparing recursive evaluation algorithms it can be shown that the cases $n = m + 1, s_j = t_{j+m+1}$ and $n = m - 1, s_j = t_{j+m}$ are identical. Finally, the particular case here is also an Overhauser spline [11].

The final case, shown in Figure 8, is $n = 0$, $m = 3$, which produces a continuous interpolatory spline.

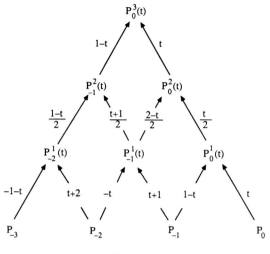

Figure 6a

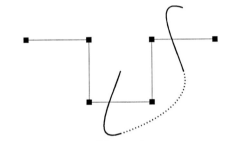

Figure 6b

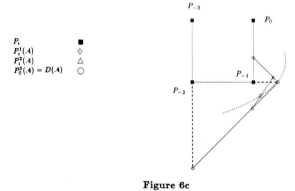

Figure 6c

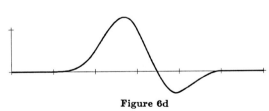

Figure 6d

Figure 6: Various figures for cubic Catmull-Rom splines with $n = 2$, $m = 1$, $t_i = i, s_i = i + 1$. The spline consists of quadratic B-splines blended with linear Lagrange curves. Figure 6a shows a diagram of the evaluation algorithm for $t \in [0, 1]$, Figure 6b shows an example of such a spline along with its control polygon, Figure 6c shows evaluation of the spline at $t = .4$, and Figure 6d shows a blending function $G_i(t)$. Note that this spline is C^1.

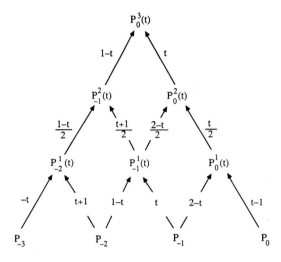

Figure 7a

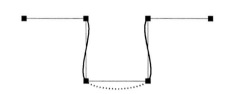

Figure 7b

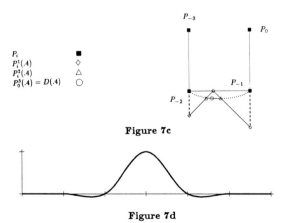

Figure 7c

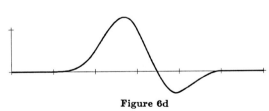

Figure 7d

Figure 7: Various figures for cubic Catmull-Rom splines with $n = 1$, $m = 2$, $t_i = i, s_i = i+2$. This spline consists of linear B-splines blended with quadratic Lagrange polynomials. Figure 7a shows a diagram of the evaluation algorithm for $t \in [0, 1]$, Figure 7b shows an example of such a spline along with its control polygon, Figure 7c shows evaluation of the spline at $t = .4$, and Figure 7d shows a blending function $G_i(t)$. This spline is C^1 and interpolatory.

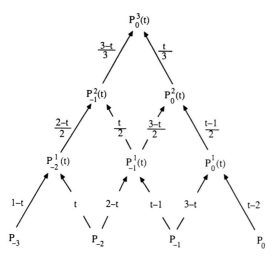

Figure 8a

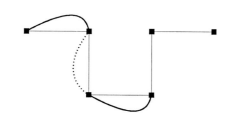

Figure 8b

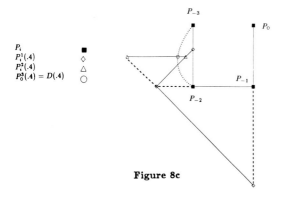

Figure 8c

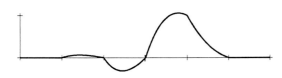

Figure 8d

Figure 8: Various figures for cubic Catmull-Rom splines with $n = 0$, $m = 3$, $t_i = i$, $s_i = i + 3$. Since $n = 0$ each segment of this curve is a cubic Lagrange polynomial. Figure 8a shows a diagram of the evaluation algorithm for $t \in [0, 1]$, Figure 8b shows an example of such a spline along with its control polygon, Figure 8c shows evaluation of the spline at $t = .4$, and Figure 8d shows a blending function $G_i(t)$. This spline is C^0 and interpolatory.

4 Concluding remarks

In this paper we have shown that a special class of Catmull-Rom splines possess a recursive evaluation algorithm similar to the de Boor algorithm for B-splines. This algorithm for Catmull-Rom splines is obtained by combining the deBoor algorithm for the evaluation of B-splines with Neville's algorithm for the evaluation of Lagrange curves. The recursive evaluation algorithm for Catmull-Rom splines gives us a possible means of fast evaluation. It also allows the construction of new curve schemes which retain some properties of Catmull-Rom curves and which may have useful shape parameters. Another benefit is that it facilitates derivation of some transformation techniques. Further it makes Catmull-Rom splines noteworthy since very few known piecewise polynomial schemes have a simple evaluation algorithm.

Although we have derived one new property of Catmull-Rom splines, other properties still need to be investigated. For example, what shape preservation properties do Catmull-Rom splines possess? What geometric effects can be produced by the introduction of shape parameters? And finally, are there simple algorithms for such processes as subdivision, degree elevation, or differentiation of Catmull-Rom splines?

Acknowledgments: The research reported here was partially supported by the Natural Sciences and Engineering Research Council of Canada, the University of Waterloo, and Control Data Corporation. The authors would also like to thank Dr. John Beatty of the University of Waterloo for his helpful remarks.

References

1. Barry, Phillip J., Urn models, recursive curve schemes, and computer aided geometric design, Ph.D. dissertation, Dept. of Mathematics, University of Utah, Salt Lake City, 1987.

2. Barry, Phillip J. and Goldman, Ronald N., Piecewise polynomial recursive curve schemes and computer aided geometric design, in preparation.

3. Barsky, Brian A., The beta-spline: a local representation based on shape parameters and fundamental geometric measures, Ph.D. dissertation, Computer Science Dept., University of Utah, Salt Lake City, 1981.

4. de Boor, Carl, On calculating with B-splines, *Journal of Approximation Theory* **6**, (1972), 50-62.

5. de Boor, Carl, *A Practical Guide to Splines*, Springer-Verlag, New York, 1978.

6. Burden, Richard L., Faires, J.Douglas, and Reynolds, Albert C., *Numerical Analysis*, Prindle, Weber, and Schmidt, Boston, 1978.

7. Catmull, Edwin and Rom, Raphael, A class of local interpolating splines, in R.E. Barnhill and R.F. Riesenfeld (eds.) *Computer Aided Geometric Design*, Academic Press, New York, 1974, 317-326.

8. Cox, M.G., The numerical evaluation of B-splines, *J. Inst. Maths. Applics.* **10**, (1972), 134-149.

9. DeRose, Anthony D. and Barsky, Brian A., Geometric continuity and shape parameters for Catmull-Rom splines, submitted for publication.

10. DeRose, Anthony D. and Holman, Thomas J., The triangle: a multiprocessor architecture for fast curve and surface generation, submitted for publication.

11. Overhauser, A.H., Analytic definition of curves and surfaces by parabolic blending, Scientific Research Staff Publication, Ford Motor Co., Detroit, Michigan, 1968.

12. Ramshaw, Lyle, *Blossoming: A Connect-the-Dots Approach to Splines*, Digital Systems Research Center, Palo Alto, California, 1987.

13. Riesenfeld, Richard F., Applications of B-spline approximation to geometric problems of computer-aided design, Ph.D. dissertation, Dept. of Systems and Information Science, Syracuse University, Syracuse, New York, 1973.

Hierarchical B-Spline Refinement

David R. Forsey and Richard H. Bartels

Computer Graphics Laboratory, Department of Computer Science
University of Waterloo, Waterloo, Ontario, Canada N2L 3G1

ABSTRACT

Refinement is usually advocated as a means of gaining finer control over a spline curve or surface during editing. For curves, refinement is a local process. It permits the change of control vertices and subsequent editing of fine detail in one region of the curve while leaving control vertices in other regions unaffected. For tensor-product surfaces, however, refinement is not local in the sense that it causes control vertices far from a region of interest to change as well as changing the control vertices that influence the region. However, with some care and understanding it is possible to restrict the influence of refinement to the locality at which an editing effect is desired. We present a method of localizing the effect of refinement through the use of *overlays*, which are hierarchically controlled subdivisions. We also introduce two editing techniques that are effective when using overlays: one is direct surface manipulation through the use of *edit points* and the other is *offset referencing* of control vertices.

CR Categories and Subject Descriptors: I.3.5 [Computer Graphics]: Computational Geometry and Object Modeling — Curve, surface, solid, and object representations; Geometric algorithms, languages, and systems; Hierarchy and geometric transformations; Modeling packages.

Key Words and Phrases: Splines, free-form surface editing, refinement, subdivision.

1. Introduction

The material in this paper derives from experience gained during the design of a prototype B-spline surface editor intended for the construction of jointed bodies to be used in a realistic animation system [7] with which one of the authors has become involved. The two issues that influenced the design of the editor in this context were: the need to mix broad-scale surface manipulations with manipulations of a finer nature and the need to superimpose fine-scale details upon broad-scale surface movements and distortions. This has led to a hierarchy of surface refinements, which we refer to as *overlays*, to a representation of control vertices in terms of *offsets* relative to a hierarchy of local reference frames, and to the investigation of mechanisms for the *direct manipulation* of points on surfaces

rather than manipulation indirectly through the movement of control vertices.

The techniques we employ are suitable for any tensor-product, parametric surface, defined in terms of control vertices and basis functions, provided that the surface supports a refinement algorithm; i.e. a re-representation process that replaces each basis function by an equivalent linear combination of one or more new basis functions. This includes, but is not restricted to, surfaces constructed from B-splines, Beta-splines, Bezier patches, and NURBS. This paper will develop the underlying ideas in the notation of B-splines, and assume that refinement is provided by the Oslo Algorithm [4].

Occasional discussions will be specific to the uniform, bicubic B-spline case, to streamline the presentation. The ideas have been implemented and tested using uniform cubic B-splines on a Silicon Graphics 4-D workstation. This simplification was made for reasons of the ease and speed with which such surfaces are supported on the hardware and in the graphics library of this workstation, not out of a limitation of the approach.

In Section 2 we will give a brief background for spline refinement. Section 3 follows with a description of overlays and their construction through the use of refinement. The representation of an overlay through the use of a local reference frame and offsets is covered in Section 4. Mechanisms for achieving direct manipulation of surface features are mentioned in Section 5. In Section 6 we touch upon some obvious ways to join our proposals with techniques introduced by Barr, Cobb, and Sederberg and Parry. Section 7 closes with some examples taken from our prototype editor.

2. Terminology and Notation

The material that we will be presenting, in its broadest formulation, relates to surfaces $S(u,v)$ which are defined by *control vertices* $V_{i,j}$ and *basis functions* $B_{i,k}(u)$, $B_{j,\ell}(v)$ of some polynomial order k and ℓ, respectively,

$$S(u,v) = \sum_i \sum_j V_{i,j} B_{i,k}(u) B_{j,\ell}(v) \ .$$

The basis functions, furthermore, should be *refinable* in the sense that each one can be re-expressed as a linear combination of one or more "smaller" basis functions

$$B_{i,k}(u) = \sum_r \alpha_{i,k}(r) N_{r,k}(u)$$

$$B_{j,\ell}(v) = \sum_s \alpha_{j,\ell}(s) N_{s,\ell}(v) \ .$$

Reflected in this property is a corresponding re-representation of the surface in terms of the smaller basis functions and a larger number of control vertices

$$S(u,v) = \sum_r \sum_s \mathbf{W}_{r,s} N_{r,k}(u) N_{s,\ell}(v) \ ,$$

where

$$\mathbf{W}_{r,s} = \sum_i \sum_s \alpha_{i,k}(r) \alpha_{j,\ell}(s) \mathbf{V}_{i,j} \ .$$

Refinement is nonlocal in the sense that, if $\mathbf{V}_{i,j}$ is one control vertex that influences a (large) region, to which some fine detail is to be added, it is not possible merely to replace $\mathbf{V}_{i,j}$ by one or more control vertices $\mathbf{W}_{r,s}$. The conversion of $\mathbf{V}$'s to $\mathbf{W}$'s proceeds by way of the conversion of B's to N's, and this results in a large-scale replacement of $\mathbf{V}$'s by $\mathbf{W}$'s. $\mathbf{V}$'s that have no influence on the region to be edited may be changed along with $\mathbf{V}$'s that do have an influence.

The foregoing material is often presented in matrix terminology; e.g. as in [5,6,9], and we will follow this convention. The matrix notation derives from the fact that each of the functions B and N is nonzero in only a small region, where it is a piecewise composite of polynomials. For example, taking each polynomial piece of $B_{i,k}(u)$ and combining it with each polynomial piece of $B_{j,\ell}(v)$, a surface patch is produced that can be represented as

$$[\mathbf{u}][\mathbf{B}_u][\mathbf{V}][\mathbf{B}_v]^T[\mathbf{v}]^T \ , \tag{2.1}$$

where the superscript T stands for the transpose of a matrix or vector. On each patch the parameters u and v vary over the unit interval, and

$$[\mathbf{u}] = \begin{bmatrix} 1 \ u \ u^2 \ \cdots \ u^{k-1} \end{bmatrix} \ ,$$

$$[\mathbf{v}] = \begin{bmatrix} 1 \ v \ v^2 \ \cdots \ v^{\ell-1} \end{bmatrix} \ .$$

The δ, γ^{th} patch is given by the control vertices

$$[\mathbf{V}] = \begin{bmatrix} \mathbf{V}_{\delta-k+1,\gamma-\ell+1} & \cdots & \mathbf{V}_{\delta-k+1,\gamma} \\ \cdot & & \cdot \\ \cdot & & \cdot \\ \cdot & & \cdot \\ \mathbf{V}_{\delta,\gamma-\ell+1} & \cdots & \mathbf{V}_{\delta,\gamma} \end{bmatrix} \ . \tag{2.2}$$

Finally $[\mathbf{B}_u]$ and $[\mathbf{B}_v]$ are the matrices formed from the polynomial coefficients appropriate for the basis pieces in the δth and γ^{th} parametric intervals respectively.

With an array of $(m+1) \times (n+1)$ control vertices

$$\begin{matrix} \mathbf{V}_{0,0} & \cdots & \mathbf{V}_{0,n} \\ \cdot & & \cdot \\ \cdot & & \cdot \\ \cdot & & \cdot \\ \mathbf{V}_{m,0} & \cdots & \mathbf{V}_{m,n} \end{matrix} \tag{2.3}$$

and basis functions of order k and ℓ respectively, a tensor-product surface consisting of $(m-k+2) \times (n-\ell+2)$ patches is defined.

The common example is the uniform, bicubic, B-spline case, for which $k = \ell = 4$ and both matrices $[\mathbf{B}]$ are equal to

$$\frac{1}{6} \begin{bmatrix} 1 & 4 & 1 & 0 \\ -3 & 0 & 3 & 0 \\ 3 & -6 & 3 & 0 \\ -1 & 3 & -3 & 1 \end{bmatrix} \tag{2.4}$$

for all polynomial segments.

The refinement process that produces basis functions N from basis functions B is derived, in the B-spline, Beta-spline, Bezier, and NURB case by breaking up one or more polynomial segments into a succession of smaller segments.

The re-expression of the surface defined by the $(m+1) \times (n+1)$ control vertices $[\mathbf{V}]$ as a surface of $(m+M+1) \times (n+N+1)$ new control vertices $[\mathbf{W}]$ is accomplished by two matrices composed of the α coefficients, $[\alpha_{left}]$ and $[\alpha_{right}]$:

$$[\mathbf{W}] = [\alpha_{left}][\mathbf{V}][\alpha_{right}]^T \ , \tag{2.5}$$

where

$$[\mathbf{W}] = \begin{bmatrix} \mathbf{W}_{\mu-k+1,\lambda-\ell+1} & \cdots & \mathbf{W}_{\mu-k+1,\lambda} \\ \cdot & & \cdot \\ \cdot & & \cdot \\ \cdot & & \cdot \\ \mathbf{W}_{\mu,\lambda-\ell+1} & \cdots & \mathbf{W}_{\mu,\lambda} \end{bmatrix} \ ,$$

$$[\alpha_{left}] = \begin{bmatrix} \alpha_{\delta-k+1,k}(\mu-k+1) & \cdots & \alpha_{\delta,k}(\mu-k+1) \\ \cdot & & \cdot \\ \cdot & & \cdot \\ \cdot & & \cdot \\ \alpha_{\delta-k+1,k}(\mu) & \cdots & \alpha_{\delta,k}(\mu) \end{bmatrix} \ ,$$

$$[\alpha_{right}] = \begin{bmatrix} \alpha_{\gamma-\ell+1,\ell}(\lambda-\ell+1) & \cdots & \alpha_{\gamma,\ell}(\lambda-\ell+1) \\ \cdot & & \cdot \\ \cdot & & \cdot \\ \cdot & & \cdot \\ \alpha_{\gamma-\ell+1,\ell}(\lambda) & \cdots & \alpha_{\gamma,\ell}(\lambda) \end{bmatrix} \ ,$$

and $[\mathbf{V}]$ is as is given in (2.2).

This matrix formulation is to be understood in the context of the δ, γ^{th} patch and the μ, λ^{th} subpatch that result from breaking the parametric ranges $0 \leq u, v \leq 1$ into a number of subranges

$$0 \leq \cdots \leq u_\mu \leq u < u_{\mu+1} \leq \cdots \leq 1$$

and

$$0 \leq \cdots \leq v_\lambda \leq v < v_{\lambda+1} \leq \cdots \leq 1 \ .$$

The simplest example derives from the uniform cubic case where each parametric range in u and v is broken at its midpoint. This converts each patch determined by the control vertices $[\mathbf{V}]$ into four equal patches according to the diagram

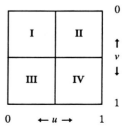

Formula (2.1), in turn, is converted into

$$[\mathbf{u}][\mathbf{B}_u][\mathbf{W}][\mathbf{B}_v]^T[\mathbf{v}]^T \ , \tag{2.6}$$

where $[\mathbf{B}_u]$ and $[\mathbf{B}_v]$ are given by (2.4), $[\mathbf{W}]$ is given by (2.5), and

$$[\alpha_{left}] = \begin{cases} [\mathbf{A}_1] & \text{for regions } \mathbf{I} \text{ and } \mathbf{III} \\ [\mathbf{A}_2] & \text{for regions } \mathbf{II} \text{ and } \mathbf{IV} \end{cases},$$

$$[\alpha_{right}] = \begin{cases} [\mathbf{A}_1] & \text{for regions } \mathbf{I} \text{ and } \mathbf{II} \\ [\mathbf{A}_2] & \text{for regions } \mathbf{III} \text{ and } \mathbf{IV} \end{cases}.$$

The matrices $[\mathbf{A}]$ are given by

$$[\mathbf{A}_1] = \begin{bmatrix} \frac{1}{2} & \frac{1}{2} & 0 & 0 \\ \frac{1}{8} & \frac{3}{4} & \frac{1}{8} & 0 \\ 0 & \frac{1}{2} & \frac{1}{2} & 0 \\ 0 & \frac{1}{8} & \frac{3}{4} & \frac{1}{8} \end{bmatrix}$$

and

$$[\mathbf{A}_2] = \begin{bmatrix} \frac{1}{8} & \frac{3}{4} & \frac{1}{8} & 0 \\ 0 & \frac{1}{2} & \frac{1}{2} & 0 \\ 0 & \frac{1}{8} & \frac{3}{4} & \frac{1}{8} \\ 0 & 0 & \frac{1}{2} & \frac{1}{2} \end{bmatrix}$$

A more thorough treatment of this material, and computational algorithms for determining the matrices $[\mathbf{B}]$ and $[\alpha]$ in the case of B-spline/Bezier surfaces (and by extension, NURBS) can be found in [2]. The computational algorithms presented there have their origin in the Oslo Algorithm first presented in [4]. For the case of Beta-splines the material in [8] is applicable.

3. Overlays

The refinement process described in Section 2 is the standard mechanism for reproducing an existing, V-defined surface using a W definition. The major complaint to be made about the process is that it frequently generates more W control vertices than we have any intention of moving. We would like to retain only those W's that interest us for editing purposes and discard the rest, retaining the unedited portion of the surface in its V definition.

It is important to remind ourselves that the refinement process produces an exact re-representation. The W-defined surface is the same as its V-defined parent. Figure 1 shows a small portion of a uniform, bicubic, V-defined surface in cross section (with circles indicating the V's), and Figure 2 shows a view of the same surface in a W definition (with black dots indicating the W's and with the V's included as circles for comparison). Refinement has been applied to the middle portion of the surface (centered about the topmost V). The right and left margins of the surface have not been included in the refinement.

If one of the W control vertices is moved, then the W surface departs from its V parent, but only in the area influenced by the W control vertex that has been changed. Outside of this area, parent and child are identical. Figure 3 shows the V surface superimposed on the W surface after one W has been moved. Because of this correspondence, we may continue to use the V definition as our basic description of the surface, save for the replacement of a small piece of the W definition. Generally more than just one W control vertex must be retained to define this small piece, but the number is small relative to the total number of W control vertices that the refinement produces. In the bicubic case, for example, 49 W control vertices must be retained in a 7×7 pattern centered around the control vertex that has been moved. In the general B-spline case, $[1+2(k-1)]\times[1+2(\ell-1)]$ W's must be retained centered about the control vertex that has been moved.

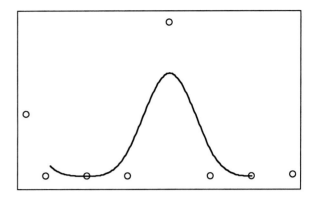

Figure 1. V surface in cross section.

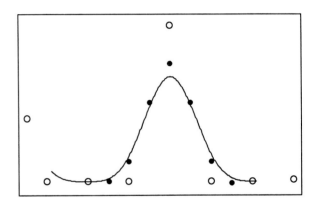

Figure 2. W surface in cross section.

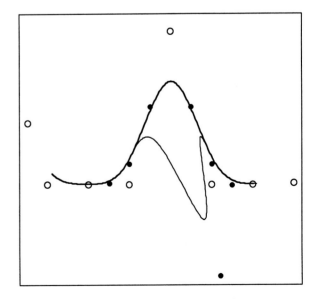

Figure 3. V surface and altered W surface.

We can regard the retained portion of the **W** definition as a separate surface to be manipulated. If we are careful to manipulate only the central **W** vertex and keep the peripheral **W** vertices static, we can localize editing/refinement processes to restricted patches of the surface. Each such localized patch subjected to such restricted editing and used as a replacement for a portion of the parent-level substrate constitutes an *overlay*.

We can repeat this approach on the interior of an overlay, regarding it, in its turn, to be the parent surface to be subjected to refinement for the creation of further overlays. The basic operation of creating an overlay consists of designating a patch on the surface at any level of refinement and executing a new refinement step to re-represent this patch. Also, we refine a surrounding number of patches sufficient to include the area influenced by any refined control vertex that we will manipulate. If this causes overlays to cross each other at some level of refinement, the overlays concerned are made into a composite overlay by combining their respective control vertices into a single collection.

In order to get a feel for the creation of an overlay, it is instructive to look at the simplest refinement step that could be carried out on a uniform, bicubic surface. Figure 4 shows a schematic plan of 7×7 control vertices, along with the 16 patches making up the surface they define. This constitutes the minimal surface portion that would change due to any movement of the central control vertex, $V_{r,s}$. If all vertices save $V_{r,s}$ are held fixed, the depicted region can be regarded as an independent surface, yet its boundary will always coincide with the larger surface from which it was derived.

If this area of surface is too large for the scale of detail we wish to introduce, the simplest thing we might do is refine each of the central four patches by halving, as was presented at the end of Section 2, Figure 5 diagrams the overlay that would result. The black dots represent the **W** control vertices, and the dashed boxes outline the smaller patches that the central **W** will influence. If only this central vertex is moved, and all the others are held fixed, the patches given by the dashed boxes can be considered an integral unit of surface whose boundary will always coincide with the 12 surrounding patches defined by the circles.

This is the style in which overlays are to be created. For editing involving the movement of several control vertices, modifying a larger area of surface, the overlay to be created must enclose the union of the separate single-vertex overlays. For editing that is to influence a smaller region, the refinement must break each patch into a greater number of subpatches. The creation of an overlay in the general B-spline case will involve other numbers of patches and **V** and **W** control vertices.

The net effect of refining and subdividing the surface, over time, will be that the surface will be broken into a collection of overlays at different levels of refinement. The obvious storage mechanism for managing overlays is a tree-structure with each level of depth in the tree corresponding to a level of refinement. The root node of the tree defines the basic **V**-defined surface, and every other node in the tree stores information that defines an overlay surface. Every node in the tree points to overlays that are derived entirely within the portion. Sibling pointers are used to access information in adjoining patches for ease in processing portions of the surface at a common level of refinement.

Successive application of refinement defines a composite surface recursively. The composite surface is given by the totality of information contained at the root and leaves of the data structure.

4. Offset Referencing

Up to this point, the formulas have been presented assuming that a single coordinate frame has provided the description of each portion of the surface at each level of refinement. This is not suitable in the context of hierarchical refinements. When editing takes place at one level of surface definition, any

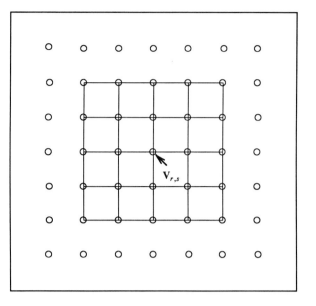

Figure 4. A 16-patch surface described by 49 control vertices.

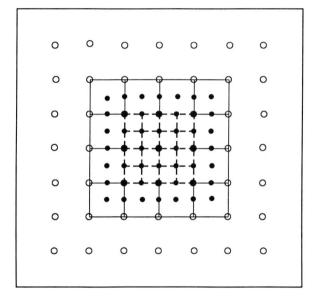

Figure 5. A 16-patch surface with refinement and overlay control vertices.

overlays resting within the edited area are expected to remain embedded in that area. They will follow editing changes only if they can be dynamically tied to that area, which amounts to saying that their control vertices must move in accord with the movement of the section of surface undergoing edit. One method of achieving this is to represent the control vertices of any overlay relative to a frame of reference fixed upon the surface being edited rather than relative to the fixed frame of reference defined by some external coordinate system. This brings into consideration a "reference-plus-offset" notation for the control vertices. By this we mean that we write each control vertex $W_{i,j}$ of any part of the surface, whether root-level parent surface or overlay at any level of refinement, in the form

Figure 6. A surface created using local refinement.

$$\mathbf{W}_{i,j} = \mathbf{R}_{i,j} + \mathbf{O}_{i,j} \; ; \; \text{i.e.} \; [\mathbf{W}] = [\mathbf{R}] + [\mathbf{O}] \; .$$

The point $\mathbf{R}_{i,j}$ is the reference, and it is to be specified from the parent surface. In our prototype editor $\mathbf{R}_{i,j}$, the reference for $\mathbf{W}_{i,j}$, is derived from the point on the surface maximally influenced by $\mathbf{W}_{i,j}$. The components of $\mathbf{R}_{i,j}$ are calculated from the tangent plane and the normal to the surface at this maximally influenced point. This is, however, only one of many possibilities, and an investigation of other choices is in order.

Editing changes to level $\mathbf{V}$ of a surface automatically cause revisions in the $\mathbf{R}$'s, and through them revisions are made dynamically to the $\mathbf{W}$'s. Editing changes to the $\mathbf{W}$-level surface are to be recorded entirely as changes to the $\mathbf{O}$'s. In the case of the root (original-level) surface, the $\mathbf{R}$'s can be derived from points on a reference exterior to the surface; e.g. on the jointed member of a skeleton.

The implications of this on (2.1) are that the surface will be given as an offset component from a reference surface:

$$[\mathbf{u}][\mathbf{B}_u][\mathbf{W}][\mathbf{B}_v]^T[\mathbf{v}]^T \qquad (4.1)$$

$$= [\mathbf{u}][\mathbf{B}_u]\left\{[\mathbf{R}]+[\mathbf{O}]\right\}[\mathbf{B}_v]^T[\mathbf{v}]^T$$

$$= \left\{[\mathbf{u}][\mathbf{B}_u][\mathbf{R}][\mathbf{B}_v]^T[\mathbf{v}]^T\right\}$$

$$+ \left\{[\mathbf{u}][\mathbf{B}_u][\mathbf{O}][\mathbf{B}_v]^T[\mathbf{v}]^T\right\} \; .$$

Changes to the surface at any level of refinement closer to the root change $\mathbf{R}$, and these appear as global changes to the overlay surface at the current level of refinement. The current level of surface, of course, has its control vertices changed in accord with changes in the $\mathbf{R}$ information, and this, in turn, changes the reference information for finer levels of surface. Likewise, changes to $\mathbf{O}$ affect the surface at the current level of refinement and all fine levels.

Rendering proceeds for any point on the surface using reference and offset information at the lowest level of the tree containing that point. Thus, offset information accumulates editing changes local to an overlay, and references reflect editing change at all higher levels; i.e., all global changes to the offset (See Figures 7 and 8).

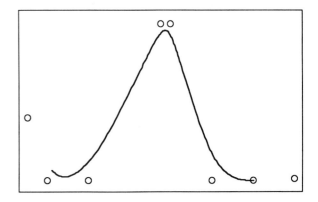

Figure 7. The V-level surface after moving one control vertex.

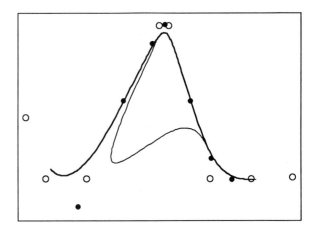

Figure 8. The W-level surface dragged along on the V surface due to offset referencing.

5. Direct Surface Manipulation and Edit Points

A composite surface of the nature indicated has a highly complicated structure of control vertices. It becomes more sensible to allow direct picking and manipulation of points on the surface than to hope that the user can make any sense of the maze of the control graph. The most fundamental relationship between surface and control vertices that can be provided is the one that relates each control vertex to the point on the surface over which it has maximal influence. A movement of that surface point can be converted, transparently to the user, to a corresponding change in that one control vertex. This generalizes to areas on the surface influenced by multiple control vertices.

The complete implementation of the pick operation to achieve these ideas would require a root-finding algorithm to convert a point $\mathbf{P}$ on the surface to u,v values on some patch. However, it is easy to determine the u,v associated with the point $\mathbf{P}$ maximally influenced by any given control vertex $\mathbf{V}_{i,j}$. For example, in the uniform cubic case, the point maximally influenced by any control vertex $\mathbf{V}_{i,j}$ is given by the formula:

$$\mathbf{P} = \tfrac{1}{6}(\tfrac{1}{6}\mathbf{V}_{i-1,j-1} + \tfrac{4}{6}\mathbf{V}_{i,j-1} + \tfrac{1}{6}\mathbf{V}_{i+1,j-1}) \qquad (5.1)$$
$$+ \tfrac{4}{6}(\tfrac{1}{6}\mathbf{V}_{i-1,j} + \tfrac{4}{6}\mathbf{V}_{i,j} + \tfrac{1}{6}\mathbf{V}_{i+1,j})$$
$$+ \tfrac{1}{6}(\tfrac{1}{6}\mathbf{V}_{i-1,j+1} + \tfrac{4}{6}\mathbf{V}_{i,j+1} + \tfrac{1}{6}\mathbf{V}_{i+1,j+1}) \ ,$$

We have carried out our preliminary studies by offering only these points of maximal influence on the surface for picking and manipulation.

The displacement of the above surface point $\mathbf{P}$ to a new position $\mathbf{Q}$ is carried out by adjusting the control vertex of maximal influence. For example, in the uniform cubic case, the control vertex $\mathbf{V}_{i,j}$ is to be replaced by the new control vertex $\overline{\mathbf{V}}_{i,j}$ according to the formula

$$\overline{\mathbf{V}}_{i,j} = \tfrac{36}{16}\left(\mathbf{Q} - \mathbf{P}\right) + \mathbf{V}_{i,j} \ .$$

Of course, $\overline{\mathbf{V}}_{i,j}$ is to be represented as the fixed reference $\mathbf{R}_{i,j}$ suitable for the V's and an offset $\mathbf{O}_{i,j} = \overline{\mathbf{V}}_{i,j} - \mathbf{R}_{i,j}$. Further, as we have pointed out, all overlays depending on the surface just changed must have their reference information updated.

In the Section 7 we present some examples taken from our prototype surface editor. This editor was written in C to run on a Silicon Graphics 4-D workstation. The software uses the Silicon Graphics library for its spline computations; consequently all example pictures represent uniform bicubic B-spline surfaces.

6. Other Manipulation Techniques

Each overlay, together with the originally defined surface on which the overlays were constructed, may be viewed as an individual spline surface, independently defined by control vertices and basis functions. The only conditions required for the integrity of the hierarchical composite is that manipulations carried out on any overlay be restricted to the interior of the overlay, and that the control-vertex information be stored in reference-plus-offset format. Within this context, however, manipulations that are traditionally performed on control vertices may be performed on offset information instead. We have presented manipulations that concentrated on the use of edit points, but many things are possible. In particular, the composite forms of manipulation suggested by Cobb [3] may be used in this context.

The result of any hierarchical editing session is a composite surface, whose individual components are simply tensor-product spline surfaces occupying known locations in space. Transformational techniques that build new surfaces from existing ones can use the composites produced by our

suggestions. In particular, Barr [1] and Sederberg and Parry [10] have proposed methods of transforming existing surfaces into deformed surfaces. Barr shows how space curves can be continuously deformed, and then shows how such deformations can be applied, approximately, to bivariate, parametric surfaces, by a process of point sampling. Sederberg and Parry embed surfaces in a trivariate spline volume, distort the volume by control-vertex manipulation, and then compute, approximately, the corresponding deformation of the embedded surface, also by a process of point sampling. Either of these techniques would work on the surfaces we have produced.

7. Examples

The surface in Figure 9 was constructed through repeated local refinement around the center of the 16-patch surface illustrated in Figure 5. The dark orange portion spans the region created in the first step of refinement as illustrated in Figure 6. The light orange portion spans a region created by a second step of refinement around the same edit point.

Parts b, c, and d of Figure 9 illustrate the effect of moving the central edit point at different levels of refinement. If the central edit point is moved at the finest level of refinement, the entire surface is affected (Figure 9b). In Figures 9c and 9d, by moving the edit point at coarser levels of refinement, more restricted regions of the surface are modified without affecting the integrity of the entire surface. Figure 10a-c illustrates how the modifications of the surface at a fine level of refinement affects edits performed at coarser levels of refinement. Edits performed at the coarsest level (Figure 10a), are retained when larger regions of the surface are modified (Figure 10b-c). After editing at a fine level, the surface can be still be modified at the coarsest level of refinement without affecting finer levels (Figure 10d). In Figure 11 lighter colored patches denote regions of the surface that have undergone greater refinement.

8. Conclusions

Tensor product B-splines are quite flexible, but they possess a deficiency when it comes to refinement. Refinement may change more control vertices than we wish to manipulate. We present a solution to this problem that uses a hierarchical data structure to localize the refinement operations. This data structure also supports, by means of offset referencing, a means of allowing a designer to manipulate a surface conveniently at various levels of detail.

Local refinement and offset referencing provide a flexible and powerful new editing tool. Local refinement controls the extent of any modification to the surface, and offset referencing allows localized edits to be retained over global changes to the surface.

9. Acknowledgements

This research was supported in part by the Natural Sciences and Engineering Research Council of Canada and in part by the Studio d'Animation Français of the National Film Board of Canada. We wish to thank Robert Forget for arranging the latter funding. Thanks are also due to Silicon Graphics for the donation of the 4-D workstation on which the system was implemented, to Alan Paeth for his IM imaging tools, Victor Klassen for his sky and image resizing software, and Stewart Kingdon for his solid texturing software. Robert Dickinson of Visual Edge Software participated in many of our formative discussions on this material.

Comments by the reviewers were most helpful, and we appreciate the care with which they read the manuscript.

10. References

1. Barr, Alan, "Global and Local Deformations of Solid Primitives", Proceedings of SIGGRAPH'84 (Minneapolis, Minnesota, July 23-27, 1984). In *Computer Graphics, 18*,3 (July, 1984) 21-30.

2. Bartels, Richard, Beatty, John, and Barsky, Brian, *An Introduction to Splines for Use in Computer Graphics and Geometric Modeling*, Morgan Kaufmann Publishers, Palo Alto, California (1987).

3. Cobb, Elizabeth, *Design of Sculptured Surfaces Using the B-Spline Representation*, University of Utah PhD Thesis, Salt Lake City, Utah (1984).

4. Cohen, Elaine, Lyche, Tom, and Riesenfeld, Richard, "Discrete B-splines and Subdivision Techniques in Computer-Aided Geometric Design and Computer Graphics," *Computer Graphics and Image Processing, 14*,2 (October, 1980) 87-111.

5. Faux, Ivor and Pratt, Michael, *Computational Geometry for Design and Manufacture*, John Wiley & Sons (1979).

6. Foley, James and van Dam, Andries, *Fundamentals of Interactive Computer Graphics*, Addison Wesley (1982).

7. Forsey, David and Wilhelms, Jane, "Techniques for Interactive Manipulation of Articulated Bodies Using Dynamic Analysis," Proceedings of Graphics Interface '88 [to appear] (1988).

8. Joe, Barry, "Discrete Beta-Splines," Proceedings of SIGGRAPH'87 (Anaheim, California, July 27-31, 1987). In *Computer Graphics, 21*,4 (July, 1987) 137-144.

9. Mortenson, Michael, *Geometric Modeling*, Wiley, New York (1985).

10. Sederberg, Tom and Parry, Scott, "Free-Form Deformation of Solid Geometric Models," Proceedings of SIGGRAPH'86 (Dallas, Texas, August 18-22, 1986). In *Computer Graphics, 20*,4 (August, 1986) 151-160.

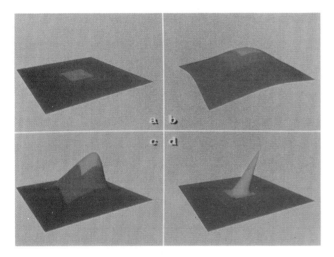

Figure 9. The effect of refinement level on surface modifications.

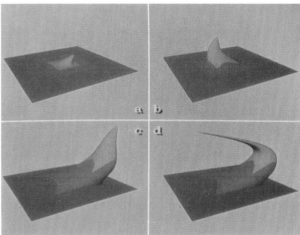

Figure 10. The use of offset referencing for surface editing

Figure 11a. A 16-patch surface is drawn into a hump by moving one edit point.

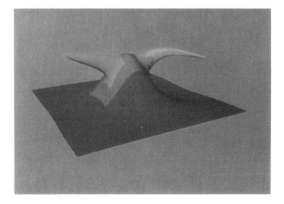

Figure 11b. Two refinement stages are used to create regions that can be drawn into horns. The horn on the right has been further refined to allow a local increase in curvature for a sharp point.

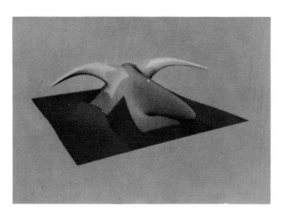

Figure 11c. The forward part of the hump is refined and drawn forward to create a snout.

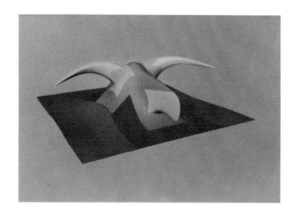

Figure 11d. The tip of the snout is refined and pulled down into a beak.

Figure 11e. Brow ridges are brought forward and down.

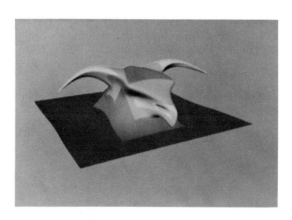

Figure 11f. The tip of the snout is refined twice and nostrils are constructed.

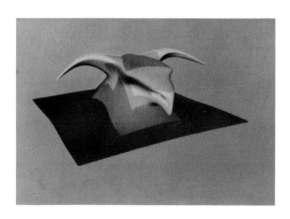

Figure 11g. The front of the snout is spread and the head is raised.

Figure 11h. The base-level surface is folded over.

INTENSITY FLUCTUATIONS AND NATURAL TEXTURING

Wolfgang Krueger

Hochschule der Kuenste, Berlin

Art + Com Projekt

A model for texturing of surfaces is introduced based on the concept of light intensity fluctuations. During the evaluation of the reflected intensity in the rendering process a non-Gaussian stochastic component is added which is governed by electromagnetic scattering theory. This component simulates the appearance of macroscopic surface irregularities in the image plane by considering not only the mean value of the intensity, given by the usual specular contribution, but also its variance and autocorrelation function. The variance generates the strength and distribution of the intensity fluctuations and the spatiotemporal autocorrelation function can be used to model the form and temporal develoment of the texture patterns. With an appropriate choice of a few parameters, soft intensity perturbations and bumpy speckle patterns as well as glint effects can be created.

Categories and Subject Descriptors: I.3.7 (Computer Graphics): Three-Dimensional Graphics and Realism- Color, shading, shadowing and texture

Autor's address: Art + Com Projekt, HdK Berlin, Hardenbergstr. 27a, D 1000 Berlin 12, West Germany

1. Introduction

One of the goals of modern computer animation is the simulation of complex natural environments |2|. Texture mapping is one of the most common techniques used to model macroscopic surface patterns |8,10,11|. These procedures usually work with artificial patterns computed with stochastic and/or analytic models. The patterns are mapped onto the object surface or are modeled on the surface patch itself. Approaches especially suitable for rendering via ray tracing incorporate the texture generating process into the reflection calculations |6,7,8,16| directly.

A wide range of naturally occurring phenomena that are visible to the naked eye are characterized by fluctuation effects. Examples are the glittering of a sunlit sea surface or of a snow-covered object, the beautiful caustic patterns produced by sunlight on the floor and the surface of a pool, the appearance of a glass window on a rainy day or a bathroom window, and the twinkling of light sources caused by atmospheric fluctuations.

In the following, a natural texturing model is introduced which is implemented in a physical ray tracing program. The optical appearance of realistic non-smooth surfaces is described by the statistical properties of the intensity of the scattered light. The model considered is especially concerned with the following aspects of simulating natural (stochastic) texture patterns:

- The model should reproduce the appearance of a texture with consideration given to the underlying natural properties of the object.
- The texture generation process should be contained in the reflection or transmission calculations, because ray tracing methods are better equipped to treat complicated shading models than to render large and/or complicated databases.
- The model should take into account the distance dependence of the texture appearance. In computer animation, one is only interested in the appearance of the texture in the image plane (display screen or other reflecting surfaces in the scenery). Modeling the texture on the surface itself often causes serious aliasing problems.
- The model should also govern the time development of the pattern.

As a first attempt to introduce intensity fluctuations of the scattered light into computer graphics a simple version of the random phase screen (RPS) method |12-15,18,20| in electromagnetic scattering theory is exploited. Section 2 briefly explains this method from a physicist's point of view. The first two moments of the probability density function (PDF) and the autocorrelation function of the intensity of the scattered light are given. Section 3 gives the statistical description of the scattered light based on the intensity moments. Section 4 shows how this statistical description can be applied in computer graphics to generate stochastic texture patterns. Several interesting limiting cases are discussed and some test pictures are presented to illustrate the implementation procedure. All textures on the pictures are modeled on a single polygon.

2. Reflection from macroscopic rough surfaces

In general, naturally occurring, that is "non-sanitized" in appearance, scattering surfaces and objects with high transparency (glass, dust, clouds, ocean water) can be divided into two basic categories:

- The fractal type, e.g. surfaces with self-similar roughness properties over many scales, which only generates diffraction and interference effects but never caustic effects (glints).
- The smoothly varying type with Gaussian-like correlation properties, which also generates geometrical optics effects associated with rays (caustic patterns).

For both types the scattered intensity can be described by the RPS model |13,15,18| which introduces spatial and temporal distortions into an incident plane electromagnetic wavefront. This distortions are assumed to have scales very large compared to the wavelength. This approach is based on the evaluation of the Huygens-Fresnel integral which approximately solves the wave equations for electromagnetic scattering theory. The RPS model can extend the results of scattering theory for randomly rough surfaces |3|. It permits evaluation of the mean intensity and also predicts higher statistical moments such as the variance and the spatiotemporal autocorrelation function of the scattered intensity in the observation plane. Those higher moments strongly depend on the surface parameters (mean height and correlation length of the surface distortions), on the relation of the sizes of the distortion elements to the size of the illuminated area, and on the distance of the observer from the scattering surface. For several classes of random irregularities, e.g. having one- or two-dimensional Gaussian-like or fractal correlation functions, analytic expressions for the intensity moments can be approximated |13,15,20|, provided assumptions such as small angle scattering and near or far field only are made. The connection of this model to catastrophe optics |4| treating caustic effects in the near field of the scattering object, e.g. rippled water surface or drops, should also be mentioned.

In the event that we are not interested in the "full blown" models of stochastic scattering theory a more tractable approximation should be used. This is the discrete scattering model which describes a limited number of uncorrelated scattering centers (macro-facets) |13,18| giving randomly phased contributions to the scattered electromagnetic field.

The phase variations are converted into non-Gaussian intensity fluctuations by a distance dependent focusing of the light rays (s. Fig. 1).

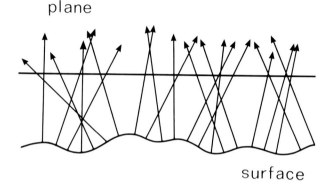

observation plane

surface

Fig. 1 Focusing of reflected rays

Generally, the reflection model used in computer graphics has the additive form $I_s = I_{amb} + I_{diff} + I_{spec}$ |5,9|, where I_{amb}, I_{diff} and I_{spec} represent the ambient, diffuse and specular part, respectively. Stochastic texture patterns can be generated by geometric and/or spectral perturbations of the specular component |6,8|. In the following, perturbations will be achieved by calculating the specular part via a probabilistic description.

The scattered electromagnetic field $\mathbf{E_s}$ at space point $\mathbf{r}=(x,y,z)$ and time t is assumed to be a superposition of independent contributions from N facets |13,18|

$$\mathbf{E_s}(\mathbf{r},t) = \sum_{i=1}^{N(\mathbf{r},t)} \mathbf{A_i}(\mathbf{r},t) \cdot \exp(-i\phi_i(\mathbf{r},t)-\omega t)) \qquad (1)$$

where the $\mathbf{A_i}(\mathbf{r},t)$ are the individual scattering amplitudes, $\phi_i(\mathbf{r},t)$ are statistically independent random phases and ω is the light frequency. For natural (incoherent) light no interference effects will appear such that the specular reflected intensity yields

$$I_s(\mathbf{r},t) = |\mathbf{E_s}(\mathbf{r},t)|^2 = \sum_{i=1}^{N(\mathbf{r},t)} |\mathbf{A_i}(\mathbf{r},t)|^2 \qquad (2)$$

Neglecting diffraction effects, the statistical mean of the specular reflected intensity (2) for very rough surfaces has the general form

$$< I_s > = I_{spec} = D \cdot S \cdot F \qquad (3)$$

as already been used in various reflection models |5,9|. The brackets denote averaging over an ensemble of undulating surfaces. The decisive quantity to calculate $<I_s>$ is the probability density function D of the local slope. For a two-dimensional Gaussian distribution it is given by |3,5,9|

$$D = \frac{1}{2 \cdot \pi \cdot m^2 \cdot \cos^4 \gamma} \cdot \exp(-\tan^2\gamma / 2 \cdot m^2) \qquad (4)$$

where γ is the tilt angle of the facet normal and m denotes the mean slope. The factor S (≤ 1) depending on the incident and scattering directions accounts for the self-shadowing of the facets |9,19|. $F(n, \theta_s)$ denotes the Fresnel reflection coefficient |5,9| depending on the light frequency via the refractive index n and on the scattering angle θ_s. The angles γ and θ_s can be determined from the incident and scattering directions and the mean surface normal |5,9|.

The variance σ_I of the scattered intensity is given by the effectively contributing number N_{eff} of facets |13,18|

$$\sigma_I^2 = \frac{< I_s^2 >}{< I_s >^2} - 1 = N_{eff}^{-1} \qquad (5)$$

where the macro-facet model considered N_{eff} is given by

$$N_{eff} = N \cdot D \cdot S \qquad (6)$$

N is the number of facets covering the visible part of the surface, D is given, for example, by (4) and S is the self-shadowing factor. Even for large N the variance may be very large because the slope distribution (4) is sharply peaked around the specular direction ($\gamma =0$).

The variance (5) describes the interesting non-Gaussian fluctuations representing geometrical optics effects, arising from the focusing or lens-like behaviour of the individual scattering elements (s. Fig. 1).

The texture pattern generated by the irregularities of the scatterer in such a non-Gaussian configuration may have a highly complex spatial and temporal structure. For random distortions this structure can be defined by the correlation function of the essential statistical parameter describing the irregularities, e.g. local height deviation, refractive index, density of scattering particles. For the macro-facet model a convenient description of the spatiotemporal correlation function of the height deviation H can be given by

$$C_{facet}(R_1,t_1;R_2,t_2) = <H(R_1,t_1) \cdot H(R_2,t_2)>$$
$$= C_r(|R_1-R_2|) \cdot C_t(|t_2-t_1|) \quad (7)$$

where R_1,R_2 are points in the surface patch. For example, for smoothly varying facets appearing on rippled water surfaces the spatial part C_r can be modeled with

$$C_r(|R_1-R_2|) = \begin{cases} \sigma_H^2 \cdot (1 - \dfrac{|R_1-R_2|^2}{\tau_r^2}) & \text{for } |R_1-R_2| \leq \tau_r, \\ 0 & \text{for } |R_1-R_2| > \tau_r \end{cases}$$
$$(8)$$

where σ_H is the mean height deviation and the correlation length τ_r represents the mean diameter of the facets such that the mean slope is given by $m = 2^{1/2} \cdot \sigma_H / \tau_r$. For crystalline or random structures C_r should be modeled by tiny polygons or random two-dimensional shapes, respectively. The temporal part C_t of C_{facet} in (7) can be taken as a constant for static glints or as a sinusoidal-like function to simulate the temporal development of a glint on a water surface.

The concept of using the spatial and/or temporal autocorrelation function to generate the texture appearance is equivalent to the usual spectral modeling |8,10,11,17| due to the Wiener theorem.

The spatial autocorrelation function C_r describes the shape of the simulated texture pattern and the parameters σ_H and τ_r provide a suitable measure of the coarseness or granularity. The rapidity or conversely, the persistence, of the patterns is governed by the temporal part C_t. In addition, a movement of the whole pattern structure can be simulated (see e.g. |18,20|).

The RPS model describes the appearance of the surface texture at the observation plane. By evaluating the Huygens-Fresnel integral it maps the correlation function C_{facet} (7) onto the autocorrelation function of the scattered intensity

$$C_s(r_1,t_1;r_2,t_2) = \frac{<I_s(r_1,t_1) \cdot I_s(r_2,t_2)>}{<I_s(r_1,t_1)> \cdot <I_s(r_2,t_2)>} - 1 \quad (9)$$

where r_1,r_2 are points in the observation plane such that one obtains $C_s=\sigma_I^2$ for $r_1=r_2$ and $t_2=t_1$. Approximated analytic results for a variety of surface or volume structures can be found in |12-15,18,20|.

The macro-facet model will be applied in the following sections to simulate natural texturing in computer graphics. It neglects all diffraction and interference effects such that the intensity autocorrelation function (9) can simply be calculated by a perspective projection of C_{facet}/σ_H^2 onto the observation plane.

3. Statistical description of the specular scattered light

In "classical" reflection models (see e.g. |5,9|) the specular part of the reflected intensity in the image plane is given by expressions equivalent to the mean value $<I_s>$ (3). For non-zero intensity variances (5) the scattered specular intensity I_{fluc}, fluctuating around the mean specular part $<I_s>$, has to be described by a probability density function (PDF). The functional form of this PDF strongly depends on the scattering environment and on the illumination considered. An appropriate form of the PDF for the scattering of natural (incoherent) light from a random configuration of macro-facets has been suggested to be the gamma distribution |14|

$$P_\Gamma(I_{fluc}) = \frac{\alpha}{<I_s>\cdot\Gamma(\alpha)} \cdot (\frac{\alpha\cdot I_{fluc}}{<I_s>})^{\alpha-1} \cdot \exp(-\frac{\alpha\cdot I_{fluc}}{<I_s>})$$

(10)

where $\Gamma(\alpha)$ is the gamma function and the parameter α is given by

$$\alpha = 1/\sigma_I^2$$

(11)

Obviously, for $\sigma_I^2=1$ this distribution degenerates to the form for a totally random Gaussian process

$$P_{rand}(I_{fluc}) = \frac{1}{<I_s>} \cdot \exp(-\frac{I_{fluc}}{<I_s>})$$

(12)

which generates "perfectly" noisy pictures (speckle). For very large α (small variances) $P_\Gamma(I_{fluc})$ degenerates into a Gaussian distribution for I_{fluc}. For very large N in (6) this is expected by virtue of the central limit theorem.

The gamma distribution (10) is appropriate for describing fluctuations of the "effective" facet number N_{eff}. Texture models simulating more complex patterns with composite scales, appearing e.g. in remote sensing models, should be constructed with K-distributions (K is the modified Bessel function) |12,15|.

4. Modeling of natural texture patterns

The simple macro-facet scattering model was chosen such that the requirements of computational tractability are fulfilled. To apply this model in computer graphics the generation of natural texture patterns is divided into two steps.

In line with the general input form used in computer graphics the scattered intensity in the image plane can be written

$$I = I_{amb} + I_{diff} + I_{fluc}$$

(13)

where I_{fluc} represents the fluctuating specular part.

In the first step the additional fluctuation term I_{fluc} in (13) will be locally evaluated with (3), (9) and (11) via the probability that I_{fluc} exceeds a given pseudo-random number RN uniformly distributed in (0,1). Then one obtains I_{fluc} by inverting

$$\int_{I_{fluc}}^{\infty} P_\Gamma(I')\, dI' = \Gamma(\alpha, \frac{\alpha\cdot I_{fluc}}{<I_s>}) = RN$$

(14)

where $\Gamma(\alpha,\beta)$ is the incomplete gamma function tabulated in |1|. Using the leading expansion terms of the error function and of $\Gamma(\alpha,\beta)$ |1|, equation (14) can be approximately inverted in two interesting limits

$$I_{fluc} \approx \begin{cases} <I_s>\cdot(1 + (2\pi\cdot\sigma_I^2)^{1/2} \cdot(RN-0.5)) & \text{for } \sigma_I^2 \ll 1, \\ <I_s>\cdot\sigma_I^2\cdot RN^{\sigma_I^2} & \text{for } \sigma_I^2 \gg 1. \end{cases}$$

(15)

From (15) it follows that for very large intensity variances (5) I_{fluc} will almost everywhere be equal to zero and only a few centers of caustic effects will appear for RN $\simeq 1$. Glint effects on water, snow, or mineral surfaces can be modeled within this range of σ_I^2. On the other hand, for small σ_I^2 the fluctuation term will almost everywhere be equal to $<I_s>$, and the intensity (15) will appear to fluctuate only softly. This case simulates "diffuse" reflection from objects with very rough surfaces or those consisting of inhomogeneous material such as building materials, ceramics, textiles, paper and biological substances.

In the special case $\alpha = 1$ (noise-to-signal ratio equal to one) equation (14) can be exactly inverted to

$$I^{speckle}_{fluc} = - <I_s>\cdot\ln(RN), \qquad (16)$$

which represents a totally "bumpy" appearance because in this case I_{fluc} takes arbitrary values from one point to the next one (see Fig. 2).

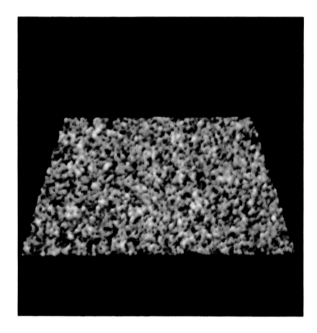

Fig. 2 Random "bumpy" pattern (smoothed speckle)

The typical dependence of the intensity variance (5) on the distance of the image from the surface, calculated via the RPS model for near and far field regions or obtained by measurements |14,18|, has the form outlined in Figure 3.

Very close to the disturbed object only phase fluctuations exist ($\sigma^2_I \simeq 0$). For larger distances rays start to propagate normally to the local phase front (s. Fig. 1). They overlap and intensity fluctuations (caustic patterns) develop for increasing σ^2_I ($>> 1$). The distance d_f represents the mean focusing distance where regions of high intensity associated with the lens-like focusing effect can be found (random networks of diffraction-broadened caustics). In the far field σ^2_I decreases slowly towards zero because many of the individual scattering elements contribute. Looking through a window on a rainy day confirms this general behaviour.

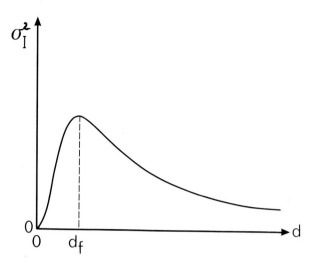

Fig. 3 Typical distance dependence of the intensity variance

For the macro-facet model the dependence of σ^2_I on the distance d can be simulated in the far field region ($d > d_f$) by assuming $N \sim d^2$. The distance dependent appearance of snow or rippled water surfaces can be modeled with such variances $\sigma^2_I(d)$.

In a second step the spatial and/or temporal connectivity of the pattern can be simulated by exploiting the autocorrelation properties (7) and (9). The most probable value of the intensity I_2 in a neighborhood of a given intensity I_1 can be obtained with

$$E(I_2|I_1) = \int_0^\infty I_2 \cdot P(I_2|I_1) \, dI_2 = c\cdot I_1 + (1-c)\cdot<I_s> \qquad (17)$$

where $P(I_2|I_1)$ is the conditional probability density. As mentioned in section 2, the reduced autocorrelation function $C = C_s/\sigma^2_I$ (≤ 1) can be approximated by $C \sim C_{facet}/\sigma^2_H$ by projecting C_{facet} onto the display screen. Equation (17) generates with (7) and (9) the specific texture pattern and also guarantees a non-aliasing effect due to the assumed smooth decay of the correlation factors.

The influence of the essential parameters (N=mean number of macro-facets, m=mean slope, τ_r=mean diameter) are outlined on Figures 4-7. All pictures only contain a single polygon. Figure 4 shows soft perturbations with m=0.5, τ_r randomly chosen and $N_{eff} \sim 100$ (see equ. (6)). Figure 5 shows the simulation of caustic glint effects with $N_{eff} \sim 0.01$. Figure 6 represents a superposition of soft perturbations ("background") and small glints.

Finally, Figure 7 is chosen to illustrate the strong influence of the incident and scattering angles on the variance σ_I via the slope distribution function D.

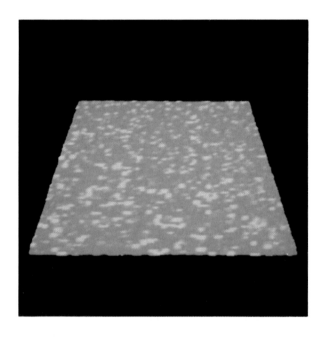

Figure 4

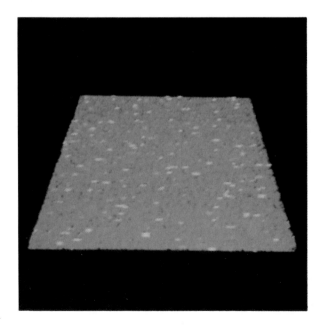

Figure 6

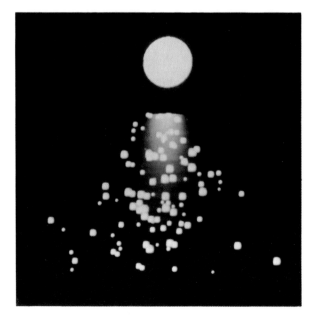

Figure 5

Figure 7

5. Conclusions

In this work a preliminary simple model for natural texturing is introduced which exploits the physical concept of light intensity fluctuations. For describing the complex random appearance of naturally occurring surfaces it seems to be important to study not only the mean specular reflected intensity but also its variance and auto-correlation moment. The intensity variance generates the amount and the distribution of the facet-like scattering elements whereas the auto-correlation function determines the spatial appearance and temporal development.

The model can be implemented in the reflection coefficient routine of rendering programs, e.g. ray tracing. The model is not very time consuming and no mapping problems arise. The set of parameters given allows a simulation of a wide class of surface structures occurring in nature, but textures which carry a large amount of information cannot be modeled by this construction.

Acknowledgements

I am grateful to the reviewers, H.-J. Andree and John A. Berton for helpful discussions and suggestions, and to ARRI TV, Munich, for technical support. A part of this work was performed at mental images, Berlin.

References

1. Abramovitz,M., Stegun,I.A. (eds.), Handbook of Mathematical Functions, Dover, New York, 1964
2. Amanatides,J., Realism in Computer Graphics: A Survey, IEEE CG&A, (Jan. 1987), pp. 44-56
3. Beckmann,P., Spizzichino,A., The Scattering of Electromagnetic Waves from Rough Surfaces, MacMillan, New York, 1963
4. Berry,M.V., Twinkling Exponents in the Catastrophe Theory of Random Short Waves, in "Wave Propagation and Scattering", Uscinski,B.J. (ed.), Clarendon Press, Oxford, 1986, pp. 11-35
5. Blinn,J.F., Models of Light Reflection for Computer Synthesized Pictures, Proceedings of SIGGRAPH'77, (San Jose, California, July 20-23, 1977), In Computer Graphics, Vol. 11, 2 (1977), pp. 192-198
6. Blinn,J.F., Simulation of Wrinkled Surfaces, Proceeding of SIGGRAPH'78, (Atlanta, Georgia, August 23-25, 1978), In Computer Graphics, Vol. 12, 3 (1978), pp. 286-292
7. Cabral,B., Max,N., Springmeyer,R., Bidirectional Reflection Functions from Surface Bump Maps, Proceedings of SIGGRAPH'87 (Anaheim, California, July 27-31, 1987), In Computer Graphics, Vol. 19, 4 (1987), pp. 273-281
8. Carey,R.J., Greenberg,D.P., Texture for Realistic Image Synthesis, Comput. & Graphics, Vol. 9, 2 (1985), pp. 125-138
9. Cook,R.L., Torrance,K.E., A Reflectance Model for Computer Graphics, Proceedings of SIGGRAPH'81 (Dallas, Texas, August 3-7, 1981), In Computer Graphics, Vol. 13, 3 (1981), pp. 307-316
10. Haruyama,S., Barsky,B.A., Using Stochastic Modeling for Texture Generation, IEEE CG&A, (March 1984), pp. 7-19
11. Heckbert,P.S., Survey of Texture Mapping, IEEE CG&A, (Nov. 1986), pp. 56-57
12. Hoenders,B.J., Jakeman,E., Baltes,H.P., Steinle, B., K - Correlations and Facet Models in Diffuse Scattering, Optica Acta, Vol. 26, (1979), pp. 1307-1319
13. Jakeman,E., Pusey,P.N., Non-Gaussian Fluctuations in Electromagnetic Radiation Scattered by a Random Phase Screen, J. Phys. A, Vol. 8, 3 (1975), pp. 369-391
14. Jakeman,E., Pusey,P.N., Photon Counting Statistics of Optical Scintillations, in "Inverse Scattering Problems in Optics", Baltes,H.P. (ed.), Springer Verlag, Berlin, 1980, pp. 73-116
15. Jakeman,E., Speckle Statistics with a Small Number of Scatterers, Opt. Engineering, Vol. 23, 4 (1984), pp. 453-461
16. Kajiya,J.T., Anisotropic Reflection Models, Proceedings of SIGGRAPH'86 (San Francisco, California, July 22-26, 1985), In Computer Graphics, Vol. 19, 3 (1985), pp. 15-21
17. Lewis,J.P., Generalized Stochastic Subdivision, ACM Trans. on Graphics, Vol. 6, (July 1987), pp. 167-190
18. Pusey,P.N., Statistical Properties of Scattered Radiation, in "Photon Correlation Spectroscopy and Velocimetry", Cummins,H.Z., Pike,E.R. (eds.), Plenum Press, New York, 1977, pp. 45-141
19. Sancer,M.I., Shadow-Corrected Electromagnetic Scattering from a Randomly Rough Surface, IEEE Trans. AP, Vol. 17, (1969), pp. 577-585
20. Zardecki,A., Statistical Features of Phase Screens from Scattering Data, in "Inverse Source Problems in Optics", Baltes,H.P. (ed.), Springer Verlag, Berlin, 1978, pp. 155-189

Reconstruction Filters in Computer Graphics

Don P. Mitchell

Arun N. Netravali

AT&T Bell Laboratories

Murray Hill, New Jersey 07974

ABSTRACT

Problems of signal processing arise in image synthesis because of transformations between continuous and discrete representations of 2D images. Aliasing introduced by sampling has received much attention in graphics, but reconstruction of samples into a continuous representation can also cause aliasing as well as other defects in image quality. The problem of designing a filter for use on images is discussed, and a new family of piecewise cubic filters are investigated as a practical demonstration. Two interesting cubic filters are found, one having good antialiasing properties and the other having good image-quality properties. It is also shown that reconstruction using derivative as well as amplitude values can greatly reduce aliasing.

CR Categories and Subject Descriptions: I.3.3 [**Computer Graphics**]: Picture/Image Generation; I.4.1 [**Image Processing**]: Digitization

General Terms: Algorithms

Additional Keywords and Phrases: Antialiasing, Cubic Filters, Filters, Derivative Reconstruction, Reconstruction, Sampling

1. Introduction

The issues of signal processing arise in image synthesis because of transformation between continuous and discrete representations of images. A continuous signal is converted to a discrete one by *sampling,* and according to the sampling theorem [SHA49], all the information in the continuous signal is preserved in the samples if they are evenly spaced and the frequency of sampling is twice that of the highest frequency contained in the signal. A discrete signal can be converted to a continuous one by interpolating between samples, a process referred to in the signal-processing literature as *reconstruction.*

Many conversions between continuous and discrete representations may occur in the course of generating an image. For example when ray tracing a texture-mapped surface, a photograph may be sampled by a digitizer to define the texture, then the texture samples are interpolated and resampled when a ray strikes the textured surface, the ray samples are interpolated and resampled to generate pixel values, and the pixels are interpolated by a display and finally resampled by retinal cells when the image is viewed. Resampling may be more explicit, as in enlarging or reducing a digital image or warping an image (e.g., with Catmull and Smith's algorithm [CAT80]). Each of these conversions can introduce conspicuous errors into an image.

Errors introduced by sampling (e.g., aliasing) have received considerable attention in the graphics community since Crow identified this as the cause of certain unwanted artifacts in synthetic images [CRO77]. Aliasing in images was discussed in the classic 1934 paper by Mertz and Gray [MER34]. Their discussion contains a description of artifacts well-known to graphics researchers today and shows that the condition for preventing aliasing was known, as a rule of thumb, long before Shannon's proof of the sampling theorem:

> The interference usually manifests itself in the form of serrations on diagonal lines and occasional moiré effects in the received picture. Confusion in the signal may be practically eliminated by using an aperture of such a nature that it cuts off all [Fourier] components with *n* numbers greater than N/2 [half the scanning rate] ....

By comparison, the problems introduced by reconstruction have been somewhat neglected in the graphics literature. Reconstruction can be responsible for aliasing and other types of distortion that mar the subjective quality of an image. This paper will focus on the effects of reconstruction and how to design filters for graphics applications.

2. Aliasing Caused by Reconstruction

Aliasing in synthetic images is a serious problem and still not completely solved. In other digital-signal-processing applications, aliasing is eliminated by prefiltering signals before sampling, as illustrated in Figure 1. Note that it is the prefiltered signal that is reconstructed in this case.

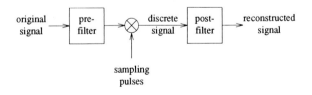

Figure 1. Sampling and Reconstruction

While prefiltering is the classic solution to aliasing problems, there is a special problem encountered in computer graphics. Many synthetic images originate from what we will call *procedural signals,* in which the signal is only implicitly defined by an algorithm for computing point samples. Operations that require an explicit representation of the signal cannot be performed, and in particular, prefiltering is impractical. This difficulty is unique to computer graphics, and ray tracing is the clearest example of it [WHI80].

To explain the role that reconstruction plays in aliasing, it will be helpful to review briefly the theory of sampling and define the operations of sampling and reconstruction more precisely. In one dimension, a signal can be represented by a continuous function $f(x)$. Producing a discrete signal by sampling is equivalent to multiplying by an infinite train of impulses known as a comb function:

$$f_s(x) = f(x) \cdot comb(x) \qquad (1)$$

where

$$comb(x) = \sum_{n=-\infty}^{\infty} \delta(x-n) \qquad (1b)$$

Unit spacing between samples is assumed in equation (1b), and $\delta(x)$ is the Dirac delta function. In this case, the sampling theorem states that $f(x)$ can be reconstructed exactly from its samples if it contains no frequencies greater than 0.5 cycles per sample. This critical frequency is called the *Nyquist frequency.*

Reconstruction is accomplished by convolving (indicated by *) the discrete signal with a reconstruction filter kernel, $k(x)$:

$$f_r(x) = f_s(x) * k(x) \qquad (2)$$

$$= \int_{-\infty}^{\infty} f_s(u) \cdot k(x-u) du \qquad (2b)$$

$$= \sum_{n=-\infty}^{\infty} f(n) \cdot k(x-n) \qquad (2c)$$

Except in the mathematically ideal case, some error is introduced in the process of sampling and reconstruction, and $f(x)$ will be somewhat different from $f_r(x)$. To analyze this error, it is useful to view the problem in the frequency domain. The Fourier transform of the signal is its spectrum $F(v)$, and the Fourier transform of the filter is its frequency response $K(v)$. Since multiplication in the spatial domain is equivalent to convolution in the frequency domain (and vice versa), sampling can be described by:

$$F_s(v) = F(v) * Comb(v) \qquad (3)$$

and reconstruction by:

$$F_r(v) = F_s(v) \cdot K(v) \qquad (4)$$

The Fourier transform of a comb function is also a comb function (with reciprocal spacing between impulses).

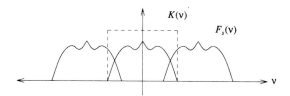

Figure 2. Sampling and Reconstruction in Frequency Domain

Figure 2 illustrates the consequences of the convolution in equation (3). The spectrum of a sampled signal $F_s(v)$ is the sum of an infinite sequence of shifted replicas of the original signal's spectrum, each

centered at the location of an impulse in the comb. Equation (4) states that, in the frequency domain, reconstruction can be interpreted as the multiplication by $K(v)$ which is intended to eliminate all the *extraneous replicas* of the signal's spectrum and keep the original *base-band* centered at the origin. $K(v)$ is indicated by the dashed curve in Figure 2.

However, Figure 2 also demonstrates a problem. The replicas of the signal spectrum overlap, and the reconstruction filter can not isolate a pure version of the base-band signal. When part of the energy in a replica of the spectrum leaks into the reconstructed signal, aliasing results. If the bandwidth of the signal were narrower or the sampling rate higher, the copies would not overlap, and exact reconstruction would be possible.

Even if the replicated spectra do not overlap, aliasing can result from poor reconstruction, as illustrated in Figure 3. When aliasing is a consequence of undersampling (or lack of prefiltering), it is referred to as *prealiasing,* and when it results from poor reconstruction, it is called *postaliasing.*

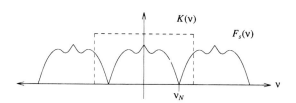

Figure 3. Postaliasing Resulting from Poor Reconstruction Filter

Figure 4 shows an extreme example of aliasing in an image. In this figure, the two-dimensional signal, $f(x,y) = \sin(x^2+y^2)$, was sampled on a 128 x 128 pixel grid. Then, these samples were reconstructed with a cubic filter (to be described later in the paper) and resampled to 512 x 512 pixels.

The rings on the left side of the image are part of the actual signal, but the rings on the right side are Moiré patterns due to prealiasing. In the center of the image is a fainter set of concentric rings resulting from postaliasing. Postaliasing occurred when the discrete image of 128 x 128 pixels was enlarged to 512 x 512 pixels by resampling. Note that this conspicuous postaliasing pattern results from "beating" between the signal and its alias. This can also be understood from Figure 3, where it can be seen that at the Nyquist frequency (indicated by v_N) the signal's spectrum and its nearest replica come close together. Power in the spectrum very near the Nyquist frequency is thus the cause of the most difficult type of aliasing to remove from an image. This problem has been noted by other graphics researchers [COO87] and by Mertz et al. [MER34].

Using the same set of samples as in Figure 4, a much better reconstruction filter can be applied (a 30-unit-wide windowed sinc filter). Figure 5 demonstrates a dramatic reduction of the postaliasing pattern, but the prealiasing is unaffected. The spectrum of this reconstruction filter is very close to the ideal step shape shown in Figures 2 and 3.

3. Other Image Defects Caused by Reconstruction

Notice in Figure 2, that a reconstruction filter $K(v)$ has two tasks. First it must remove the extraneous replicas of the signal spectrum (to prevent aliasing). Second, it should pass the original signal base band, but the signal can be distorted if this is not done perfectly. This second type of reconstruction error will be referred to as *base-band attenuation.*

From the previous section, one might assume that the literature of signal processing provides a complete solution to the reconstruction problem in graphics; however, there is a serious difficulty with the ideal sinc filter that is not obvious from studying its frequency response. Figure 6 shows a simple figure reconstructed with the same filter used in Figure 5. The rippling pattern radiating from the edges is called *ringing*. Ringing is strongly suggested by the form of the impulse response of the sinc filter, as shown in Figure 7:

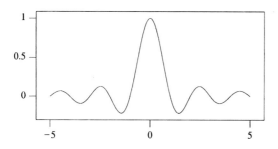

Figure 7. Impulse Response of Ideal Sinc Filter

Classical digital filter design places a heavy emphasis on the frequency response of a filter. That works well in the audio domain, but when considering the appearance of images, it is important to also pay attention to the shape of the impulse response.

The response of human viewers to various spatial effects of filters is not yet a well-understood science and is largely subjective in nature. Filters that have some aliasing problems or certain types of base-band attenuation may turn out to give visually-pleasing results. Schreiber and Troxel have discussed the spatial effects of reconstruction filters [SCH85], and they mention some of the important defects that can occur when judging the quality of an image subjectively: *sample-frequency ripple, anisotropic effects, ringing, blurring, and aliasing.* Each of these effects will be considered in detail in the following section.

Unfortunately, it is often necessary to trade off one type of distortion for another, and the design of a single filter perfect for all applications is almost certainly impossible. As Figure 6 illustrated, perfect antialiasing resulted in the serious defect of ringing. However, Brown realized that a moderate amount of ringing can improve the subjective quality of an image by enhancing the appearance of sharpness [BRO69]. He found that a single transient lobe of ringing was effective at sharpening, but multiple transients (as in Figure 6) always degrade image quality.

Many of the concepts presented so far have been illustrated in one dimension for simplicity. However, image reconstruction takes place in two dimensions and involves the convolution of a 2D lattice of samples with a filter $k(x,y)$. In this paper, we will consider only *separable* filters, where the samples are convolved with the product $k(x)k(y)$. Separable filters are computationally more efficient than nonseparable because the filtering operation can be performed in separate passes vertically and horizontally. If the filter kernel is N samples wide, the reconstruction can be performed with $O(N^2)$ multiplications for the general filter $k(x,y)$ but with $O(N)$ if the filter is separable.

4. Piecewise Cubic Reconstruction Filters

Rather than discuss the issues of filter design abstractly, this paper will apply them to the study of a family of filters defined by piecewise cubic polynomials. Cubic filters are sufficiently complex to have a broad range of behaviors, but they are simple enough to be computationally attractive. Hou and Andrews have studied the filtering properties of the cubic B-spline [HOU78], and two studies have been made of the one-parameter family of cardinal cubic splines [KEY81,PAR83].

The general form for a symmetric cubic filter is:

$$k(x) = \begin{cases} P|x|^3 + Q|x|^2 + R|x| + S & \text{if } |x| < 1 \\ T|x|^3 + U|x|^2 + V|x| + W & \text{if } 1 \le |x| < 2 \\ 0 & \text{otherwise} \end{cases} \qquad (6)$$

Several obvious constraints can be placed on this function to reduce the

number of free parameters. First, the filter should be smooth in the sense that its value and first derivative are continuous everywhere. Discontinuities in $k(x)$ will lead to high-frequency leakage in the frequency response of the filter which can allow aliasing. In addition, the problem of *sample-frequency ripple* can be designed out of the filter by requiring (for all x):

$$\sum_{n=-\infty}^{\infty} k(x-n) = 1 \qquad (7)$$

This means that if all the samples are a constant value, the reconstruction will be a flat constant signal. Figure 8 demonstrates this defect by using an unnormalized Gaussian filter to reconstruct a 512 x 512 image from 64 x 64 samples. In the frequency domain, sample ripple can be viewed as an alias of the image's DC component. It can be shown that the condition given by equation (7) means that the frequency response of these cubic filters will be zero at all integer multiples of the sampling frequency except zero, eliminating all extraneous replicas of the DC component.

With these constraints, the number of free parameters are reduced from eight to two, resulting in the following family of cubic filters:

$$k(x) = \frac{1}{6} \begin{cases} (12-9B-6C)|x|^3 + & \\ (-18+12B+6C)|x|^2 + (6-2B) & \text{if } |x| < 1 \\ (-B-6C)|x|^3 + (6B+30C)|x|^2 + & \text{if } 1 \le |x| < 2 \\ (-12B-48C)|x| + (8B+24C) & \\ 0 & \text{otherwise} \end{cases} \qquad (8)$$

Some values of (B, C) correspond to well-known cubic splines. (1,0) is the cubic B-spline, (0, C) is the one-parameter family of cardinal cubics with (0, 0.5) being the Catmull-Rom spline, and (B, 0) are Duff's tensioned B-splines [DUF86].

In two or more dimensions, visible artifacts can be caused by angle-dependent behavior or *anisotropic effects.* Figure 9 illustrates this problem by reconstructing with the separable filter $k(x)k(y)$ using parameter values of (0,0). Even though sample-frequency ripple has been designed out of $k(x)$, in two dimensions the pixel structure is highly conspicuous because the impulse response and the sampling lattice are not radially symmetric.

The phenomenon of *ringing* has already been seen in Figure 6. Filters in the cubic filter family can also exhibit this problem as seen in Figure 10, where parameter values of (0,1) were used. Ringing results when $k(x)$ has negative side lobes, and although some ringing can enhance sharpness, a filter that becomes negative is problematic. In Figure 10, a typical problem is seen where portions of the image near an edge have become negative and have been clamped to zero. This results in pronounced black spots (e.g., at the top of the statue's head). Similar clamping occurs to white, but is less noticeable because of the eye's non-linear response to contrast. Schreiber and Troxel have suggested that subjectively even sharpening can only be produced by introducing ringing transients in a suitably nonlinear fashion [SCH85]. These conspicuous clamping effects could also be eliminated by reducing the dynamic range of the image or raising the DC level of the image.

Parameter values of (3/2, -1/4) result in an image that is unnecessarily *blurry,* as seen in Figure 11. The cubic B-spline also suffers from this problem. In viewing many reconstructions with filters in this family, ringing, anisotropy, and blurring are the dominant behaviors, and in a small region of the parameter space, a satisfactory compromise seems to exist which is seen in Figure 12, using parameter values of (1/3, 1/3). This is quite good, considering that the image is being magnified from 64 x 64 pixels. There is some degree of sharpening, and almost no visible evidence of the sampling lattice.

To get a better idea of which regions of the parameter space yield which type of behavior, a simple subjective test was designed. On a neutral background, four images were displayed typifying the effects of ringing, blurring, anisotropy, and an example of the most satisfactory behavior. In the center of the display, images reconstructed from filters with random values of (B, C) were displayed, and the test subject was asked to choose which of the four behaviors it exemplified. Nine expert observers (researchers working in graphics or image processing) took part and over 500 samples were taken. It would not be credible to suggest that a single ideal parameter pair can be deduced from subjective testing. The motivation for this experiment was simply to draw approximate boundaries between regions of differing behavior as shown in Figure 13. The test subjects were quite consistent with one another in their judgements.

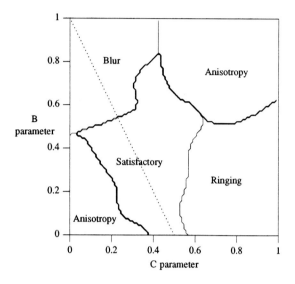

Figure 13. Regions of Dominant Subjective Behavior

To help choose a good filter from the two-parameter space, some quantitative analysis can be done to remove one more degree of freedom. Keys and Park et al. studied the cardinal cubic splines because these cubics exactly interpolate at the sample positions [KEY81,PAR83]. Using standard numerical analysis, Keys concluded that the Catmull-Rom spline was best. Park et al. reached the same conclusion using an equivalent analysis in the frequency domain. Figure 14 illustrates this technique:

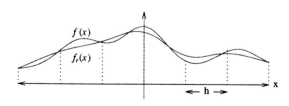

Figure 14. $f(x)$ and $f_r(x)$

As the sample spacing h diminishes, the function and its reconstruction become closer. The difference $f(x) - f_r(x)$ can be expanded into a power series in h to study how parameters affect various orders of behavior. Details of this type of analysis can be found in Keys' paper, and when applied to the two-parameter family, the following is obtained:

$$f(x) - f_r(x) = (2C + B - 1) h f' r(x) + O(h^2)$$ (9)

$r(x)$ is a polynomial factor. When $2C + B = 1$ (indicated by dotted line

in Figure 13), quadratic convergence of fit is achieved. This line contains the cubic B-spline and the Catmull-Rom spline (which actually has cubic convergence). Within the interval of $B = 5/3$ to $B = 0$, good subjective behavior is found with a simple trade-off between blurring and ringing. Outside this interval, $k(x)$ becomes bimodal or exhibits extreme ringing. The filter (1/3, 1/3) used to generate Figure 12 is recommended by the authors, but other observers may prefer more or less ringing.

5. Postaliasing Revisited

A systematic consideration of subjective appearance along with quantitative analysis has yielded an excellent piecewise cubic filter. However, the issue of postaliasing, defined in section 2, has been ignored. In fact the (1/3, 1/3) filter has only fair antialiasing properties and was used to generate Figure 4. Postaliasing is usually not strong enough to cause visible "jaggies" on edges unless a very poor filter is used (e.g., a box filter); however, an image with periodic patterns can have conspicuous postalias Moiré effects unless careful precautions are taken. Synthetic images that contain brick walls, ocean waves, or the ubiquitous checkerboard pattern are examples of images that might have this difficulty. There are several approaches to fixing this problem.

If the signal is bandlimited and samples carry information about the derivative as well as about signal amplitude, a better job of reconstruction can be done [PET64]. Given samples (at unit spacing) of a signal and of its derivative, a reconstruction can be done in the following form:

$$f(x) = \sum_{n=-\infty}^{\infty} \left[f_n g(x-n) + f'_n h(x-n) \right]$$ (10)

In an extension of the sampling theorem, if the signal contains no energy above the sampling frequency (twice the allowed bandwidth of sampling without derivatives), then it can be perfectly reconstructed by the filter kernels:

$$g(x) = \frac{\sin^2 \pi x}{\pi^2 x^2}$$ (11)

$$h(x) = \frac{\sin^2 \pi x}{\pi^2 x}$$ (11b)

This is analogous to the ideal sinc reconstruction formula in the standard case where no derivative information is present. A common approximation to these ideal reconstruction formulae is Hermite cubic interpolation:

$$g(x) = \begin{cases} 2|x|^3 - 3|x|^2 + 1 & \text{if } |x| \le 1 \\ 0 & otherwise \end{cases}$$ (12)

$$h(x) = \begin{cases} x^3 - 2x|x| + x & \text{if } |x| \le 1 \\ 0 & otherwise \end{cases}$$ (12b)

Figure 15 shows the aliasing test pattern (still starting with 128 x 128 samples) reconstructed with the Hermite cubic postfilter. The effect is dramatic when compared to Figure 4. The postaliasing artifact in the middle of the image is nearly gone, and the prealiasing pattern on the right is less intense.

The theory of *derivative reconstruction* may have some practical value in computer graphics. For example, it may be possible to extend Whitted's ray-tracing shading model [WHI80] to generate derivatives with respect to the screen coordinates. This is not an easy problem, but we have demonstrated the feasibility of this extension by deriving the formulae for Lambert and Phong shading on quadric surfaces. It is possible that the density of rays used to reconstruct an image could be reduced in this manner by gathering more useful information from each visible surface calculation.

A second approach to improving postaliasing properties is suggested by the success of stochastic sampling on the prealiasing problem

[COO86,DIP85,MIT87]. However, preliminary experiments conducted by the authors with *stochastic-phase reconstruction* have yielded very poor results. The amount of noise needed to obscure postaliasing seriously degraded image quality.

Finally, it was observed in section 2 that signal energy very near the Nyquist frequency is most responsible for conspicuous Moiré patterns. It is possible to cut out this component by *notch-filter reconstruction*. The frequency response of the two-parameter cubic filter in equation (8) is:

$$K(v) = \frac{3-3B}{(\pi v)^2}\left[sinc^2(v) - sinc(2v)\right] \quad (13)$$
$$+ \frac{2C}{(\pi v)^2}\left[-3sinc^2(2v) + 2sinc(2v) + sinc(4v)\right]$$
$$+ B\, sinc^4(v)$$

This function goes to zero at $v = 1/2$ when $B = 3/2$. In fact, the frequency response is zero at all integer and half-integer multiples of the sampling rate except zero. The filter (3/2, -1/4) is quadratically convergent, and the result of reconstruction with it can be seen in Figure 16, in which the postaliasing artifact is almost completely eliminated. Unfortunately, this filter is quite blurry as was seen in Figure 11. The behavior of this notch filter can be seen in its frequency response in Figure 17 compared with the cubic B-spline filter (1, 0) in Figure 18. The log magnitudes of the frequency responses are plotted below:

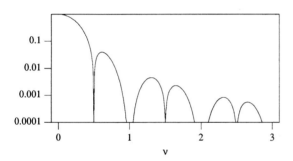

Figure 17. Frequency Response of Cubic Notch Filter

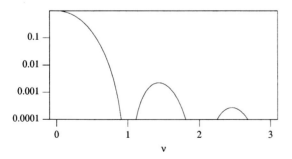

Figure 18. Frequency Response of Cubic B-Spline Filter

6. Conclusions

Designing reconstruction filters for computer graphics applications requires a balanced analysis of formal quantitative properties and subjective image quality. There are many trade-offs, and it may be impossible to find a filter that yields good image quality and has good antialiasing properties.

A new family of cubic filters has been analyzed, and two interesting filters have been found. The (1/3, 1/3) filter yields excellent image quality, and the notch filter (3/2, -1/4) strongly suppresses postaliasing patterns.

If derivative values can be generated by a procedural signal, an image with less aliasing is possible by reconstruction with Hermite interpolation or some other suitable filter.

More work remains to be done. While the authors do not believe simple filters will be found that improve much on the cubic filters derived here, there are other avenues for progress. Adaptive filters might allow good image quality with strong antialiasing only where it is needed in problem areas. The effects of the reconstruction in the display and eye might be allowed for given models of the visual system [NET88].

Finally, the problem of reconstruction from nonuniform sampling is not entirely solved. Reasonable filters have been proposed [MIT87], but more analysis could be done. "Ideal" nonuniform reconstruction filters are known which are analogous to the sinc filter used with uniform samples. A greater challenge will be to understand the subjective issues involved in designing filters that are well suited to computer graphics.

7. Acknowledgements

We would like to thank our colleagues who volunteered to help with subjective testing. We would also like to thank Jim Bergen from the David Sarnoff Laboratory, Jim Johnston from Bell Labs Signal Processing Research Department., and William Schreiber from MIT's Advanced Television Research Program for their views on filter design. We would also like to thank Larry O'Gorman, Bruce Naylor, Rob Pike, David Thomas and Pamela Zave and the SIGGRAPH reviewers for their helpful comments.

8. References

[BRO69]   Brown, Earl F., "Television: The Subjective Effects of Filter Ringing Transients", *Journal of the SMPTE*, Vol. 78, No. 4, April 1969, pp. 249-255.

[CAT80]   Catmull, Edwin, Alvy Ray Smith, "3-D Transformations of Images in Scanline Order", *Computer Graphics*, Vol. 14, No. 3, pp. 279-285.

[COO86]   Cook, Robert L., "Stochastic Sampling in Computer Graphics", *ACM Trans. Graphics*, Vol. 5, No. 1, January 1986.

[COO87]   Cook, Robert L., *personal communication*, August, 1987.

[CRO77]   Crow, Franklin C., "The Aliasing Problem in Computer-Generated Shaded Images", *Comm. ACM*, Vol. 20, No. 11, November 1977, pp. 799-805.

[DIP85]   Dippe, Mark A. Z. and Erling Henry Wold, "Antialiasing Through Stochastic Sampling", *Computer Graphics*, Vol. 19, No. 3, July 1985, pp. 69-78.

[DUF86]   Duff, Tom, "Splines in Animation and Modeling", *State of the Art in Image Synthesis*, SIGGRAPH 86 Course Notes.

[HOU78]   Hou, Hsieh S., Harry C. Andrews, "Cubic Splines for Image Interpolation and Digital Filtering", *IEEE Trans. Acoustics, Speech, and Signal Processing*, Vol. ASSP-26, No. 6, December 1978, pp. 508-517.

[KEY81]   Keys, Robert, G., "Cubic Convolution Interpolation for Digital Image Processing", *IEEE Trans. Acoustics, Speech, and Signal Processing*, Vol. ASSP-29, No. 6, December 1981, pp. 1153-1160.

[MER84] Mertz, Pierre, and Frank Grey, "A Theory of Scanning and its Relation to the Characteristics of the Transmitted Signal in Telephotography and Television," *Bell System Tech. J.,* Vol. 13, pp. 464-515, July 1934.

[MIT87] Mitchell, Don P., "Generating Antialiased Images at Low Sampling Densities", *Computer Graphics,* Vol. 21, No. 4, July 1987, pp. 65-72.

[NET88] Netravali, Arun N., Barry G. Haskell, *Digital Pictures: Representation and Compression,* New York, Plenum, 1988.

[PAR83] Park, Stephen K., Robert A. Schowengerdt, "Image Reconstruction by Parametric Cubic Convolution", *Computer Vision, Graphics, and Image Processing,* Vol. 23, No. 3, September 1983, pp. 258-272.

[PET64] Petersen, Daniel P., David Middleton, "Reconstruction of Multidimensional Stochastic Fields from Discrete Measurements of Amplitude and Gradient", *Information and Control,* Vol. 7, pp. 445-476.

[SCH85] Schreiber, William F., Donald E. Troxel, "Transformation Between Continuous and Discrete Representations of Images: A Perceptual Approach", *IEEE Trans. Pattern Analysis and Machine Intelligence,* Vol. PAMI-7, No. 2, March 1985, pp. 178-186.

[SHA49] Shannon, Claude E., "Communication in the Presence of Noise.", *Proc. IRE* Vol. 37, 1949, pp. 10-21.

[WHI80] Whitted, Turner, "An Improved Illumination Model for Shaded Display", *Comm. ACM,* Vol. 23, No. 6, June 1980, pp. 343-349.

Figure 4. Prealiasing and Postaliasing Example

Figure 5. Nearly Ideal Postfiltering

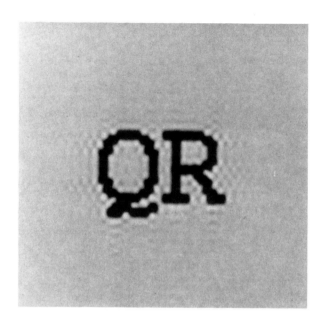

Figure 6. Ringing Caused By Sinc Postfilter

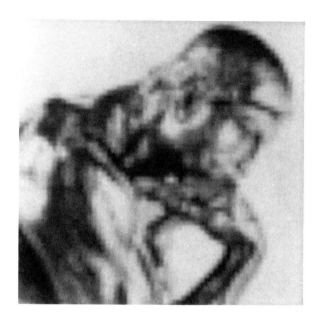

Figure 9. Anisotropic Artifacts

Figure 8. Sample-Frequency Ripple

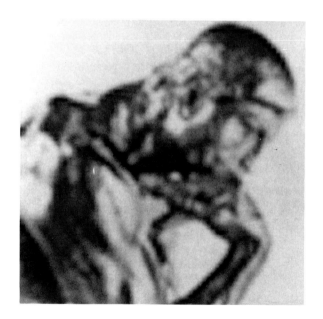

Figure 10. Excessive Ringing and Clamping Artifacts

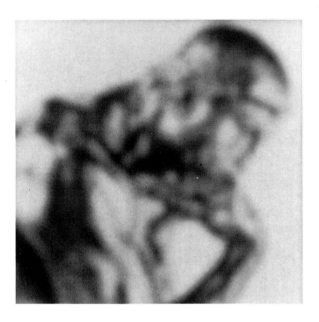

Figure 11. Excessive Blurring

Figure 15. Using Derivative Reconstruction

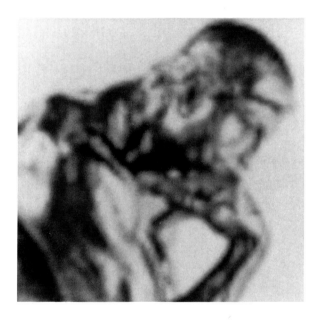

Figure 12. Best-Looking Cubic Reconstruction

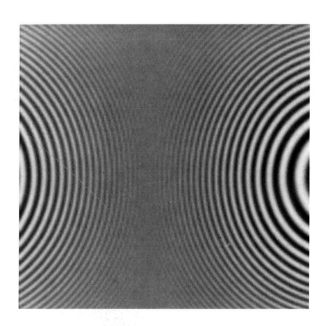

Figure 16. Using Notch-Filter Reconstruction

Constant-Time Filtering with Space-Variant Kernels

Alain Fournier
Eugene Fiume

Department of Computer Science
Sandford Fleming Building
University of Toronto
Toronto, Ontario
M5S 1A4
BITNET: {elf | alain}@dgp.utoronto
CSNET/UUCP: {elf | alain}@dgp.toronto.edu

Abstract

Filtering is an essential but costly step in many computer graphics applications, most notably in texture mapping. Several techniques have been previously developed which allow prefiltering of a texture (or in general an image) in time that is independent of the number of texture elements under the filter kernel. These are limited, however, to space-invariant kernels whose shape in texture space is the same independently of their positions, and usually are also limited to a small range of filters.

We present here a technique that permits constant-time filtering for space-variant kernels. The essential step is to approximate a filter surface in texture space by a sum of suitably-chosen basis functions. The convolution of a filter with a texture is replaced by the weighted sum of the convolution of the basis functions with the texture, which can be precomputed. To achieve constant time, convolutions with the basis functions are computed and stored in a pyramidal fashion, and the right level of the pyramid is selected so that only a constant number of points on the filter kernel need be evaluated.

The technique allows the use of arbitrary filters, and as such is useful to explore interesting mappings and special filtering techniques. We give examples of applications to perspective and conformal mappings, and to the use of filters such as gaussians and sinc functions.

CR Categories: I.3.3 [**Computer Graphics**]: Picture/Image Generation — *display algorithms*; I.3.5 [**Computer Graphics**]: Computational Geometry and Object Modeling — *Surface representation*; I.4.3 [**Image Processing**]: Enhancement — *filtering, smoothing*.

1. Introduction

In many applications of computer graphics such as raster image transformations, environment mapping and texture mapping, *filtering* is a basic operation. To use consistent and familiar terminology (see glossary at end of paper), we will call the image on which the filtering is applied the *texture* and the coordinates for the texture space (u,v). The central operation of filtering is to compute for a filter function $F(u,v)$, a texture $T(u,v)$, and a position in texture space (u_c, v_c), the *convolution*

$$S_c = \iint T(u,v) \ F(u_c-u, v_c-v) \ du \ dv. \qquad (1)$$

Usually an entire array of such sample values is needed, and the positions of these values are determined from a mapping from another space. Again by convention we will call that space the *screen* and denote screen coordinates by (x,y). The *kernel* of the filter is the domain of F centered at a particular sample pair (u_c, v_c). The texture to screen mapping is

$$\tau(u,v) = (x,y),$$

and the inverse mapping (if defined) is

$$\tau^{-1}(x,y) = (u,v).$$

By the same token, the filter kernel in texture space is normally obtained by mapping a given kernel from screen space:

$$F(u,v) = F(\tau^{-1}(x,y)).$$

The main concerns in applications are the quality and properties of the filters used, the accuracy of the computation of the convolution, and the efficiency of the computation. The latter is especially important, since convolution can be a costly proposition. In the simple case of a discrete texture, and a kernel with a *finite width of support* (that is non-zero only over a finite area), the cost is proportional to the number of *texels* (texture elements) under the kernel. Since that can be most or all of the texture if the kernel is large with respect to the texture, the cost per sample can be very high.

A further distinction is important. In applications where the mappings are affine,[0] each filter is a translation of the same function. In this case more efficient methods are applicable, and we will survey some in the next section. The kernel of the filter is then said to be *space-invariant*. The majority of applications, however, involve non-affine mappings, which cause a filter kernel to vary from sample point to sample

---

0.   In an affine mapping parallelism is preserved, but not necessarily distances and angles. Perspective projection is not affine.

point. Such kernels are thus *space-variant*, and dealing with them is more difficult, but unfortunately unavoidable.

2. Previous Techniques

A series of papers by Greene and Heckbert [GrHe86], Greene [Gree86], and Heckbert [Heck86a, Heck86b] have surveyed the recent results, especially as they relate to texture mapping, and the reader is referred to them. Table 1 is directly derived from a table in [Heck86b]. The additional references are to [DuSS78, Crow81, Will83].

Method	Filter	Shape	Time	Storage	Reference
Direct Convolution	Any	Any	# of texels	1	Any
Point Sampling	Delta	Point	1	1	Any
Point sampled Pyramid	Box	Square	1	4/3	Dungan
MIP map	Box	Square	8	4/3	Williams
EWA on Pyramid	Any	Ellipse	# of texels	4/3	Greene
Summed Area Table	Box	Rectangle	4 or 16	2 to 4	Crow
Repeated Integration	Spline	Rectangle	~Order^2	~Order	Heckbert

EWA stands for *Elliptical Weighted Average*, and was developed for space-variant filtering for Omnimax images. There are variations on these basic techniques. MIP maps have been modified to allow for rectangular areas. In the other direction, Naiman and Fournier [NaFo87] used a summed-area filter in the special case where the picture is decomposed into single-valued rectangles.

There is no need to reproduce here the excellent discussions found in Greene and Heckbert about the pluses and minuses of these various methods. An important fact is that the techniques achieving constant time are severely limited in the type of filters they can use (with the exception of repeated integration) or in the shape of the area considered. The most flexible methods in this respect (direct convolution and EWA on a pyramid) can take an arbitrarily large amount of time for kernels that are large in texture space.

Our original motivation was to find a suitable filtering technique when using *conformal texture mapping* [FiFC87]. In this type of mapping the kernel in texture space is space-variant, and can often be severely distorted. Figure 1 shows how circles of equal size in screen space map to texture space under a conformal mapping which maps a square to a non-convex pentagon.

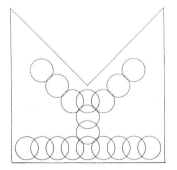 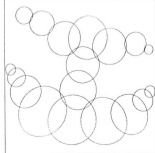

Figure 1. Distortion of kernels under conformal mapping

The number of texels under the kernel can also vary greatly. This is especially true in animation. Moreover, in animation

the same texture can be used in hundreds of frames. Even a small gain in cost per frame can therefore more than offset even a large precomputing cost.

It is clear from the preceding table that a technique which could accommodate any type and shape of filter but whose cost would be largely independent of the number of texels under the filter would be useful.

3. The Technique

3.1. Filter Surface Approximation

If we look at $F(u_c-u, v_c-v)$ as a surface in texture space, it can be approximated piece-wise in the traditional manner by the union of *patches*, each being a weighted sum of the cartesian product of M basis functions over some knots:

$$F(u_c-u, v_c-v) \approx \bigcup_{all\ patches} \sum_{i=0}^{M} \sum_{j=0}^{M} B_i(u) B_j(v) b_{ij}. \quad (2)$$

Patches are normally selected from an array, and will be indexed by (k,l). The parameters u and v for patch (k,l) vary from u_k to u_{k+1} and v_l to v_{l+1}. In general the values of the parameters at knot k will be k, and the basis functions will be translates of each other so that in effect u and v range from 0 to 1. The b_{ij} are coefficients determined from the values of $F(u_c-u, v_c-v)$ at the knots. The convolution over the patches can then be approximated by

$$S_a = \sum_{all\ patches} \int_{u=u_k}^{u_{k+1}} \int_{v=v_l}^{v_{l+1}} T(u,v) \sum_{i=0}^{M} \sum_{j=0}^{M} B_i(u) B_j(v) b_{ij}\, du\, dv.$$

Since the b_{ij} are independent of u and v over a patch, and since summation distributes over integration for well-behaved $T(u,v)$ and B_i and B_j,

$$S_a = \sum_{all\ patches} \sum_{i=0}^{M} \sum_{j=0}^{M} b_{ij} \int_{u=u_k}^{u_{k+1}} \int_{v=v_l}^{v_{l+1}} T(u,v) B_i(u) B_j(v)\, du\, dv.$$

The M^2 double integrals of the form

$$C_{ij} = \int_{u=u_k}^{u_{k+1}} \int_{v=v_l}^{v_{l+1}} T(u,v) B_i(u) B_j(v)\, du\, dv \quad (3)$$

can therefore be precomputed and stored for a given texture. For each position of the filter, the filter surface is approximated by a collection of patches for which the b_{ij} are determined, then multiplied by the stored C_{ij} and summed to give the approximation S_a to the convolution S_c:

$$S_c \approx S_a = \sum_{all\ patches} \sum_{i=0}^{M} \sum_{j=0}^{M} b_{ij} C_{ij}. \quad (4)$$

For each patch contributing to the piece-wise approximation to the filter surface in texture space, the cost of computation and storage is therefore a function of the number of basis functions (the *order* of the polynomials in the case of polynomial basis functions) and the number of primaries used for the image values.

3.2. NIL Maps

To keep the total cost for each application of the filter independent of the number of texels under the filter, we have to make sure that the number of patches used is independent of the number of texels. The number of patches needed is a function of how well the filter surface is approximated by the basis functions, and of how much approximation error we are willing to tolerate. Once this is established, however, to effectively guarantee this number of patches we must have an approximately-equal number of knots under the filter width of response. This suggests immediately a *pyramidal* approach, in which we build up precomputed C_{ij} for increasingly closer knots, until we reach the spacing of the texels if we have a discrete texture, or some other practical limit for an analytic texture. The hierarchical construction thus obtained closely resembles *MIP* maps described in [Will83] and we call them *NIL maps*, where NIL stands for *nodus in largo*, which can be loosely translated as "knot large". When using the pyramid, the goal is then to select the level (or levels) of the pyramid which will give the fewest knots, and therefore patches under the filter, while guaranteeing a good approximation of the filter surface for the purpose of convolution.

3.3. Computing the Answer

Once the C_{ij} have been computed and stored for each level (*i.e.* knot spacing) of the NIL maps, the result of the convolution for a given filter position is computed according to the following steps:

- map the filter position from screen to texture space

- find the level in the NIL maps so that the number of patches used is sufficient for a good approximation of the surface while making sure that the number of patches is bounded by a small constant. Note that the level does not have to be the same for all patches.

- for each patch selected to contribute, compute the relevant b_{ij} from the filter values at the knots, and compute the S_a according to Eq. 4 summing all the contributions to obtain the final result.

3.4. Cost in Time and Space

The storage cost can be determined as follows. At the highest level (where there are as many patches as there are texels), the number of C_{ij} is M^2 times the number of texels. The precision needed is dependent of the type of basis functions used, but most reasonable choices are functions whose values do not go far beyond [0,1], and therefore each C_{ij} will have values of the order of the texel values. Thus the same precision is required to store the C_{ij} as to store the texel values. To avoid too large an error accumulated in round-offs when adding M^2 terms, it is prudent to add $\log_2(M^2p)$ bits per value for storage. The number of levels needed is $p+1$, if the size of the original texture is $S = 2^p \times 2^p$. Each level requires one-fourth of the size of the preceding one, and therefore the total storage needed is

$$O\left[M^2 \times S \times \sum_{i=0}^{p} \frac{1}{2^{2i}} \right] = O\left[M^2 \times S \times \frac{4}{3} \right].$$

The cost per patch after pre-processing is easily obtained. It is proportional to the number of b_{ij} coefficients to be evaluated, and to the number of C_{ij} to be retrieved. In both cases this number is M^2 if M is the number of basis functions used. For polynomial bases, M is the order of approximation.

The theoretical goal of constant-time space-variant filtering is reached if the number of patches used is effectively bounded by a number independent of the number of texels under the filter. A variety of algorithms can guarantee this, and we will describe in the next section a rather simple one. The additional cost of the search through the NIL maps can only be determined for a specific algorithm, but will be most likely directly related to the number of levels in the pyramid.

4. Modalities

4.1. Choosing the Basis Functions and the Order

The main criterion governing the choice of the basis functions is how well and how easily the filter surface is approximated. The ways to determine the quality of approximation, however, are not the usual criteria of smoothness, visual fidelity or ease of control. If we view the filter as a reconstruction waveform, the approximated surface should be such that the various characteristics of the filter, both good and bad (amplitude of side lobe, stopband attenuation, resolution and interpolation errors), should be respected as much as possible. Most of these characteristics are computed in the frequency domain, and some include the power spectrum of the signal to which the filter is applied, which is not known in general. It is more useful and convenient to use a metric in the spatial domain for the approximation error. We use the *mean square* metric, namely the expression:

$$ER = \sum_{all\ patches} \int_{u=u_k}^{u_{k+1}} \int_{v=v_l}^{v_{l+1}} \left[F(u_c-u,v_c-v) - \hat{F}(u,v) \right]^2 du\ dv,$$

where

$$\hat{F}(u,v) = \sum_{i=0}^{M} \sum_{j=0}^{M} B_i(u)\, B_j(v)\, b_{ij}.$$

ER is normalized by dividing by

$$SQ = \sum_{all\ patches} \int_{u=u_k}^{u_{k+1}} \int_{v=v_l}^{v_{l+1}} \left[F(u_c-u,v_c-v) \right]^2 du\ dv.$$

Such a metric is commonly used when computing sampling errors [RoKa76] or evaluating filtering methods [KaUl81, KiON87]. In those cases the difference involved is between the image function (making some assumptions when it is unknown) and its sampled/approximated version. Here our metric is to indicate how well the filter is approximated, independently of the filtered image (*i.e.* texture). Such a metric is especially useful in this case because as the integral of the square of the difference between the filter and its approximation, it is directly related by Parseval's theorem to the energy difference due to the approximation error. This energy plays the main role in the various formulas for the characterization of the quality of filters[Prat78].

Since the method involves a piecewise approximation, we cannot seek a global least-square solution, but a formulation which gives a local least-square approximation is good as long as the computation of the b_{ij} is not too costly. The cost of the computations of the basis functions themselves is not as important an issue since it only intervenes in the preprocessing step. Polynomial bases are an obvious choice since they are well behaved and familiar. They have the added advantage that many of the popular filter formulations are polynomial, and therefore the approximation can be expected to be good (it is not necessarily exact, even if the degree of the polynomial describing the filter is less than or equal to the degree of the basis, since the screen-texture mapping itself can be arbitrary). It is also important for storage purposes that the values of the basis functions are not far from a [0,1] range since this influences the amount of storage needed for the NIL maps. For our examples we have chosen an interpolating formulation. The advantage is that in this case the b_{ij} of equation 2 are simply the values of the filter at the knots and this simplifies the use of the NIL maps.

In the choice of the order for the basis functions, there is an obvious trade-off between the storage and computation cost, which are proportional the the square of the order (we will assume it is the same in the u and v direction) and the number of patches required for a given quality of interpolation. It is interesting to examine the characteristics of the first few orders.

M	Patch Type	Terms/ Patch	Patches Required	Terms Required	% Error
1	Box	1	NR	--	31.5
2	Bilinear	4	27	108	13.1
3	Biquadratic	9	22	198	11.2
4	Bicubic	16	13	208	8.8

The entry in the "Patches Required" column is the number of patches required to approximate a bivariate Gaussian filter in the -2σ to 2σ range with a mean square error less than 5% of the mean square value of the filter. The 5% error threshold was not reached for the order 1 approximation because the necessary level of subdivision was more than the resolution of the original texture used. The entry in the "% Error" column is the percentage error when 9 patches of equal size are used to approximate the same filter. These errors should be compared to a *resolution error* of 54.6% and an *interpolation error* of 2.0% (relative to the ideal filter) for a Gaussian of $\sigma=1$ pixel [Prat78]. The latter are mean square errors in frequency space, but the order of magnitude is useful and indicates that it is easy to achieve approximation errors that are much smaller than the one due to the filter itself. Figures 2, 3, 4 and 5 illustrate how the surface is approximated by the patches of order 1, 2, 3 and 4 respectively. It should be noted that these surfaces are not explicitly computed in the normal process.

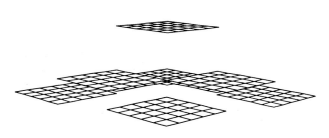

Figure 2. Gaussian approximated by 9 order 1 patches (boxes)

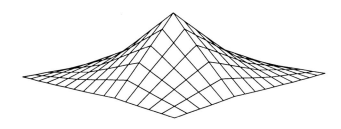

Figure 3. Gaussian approximated by 9 order 2 (bilinear) patches

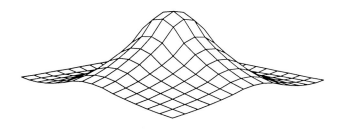

Figure 4. Gaussian approximated by 9 order 3 (biquadratic) patches

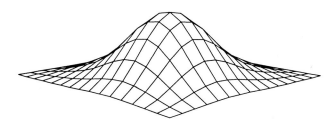

Figure 5. Gaussian approximated by 9 order 4 (bicubic) patches

It is clear from the table than in practice order 2, a bilinear patch approximation, is sufficient, since after that the gain in precision is probably not sufficient to compensate for the increased cost in computation and storage. Most of the examples we give were computed with a Catmull-Rom interpolating bicubic spline formulation[CaRo74] mainly for illustration purposes. It would be serious overkill for a production system.

4.2. Choosing the right level

As indicated before, it is crucial for the efficiency of the method that, when applying a filter, the number of patches used to approximate the surface is bounded by a small constant, independently of the kernel size in texture space. We use the following algorithm, but we stress that there are many ways to meet the same goal.

For a given type of filter in screen space, a set of N_g representative points on the filter surface, called *filter grid points*, and a number N_p is chosen. They are chosen so that if the filter surface is approximated by N_p patches of equal size including all the filter grid points, then the square error is less than a given threshold. For most filters the grid points will be equally spaced and form a square grid in screen space (whence their names), but it is not required. There should be at least four grid points defining a quadrilateral enclosing the kernel in screen space. In the simplest case the grid points reduce to these four boundary points. In the case of a kernel with an infinite width of support, these points define the boundary at which the filter can be safely truncated. We will see that there is not much penalty involved in making this boundary very loose. We will call s the level within the NIL map pyramid, s ranging from 0, which contains only one patch, to p, with $2^p \times 2^p$ patches. In the case of discrete textures p is the level of the original image. The steps of the algorithm are as follows:

(1) *Determine the global level.*

- map the four corner grid points to texture space.

- determine in texture space the smallest enclosing rectangle and compute its area A in texel square units.

- determine the level s such that the rectangle is covered by N_p patches. To do this, observe that at level s each patch has area $2^{p-s} \times 2^{p-s}$. Thus

$$s = p - \left\lceil \frac{1}{2} \log_2 \frac{A}{N_p} \right\rceil. \tag{5}$$

- compute the indices of the patches to be selected at that level. At level s they are the coordinates of the corners of the minimum enclosing rectangle taken from p bits to the top s bits.

We now have found the levels such that the filter kernel is covered by at least N_p patches. The screen to texture mapping, however, might have distorted the kernel in such a way that the filter would be poorly approximated, especially in the case of low order bases. The role of the filter grid points is to allow a refinement of the selected patches.

(2) *Refine the selected patches*

- for each of the selected patches **Refine**(patch)

- **Refine**(patch) is a recursive procedure:
    if the patch contains more than 2 of the filter grid points and if it is not at level p then split it in 4 by selecting the 4 corresponding patches at the next $s+1$ level. For each of these new patches **Refine**(patch).

Figure 6 illustrates the determination of the global level, and Figure 7 the refinement of the patches. In this example $N_g = 9, N_p = 4, p = 5, A = 195$ and $s = 2$.

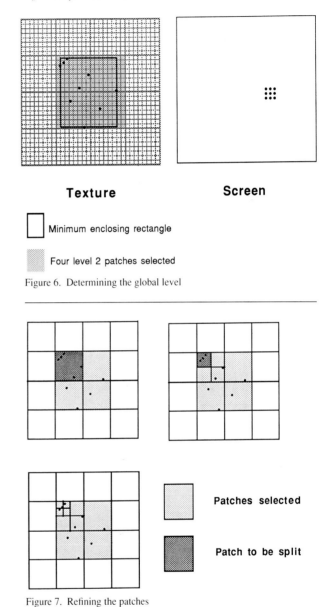

Texture   **Screen**

Minimum enclosing rectangle

Four level 2 patches selected

Figure 6. Determining the global level

Patches selected

Patch to be split

Figure 7. Refining the patches

We can establish the range of the number of patches actually selected. The smallest number is obtained when none of the initial patches are actually split. In this case about N_p patches are then used. The exact number depends on the effect of rounding the log in equation 5, but cannot be more than $4N_p$.

The worst case arises when patches have been split from level 0 down to level p. In this case, the last split occurred because there were at least 3 grid points in the patch. If there were more than 3 grid points involved at any level, then we would not have maximal splitting for all grid points, because the extra points are not credited for the creation of new patches. Therefore the worst case occurs when there are only 3 grid points present in the patch from level 0. They would then create $3p$ new patches from level 0 to level p. No other triple can create that many patches, since the first splitting, from level 0 to level 1, is already credited to the first triple. To simplify the analysis, we will then use the upper bound, which is obtained assuming that all the triples cause the maximum number of new patches. Figure 8 shows the situation for a patch at level 0 split down to level $p = 5$ by 3 filter grid points.

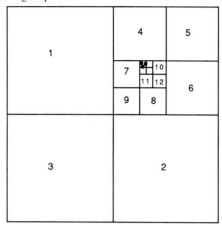

Figure 8. Maximum splitting of a patch

Therefore a maximum of $3p \dfrac{N_g}{3}$ new patches are created, and the maximum total number of patches is $4 N_p + p N_g$. We are therefore guaranteed a constant upper bound for a given resolution. The term p is proportional to the log of the resolution, and will not be very high (10 or 11 at most).

4.3. Discrete Textures

In most computer graphics applications (but not all) the texture is discrete and finite. A convenient formulation is to represent it by a finite array of delta pulses[Prat78] :

$$\sum_{m=0}^{2^p-1} \sum_{n=0}^{2^p-1} T(m\Delta u, n\Delta v) \; \delta(u-m\Delta u, v-n\Delta v).$$

Each discrete value can be written as $T_l(m,n)$. The double integral of the convolution then reduces to the sum

$$S_c = \sum_{m=0}^{2^p-1} \sum_{n=0}^{2^p-1} T_l(m,n) \; F(u_c-m\Delta u, v_c-n\Delta v).$$

It is generally assumed that the texel value represents a sample in the middle of the texel, that is $T_l(m,n)$ has effective coordinates $((m+0.5)\Delta u, (n+0.5)\Delta v)$. The C_{ij} for patch (k,l) at level s are then computed as

$$C_{ij} = \sum_{u=u_k}^{u_{k+1}} \sum_{v=v_l}^{v_{l+1}} T_l(m,n) \; B_i(u) B_j(v).$$

To normalize the C_{ij}, the sum of the coefficients multiplying the $T_l(k,l)$, that is products of the form $B_i(u)B_j(v)$, has to be computed and used to divide the entries in the corresponding NIL maps. The entries are thus of the same order of magnitude and require a precision similar to the one required by the texel values. In this respect they are similar to MIP map entries, and are less demanding than entries in a summed-

area table or a table using repeated integration, which require a higher precision.

4.4. Analytic Textures

In the case of textures given as continuous $T(u,v)$ functions, a double integral must be performed for the computation of the C_{ij} (Eq. 3). Since the double integral is taken over a square region in texture space, it is advantageous to use Green's theorem. It states that given functions $P(u,v)$ and $Q(u,v)$ which are continuously differentiable on $\mathbf{R}^2$, and given a closed path γ

$$\int_\gamma Pdu + Qdv = \iint_{\mathbf{R}^2} \left[\frac{\partial Q}{\partial u} - \frac{\partial P}{\partial v} \right] du \; dv.$$

The partial derivatives also must be continuous on $\mathbf{R}^2$. It is simpler at this point to use a $[0,1]$ range for u and v within a patch. The C_{ij} for patch (k,l) at level s are written as:

$$C_{ij} = \int_{u=0}^{1} \int_{v=0}^{1} T((k+u)r,(l+v)r) \; B_i(u) B_j(v) \; du \; dv$$

where r is the ratio between the size of patches at level p and the size at level s. Hence $r = 2^{p-s}$. If we can find a function $P(u,v)$ such that

$$\frac{\partial P(u,v)}{\partial v} = T((k+u)r, (l+v)r) \; B_j(v),$$

which means that

$$P(u,v) = \int T((k+u)r, (l+v)r) \; B_j(v) \; dv,$$

then by Green's theorem,

$$C_{ij} = -\int_\gamma B_i(u) \; P(u,v) \; du,$$

where γ is the path around the square $(0,0),(1,0),(1,1),(0,1)$. This reduces to the two terms:

$$C_{ij} = -\int_{u=0}^{1} B_i(u) \; P(u,0) \; du + \int_{u=0}^{1} B_i(u) \; P(u,1) \; du.$$

There are many commonly-used texture functions for which these integrals have closed-form solutions, and which therefore can be computed analytically at little cost.

It is important to note that with analytical textures the C_{ij} do not have to be precomputed, but can be computed "on the fly". There is also no ultimate resolution. A "bottom" level still has to be kept in the algorithm used to find the right level in the NIL maps (which are now "virtual" NIL maps) to limit the number of patches created. In the case where no closed-form solution for the integrals is available, or if the functions involved are expensive to compute, or if the mapping will be done often enough so that most of the levels and most of the patches will be used, precomputing the real NIL maps can still be the most efficient solution.

4.5. Interpolation of Textures

A situation intermediate between discrete textures and procedural textures arises when a continuous $T(u,v)$ is computed from a set of discrete $T_l(m,n)$. This is of course what is produced by a reconstruction filter, but in this case we still want the convolution of our filter with the reconstructed surface.

We will examine briefly the common case where the interpolation is done with a piece-wise polynomial interpolant. In this case the only difference from the preceding section is that Green's theorem has to applied piece-wise (since the functions involved have to be continuous over the region), and we have now two different situations: when the patches of the NIL maps are larger than the patches of the interpolant, which correspond to the case $s<p$, or $r = 2^{p-s}>1$, and when the patches of the interpolant are larger than the patches of the NIL maps, that is when $s>p$ and $r = 2^{p-s}<1$.

In the $s<p$ case the computation of the C_{ij} proceeds as in the discrete case, except that there is an effective integration over each interpolant patch within the NIL map patch. To give a specific example, assume that we have a discrete texture $T_I(m,n)$, which is bilinearly interpolated. To simplify the formula we will assume, as opposed to what we have done for discrete textures, that the $T_I(m,n)$ values are at the lower left corner of texel (m,n). The interpolated value is

$$T_i(m+u_t,n+v_t) = T_I(m,n)(1-u_t)(1-v_t) + T_I(m,n+1)(1-u_t)v_t$$
$$+ T_I(m+1,n)u_t(1-v_t) + T_I(m+1,n+1)u_tv_t.$$

It is important to distinguish the parameters of the interpolant within the texel (u_t,v_t) from the parameters of the NIL map patches (u_p,v_p). The relationship between them is:

$$kr + u_pr = m + u_t$$
$$lr + v_pr = n + v_t$$

for patch (k,l) at level s, $r = 2^{p-s}$, and texel (m,n). If $r>1$, it is best to let (u_t,v_t) range from 0 to 1, and express (u_p,v_p) as functions of them. If $s<1$, then it is best to use (u_p,v_p) and express (u_t,v_t) as functions of them.

One can then compute $P(u,v)$. For example, for the term C_{00} it is (to simplify (u_t,v_t) are written as (u,v)):

$$P(u,v) = T_I(m,n) (1-u) (av+bv^2+cv^3)$$
$$+ T_I(m,n+1) (1-u) (dv^2+ev^3)$$
$$+ T_I(m+1,n) u (av+bv^2+cv^3)$$
$$+ T_I(m+1,n+1) (dv^2+ev^3)$$

where a,b,c,d,e are expressions of r,k,l,m,n. The line integrals for C_{00} are:

$$-\int_0^1 (1+k - \frac{m+u}{r}) P(u, 0)\, du + \int_0^1 (1+k - \frac{m+u}{r}) P(u, 1)\, du.$$

In the case where $s>p$, the NIL maps are not actually precomputed but computed as needed. For the example above, the functions are the same but the variables used are now (u_p,v_p), which range from 0 to 1. The substitutions are

$$u_t = k r + u_pr - m,$$
$$v_t = l r + v_pr - n.$$

This allows an arbitrary magnification of the texture with correct filtering of the interpolated surface.

5. Examples of Applications

5.1. Approximating Filters

A Gaussian kernel,
$$F(x,y) = \frac{1}{2\pi\sigma^2} e^{-\frac{x^2+y^2}{2\sigma^2}},$$

has many qualities for filtering, but its main drawback is its infinite width of support. Using the NIL maps it is not such a problem, since a wide support can be used at little increased cost in number of patches. Figures 2 to 5 depict approximations of a Gaussian with polynomial bases of order 1 to 4. The top row of Figure 9 shows 128×128 pictures produced by filtering the original mandrill texture, using NIL maps with Catmull-Rom bicubic bases and an identity mapping between screen and texture. The σs are 1.0 and 0.3; the width of support is 4×4 pixels. It is easy to see the blurring of the image caused by the widening of the kernel. The second row of Figure 9 shows an approximation of a separable sinc filter:

$$F(x,y) = \frac{\omega^2}{\pi^2} \frac{\sin(\omega x)}{\omega x} \frac{\sin(\omega y)}{\omega y}.$$

This is the ideal reconstruction filter for textures that have had rectangular band-limiting, but is not used in practice because of its infinite width of support and negative lobes. The method used here is not affected by negative lobes, and the sinc filter can be used almost as easily as the Gaussian. The main difference is that the approximation errors are greater with low order bases. The examples given are for ω equal to $\pi/2$ and $\frac{3\pi}{2}$. The first zero is then at 2 and $\frac{2}{3}$ pixel respectively. The other parameters are the same as for the Gaussian filter. It is easy to see how much sharper and more detailed the pictures are compared to the Gaussian filter.

A *difference of Gaussians* or DOG has been used in image processing (mostly as an approximation of the Laplacian of a Gaussian) and to model some properties of the human visual system. Figure 10 shows pictures obtained by approximations of a Gaussian of $\sigma = 0.5$, another Gaussian of $\sigma = 1.0$, and the difference of the preceding two suitably normalized. Figure 11 shows the approximated surface.

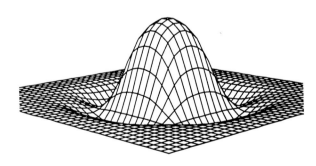

Figure 11. Approximation of a DOG

The last example is of a "rotated Gaussian". The kernel of a Gaussian filter has been rotated and stretched to simulate the effect of the texture rotating around a centre. The resulting image shown in Figure 12 simulates convincingly the motion blur which would be created by the texture rotating while a camera shutter is open. The kernel under the rotation takes the shape of a sickle shown in Figure 13, and this example illustrates how well a non-convex kernel is handled by the method.

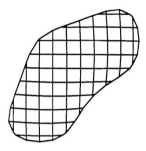

Figure 13. Kernel transformed by rotation

It is interesting to note that paradoxically a box filter is not well approximated by this method because of the discontinuities. Figure 14 shows a box filter approximated by Catmull-Rom bicubic. The error in the approximation is clearly visible. Of course one would not want to use this method for box filters anyway.

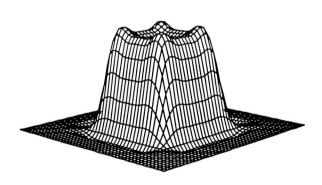

Figure 14. Approximation of a box filter by Catmull-Rom bicubic

5.2. Space-Variant Mappings

The perspective mapping is the most common and the most important space-variant mapping in computer graphics. Figure 15 shows the same old monkey in perspective (the plane of the texture is inclined 60 degrees from the vertical), and filtered by a sinc and a Gaussian filters with the same parameters as used in the preceding section. The picture in the middle was produced by a display system using MIP maps. It is easy to note how sharp are the pictures produced with the sinc filter with a small ω. Most techniques would considerably blur the top of the picture in these cases. Figure 16 depicts a slice through the top of the surface approximated for the Gaussian filter, illustrating the deformation of the kernel under the perspective transformation. This is a filter

for a pixel in the lower left region of the picture.

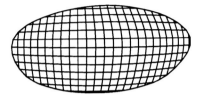

Figure 16. Distortion of a Gaussian kernel under perspective

Another challenging example is *conformal mapping*. The mapping in this example takes a rectangle (again the original mandrill) to a dodecagon while conserving all angles and continuity. For more details on the mapping see [FiFC87]. In this case the mapped kernels vary in shape and size from point to point. Figure 17 shows the results, again with the same two filters. It is easy to follow the lines of the long hairs around the mouth and to see the compression of the texture around the eyebrows, as well as the expansions near some of the vertices of the dodecagon.

6. Conclusions

The basic goal of achieving constant-time filtering with arbitrary space-variant kernels has been met. The most notable aspects of the technique are that it does not involve approximations of the convolution, but only approximations of the filters' surfaces, that it can be applied to discrete as well as analytic textures, and that it allows the use of sophisticated filters without having to pay too high a price.

While the examples we give are relatively simple, it is important to remember that the mappings can be composed, and a mixture of conformal, perspective and/or environment mappings would be handled in the same way.

Since the method is at first glance rather complex, and involves the computation and storage of $\frac{4}{3}M^2$ terms per texel, a legitimate question is whether it is practical in simple cases. First, the technique can be simple. The error results show clearly that bilinear approximation is probably sufficient for most cases, and in this case an approximation with 16 patches requires 64 terms. There is therefore a gain over a direct convolution if the filter covers more than 64 texels on average. This is met, for example, if we filter a 256×256 texture down to a 128×128 image with a 4×4 pixel width of support. If we compare to MIP maps, the computation and storage costs are multiplied by M^2. The gain is in the additional flexibility and filtering quality. Even in the case where $M = 1$, where the storage is the same as in straight MIP maps, the adaptive subdivision inherent in the methods improves the result.

As mentioned before, in animation a small gain per frame quickly recoups even a large preprocessing cost, and for any texture whose on-screen size varies by a few binary orders of magnitude during a sequence there will be a net saving no matter which order is used.

Glossary

Symbol	Meaning	Relations
u,v	Texture coordinates	$0 \leq u,v < 2^p$
x,y	Screen Coordinates	
p	Texture Resolution	
s	Level in NIL map	
r	Linear ratio between levels p and s	$r = 2^{p-s}$
(i,j)	Indices for basis functions	
(k,l)	Indices for patches	
(m,n)	Indices for texels	
(u_t,v_t)	Coordinates at level p	$0 \leq u_t,v_t < 2^p$
u_p	Coordinate in patch (k,l) at level s	$kr+u_p r = m+u_t$
v_p	Coordinate in patch (k,l) at level s	$lr+v_p r = n+v_t$
$T(u,v)$	Texture function	
$T_I(m,n)$	Discrete texture samples	
$F(u,v)$	Filter in texture space	
(u_c,v_c)	Center of filter in texture space	
τ	Texture to screen mapping	$(x,y) = \tau(u,v)$
τ^{-1}	Screen to texture mapping	$(u,v) = \tau^{-1}(x,y)$
M	Order of polynomial basis	Degree $= M-1$
$B_i(u)$	Basis function	$0 \leq i < M$
b_{ij}	Coefficients of $B_i(u)B_j(v)$ for given filter	
C_{ij}	Precomputed convolution terms	
S_c	Convolution of texture with filter	Eq. (1)
S_a	Approximation to S_c	Eq. (4)

Acknowledgements

We acknowledge the support of NSERC through operating grants, a University Research Fellowship and an equipment grant which considerably facilitated this research. The first author was visiting at Xerox PARC and the second author was visiting at CUI, University of Geneva, when this work began, and they are grateful for the support these institutions provided.

References

Crow81.
F.C. Crow, "Summed-Area Tables for Texture Mapping," *Computer Graphics*, vol. 18(3), pp. 207-212, July 1984.

FiFC87.
E. Fiume, A. Fournier, and V. Canale, "Conformal Texture Mapping," *Proceedings of Eurographics '87*, pp. 53-64, August 1987. Elsevier Science Publishers (North Holland) (August 24-28, 1987, Amsterdam, The Netherlands).

GrHe86.
N. Greene and P. S. Heckbert, "Creating Raster Omnimax Images from Multiple Perspective Views Using the Elliptical Weighted Average Filter," *IEEE Computer Graphics and Applications*, vol. 6, no. 6, pp. 21-27, June 1986.

Gree86.
N. Greene, "Environment Mapping and Other Applications of World Projections," *IEEE Computer Graphics and Applications*, vol. 6(11), pp. 21-29, November 1986.

Heck86a.
P.S. Heckbert, "Filtering By Repeated Integration," *Computer Graphics*, vol. 20(4), pp. 315-321, August 1986.

Heck86b.
P.S. Heckbert, "Survey of Texture Mapping," *IEEE Computer Graphics and Applications*, vol. 6(11), pp. 56-67, November 1986.

KaUl81.
J. Kajiya and M. Ullner, "Filtering High Quality Text for Display on Raster Scan Devices," *Computer Graphics*, vol. 15, no. 3, pp. 7-15, 1981. (ACM SIGGRAPH'81 Conference Proceedings, July 1981, Dallas, Texas)

KiON87.
K. Kishimoto, K. Onaga, and E. Nakamae, "Theoretical Assessments of Mean Square Errors of Antialiasing Filters," *Computer Vision, Graphics and Image Processing*, vol. 37, pp. 428-437, 1987.

NaFo87.
A. Naiman and A. Fournier, "Rectangular Convolution for Fast Filtering of Characters," *Computer Graphics*, vol. 21, no. 4, pp. 233-242, 1987. (ACM SIGGRAPH'87 Conference Proceedings, July 27-31, 1987, Anaheim, California).

Prat78.
W.K. Pratt, *Digital Image Processing*, Wiley-Interscience, 1978.

Will83.
L. Williams, "Pyramidal Parametrics," *Computer Graphics*, vol. 17(3), pp. 1-11, July 1983.

DuSS78.
W. Dungan, A. Stenger, and G. Sutty, "Texture Tiles Consideration for Raster Graphics," *Computer Graphics*, vol. 12, no. 3, pp. 130-134, 1978. (ACM SIGGRAPH'78 Conference Proceedings, July 1978, Atlanta, Georgia)

CaRo74.
E. Catmull and R. Rom, "A Class of Local Interpolating Splines," in *Computer-Aided Geometric Design*, ed. R. F. Riesenfeld, pp. 317-326, Academic Press, 1974.

RoKa76.
A. Rosenfeld and A. C. Kak, *Digital Picture Processing*, Academic Press, 1976.

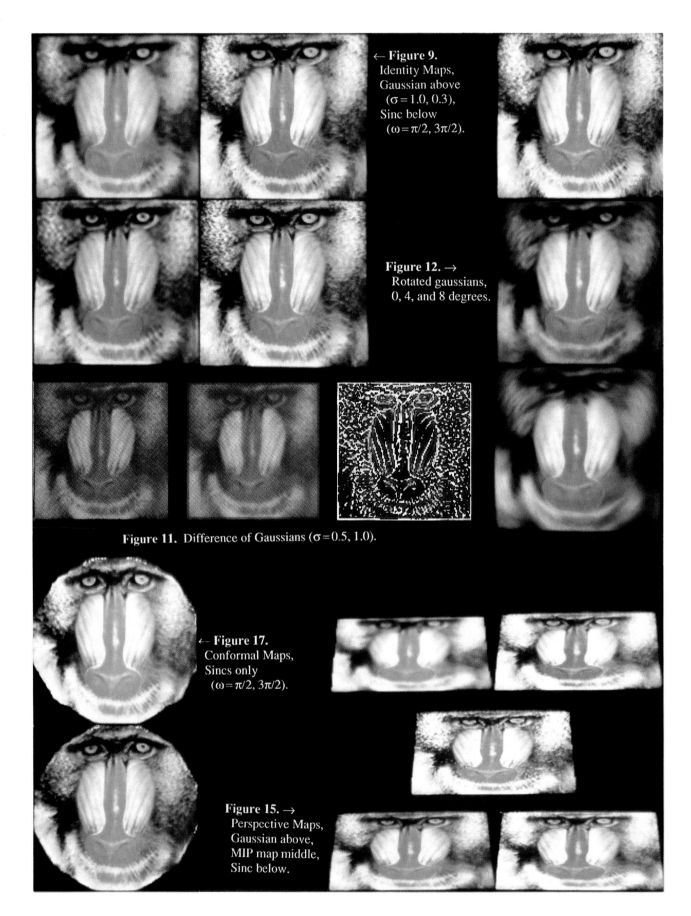

← Figure 9.
Identity Maps,
Gaussian above
($\sigma = 1.0, 0.3$),
Sinc below
($\omega = \pi/2, 3\pi/2$).

Figure 12. →
Rotated gaussians,
0, 4, and 8 degrees.

Figure 11. Difference of Gaussians ($\sigma = 0.5, 1.0$).

← Figure 17.
Conformal Maps,
Sincs only
($\omega = \pi/2, 3\pi/2$).

Figure 15. →
Perspective Maps,
Gaussian above,
MIP map middle,
Sinc below.

High-Performance Polygon Rendering

Kurt Akeley
Tom Jermoluk

Silicon Graphics, Inc.
2011 North Shoreline Boulevard
Mountain View, CA 94039-7311

ABSTRACT

This paper describes a system architecture for realtime display of shaded polygons. Performance of 100,000 lighted, 4-sided polygons per second is achieved. Vectors and points draw at the rate of 400,000 per second. High-speed pan and zoom, alpha blending, realtime video input, and antialiased lines are supported. The architecture heavily leverages parallelism in several forms: pipeline, vector, and array processing. It is unique in providing efficient and balanced graphics that support interactive design and manipulation of solid models. After an overview of algorithms and computational requirements, we describe the details of the implementation. Finally, the unique features enabled by the architecture are highlighted.

CR Categories and Subject Descriptors: B.2.1 [Arithmetic and Logic Structures]: Design Styles - Parallel, Pipeline; C.1.2 [Processor Architectures]: Multiprocessors - Parallel processors, Pipeline processors; I.3.1 [Computer Graphics]: Hardware Architecture - Raster Display Devices.

Additional Key Words and Phrases: Graphics Systems.

©1988   ACM-0-89791-275-6/88/008/0239 $00.75

1. Introduction

Traditional 3D graphics workstations have concentrated on the hardware that transforms points and lines from object-space to screen-space. As users' needs for display of realistic solid objects have increased, demands on graphics architectures have changed significantly. New challenges include increases in transformation rate, incorporation of realtime illumination calculations, and dramatic increases in pixel fill rates.

Contemporary workstations have attempted to satisfy these new demands using a variety of architectures. Swanson and Thayer [11] describe a system which incorporates parallel pixel processors in its raster subsystem. A parallel geometry system is described by Torborg [12]. The lineage of these and other contemporary graphics systems can be traced to works by Clark [3], Clark and Hannah [2], and eventually to Fuchs and Johnson [5].

Our specific goals for the performance and capability of the new architecture were:

- *100,000 polygons per second.* The polygons are RGB, 4-sided, 10x10 pixels, lighted, Gouraud shaded [6], arbitrarily rotated, Z-buffered, clip tested, projected, and rendered into one of multiple, possibly overlapping, windows at an instantaneous rate of 100,000 per second.

- *10 frames per second.* Realtime systems must be able to draw and display at rates exceeding 10 Hz.

- *Window support.* User productivity is optimized by a system that supports multiple fully independent windows.

First we describe our view of the general algorithmic problem of rendering 100,000 polygons per second, paying particular attention to the computational requirements of each step of the process. Then we describe a novel architecture to achieve the goals. Finally we present several unique features that were realized from the implementation.

2. Problem Description

The floating-point performance and pixel fill rates required for interactive display of solids are both exceptional. By examining each component of the problem we show that at least 40 million floating-point operations per second, and fill rates exceeding 10 million pixels per second, are required to render 100,000 polygons per second. The problem components are:

1. Transfer vertex data from memory to the graphics subsystem.

2. Transform vertex coordinates.

3. Transform vertex normals.

4. Light each vertex.

5. Clip each vertex.

6. Project each vertex.

7. Map vertex coordinates to the screen.

8. Fill the resulting screen-space polygons, interpolating color and depth.

9. Clip all drawing against the visible window boundaries.

10. Be prepared to quickly swap drawing contexts at any time.

11. Continually scan the frame buffer at screen refresh rates, interpreting each pixel appropriately as a function of the process to which it belongs.

2.1 Transfer Data

Achieving our goal of 100,000 4-vertex polygons per second requires that 400,000 vertex specifications per second be transferred to the graphics subsystem. A lighted vertex specification includes 6 floating-point values: 3 (x,y,z) specify the vertex position, and 3 (nx,ny,nz) specify the vertex normal direction. The required data rate is therefore:

$$400,000 \text{ } (xform/sec) \times 6 \text{ } (words/xform) \times 4 \text{ } (bytes/word) \approx 10 \text{ } Mbytes/sec$$

2.2 Transform Vertexes

Homogeneous 3D vertexes include 4 components, and are transformed by multiplication by a 4x4 matrix. This vector operation requires 16 floating-point multiplications and 12 floating-point additions. The computation rate is therefore:

$$400,000 \text{ } (xform/sec) \times (16 + 12) \text{ } (flop/xform) \approx 11 \text{ } Mflops$$

If it is known that the w component of the vertex to be transformed is 1.0 (a common case with 3D homogeneous data) then 4 multiplications can be eliminated, resulting in a computation rate of:

$$400,000 \times (12 + 12) \approx 9.5 \text{ } Mflops$$

2.3 Transform Normals

Plane equations are properly transformed by the inverse-transpose of the vertex matrix. This transformation has the same expense as the full vertex transformation. It is unnecessary, however, for lighting calculations.

Vertex normals are plane equations stripped of distance information. Because normals are not position sensitive, translation information in the vertex matrix need not be included in a normal matrix. Also, because vertex normals are normalized to unit length before they are used, uniform scale information need not be applied to a normal matrix. Thus only rotations and non-uniform scales of the vertex matrix are applied, by inverse-transpose, to the normal matrix.

A 3 by 3 normal matrix supports all the required information, and is used to transform the 3-component lighting normals. This transformation requires 9 floating-point multiplications and 6 floating-point additions, for a total computation rate of:

$$400,000 \times (9 + 6) \approx 6 \text{ } Mflops$$

As was indicated above, normals must be unit length before they are used in lighting calculations. Although it will in some cases be possible to avoid explicit normalization,[1] we compute the expense of this operation. Sum of squares requires 3 floating-point multiplications and 2 floating-point additions. We conservatively estimate the cost of reciprocal square root calculation to be twice that of simple reciprocal calculation: 8 floating-point operations. Finally, each of the three components is multiplied by the newly computed factor. The approximate required computation rate for normalization is:

$$400,000 \times (3 + 2 + 16 + 3) \approx 9.5 \text{ } Mflops$$

2.4 Light Vertexes

Because the target polygons are Gouraud shaded, lighting calculations are required only at the vertexes of polygons, never in their interiors. Transformed vertex and normal information, current light positions and colors, surface properties, and specific lighting-model properties for each vertex are resolved to a single RGB triple. These triples will be interpolated across the interiors of projected polygons.

---

1. *Normals specified with unit length, no non-uniform scales.*

The lighting model that we chose for our performance requirement estimates is:

- A single light - infinitely distant

- A viewer - infinitely distant

- Ambient, diffuse, and specular reflection components

The equation

$$C_{object} = C_{ambient} + C_{diffuse}C_{light}(N \cdot L) + C_{specular}C_{light}(N \cdot H)^n$$

is executed 3 times, once each for red, green, and blue (all C's are RGB vectors). Dot products are evaluated only once. Including tests for overflow, each optimized lighting computation requires 12 floating-point multiplications, 10 floating-point additions, 5 floating-point comparisons, and a table lookup. The total compute power required is:

$$400,000 \times (12 + 10 + 5 + 1) \approx 11 \text{ } Mflops$$

2.5 Clip

Polygons are correctly clipped in all cases using the Sutherland-Hodgman Algorithm [10]. This algorithm requires one floating-point compare per clipping plane, 6 compares per vertex in a 3D system. Additional floating-point operations are required only in the event of actual clipping, i.e. infrequently. In either case the algorithm execution time is dominated by data movement and branching, not by floating-point operations.

Using proper optimization to avoid unnecessary clipping, the floating-point demands for clipping are:

$$400,000 \times 6 \approx 2.5 \text{ } Mflops$$

2.6 Project

Each vertex is projected in homogeneous space by division of its x, y, and z components by its w component. This is accomplished most efficiently by first computing $1/w$, then multiplying each of x, y, and z by this factor. We asserted previously that computing a reciprocal requires 8 floating-point operations. Thus perspective division requires a total of 11 floating-point operations, at an aggregate rate of:

$$400,000 \times (8 + 3) \approx 4.5 \text{ } Mflops$$

2.7 Viewport and Fix

Projected vertexes are mapped to screen coordinates with a simple affine calculation. Each of the three vertex components is scaled by an independent scale factor, offset by an independent offset, and converted to integer screen coordinates. The total floating-point calculation rate is:

$$400,000 \times (3 + 3 + 3) \approx 3.5 \text{ } Mflops$$

The total floating-point performance required to convert object-space coordinate vertexes and normals to screen-space coordinates and colors is:

Operation	Mflops
Vertex Transformation	9.5
Normal Transformation	6
Normal Normalization	9.5
Lighting	11
Clipping	2.5
Projection	4.5
Viewport	3.5
Total	46.5

2.8 Fill and Smooth Shade Screen Space Polygons

Screen-space vertexes, now interpreted as polygon vertexes, are used to specify the boundaries of frame buffer regions to be smooth shaded. Although the details of this shade/fill operation are implementation dependent, we can safely describe some of the problems that will be encountered. They are:

- *Test for convexity.* A substantially more complex algorithm is required to fill concave polygons.

- *Decompose to trapezoids.* It will almost always be desirable to reduce the full polygons to collections of screen-aligned trapezoids, whose parallel edges are in the direction of preferred fill in the frame buffer.

- *Calculate slopes.* Slopes for all parameters to be interpolated must be computed. Substantial integer precision must be maintained if interpolation errors are to be avoided.

- *Write to the frame buffer.* A huge memory bandwidth is required to fill polygons at the rate of 100,000 per second. Our benchmark 10 pixel by 10 pixel polygons fill at 10 Million pixels per second. A substantially higher fill rate is desirable for larger polygons. Screen clear, really just filling a large, screen-aligned polygon, demands the highest fill rate.

2.9 Clip all Drawing Against Visible Window Boundaries

The clipping and viewport operations described above will limit polygon filling to a screen-aligned rectangular region, or *window*. They are not sufficient, however, if the window is non-rectangular, either because it is obscured by another window, or because it wasn't rectangular to begin with. In some systems the problem of obscured windows is deferred by always rendering into rectangular regions, then assembling the final screen image on the fly. While attractive in many respects, this solution does nothing to solve the fundamental problem of non-rectangular windows, and is expensive in terms of memory consumption.

2.10 Change Contexts

The entire graphics system must be prepared, at any moment, to save the drawing state of the current context and restore the state of a previously interrupted context. This operation must happen quickly in most cases, but must also be able to support a huge number, perhaps hundreds, of independent contexts. Support for a *working set* of processes is therefore desirable.

2.11 Scan Frame Buffer

Although the bandwidth required to scan a high-resolution frame buffer at 60 Hertz is enormous (pixel rates of 110 to 125 MHz are standard today) the availability of inexpensive Video RAMs allows this bandwidth to be supported with little engineering effort. We don't emphasize this problem here. Rather, we concentrate on the issue of multiple windows as it pertains to frame buffer output.

It is desirable that imaging to separate windows be as independent as possible. Most important, perhaps, is that windows be able to select and alter their buffer modes independently. Single and double buffer images must coexist, and double buffer images must swap buffers independently. Further, if pixels can be interpreted in different ways, it is important that the interpretation in each window also be independent.

An important exception is color mapping, the process of interpreting pixel values as indexes into a table of RGB triples. While it would seem that each process should have its own table, it is sometimes desirable to share table entries between processes. Thus a single table, large enough to supply separate areas to processes that desire independence, yet shared by all processes, is an appropriate solution.

3. Architectural Solution

Our graphics subsystem is a part of a complete workstation whose host processor comprises multiple RISC-based CPUs. The CPUs and the graphics interface share a high-speed 64-bit synchronous bus of proprietary design. While the primary design goal of the bus was multiprocessor support, it includes special support for data transfer to the graphics subsystem.

The graphics system itself is partitioned into four pipelined subsystems. In order of data flow these are:

1. *Geometry subsystem.* Supports all floating-point operations. Transforms data from object-space coordinates to screen-space coordinates.

2. *Scan conversion subsystem.* Interprets screen-space coordinate vertexes as points, lines, and polygons, and generates appropriate fill instructions. Interpolates color and depth data across lines and polygons.

3. *Raster subsystem.* Maintains a 1280 by 1024 frame buffer of 96-bit pixels. Executes pixel algorithms such as replace, depth conditional replace (Z-buffer), and blend.

4. *Display subsystem.* Continually scans the frame buffer to supply video data to the monitor. Each pixel is interpreted individually as a function of the window to which it belongs.

Each of these four subsystems, as well as the host interface, is described in detail below.

3.1 Data Transfer

As we have seen, the graphics subsystem consumes data at roughly 10 Mbytes per second. The 64 Mbyte per second synchronous bus that connects the host processors to the graphics subsystem is able to handle this load. Thus large blocks of geometric data can be transferred across this bus to the graphics subsystem. Such transfers, however, are not consistent with the programming model desired for the machine.

The target graphics library includes commands such as *vertex(x,y,z)* and *normal(nx,ny,nz)*. Each command is implemented as a subroutine in the language of the calling application program. Each specifies data from an arbitrary structure. Graphics programs using commands such as these can operate directly from application data bases. Programs need not be 'compiled' into display lists, and therefore can traverse data under complete application control. Finally, because all traversal code and data reside in main memory, there is essentially no limit to the size of either.

We seek a solution that retains the desired properties of *immediate-mode* graphics, and supports extremely high-performance graphics. Our answer is to create new commands that operate on 2, 3, and 4-component vectors, rather than on scalar values. Thus *vertex(x,y,z)* becomes *vertex(xyz)*, where *xyz* is the address of three adjacent floating-point values. Hardware support allows each host processor to make a single memory reference when dealing with such a vector. The memory and synchronous bus deliver the data to the graphics subsystem in a single burst, making optimum use of the available bus bandwidth. Vectors that straddle page boundaries are detected and handled automatically.

By providing support for program controlled data transfer to the graphics subsystem at rates far in excess of 10 Mbytes per second, we allow for both future increases in graphics performance, and for desirable inefficiencies in program execution. One such inefficiency is shared graphics libraries. While such libraries exact a performance penalty at each call, they greatly reduce code size, both on disk and in memory, and also support object code compatibility between machines with different graphics subsystems.

3.2 Geometry Subsystem

The geometry subsystem comprises a single conversion and FIFO module, followed by 5 identical floating-point processors (Geometry Engines®). These 6 processors are organized as a single pipeline. Each executes a specific subset of the rendering algorithm, minimizing microcode space requirements.

3.2.1 Conversion and FIFO Module This module accepts coordinate data in 4 formats: 16-bit integer, 24-bit integer, 32-bit IEEE floating-point, and 64-bit IEEE double precision floating-point. Color data are accepted as packed integers as well as in the coordinate formats. All data are converted to 32-bit IEEE floating-point format for consumption by the Geometry Engines. Hardware format conversion supports direct transfer of data from user structures to the graphics subsystem without performance penalty.

A 512-word FIFO precedes the conversion module. The hardware interrupts when a *high water* mark is passed, allowing user programs to transfer data to the graphics subsystem without concern for flow control. On interrupt, the operating system blocks the user program until the FIFO empties past a *low water* mark. Thus transfer rate is adversely affected by flow control protocol only when it has already exceeded the ability of the graphics system to accept data.

3.2.2 Geometry Engine Each of the five Geometry Engines is an identical module capable of 20 million single-precision floating-point operations per second (Mflops). Each includes separate high-speed microcode and data memories. The engines accept and output commands accompanied by up to 4 data words. Command interpretation is accomplished by program jump, followed by normal program counter operations. Hardware support in each engine includes:

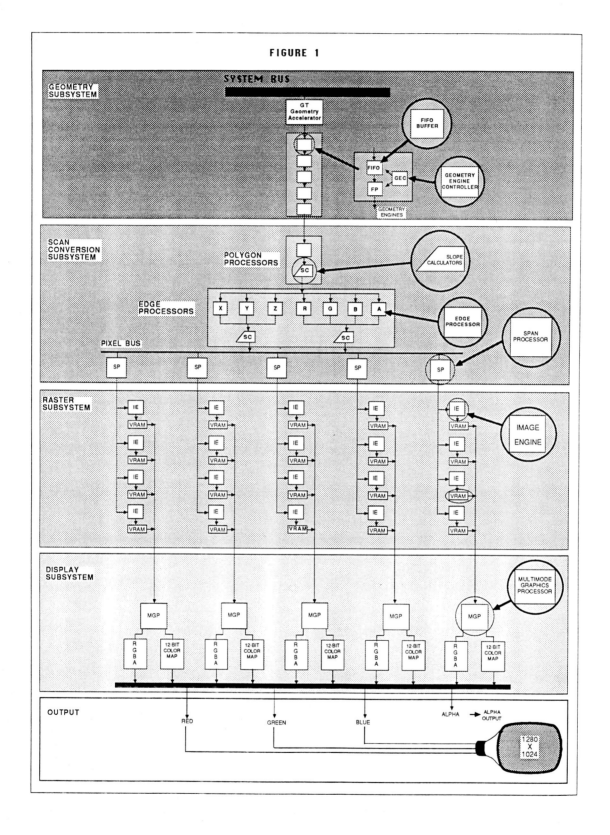

FIGURE 1

- *Flow control*. Microcode ignores the issues of command availability, and of the subsequent engine's ability to accept commands. Hardware blocking is provided for both cases.

- *FIFO input buffer*. Each engine includes 4 command buffers at its input. Buffers store up to 4 data words and a command address.

- *Pipeline support*. Although the Geometry Engine has 6 internal pipeline stages, individual microcode instructions specify complete operations, including data sources, operations to be performed, and data destinations.

- *Concurrent command execution*. The flow control and branch hardware support concurrent command (as well as instruction) execution.

The above, taken together, allow each engine to operate efficiently. The pipeline sustains the required 40-50 Mflops floating-point rate with 5 modules whose aggregate peak rate is 100 Mflops, an efficiency approaching 50 percent. This efficiency is not achieved in more general purpose vector processors, especially when the vectors are of 3 to 4 element length.

Graphics tasks are distributed among the 5 Geometry Engines as follows:

1. Matrix and normal transformation. Matrix and normal stacks. Normal normalization.

2. Lighting calculations.

3. Clip testing.

4. Perspective division. Clipping (when required).

5. Viewport transformation. Color clamping to a maximum value. Depthcue calculations.

3.3 Scan Conversion Subsystem

Screen coordinates sent from the geometry subsystem to the Scan Conversion Subsystem specify the vertexes of points, lines, and polygons. The Scan Conversion Subsystem performs the calculations required to reduce vertex data to individual pixels. Each pixel is assigned an x, y, and z coordinate and an r, g, b, and α color value. Color and z data are always interpolated linearly between vertexes and between the edges of polygons.

The task of scan-converting polygons is partitioned into three separate processors within the Scan Conversion Subsystem. The first two of these processors, the Polygon and Edge processors, use a pseudo floating-point representation to maintain coordinate integrity when calculating slopes. In addition, the y coordinates of polygon edges are computed to 1/8 pixel tolerance. All depth and color component iterations are first corrected to the nearest pixel center, then iterated in full-pixel steps. As a result, iterated color and depth values remain planar across polygonal surfaces, and subsequent Z-buffer calculations result in clean intersections.

Vertex data are not passed directly from the geometry subsystem to the Scan Conversion Subsystem, but rather are accumulated in one of two 256-vertex buffers. Vertex representations in this buffer are always the same, regardless of the operating mode of the system. Hardware on both the Geometry and Scan sides of the buffer is optimized to operate on these vertexes. Thus, the Polygon Processor receives entire polygons, rather than individual vertexes. It operates on vertexes directly from this buffer, avoiding unnecessary copying and interpretation.

The Polygon Processor both sorts vertexes from left to right and checks for convexity in one simple, pipelined operation. The sorted vertexes are decomposed into trapezoids. Slopes of y, z, r, g, b, and α are computed relative to delta x. Coordinates and slopes for each edge are passed to the Edge Processor. Trapezoid edges are handles at the rate of 1 per microsecond.

The Edge Processor iterates along the top and bottom edges of the trapezoid, generating at each iteration the top and bottom coordinates of a single *span*.[2] Spans are always iterated bottom to top. Therefore hardware

---

2. *We refer to vertical lines of pixels as* spans, *horizontal lines as* scans.

SCAN CONVERSION SUBSYSTEM

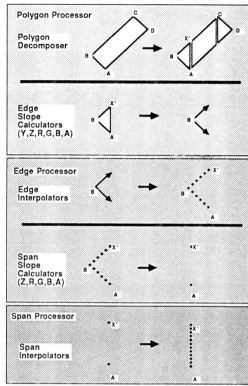

FIGURE 2

is provided to swap span ends as necessary, both avoiding a complex test at trapezoid decomposition time, and correctly handling *bow-tie* polygons, which occur frequently at surface silhouettes.

The color, y, and z edge components comprise 2 vectors which are iterated in parallel by multiple, proprietary engines. Spans are generated at the rate of 2 per microsecond.

The y components of span endpoints are computed to 1/8 pixel accuracy. Color and depth slopes are computed using delta y to this accuracy. This slope is then used to iterate to the nearest pixel center. The final span definition comprises the corrected initial color and depth values, the color and depth slopes, the integer x and y values of the bottom pixel, and the span length.

The Edge Processor delivers each span to one of five Span Processors. Each Span Processor manages every fifth column of pixels in the frame buffer. Since spans generated from a single polygon are always adjacent, the span processing load is evenly distributed across the five Span Processors. Each Span Processor iterates through its span using the initial and slope values provided, treating color and z span components as a vector. Pixel specifications are generated at the rate of 8 per microsecond. Thus the aggregate fill rate of the 5 Span Processors is 40 million pixels per second (Z-buffered).

3.4 Raster Subsystem

The Raster Subsystem contains 20 Image Engines TM, each of which is an independent state machine that controls 1/20th of the frame buffer memory. Groups of 4 Image Engines are driven by each Span Processor. The array of Image Engines tiles the frame buffer in a 5-wide, 4-high, pattern.

Bitplane memory is organized into 5 banks, comprising a total of 96 bits per pixel. The banks are arranged as follows:

- *Image banks*. Two banks of 32 bits each, organized as 8 bits each of red, green, blue, and alpha data.

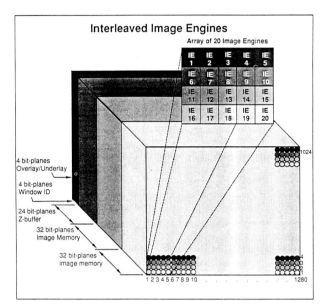

FIGURE 3

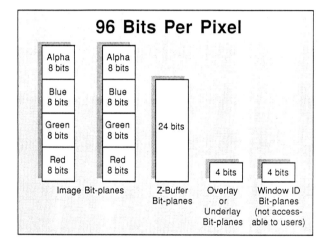

FIGURE 4

- *Depth bank.* One bank of 24 bits. Stores 24-bit integer depth information when used in conjunction with the Image Engine Z-buffer pixel algorithm. It is also available for image data.

- *Overlay bank.* One bank of 4 bits. Two bits are reserved for the window manager.

- *Window ID bank.* One bank of 4 bits, used by the window manager to tag pixels based on the drawing process to which they belong.

Image Engines operate as specialized memory controllers, supporting video RAM refresh, display refresh, and a handful of pixel access algorithms. These algorithms include:

- *Replace.* Replace the destination color with the source color.

- *Z-buffer.* Compare the source and destination z values. If the test passes[3] replace the destination color and z with the source color and z,

- *Z-buffer blend.* Like Z-buffer, but replace the destination color with a linear combination of the source and destination colors.

- *High-speed clear.* Simple replace available only for large, screen-aligned rectangles.

Although the Image Engines are simple machines, their parallel operation and multiple algorithms result in extremely powerful pixel fill operation. Their aggregate performance for the various pixel algorithms is:

Pixel Algorithm	Fill Rate Mpixel/sec
Replace	80
Z-buffer	40
Z-buffer with blending	10
High-speed clear	160

3.5 Display Subsystem

The Display Subsystem receives pixel data from the frame buffer, interprets it, and routes the resulting red, green, blue, and alpha data to the Digital-to-Analog converters for display. Five Multimode Graphics Processors (MGPs) operate in parallel, one assigned to the pixels controlled by each Span Processor. These MGPs receive all 64 image bank bits, the 4 auxiliary bank bits, and the 4 window ID bits for each pixel. They interpret the image and auxiliary bits as a function of the window ID bits, using an internal 16-entry table.

3.6 Context Switching

The graphics subsystem is designed to support context switching with minimal overhead. Because significant quantities of state are accumulated in each of the 5 Geometry Engines, each maintains complete context for 16 independent processes in its local data memory. The Geometry Engines are also able to dump and restore context to and from a host processor, allowing more than 16 processes to share the hardware. Thus a *working set* of up to 16 processes is supported, with essentially no limit to the total number of processes.

Because the Edge, Span, and Image Processors are unable to return state information, the few states stored in these processors are shadowed by the Polygon Processor. The Polygon Processor state, including shadow state, is minimal, and is therefore maintained by a host CPU.

4. Performance

We achieved our polygon performance and quality objectives, including operation in a window environment. The subsystems used to achieve this goal are carefully balanced in performance, resulting in a cost effective solution. Vertexes are transformed and lighted at the rate of 400,000 per second, just matching the desired rate of 100,000 4-vertex polygons per second. The Polygon Processor sorts the vertexes of 4-vertex polygons, and computes slopes for 4 edges, in just under 10 microseconds, again just meeting the required performance. The edge processor iterates along edges and generates spans at the rate of 2 spans per microsecond, slightly faster than required to generate 14 spans in 10 microseconds. Spans are iterated and pixels generated at the aggregate rate of 40 million per second, four times the rate needed to meet the performance objective, but invaluable for smoothing the performance transition between small and large polygons.

Some performance notes for various operations follow:

- *Polygons.* Because the system is balanced to render lighted, smooth shaded polygons, there is no performance benefit for not using these features. Thus flat shaded, smooth shaded but unlighted, and lighted 4-side polygons all render at the target rate of 100,000 per second. Small triangles render at 120,000 per second, again regardless of mode. Large polygons render at rates limited by the 40 million pixel per second fill rate.

- *Vectors.* The draw rate of short vectors is transformation limited, resulting in 400,000 connected vectors per second, or 200,000 unconnected vectors per second. Long vector rates are limited by the 8 million pixel per second fill rate (16 million with the Z-buffer disabled).

- *Window clear.* The performance of even moderately complex animations can be limited by the time required to clear the window. The special 160 million pixel per second fill rate, available only for window clear, allows a screen-size window to be cleared in 8.2

---

3. *Any combination of greater than, equal to, and less than can be specified .*

milliseconds. Thus full screen animations running at 10 Hz lose only 8% of their draw time to screen clear. Even 30 Hz animations lose only 25% of their draw time.

- *Pixel access.* An important ancillary function of 3D graphics is high-speed host access to the frame buffer. This is useful for image display and storage, image convolution, paint programs, and many other applications. The new raster architecture supports host read and write rates of 5 million pixels per second.

5. Special Features

Our design goal achieved, let us now consider some other features of the new graphics architecture.

5.1 Pan and Zoom

Typical raster systems handle pan and zoom as a display process by altering the fetching of data for the monitor. Frame buffer scan lines are output multiple times to achieve vertical zoom, and are output at reduced rates to achieve horizontal zoom. Initial pixel addresses are altered to achieve horizontal and vertical pan. In all cases the video data rate is either reduced or unaffected. Thus, while the implementation is complex, it makes no performance demands on the hardware.

This typical pan and zoom implementation, however, has some undesirable properties:

- It either operates on the entire screen, which is unacceptable in a window environment, or it becomes unmanageably complex.

- The effort and cost expended solving pan and zoom in this manner do not contribute to the machine in any other way.

The second point is of particular interest. We prefer solutions that have a synergistic effect on the performance of the entire machine.

Recall the bus that connects the Edge Processor to the five Span Processors. This *pixelbus* transmits span definitions during polygon fill, but is also designed to support pixel transfers during line fill. (The Edge Processor fills lines as though each was a single trapezoid edge, generating pixels at the rate of 8 (Z-buffered) or 16 million per second.)

The addition of a small pixel cache on the *pixelbus* allows pixels to be read and written in blocks large enough to achieve performance roughly equal to the peak *pixelbus* rates:

Operation	Mpixel/sec
read	5.3
write	16.0

Because write cycles greatly outnumber read cycles when the zoom factor is large, fill rates approach the higher write rate as the zoom factor is increased. The fill rates for a variety of zoom factors are:

Zoom Factor	Mpixel/sec
1	4.0
2	9.1
3	12.0
4	13.5
8	15.3

With this performance it is possible to zoom 1/4 of the screen by a factor of 2 at the rate of 7 frames per second. Smaller areas, common in window-capable systems, easily zoom at 30 frames per second. Because the effects of pan and zoom are limited to a single window, or to multiple windows with independent factors if desired, the full screen with all its windows remains a useful resource.

High-speed pixel copy leverages *pixelbus* throughput, which was also required for line drawing. By emphasizing high-speed pixel read and write, we improve the performance of transfers between host memory and the frame buffer, and also support real-time video input.

5.2 Window ID Masking

Each pixel in the frame buffer includes a 4-bit ID field that is unique to the process that controls that pixel. Previous architectures [9] have used this per-pixel window ID field to control interpretation of pixel contents at display time.[4] Such an ID, read out and interpreted as a part of the display process, easily supports independent buffer mode specification on a per-pixel basis. Windows can independently select single or double buffer operation, and double buffer windows can swap buffers independently. Colorindex or RGB operation is also selected independently on a per-window basis. Thus, while the notion of a pixel ID is not new, its use as a drawing mask is.

The new graphics hardware includes pipelined hardware that tests the ID of each pixel against the ID of the current drawing process. If the test fails, the draw operation is aborted with no change to the frame buffer contents. Otherwise, the drawing operation is completed in the currently specified manner. Because the compare operation is truly pipelined, there are no drawing order requirements imposed by the test. All drawing operations to the frame buffer, including lines, are ID masked with no performance penalty.[5]

ID masking supports both partially obscured windows and non-rectangular windows (such as round clocks or templates) in a simple and consistent manner. It imposes no constraints on window size or shape, and never results in loss of performance.

5.3 Realtime Video

The new graphics architecture is capable of capturing both NTSC and PAL images in real time. These images are transferred to an arbitrary window on the screen via the *pixelbus* at the rate of 16 million pixels per second. Once in the frame buffer, they can be operated on just like images from any other source. Frame grab rate is controlled by the drawing program, allowing the simple program loop:

```
while (TRUE)
    grab a frame
    modify the image
    swap buffers
```

to operate as expected. Multiple buffers within the grabbing hardware insure that no frames are missed as long as the sum of the *grab a frame* period and the *modify the image* period does not exceed 1/30 of a second. The resulting NTSC or PAL image can be output in the same video format, allowing the hardware to act as a realtime video filter. Genlock and the alpha channel output allow additional video sources to be merged in a useful manner.

5.4 Alpha Blending

Each of the twenty Image Engines includes both ALU and microcode support for an alpha blending algorithm. This blending algorithm, used while operating in RGB mode, causes the destination pixel values to be a linear combination of the previous destination values and the new source values.

$$C_{dst} = F_{dst}C_{dst} + F_{src}C_{src}$$

$$F \in 0, 1, alpha, 1-alpha, C_{src}, 1-C_{src}, C_{dst}, 1-C_{dst}$$

The algorithm operates identically on red, green, blue, and alpha color components, each of which is stored as an 8-bit value in the frame buffer. Algorithm options are specified in table format. All of the operations described by Porter and Duff [8], as well as others, are available.

The frame buffer provides complete support for image compositing, including output of the alpha channel for external image merging. In addition, such a blending function at the tail end of a geometric graphics system provides capabilities well beyond traditional image compositing. Specifically, because blending is supported in conjunction with Z-buffer operation, geometrically specified *solids* can be blended to simulate the effects of transparency. With some attention to the order in which image components are specified, useful engineering images can be created.

5.5 Antialiased Lines

While the problem of realtime antialiasing of geometric images (as discussed by Crow [4]) has yet to be solved by a workstation, it has become possible to solve limited subsets of this problem. Our specific

---

4. *Silicon Graphics has applied for patent protection for this technology.*

5. *Silicon Graphics has applied for patent protection for this technology.*

implementation solves the problem of realtime rendering of antialiased lines against a constant color background. It is related to the algorithm described by Gupta and Sproull [7].

We require subpixel position information to properly antialias a line. This information is unavailable in graphics systems that rely on the Bresenham [1] algorithm for line iteration. It is available in a system that iterates using a digital differential analyzer (DDA). The DDA approach has been avoided in the past because of the division required. Since hardware has been provided to compute both color and depth slopes, the cost of computing line slopes, and thus of DDA iteration, has become insignificant.

Our antialias line algorithm forces line end points to pixel-centered positions, then uses sub-pixel information to smooth interior pixels. Each line is drawn twice, the second time offset one pixel position in the direction opposite the major line direction. During each pass the 3 most significant fraction bits of y, if the line is x major, or x, if the line is y major, as well as the pass (first or second) are used to drive a table lookup of pixel coverage information (see Picture 1). The table output is a 4-bit colorindex, which is concatenated with the 8 most significant bits of the current drawing colorindex to form the new pixel value. Thus constant color lines access 1 of 16 colormap locations as a function of pixel coverage. When appropriate values are loaded into the colormap, attractive antialiased lines result.

Of course the current colorindex, and thus the upper 8 bits of that index, can be iterated while the antialiased line is being drawn. When this iteration is controlled as a function of depth, and appropriately scaled ramps of 16 entries are created in the colormap, depthcued antialiased lines are drawn. Antialiased lines of different colors can be drawn by simply changing the current colorindex between lines, again with appropriate ramp specifications.

Line intersections are handled in one of three ways:

- *Depth Buffered.* Z-buffer conditional pixel fill can be used to force the nearest (or farthest) line's color to dominate pixels where lines intersect.

- *Color Buffered.* The same Z-buffer hardware can be retargeted to branch on colorindex, rather than depth, information. This insures that the intensity of a pixel is never diminished. This algorithm works well with single-color images that include many intersections.

- *Painter's algorithm.* Each pixel takes the last value that is written to it.

6. Summary

We have presented a parallel architecture for high speed polygon rendering. The system achieved its goal of 100,000 polygons per second through an efficient and balanced implementation of a novel architecture. In addition, several features new to workstation graphics were introduced. The implementation of the graphics subsystem consists of a 5-board set utilizing 50 copies of 7 proprietary chips and 7 additional commercial microprocessors.

Benchmark testing of a completed system immediately prior to publication yielded the following results:

- *101,000 quadrilaterals per second.* 100 pixel, arbitrarily rotated, lighted, Z-buffered.

- *137,000 triangles per second.* 50 pixel, arbitrary strip direction, lighted, Z-buffered.

- *394,000 lines per second.* 10 pixel, arbitrarily directed, depthcued, Z-buffered.

- *210,000 antialiased lines per second.* 10 pixel, arbitrarily directed, Z-buffered.

- *8.3 millisecond full-screen clear.* Both color and Z-buffer banks cleared.

7. Acknowledgements

We appreciate and thank the entire Silicon Graphics team.

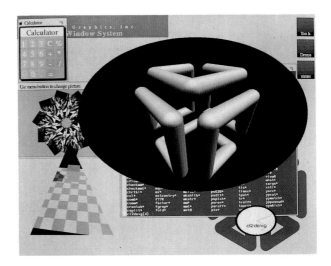

Figure 5

Silicon Graphics Superworkstation windowing system simultaneously exhibits high-performance 3D graphics, multi-mode graphics, and arbitrarily shaped windows.

8. References

1. Bresenham, J. Algorithm for Computer Control of a Digital Plotter. *IBM Systems Journal 4*, 1 (1965), 25-30.

2. Clark, Jim and Hannah, Marc. Distributed Processing in a High-Performance Smart Image Memory. *Lambda 1*, 3 (4th Quarter 1980), 40-45.

3. Clark, Jim. The Geometry Engine, A VLSI Geometry System for Graphics. *Computer Graphics (ACM) 16*, 3 (1982), 127.

4. Crow, Frank. The Aliasing Problem in Computer-Generated Shaded Images. *Communications of the ACM 20*, November 1977, 799-805.

5. Fuchs, Henry and Johnson, B. An Expandable Multiprocessor Architecture for Video Graphics. Proceedings of the 6th ACM-IEEE Symposium on Computer Architecture (April 1979), 58-67.

6. Gouraud, H. Continuous Shading of Curved Surfaces. *IEEE Transactions on Computers C-20*, 6 (June, 1971), 623-629.

7. Gupta, Satish and Sproull, Robert. Filtering Edges for Gray-Scale Displays. Technical Report, Carnegie-Mellon University, Computer Science Department, 1981.

8. Porter, Thomas and Duff, Tom. Compositing Digital Images. Proceedings of SIGGRAPH'84 (Minneapolis, Minnesota, July 23-27, 1984). In *Computer Graphics 18*, 3 (July 1984), 253-259.

9. Silicon Graphics. IRIS 4D/70 Superworkstation Technical Report. Silicon Graphics, Mountain View, CA 1987.

10. Sutherland, Ivan and Hodgman, Gary. Reentrant Polygon Clipping. *Communications of the ACM 17*, 1 (January 1974), 32.

11. Swanson, Roger and Thayer, Larry. A Fast Shaded-Polygon Renderer. Proceedings of SIGGRAPH'86 (Dallas, Texas, August 18-22, 1986). In *Computer Graphics 20*, 4 (August 1986), 95-101.

12. Torborg, John. A Parallel Processor Architecture for Graphics Arithmetic Operations. Proceedings of SIGGRAPH'87 (Anaheim, California, July 27-31, 1987). In *Computer Graphics 21*, 4 (July 1987), 197-204.

Virtual Graphics

Douglas Voorhies, David Kirk, Olin Lathrop

Apollo Computer Inc.
330 Billerica Road
Chelmsford, Mass. 01824

ABSTRACT

Graphics can be implemented as a virtual system resource. This abstraction appears to each application on a multiprocessing workstation as a dedicated rendering and display pipeline. A variety of simple mechanisms support the simultaneous display of different types of images and eliminate the need for low-level device driver software. They permit applications to embed graphics instructions directly in their code. The abstraction allows for cleaner software design, higher performance, and effective concurrent use of the display by several applications.

INTRODUCTION

There is a conflict between the multiple-process orientation of workstations and the single-task orientation of graphics hardware. Timesliced CPUs with virtual memory support many concurrent processes [2,9], and increasingly, those processes demand fast, sophisticated graphics for high interactivity and for complex data visualization. Moreover, windowing systems are raising the users' expectations for concurrency [10].

Previously, graphics hardware has not been structured to match this environment. (See Figure 1). Usually it is coupled to the CPU by an ad-hoc protocol. Although current graphics hardware connects to a high-bandwidth internal bus, its interface still presents the old paradigm of a dedicated graphics display serving one application from the far end of a communications line [5]. Despite the graphics hardware holding considerable per-process drawing state information, there is rarely any state management design discipline or effective swapping mechanism present [7]. Consequently, layers of graphics systems software are needed to manage access and context. Additional low-level software complexity arises from the need to throttle the CPU's request rate so as not to exceed the graphics hardware's input capacity. Finally, a single screen-wide display mode such as a color lookup table or pixel format satisfies only one class of applications at a time. Thus, the single-task orientation of graphics hardware has left the meta-rendering problem of updating and displaying multiple images unaddressed.

CPU/graphics interfaces are ad-hoc because they fall between two cultures. To the CPU and OS, graphics is a peripheral, and to graphics, the CPU and memory are a command source. Ad-hoc I/O interfaces are usually "dressed up" by intervening software for elegance and for device independence. While device independence is a requirement in many cases, applications are increasingly seeking the maximum performance from expensive hardware. For them, the intervening software is an obstacle. As we have learned, with more careful integration, this software can be eliminated.

In this paper we develop an approach which makes current user-interface and graphics rendering technology (both hardware and software) more effective on a workstation.

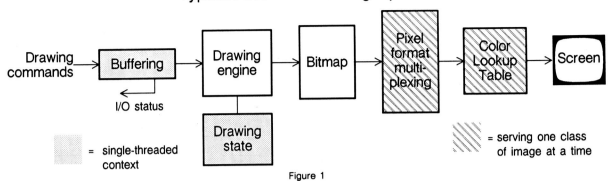

Figure 1

We offer an effective abstraction, "virtual graphics", which cleans up the ad-hoc hardware/software interface and tackles the problems of both time-slicing drawing hardware and simultaneously displaying varied images.

"VIRTUAL GRAPHICS"

By "virtual graphics" we mean every application has the illusion of owning a dedicated rendering co-processor. Each screen window is independently displayed. Applications need not deal with sharing access, switching contexts, modulating command flows, I/O status checking, screen-wide pixel formats, or sharing color lookup tables.

"Virtual" means that implementation details are hidden beneath an abstract interface, allowing higher levels to be simpler [3]. Virtual graphics hides the single-threaded nature of the rendering and display hardware. Because the interface is simplified, multiple threads of graphics rendering can be handled efficiently. Since each applications' windows are updated more smoothly, the benefits extend to the user as well.

Although windowing systems, such as X-windows [14] or Apollo's Display Manager, have already begun to address the screen allocation problem, they do so by making window shape and size variable at display time. This, in turn, places demands on the drawing and display hardware to support window-oriented update and display.

To create the appearance of a dedicated resource to multiple requestors, the hardware must either have sufficient **parallelism** to actually perform all work simultaneously, or be able to rapidly **switch** between tasks. The success of both CPU timesharing and the virtual

memory page sharing have proven rapid switching of an expensive resource to be effective [11]. Since CPUs and high-end graphics hardware cost roughly the same, concurrency through rapid switching is the most practical solution.

The key to managing state is to switch low-level contexts rapidly. It is very difficult to emulate fast task switching at a high abstraction level if lower levels cannot exchange their state quickly. Useful techniques include the simple switching of the context (by moving a pointer) or the complete swapping of the context (by a saving and restoring copy).

IMPLEMENTATION

At Apollo we have implemented a high-end graphics system for the DN10000. It offers virtual graphics by combining six simple mechanisms (see Figure 2):

1. The integration of graphics via a co-processor interface
2. The exception-based detection of graphics ownership violations
3. The efficient swapping of drawing context
4. The exception-based management of command flow rate
5. The clipping of drawing to window boundaries
6. The switching of pixel formats and lookup tables per pixel

These mechanisms are not very powerful separately, but together they remove the barriers between the applications and the graphics hardware. Applications become unaware

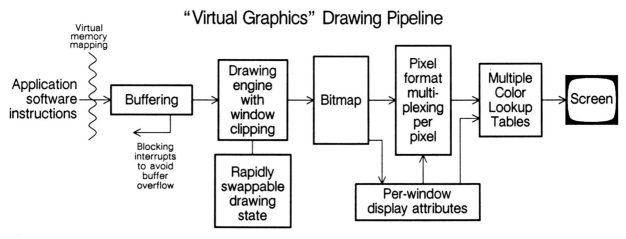

Figure 2

that they are sharing the hardware device, or its drawing context, or the screen.

Co-processor interface

The graphics hardware is mapped into the application's memory space. Memory-mapping allows control to be cleanly presented in higher-level languages. It permits the application to use *Store* instructions to set all drawing parameters and initiate all drawing operations. Drawing is simply done by initializing all relevant parameters and then requesting an operation.

Graphics is a co-processor since the *Store* subsumes both an 8-bit graphics opcode and 32-bit data operand in its address and data. The parameters and operations are selected by 8 low address bits, and the data is the 32-bit operand. By packing all the commands into one page, the cost of setting up the mapping is minimized.

Exception-based detection of graphics ownership violations

State ownership and graphics access are built upon virtual memory access management mechanisms. Both the graphics drawing commands and the bitmap itself are mapped into the physical memory space. By allowing only one requesting process at a time to map the *graphics command page*, access to the graphics becomes single-threaded. Even in a shared-memory and multiple CPU system, access remains exclusive. Whenever the *graphics*

command page is mapped, that process's context is presumed to be active in the drawing hardware.

The fault handler grants access to processes following a "fairness" policy. A graphics access fault differs from page faults in that the requesting process does not necessarily get access as soon as possible. The access policy software permits only one requesting process to "own" the graphics; the others wait their turn. In this respect it resembles the "fair" allocation of CPU timeslices to processes.

The bitmap may also be mapped into the process's virtual address space. In order to insure a consistent view of the bitmap by both direct reads and writes as well as by the drawing hardware, an interlock is needed. Here again, virtual memory mapping can detect both direct bitmap access as well as command page access. Only one or the other is mapped at a time. Execution of a direct bitmap read/write is delayed until all drawing has completed, and a request for drawing is assumed to signal the end of direct bitmap access.

Fast drawing context swapping in hardware

Drawing context can be swapped quickly by a VLSI state machine within the graphics hardware. In our implementation, the state is large because this rendering hardware is highly parallel and strives for unusually high image quality. The per-process drawing state is kept in 144 hardware registers (576 bytes) during use. When swapping, the live state (524 bytes) is exchanged with a copy in a local graphics context RAM. The remaining per-process state (52 bytes) stays in that RAM while in use, and so may be switched by updating a reference pointer.

This local RAM has space for six graphics contexts, including the active one; these copies function as a cache over additional ones in main memory. The state machine can perform a swap to and from the local RAM in 16 μsec., which is less time than a CPU process swap takes. Those occasional swaps involving a context not in the local RAM are handled by CPU copying to and from the main memory contexts, and take under 200 μsec..

Since all drawing commands atomically update the drawing engine state, swaps are legal between any commands. Drawing commands are never interrupted or aborted, since some (such as RASTER-OP [12]) may not be idempotent or may use temporary storage in mid-execution. Swaps are initiated by issuing SAVE and RESTORE commands between the drawing commands of one process and the next. The fault handler inserts these commands between the commands of the old and new owning processes.

Exception-based command flow control

Flow control can best be handled by an exception mechanism. Usually, graphics hardware handles requests faster than a CPU can generate them, but whenever this is untrue, the CPU must wait until the graphics hardware has caught up. In our implementation, a command FIFO with 512 entries buffers between the bursty request and execution traffic. It permits a requesting CPU and the drawing hardware to proceed asynchronously. When a FIFO is nearly full, all further requests trigger interrupts [1], which force the requesting process to wait until the FIFO signals it has reached half full. (An interrupt is issued upon **each** request to insure the nearly-full condition is communicated successfully, since processes may migrate between CPUs at any time.) This throttling of the requesting process is separate from the access mechanism, although it may be factored into the access policy decisions.

Since the CPU is increasingly the bottleneck in graphics-based applications, it is advantageous to slow it down only in the exceptional case of being limited by the graphics hardware. CPU busy-flag tests, "done" interrupts, and other hardware/software locks are eliminated by handling flow control transparently, streamlining and simplifying the co-processor interface.

Window-boundary clipping during drawing

Drawing into a window usually requires 2-D clipping to the window boundaries. This can be cumbersome, especially if the window is partially occluded [6,16]. The burden of screen clipping makes it more difficult for applications to fully participate in a shared screen, and slows down their rendering if they do. Since we added rectangle clip logic in hardware, drawing can simply ignore window boundaries, or only trivially reject primitives prior to drawing.

In our implementation, every potential pixel write is compared with up to seven rectangles using 28 parallel X or Y comparators. These 28 rectangle coordinates are part of the per-process state swapped when changing drawing contexts. Two clipping tactics are supported. Simple windows are handled by one "clip outside" rectangle occluded by up to six "clip inside" rectangles. More complex windows are drawn in multiple passes, with each pass clipped to the union of seven "draw inside" rectangles. In both modes, the clip decision is made in parallel with address synthesis, and imposes no speed penalty.

Pixel format switching per pixel

Even if multiple windows can be drawn rapidly, having only a single pixel format or single color lookup table for the whole screen thwarts their concurrent display. For example, a page-layout system may wish to mix full-color photographs with false-color text. Another application may wish to alter the color lookup table to highlight part of its image. And a third may want to double-buffer a false-color CAD image. If they are to effectively share the screen, the video display mode must change on-the-fly at each window boundary. Switching the display hardware mode at pixel rates satisfies the requirement of most window managers to arbitrary window position, size, and complexity [15].

By appending each bitmap pixel with a 4-bit tag, the video logic obtains control information synchronously with the raw bitmap pixel data. Using this tag as an index into a 16-entry *display attributes table* expands the tag into its current display mode [17]. See Figure 3. This table

Per-pixel Display Mode Implementation

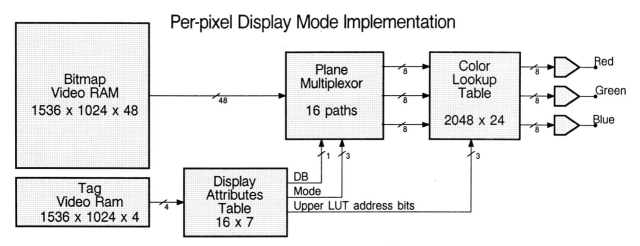

Figure 3

lookup is analogous to the color lookup table for pixel data. Per-pixel display attributes in our implementation include:

- Color Lookup Table (LUT) selection (1 of 8)
- Plane multiplexing mode:
  - 8-bit false color
  - 10-bit false color
  - 12-bit real color
  - 24-bit real color
  - Mixed false and real color
  - Substitute a cursor color
- Overlays on/off
- Double buffer select

Typically, all pixels in a particular window are displayed in the same mode. The actual number of windows is not limited by the 16 *display attributes table* size, since several windows will often share the same attributes (e.g. text windows). Further, the limitation of 8 x 256 LUT entries is ameliorated by allocating color blocks smaller than 256 on demand, and by sharing LUT blocks (e.g. a shared real color Gamma function).

BENEFITS

Together, these six mechanisms and the regular graphics hardware appear to each application as a fast dedicated rendering and display pipeline. Applications are unaware of sharing the screen area, drawing context timeslicing, screen display mode cooperation, or flow control. Consequently, graphics is presented to applications as a

clean and useful abstraction. The abstraction allows instructions embedded within an application to request drawing directly. Neither active coordination with other applications nor intervening layers of graphics system software are required. Moreover, this memory-mapped interface is easily used by high level languages.

The most challenging part of virtual graphics is access management. We chose to base our implementation on virtual memory management, thus reducing it to an already-solved problem.

Performance is improved by the reduction in both software layering and context management overhead. Indeed, there is **no** state-management overhead when there is only one active drawing process, and minimal overhead when there are six or less active processes.

A more subtle performance gain is achieved through the asynchrony of the CPU and graphics executions allowed by the FIFO. Inserting swap requests in the drawing instruction sequence inherently synchronizes drawing context and operations. When a process gains access to the FIFO, it does not need to wait for its state to be swapped in. Drawing instructions can be issued immediately, even though they presume post-swap context, because they are preceeded in the FIFO by the swap request. Since the FIFO preserves the sequence, the swap will emerge from the FIFO and occur before these instructions emerge. This is possible because the graphics context is swapped synchronous with drawing and asynchronous from the CPU by a post-FIFO mechanism.

HARDER PROBLEMS

Our six mechanisms do not address several more difficult graphics resource management limitations. Any sharing abstraction breaks down when its underlying resources have insufficient capacity or are too slow to multiplex their context. For example, thrashing occurs in a virtual memory system if there is insufficient physical memory. Also, software locks are needed for single-threaded peripherals such as tape drives. Similarly, virtual graphics, while effective for common rendering, cannot hide finite resources and cannot transparently share what it cannot swap.

Screen space is the most visible finite resource. There is an obvious extension of virtual memory to virtual windows [8], which allows drawing to proceed oblivious to window occlusion, and allows a potentially larger bitmap. However, crossing discontiguous page boundaries is awkward, and gathering the scattered windows at video rates is either very expensive or requires a massive copy. Such copying cuts into drawing bandwidth, and may in turn cause jerky screen update. Moreover, a fixed-size video-RAM array offers much lower cost; and, because it can be tightly interconnected to a dedicated drawing engine, it can achieve higher potential performance.

Off-screen images, such as image preparation areas, down-loaded fonts, texture maps, or tile patterns, represent a huge context which defies rapid swapping. Many bitmaps have some off-screen area where the drawing hardware can work at full speed, but it is expensive and must be allocated very carefully. Moreover, high-level software locks are often needed to single-thread access to large blocks of the limited space. Virtual graphics can do little to manage these large images.

Similarly, color and display attribute lookup tables sizes are finite, and the number of entries needed for all the windows may ocassionally exceed what the hardware can support. In time, however, technology will push the limit beyond common user needs. Other features, such as per-window pan and zoom, remain particularly difficult to implement without copying pixels. High display rates and the horizontal shifting efficiency of video RAMs [13] limit flexibility in video back-end hardware. Fortunately, with improving redraw speeds, video panning and pixel-replicating zoom are becoming obsolete.

Finally, with increasingly asynchronous CPU and drawing execution and with more automatic state management, software has less control. These features optimize output-only rendering while penalizing operations which require the CPU to know the state of the bitmap or drawing operation. For example, if an application wishes to read the bitmap, or be signaled at the end of a drawing operation, or ascertain the current interpolated colors, then the long pipeline must be drained and synchronization reestablished. Since most of such "upstream" communication is to support human input, the frequency is quite low. Response time, however, must remain adequate, and any forced re-synchronization conflicts with concurrent update.

CONCLUSIONS

The abstraction of virtual graphics elevates graphics to a first-class system resource. Its implementation pushes the multiplexing of control and context from the device driver level down into the hardware. Hardware accelerates context swaps, FIFO full detection, and window clipping. By moving these mechanisms into the hardware, we eliminate a layer of software and achieve a significant reduction in multiplexing overhead. Faster multiplexing can quantitatively improve performance as well as qualitatively smooth the drawing of multiple windows.

The software sees a dedicated graphics co-processor. Because the ad-hoc jumble of low-level driver software has been replaced, applications can simply access the hardware by embedding graphics instructions directly in their code. Additionally, several applications each retain a clean view despite simultaneously running on multiple processors.

The user sees a screen supporting multiple images, each displayed properly and updated smoothly. Thus virtual graphics enhances the concurrency and effectiveness of modern workstations by addressing the meta-rendering problem of multiple image update.

ACKNOWLEDGEMENTS

We wish to thank Inwhan Choi, Robert Feldstein, Thomas Fincher, Jeffery Kurtze, Eliot Polk, and Robert Taylor for their insightful contributions and refinements during the implementation of this architecture. We also appreciate Dr. Terence Lindgren for his helpful observations in the presentation of these ideas.

REFERENCES

[1] Asal, M., Short, G., Preston, T., Simpson, R., Roskell, D., and Guttag, K., "The Texas Instruments 34010 Graphics System Processor", *IEEE Computer Graphics and Applications*, Vol. 6, No. 10, October 1986, pp. 24-39

[2] Barton, R. S., "A New Approach to Functional Design of a Digital Computer", *Proc. AFIPS Western Joint Comp. Conf.*, 1961, Vol. 19, pp. 393-396.

[3] Buzen, J. P. and Gagliardi, U. O., "The Evolution of Virtual Machine Architecture", *Proc. of AFIPS*, NCC 1973

[4] Cohen, E. S., Smith, E. T., and Iverson, L. A., "Constraint-based Tiled Windows", *IEEE Computer Graphics and Applications*, Vol. 6, No. 5, May 1986, pp. 35-45.

[5] England, N., "A Graphics System Architecture for Interactive Application-Specific Display Functions", *IEEE Computer Graphics and Applications*, Vol. 6, No. 1, January 1986, pp. 60-70.

[6] Foley, J. and van Dam, A., *Fundamentals of Interactive Computer Graphics*, Addison-Wesley, Reading, Mass., 1982

[7] Guttag, K., Van Aken, J., and Asal, M., "Requirements for a VLSI Graphics Processor", *IEEE Computer Graphics and Applications*, Vol. 6, No. 1, January 1986, pp. 32-47.

[8] Ilgen, S. and Scherson, I. D., "Real Time Virtual Window Management for Bit Mapped Raster Graphics", *Proc. 5th International Conf. on Computer Graphics in Japan*, Springer-Verlag, Tokyo, 1987, pp. 145-158.

[9] Kilburn, T., Edwards, D. B. G., Lanigan, M. J., and Sumner, F. H., "One-level Storage System", *IRE Trans. on Electronic Computers*, Vol EC-11, No. 2, pp. 223-235.

[10] Lantz, K. A., Tanner, P. P., Binding, C., Huang, K., and Dwelly, A., "Reference Models, Window Systems, and Concurrency", *Computer Graphics*, Vol. 21, No. 2, April 1987, pp. 87-97.

[11] Meyer, R. A. and Seawright, L. H., "A Virtual Machine Timesharing System", *IBM Sys. Journal*, Vol. 9, No. 3, 1970

[12] Newman, W. M. and Sproull, R. F., *Principles of Interactive Computer Graphics*, 2nd ed., McGraw-Hill, New York, 1979, pp. 262-265.

[13] Pinkham, R., Novak, M., and Guttag, K., "Video RAM Excels at Fast Graphics", *Electronic Design*, Vol. 31, No. 17, Aug. 18, 1983, pp. 161-182

[14] Scheifler, R. W. and Gettys, J., "The X-Window System", *ACM Trans. on Graphics*, Vol. 5, No. 2, April 1986, pp. 79-109

[15] Shires, G., "A New VLSI Graphics Coprocessor — The Intel 82786", *IEEE Computer Graphics and Applications*, Vol. 6, No. 10, October 1986, pp. 49-55.

[16] Sproull, R. F. and Sutherland, I. E., "A Clipping Divider", *Fall Joint Computer Conf. 1968*, Thompson Books, Wash. D.C., pp. 765-775.

A Display System for the
Stellar™ Graphics Supercomputer Model GS1000™

Brian Apgar, Bret Bersack, Abraham Mammen

Stellar Computer Inc.
85 Wells Ave.
Newton, MA 02159

Abstract

This paper describes a high performance display system that has been incorporated into the overall architecture of the Stellar Graphics Supercomputer Model GS1000. The display system is tightly coupled to the CPU, memory system and vector processing unit of this supercomputer, and is capable of rendering 150,000 shaded triangles/sec, and 600,000 short vectors/sec. The goal of the architecture is to share hardware resources between the CPU and display system and achieve a high bandwidth connection between them. This coupling of the display system and the processor, the architecture of the rendering processor, and the two ASICs that are used to implement the rendering processor are described.

In addition, the display system architecture is contrasted to other approaches to high performance graphics, and design trade-offs and possible extensions are described. The implementation of popular display algorithms on the architecture is discussed, and their performance specified. The reader is advised that Stellar Computer Inc. is seeking patent protection for work described in this paper.

Introduction

In the past decade, the use of supercomputers for the solution of large, complex scientific and engineering problems has become increasingly important. As the performance of supercomputers and the size of the problems studied on them has grown, the need for aids to human comprehension of the results and ways to 'steer' the solution process has increased. At the same time, computer graphics has become an important part of a wide range of technical applications including mechanical CAD, medicine, molecular modelling, and computational fluid dynamics. As the complexity of the problems under study in both supercomputing and graphics increases, it is clear that much can be gained by the integration of supercomputing and computer graphics technologies. This is the focus of the NSF initiative on Visualization in Scientific Computing (ViSC). [15]

For use in such applications, a display system must be able to render a large number of objects at speeds that allow animations of time-varying phenomena. We believe this requires tens of thousands of polygons and hundreds of thousands of vectors rendered at interactive speeds. To maximize the information content of the created images, high quality rendering techniques are necessary. These include anti-aliasing, shading, light modeling, transparency, and texture mapping.

Current Approaches to High Performance Graphics

There are four areas that are important for the performance of a display system: the display interface, geometry computations, pixel computations, and the pixel memory system.

Display Interface

In many current systems the display system is a specialized processor that is connected to a general purpose host computer over a network, parallel interface, or memory bus [13,14,18]. An application running on a host processor is the source for all the graphics commands; it sends them through the interface to the display processor. If this interface does not have sufficient bandwidth, it can limit the performance of the system. Some systems use a display list memory local in the display processor. This approach works well if the object description is not frequently modified. The object may be tumbled at high rates but cannot be extensively modified for each new frame.

Geometry Computations

The geometry computations include object coordinate transformation, clipping, lighting, and device coordinate scaling. Since the different steps of the geometry computations for a single primitive are largely independent and different primitives are commonly independent of one another, parallel techniques can be used to achieve the geometry processing speeds needed for high performance graphics. Two approaches are a pipeline structure and parallel processing of primitives [5,19].

The pipeline performs each of the steps if the geometry computation in different stages of a hardware structure; this causes the different steps of several primitives to be executed in parallel. To process entire primitives in parallel, the primitives are distributed to multiple independent geometry processors. As a result objects are not necessarily rendered in the same order that the commands for them were issued. In most cases this is of no concern, but some operations (such as changing the draw colors or light sources) require execution order to be maintained. This is done by tagging graphics commands with order dependence information. All of the processors must keep track of any commands requiring sequential execution.

Pixel Computation

Pixel computations consist of the scan conversion of the primitives and the computation of the color values and Z coordinates.

Lines are efficiently scan converted using the Bresenham algorithm [3]. This algorithm is easily implemented in hardware that can produce a new pixel address every clock cycle. Variations of the algorithm can handle the shading of polygons. [18] The polygon setup, scan conversion of the polygon edges, and interpolation of color and Z values can be pipelined to achieve high performance. The algorithm can be implemented using a digital differential analyzer (DDA) that uses iterative addition, which works well if the object to be scan converted and the pixel computations are relatively simple. This is the case for linear color interpolation over a polygon.

©1988   ACM-0-89791-275-6/88/008/0255 $00.75

Since the computations for a given pixel are independent of the computations for all other pixels (for most rendering algorithms) pixel parallelism may be used. This can easily be extended to a processor for each pixel, as in the Pixel-planes system.[8,9] Objects are scan converted by evaluating functions for their boundaries, and only those pixels that are inside the boundaries are written. For simple polygons, the edges are defined by linear equations. For Gouraud shading of a flat polygon with Z-buffering, both the color values and Z coordinate are computed from linear functions. The power of this technique is that any bounding function can be used, limited only by the numeric capabilities of the pixel processors. Second order functions can be used to render conic sections, and this can be used for direct rendering of constructive solid geometry operations. [10] The system is controlled in a single instruction stream, multiple data stream (SIMD) fashion i.e., a single control word is supplied to all of the processors.

Pixel Memory
To supply the pixel memory bandwidth that is needed in high performance display systems, several approaches have been used.

To get high pixel rates, frame buffers have been designed to access multiple pixels at a time. A frame buffer memory location that holds 16 pixels can be organized as 4x4 or 16x1 tiles.[11] The scan conversion hardware can generate a single pixel at a time, as long as all the pixels are completed in the memory cycle time of the frame buffer. A pixel cache can be used to match the different speeds of the frame buffer memory and the scan converter.

A frame buffer can be divided into separate banks that allow multiple accesses to occur simultaneously. Scan conversion hardware can be incorporated into each of the frame buffer memory banks so that scan conversion can also be done in parallel. One implementation organizes the frame buffer memory horizontally and vertically as a 5x4 array of banks.[1,6] Each bank holds every fifth horizontal pixel and every fourth vertical pixel and has its own dedicated scan conversion chip. This allows 20 pixels each in a different bank to be accessed and processed at the same time.

If a processor is dedicated to each screen pixel, it is possible to incorporate the frame buffer memory storage in the processors. This is the approach used in the Pixel-planes system; it allows all of the pixels on the screen to be accessed and processed in parallel. Since the pixels are stored in the chips, the chips can also support the reading out of the pixels for video generation.

Limitations
In the systems discussed, specialized hardware was used in the display processor to achieve high performance for some applications. However, this specialized hardware may have fundamental limitations that make it less effective for a broad range of graphics functions.

A pipelined geometry processor works well when the computations to be performed are simple and can be broken into a fixed set of stages. It is not well suited for computations that vary greatly in their complexity or involve many cases such as lighting computations. For the simple case of Gouraud shading [12] (diffuse lighting with a single directional light) approximately 6 floating point operations per vertex are needed. In Stellar's implementation of Bishop Weimer Fast Phong Shading [2,16], a light local to the object with specular lighting requires more than 500 floating point operations per vertex. If a pipeline is optimized for the most common simple cases, the performance will drop suddenly for an occasional complex case, or worse: it cannot be supported at all.

Pixel computation based on hardware implementations of DDA techniques are good for lines and smooth shading of polygons. The Pixel-planes technique of general purpose function evaluation is better suited for more complex objects such as spheres and CSG primitives. Operations requiring non-linear functions or multiplication at the pixel level, such as specular lighting models and texture mapping, cannot be easily implemented with DDA scan conversion methods.

The use of dedicated frame buffer memory in a display processor can present several difficulties. For simple rendering operations, each pixel only needs storage for color values. To support pixel space functions, such as double buffering and Z-buffering, additional dedicated storage is needed at each pixel. Functions such as anti-aliasing, transparency, shadows, and depth sorting can be implemented by using additional storage at each pixel. If frame buffer memory is added to a system to support these functions, a significant cost is added to the system for a feature that may only be used occasionally. Further, hardware restrictions imposed by the display processor may prevent additional per-pixel storage for new algorithms and functions. Dedicated frame buffer memories are also designed to optimize accesses by the rendering hardware; host processor access to the pixels can be poor. Specialized application operations on pixels that are not supported by the display processor are inconvenient or impossible.

Other researchers have recognized the restrictions of special purpose graphics architectures and have built machines using general purpose programmable processors. One approach connects frame buffer memory, display processors and graphics I/O devices to a shared high speed bus.[7]

System Hardware and Functions
The Stellar design goal was to tightly integrate a high performance display system with the CPU and vector processor of a supercomputer. We recognized that high memory bandwidth and floating point performance were both critical needs of vector processing and graphics. We designed a system that shared a single memory system and vector processor between the CPU, vector processor, and display system. This reduced the need for specialized hardware, and achieved a high bandwidth connection between the display system and the CPU and vector processor. The GS1000 system consists of several major sections that are shown in Figure 1. [17]

Multi-Stream Processor and DataPath[TM] Architecture
The Multi-Stream Processor is single uniform 25 MIPS processor that simultaneously executes instructions from 4 independent instruction "streams". The core of the machine is the DataPath. The DataPath acts as an interconnect path between all of the functional units, and supplies the register storage for the processor. Independent sets of registers for each stream are held within the Data Path. These include 32 integer registers, 8 scalar floating point registers, and 6 vector registers of 32 elements each. Both the memory system and the cache are connected to the Data Path by dedicated 512-bit wide busses, and the Vector Floating point Processor (VFP) is connected by a 384-bit wide path.

The Data Path also contains a pixel buffer, which consists of 8 pixel registers. Each pixel register holds 16 32-bit pixels. Associated with the pixel buffer is logic for horizontal alignment of pixels, raster ops, and a register for controlling these functions called the drawing state register. The CPU supports pixel load/store instructions that transfer pixels between the pixel registers and memory. They are used to support a wide variety of pixel graphics functions to arrays of pixels stored in virtual memory or the video memory. This includes 2D line drawing, polygon filling, and pixel block transfers (pix-BLTs) with raster operations. Pixels can be written at 160 Million pixels/second or copied at 60 Million pixels/second.

Memory System
The memory system consists of a cache, Translation Look-aside Buffer (TLB), main memory, and video memory. It is designed to support the high memory bandwidth needs of the Multi-Stream Processor, the Vector Floating-point Processor and the Rendering Processor.

The TLB holds 16K entries mapping virtual to physical page addresses. The cache holds 1Mbyte and is shared between the four streams of the Multi-Stream Processor.

Memory consists of two parts, Main memory and Video memory which share a 512-bit connection to the DataPath. Each main memory location holds 16 32-bit words that can be used for program and data storage, or can hold 16 pixels organized either as

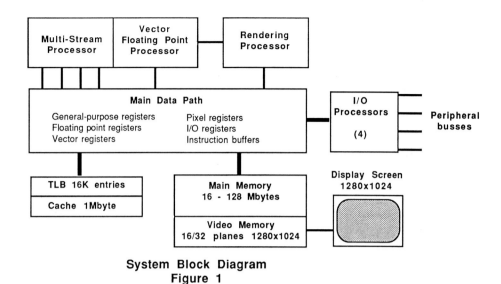

System Block Diagram
Figure 1

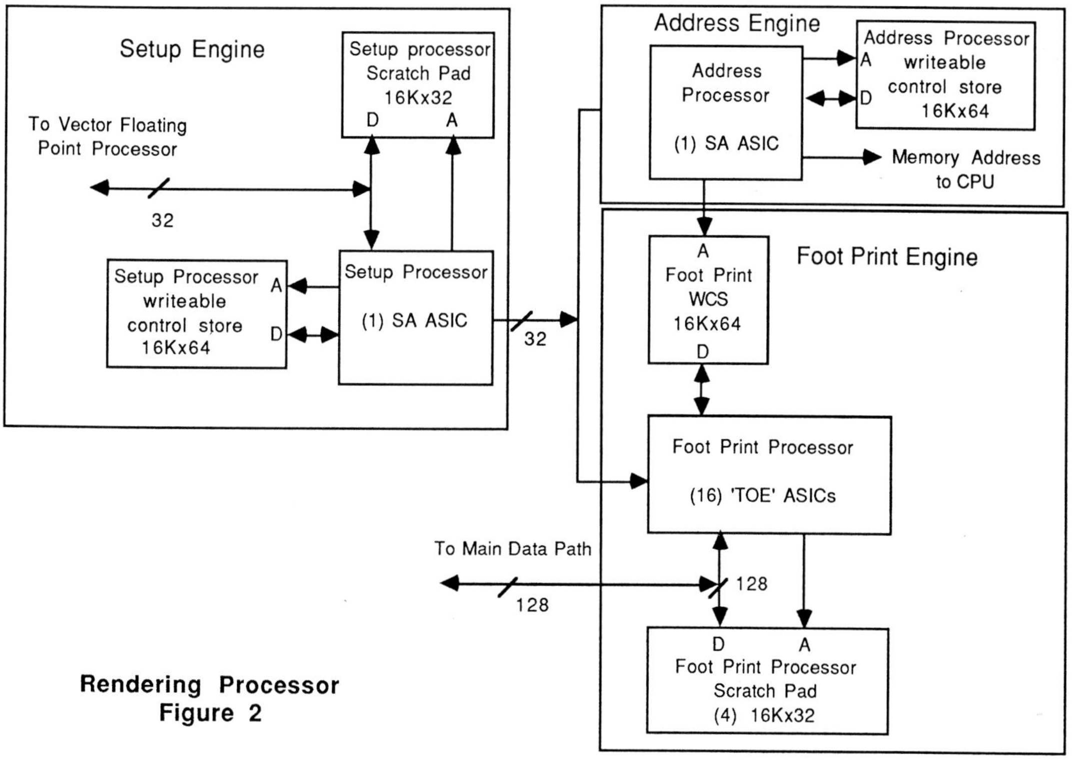

Rendering Processor
Figure 2

4x4 blocks or 16x1 strokes. The video memory is organized as a 1280x1024 array of 32-bit pixels with each video memory location holding a 16x1 stroke. Video memory is identical to main memory except that it is implemented with video rams, holds the screen image that is used for video generation, and allows write enabling down to groups of 4 planes within a pixel.

Both Main memory and Video memory support two types of memory cycles. The standard cycle reads or writes a single 512-bit memory location every 200ns. Pixel transfers to/from the pixel buffer may use an overlapped memory cycle that moves 1024-bits in 200ns.

Virtual Pixel Maps[TM] Rendering Technique

Pixels are stored as rectangular arrays in virtual memory called Virtual Pixel Maps (VPM), which are identified by a pixel map bit in the TLB. The CPU may access the pixels in a VPM with any general purpose load/store instruction or with the special pixel load/store instructions. The Rendering Processor performs all of its operations on VPMs.

A VPM may be up to 2^{16} x 2^{16} pixels in size. Up to the 4Gbyte virtual address limit, any number of pixel maps may be defined and used. Multiple VPMs are used to support rendering operations that require more than 32 bits per pixel. For rendering operations the 4x4 format is used because it yields higher pixel efficiency for small graphics objects (more useful pixels per memory access).

The Rendering Processor supports rendering with 12 plane pseudo-color and 24 plane true color. A single VPM is used for rendering in pseudo-color. The Z-buffer occupies 16 bits of each pixel; the color value uses 12 bits, and 4 bits are unused. Two VPMs are used for true-color. The 24-bit color value and 8 unused bits occupy the first pixel map, and a 32-bit Z-buffer is held in the second. We are presently implementing rendering functions that use several VPMs to support anti-aliasing of solids, texture mapping, and transparency.

Vector Floating Point Processor

The Vector/Floating Point Processor (VFP) performs scalar and vector floating point operations for the entire machine. Operands are loaded from cache/memory to vector registers using VLOAD instructions, and results are stored with VSTORES. Vector registers are 'broad-side loaded' in 2 or 4 memory accesses, depending on the precision of the operand. They can hold single or double precision floating point values or 32-bit signed integers. Vectors are processed with register-to-register vector instructions. The VFP supports a general set of vector multiply, add, subtract, multiply-add, compress, mask, merge functions. In addition it supports vector instructions specialized to graphics geometry computations. These include instructions for coordinate transformation, clip checking, matrix concatenation, lighting dot products, square root approximation, and device coordinate conversion. Loads and stores of vector registers are overlapped with vector operations as long as there are no register conflicts. The VFP is pipelined to produce one floating add, multiply or multiply-add result every clock cycle for a peak throughput of 40 MFLOPS.

Graphics Geometry Processing

All the geometry computations are implemented by a software package written in C and assembly code that provides the graphics device interface for the machine. It is a high level device interface that is exported through the X11 Window System[TM] on our system. It is called the X Floating Point Device Interface (XFDI), and it supports a large number of graphics primitives, and controls their attributes. The primitives are: points, lines, line meshes, line polyhedral meshes, triangles, triangle meshes, triangle polyhedral meshes, and spheres.

The XFDI performs coordinate transformation, clipping, lighting computations, and device coordinate conversion for all the primitives that it supports. All of the geometry computations are done in single precision floating point using the VFP. The XFDI can transform a 3D point in approximately 800ns with the VFP operating at over 35 MFLOPS during the computations.

In addition to the standard attributes for these primitives, the XFDI supports flat, Gouraud and Phong shading with diffuse and specular lighting. Up to 16 colored light sources are allowed, and they may be point or directional lights. For specular lighting, the viewer may either be at infinity or local to the object. Clipping can be done to the standard six clipping planes and to 16 arbitrary clipping planes (used to create cut-away views of complex objects.)

Connection to the Rendering Processor

The VFP supports three vector instructions for communicating with the Rendering processor. The send-to-renderer instruction transfers data (at a rate of 32 bits per clock cycle) from a vector register to the Setup Engine scratch pad memory. The XFDI uses this instruction to send argument and attribute information for a group of primitives to the renderer. The arguments can include the X, Y, and Z coordinates of the vertices, the vertex color values computed from the light sources, and the coefficient values needed to compute the linear equations for the color and Z coordinates. The attributes can include the draw color, the definitions of the current pixel maps, and the light source intensities. The receive-from-renderer instruction, which is used primarily for diagnostics, transfers data in the reverse direction. The execute-renderer instruction causes the Setup Engine to begin execution of the micro-code for the desired primitives. All three instructions are hardware interlocked so the VFP is prevented from proceeding if the Setup Engine is busy.

Rendering Processor

The Rendering Processor (RP) performs all of the per-pixel rendering computations in the system. It receives rendering commands and parameters from the vector unit, calculates individual pixel values, and writes the new values into pixel maps stored in virtual memory. The RP is shown in Figure 2. It consists of three independent engines that operate as a rendering pipeline: the Setup Engine, the Address Engine, and the Foot Print Engine. The Setup Engine performs initialization and preliminary computations on the primitives to be rendered and sends commands and data to the other engines. The Address Engine determines which 4x4 blocks of pixels are covered by a primitive, and sequentially "walks" the Foot Print Engine over those blocks while coordinating the virtual memory accesses. The blocks of pixels are transferred between memory and the pixel buffer, where they can be read or written by the Foot Print Engine. The Foot Print Engine evaluates the bounding functions for the primitive, computes the pixel values and Z coordinates, and performs the depth buffering comparison.

Core Processor Functions

The RP is implemented using two specially designed application-specific integrated circuits (ASICs). The Setup-Address (SA) ASIC is used once in the Setup Engine and once in the Address Engine. It contains over 40,000 used gates in a 299-pin package. The Toe ASIC is used 16 times to implement the footprint engine. It contains over 25,000 used gates in a 155-pin package. Both ASICs use scan-path techniques for testing and fault isolation. The SA and Toe ASICs each contain a micro-coded 32-bit integer processor whose core arithmetic features are shown in Figure 3.

The processor ALU performs integer arithmetic, logical, and shifting operations on two 32-bit operands, generating a 32-bit result. The multiplier performs signed, unsigned, and mixed mode 16x16 integer multiplies to produce a 32-bit product. With the accumulator register, the multiplier and ALU can implement 16x32 and 32x32 multiplication.

The general register file is a 32-word by 32-bit triple-port memory. It provides operands to the other functional units and receives their results. The memory address register is used to access external scratch memories, and the input/output data registers are used to transfer data to these memories or the pixel buffer.

Setup Processor Hardware

In addition to the core functions, the SA ASIC has hardware for functions specific to the Setup Processor. This includes a micro-sequencer, the interface to the VFP, and an interface to the Address and Foot Print Engines.

The instruction sequencer generates the micro-code execution address for the Setup Engine control store. A standard set of micro-code branch and subroutine call/return functions are provided. The interface to the VFP supports the renderer communication instructions. The Address/Foot Print interface consists of a transfer RAM and handshaking logic. The transfer RAM buffers data to be sent from the Setup Engine to the Address and Foot Print processors.

Setup Engine Operation

After the XFDI performs an execute-renderer instruction, the Setup Engine starts working on the first primitive in the argument buffer. The setup computation involves determining the orientation of the primitive and calculating the coefficients and starting values for the equations used for rendering the primitive. After the setup results for a single primitive are written into the transfer RAM, the Address and Foot Print Engines will start working on that primitive, and the Setup Engine can go on to the next primitive in the argument buffer. When the argument buffer is exhausted, the Setup Engine returns to its idle loop to wait for new commands.

Address Processor Hardware

The SA ASIC also has hardware for functions that are specific to the Address Processor. This includes the same micro-sequencer used by the Setup Processor, an interface to the Setup Engine, a CPU/memory interface, and logic for controlling the Foot Print Engine.

The Setup Engine interface controls the burst transfer of data from the transfer RAM in the Setup Processor. The CPU/memory interface controls the accesses to virtual memory during rendering. The interface consists of a memory access controller and a queue for holding active memory requests. The memory controller manages the queue and requests the necessary memory accesses specified by the queue entries. It also synchronizes Foot Print Engine execution with the completion of the requested memory cycles. The Foot Print Engine interface controls the micro-code execution of the Foot Print Engine and consists of a jump address queue and a micro-sequencer. The queue holds the starting micro-addresses of code sequences to be executed by the Foot Print Engine.

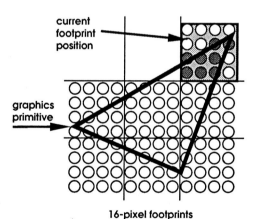

16-pixel footprints

Pixel Blocks Covering a Triangle
Figure 4

Address Engine Operation

The Address Engine begins a primitive by fetching the relevant data from the transfer RAM in the Setup Engine. The Address Engine evaluates the bounding function(s) of the primitive, sequentially determining the virtual address of each 4x4 block that the primitive hits (See Figure 4.) For triangles and lines, the bounding functions are the linear equations defining the sides or ends of the primitive. For spheres the equation of a circle defines the boundary. Each block is associated with a Foot Print Engine micro-code sequence. The virtual addresses, along with commands for the appropriate memory operations, are inserted into the memory request queue. The starting addresses of the Foot Print sequences are written into the jump queue.

Foot Print Engine Hardware

In addition to the core functions, the Toe ASIC contains an interface to the Setup Engine and pixel write enable logic. The Setup Engine interface controls the burst transfer of data from the transfer RAM. The 16 Toes share an input bus that is used to broadcast the transfer data. The write enable logic generates pixel write enables based on the computed values of the bounding equations and Z comparison. The write enables determine which new color and Z values will be written to the pixel map.

The Foot Print Engine is a 4x4 array of Toe ASICs (See Figure 5), arranged so each Toe handles one pixel per memory block. The array is a single-instruction multiple-data (SIMD) machine with all the Toes executing instructions in lockstep from a single control store. The Toe ASIC supports conditional execution of instructions so that data-dependent operations can be individually controlled at the pixel level without using micro-code branches. Pixel data is transferred between the Foot Print Engine and the pixel registers in the DataPath over a 128-bit wide bus. It takes four 50ns cycles to completely transfer a pixel register; each cycle involves only one Toe in each column. Each column of Toes also shares a 16K x 32-bit scratch RAM. Only one Toe in a column may address it or write data to it at a time, but all four may receive data that is accessed by one of the four. This makes the scratch RAM very useful for constant values that are independent of the pixel position.

Foot Print Engine Operation

Under the control of the Address Engine, the Foot Print Engine begins a primitive by fetching the initial values and coefficients for all the rendering equations from the transfer RAM. These initial values were computed for the pixel at position (1,1) in the first block of the primitive. Each Toe adjusts the values (by adding or subtracting the appropriate coefficients, as shown in Figure 6) to obtain the correct values for its position in the array.

0,0 $C-A-B$	1,0 $C-B$	2,0 $C+A-B$	3,0 $C+2A-B$
0,1 $C-A$	1,1 C	2,1 $C+A$	3,1 $C+2A$
0,2 $C-A+B$	1,2 $C+B$	2,2 $C+A+B$	3,2 $C+2A+B$
0,3 $C-A+2B$	1,3 $C+2B$	2,3 $C+A+2B$	3,3 $C+2A+2B$

$$F(X,Y) = AX + BY + C$$

Foot Print Function Adjustment
Figure 6

After the first block is done, the Address Engine walks the Foot Print Engine to the other blocks in horizontal or vertical steps, at each step moving 4 pixels in either X or Y. For a horizontal step, each Toe updates each function by **4A**, while for vertical steps the functions are updated by **4B**. The functions are evaluated by finite differences taking advantage of the coherence of the objects being rendered.

Performance and System Operation

We will illustrate the performance of the system by presenting overall measured performance of a test application running through the X11 Window System, and the performance of the rendering processor for a variety of functions. This will show how well we have matched the geometry computation speed of the XFDI to the pixel rendering performance of the rendering processor.

The performance measured through the X11 Window System was done with a simple animation application that we have written for XFDI testing purposes. It uses X and XFDI calls to perform all of its graphics operations; all the functions that are used are available to user applications. It is important to note that the XFDI performance measurements were done in a multi-user UNIX® environment. In addition to X11, all the typical UNIX processes were active including those for network services. We feel that meaningful performance measurements must be made in the same environment in which the system will be used. Standalone measurements using specialized 'demo' programs yield results that are almost never possible for real applications to achieve.

The rendering processor performance was measured using an exact functional simulation model. This model was used during the hardware design process to validate the chip designs for the rendering processor, and to debug renderer micro-code. It is a register transfer level (RTL) model written in C that functionally models all register state internal to the renderer and all signals that cross chip boundaries and internal blocks within chips.

In the performance charts below, numbers are specified at a 50ns machine cycle. At the time the measurements were made, we had 20 running systems based on our first pass of our ASICs. These first pass machines have several minor design errors that have been fixed with external logic. This external logic prevents us from running these machines at their design speed of 50ns. As this paper is completed, second pass ASICs which will run at 50ns are returning from our silicon vendor. We have already received second pass Toe and SA ASICs and they have passed their chip level tests. The actual measurements were made on a first pass system running at 80ns. Since our system is synchronous, we can confidently extrapolate the performance to second pass systems running at 50ns.

XFDI Performance

The XFDI performance was measured using a data base for a torus and a test program that could render it in a variety of ways. The torus was rendered between 200 and 1000 times, and the elapsed time was measured using system time calls. When rendered as a shaded surface the torus contains 1624 triangles, or as lines, 1638 lines. As the paper is being completed, we are actively tuning the geometry computation code in the XFDI. The cases for which we can quote performance are shown in figure 7. We are still tuning some of these cases and expect further improvements.

Rendering Processor Performance

Triangles

For Gouraud or Flat shading without Z-buffering, the RP needs only to write the color values of the triangle. For large triangles, the RP is able to sustain 80 million pixels per second for either shading cases with both true-color and pseudo-color. When Z-buffering is in effect, the Z coordinates are read, and the color and Z coordinates are written. 40 million pixels per second are sustained for large pseudo-color triangles, and 25 million pixels per second for true-color.

When triangles are small, the rendering efficiency determines the performance. When the Foot Print processor walks over a small triangle, the 4x4 foot print often overlaps the triangle edges. This reduces the useful pixels produced with each Foot Print step and reduces the effective pixel throughput. We define the triangle rendering efficiency to be the ratio of the triangle area in pixels to the total number or pixels that are accessed in rendering it. On average, this is independent of the triangle orientation and depends on the ratio of the area to the perimeter of the triangle. For 100 pixel area triangles, we see rendering efficiencies ranging from 15% to 60%. We have found 45% rendering efficiency to be average and quote the triangle rendering performance for this case. For a 100 pixel triangle, this means that 14 Foot Print steps are required.

Lines

We quote our line rendering performance for 10 pixel long vectors. At this length, we see an average of 2.5 pixels written for each Foot Print step, for a total of 5 steps required. In figure 8 the Rendering Processor performance for a few cases are shown.

XFDI Performance	
Case	Performance
True and pseudo-color solid lines 10 pixels long	551,194 lines/sec
Pseudo-color Gouraud shaded Z-buffered 100 pixel triangles	163,710 triangles/sec
Pseudo-color Gouraud shaded Z-buffered 100 pixel triangles	
1 directional light	143,616 triangles/sec
2 directional lights	134,123 triangles/sec
4 directional lights	119,053 triangles/sec
Pseudo-color Phong shaded Z-buffered 100 pixel triangles 1 directional light, diffuse lighting	39,203 triangles/sec
Pseudo-color Phong shaded Z-buffered 100 pixel triangles 1 directional light, specular lighting	25,144 triangles/sec

Figure 7

Rendering Processor Performance		
Case	Clock Cycles	Rate
10 pixel Lines, pseudo-color	33	600,000/sec
Gouraud shaded, Z-buffered, pseudo-color 100 pixel triangles	129	155,000/sec
Gouraud shaded, Z-buffered, true-color 100 pixel triangles	195	100,000/sec
Phong shaded, Z-buffered, pseudo-color 100 pixel triangles 1 directional light	491	40,700/sec

Figure 8

Discussion

Geometry

We feel that the implementation of the geometry computations with a general purpose vector processor is very effective in this system. It is much easier to implement complex functions such as arbitrary clipping planes and general lighting models for the vector processor than for a specialized micro-coded engine. All the tools of a general purpose programming environment, such as high level languages, compilers and debuggers, are available. As more light sources and clipping planes are added, performance degrades predictably with the increased complexity of the geometry computations.

There are improvements that can be made. When the measured performance is compared to the rendering processor performance, it is clear that additional vector processing throughput would be useful. We are confident that our architecture will allow this to be easily improved in future systems. There are new floating point parts already available that could allow us to double the vector processing performance.

Pixel Memory

Rendering to pixel maps stored in virtual memory works very well, and provided several advantages over rendering to specialized frame buffer memory. It allows fast and flexible application access to pixels, and it allows us to support pixel space rendering algorithms that require very deep pixels.[4,20]

There are aspects that we feel can be improved. If we could eliminate the video memory, and generate video directly from main memory, we could avoid copying pixels from VPMs to the video memory. At the present time it is not possible to get sufficient main memory bandwidth to generate video directly from main memory. This requires us to copy pixels from VPMs to the video memory so they can be displayed, while systems with specialized frame buffers do not require this copy. In the present system, we are able to copy at over 60 million pixels per second, yet there are easy changes that can at least double this rate. A main memory location holds pixels in a 4x4 block, while video memory organizes them as a 16x1 stroke. Video memory is organized to simplify video generation, but this requires pixels to be reorganized through the pixel buffer during the copy. If pixels in the video memory could be organized as 4x4 blocks, the reorganization would not be needed and the copy rate could double.

Pixel Processing
The pixel processing capabilities of the Rendering Processor are very flexible and powerful. The presence of a multiplier at each Toe allows functions such as transparency and texture mapping to be easily supported. We feel that in the future, the trend will be to increase the numeric capability at the pixel level.

Simulations have shown that the Foot Print processor architecture can be scaled to approximately 3 times the present performance by using an 8x8 array of Toes. Four times the memory bandwidth would be needed to support this, but such bandwidth seems possible. Toe arrays larger than 8x8 would suffer from poor efficiency and could not be cost-justified. A MIMD architecture may then be needed to go faster. During rendering, the present system transfers data over the 512-bit wide memory path every 200ns, using non-interleaved memory cycles. We do use a simple form of interleaving for transferring data every 100ns during pixel copies. We feel that it will be possible in future systems to transfer memory data every 50ns using both interleaving and page mode DRAMs.

Although we were successful at eliminating specialized hardware for geometry computations and frame buffer memory, the Rendering Processor is still used only for graphics. It is implemented with general purpose computational elements that can evaluate any functions limited only by its fixed numeric precision. Since it is micro-programmed for graphics rendering functions, it remains a specialized processor. It is not clear that it will be possible in future systems to design a processor that can be used both for pixel rendering computations and other application specific computations.

Conclusion
We have presented a display system architecture intimately coupled with the CPU of our graphics supercomputer. The architectural principle of sharing resources between a display system and CPU is discussed, and a particular implementation is described. The performance of the system is shown to be competitive with specialized architectures. Limitations of the implementation are described, and possible extensions and areas for further study are put forth.

Acknowledgements
The authors would like to thank Professors Andries van Dam and Henry Fuchs for their suggestion to write this paper, for their review and comments while it was written, and most of all for their support and ideas during the architecture and design of the graphics system described here. We want to thank Bill Poduska and Mike Sporer for the key ideas behind the architecture, and Paul Jones and Mike Sporer for technical leadership during the project. Finally, the work described here is the creation of a large group of exceptional individuals working in Stellar's CPU hardware, Hardware Tools, Graphics hardware, and Software groups. Special thanks to Clare Campbell for assistance in manuscript preparation.

STELLAR, GS1000, DATAPATH, VIRTUAL PIXEL MAPS are trademarks of Stellar Computer Inc.

UNIX is a registered trademark of AT&T.

X Window Systerm is a trademark of MIT.

References

[1] Baskett, Forest, Tom Jermoluk, Doug Solomon. The 4D-MP Graphics Superworkstation: Computing + Graphics = 40 MIPS + 40 MFLOPS and 100,000 Lighted Polygons per Second. Digest of papers COMPCOM '88 (San Francisco, California, February 29 - March 4 1988) pp. 468-471

[2] Bishop, Gary and David Weimer, Fast Phong Shading. Proceedings of SIGGRAPH'86 (Dallas, Texas, August 18-22). In *Computer Graphics 20,* 4 (August 1986) pp. 103-106

[3] Bresenham, Jack. Algorithm for Computer Control of Digital Plotter. *IBM System Journal 4,* 1 (1965)

[4] Carpenter, Loren. The A-buffer, an Antialiased Hidden Surface Method. Proceedings of SIGGRAPH'84 (Minneapolis, Minnesota, July 23-27). In *Computer Graphics 18,* 3 (July 1984) pp. 103-108

[5] Clark, Jim. The Geometry Engine: A VLSI Geometry System for Graphics. Proceedings of SIGGRAPH'82 (Boston, Massachusetts, July 26-30). In *Computer Graphics 16,* 3 (July 1982) pp. 127-133

[6] Clark, Jim. and M. Hannah. Distributed Processing in a High Performance Smart Image Memory. *LAMBDA* 4th Quarter, 1980. pp. 40-45

[7] England, Nick. A Graphics System Architecture for Interactive Application Specific Display Functions. *IEEE Computer Graphics and Applications 6,* 1 (January 1986) pp. 60-70

[8] Fuchs, Henry and John Poulton. Pixel-planes: A VLSI-Oriented Design for a Raster Graphics Engine. *VLSI Design 2,* 3 3rd quarter 1981, pp. 20-28.

[9] Fuchs, Henry, Jack Goldfeather, Jeff Hulquist, Susan Spach, John Austin, Frederick Brooks, John Eyles, and John Poulton. Fast Spheres, Shadows, Textures , Transparencies, and Image Enhancements in Pixel-planes. Proceedings of SIGGRAPH'85 (San Francisco, California July 22-26). In *Computer Graphics 19,* 3 (July 1985) pp. 111-120

[10] Goldfeather, Jack, Jeff Hulquist, and Henry Fuchs. Fast Constructive Solid Geometry Display in the Pixel-Powers Graphics System. Proceedings of SIGGRAPH'86 (Dallas, Texas, August 18-22). In *Computer Graphics 20,* 4 (August 1986) pp. 107-116

[11] Goris, Andy, B. Fredrickson, H. Baeverstad Jr., "A Configurable Pixel Cache for Fast Image Generation", Computer Graphics and Applications, Vol. 7, No. 3

[12] Gouraud, H. "Computer Display of Curved Surfaces" Dept. of Computer Science, U. of Utah, UTEC-CSc-71-113, June 1971

[13] "*GRAPHICON* 700 Specifications", A marketing specification sheet from General Electric Company, Silicon Systems Technology Department, P.O. Box 13049 Research Triangle Park, NC 27709

[14] Levinthal, Adam and Thomas Porter. Chap - A SIMD Graphics Processor. Proceedings of SIGGRAPH'84 (Minneapolis, Minnesota, July 23-27). In *Computer Graphics 18,* 3 (July 1984) pp. 77-82

[15] McCormick, Bruce, Thomas DeFanti, Maxine Brown editors. Visualization in Scientific Computing. *Siggraph Computer Graphics newsletter 21,* 5 (October 1987)

[16] Phong, Bui Tuong. Illumination for Computer Generated Pictures. *Communications of the ACM18,* 6 (June 1975) pp. 311-317

[17] Sporer Michael, Franklin Moss, and Craig Mathias. An Introduction to the Architecture of the Stellar Graphics Supercomputer. Digest of papers COMPCOM '88 (San Francisco, California, February 29 - March 4 1988) pp. 464-467

[18] Swanson, Roger and Larry Thayer. A Fast Shaded-Polygon Renderer. Proceedings of SIGGRAPH'86 (Dallas, Texas, August 18-22). In *Computer Graphics 20,* 4 (August 1986) pp. 95-101

[19] Torborg, John . A Parallel Processor Architecture for Graphics Arithmetic Operations. Proceedings of SIGGRAPH'87 (Anaheim, California, July 27-31). In *Computer Graphics 21,* 4 (July 1987) pp. 197-204

[20] Williams, Lance. Casting Curved Shadows on Curved Surfaces. In *Computer Graphics 12,* 2 (1978) pp.270-274

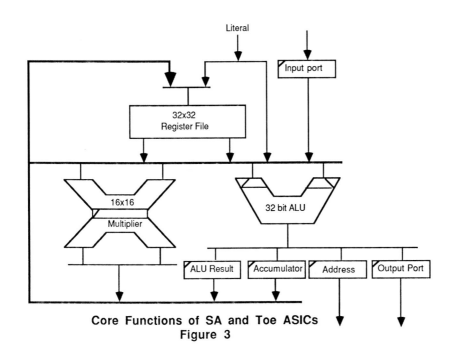

Core Functions of SA and Toe ASICs
Figure 3

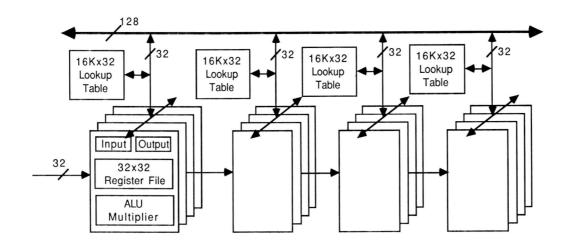

Foot Print Engine
Figure 5

Terrain Simulation Using a Model of Stream Erosion

Alex D. Kelley [1]
Michael C. Malin [2]
Gregory M. Nielson[1]

[1] Department of Computer Science   [2] Department of Geology
Arizona State University
Tempe, Arizona 85287

Abstract

The major process affecting the configuration and evolution of terrain is erosion by flowing water. Landscapes thus reflect the branching patterns of river and stream networks. The network patterns contain information that is characteristic of the landscape's topographic features. It is therefore possible to create an approximation to natural terrain by simulating the erosion of stream networks on an initially uneroded surface. Empirical models of stream erosion were used as a basis for the model presented here. Stream networks of various sizes and shapes are created by the model from a small number of initial parameters. The eroded surface is represented as a surface under tension, using the tension parameter to shape the profiles of valleys created by the stream networks. The model can be used to generate terrain databases for flight simulation and computer animation applications.

CR Categories and Subject Descriptors: I.3.3 [**Computer Graphics**]: Picture/Image Generation - Display Algorithms; I.3.5 [**Computer Graphics**]: Computational Geometry and Object Modeling - curve, surface and object representations; geometric algorithms; modeling packages; I.3.7 [**Computer Graphics**]: Three-dimensional Graphics and Realism - animation; color, shading, texture.

Additional Keywords and Phrases: Drainage Network Simulation, Erosion Models, Surfaces Under Tension, Database Amplification, Structural Models.

1. Introduction

During the past decade, considerable progress has been made toward developing efficient models for generating approximations to natural terrain. However, models that are both realistic and efficient have not been perfected. Models used in real-time applications (e.g., flight simulation) often sacrifice realism for efficiency, and the most realistic models may take many hours to compute a single scene.

Fractal techniques [8] are considered by many to be the most efficient method for creating realistic-appearing terrain.

Their efficiency stems from their ability to generate complex detail by "amplifying" a small database of structural or statistical primitives. In the case of terrain, this information may be derived directly from digital elevation maps of actual topography. In such cases, however, care must be taken to insure proper sampling of the geographic data: too little "seed" information will result in a conspicuous self-similarity, characterized by unrealistically complex and irregular terrain. In natural landscapes, different erosional and weathering processes shape the surface at different scales, thereby restricting self-similarity to a finite range in scale.

This paper describes an alternative approach from which images of realistic-looking terrain may be produced while retaining a degree of database amplification as present in fractal models. Its basic tenet is that greater realism can be achieved from somewhat more deterministic approximations of the relief of natural landscapes. As relief is primarily created through water erosion, the model developed here creates topographic structure by tracking the "negative space" formed by a *drainage system* comprised of a stream and its tributaries. Such systems are sometimes called *stream networks, channel networks* or *drainage networks*. The model shares an "amplifying" quality with fractals, in that tributaries may be added to a stream at a variety of scales. By increasing or decreasing the number of tributaries, terrain may be modeled at variable degrees of detail.

The primary sources of information for this work are empirical erosion models used in geomorphology. These models provide simple equations for simulating the features of drainage systems. The stream networks thus created then provide a coarse framework for surface fitting, which is accomplished by triangulation and interpolation using a bivariate analog of the spline under tension [19]. The tension parameters, useful for controlling the shape of the modeled terrain, are selected based upon the values of certain features of the stream network.

An additional goal of this model is to create a numerical system that can be used as a test bed for examining the physics by which erosion occurs on the earth and other planets [13]. Given the complexity of such problems, the amount of data produced by numerical simulations are nearly uninterpretable using conventional methods of analysis. By employing computer graphics, it is possible to synthesize these data into visual form, thus taking advantage of the visual bandwidth into the human brain.

©1988   ACM-0-89791-275-6/88/008/0263 $00.75

2. Background

2.1. Basic Terminology

The following is a glossary of mostly geological terms, used throughout the remainder of the paper:

baselevel -- the level below which a land surface cannot be reduced by running water.

constant of channel maintenance -- the minimum area necessary to support the development of a stream.

divide angle -- the angle (measured in the horizontal plane) between a drainage divide and an adjacent stream.

drainage area -- the amount of surface area draining into an individual section of channel.

drainage basin -- the area occupied by a stream network defined by the ridge crests that surround the network.

drainage density -- the total length of channel per unit area. This parameter is the reciprocal of the constant of channel maintenance.

drainage divide -- a boundary between streams, separating the area drained by these streams; this is usually a ridge.

drainage polygon -- a polygon representing a portion of the surface area drained by one side of a section of channel.

exterior link -- a section of tributary channel that extends from a source of water to a junction with another stream.

interior link -- a section of channel between two tributaries.

junction -- the point of confluence of two streams.

junction angle -- the angle (measured in the horizontal plane) formed by the confluence of two streams.

link -- a section of channel extending between two tributaries or between a source and its first junction with a stream.

link gradient -- the change in elevation between two junctions, divided by the horizontal distance between them.

longitudinal profile -- the change in elevation as a function of position along a stream.

main trunk stream -- the stream to which all water collected by the tributaries is funnelled.

outlet link -- a link through which all water is discharged from the network. This link is the lowest end of the network.

sources -- the farthest points upstream in a drainage system.

valley sidewall slope -- the slope measured from the edge of a channel to a brink where the slope begins to taper off.

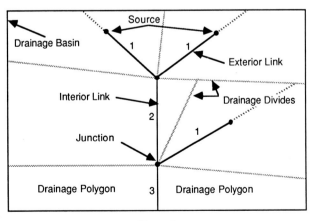

Figure 1.
Schematic Diagram Illustrating Terminology
Introduced in Section 2.1.

Several of these terms are illustrated in Figure 1. The links are numbered according to *Shreve Ordering* [23]. These numbers reflect the cumulative increase in the amount of water as links come together. Exterior links are assigned a magnitude of 1. When links of magnitude n and m come together the resulting link has magnitude (n + m). Research in geomorphology has shown that there are relationships between stream order and many of the properties of drainage systems [20]. Several empirical models of planimetric features employed in the present simulation are derived from these relationships.

2.2. Previous work

Stream network simulations have been developed by researchers in geomorpholgy over the last two decades. The majority are two dimensional, falling into two broad categories herein termed the stream convergence and headward growth models. A survey published by Abrahams [1] is an excellent starting point for the reader interested in learning more about drainage network research.

In stream convergence models [15,22], a stream is initiated by randomly choosing a source location within a grid. Its growth and direction is controlled by successive random moves into adjacent grid areas. It continues to grow until it joins another stream or goes outside the grid. Stream convergence models produce various statistics that are similar to those of natural networks, but they do not simulate their physical appearance. Streams often wander excessively and drainage basins exhibit highly irregular geometries.

Headward growth models [11,5] better simulate the physical appearance of natural networks and often produce statistics closer to reality than stream convergence models. The growth of a stream is initiated through headward random walks on a grid representing uneroded area. Branching of an original stream occurs upon reaching a pre-defined length. If a stream threatens to cross an existing stream, its growth is terminated.

An alternate type of model simulates erosion of the entire landscape using transport equations for the removal of solid material [14]. These models show greater promise in understanding the geomorphic processes and mechanisms that control the evolution of natural drainage systems. The principal difficulty with this approach is the selection of appropriate transport equations for the channel and hillslope subsystems.

3. Modeling the Drainage Network

Caution must be exercised in comparing the model presented here with the simulation models described above, as an approach directly analogous to these other works has not employed. Rather, the model presented below is structural [9] in the sense that a three-dimensional skeleton of terrain is developed. Aside from fitting points representing the stream network, parameters controlling the appearance of the surface (e.g., texture, tension, etc.) may be freely adjusted. Structural models have been previously used as a basis for modeling plants and trees [3,24].

The model presented herein incorporates empirical methods for determining tributary arrangement along principal streams, interior and exterior link lengths, drainage density, stream junction angles, drainage divides, longitudinal profile, and valley sidewall slope.

3.1. Drainage Network Initialization

The data structure used to describe the drainage network is a tree, where each node represents an individual channel link and the surface area that contributes water to it. The components of each node are used to store the link's endpoints, length, Shreve order, drainage polygons, and drainage area. The tree is constructed by recursively adding sub-branches, hereinafter referred to as *tributary links*.

To initialize the root of the tree, points projected onto the horizontal plane that describe the initial outline of the drainage basin and position of the main trunk stream are specified by the user. An example of an initial drainage system is shown in Figure 2. The procedure for computing the elevations at these data points is described at the end of Section 3.2. To initialize the left and right drainage polygons, the drainage basin is partitioned along the line segment representing the maintrunk stream. Since the maintrunk stream is initially represented by a single link, the Shreve order assigned to this root node is 1.

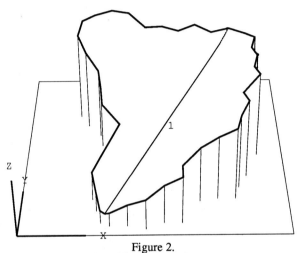

Figure 2.
An Initial Drainage System.

3.2. The Addition of Tributaries

A recursive algorithm is used to generate additional links within the drainage network. The addition of a tributary link occurs when the channel maintenance of a candidate link is greater than the mean value specified for the entire drainage basin. The constant of channel maintenance is defined by the quantity:

$$C = A / L \qquad (1)$$

where A is the total drainage area and L is the total length of channel. On a regional scale, surface material is the main factor controlling this parameter [1]. For example, in humid-temperate climates, typical values range between 0.33 and 0.25 for resistant materials (e.g., sandstone). In contrast, if the surface material is weak (e.g., clay), the same climate produces values that range from 0.00077 - 0.00091 [21].

Adding a new tributary link results in the insertion of two additional nodes into the tree. The second node, herein termed the *upstream link*, is created by subdividing the the original, or *parent link*, into two sublinks at the point of junction (the shortened parent link is then called the *downstream link*). Initializing the branch nodes as well as modifying the parameters within the parent node involves the computation of Shreve orders, junction position, tributary arrangement, junction angle and drainage divides.

The Shreve order at each of the three links is computed in the following manner. As all tributaries are initially exterior

links, their magnitudes are 1. The upstream link inherits the original Shreve order of the parent link. The downstream link receives water from both the upstream link and the magnitude 1 tributary. Thus its magnitude is the original (ancestral) Shreve order plus 1. Stream orders throughout the network increment with the contribution of each new tributary, as appropriate.

The following equation determines the junction position where the tributary link enters the parent link:

$$\text{Junction} = \text{MeanJunction} + \text{Rand( )} * \text{DeltaJunction} \qquad (2)$$

where Rand( ) is a procedure returning a pseudorandom number uniformly distributed between -1.0 and +1.0. Each link in the network has "parametric length" 1. Therefore, the values of MeanJunction and DeltaJunction are set to insure that Junction is greater than 0.0 and less than or equal to 1.0. For example, if MeanJunction is 0.5 and DeltaJunction is 0.0, the junction position will subdivide the parent link into two sublinks of equal length.

The placement of junctions has a direct effect on the resulting length of interior and exterior links. A small MeanJunction is likely to result in smaller interior links than exterior links. Conversely, if MeanJunction is large, exterior links are likely to be smaller than interior links. DeltaJunction and the pseudorandom number are used to provide a stochastic perturbation on the resulting link lengths. Investigation into the ratios of exterior link lengths to interior link lengths have found them to vary considerably between regions, although the ratio is usually greater than 1 [1].

The decision on which side of the parent link to place the tributary link is based on field observations of tributary arrangements in natural networks [7]. These observations show that in the lower reaches of a stream, the initial tributaries have a greater probability of occurring on the obtuse or outer side of the stream. Along the middle reaches of the stream, a tributary is more likely to develop on the side opposite the next tributary encountered downstream. Both of these observations are attributed to space filling constraints imposed on tributary development.

In order to model these empirical relationships, a stream is partitioned into three reaches (lower, middle, and upper) of equal length. Each junction's position is evaluated with respect to this partitioning and the tributary arrangement in the lower and middle reaches are biased accordingly. In the upper reaches of the stream, the model assigns both sides an equal probability, although some evidence has shown that the shape of the basin at the upstream end will tend to promote tributary development on one side over the other [1].

The tributary and upstream links are next assigned a junction angle, which is estimated using the Howard geometric model [12]:

$$\text{Junction Angle} = E_1 + E_2 \qquad (3)$$

where

$$\cos E_1 = S_3/S_1 \qquad (4)$$

$$\cos E_2 = S_3/S_2 \qquad (5)$$

The entrance angles E_1 and E_2 (Figure 3) are projected onto the horizontal plane. S_1, S_2 and S_3 are the stream gradients (slope tangents) of the tributary, upstream and downstream links, respectively. The magnitude of each of the three links is used to estimate the stream gradients, derived using a simplified form of Flint's [6] equation:

$$S = p(2u - 1)^q \qquad (6)$$

where S is the gradient of a link of magnitude u, p is the mean link length of exterior links, and q is a negative exponent that is specific to a particular network. In the networks he studied, Flint found q to range between -0.37 and -0.837. Other field studies have shown q to have an average value of -0.6.

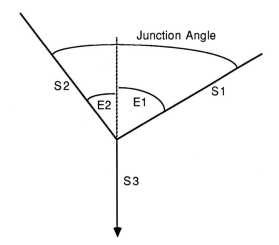

Figure 3.
Schematic Diagram of Howard's Junction Angle Model.

The orientation of the tributary and upstream links are set according to the junction angle. The source point of the tributary is computed by estimating the length of this exterior link. This is performed using Equation 2, replacing MeanJunction and DeltaJunction with MeanLength and DeltaLength, respectively. Similarly, the value of these parameters are set so that the exterior link length is greater than 0.0 and less than or equal to 1.0. If the result is 1.0, the tributary link will extend to a corresponding edge of the drainage polygon.

The drainage polygons of upstream, tributary, and downstream links are initialized by partitioning the original drainage polygons belonging to the parent link. As shown in Figure 1, the dotted lines represent the three drainage divides that separate the area drained by each of the three links connected at a junction. The orientation of each drainage divide is computed using a model that relates divide angles to the link and valley sidewall slopes [2]. Each of the three divides is extended from the junction to a corresponding edge of the left or right drainage polygon.

The planimetric features discussed thus far are computed by projecting the drainage system onto the horizontal plane. The third dimension is now added by computing the elevation at each data point. The height at the source and junctions are computed by approximating the longitudinal profile of individual streams. The remaining elevations at the ridge crests are computed using a model for valley sidewall slopes.

The longitudinal profile of a stream is determined using Equation 6 to approximate the gradients (slope tangents) at each link in the stream. First, the baselevel of the junction at the end of the outlet link is assigned to a specified elevation. Then, working upstream, the gradient at each link is computed and the

elevation at each junction set according to the following scheme: If z_1 is the elevation at junction j_1 and z_2 the elevation at the next upstream junction j_2,

$$z_2 = z_1 + S * L \qquad (7)$$

where S is the link gradient computed in Equation 6 and L is the projected horizontal distance from j_1 to j_2. Starting from the outlet link, the initial value of z_1 is the baselevel elevation. To set the elevation of the upstream junction at the next link in the stream, z_1 is assigned the value of z_2 from the previous link. The resulting curve of each stream exhibits the characteristic concave upward profile [17].

Valley sidewalls are represented by the left and right drainage polygons associated with each link in the network. As shown in Figure 2, a stream link occupies the lower edge shared by the left and right drainage polygons. Excluding the endpoints of this edge, the height at the remaining vertices of the drainage polygons are computed using a model for valley sidewall slopes. The slope angle (measured from the stream link to each vertex) is determined from Equation 2, replacing MeanJunction with MeanValley Sidewall Slope and DeltaJunction with DeltaValley Sidewall Slope. In this case, these parameters are set to insure that the angle of elevation ranges between zero and ninety degrees.

4. Modeling the Surface

The result from applying the methods described in Section 3 is a three-dimensional polygonal representation of the drainage basin, shown in Figure 4. To complete the description of the modeled terrain, a surface under tension is constructed from the polygonal representation using a method of scattered data interpolation. The tension parameter is used to control the shape of the valley sidewall profiles.

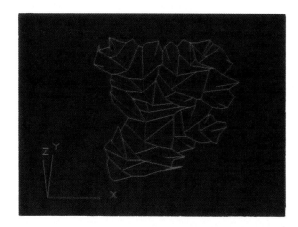

Figure 4.
Polygonal Representation of Modeled Terrain.

4.1. Surface Fitting

In general terms, a scattered data method accepts independent data values (x_i, y_i), $i = 1,...,n$ and associated dependent values f_i, $i=1,...,n$ and produces a surface $S(x,y)$ such that $S(x_i, y_i) = f_i$, $i=1,...,n$. A variety of scattered data interpolation methods are discussed in Franke [10]. For this application, it is important that the fitting technique have certain properties. First, the influence of the data should be local in that a change in one data value, (x_k, y_k), f_k should only affect the surface in the neighborhood of that point and the change should have essentially no impact at greater distance. It is also important that the method be computationally efficient and be able to handle large data sets. Both these properties are usually shared by a class of scattered data methods which attempt to mimic the classical univariate spline by using a piecewise defined surface with some smoothing interconnecting conditions between surface segments. A decomposition of the domain into triangles is the most common approach.

The method selected here is a surface under tension technique proposed by Nielson and Franke [19]. There are three stages to their method. First, the domain is triangulated using the data points (x_i, y_i), i=1,...,n as vertices. Next, the gradient of the surface, S, is estimated and finally, a triangular surface patch is used to define $S(x,y)$ over each triangle. The first stage is performed by triangulating each drainage polygon in the network. Edges inferred by the links and divides of the drainage network remain edges in the triangulation. The gradients are estimated by solving the problem of minimizing the quantity:

$$\sum_{ij \in E} \int_{e_{ij}} \left[\frac{\partial^2 S}{\partial e_{ij}^2}\right]^2 + v_{ij} \int_{e_{ij}} \left[\frac{\partial S}{\partial e_{ij}}\right]^2 \quad (8)$$

where E is a list of all the edges in the triangulation. This quantity is similar to the norm that is used to characterize the univariate spline under tension [4]. The solution here is only defined over a domain consisting of the edges of the triangulation and is referred to as a *minimum norm network*. The parameters v_{ij} are tension parameters and can be used to adjust the shape of the network. As the tension parameter associated with an edge is increased, the arc of the network related to this edge converges to a straight line segment. In order to extend the surface to the entire domain, a triangular surface patch is used over each triangle. This surface patch is chosen so that it will match all of the boundary information provided by the minimum norm network and also reflect the affects that the tension parameters v_{ij} have on the network.

A wireframe representation of the modeled terrain is shown in Figure 5. This surface under tension was evaluated at evenly spaced locations within a 50 x 50 grid and transformed into triangles. Points outside the boundary of the surface were assigned a zero elevation value. The tension value assigned to the endpoints of the stream links was 5.0, while the remainder of the data points along the ridge crests were assigned a tension value of 0.0. This resulted in a convex curved profile at the valley sidewalls. More analytical treatment of the use of tension in simulating valley sidewall profiles will be eventually incorporated into the model.

To simulate surface roughness features, each sampled elevation may be displaced by a small random perturbation. Additional elevations for the terrain shown in Figure 5 were evaluated along the boundary edges of each stream in the network. The width of a stream is computed using a model which relates channel width to the order of the individual links [20].

5. Rendering the Surface

A fully rendered image of simulated terrain is shown in Figure 6. Perspective views of the terrain surface can be generated using conventional perspective and hidden point removal techniques. In the implementation used here, hidden surface removal is performed using a depth sort algorithm [18].

Surface colors were selected from tables which approximate the color of foliage, snow, water and rock types. The choice of color assigned to each triangle is based on its location, elevation, and gradient. For example, steep triangles (measured by the direction of the normal) are assigned the color of a rock type. The surface color is modulated using a simple diffuse lighting model with no specular component.

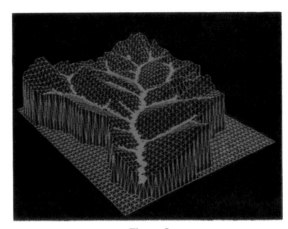

Figure 5.
Wireframe Representation of Modeled Terrain.

Figure 6.
Shreve Valley.

6. Implementation

The program for the model outlined in this paper is run under Berkeley 4.2 Unix on a SUN 3/160, with no floating point accelerator and 12 Mb of memory. The majority of the modeling software was written in C, except for several FORTRAN-77 subroutines used to compute the minimum norm network. The rendering programs are written in C and run under VMS 4.2 on a VAX 11/750 with floating point accelerator and 6 Mb of memory.

Modeling consists of computing the polygonal representation, triangulation, minimum norm network, and surface evaluation. Computation time for the stream network shown in Figure 6 was 8 minutes, about 90% of which was consumed by the surface evaluation and minimum norm network computations. The surface was evaluated at 26,671 locations and transformed into 41,339 triangles. This series of computations need be performed only once. Rendering the 512 x 512 x 24-bit image took 4 minutes.

7. Conclusion & Future Work

A method for modeling terrain at the scale in which fluvial processes shape its surface has been demonstrated. Terrain is modeled by simulating the erosion caused by stream networks on an initially uneroded surface. The model has an "amplifying" quality because an initial stream network evolves into a much larger network. Furthermore, very little information is required to represent the initial drainage system. Empirical models from geomorphology are used as a basis for the modeling. Planimetric attributes are parameterized and therefore do not require explicit modeling.

The model may be amplified in many ways. Although the tension parameter appears to be useful in controlling the transverse profiles of valleys, the model currently does not incorporate an explicit or physically based model of changes in hillslope profiles. Thus, the hillslopes are too simplistic.

A deficiency of the model is that it addresses only one, albeit major, mechanism for shaping landscapes. Several others contribute to the total picture. At smaller scales, various weathering processes are important factors controlling the shape and texture of rock surfaces. Stochastic subdivision methods [16] are a possible source for modeling these smaller features. The model can probably be animated to show the evolution of a landscape once these suggested areas of future work have been addressed.

Acknowledgments

ADK and MCM were supported by NASA Grant NAGW-1 and NSF Grant EAR-8313091. GMN was supported by the U.S. Department of Energy under contract DE-FG02-87ER25041 to Arizona State University and by a NATO Research Grant RG.0097/88. We wish to thank Mike Caplinger for his help in defining and implementing the rendering software used to produce Figure 6. Richard Franke wrote the original code which performed the minimum norm network computations.

References

1. Abrahams, A. "Channel Networks: A Geomorphological Perspective", *Water Resour. Res., 20,* 2 (February 1984), 161-168.

2. Abrahams, A. "Divide Angles and Their Relation to Interior Link Lengths in Natural Channel Networks", *Geographical Analysis, 12,* 2 (April 1980), 161-168.

3. Bloomenthal, J. "Modeling the Mighty Maple", *Computer Graphics 19,* 3 (July 1985), 305-311.

4. de Boor, C., *A Practical Guide to Splines,* Springer-Verlag, 1978.

5. Dunkerly, D. "Frequency Distributions of Stream Link Lengths and the Development of Channel Networks", *J. Geol. 85,* (1977), 459-470.

6. Flint, J. "Stream Gradient as a Function of Order, Magnitude, and Discharge", *Water Resour. Res., 10,* 5 (October 1974), 969-973.

7. Flint, J. "Tributary Arrangements in Fluvial Systems", *Am. J. Sci. 280,* (January 1980), 26-45.

8. Fournier, A., Fussell, D., and Carpenter, L. "Computer Rendering of Stochastic Models", *Commun. ACM , 25,* 6 (June 1982), 371-384.

9. Fournier, A. "Prolegomenon", Siggraph '87 Course Notes: The Modeling of Natural Phenomena", July 1987.

10. Franke, R., "Scattered Data Interpolation: tests of some methods, *Math. Comp.* 38 (1982), 181-200.

11. Howard, A. "Simulation of Stream Networks by Headward Growth and Branching", *Geogr. Anal., 3,* (1971), 29-50.

12. Howard, A. "Optimal Angles of Stream Junction: Geometric, Stability to Capture, and Minimum Power Criteria", *Water Resour. Res., 7,* 4 (August 1971), 863-873.

13. Kelley, A., Malin, M. "Three-Dimensional Digital Simulation of Drainage Basin Development: Modeling the Martian Valley Networks", *Reports of Planetary Geology and Geophysics Program - 1987, NASA Tech Mem.* (in press).

14. Kirkby, M. "A Two-Dimensional Simulation Model of Slope and Stream Evolution", In *Hillslope Processes,* edited by A. D. Abrahams, Allen and Unwin, Boston, 1986, 203-222.

15. Leopold, L. and Langbein, W. "The Concept of Entropy in Landscape Evolution", *Geol. Surv. Prof. Pap. 500-A,* 1962.

16. Lewis, J. "Generalized Stochastic Subdivision", *ACM Trans. Graphics, 6,* 2 (July 1987), 167-190.

17. Morisawa, M., *Streams: Their Dynamics and Morphology,* McGraw-Hill Inc. 1968.

18. Newell, M. E., Newell, R. G.and Sancha, T. L. "A Solution to the Hidden Surface Problem", *Proc. ACM Nat. Conf.,* (1972), 236-243.

19. Nielson, G. and Franke, R. "A Method for Construction of Surfaces Under Tension", *Rocky Mountain Journal of Mathematics 14,* 1 (Winter 1984), 203-221.

20. Richards, K. "A Note on Changes in Channel Geometry at Tributary Junctions", *Water Resour. Res., 16,* 1 (February 1980), 241-244.

21. Ritter, D., *Process Geomorphology,* Wm. C. Brown, Dubuque, Iowa, 1978.

22. Schenck H. "Simulation of the Evolution of Drainage-Basin Networks with a Digital Computer", *J. Geophys. Res., 68,* 20 (October 1963), 5739-5745.

23. Shreve, R., "Statistical Law of Stream Numbers", *J. Geol.,* 74, (1966), 17-37.

24. Smith, A. "Plants, Fractal, and Formal Languages", *Computer Graphics 18,* 3, (July 1984), 1-10.

Modeling Inelastic Deformation:
Viscoelasticity, Plasticity, Fracture

Demetri Terzopoulos
Kurt Fleischer

Schlumberger Palo Alto Research
3340 Hillview Avenue, Palo Alto, CA 94304

Abstract

We continue our development of physically-based models for animating nonrigid objects in simulated physical environments. Our prior work treats the special case of objects that undergo perfectly elastic deformations. Real materials, however, exhibit a rich variety of inelastic phenomena. For instance, objects may restore themselves to their natural shapes slowly, or perhaps only partially upon removal of forces that cause deformation. Moreover, the deformation may depend on the history of applied forces. The present paper proposes inelastically deformable models for use in computer graphics animation. These dynamic models tractably simulate three canonical inelastic behaviors—viscoelasticity, plasticity, and fracture. Viscous and plastic processes within the models evolve a reference component, which describes the natural shape, according to yield and creep relationships that depend on applied force and/or instantaneous deformation. Simple fracture mechanics result from internal processes that introduce local discontinuities as a function of the instantaneous deformations measured through the model. We apply our inelastically deformable models to achieve novel computer graphics effects.

Keywords: Modeling, Animation, Deformation, Elasticity, Dynamics, Simulation

CR Categories and Subject Descriptors: G.1.8—Partial Differential Equations; I.3.5—Computational Geometry and Object Modeling (Curve, Surface, Solid, and Object Representations); I.3.7—Three-Dimensional Graphics and Realism (Animation); I.6.3 Simulation and Modeling (Applications)

©1988   ACM-0-89791-275-6/88/008/0269 $00.75

1. Introduction

Modeling and animation based on physical principles is establishing itself as a computer graphics technique offering unsurpassed realism [1, 2]. Physically-based models of natural phenomena are making exciting contributions to image synthesis. A popular theme is the use of Newtonian dynamics to animate articulated or arbitrarily constrained assemblies of rigid objects in simulated physical environments [3–8]. The animation of continuously stretchable and flexible objects in such environments is also attracting increasing attention. It is extremely difficult to animate nonrigid objects with any degree of realism using conventional, kinematic methods. A better approach to synthesizing physically plausible nonrigid motions is to model the continuum-mechanical principles governing the dynamics of nonrigid bodies.

Initial models of flexible objects were concerned with static shape [9, 10]. Subsequent work produced models for animating nonrigid objects in simulated physical worlds [11–14]. In [11] we employ elasticity theory to model the shapes and motions of deformable curves, surfaces, and solids. Technically as well as computationally, this approach is more demanding than conventional methods for modeling free-form shape, but the results are well worth the extra effort. Our simulation algorithms have proven capable of synthesizing realistic motions arising from the complex interaction of elastically deformable models with diverse forces, ambient media, and impenetrable obstacles.

Prior work on deformable models in computer graphics treats only the case of objects undergoing perfectly elastic deformation. A deformation is termed elastic if the undeformed or reference shape restores itself completely, upon removal of all external forces. A basic assumption underlying the constitutive laws of classical elasticity theory is that the restoring force (stress) in a body is a single-valued function of the deformation (strain) of the body and, moreover, that it is independent of the history of the deformation. It is possible to quantify elastic restoring forces in terms of potential energies of deformation, a characterization that we employ in the formulation of our models. Like an ideal spring, an elastic model stores potential energy during deformation and releases the energy entirely as it recovers the reference shape. By contrast, a perfect (Newtonian) fluid stores no deformation energy, hence it exhibits no resilience.

In the present paper, we develop computer graphics models which make inroads into the broad spectrum of *inelastic* deformation phenomena intermediate between perfectly elastic solids, on the one hand, and viscous fluids, on the other. Generally, a deformation is inelastic if it does not obey the idealized (Hookean) constitutive laws of classical elasticity. Inelastic deformations occur in real materials for temperatures and forces exceeding certain limiting values above which irreversible dislocations at the atomic level can no longer be neglected.

Why model inelastic behavior? Aside from an artistic motivation to achieve a rich variety of novel graphics effects, we wish to incorporate into our deformable models the mechanical behaviors commonly associated with high polymer solids—organic compounds containing a large number of recurring chemical structures—such as modeling clay, thermoplastic compound, or silicone putty [15]. These behaviors are responsible for the universal utility of these sorts of modeling materials in molding complex shapes (e.g, in the design of automobile bodies). We are interested in assimilating some of the natural conveniences of this traditional art into the computer-aided design environment of the future. We envision users, aided by stereoscopic and haptic input-output devices, carving "computer plasticine" and applying simulated forces to it in order to create free-form shapes interactively.

Our physically-based models incorporate three canonical genres of inelastic behavior—*viscoelasticity*, *plasticity*, and *fracture*. Viscoelastic material behavior includes the characteristics of a viscous fluid together with elasticity. Silicone ("Silly") putty exhibits unmistakable viscoelastic behavior; it flows under sustained force, but bounces like a rubber ball when subjected to quickly transient forces. Inelastic materials for which permanent deformations result from the mechanism of slip or atomic dislocation are known as plastic. Most metals, for instance, behave elastically only when the applied forces are small, after which they yield plastically, resulting in permanent dimensional changes. Our models can also simulate the behavior of thermoplastics, which may be formed easily into desired shapes by pressure at relatively moderate temperatures, then made elastic or rigid around these shapes by cooling. As materials are deformed beyond certain limits, they eventually fracture. Cracks develop according to internal force or deformation distributions and their propagation is affected by local variations in material properties.

Fig. 1 illustrates some of the capabilities of our inelastic models in Flatland, a restricted physical world. Flatland models are deformable planar curves capable of rigid-body dynamics or general "elastoviscoplastodynamics" (!) with possible fractures. An efficient numerical algorithm provides real-time response (on Symbolics 3600 series Lisp Machines), enabling us to interact with the models by subjecting them to user-controlled forces, aerodynamic drag, gravity, collisions, etc. (see [11] for more details on formulating forces). Fig. 1a–c shows the strobed motion of an inelastic flatland model that has zero, medium, and high viscoelasticity as it collides into frictionless walls. The strobe frames in Fig. 1d illustrate the interactive molding

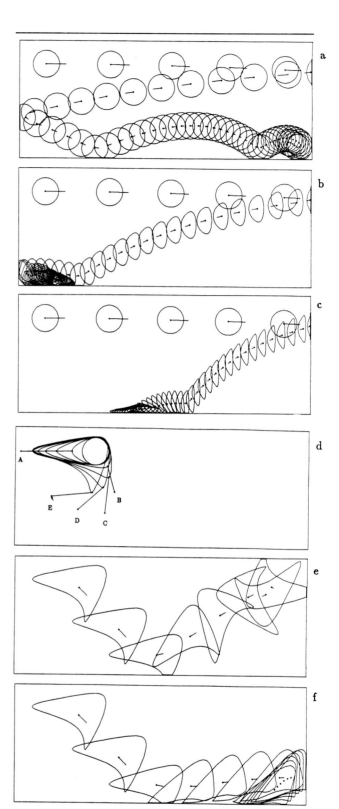

Figure 1. Simulations in Flatland. Models are strobed while undergoing motion subject to gravity, drag, collisions, and user-controlled forces. Velocity vector of the center of mass (dot) is indicated. (a) Elastic model. (b) Viscoelastic model. (c) Highly viscoelastic model. (d) A viscoelastic model is deformed. (e) Resulting shape is made elastic and bounced. (f) Same shape made viscoelastic and bounced.

of inelastic models through the application of simple forces. The user starts with a circular viscoelastic model fixed at its center. The model simulates thermoplastic material. The user applies a sustained spring force from point A. The spring (under position control from a "mouse") is shown in the figure as a line between two points. The spring force deforms the model, stretching it to the left (an effect known as stress relaxation). Next, the user releases the spring from A, then reactivates it at B and sweeps through C, D, and E, pulling the material along. The final shape is set by "cooling" the thermoplastic. The model is then made perfectly elastic and it can be bounced (Fig. 1e). Finally the model is made inelastic and bounced again (Fig. 1f). Later we present further details and examples of more complex three-dimensional inelastic models.

The inelastic models described in this paper generalize our prior elastic models and inherit their animate characteristics, thereby unifying the description of shape and motion. We show how to model inelastic deformation in the context of two varieties of deformable models which we have developed in prior papers [11, 14]. Both formulations allow elastic deformation away from a reference shape represented within the model. In our inelastic generalizations, internal viscous and plastic processes dynamically feed part of the instantaneous deformation back into the reference shape component. Simplified fracture mechanics result from internal processes which introduce local discontinuities dynamically as a function of the instantaneous deformations measured through the model.

We conclude the introduction with a perspective on our work as it relates to the engineering analysis of materials and structures. First, here is a caveat: We make no particular attempt to model specific materials accurately. Usually the general behavior of a material will defy accurate mathematical description, and engineering models tend to be complicated. Sophisticated finite element codes are available for analyzing the mechanics of nonrigid structures constructed from specific materials such as steel and concrete [16]. Computer graphics has become indispensable for visualizing the overwhelming amount of data that can be produced during the preprocessing and postprocessing stages of finite element analysis [17–19].

Although we adopt certain numerical techniques from finite element analysis, our computer graphics modeling work has a distinctly different emphasis. We have sought to develop physically-based models with associated numerical procedures that can be utilized to create realistic animations. Hence, our deformable models are convenient for computer graphics applications, where a keen concern with tractability motivates mathematical abstraction and computational expediency. This paper develops inelastic models that idealize regimes of material response under certain types of environmental conditions, whose parameters describe qualitatively familiar behaviors, such as stretchability, bendability, resilience, fragility, etc.

The organization of the remainder of the paper is as follows: Section 2 describes inelastic deformation phenomena in more detail using idealized mechanical units. Sections 3 and 4 review our basic elastic models and explain how we incorporate inelastic behaviors into the partial dif-

ferential equations that govern their motions. Section 5 summarizes our implementation. Section 6 presents more simulation results and Section 7 draws conclusions.

2. Inelastic Deformation

A formal treatment of inelastic deformation is beyond the scope of this paper. For theory on viscoelasticity, plasticity, and fracture, refer to, e.g., [20–22]. The basic inelastic behaviors may be understood readily, however, in terms of assemblies of idealized uniaxial (one-dimensional) mechanical units. The ideal linear elastic unit is the spring (Fig. 2a). The spring satisfies Hooke's law—elongation or contraction e (strain) is proportional to applied tension or compression force f (stress): $ke = f$, where k is the spring constant. The elastic unit is supplemented by two other uniaxial units, the viscous and plastic units (Fig. 2b,c). By assembling these units in specific configurations, we can simulate simple, uniaxial viscoelasticity and plasticity. Our inelastically deformable models incorporate the laws governing these units, suitably generalized and extended over a multidimensional continuum.

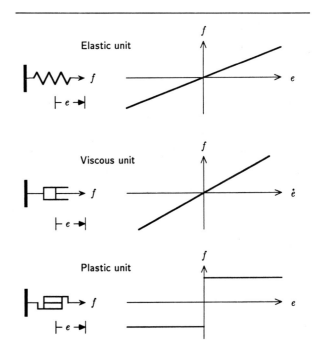

Figure 2. Uniaxial deformation units and their response to applied forces. (a) Elastic spring. (b) Viscous dashpot. (c) Plastic slip unit.

2.1. Viscoelasticity

Viscoelasticity is a generalization of elasticity and viscosity. It is characterized by the phenomenon of creep which manifests itself as a time dependent deformation under constant applied force. In addition to instantaneous deformation, creep deformations develop which generally increase with the duration of the force. Whereas an elastic model, by definition, is one which has the memory only of its reference shape, the instantaneous deformation of a viscoelastic model is a function of the entire history of applied force. Conversely, the instantaneous restoring force is a function of the entire history of deformation.

The ideal linear viscous unit is the dashpot (Fig. 2b). The rate of increase in elongation or contraction e is proportional to applied force f: $\eta\dot{e} = f$, where η is the viscosity constant (the overstruck dot denotes a time derivative). The elastic and viscous units are combined to model linear viscoelasticity, so that the internal forces depend not just on the magnitude of deformation, but also on the rate of deformation. Fig. 3a illustrates a four-unit viscoelastic model, a series assembly of the so called Maxwell and Voigt viscoelastic models. The stress-strain relationship for this assembly has the general form

$$a_2\ddot{e} + a_1\dot{e} + a_0 e = b_2\ddot{f} + b_1\dot{f} + b_0 f, \qquad (1)$$

where the coefficients depend on the spring and viscosity constants. The response of the models to an applied force (Fig. 3b) is shown graphically in Fig. 3c.

gation or contraction as soon as the applied force exceeds a yield force. During plastic yield, the apparent instantaneous elastic constants of the material are smaller than those in the elastic state. Removal of applied force causes the material to unload elastically with its initial elastic constants. This behavior may be termed elastoplastic.

Viscoplasticity, a generalization of plasticity and viscosity, can be modeled by assembling dashpots with plastic units. Analogously, elastoplasticity generalizes elasticity and plasticity and is modeled by assembling springs with plastic units. Fig. 4b presents graphically the response of a simple elastoplastic model (Fig. 4a). The model is linearly elastic from O to A. After reaching the yield point A, the model exhibits linear work hardening. Upon unloading from B, the elastic region is defined by force amplitude $f_B - f_C = 2f_A$. Subsequent loads now move the model along BC. Loading past point B causes further plastic deformation along BE. The reverse plastic deformation occurs along CD. After a closed cycle in force and displacement OABCDO, the model returns to its initial state and subsequent behavior is not affected by the cycle.

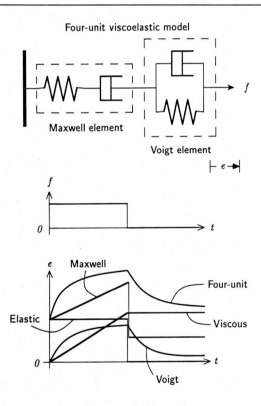

Figure 3. Uniaxial viscoelastic model. (a) The four-element model is a series connection of a Maxwell viscoelastic unit and a Voigt viscoelastic unit. (b) Force applied to the model. (c) Response of various components.

2.2. Plasticity

In plasticity, unique relationships between displacement and applied force do not generally exist. The ideal plastic unit is the slip unit (Fig. 2c). It is capable of arbitrary elon-

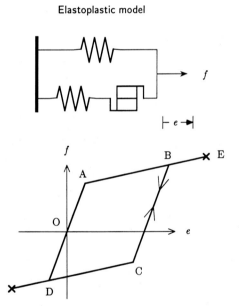

Figure 4. Uniaxial elastoplastic model. (a) The three-unit model. (b) Response to applied force (see text).

2.3. Fracture

Solid materials cannot sustain arbitrarily large stresses without failure, as is represented at point E in the elastoplastic model of Fig. 4. Beyond this limiting elongation, the elastoplastic model fractures. Fractures are localized position discontinuities that arise due to the breaking of atomic bonds in materials. They usually initiate from stress singularities that arise at corners of irregularities or cavities present in solids. Solids exhibit three modes of fracture opening: a tensile mode and two shear modes, one planar and one normal to a plane.

As fractures develop they release internal potential energy of deformation (strain energy). For fractures to propagate through the material, the energy release rate as the fracture lengthens must be greater than a critical value. For brittle materials such as glass, fractures will develop unstably if the energy released is equal to the energy needed to create the free surface associated with the fracture. In this case, minor variations in material properties in the continuum can greatly influence the propagation. For materials like steel, however, the effects of plasticity at fracture tips must be taken into account. We do not consider this effect; its mathematical treatment is under development in the large body of literature on fracture mechanics (see [22]).

3. Basic Deformable Models

This section briefly reviews two formulations of deformable models, a *primary formulation* and a *hybrid formulation*, each of which can serve as a foundation for modeling inelastic behavior. In both formulations u denotes the intrinsic or material coordinates of points in a body Ω. For a solid body $u = (u_1, u_2, u_3)$ has three coordinates. For a surface $u = (u_1, u_2)$ and for a curve $u = (u_1)$. In these three cases, respectively, and without loss of generality, Ω will be the unit interval $[0, 1]$, the unit square $[0, 1]^2$, and the unit cube $[0, 1]^3$.

The primary formulation of deformable models [11] describes deformations using the positions $\mathbf{x}(u, t)$ of points in the body relative to an inertial frame of reference Φ in Euclidean 3-space (Fig. 5). Position is a 3-component vector-valued function of the material coordinates and time. Deformations are measured away from a reference shape which is represented in differential geometric form. For elastic deformations, this representation gives rise to internal deformation energies $\mathcal{E}(\mathbf{x})$ which produce restoring forces that are invariant with respect to rigid motions in Φ.

The hybrid formulation [14] represents the same deformable body as the sum of a reference component $\mathbf{r}(u, t)$ and a deformation component $\mathbf{e}(u, t)$. Both components are expressed relative to a reference frame ϕ whose origin coincides with the body's center of mass $\mathbf{c}(t)$ and which translates and rotates along with the deformable body (Fig. 5). We denote the positions of mass elements in the body relative to ϕ by

$$\mathbf{q}(u, t) = \mathbf{r}(u, t) + \mathbf{e}(u, t). \qquad (2)$$

We measure deformations with respect to the reference shape $\mathbf{r}$ represented in parametric form. Elastic deformations are again representable by an energy $\mathcal{E}(\mathbf{e})$, but this energy depends on the position of ϕ. Hence, for the deformable model to have a rigid-body motion mode in addition to an elastic mode, the reference component must be evolved over time according to the laws of rigid-body dynamics [23]. We obtain a model with explicit deformable and rigid characteristics; hence the name "hybrid."

Appendix A gives the equations of motion for both formulations. The primary and hybrid formulations offer different practical benefits at extreme limits of deformable behavior. The primary formulation handles free motions implicitly, but at the expense of a nonquadratic energy functional $\mathcal{E}(\mathbf{x})$ (nonlinear restoring forces). The equation of motion (9) with such a functional is numerically solvable without much difficulty for extremely nonrigid models such as rubber sheets, but the numerical conditioning deteriorates with increasing rigidity due to exacerbated nonlinearity. The hybrid formulation permits the use of a quadratic energy functional $\mathcal{E}(\mathbf{e})$ (linear restoring forces). Despite their greater complexity, the equations of motion (13) offer a significant practical advantage for fairly rigid models with complex reference shapes. Conditioning improves as the model becomes more rigid, tending in the limit to well-conditioned, rigid-body dynamics. See [14] for more details.

4. Incorporating Inelastic Behavior

This section describes how we incorporate inelastic behavior using the hybrid formulation of deformable models and also briefly indicates how we obtain similar effects using the primary formulation. First we will specify the internal restoring forces that govern deformation. Recall that the hybrid formulation expresses this deformation $\mathbf{e}(u, t)$ with respect to a reference component $\mathbf{r}(u, t)$. We obtain viscoelastic, plastic, and fracture behavior by designing internal processes that lawfully update $\mathbf{r}$ and modify material properties according to applied force and instantaneous deformation.

In the hybrid equations of motion (13), the restoring force due to deformational displacement $\mathbf{e}(u, t)$ is represented in (13c) by $\delta_\mathbf{e}\mathcal{E}$, a variational derivative [24] with respect to $\mathbf{e}$ of an elastic potential energy functional $\mathcal{E}$. The general form of $\mathcal{E}$ is

$$\mathcal{E}(\mathbf{e}) = \int_\Omega E(u, \mathbf{e}, \mathbf{e}_u, \mathbf{e}_{uu}, \ldots)\, du, \qquad (3)$$

an integral over material coordinates of an elastic energy density E, which depends on $\mathbf{e}$ and its partial derivatives

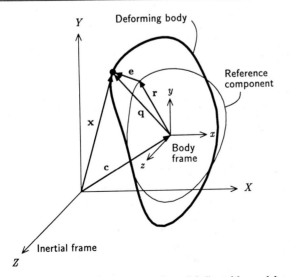

Figure 5. Geometric representation of deformable models.

with respect to material coordinates.

A convenient choice for $\mathcal{E}$ is the controlled-continuity generalized spline kernels [25]. These splines are of the form (3) with the integrand defined by

$$E = \frac{1}{2} \sum_{m=0}^{p} \sum_{|j|=m} \frac{m!}{j_1! \ldots j_d!} w_j \left| \partial_j^m \mathbf{e} \right|^2, \qquad (4)$$

where $j = (j_1, \ldots, j_d)$ is a multi-index with $|j| = j_1 + \ldots + j_d$, where d is the material dimensionality of the model ($d = 1$ for curves, $d = 2$ for surfaces, and $d = 3$ for solids), and where the partial derivative operator

$$\partial_j^m = \frac{\partial^m}{\partial u_1^{j_1} \ldots \partial u_d^{j_d}}. \qquad (5)$$

Thus, E is a weighted combination of partial derivatives of $\mathbf{e}$ of all orders up to p, with the weighting functions $w_j(\mathbf{u})$ in (4) controlling the elastic properties of the deformable model over $\mathbf{u}$. The allowable deformation becomes smoother for increasing p.

The variational derivative in Ω of $\mathcal{E}$ with the spline density (4) is

$$\delta_{\mathbf{e}} \mathcal{E} = \sum_{m=0}^{p} (-1)^m \Delta_{w_m}^m \mathbf{e}, \qquad (6)$$

where

$$\Delta_{w_m}^m = \sum_{|j|=m} \frac{m!}{j_1! \ldots j_d!} \partial_j^m \left(w_j \partial_j^m \right) \qquad (7)$$

is a spatially-weighted iterated Laplacian operator of order m. For convenience, we use cyclic boundary conditions on Ω and we introduce predetermined fractures to create free boundaries as necessary. To create a free surface, for example, we start with a torus and section it around the large and small circumference to obtain a single sheet.

For a surface with $p = 2$ (the highest order of p that we have used to date), the variational derivative of (18) is

$$\delta_{\mathbf{e}} \mathcal{E}(\mathbf{e}) = w_{00}\mathbf{e} - \frac{\partial}{\partial u_1}\left(w_{10}\frac{\partial \mathbf{e}}{\partial u_1}\right) - \frac{\partial}{\partial u_2}\left(w_{01}\frac{\partial \mathbf{e}}{\partial u_2}\right)$$
$$+ \frac{\partial^2}{\partial u_1^2}\left(w_{20}\frac{\partial^2 \mathbf{e}}{\partial u_1^2}\right) + 2\frac{\partial^2}{\partial u_1 \partial u_2}\left(w_{11}\frac{\partial^2 \mathbf{e}}{\partial u_1 \partial u_2}\right)$$
$$+ \frac{\partial^2}{\partial u_2^2}\left(w_{02}\frac{\partial^2 \mathbf{e}}{\partial u_2^2}\right), \qquad (8)$$

where $\mathbf{u} = (u_1, u_2)$ are the surface's material coordinates. The function w_{00} penalizes the total magnitude of the deformation; w_{10} and w_{01} penalize the magnitude of its first partial derivatives; w_{20}, w_{11}, and w_{02} penalize the magnitude of its second partial derivatives; etc.

The controlled-continuity spline kernel (4) allows our models to simulate the piecewise continuous deformations characteristic of fractures, creases, curvature discontinuities, etc. The distributed parameter functions w_j offer local continuity control throughout the material domain Ω. Discontinuities in the deformation of order $0 \leq k < p$ will occur freely at a material point $\mathbf{u}_0$ when $w_j(\mathbf{u}_0)$ is set to 0 for $|j| > k$ [25].

When the stresses or deformations exceed preset fracture limits, we locally nullify the w_j to introduce discontinuities. We have experimented with several simple schemes for propagating fractures in our models; for instance, at each time step we can insert a position discontinuity (order $k = 0$) at the material point $\mathbf{u}_*$ at which there occurs the greatest elastic displacement beyond the limiting elongation over Ω. The yield limit may vary greatly over material coordinates in real materials, especially if there happen to be localized weaknesses, say, from imperfections. We have experimented successfully with yield functions that vary stochastically around some mean yield limit. Promising variations on this theme abound.

As a simple case of viscoelasticity, consider the Maxwell unit depicted in Fig. 3. We allow $\mathbf{e}(\mathbf{u}, t)$, as governed by (6), to play the role of a multidimensional elastic spring in the continuum generalization of this unit, while $\mathbf{r}(\mathbf{u}, t)$ plays the role of the dashpot. The viscous behavior of the dashpot is simulated by an internal process which evolves the reference component as follows: $\dot{\mathbf{r}}(\mathbf{u}, t) = (1/\eta(\mathbf{u}))\mathbf{e}(\mathbf{u}, t)$. We extend this to simulate the four-element viscoelastic model shown in the figure, according to (1). Thus, the viscoelastic process establishes a feedback path from $\mathbf{e}$ into $\mathbf{r}$. During each time interval, a portion of the instantaneous elastic displacement is transferred into the reference component, thereby maintaining a deformation history. This is analogous to the incremental strain theory or flow theory of elasticity. More complex viscoelastic behaviors are produced readily by introducing nonlinear functions into the feedback loop. Bizarre yet interesting behavior—such as negative viscosity—is possible by choosing physically unrealizable parameters.

We have incorporated a multidimensional extension of the uniaxial elastoplastic model of Fig. 4. Here, the reference component $\mathbf{e}$ absorbs the extension of the plastic unit as soon as the applied force exceeds the yield limit. In the multidimensional case, we can incorporate a *yield condition* which can either be dependent on the stresses internal to the model (such as the Tresca or von Mises yield conditions [21]) or on the internal deformation $\mathbf{e}$. The model behaves elastically until the yield condition is exceeded locally. Then the material parameters w_j are reduced locally to simulate linear strain hardening.

The primary formulation of elastically deformable models involves deformation energy functionals that contain fundamental tensors of curves, surfaces, and solids (see [11]). For example, the elastic functional for a solid model was of the form $\mathcal{E}(\mathbf{x}) = \int_\Omega |\mathbf{G} - \mathbf{G}^0|_{\mathbf{W}}^2 \, du$, a squared normed difference between the first-order or metric tensors (matrices) $\mathbf{G}(\mathbf{x})$ of the deformed body and $\mathbf{G}^0$ of the undeformed body. The weighted norm $| \cdot |_{\mathbf{W}}$ provides functions $w_i(\mathbf{u})$ that determine material properties. The approach for introducing inelastic behavior is essentially the same as for the hybrid model: We evolve the metric tensor $\mathbf{G}^0$ (and other tensors in $\mathcal{E}(\mathbf{x})$ associated with the undeformed body) according to the model's internal stresses or deformations. For plasticity and fracture, this includes dynamic adjustments to the material property functions.

5. Implementation Overview

Our implementation of inelastic models is built on a substrate of numerical algorithms that we have developed for simulating elastically deformable models [11, 14]. This section provides an overview of the solution methodology. We refer the reader to our prior papers for mathematical details and discussion.

The first step is to discretize the continuum equations (9) or (13c) in material coordinates (these partial differential equations are of the hyperbolic-parabolic type, second-order in time and, so far, up to fourth-order in material coordinates). This step, known as semidiscretization, may be performed using finite-difference or finite-element methods on a discrete mesh of nodes [26]. The result is a large system of simultaneous ordinary differential equations.

The second step is to integrate the semidiscrete system through time, thus simulating the dynamics of deformable models. At each time step (or every few time steps) the resulting simulation data may be rendered to create successive frames of the animation. We use a semi-implicit time integration procedure which evolves the elastic displacements (and rigid-body dynamics in the hybrid model) from given initial conditions. In essence, the evolving deformation yields a recursive sequence of (dynamic) equilibrium problems, each requiring the solution of a *sparse*, linear system whose dimensionality is proportional to the number of nodes comprising the discrete model.

The size of these linear systems can vary greatly depending on the application. The simulations presented in the next sections range from hundreds to tens of thousands of state variables. Since deformable models involve so many variables (very many more than for typical rigid or articulated body simulations) it is crucial to choose the applicable numerical solution methods judiciously in order to achieve efficiency ([27] is a nice survey of standard numerical techniques).

For up to moderately-sized problems, we have used direct methods; specifically, a Choleski-type matrix factorization procedure with forward-reverse resolution. We use an efficient, profile storage scheme [28] which exploits the sparsity of the linear system (a sparse stiffness matrix results from discretizing the variational derivative $\delta_e \mathcal{E}$ using finite-element or finite-difference approximations; e.g., discretizing (8) using central differences yields equations having at most 13 nonzero coefficients). For large problems involving surfaces or solids, we must resort to iterative methods such as successive over-relaxation (SOR) or the conjugate gradient (CG) method. We have also made use of an alternating-direction-implicit method (ADI) which iterates fast, one-dimensional Choleski solvers [27]. Multigrid methods based on SOR have served well in the largest of our simulations [29].

6. Simulation Examples

The Flatland simulations in Fig. 1 involve a 50-node discrete model (100 deformation equations) and the Choleski solution on the hybrid equations of motion in two dimensions. The collisions are computed by a simple projection method which does not conserve the area of the model. We have animated both physically realizable and unrealizable behaviors in Flatland, including buckling and collapse under load, swelling after impact, etc. It should be possible

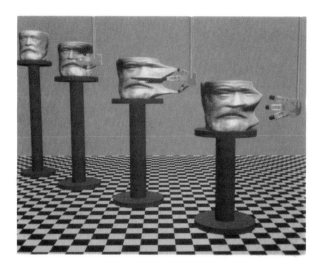

Figure 6. Hugo. (a) A "plasticine" bust of Victor Hugo. (b, back to front) Grabby hand pinches; grabby hand pulls; deformed Hugo.

to animate such inelastic dynamics in real-time in three dimensions on a supercomputer.

Next, we demonstrate a physically-based interaction with a 3D simulated "plasticine" bust (Fig. 6a). Employing the hybrid formulation, we initialized the reference component of the model with sampled three-dimensional data (made available by the University of Utah [30]) from a laser scanned sculpture of Victor Hugo. Fig. 6b shows first the undeformed model, followed by a simulation of a robot hand pinching the deformable material with sticky fingers, pulling, then releasing to show the residual plastic deformation. Because of the relatively large size of the discrete model (180×127 mesh; 68580 equations), we applied a multigrid solution method similar to the one described in [31].

The last two examples simulate fracture propagation in surfaces. We used the primary deformable model for-

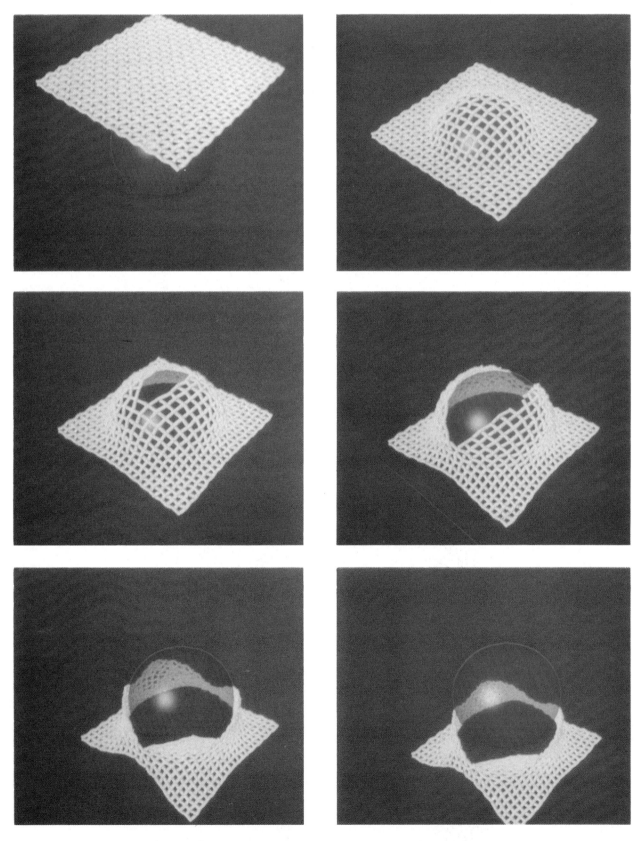

Figure 7. A net falling over a spherical obstacle. Fractures develop and propagate as the deformation exceeds the elastic limit.

mulation and the ADI solution method to run these simulations. Fig. 7 presents an animation of a net (23×23 mesh; 1587 equations) falling over an impenetrable obstacle in a gravitational field, in the spirit of the flying carpet animation in [11]. The difference here is that the "fibers" of the mesh are subject to fracture limits based on the deformation in the material. When a fiber stretches beyond the fracture limit it is broken by the fracture process which inserts a discontinuity as described in Section 4. The yield limit is uniform over the mesh, which causes linear tears as one might obtain with cloth.

Fig. 8 shows surface models (30×30; 2700 equations) which are sheared by opposing forces. In these examples, we perturbed the fracture tolerance around the material's mean tolerance stochastically in order to introduce some unpredictability in the propagation of fractures.

We rendered the color images in this section using the modeling testbed system described in [32].

Figure 8. (a) January 12, 1988. (b) April 15, 1988.

7. Conclusion

We have developed physically-based models of objects capable of inelastic deformation for use in computer graphics. We have applied these dynamic models to create interesting viscoelasticity, plasticity, and fracture effects. Our models are designed to be computationally tractable for the purposes of animation. This paper has only touched upon the vast volume of accumulated facts about the mechanics of materials. The modeling of inelastic deformation remains open for further exploration in the context of computer graphics.

Acknowledgements

We thank Rob Howe for providing the CAD model of the robot hand.

A.   Equations of Motion

A deformable model is described completely by the positions $\mathbf{x}(u,t)$, velocities $\dot{\mathbf{x}}(u,t)$, and accelerations $\ddot{\mathbf{x}}(u,t)$ of its mass elements as a function of material coordinates u and time t. In this appendix, overstruck dots denote time derivatives d/dt or $\partial/\partial t$ as appropriate.

Lagrange's equations of motion [23] for $\mathbf{x}$ in the inertial frame Φ take on a relatively simple form [11]:

$$\mu\ddot{\mathbf{x}} + \gamma\dot{\mathbf{x}} + \delta_{\mathbf{x}}\mathcal{E} = \mathbf{f}. \qquad (9)$$

During motion, the net external forces $\mathbf{f}(\mathbf{x},t)$ balance dynamically against the inertial force due to the mass density $\mu(u)$, the velocity dependent damping force with damping density $\gamma(u)$ (here a scalar, but generally a matrix), and the internal restoring force. The latter is expressed as a variational derivative $\delta_{\mathbf{x}}$ [24] of a nonnegative deformation energy $\mathcal{E}(\mathbf{x})$ whose value increases monotonically with the magnitude of the deformation. Eq. (9) is a partial differential equation (due to the dependence of $\delta_{\mathbf{x}}\mathcal{E}$ on $\mathbf{x}$ and its partial derivatives with respect to u—see below). Given appropriate conditions for $\mathbf{x}$ on the boundary of Ω and initial conditions $\mathbf{x}(u,0)$, $\dot{\mathbf{x}}(u,0)$, we have a well-posed initial-boundary-value problem.

In the hybrid formulation of the deformable model deformation is decomposed into a reference component $\mathbf{r}(u,t)$ and a deformation component $\mathbf{e}(u,t)$ in a noninertial frame ϕ located at the model's center of mass (See Fig. 5.)

$$\mathbf{c}(t) = \int_{\Omega} \mu(u)\mathbf{x}(u,t)\,du. \qquad (10)$$

The orientation of ϕ relative to Φ is $\boldsymbol{\theta}(t)$. Given

$$\mathbf{v}(t) = \dot{\mathbf{c}}(t); \qquad \boldsymbol{\omega}(t) = \dot{\boldsymbol{\theta}}(t), \qquad (11)$$

respectively the linear and angular velocity of ϕ relative to Φ, the velocity of mass elements relative to Φ is

$$\dot{\mathbf{x}}(u,t) = \mathbf{v}(t) + \boldsymbol{\omega}(t) \times \mathbf{q}(u,t) + \dot{\mathbf{e}}(u,t), \qquad (12)$$

where $\mathbf{q}$ is given by (2).

In [14] we apply Lagrangian mechanics based on the kinetic and potential energies which govern our model to transform (9) into three coupled, partial differential equations for the unknown functions $\mathbf{v}$, $\boldsymbol{\omega}$ and $\mathbf{e}$ under the action of an applied force $\mathbf{f}(u,t)$. These equations are given

by

$$\frac{d}{dt}(m\mathbf{v}) + \frac{d}{dt}\int_\Omega \mu\dot{\mathbf{e}}\,du + \int_\Omega \gamma\dot{\mathbf{x}}\,du = \mathbf{f}^{\mathbf{v}}, \quad (13a)$$

$$\frac{d}{dt}(\mathbf{I}\boldsymbol{\omega}) + \frac{d}{dt}\int_\Omega \mu\mathbf{q}\times\dot{\mathbf{e}}\,du + \int_\Omega \gamma\mathbf{q}\times\dot{\mathbf{x}}\,du = \mathbf{f}^{\boldsymbol{\omega}}, \quad (13b)$$

$$\frac{d}{dt}(\mu\dot{\mathbf{e}}) + \mu\dot{\mathbf{v}} + \mu\boldsymbol{\omega}\times(\boldsymbol{\omega}\times\mathbf{q})$$

$$+2\mu\boldsymbol{\omega}\times\dot{\mathbf{e}} + \mu\dot{\boldsymbol{\omega}}\times\mathbf{q} + \gamma\dot{\mathbf{x}} + \delta_{\mathbf{e}}\mathcal{E} = \mathbf{f}^{\mathbf{e}}. \quad (13c)$$

Here $m = \int_\Omega \mu\,du$ is the total mass of the body, and the time-varying, 3×3 symmetric matrix $\mathbf{I}$ with entries $I_{ij} = \int_\Omega \mu(\delta_{ij}\mathbf{q}^2 - q_i q_j)\,du$, where $\mathbf{q} = [q_1, q_2, q_3]$ and δ_{ij} is the Kronecker delta, is known as the inertia tensor. The applied force transforms to a deformational term $\mathbf{f}^{\mathbf{e}}(u,t) = \mathbf{f}(u,t)$, as well as net translational $\mathbf{f}^{\mathbf{v}}(t) = \int_\Omega \mathbf{f}(u,t)\,du$ and net torque $\mathbf{f}^{\boldsymbol{\omega}}(t) = \int_\Omega \mathbf{q}(u,t)\times\mathbf{f}(u,t)\,du$ terms on the center of mass.

The ordinary differential equations (13a) and (13b) describe $\mathbf{v}$ and $\boldsymbol{\omega}$, the translational and rotational motion of the body's center of mass. The terms on the left hand sides of these equations pertain to the total moving mass of the body as if concentrated at $\mathbf{c}$, the total (vibrational) motion of the mass elements about the reference component $\mathbf{r}$, and the total damping of the moving mass elements. The partial differential equation (13c) describes (relative to ϕ) the deformation $\mathbf{e}$ of the model away from $\mathbf{r}$. Each term is a dynamic per-mass-element force: (i) the basic inertial force, (ii) the inertial force due to linear acceleration of ϕ, (iii) the centrifugal force due to the rotation of ϕ, (iv) the Coriolis force due the velocity of the mass elements in ϕ, (v) the transverse force due to the angular acceleration of ϕ, (vi) the damping force, and (vii) the restoring force due to deformation away from $\mathbf{r}$.

References

1. **Barr, A., Barzel, R., Haumann, D., Kass, M., Platt, J., Terzopoulos, D., and Witkin, A.**, Topics in physically-based modeling, ACM SIGGRAPH '87 Course Notes, Vol. 17, Anaheim, CA, 1987.

2. **Fournier, A., Bloomenthal, J., Oppenheimer, P., Reeves, W.T., and Smith, A.R.**, The modeling of natural phenomena, ACM SIGGRAPH '87 Course Notes, Vol. 16, Anaheim, CA, 1987.

3. **Armstrong, W.W., and Green, M.**, "The dynamics of articulated rigid bodies for purposes of animation," *The Visual Computer*, 1, 1985, 231–240.

4. **Wilhelms, J., and Barsky, B.A.**, "Using dynamic analysis to animate articulated bodies such as humans and robots," *Proc. Graphics Interface '85*, Montreal, Canada, 1985, 97–104.

5. **Girard, M., and Maciejewski, A.A.**, "Computational modeling for the computer animation of legged figures," *Computer Graphics*, 19, 3, 1985, (Proc. SIGGRAPH), 263–270.

6. **Barzel, R., and Barr, A.**, Dynamic Constraints, 1987, in [1].

7. **Hoffmann, C.M., and Hopcroft, J.E.**, "Simulation of physical systems from geometric models," *IEEE Journ. Robotics and Automation*, RA-3, 3, 1987, 194–206.

8. **Issacs, P.M., and Cohen, M.F.**, "Controlling dynamic simulation with kinematic constraints, behavior functions, and inverse dynamics," *Computer Graphics*, 21, 4, 1987, (Proc. SIGGRAPH) 215–224.

9. **Weil, J.**, "The synthesis of cloth objects," *Computer Graphics*, 20, 4, 1986, (Proc. SIGGRAPH), 49–54.

10. **Feynman, C.R.**, Modeling the Appearance of Cloth, MSc thesis, Department of Electrical Engineering and Computer Science, MIT, Cambridge, MA, 1986.

11. **Terzopoulos, D., Platt, J., Barr, A., and Fleischer, K.**, "Elastically deformable models," *Computer Graphics*, 21, 4, 1987, (Proc. SIGGRAPH) 205–214.

12. **Haumann, D.**, Modeling the physical behavior of flexible objects, 1987, in [1].

13. **Weil, J.**, "Animating cloth objects," *unpublished manuscript*, 1987.

14. **Terzopoulos, D., and Witkin, A.**, "Physically-based models with rigid and deformable components," *Proc. Graphics Interface '88*, Edmonton, Canada, June, 1988.

15. **Alfrey, T.**, *Mechanical Behavior of High Polymers*, Interscience, New York, NY, 1947.

16. **Kardestuncer, H., and Norrie, D.H.**, (ed.), *Finite Element Handbook*, McGraw–Hill, New York, NY, 1987.

17. **Christiansen, H.N.**, "Computer generated displays of structures in vibration," *The Shock and Vibration Bulletin*, 44, 2, 1974, 185–192.

18. **Christiansen, H.N., and Benzley, S.E.**, "Computer graphics displays of nonlinear calculations," *Computer Methods in Applied Mechanics and Engineering*, 34, 1982, 1037–1050.

19. **Shephard, M.S., and Abel, J.F.**, Interactive computer graphics for CAD/CAM, 1987, in [16], Section 4.4.3.

20. **Christensen, R.M.**, *Theory of viscoelasticity, 2nd ed.*, Academic Press, New York, NY, 1982.

21. **Mendelson, A.**, *Plasticity—Theory and Application*, Macmillan, New York, NY, 1968.

22. **Sih, G.C.**, *Mechanics of Fracture*, Martinus Nijhoff, The Hague, 1981.

23. **Goldstein, H.**, *Classical Mechanics*, Addison–Wesley, Reading, MA, 1950.

24. **Courant, R., and Hilbert, D.**, *Methods of Mathematical Physics*, Vol. I, Interscience, London, 1953.

25. **Terzopoulos, D.**, "Regularization of inverse visual problems involving discontinuities," *IEEE Trans. Pattern Analysis and Machine Intelligence*, PAMI-8, 1986, 413–424.

26. **Lapidus, L., and Pinder, G.F.**, *Numerical Solution of Partial Differential Equations in Science and Engineering*, Wiley, New York, NY, 1982.

27. **Press, W.H., Flannery, B.P., Teukolsky, S.A., and Vetterling, W.T.**, *Numerical Recipes: The Art of Scientific Computing*, Cambridge University Press, Cambridge, UK, 1986.

28. **Zienkiewicz, O.C.**, *The Finite Element Method; Third edition*, McGraw–Hill, London, 1977.

29. **Hackbusch, W.**, *Multigrid Methods and Applications*, Springer–Verlag, Berlin, 1985.

30. **Hansen, C., and Henderson, T.**, UTAH Range Database, Dept. of Computer Science, University of Utah, Salt Lake City, Utah, TR No. UUCS-86-113, 1986.

31. **Terzopoulos, D.**, "Multilevel computational processes for visual surface reconstruction," *Computer Vision, Graphics, and Image Processing*, 24, 1983, 52–96.

32. **Fleischer, K., and Witkin, A.**, "A modeling testbed," *Proc. Graphics Interface '88*, Edmonton, Canada, June, 1988.

Constraint Methods for Flexible Models

John C. Platt
Alan H. Barr
California Institute of Technology
Pasadena, CA 91125

Abstract

Simulating flexible models can create aesthetic motion for computer animation. Animators can control these motions through the use of *constraints* on the physical behavior of the models. This paper shows how to use mathematical constraint methods based on physics and on optimization theory to create controlled, realistic animation of physically-based flexible models. Two types of constraints are presented in this paper: reaction constraints (RCs) and augmented Lagrangian constraints (ALCs). RCs allow the fast computation of collisions of flexible models with polygonal models. In addition, RCs allow flexible models to be pushed and pulled under the control of an animator. ALCs create animation effects such as volume-preserving squashing and the molding of taffy-like substances. ALCs are compatible with RCs. In this paper, we describe how to apply these constraint methods to a flexible model that uses finite elements.

KEYWORDS: Elasticity, Modeling, Dynamics, Constraints, Simulation
CR categories: G.1.6 — Constrained Optimization; I.3.7—Three-Dimensional Graphics and Realism (Animation)

1 Introduction

A primary goal of simulating flexible models is to animate physically realistic motions. Examples include simulating the musculature of a human body to create realistic walking; simulating the flow of viscous liquids, such as lava over volcanic rocks; or simulating a sculptor molding clay.

This paper takes a step towards these goals, by adding constraint properties to flexible models; and other properties, such as moldability and incompressibility. Using these properties, we can now simulate materials, such as clay, taffy, or putty, that have been very difficult to simulate using previous computer graphics models.

1.1 Desirable Properties of Flexible Models

In order to create pleasing and supple motions discussed above, we incorporate many of the following properties for our flexible models:

- *Physical Realism* — Flexible models should be able to move in natural, intuitive ways. Using the theory of elasticity to animate flexible models is very helpful in creating natural motion.

- *Controllability* — Flexible models should be able to follow an animation script. Models should be able to follow pre-defined paths exactly, while still wriggling in an interesting manner and interacting with other models.

- *Non-interpenetration* — Flexible models should be able to bounce off other models while using a small amount of computer time.

- *Limited Compressibility* — Flexible models should be able to have constant volume, even while being squashed. Models that squash without retaining their volume look as if they are made of sponge: they do not bulge out enough at the sides.

- *Moldability* — Flexible models should be moldable: external forces should mold the rest shape of the model. Models should follow the theory of *plasticity*, which describes materials that do not return to their rest shape after large deformation.

1.2 Force-Based Constraint Methods

Constraint methods that add external forces to physical systems yield physically realistic motion and allow simulation with simple, commercially available, differential equation solvers.

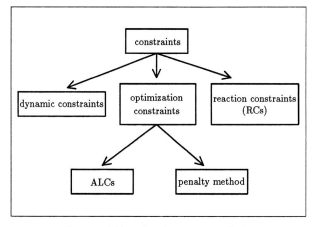

Figure 1: A hierarchy of constraint methods

There are at least three force-based constraint methods that allow the creation of flexible models with the properties listed in the last section.

- *Dynamic constraints* [3] use inverse dynamics to create critically damped forces which fulfill the constraints. Dynamic constraints are easy to use on systems which have simple dynamics. Elastic models have many state variables, however; this makes the dynamics hard to invert. We do not apply dynamic constraints to elastic models in this paper.

©1988   ACM-0-89791-275-6/88/008/0279 $00.75

- *Reaction constraints*, presented in this paper, use a modified projection method for simple constraints, such as guiding flexible models along a path and preventing flexible models from penetrating a polygon. Reaction constraints supply reaction forces that cancel other forces that would violate the constraint. Reaction constraints require no extra differential equations, but they are limited in scope.

- *Optimization constraints* use ideas from optimization theory to constrain physical systems. Physical systems perform optimization, because the total energy of any physical system with dissipation decreases.

There are two types of optimization constraints. The simplest kind of optimization constraint is the well-known *penalty method*, where an extra energy that penalizes incorrect behavior is added to the physical system. The penalty method is analogous to adding rubber bands that attract the physical system to the constraints. One large disadvantage of the penalty method is that the constraints are enforced in the presence of external forces only as the ratios of the strengths of the rubber band to the external forces increases to infinity.

The ALC method is a constrained optimization method that adds differential equations that compute Lagrange multipliers of the physical system. These additional differential equations cause the system to eventually fulfill multiple constraints, even in the presence of external forces.

1.3 Previous Work

As discussed in the last section, this paper combines physically-based modeling techniques with constrained optimization methods.

There has been a growing interest in physical models in the field of computer graphics. Elastic models have been proposed previously [7] [11] [15] [17] that simulate deformable models quite well. Of these, [7] and [15] were based directly on variational principles, which are easily modified by constrained optimization techniques.

The physically-based elastic models are based on classical elasticity theory. A recommended explanation of elasticity may be found in Truesdell [16]; Fung [8] is another useful reference for both elasticity and plasticity.

In order to make controllable modeling and animation, researchers in computer graphics have previously studied constraint methods [2] [9] [18]. Witkin, et al. [20] applied the penalty method to parametrized constraints. Barzel and Barr [3] and Isaacs and Cohen [13] developed dynamic constraints. We extend their work to flexible models.

RCs are related to techniques that enforce boundary conditions of partial differential equations [21].

ALCs are based on the method of multipliers first developed by Arrow, et al. [1]. A comprehensive review paper was written by Bertsekas [4].

1.4 Preview

Sections 1–5 of this paper discusses optimization and various constraint methods. Section 2 explains why optimization theory is applicable to flexible models. Section 3 discusses the penalty method. Section 4 presents RCs and section 5 presents ALCs. Section 6 shows the application of the general constraint methods in the first part of the paper to flexible models. Section 7 shows various animation effects made by the constraints.

The appendices of this paper contain the mathematical details of how to apply RCs and ALCs to flexible models. The appendices describe the finite element flexible model, the equations necessary for animation control and collision, the equations for incompressibility and plasticity, and an explanation of why ALCs work.

2 Flexible Models Minimize Functions

This section illustrates that simulating physically-based flexible models is an optimization procedure. An optimization procedure finds a vector $\underline{x}$ to

$$\text{locally minimize } f(\underline{x}) \tag{1}$$

where $\underline{x}$ is a position in a high-dimensional space; and $f(\underline{x})$ is a scalar function, which can be imagined as the height of a landscape as a function of position $\underline{x}$ (see figure 2). In figure 2, the arrows represent the action of an optimization procedure, where $\underline{x}_0$ is the state of the system before the optimization procedure and $\underline{x}_{\min}$ is the state of the system afterwards.

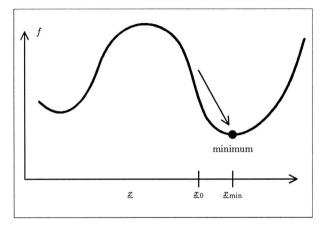

Figure 2: An optimization landscape

Physically-based flexible models minimize a particular function f. Consider the simplest flexible model, a spring. The energy of the spring comes in two forms: kinetic energy (the energy of motion) and potential energy (the energy stored in the tension of a spring). As a spring oscillates, the kinetic energy turns into potential energy, and back into kinetic energy. Because of friction, however, a spring eventually slows down and stops, with all of the energy having been converted into heat. The total energy of the spring always decreases. In general, any physical system with dissipation always loses energy, yet the total energy is always bounded below. Hence, physically-based flexible models will minimize their total energy as time increases. Even non-dissipative physical systems extremize energy over all paths in space-time.

Since simulating a flexible model is an optimization procedure, we can use optimization concepts to modify the flexible model. A useful concept is that optimization procedures, like computer graphics models, can be constrained.

A *constrained optimization procedure* finds a minimum of a function on a specified subspace. The prototypical constrained optimization problem can be stated as

$$\text{locally minimize } f(\underline{x}), \text{ subject to } g(\underline{x}) = 0, \tag{2}$$

where $g(\underline{x}) = 0$ is a scalar equation describing a subspace of the state space. During constrained optimization, the state vector $\underline{x}$ should be attracted to the subspace $g(\underline{x}) = 0$, then slide along the subspace until it reaches the locally smallest value of $f(\underline{x})$ on $g(\underline{x}) = 0$ (see figure 9). Solutions to a constrained optimization problem are restricted to a subset of the solutions of the corresponding unconstrained optimization problem.

Since physically-based flexible models minimize a function, we use constrained optimization algorithms as physical constraint methods. Applying constrained optimization algorithms to a physical system still decreases the total energy of the system, while enforcing external constraints; thus, optimization constraints do not destabilize physical systems.

There are other optimization procedures than simply simulating a physical system. The simplest optimization algorithm is *gradient descent*, where the values of $\underline{x}$ ski downhill, in the opposite direction of the gradient ∇f (see figure 3). ∇f points in the direction of the maximum increase in f.

$$\dot{x}_i = -\frac{\partial f}{\partial x_i} \tag{3}$$

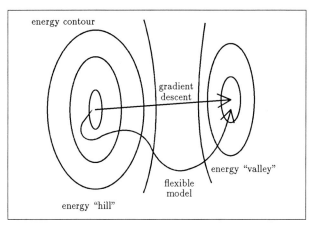

Figure 3: Both Gradient Descent and Flexible Models Minimize a Function

3 The Penalty Method

This section discusses a traditional constrained optimization technique called the penalty method; the method has previously been used in constraining computer graphics models [15][20].

The physical interpretation of the penalty method is a rubber band that attracts the physical state to the subspace $g(\underline{x}) = 0$. The penalty method adds a quadratic energy term that penalizes violations of constraints [12]. Thus, the constrained minimization problem (2) is converted to the following unconstrained minimization problem:

$$\text{minimize } \mathcal{E}_{\text{penalty}}(\underline{x}) = f(\underline{x}) + c(g(\underline{x}))^2. \quad (4)$$

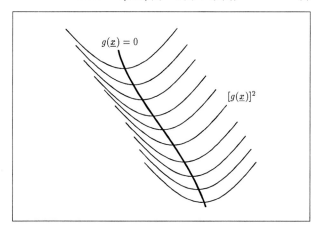

Figure 4: The penalty method makes a trough in state space

The penalty method can be extended to fulfill multiple constraints by using more than one rubber band. Namely, the constrained optimization problem

$$\text{minimize } f(\underline{x}), \text{ subject to } g_\alpha(\underline{x}) = 0; \quad \alpha = 1, 2, \ldots, n; \quad (5)$$

is converted into unconstrained optimization problem (see figure 4)

$$\text{minimize } \mathcal{E}_{\text{penalty}}(\underline{x}) = f(\underline{x}) + \sum_{\alpha=1}^{n} c_\alpha (g_\alpha(\underline{x}))^2. \quad (6)$$

The penalty method has a few convenient features.

- *Inexact Constraints* — There are situations in which it is not necesssary to exactly fulfill constraints; sometimes it is desirable to compromise between constraints.

- *Ease of Use* — Adding a rubber band to a physical system is simple and requires no extra differential equations.

However, the penalty method has number of disadvantages.

- *Inexact Constraints* — For finite constraint strengths c_α, the penalty method does not fulfill the constraints precisely. Under many circumstances, however, constraints should be fulfilled exactly. Using multiple rubber band constraints is like building a machine out of rubber bands; the machine would not hold together perfectly.

- *Stiffness of Equations* — Second, as the constraint strengths increase, the differential equations become *stiff*; that is, there are widely separated time constants. Most numerical methods must take time steps on the order of the fastest time constant, while most modelers are interested in the behavior at the slowest time constant. As a result of stiffness, the numerical differential equation solver takes very small time steps, using a large amount of computing time without getting much done.

4 Reaction Constraints

When flexible models are constrained to be on the outside of another model, or when they are constrained by an animator, they should fulfill these constraints quickly and exactly. As discussed in the last section, the penalty method has difficulties with swiftly fulfilling precise constraints.

RCs are a constraint method that retains the advantages of the penalty method while avoiding many of the disadvantages. RCs can force a point to follow a path, or to lie on the outside of a polygonal model. RCs are fast and simple to use, and do not require additional differential equations to be added to the physical system. However, only one RC can be applied to a mass point at any time.

RCs cancel forces that violate constraints and add forces that would critically damp the distance from the state to the constraint surface. RCs are a combination of the projection method [12] and dynamic constraints.

RCs work on individual mass points. Since elastic models are frequently discretized into mass points, RCs are applicable to constraining elastic models on a point-by-point basis.

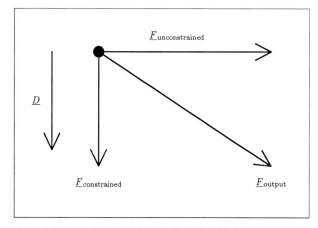

Figure 5: The reaction constraint cancels undesirable force components.

A reaction constraint is a procedure that processes the net force at a point, $\underline{F}_{\text{input}}$ created by physics or other constraint techniques, in order to yield a constrained force at a point $\underline{F}_{\text{output}}$, needed to fulfill a particular constraint. The RC first projects out undesirable components of $\underline{F}_{\text{input}}$ to yield $\underline{F}_{\text{unconstrained}}$ (see figure 5). Next, $\underline{F}_{\text{constrained}}$ is computed to yield critically damped motion that fulfills the constraint. Finally, the control force $\underline{F}_{\text{output}}$ is the sum of the constrained and unconstrained forces:

$$\underline{F}_{\text{output}} = \underline{F}_{\text{constrained}} + \underline{F}_{\text{unconstrained}} \quad (7)$$

To fulfill Newton's second law, the reaction force $\underline{F}_{\text{input}} - \underline{F}_{\text{output}}$ should be applied to the object that is interacting with the flexible model.

Let the vector $\underline{D}$ be the deviation in the position of the mass point. That is, the vector $\underline{D}$ points from the mass point towards where the mass point should be. The constrained force that eventually sets $\underline{D}$ to zero is

$$\underline{F}_{\text{constrained}} = k\underline{D} + c\frac{d}{dt}\underline{D} \qquad (8)$$

where k is the strength of the constraint and c is the damping. If $c = \sqrt{2k}$, then the mass point fulfills the constraint with critically damped motion. If the damping is too low, then the constraint force overshoots. For critically damped motion, if k is increased, then the time needed to fulfill the constraint is decreased.

In the appendices, we describe the equations necessary for implementing two useful reaction constraints (see figure 6):

- *Path Following* — In constraining flexible models, we frequently want to constrain a mass point to follow a specified spatial path parameterized by time, without speeding up or slowing down. The pre-defined path is a useful constraint in animation, where flexible models need to be picked up and moved around. If only a few mass points of the flexible models are constrained, then the rest of the model is free to wriggle in a physically realistic manner. The equations for the path-following reaction constraint are contained in Appendix A.

- *Attraction to a Plane* — Another useful constraint is to force a mass point to lie on a plane. A mass point inside of a polygonal model can be forced outside of the polygonal model by using a planar reaction constraint. The equations for the planar reaction constraint are contained in Appendix B.

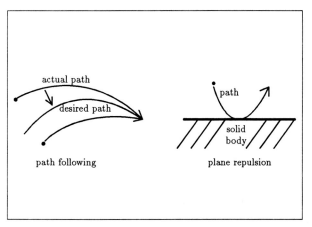

Figure 6: Examples of Reaction Constraints

Using reaction constraints is an easy way to implement simple constraints. Similar to the penalty method, no extra differential equations are required. Unlike the penalty method, the constraint is fulfilled in the presence of outside forces. If a flexible model is being lifted by a reaction force against gravity, then the lifting path is followed, even if gravity increases by a factor of ten. The reaction constraint thus reduces the amount of parameter adjustment needed in modeling elastic objects.

Reaction constraints are an extension of the projection method of constrained optimization, where any motion outside an allowed region is projected back into the region. Reaction constraints are more appropriate for physical models than the projection method, because the projection method needs to manipulate the physical state variables directly. Reaction constraints manipulate only forces, hence are compatible with both dynamic constraints [3] and with ALCs. In addition, reaction constraints do not need special numerical routines.

Reaction constraints are much faster than the penalty method for collisions. The penalty method tries to cancel a large penetration force by adding a force that is a rapidly changing function of position. Small numerical step sizes are needed for the penalty method in order to prevent unstable oscillation. However, reaction constraints cancel a pen-

etration force, independent of the depth of the penetration. Reaction constraints, therefore, can take much larger step sizes.

5 Augmented Lagrangian Constraints

In the animation of flexible models, more than one constraint per mass point is needed. Constraints may be more complex than simple path following or repulsion from a plane. In addition, we wish to enforce real properties of flexible models, such as incompressibility and moldability.

This section presents a type of constraint, called an augmented Lagragian constraint, that enforces the complex, multiple constraints needed for flexible models. The differential equations used in ALCs were first developed by Arrow in 1958 [1].

5.1 Lagrange Multipliers

Lagrange multiplier methods, like the penalty method, convert constrained optimization problems into unconstrained extremization problems. Namely, a solution to the equation (2) is also a critical point of the energy

$$\mathcal{E}_{\text{Lagrange}}(\underline{x}) = f(\underline{x}) + \lambda g(\underline{x}). \qquad (9)$$

λ is called the Lagrange multiplier for the constraint $g(\underline{x}) = 0$ [12].

A direct consequence of equation (9) is that the gradient of f is collinear to the gradient of g at the constrained extrema (see Figure 7). The constant of proportionality between ∇f and ∇g is $-\lambda$:

$$\nabla \mathcal{E}_{\text{Lagrange}} = 0 = \nabla f + \lambda \nabla g. \qquad (10)$$

We use the collinearity of ∇f and ∇g in the design of the ALC.

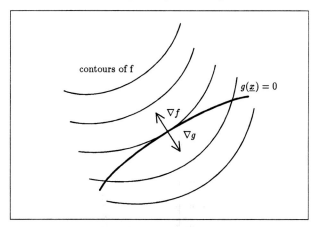

Figure 7: At the constrained minimum, $\nabla f = -\lambda \nabla g$

A simple example shows that Lagrange multipliers provide the extra degrees of freedom necessary to solve constrained optimization problems. Consider the problem of finding a point (x, y) on the line $x+y = 1$ that is closest to the origin. Using Lagrange multipliers,

$$\mathcal{E}_{\text{Lagrange}} = x^2 + y^2 + \lambda(x + y - 1) \qquad (11)$$

Now, take the derivative with respect to all variables, x, y, and λ.

$$\frac{\partial \mathcal{E}_{\text{Lagrange}}}{\partial x} = 2x + \lambda = 0 \qquad (12)$$

$$\frac{\partial \mathcal{E}_{\text{Lagrange}}}{\partial y} = 2y + \lambda = 0 \qquad (13)$$

$$\frac{\partial \mathcal{E}_{\text{Lagrange}}}{\partial \lambda} = x + y - 1 = 0 \qquad (14)$$

With the extra variable λ, there are now three equations in three unknowns. In addition, the last equation is precisely the constraint equation.

5.2 Gradient Descent Does Not Work with Lagrange Multipliers

Applying gradient descent in equation (3) to the energy in equation (9) yields

$$\dot{x}_i \;=\; -\frac{\partial \mathcal{E}_{\text{Lagrange}}}{\partial x_i} = -\frac{\partial f}{\partial x_i} - \lambda \frac{\partial g}{\partial x_i}, \qquad (15)$$

$$\dot{\lambda} \;=\; -\frac{\partial \mathcal{E}_{\text{Lagrange}}}{\partial \lambda} = -g(\underline{x}). \qquad (16)$$

Note that there is an auxiliary differential equation for λ, which is necessary to apply the constraint $g(\underline{x}) = 0$. Also, recall that when the system is at a constrained extremum, $\nabla f = -\lambda \nabla g$, hence, $\dot{x}_i = 0$.

Solutions to the constrained optimization problem (2) are saddle points of the energy in equation (9), which has no lower bound [1]. If the vector $\underline{x}$ is held fixed where $g(\underline{x}) \neq 0$, the energy can be decreased to $-\infty$ by sending λ to $+\infty$ or $-\infty$.

Gradient descent does not work with Lagrange multipliers, because a critical point of the energy in equation (9) need not be an attractor for equations (15) and (16). A stationary point must be a local minimum in order for gradient descent to converge.

5.3 The Basic Lagrange Constraint

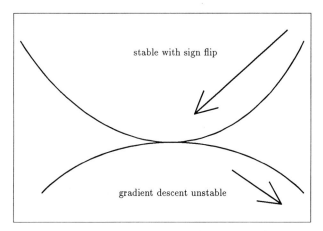

Figure 8: The sign flip from equation (16) to equation (18) makes Lagrange multipliers stable

We present an alternative to differential gradient descent that estimates the Lagrange multipliers, so that the constrained minima are attractors of the differential equations, instead of "repulsors." The differential equations that solve (2) are

$$\dot{x}_i \;=\; -\frac{\partial f}{\partial x_i} - \lambda \frac{\partial g}{\partial x_i}, \qquad (17)$$

$$\dot{\lambda} \;=\; +g(\underline{x}). \qquad (18)$$

Equations (17) and (18) are similar to equations (15) and (16). As in equations (15) and (16), solutions to problem 2 are stationary points of equations (17) and (18). Notice, however, the sign inversion in the equation (18), as compared to equation (16). The equation (18) is performing gradient *ascent* on λ. The sign flip makes the method stable, as shown in Appendix G (see figure 8)

The system of differential equations (17) and (18) gradually fulfills the constraints. Notice that the function $g(\underline{x})$ can be replaced by $kg(\underline{x})$, without changing the location of the constrained minimum. As k is increased, the state begins to undergo damped oscillation about the constraint subspace $g(\underline{x}) = 0$. As k is increased further, the frequency of the oscillations increase, and the time to convergence increases.

5.4 Extensions to the Algorithm

One extension to equations (17) and (18) is an algorithm for constrained minimization with multiple constraints. Adding an extra differential

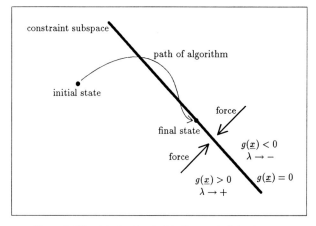

Figure 9: The state is attracted to the constraint subspace

equation for every equality constraint and summing all of the constraint forces creates the energy

$$\mathcal{E}_{\text{multiple}} = f(\underline{x}) + \sum_{\alpha} \lambda_\alpha g_\alpha(\underline{x}), \qquad (19)$$

which yields differential equations

$$\dot{x}_i \;=\; -\frac{\partial f}{\partial x_i} - \sum_{\alpha} \lambda_\alpha \frac{\partial g_\alpha}{\partial x_i}, \qquad (20)$$

$$\dot{\lambda}_\alpha \;=\; +g_\alpha(\underline{x}). \qquad (21)$$

Another extension is constrained minimization with inequality constraints. As in traditional optimization theory [12], one uses additional slack variables to convert inequality constraints into equality constraints. Namely, a constraint of the form $h(\underline{x}) \geq 0$ can be expressed as

$$g(\underline{x}) = h(\underline{x}) - z^2. \qquad (22)$$

Since z^2 must always be positive, then $h(\underline{x})$ is constrained to be positive. The slack variable z is treated like a component of $\underline{x}$ in equation (17). An inequality constraint requires two extra differential equations, one for the slack variable z and one for the Lagrange multiplier λ.

Alternatively, the inequality constraint can be represented as an equality constraint. For example, if $h(\underline{x})$ is constrained to be greater than zero, then the optimization can be constrained with

$$g(\underline{x}) = \begin{cases} [h(\underline{x})]^2, & \text{if } h > 0 \\ 0, & \text{otherwise.} \end{cases} \qquad (23)$$

Combining the basic Lagrangian constraints with the penalty method yields augmented Lagrangian constraints (ALCs). ALCs have better convergence properties than basic Lagrangian constraints, as shown in Appendix G. The basic Lagrangian constraints are completely compatible with the penalty method. If one adds a penalty force to equation (17) that corresponds to an quadratic energy

$$E_{\text{penalty}} = \frac{c}{2}(g(\underline{x}))^2, \qquad (24)$$

then the set of differential equations for an ALC is

$$\dot{x}_i \;=\; -\frac{\partial f}{\partial x_i} - \lambda \frac{\partial g}{\partial x_i} - cg \frac{\partial g}{\partial x_i}, \qquad (25)$$

$$\dot{\lambda} \;=\; g(\underline{x}). \qquad (26)$$

The extra force from the penalty does *not* change the position of the stationary points of the differential equations, because the penalty force is zero when $g(\underline{x}) = 0$, independent of the value of c.

There is a minimum necessary penalty strength c required in some cases for the ALC to converge (see appendix G). The minimum penalty strength in the ALC is usually much less than the strength needed by the penalty method for an accurate solution [4]. ALCs are applicable to more general constraints than RCs, especially when more than one non-linear constraint is associated with each mass point.

6 Constraining Flexible Models with Augmented Lagrangian Constraints

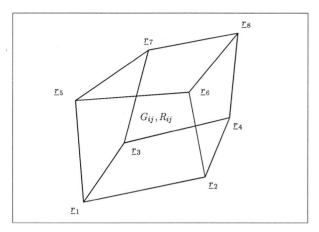

Figure 10: An element of flexible material

ALCs are ideal for the non-linear constraints that arise from adding new properties to flexible models. The augmented Lagrangian constraints are applied to the differential equations that govern an element of material. Flexible models are created by aggregating these elements in a grid, which may be difficult in the case of complex rest shapes [19].

The internal forces on a element are fully derived in Appendix C. The forces depend on the average metric tensor, $G_{ij}(\underline{r}_1, \underline{r}_2, \ldots \underline{r}_8)$, which describes the current shape of an element, and is computed for each element of material using the finite element method (see figure 10) [19]. Each element of material also has a rest state, which is described by R_{ij}. For a Hookean elastic material, the internal force encourages the metric tensor of each element to be close to the metric tensor of the rest state [15].

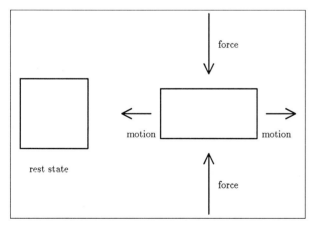

Figure 11: Incompressibility preserves the volume of an element

Hookean elasticity, however, does not fully describe the range of materials that are desirable to animate. For example, a Hookean elastic model can be easily compressed. If an elastic model undergoes violent deformation, as is common in computer graphics, then it will behave more like a sponge than like gelatin. If an incompressible material is desired (see figure 11), then ALCs are added to the equations for an elastic element.

The volume squared of one element is the determinant of the metric tensor G_{ij} of that element [6]. To constrain the volume of an element to be a constant V_0, we apply the augmented Lagrangian method, using the constraint

$$g = \det G_{ij} - V_0^2 = 0. \tag{27}$$

The complete differential equation for an incompressible element is given in Appendix E.

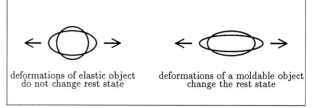

deformations of elastic object do not change rest state deformations of a moldable object change the rest state

Figure 12: The rest shape of plastic materials changes after strong deformation.

Many materials, such as taffy and putty, are moldable. Moldable materials do not return to their rest shape after being strongly deformed (see figure 12). Augmented Lagrangian constraints can be applied to each element's rest state so that it roughly approximates the theory of strongly deformed materials.

A moldable element has a rest metric R_{ij} that is constrained to be close to the metric G_{ij} [8]. Mathematically, there is an inequality constraint, based on the von Mises' yield criterion from the theory of plasticity [8],

$$P = (G_{ij} - R_{ij})(G_{ij} - R_{ij}) - P_0 < 0. \tag{28}$$

Using the method described in equation (23), we use the constraint function

$$\eta = \begin{cases} 1/2P^2; & \text{if } P > 0, \\ 0; & \text{if } P \leq 0. \end{cases} \tag{29}$$

For plasticity, there are differential equations for R_{ij} derived from applying equations (20) and (21) to the constraint in equation (29). The general differential equations for a moldable element are given in Appendix F.

The general equations for applying an ALC to a flexible model are given in appendix D. To apply an ALC to a flexible model, forget that the position and velocity are related, and simply apply equations (25) and (26) directly. In general, using ALCs on flexible models results in equations of the form

$$\dot{x}_i = v_i - u_i(\underline{x}, \underline{v}) \tag{30}$$
$$\dot{v}_i = F_i - \epsilon v_i - w_i(\underline{x}, \underline{v}) \tag{31}$$

where u_i and v_i are functions determined by applying various ALCs. Equations (30) and (31) do not appear to be in the form of a standard physical system. However, we can change the differential equations in (30) and (31) into one second-order differential equation:

$$\ddot{x}_i + \epsilon \dot{x}_i = F_i - \epsilon u_i - w(\underline{x}, \underline{x} + \underline{u}) - \frac{d}{dt} u_i(\underline{x}, \underline{v}). \tag{32}$$

The left-hand side of equation (32) is a standard form for a physical system; therefore, ALCs add only forces to flexible models.

7 Results

We have simulated all of the constraints discussed in this paper using standard differential equations solvers [14]. Since differential equations are simulated over a time interval, the results are in the form of animation. The figures in this section are individual frames from a sequence.

Figures 13 and 14 show frames from an animation of a compressible elastic cube of gelatin which is lifted up and then bounced off a table. The lifting of the cube is done with a path-following reaction constraint, and the table is implemented with a reaction constraint that keeps the cube above a plane. Notice that since the cube in compressible, its volume can vary through the course of the simulation.

Figure 15 shows a compressible seat cushion being squashed with a sphere. The sphere is a physical model with mass. An RC prevents the sphere from penetrating the cushion.

Figure 16 shows an incompressible moldable cube striking a surface. Instead of bouncing off the surface, the moldable cube sticks to the surface, with its sides near the surface bulging out. Incompressiblity forces the sides to bulge, and the moldability updates the rest shape so that the shape is no longer a cube. Both the incompressibility and the moldability are enforced with augmented Lagrangian constraints.

Figures 17–20 illustrate the moldability of the models. A sphere squashes the model in figure 17; but the elastic models bounces back to its rest shape in figure 18. In figure 19, a moldable model starts with the same rest shape, and is squashed by the sphere; but in figure 20, the moldable model has a dented edge.

8 Conclusions

In the past, researchers have made models that simulate the behavior of flexible materials. These models automatically move in a physically realistic way, without specifying the exact positions and velocities of the model at all times. The "hands-off" nature of the physically-based models, however, makes them hard for an animator to control.

By adding physical modeling constraints to the elastic models, a compromise can be reached between completely specifying the motion of a model and allowing a simulation package to run freely. Constraint methods are useful for controlling the flexible models, while retaining the physically realistic motion created by the physics.

This paper presents two constraint techniques, based physics and optimization theory, for constraining the physical simulation of flexible models: reaction constraints and augmented Lagrange constraints. Both reaction constraints and augmented Lagrange constraints eventually fulfill specified constraints exactly, unlike the penalty method.

Reaction constraints, based on the projection method, are a simple way of enforcing path following or repulsion from a polygon. Reaction constraints require no extra differential equations, because they project away undesirable components of the force. Only one reaction constraint can be applied to a mass point at a time. Reaction constraints are useful for guiding flexible models along a path and for reducing the amount of computation time needed for collisions.

ALCs are a differential version of the method of multipliers from optimization theory. ALCs are a general technique for constrained optimization. In this paper, we use ALCs for constraining flexible models to be incompressible and moldable.

Compressible elastic models look as if they are made out of sponge. To simulate other materials, such as rubber, an augmented Lagrange incompressibility constraint should be added to the elastic model.

Many natural substances, such has clay and taffy, do not return to their rest shape after strong deformations. Purely elastic models are inadequate for these substances. Using ALCs to keep the rest shape near the current shape is an effective model for these moldable substances. In addition, by applying forces to these plastic substances, we can mold interesting shapes without numerically specifying the rest shape.

Acknowledgements

We wish to thank Jed Lengyel for rest state models and John Snyder for rendering software. This paper was supported by grants from Apple Computer, Hewlett-Packard Company, Symbolics Inc., and an AT&T Bell Labs Fellowship.

References

[1] Arrow, K., Hurwicz, L., Uzawa H., *Studies in Linear and Non-linear Programming,* (Stanford University Press, Stanford, CA, 1958).

[2] Badler, N., "Multi-Dimensional Input Techniques and Articulated Figure Positioning By Multiple Constraints," *1986 Workshop on Interactive 3D Graphics* (Chapel Hill, NC, 1986).

[3] Barzel, R., Barr, A., "Modeling with Dynamic Constraints," in *Topics in Physically Based Modeling*, SIGGRAPH Tutorial 17 Notes, (1987).

[4] Bertsekas, D., "Multiplier Methods: a Survey," *Automatica,* **12**, 133–145, (1976).

[5] de Boor, C., *A Practical Guide to Splines,* (Springer-Verlag, NY, 1978).

[6] do Carmo, M., *Differential Geometry of Curves and Surfaces,* (Prentice-Hall, Englewood Cliffs, NJ, 1974).

[7] Feynman, C., *Modeling the Appearance of Cloth*, MSc Thesis, EECS Dept. , (MIT, Cambridge, MA, 1986).

[8] Fung, Y., *Foundations of Solid Mechanics,* (Prentice-Hall, Englewood Cliffs, NJ, 1965).

[9] Girard, M., Maciejewski, A. "Computational Modelling for the Computer Animation of Legged Figures," *Proc. SIGGRAPH 1985* 263–270, (1985).

[10] Goldstein, H, *Classical Mechanics,* (Addison-Wesley, Reading, MA, 1950).

[11] Haumann, D., "Modeling the Physical Behavior of Flexible Objects", in *Topics in Physically-Based Modeling*, SIGGRAPH Tutorial 17 Notes, 1987.

[12] Hestenes, M., *Optimization Theory,* (Wiley & Sons, NY, 1975).

[13] Isaacs, P., Cohen, M., "Controlling Dynamic Simulation with Kinematic Constraints, Behavior Functions and Inverse Dynamics," *Proc. SIGGRAPH 1987*, 215–224, (1987).

[14] Press, W., Flannery, B., Teukolsky, S., Vetterling W., *Numerical Recipes,* (Cambridge University Press, Cambridge, 1986).

[15] Terzopoulos, D., Platt, J., Barr, A., Fleischer, K., "Elastically Deformable Models," *Proc. SIGGRAPH 1987*, 205–214, (1987).

[16] Truesdell, C., "The Non-Linear Field Theory of Mechanics," in *Encyclopedia of Physics*, S. Flügge, ed., **III/3** (Springer-Verlag, Berlin, 1965).

[17] Weil, J., "The Synthesis of Cloth Objects," *Proc. SIGGRAPH 1986*, 49–54 (1986),

[18] Wilhelms, J., Barsky, B., "Using Dynamic Analysis to Animate Articulated Bodies such as Humans and Robots," *Proc. Graphics Interface '85*, 97–104 (Montreal, 1985)

[19] White, R., *An Introduction to the Finite Element Method with Applications to Non-linear Problems,* (John Wiley & Sons, NY, 1985).

[20] Witkin, A., Fleischer, K., Barr, A., "Energy Constraints on Parametrized Models," *Proc. SIGGRAPH 1987*, 225–232, (1987).

[21] Zienkiewicz, O., *The Finite Element Method,* Third Edition, (McGraw-Hill, London, 1977).

Appendices

A   Equations for a Path Following RC

The deviation vector $\underline{D}$ to a path is the difference between where the mass point is and where it should be on the path at that time. Let $(\underline{x}(t), \underline{v}(t))$ be the current position and velocity of the mass point, and $(\underline{x}^*(t), \underline{v}^*(t))$ be the desired position and velocity of the mass point. Then,

$$\underline{D} = \underline{x}^*(t) - \underline{x}(t) \qquad (33)$$

$$\frac{d}{dt}\underline{D} = \underline{v}^*(t) - \underline{v}(t) \qquad (34)$$

Since we want to control the velocity along the path, we do not allow any unconstrained force:

$$\underline{F}_{unconstrained} = 0 \qquad (35)$$

The final control force is:

$$\underline{F}_{output} = c(\underline{v}^*(t) - \underline{v}(t)) + k(\underline{x}^*(t) - \underline{x}(t)), \qquad (36)$$

Notice how the control force in this case is independent of the input force, $\underline{F}_{input}$.

B Equations for a Planar RC

Consider the plane with normalized plane equation $P(\underline{x}(t)) = Ax(t) + By(t) + Cz(t) + D = 0$. Let the homogeneous operator be $Q(\underline{x}(t)) = Ax(t) + By(t) + Cz(t)$. The normal, $\hat{n}$, to the plane is $(A\ B\ C)^T$. We want the distance of the mass point to the plane to be zero:

$$\underline{D} = -\hat{n}P(\underline{x}), \tag{37}$$

$$\frac{d}{dt}\underline{D} = -\hat{n}Q(\underline{v}). \tag{38}$$

where the vector $\underline{x}$ is the position of the mass point and the vector $\underline{v}$ is the velocity.

The components of the input force normal to the plane need to be controlled. The force tangent to the plane should be unconstrained.

$$\underline{F}_{\text{unconstrained}} = F_{\text{input}} - (F_{\text{input}} \cdot \hat{n})\hat{n}. \tag{39}$$

Using equation (8) yields

$$\underline{F}_{\text{constrained}} = -(kP(\underline{x}) + cQ(\underline{v}))\hat{n}. \tag{40}$$

The output of a planar RC is

$$\underline{F}_{\text{output}} = F_{\text{input}} - (kP(\underline{x}) + cQ(\underline{v}) + \underline{F}_{\text{input}} \cdot \hat{n})\hat{n}. \tag{41}$$

To constrain a point to lie on one side of the plane, $P(\underline{x}) < 0$, we apply the reaction constraint only if the mass point is on the wrong side of the plane and if the input force is not lifting the point away from the plane:

$$P(\underline{x}) < 0 \quad \text{and} \quad \underline{F}_{\text{input}} \cdot \hat{n} > \underline{F}_{\text{constrained}} \cdot \hat{n}. \tag{42}$$

The one-sided planar RC can be extended to prevent any mass points from entering a solid polygonal model. From inside of the model, choose the closest polygon, then apply the one-sided planar RC to force the mass point to the surface of that polygon.

C Finite Elements for Elasticity

Following [15], there is a potential energy for each flexible element that encourages the metric tensor to be near the rest metric:

$$U = s\sum_{i,j}(G_{ij} - R_{ij})^2, \tag{43}$$

where s is the stiffness of the material. The energy in equation (43) describes an isotropic material with a Poisson ratio of zero. The force on the the points that make up the element is the derivative of the potential energy [10]:

$$\underline{F}_k^{\text{elastic}} = s\sum_{i,j}(G_{ij} - R_{ij})\frac{\partial G_{ij}}{\partial \underline{r}_k}, \tag{44}$$

where $\underline{r}_k$ is the position of the kth corner. In addition, there is a viscous damping force that resists changes in the metric tensor:

$$\underline{F}_k^{\text{viscous}} = l\sum_{i,j}\dot{G}_{ij}\frac{\partial G_{ij}}{\partial \underline{r}_k} = l\sum_{i,j,m}\frac{\partial G_{ij}}{\partial \underline{r}_m}\cdot \underline{v}_m \cdot \frac{\partial G_{ij}}{\partial \underline{r}_k}, \tag{45}$$

where $\underline{v}_m$ is the velocity of the mth corner, and l is the viscous damping of the element. If $s \gg l$, then the material acts like a solid. If $l \gg s$, then the material acts like a fluid [16]. Using Newton's Second Law, the differential equations for an unconstrained viscoelastic element is

$$\frac{d}{dt}r_i = \underline{v}_i \tag{46}$$

$$\frac{d}{dt}v_i = \underline{F}^{\text{elastic}} + \underline{F}^{\text{viscous}} \tag{47}$$

The viscoelastic forces and the constraint force depend on G_{ij}. Following the finite element method, the G_{ij} in each element is assumed to be the integrated average of G_{ij} over the entire element. Let $\underline{a}$ be

the material coordinates of a point in the element and let $\underline{r}(\underline{a})$ be the position of the points $\underline{a}$. Then, from the definition of metric tensor,

$$G_{ij} = \int \frac{\partial \underline{r}}{\partial a_i}\frac{\partial \underline{r}}{\partial a_j}.dV \tag{48}$$

Assuming a position in the element is a linear interpolation of the positions of the corners of the element (see figure 11), the average G_{ij} can be analytically computed from the positions of the corners. To compute G_{ij}, estimates of the spatial derivatives are required:

$$\underline{\alpha}_i = \underline{r}_{2i} - \underline{r}_{2i-1}, \quad i = 1,2,3,4 \tag{49}$$

$$\underline{\beta}_1 = \underline{r}_3 - \underline{r}_1, \underline{\beta}_2 = \underline{r}_4 - \underline{r}_2, \quad \underline{\beta}_3 = \underline{r}_7 - \underline{r}_5, \underline{\beta}_4 = \underline{r}_8 - \underline{r}_6, \tag{50}$$

$$\underline{\gamma}_i = \underline{r}i + 4 - \underline{r}_i, \quad i = 1,2,3,4 \tag{51}$$

Averages of the spatial derivatives are also required:

$$\underline{a} = \sum_{i=1}^{4}\alpha_i, \quad \underline{b} = \sum_{i=1}^{4}\beta_i, \quad \underline{c} = \sum_{i=1}^{4}\gamma_i. \tag{52}$$

Finally, the various components of G_{ij} can be computed, assuming the element has unit length, width, and height in material coordinates.

$$G_{00} = \frac{1}{18}(2\underline{a}\cdot\underline{a} - \underline{\alpha}_1\cdot\underline{\alpha}_4 - \underline{\alpha}_2\cdot\underline{\alpha}_3) \tag{53}$$

$$G_{11} = \frac{1}{18}(2\underline{b}\cdot\underline{b} - \underline{\beta}_1\cdot\beta_4 - \underline{\beta}_2\cdot\underline{\beta}_3) \tag{54}$$

$$G_{22} = \frac{1}{18}(2\underline{c}\cdot\underline{c} - \underline{\gamma}_1\cdot\underline{\gamma}_4 - \underline{\gamma}_2\cdot\underline{\gamma}_3) \tag{55}$$

$$G_{01} = G_{10} = \frac{1}{24}[\underline{a}\cdot\underline{b} - (\underline{\alpha}_1 + \underline{\alpha}_2)\cdot(\underline{\beta}_1 + \underline{\beta}_2) + (\underline{\alpha}_3 + \underline{\alpha}_4)\cdot(\underline{\beta}_3 + \underline{\beta}_4)] \tag{56}$$

$$G_{02} = G_{20} = \frac{1}{24}[\underline{a}\cdot\underline{c} - (\underline{\alpha}_1 + \underline{\alpha}_3)\cdot(\underline{\gamma}_i + \underline{\gamma}_2) + (\underline{\alpha}_2 + \underline{\alpha}_4)\cdot(\underline{\gamma}_3 + \underline{\gamma}_4)] \tag{57}$$

$$G_{12} = G_{21} = \frac{1}{24}[\underline{b}\cdot\underline{c} - (\underline{\beta}_1 + \underline{\beta}_3)\cdot(\underline{\gamma}_1 + \underline{\gamma}_3) + (\underline{\beta}_2 + \underline{\beta}_4)\cdot(\underline{\gamma}_2 + \underline{\beta}_4)] \tag{58}$$

As in the continuous case, the diagonal terms of the metric tensor G_{ij} in equations (53)–(58) depend on various distances in the cube, while the off-diagonal terms depend on angles. Also, the G_{ij} are quadratic functions of the $\underline{r}_i$. Thus, $\partial G_{ij}/\partial r_i$ are complicated, although linear, functions of r_i.

The finite element is equivalent to a set of mass points with non-linear springs between them.

D Equations for a Flexible Model ALC

This appendix illustrates how to apply ALCs to physical systems. As stated in section 2, physical systems perform optimization, but not gradient descent. ALCs, however, are easily added to physical systems.

Consider a typical flexible model, with forces $F_i(\underline{x})$ and damping c. The differential equation for this system is

$$\dot{x}_i = v_i, \tag{59}$$

$$\dot{v}_i = F_i - \epsilon v_i. \tag{60}$$

Let us constrain the flexible model in equations (59) and (60) to lie on the subspace $g(\underline{x}) = 0$. There are $2N$ optimizing state variables: $\underline{x}_i$ and $\underline{v}_i$. We can apply an augmented Lagrangian λ to the equation for x to fulfill $g(\underline{x}) = 0$. We can also add a penalty term $(dg/dt)^2$ to the v equation to provide extra damping in the direction of violation of the constraint. (Notice that this extra damping force is zero when the constraint is fulfilled.) The final form of an ALC applied to a physical model is

$$\dot{x}_i = v_i - (\lambda + kg)\frac{\partial g}{\partial x_i}, \tag{61}$$

$$\dot{v}_i = F_i - \epsilon v_i - c\frac{\partial g}{\partial x_i}\frac{\partial g}{\partial x_j}v_j, \tag{62}$$

$$\dot{\lambda} = g(\underline{x}). \tag{63}$$

As section in 4, multiple constraints are performed by creating an auxiliary differential equation for each constraint and summing all of the constraint forces.

E   Equations for Incompressibility

The constraint for an incompressible element is

$$g = \det(G_{ij}) - V_0^2 = 0. \tag{64}$$

The derivative of the constraint g with respect to the spatial variables $\underline{r}_i$ is needed for an ALC. Let C_{ij} be the matrix of cofactors of G_{ij}. Then, the derivative is

$$\frac{\partial g}{\partial r_l} = C_{ij}\frac{\partial G_{ij}}{\partial r_l}. \tag{65}$$

Then, the differential equations for an incompressible element with other forces $\underline{F}_l$ are

$$\frac{d}{dt}r_l = \underline{v}_l - (\lambda + kg)\frac{\partial g}{\partial r_l}, \tag{66}$$

$$\frac{d}{dt}v_l = \underline{F}_l - \frac{\partial g}{\partial r_l}\frac{\partial g}{\partial r_i}\underline{v}_i, \tag{67}$$

$$\dot{\lambda} = g. \tag{68}$$

F   Equations for a Moldability

The constraint for a moldable element is:

$$P = (G_{ij} - R_{ij})(G_{ij} - R_{ij}) - P_0 < 0 \tag{69}$$

$$\eta = \begin{cases} 1/2P^2; & \text{if } P > 0, \\ 0; & \text{if } P \le 0. \end{cases} \tag{70}$$

Again, the derivative of the constraint function with respect to the state variables is needed by an ALC. For stretchable models, however, the rest metric is also a function of time. We thus need the derivative of η with respect to R_{ij}. Let $Q = P$ if $P > 0$ and $Q = 0$, otherwise. Then,

$$\frac{\partial \eta}{\partial r_l} = Q(G_{ij} - R_{ij})\frac{\partial G_{ij}}{\partial r_l} \tag{71}$$

$$\frac{\partial \eta}{\partial R_{ij}} = -Q(G_{ij} - R_{ij}). \tag{72}$$

Using these derivatives yield the differential equations for a moldable element with other forces $\underline{F}_l$:

$$\frac{d}{dt}r_l = \underline{v}_l - (\sigma + c\eta)\frac{\partial \eta}{\partial r_l} \tag{73}$$

$$\frac{d}{dt}v_l = \underline{F}_l - \frac{\partial \eta}{\partial r_l}\frac{\partial \eta}{\partial r_i}\underline{v}_i \tag{74}$$

$$\dot{R}_{ij} = -\frac{\partial \eta}{\partial R_{ij}} \tag{75}$$

$$\dot{\sigma} = \eta. \tag{76}$$

G   Why ALCs Work

The damped oscillations of equations (20) and (21) can be explained by differentiating equation (20) and then substituting (21):

$$\ddot{x}_i + \sum_j \left(\frac{\partial^2 f}{\partial x_i \partial x_j} + \sum_\alpha \lambda_\alpha \frac{\partial^2 g_\alpha}{\partial x_i \partial x_j} \right)\dot{x}_j + \sum_\alpha g_\alpha \frac{\partial g_\alpha}{\partial x_i} = 0. \tag{77}$$

Equation (77) is the equation for a damped mass system, with an inertia term, $\ddot{x}_i$; a damping matrix,

$$A_{ij} = \frac{\partial^2 f}{\partial x_i \partial x_j} + \sum_\alpha \lambda \frac{\partial^2 g_\alpha}{\partial x_i \partial x_j}; \tag{78}$$

and an internal force, $\sum_\alpha g_\alpha \partial g_\alpha / \partial x_i$, which is the derivative of the internal energy,

$$U = \frac{1}{2}\sum_\alpha (g_\alpha(\underline{x}))^2. \tag{79}$$

If the system is damped and the state remains bounded, the state falls into a constrained minima.

As in physics, we can construct a total energy of the system, which is the sum of the kinetic and potential energies.

$$E = T + U = \sum_i \frac{1}{2}(\dot{x}_i)^2 + \sum_\alpha \frac{1}{2}(g_\alpha(\underline{x}))^2. \tag{80}$$

If the total energy is decreasing with time, and the state remains bounded, then the system will dissipate any extra energy, and will settle down into the state where

$$g_\alpha(\underline{x}) = 0, \tag{81}$$

$$\dot{x}_i = \frac{\partial f}{\partial x_i} + \sum_\alpha \lambda \frac{\partial g_\alpha}{\partial x_i} = 0, \tag{82}$$

which is a constrained extremum of the original problem in equation (2).

The time derivative of the total energy in equation (80) is

$$\dot{E} = \sum_i \ddot{x}_i \dot{x}_i + \sum_\alpha g_\alpha(\underline{x})\frac{\partial g_\alpha}{\partial x_i}\dot{x}_i = -\sum_{i,j} \dot{x}_i A_{ij} \dot{x}_j. \tag{83}$$

If damping matrix A_{ij} is positive definite, the system converges to fulfill the constraints [1].

ALC always converges for quadratic programming, a special case of constrained optimization. A quadratic programming problem has a quadratic function $f(\underline{x})$ and piecewise linear continuous functions $g_\alpha(\underline{x})$, such that

$$\frac{\partial^2 f}{\partial x_i \partial x_j} \text{ is positive definite and } \frac{\partial^2 g_\alpha}{\partial x_i \partial x_j} = 0. \tag{84}$$

Under these circumstances, the damping matrix A_{ij} is positive definite for all $\underline{x}$ and λ, so that the system converges to the constraints.

It is possible, however, to pose a problem that has contradictory constraints. For example,

$$g_1(x) = x = 0 \text{ and } g_2(x) = x - 1 = 0. \tag{85}$$

In the case of conflicting constraints, the ALC compromises, trying to make each constraint g_α as small as possible However, the Lagrange multipliers λ_α go to $\pm\infty$ as the constraints oppose each other. It is possible, however, to arbitrarily limit the λ_α at some large absolute value.

For a given constrained optimization problem, it is frequently necessary to alter the ALC to have a region of positive damping surrounding the constrained minima. Arrow [1] combines the multiplier method with the penalty method to yield a modified multiplier method that is locally convergent around constrained minima [1].

The damping matrix is modified by the penalty force to be

$$A_{ij} = \frac{\partial^2 f}{\partial x_i \partial x_j} + \sum_\alpha \lambda_\alpha \frac{\partial^2 g_\alpha}{\partial x_i \partial x_j} + c_\alpha \frac{\partial g_\alpha}{\partial x_i}\frac{\partial g_\alpha}{\partial x_j} + cg\frac{\partial^2 g_\alpha}{\partial x_i \partial x_j}. \tag{86}$$

Arrow [1] proves a theorem that states that there exists a $c^* > 0$, such that if $c > c^*$, the damping matrix in equation (86) is positive definite at constrained minima. Using continuity, the damping matrix is positive definite in a region R surrounding each constrained minimum. If the system starts in the region R and remains bounded and in R, then the convergence theorem is applicable, and the augmented Lagrangian method converges to a constrained minimum.

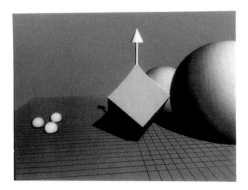

Figure 13: A compressible gelatinous cube is picked up with an RC.

Figure 14: A compressible gelatinous cube hits the table.

Figure 15: A sphere squashes a seat cushion.

Figure 16: A lump of moldable incompressible clay hits the table.

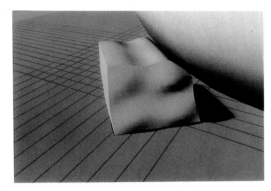

Figure 17: An elastic model is squashed.

Figure 18: An elastic model returns to its rest shape.

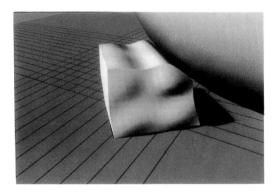

Figure 19: A moldable model is squashed.

Figure 20: A moldable model assumes a new rest shape after strong deformation.

Collision Detection and Response for Computer Animation

Matthew Moore and *Jane Wilhelms*

Computer Graphics & Imaging Laboratory
Computer & Information Sciences Board
University of California at Santa Cruz
Santa Cruz, California 95064

Abstract

When several objects are moved about by computer animation, there is the chance that they will interpenetrate. This is often an undesired state, particularly if the animation is seeking to model a realistic world. Two issues are involved: *detecting* that a collision has occurred, and *responding* to it. The former is fundamentally a kinematic problem, involving the positional relationship of objects in the world. The latter is a dynamic problem, in that it involves predicting behavior according to physical laws. This paper discusses collision detection and response in general, presents two collision detection algorithms, describes modeling collisions of arbitrary bodies using springs, and presents an analytical collision response algorithm for articulated rigid bodies that conserves linear and angular momentum.

CR Categories and Subject Descriptors: I.3.5: [Computer Graphics]: Computational Geometry and Object Modeling - Geometric algorithms; I.3.7: [Computer Graphics]: Three Dimensional Graphics and Realism - Animation.

Key Words and Phrases: computer animation, collision detection, collision response, analytical solution, dynamical simulation.

1. OVERVIEW

Computer animation provides a number of methods for controlling object motion.[28] The object's positions and orientations as functions of time may be interpolated from keyframes or parameter specification,[27] or may be the output of special computer programs written by the user,[23] or may be produced by physical simulation of the effect of internal, model-derived, and user-specified forces and torques.[1, 12, 16, 29, 32] In any such scheme, the main questions when animating a single object are how to achieve realistic motion and how to economize on the human animator's time. When several objects are animated at once, the addi-

tional problem of detecting and controlling object interactions is encountered. When no special attention is paid to object interactions, the objects will sail majestically through each other, which is usually not physically reasonable and produces a disconcerting visual effect. Whenever two objects attempt to interpenetrate each other, we call it a collision.

The most general requirement that arises from this is an ability to *detect* collisions. Most animation systems at present do not provide even minimal collision detection, but require the animator to visually inspect the scene for object interaction and respond accordingly. This is time-consuming and difficult even for keyframe or parameter systems where the user explicitly defines the motion; it is even worse for procedural or dynamical animation systems where the motion is generated by subroutines and laws defining their behavior. Though automatic collision detection is somewhat expensive both to code and to run, it is a considerable convenience for animators, particularly when more automated methods of motion control, such as dynamics or behavioral control, are used.[24, 31] This paper describes two collision detection algorithms. One algorithm deals with triangulated surface representations of objects, and is appropriate for flexible or rigid surfaces. The other algorithm applies to objects modeled as rigid polyhedra. Both algorithms are simple, robust, and not dreadfully expensive.

The related issue is *response* to collisions once they are detected. Even keyframe systems could benefit from automatic suggestions about the motion of objects immediately following a collision; animation systems using dynamical simulation inherently must respond to collisions automatically and realistically. Linear and angular momentum must be preserved, and surface friction and elasticity must be reasonable. This article presents two methods that satisfy these criteria. One is the obvious method, based on temporary springs introduced at collision points. The other method is an analytical linear system solution. The former method is more general, working equally well for flexible, rigid, and articulated bodies. The latter, limited to rigid and articulated objects, is typically faster. Furthermore, while the spring solution assumes the ability to use the dynamics equations of motion to predict the motion immediately after impact, the analytical solution could be used within a kinematic animation system.

©1988   ACM-0-89791-275-6/88/008/0289 $00.75

2. COLLISION DETECTION

Collision detection involves determining when one object penetrates another. It is clearly an expensive proposition, particularly when large numbers of objects are involved and the objects have complex shapes. Collision detection has been extensively pursued in the fields of CAD/CAM and robotics,[2,3,6,7,11,30] and it is with some diffidence that we offer any more algorithms. Some published algorithms[2,3] solve the problem in more generality (and at higher cost) than we have found to be necessary for computer animation. Others[6] do not easily produce the collision points and normal directions necessary if collision response is to be calculated. Voxel-based methods have also been used,[30] but would not be appropriate for all applications. Finally, many collision detection algorithms are quite intricate and must deal with many special cases, which we wished to avoid for software engineering reasons. Two collision algorithms are discussed here: the first is designed to test the interpenetration of surfaces modeling flexible objects; the latter is designed to test for interpenetration of convex polyhedra.

2.1. Collision Detection for Flexible Surfaces

Surfaces are modeled as a grid of points connected to form triangles.[19] Collisions between surfaces are detected by testing for penetration of each vertex point through the planes of any triangle not including that vertex (thus, self-intersection of surfaces is detected). The surfaces are assumed to be initially separate. For each time step of animation, the positions of points at the beginning and the end of the time step must be compared to see if any point went through a triangle during that time step. If so, a collision has occurred. The algorithm is $O(nm)$ for n triangles and m points.

A correct test must consider edges and triangles, as polyhedral objects can collide edge-on without any vertices being directly involved. However, in many cases merely testing points versus triangles produces acceptable results. This algorithm only tests points versus triangles. It is worth noting that the mathematics for testing intersection of a moving point with a fixed triangle is the same as for testing a fixed edge versus a fixed triangle. Thus the fully general edge versus triangle tests could be done at fixed instants in time, with the same advantages and disadvantages that will be discussed for the second collision detection algorithm.

The question of whether a moving point has intersected a surface can be divided into two cases. The easy case requires the surface to be fixed in space, whereas the hard case allows the surface to be moving also. When the surface triangle is fixed, the parametric vector equation

$$P + (P'-P)t = P_0 + (P_1-P_0)u + (P_2-P_0)v$$

where P and P' are the beginning and ending positions of the point and the P_i's define the triangle, is set up and solved for the variables u,v,t. u and v are parametric variables for the plane defined by the triangle, whereas t is a time variable which is 0 at the beginning of the simulation step in question, and 1 at the end. The left hand side is the parametric equation for the path of the point, and the right hand side is the parametric equation for any point on the plane. This vector equation represents three scalar equations in three unknowns and is solved by matrix inversion. If $0 \le t \le 1$ and $u \ge 0$ and $v \ge 0$ and $u+v \le 1$, then the point has intersected the triangle during the time step.

The hard case is solved by setting up the parametric vector equation

$$P + V t = P_0 + V_0 t + ((P_1-P_0)+(V_1-V_0)t)u$$
$$+ ((P_2-P_0)+(V_2-V_0)t)v$$

where P is the point (with velocity V per time step), the P_is define the triangle vertices (with velocity V_i per time step), and t,u,v are the parametric variables. Rearranging, we can write this as three linear equations in three unknowns.

$$a\,u + b\,v + c\,t = d$$
$$e\,u + f\,v + g\,t = h$$
$$i\,u + j\,v + k\,t = l$$

where

$$a = (P_{1x}-P_{0x})+t(V_{1x}-V_{0x})$$
$$b = (P_{2x}-P_{0x})+t(V_{2x}-V_{0x})$$
$$c = -V_x$$
$$d = P_x - (P_{0x}+tV_{0x})$$
$$e = (P_{1y}-P_{0y})+t(V_{1y}-V_{0y})$$
$$f = (P_{2y}-P_{0y})+t(V_{2y}-V_{0y})$$
$$g = -V_y$$
$$h = P_y - (P_{0y}+tV_{0y})$$
$$i = (P_{1z}-P_{0z})+t(V_{1z}-V_{0z})$$
$$j = (P_{2z}-P_{0z})+t(V_{2z}-V_{0z})$$
$$k = -V_z$$
$$l = P_z - (P_{0z}+tV_{0z})$$

The P_ws and V_ws are the position and velocity components of the point, and the P_{iw}s and V_{iw}s are the position and velocity components of the triangle vertices. The velocities are per time step.

The linear system above can be solved for t and expanded to

$$0 = a(ja-ib)(ha-ed) - a(ja-ib)(ga-ec)t$$
$$+ (fa-eb)(ka-ic)t - (la-id)(fa-eb)$$

Substitution of the actual expressions for a through l gives a 5'th order polynomial in t. If further substitutions were made, the equations could be written in the form

$$c_5 t^5 + c_4 t^4 + c_3 t^3 + c_2 t^2 + c_1 t^1 + c_0 = 0$$

Polynomials of order 5 and above cannot be solved analytically,[10] so a binary search technique is used to find approximate values for t.[5] Binary search is used because it is guaranteed to converge, and because, using economizing techniques described below, this algorithm is not used often enough to warrant large efforts at optimization. The interval from $t=0$ to $t=1$ is subdivided into a number of sub-intervals, and the left-hand side is evaluated at each dividing point. If the sign of that value is different for the two endpoints of some subinterval, then some t for which the equation is true must lie within that interval. A binary search of values of t within that interval brings the brackets around that value of t closer together, until a limit is reached (after 10 iterations, in our system) and an approximate value of t is found. Each value of t thus arrived at is used to get values for u and v by back substitution, and then the standard $0 \le t \le 1$ and $u \ge 0$ and $v \ge 0$ and $u+v \le 1$ test is used to determine whether a collision has occurred.

To minimize the cost of executing the above calculations, a preliminary step is used. Every point is compared to every triangle. The perpendicular distance of the point from the plane defined by the triangle is first derived, by substituting into the plane equation,[25] for the beginning and the end of the time step. If the sign of the perpendicular distance has not changed intersection is assumed not to have occurred. If the sign has changed, then the more expensive tests outlined above must be done, but in practice this test eliminates most point-triangle pairs.

A special kind of bounding box can also be used to minimize computation. This bounding box includes the beginning and ending position of the triangle. This box is then grown by the distance between the beginning and ending positions of the point being tested. (This is necessary to avoid the point passing unnoticed completely through the box during the time step. A similar growth technique is used in the Lozano-Perez path planning algorithm.)[15]

The basic algorithm is $O(nm)$, for n triangles and m points. Use of an octree[19] and bounding boxes can reduce the time to $O(m \log m)$ to construct the octree, and $O(n \log m)$ to search it (assuming that the tree is almost balanced and that the bounding boxes are small compared to the space covered by the tree).

The search finds all point - bounding box pairs that must be examined more closely for possible intersection. All of the points in the model are inserted into an octree, which is created anew for each round of collision detection. This octree is based on the points themselves, with each point P having up to 8 subtrees containing points in each of the octants of space defined by the $P's$ position. This is an obvious generalization of the well known binary search tree.[13, 14] A pseudo-random number generator is used to scramble the order of insertion; in this way, Knuth assures us,[13] the tree will be almost balanced, i.e. the height of the octree will be $O(\log m)$ almost always.

Each triangle's bounding box is grown by the distance between the starting and ending positions of the fastest point being tested. Each bounding box is then recursively compared against the octree to find the points inside it. If a point is inside the box, all of its subtrees must be searched recursively. If a point is outside the box, at least half of its subtrees do not need to be searched. If a point is found to be inside a box, then the algorithm above must be run to determine if the point intersected the associated triangle during the time step.

Figure 1 illustrates a two-dimensional version of this procedure. The points A through I were inserted into an initially empty quadtree in alphabetical order, so that A is the root element of the tree. The tree is to be searched for all points inside the dotted box. A is inside, so all of it's subtrees must be searched. B is above and to the right of the dotted box, so only its lower left subtree must be searched. This finds C, which is inside the box. If C had subtrees, they would all have to be searched. The next subtree of A starts with F. F is above the bounding box, so both of its lower subtrees must be searched. One is empty, and the other contains only I, which is also outside the box. A's third subtree contains only E, which is below the box. If E had subtrees, only the upper ones would need to be searched. A's fourth and last subtree contains only G, which is outside the box. If G had subtrees, only the two right hand ones would be searched. A large, bushy quadtree would be very fast to search (if the dotted box were small relative to the area covered by the tree) because the unsearched subtrees would often contain large numbers of points.

2.2. Collision Detection for Convex Polyhedra

The detection of collisions between solids (or closed surfaces) can be treated somewhat differently, for the objects have a distinguishable *inside* and *outside*. The problem is somewhat more complex than might be initially thought. Edges as well as vertex points may be involved in collisions.

This method for detecting collisions is based on the Cyrus - Beck clipping algorithm.[25] Collisions of articulated objects can be detected by applying this algorithm to all pairs of the polyhedra making up the two objects. The two polyhedra are assumed to be convex; concave polyhedra can be decomposed into collections of convex ones. The basic algorithm is $O(n^2 m^2)$ for n polyhedra and m vertices per polyhedron. Methods for reducing these exponents are discussed below.

The two-dimensional Cyrus - Beck algorithm[25] tells whether a point is inside a convex polygon. It takes the dot product of each side's outward normal vector ($\mathbf{n}$) with a vector from some point ($\mathbf{v}$) on the side to the point in question ($\mathbf{p}$). If that dot product is negative for all edges of the polygon, then the point is inside; if not, it is outside (see Figure 2).

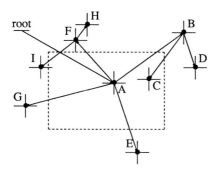

Figure 1
Searching a Quadtree

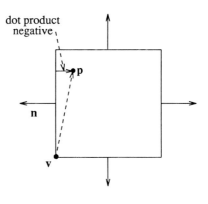

Figure 2
Cyrus - Beck Clipping

The collision detection algorithm is developed as a three-dimensional analogy to Cyrus - Beck clipping. The algorithm works by testing whether representative points of one polyhedron are inside the other polyhedron. First points from polyhedron B are tested against polyhedron A, and then the process is reversed and points from A are tested for inclusion in B. These two steps combine to cover all special cases and give a reliable answer. The algorithm given below terminates when a single point of interpenetration is found, which is sufficient for collision detection. If collision response is also required, the algorithm below should be modified to find all points of interpenetration. The rest of this section describes the test of points from B against A.

Let A consist of a set of planar polygonal faces (p_i). Each polygon contains a set of vertices (u_{ij}) and an outward pointing normal vector n_i. Let B consist of a set of vertices (v_i), a set of edges (e_i), and a set of planar polygonal faces (f_i). All coordinates of B have been transformed into the reference frame of A.

The first step tests for the presence of vertices of B inside of A. Each vertex of B is compared to every face of A; if any vertex is on the inward side of all such faces, it is inside A and the algorithm terminates having detected a collision. For each vertex i of B and for each face j of A, form the dot product $(v_i - u_{j1}) \cdot n_j$. If this dot product is negative the vertex is on the inward side of the face.

The second step tests for penetration of the edges of B through the faces of A. Each edge of B is divided into a number of smaller line segments by intersecting it with the infinite planes corresponding to every face of A. See Figure 3. This subdivision is done as follows. Let some edge of B connect the vertices v_i and v_j, and let us compare it against some face of A that has an outward pointing normal n_k and a vertex point u_{k1}. First the perpendicular distance of each vertex from the plane defining the face is calculated, by substitution into the plane equation.[25] If the perpendicular distances differ in sign, then the edge intersects the plane, and the intersection point P can be calculated.

$$d_i = (v_i - u_{k1}) \cdot n_k$$
$$d_j = (v_j - u_{k1}) \cdot n_k$$
$$t = \frac{|d_i|}{|d_i| + |d_j|}$$
$$P = v_i + t\,(v_j - v_i)$$

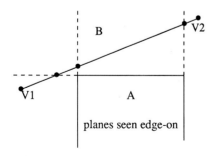

Figure 3
Edge Subdivision

This will result in a collection of intersection points P lying along the edge. Intersection points with $t < 0$ or $t > 1$ do not lie on the actual edge and are discarded. The remaining intersections are sorted into order according to their t values, forming a sequence of points from one vertex to the other along the edge. Each adjacent pair of points in this sequence, including those made by the vertices and the first and last subdivision points, defines a sub-segment of the edge. The midpoint of each resulting line segment is checked for being inside A by the same method that was used for vertices, above. Again, if any of these midpoints is inside A the algorithm terminates with a detected collision.

The third step tests for the infrequent case where two identical polyhedra are moving through each other with faces perfectly aligned. Here, the centroid point of each face of B is tested against A by the method used for vertices, above. If any of these centroids is inside A the algorithm terminates with a detected collision.

If the algorithm survives the above three steps without detecting a collision, and also does not detect one when reversing and comparing A against B, then the two polyhedra do not interpenetrate.

The above algorithm can be speeded up by a variety of tricks. A bounding box or bounding sphere test can be applied to every pair of polyhedra, yielding an immediate "no collision" result in most cases. Many of these bounding box tests can even be eliminated by octree or voxel methods. [4,9] When a point is to be tested against a polyhedron, it can first be compared to the polyhedron's bounding box, which will probably eliminate the need to compare it against all of the faces. The bounding box can be aligned with the coordinate axes of the polyhedron's local frame to make this point elimination test particularly fast.

It should be noted that this algorithm, or indeed any algorithm which point samples the positions of objects over time, could fail if one object moved entirely through another during a single time step. This is a rather unusual occurence in procedural or dynamic animation because simulation time steps are normally small relative to the velocities of the objects. The correct solution to this problem is to generalize to four dimensions;[3] the starting and ending positions of the polyhedra define 4-D hyper-polyhedra which are checked for interpenetration by higher-dimensional analogues to the algorithm given above. The more practical approach is either to ignore the problem (as we do) or to restrict the animation step size so that the change in any object's position in any step is small relative to the object's size.

3. COLLISION RESPONSE

In keyframed and procedural animation systems, collision detection is the main requirement; collision response usually consists of informing the animator or the motion control program that a collision has occurred, and trusting them to handle it. In animation systems using dynamics to generate motion, the system itself must respond to a collision by determining new linear and angular velocities for the colliding objects. These new velocities must conserve linear and angular momentum, or else the resulting "funny bounce" will be very obvious to viewers of the animation. The elasticity of the surfaces must also be taken into account, as this determines how much kinetic energy is lost in the collision; no-one will believe that a bean bag should bounce off of a hard surface as if it were a golf ball.

3.1. Collision Response Using Springs

The most intuitive way to handle collisions is with springs. Dynamic simulation systems must already have a method for applying external forces to objects. Thus, when a collision is detected, a very stiff spring is temporarily inserted between the points of closest approach (or deepest interpenetration) of the two objects. The spring law is usually K/d, or some other functional form that goes to infinity as the separation d of the two objects approaches 0 (or the interpenetration depth approaches some small value). K is a spring constant controlling the stiffness of the spring. The spring force is applied equally and in opposite directions to the two colliding objects. The direction of the force is such as to push the two objects apart (or to reduce their depth of interpenetration).

Our particular implementation handles variable elasticity by making a distinction between collisions where the objects are approaching each other and collisions where the objects are receding from each other. For $\varepsilon = 1$, i.e. perfectly elastic (hard) collisions, the spring constant K will be the same whether the objects are approaching or receding. For $\varepsilon = 0$, i.e. totally inelastic (soft) collisions, the spring will act as noted above as long as the objects are approaching each other, but as soon as they start to move apart the spring force will decrease to 0. For elasticities between 0 and 1, the two spring constants will be related by $K_{recede} = \varepsilon K_{approach}$.

The spring method is easy to understand and easy to program. It applies equally well to rigid bodies (articulated or not) and to flexible bodies, whether modeled as point masses connected by springs, or by energy of deformation techniques.[29] The main problem with this method is that it is computationally expensive; stiffer springs mean stiffer equations, which require smaller time steps for accurate numerical integration.[8] The numerical effort required goes up with the violence of the collision; as the springs are compressed more and more, the equations become stiffer and stiffer, and smaller and smaller time steps are needed. This was the motivation for seeking a better method of collision response.

3.2. Collision Response Using an Analytical Solution

An analytical solution for the collision of two arbitrary articulated rigid objects is available. The analytical solution depends upon the conservation of momentum during a collision, and results in a new angular and linear velocity for each body. Thus, the solution bypasses the question of collision forces and can be used independent of dynamic simulation, assuming information concerning the bodies mass and mass distribution can be provided.

Some combination of spring and analytical collision response may be desirable for a dynamic animation system. Analytical solutions are typically faster for strong collisions, because the solution need only be found once. However, for gentle collisions, such as a body resting quietly atop another body, springs may be desirable.[26] In such a case, gravity may consistently cause the two objects to interpenetrate and, thus, the analytical solution would have to be applied time and time again. A simple spring that counteracts gravity will be faster and more stable in this case.

This section develops the solution in stages. First, an analytical solution for the collision of two rigid bodies is presented; this result is due to MacMillan.[17] MacMillan's solution is extended to tree-like articulated rigid objects with revolute joints. Then, the restriction to tree-like objects is removed, and finally the method is extended to encompass joints with one or two sliding degrees of freedom.

3.2.1. Single Rigid Bodies

MacMillan gives a general solution for the collision of two arbitrary rigid objects. Each object has a linear velocity vector v_i, an angular velocity vector ω_i, a mass m_i, a center of mass vector c_i, and an inertial tensor matrix I_i which is relative to the center of mass. All of these quantities, for both objects, are expressed in the same inertial reference frame. In addition, each object has a vector ρ_i which points from its center of mass to the collision point. The solution also requires three orthogonal unit vectors i,j,k that define the "collision frame". k will be perpendicular to the plane of collision and i and j will be in that plane. The definition of the plane of collision is somewhat arbitrary; for convenience we will define it as follows. If a vertex of one object is colliding with a face of the other, then that face defines the plane of collision. If an edge of one object is colliding with an edge of the other, these two edges define the plane of collision. If two vertices are colliding, k is directed along the line joining them. See Figure 4.

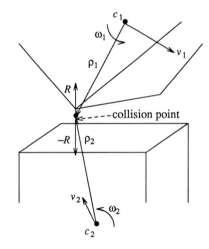

Figure 4.
Collision Problem - Two Rigid Objects

It is desirable to assume that there is only one collision point in any given collision; this restriction is not totally necessary, but it simplifies the formulations given below. It is reasonable to say that whenever two objects collide in the real world, there is one point at which they collide first (other collisions may follow within microseconds). Thus, the collision detection algorithm must furnish a single collision point between two objects. Because of the time-stepped nature of dynamics simulations, this will only be an approximate collision point; a good heuristic is to take the point of greatest interpenetration of any two objects in the simulation, provided that the relative velocities of the two objects at that common point are such that the interpenetration depth is increasing. If adaptive step size control is available, this heuristic can be refined by stating that interpenetration to greater than some threshold depth is unacceptable, and causes backtracking and reduction of the step size. This allows the simulation to close in on a collision point very close to the surfaces of the objects by a process similar to binary search. Multiple collision points can be handled by a straightforward extension to the algorithms given below, by inventing multiple collision impulses and incorporating them into the matrix.

The solution involves solving a set of 15 linear equations in 15 unknowns. The fifteen unknowns are: the new linear velocity vector for each object ($\bar{v}_1$, $\bar{v}_2$); the new angular velocity vector for each object ($\bar{\omega}_1$, $\bar{\omega}_2$); and the impulse vector R. An impulse has units of momentum and can be thought of as a huge force applied for a tiny time. Because the collision is assumed to occur in a negligible time (approximately instantaneous), only the collision impulse itself matters; any other forces being applied to the objects will be too small to have an effect. By convention, the impulse is directed from object 2 to object 1.

Twelve linear equations can be written down immediately, expressing the change in linear and angular momentum that each object experiences as a result of the collision impulse R.

$$m_1 \bar{v}_1 = m_1 v_1 + R$$
$$m_2 \bar{v}_2 = m_2 v_2 - R$$
$$I_1 \bar{\omega}_1 = I_1 \omega_1 + \rho_1 \times R$$
$$I_2 \bar{\omega}_2 = I_2 \omega_2 - \rho_2 \times R$$

The last three linear equations come from some assumptions about the collision conditions; the assumptions that we will use are that the elasticity, ε, is zero (so that the two colliding objects come to rest relative to each other, at least at the collision point) and that the surfaces are frictionless (so that the impulse must be perpendicular to the collision plane). Other assumptions are possible and are discussed below. Our assumptions require the dot products of R with the collision frame unit vectors i and j to be zero, and the difference in the velocity of the collision point, as seen from each of the two objects, to be zero in the k direction. We can write:

$$R \cdot i = 0$$
$$R \cdot j = 0$$
$$(\bar{v}_2 + \bar{\omega}_2 \times \rho_2 - \bar{v}_1 - \bar{\omega}_1 \times \rho_1) \cdot k = 0$$

These equations can be solved by standard Gauss-Jordan elimination with maximal pivoting,[5] LU-decomposition,[22] or by more advanced sparse matrix methods.[20, 21] It is possible at this point in the algorithm to find the solution for an elastic collision. The actual elasticity of the collision can be taken as the lower of the elasticities of the two colliding surfaces. A new collision impulse R_{actual} can then be calculated as $R_{actual} = (1 + \varepsilon_{actual}) R$. This new collision impulse is then plugged back into the defining equations above, to solve for the $\bar{v}_i$ and $\bar{\omega}_i$ vectors that are required. The $\bar{v}_i$ vectors come out easily; the $\bar{\omega}_i$ vectors require inverting the I_i inertial tensor matrices.

Next consider including friction. If the objects are infinitely rough and $\varepsilon = 0$, the collision condition requires that the objects come to rest (relative to each other) at the collision point. This corresponds to the vector equation:

$$\bar{v}_2 + \bar{\omega}_2 \times \rho_2 - \bar{v}_1 - \bar{\omega}_1 \times \rho_1 = 0$$

In between perfectly smooth and perfectly rough collisions lies the great middle ground of partially rough friction. Modeling partial (i.e. realistic) friction can become quite complex; the simple treatment given here is from MacMillan[17] and McLean[18] and is sufficient to produce visually reasonable results.

The coefficient of friction, γ, is the maximum allowed ratio of force parallel to the collision plane versus force perpendicular to that plane. Although properly speaking, γ is a property of pairs of surfaces, we assign a γ value to each surface, and then use the larger of the γ values of the colliding objects. When the two objects have finite γ and $\varepsilon = 0$, the collision can be solved in two steps. First the collision is solved as if it were infinitely rough. Then the resulting collision impulse, R, is examined. If the allowed ratio, γ, of the components of R parallel and perpendicular to the collision plane is not exceeded (i.e. if $\gamma R \cdot k \geq | R - k(R \cdot k) |$), all is well and the solution stands, because the objects should stick.

Otherwise, the objects should slide. The system of equations must be set up and solved again with different collision conditions. These new conditions will give a smaller restraining parallel force, because only a limited amount of friction can act against sliding motion. Two constants α and β are calculated, such that the collision impulse will exactly fulfill $\gamma R \cdot k = | R - k (R \cdot k) |$, or in other words such that the ratio of the parallel and perpendicular components of R is exactly γ, and the direction of the parallel component of R is the same as before. This gives the maximum parallel force allowed by the necessary perpendicular force and the coefficient of friction. The collision conditions are then:

$$R \cdot i = \alpha R \cdot k$$
$$R \cdot j = \beta R \cdot k$$
$$(\bar{v}_2 + \bar{\omega}_2 \times \rho_2 - \bar{v}_1 - \bar{\omega}_1 \times \rho_1) \cdot k = 0$$

α and β are calculated as follows, with Q the component of R perpendicular to the collision plane, and P the unit direction vector of the component of R parallel to the collision plane:

$$Q = k (R \cdot k)$$
$$P = \frac{R - Q}{| R - Q |}$$
$$\alpha = \gamma (P \cdot i)$$
$$\beta = \gamma (P \cdot j)$$

To reiterate, the full algorithm for solving a general collision of two rigid objects is to transform the required quantities (incoming velocities, tensor matrices, ρ_i, etc) from the objects' local coordinate frames to a common inertial frame, define the collision frame's orthogonal unit vectors i, j, and k, choose appropriate collision conditions, set up and solve the system of equations as outlined above, and transform the new linear and angular velocities back to the objects' local frames. This may seem like a drastic amount of work when compared with inserting a simple spring between the two objects, and it does require more lines of computer code, but this method is usually applied only once for each collision, whereas springs generally must be applied over a large number of very small time steps. This analytical method is cheaper computationally unless the collision is very gentle indeed, and the cost of this collision solution does not depend upon the violence of the collision, certainly a desirable property.

3.2.2. Articulated Rigid Bodies - Tree-Structured, Revolute Joints

Now we extend MacMillan's solution to tree-like articulated rigid objects with revolute joints. The various rigid objects that make up the tree-like linkages will be numbered from 1 to n. Objects 1 and 2 will be the colliding objects, and the rest will be linked to one or both of them, either directly or through some number of intermediaries. Note that this solution allows the links of an articulated object to collide with other links of the same object or with another object entirely. Each rigid object will again have a linear velocity vector v_i, an angular velocity vector ω_i, an inertial tensor matrix I_i, a mass m_i, and a center of mass c_i, all expressed in a common inertial reference frame.

The revolute joints connecting the various rigid objects will be assumed to be ideal, that is, perfectly elastic and with no mechanical tolerance. The single joint that connects object i to object j will be described by the vector ρ_{ij} that points from c_i to the joint, and the vector ρ_{ji} that points from c_j to the joint. As well as the collision impulse R, this solution will calculate an attachment impulse R_{ij} for each joint. Unlike the collision impulse, the attachment impulses R_{ij} are unconstrained as to direction. By convention, the attachment impulse R_{ij} points from object j to object i, and $R_{ij} = -R_{ji}$. R_{ij} will be $(0,0,0)$ if objects i and j are not connected by a joint. See Figure 5.

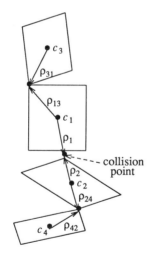

Figure 5.
Articulated Collision Problem

For a collision involving n rigid objects there are $6n$ unknowns corresponding to the resulting linear and angular velocities of the objects, 3 unknowns for the collision impulse, and either $3(n-1)$ unknowns corresponding to the attachment impulses if the objects are all part of one articulated linkage, or $3(n-2)$ unknowns if two different articulated objects are

colliding. Thus, the total size of the linear system to be solved is approximately $9n$ for n rigid objects involved in the collision. The sparsity of the matrix increases as n increases, so that if sparse matrix methods are used the solution should be around $O(n)$.[20, 21]

Once again, the unknowns to be solved for are $\bar{v}_i$ and $\bar{\omega}_i$ for $i = 1...n$, R, and R_{ij} for all pairs of objects i and j connected by a joint. The equations for objects 1 and 2, and for the collision impulse, still look familiar. The extra summation terms reflect the change in linear and angular momentum resulting from any attachment impulses felt by those objects.

$$m_1 \bar{v}_1 = m_1 v_1 + R + \sum_{i=1}^{n} R_{1i}$$

$$m_2 \bar{v}_2 = m_2 v_2 - R + \sum_{i=1}^{n} R_{2i}$$

$$I_1 \bar{\omega}_1 = I_1 \omega_1 + \rho_1 \times R + \sum_{i=1}^{n} \rho_{1i} \times R_{1i}$$

$$I_2 \bar{\omega}_2 = I_2 \omega_2 - \rho_2 \times R + \sum_{i=1}^{n} \rho_{2i} \times R_{2i}$$

The conditions on the collision impulse R are still the same.

$$R \cdot i = 0$$

$$R \cdot j = 0$$

$$(\bar{v}_2 + \bar{\omega}_2 \times \rho_2 - \bar{v}_1 - \bar{\omega}_1 \times \rho_1) \cdot k = 0$$

For the objects that are not directly colliding (for object $i = 3..n$), the momentum conservation equations are

$$m_i \bar{v}_i = m_i v_i + \sum_{j=1}^{n} R_{ij}$$

$$I_i \bar{\omega}_i = I_i \omega_i + \sum_{j=1}^{n} \rho_{ij} \times R_{ij}$$

Each joint requires three more linear equations to make the system of equations complete and solvable. These are derived from the basic requirement of a revolute joint: the velocity of the joining point, when seen as part of either of the rigid objects which it connects, must be the same. Otherwise, the joint would tend to pull apart. For each joint connecting objects i and j, three more equations can be written.

$$\bar{v}_i + \bar{\omega}_i \times \rho_{ij} = \bar{v}_j + \bar{\omega}_j \times \rho_{ji}$$

Once again, the algorithm requires that the necessary information about all of the objects be transformed from their local reference frames to a common inertial reference frame. The collision frame orthogonal unit vectors i, j, and k must be determined. The (potentially rather large) linear system is set up and solved for the variables $\bar{v}_i$, $\bar{\omega}_i$, R, and R_{ij}, by standard methods.[5, 22, 20, 21] The actual elasticity of the collision is determined as above, and actual impulses are determined by multiplying R and the R_{ij}'s by $(1 + \varepsilon_{actual})$. The actual impulses are then put back into the equations above to get the final solution for linear and angular velocities. The last step is to transform the solution back to the object's local frames.

3.2.3. Articulated Rigid Bodies - Revolute Joints

The above solution for tree-like articulated rigid objects can be extended by removing the requirement for tree-like linkage. Since the two articulated objects that are colliding are defined to be connected objects, some subset of the attachment points will define tree-like linkages. The first step is to set up the problem as above for the objects and for those joints. Then the extra joints are added; each contributes another attachment impulse R_{ij}, and thus adds three variables to the problem. Each joint also allows three more linear equations to be written down, the familiar velocity matching condition.

$$\bar{v}_i + \bar{\omega}_i \times \rho_{ij} = \bar{v}_j + \bar{\omega}_j \times \rho_{ji}$$

This larger system once again contains as many variables as equations, and so can be solved by standard techniques. The actual collision and attachment impulses are calculated and applied in the same way as above, and the solution values are transformed back to the objects' local coordinate systems. It is even possible to have more than one joint connecting two objects i and j, although in that case the notation used above would have to be expanded slightly. If two joints connect objects i and j, the objects will have only one degree of freedom of motion relative to each other; they will be able to twist around the line connecting the two joints. If a third joint is added connecting i and j, which is not colinear with the other two, the two objects will be locked in position relative to each other, and will form in effect a single rigid object. This is probably not a desirable state of affairs, but the solution algorithm does permit it.

3.2.4. Articulated Bodies - Sliding Joints

A sliding joint is one in which the joining points on the two objects are allowed to move freely with respect to each other in one or two dimensions, but are at the same time constrained to a fixed relationship in the other dimensions. A linear sliding joint allows sliding motion in one degree of freedom, while controlling two others; a planar sliding joint controls one degree of freedom, allowing sliding motion in the other two. For now, assume that these joints allow three revolute degrees of freedom as well.

For a linear sliding joint, assume that objects i and j are connected, and that a joint coordinate system is defined by three orthogonal unit vectors d_i, d_j, and d_k. These vectors are stated in the local coordinate system of object i and rotate with it. Further assume that the attachment point on object j is allowed to move freely in the d_i direction, but must maintain some particular value for its position along d_j and d_k as seen from object i. Note that the "attachment point" on object i is in fact a line; this requires us to calculate ρ_{ij}, the actual attachment point on object i, separately for each collision. Note also that the joint coordinate system orthogonal unit vectors must be rotated into the common inertial frame.

Notice that the attachment impulse R_{ij} is required to lie in the d_j, d_k plane. As it is possible to write down three linear constraining equations about this joint, such a joint can be treated within the linear systems described above. One equation expresses the constraint that R_{ij} must lie in a plane; the other two equations constrain the attachment point velocities to match in two of the three joint coordinate system directions.

$$R_{ij} \cdot d_i = 0$$
$$(\bar{v}_j + \bar{\omega}_j \times \rho_{ji} - \bar{v}_i - \bar{\omega}_j \times \rho_{ij}) \cdot d_j = 0$$
$$(\bar{v}_j + \bar{\omega}_j \times \rho_{ji} - \bar{v}_i - \bar{\omega}_j \times \rho_{ij}) \cdot d_k = 0$$

The argument for a planar sliding joint is similar. In this case the attachment point on object j is allowed to move freely in the d_i and d_j directions, constraining the collision impulse to exactly the d_k direction, but leaving its magnitude unknown. The attachment point velocities must still match in the d_k direction, but are allowed to vary in the other two directions. The equations are as follows.

$$R_{ij} \cdot d_i = 0$$
$$R_{ij} \cdot d_j = 0$$
$$(\bar{v}_j + \bar{\omega}_j \times \rho_{ji} - \bar{v}_i - \bar{\omega}_j \times \rho_{ij}) \cdot d_k = 0$$

The sliding joints described above allow the two objects that they connect either 4 (linear) or 5 (planar) degrees of freedom of movement relative to each other. Sliding joints that provide fewer degrees of freedom can be constructed by adding one or more extra joints of the above types. For instance, suppose that a planar sliding joint is desired such that one object can slide relative to the other, but the objects cannot rotate relative to each other. This can be accomplished by defining three planar sliding joints (all using the same plane) with the sliding points not colinear. A piston type joint (one degree of translational freedom and one degree of rotational freedom) can be described by two linear sliding joints of the above type, with the connection points constrained to slide along the same line.

3.3. Collisions of Dynamic Objects with Non-Dynamic Objects

A complication seems to arise when dynamically controlled objects collide with objects that are controlled in other ways (such as keyframe interpolation). In these cases the velocities of the non-dynamic objects involved in the collision cannot change. Thus, $\bar{v}_i = v_i$ and $\bar{\omega}_i = \omega_i$ for the objects that are not under dynamic control, and $\bar{v}_i$ and $\bar{\omega}_i$ are not variables in the linear system formulations above. The systems can be reformulated with fewer rows and columns, and the solution proceeds just as before. The result is collisions that do not conserve linear or angular momentum. The keyframe or procedurally controlled objects move along their assigned paths with lordly disdain, brushing aside the dynamically controlled objects as if they had negligible mass.

More complex responses from the non-dynamic objects are possible. Programs that control objects could be written to take the results of dynamic collisions into account. In effect, the procedural object could become dynamic for the duration of the collision, and its velocity could change. The program would have to be alert to this possibility. This would be fairly simple to implement using the analytic solution, which does not require setting up and solving the complete dynamics equations of motion. Alternatively, collisions between dynamic and keyframed objects could be defined as exceptional events that require that the human animator be notified.

4. CONCLUSIONS

Collision detection is important for any animation system. The coding requirements are not excessive, and, while a naive approach to collision detection can consume large amounts of computer time, several tricks are available to keep the cost reasonable.

Dynamical simulation systems must resolve collisions after detecting them. The obvious method of inserting temporary springs is general and easy to program, but exacts a severe execution time penalty, particularly for violent collisions. This makes an analytical collision resolution algorithm attractive. On the other hand, for objects resting against each other but encouraged by forces to interpenetrate, the spring solution is more appropriate. A dynamical simulation system should have a combination of both methods available.

ACKNOWLEDGEMENTS

This work was supported by National Science Foundation grant number CCR-8606519. We wish to thank Robert Skinner, David Forsey, and Peter Valtin for contributing to the dynamical animation software that we used to implement these algorithms. We would also like to thank our reviewers for their incisive and helpful comments and references.

References

1. William W. Armstrong and Mark W. Green, "The Dynamics of Articulated Rigid Bodies for Purposes of Animation," *Proceedings of Graphics Interface '85*, pp. 407-415, Canadian Information Processing Society, Toronto, Ontario, Canada, May 1985.

2. John W. Boyse, "Interference Detection Among Solids and Surfaces," *Communications of the ACM*, vol. 22:1, pp. 3-9, January, 1979.

3. John Canny, "Collision Detection for Moving Polyhedra," *MIT A.I. Lab Memo 806*, October, 1984.

4. Ingrid Carlbom, "An Algorithm for Geometric Set Operations Using Cellular Subdivision Techniques," *IEEE Computer Graphics and Applications*, vol. 7, pp. 44-55, Computer Society of the IEEE, Los Alamitos, CA, May 1987.

5. Brice Carnahan and James O. Wilkes, *Digital Computing and Numerical Methods*, John Wiley and Sons, Inc., New York, 1973.

6. Scott E. Fahlman, "A Planning System for Robot Construction Tasks," *Artificial Intelligence*, vol. 5, pp. 1-49, 1974.

7. Wm. Randolph Franklin, "Efficient Polyhedron Intersection and Union," *Proceedings of Graphics Interface 1982*, pp. 73-80, 1982.

8. C. William Gear, *Numerical Initial Value Problems in Ordinary Differential Equations*, Prentice-Hall, Englewood Cliffs, NJ, 1971.

9. Jeffrey Goldsmith and John Salmon, "Automatic Creation of Object Hierarchies for Ray Tracing," *IEEE Computer Graphics and Applications*, vol. 7, pp. 14-20, Computer Society of the IEEE, Los Alamitos, CA, May 1987.

10. I. N. Herstein, *Topics in Algebra*, Xerox College Publishing, Lexington, MA, 1964.

11. J.E. Hopcroft, J.T. Schwartz, and M. Sharir, "Efficient Detection of Intersections among Spheres," *The International Journal of Robotics Research*, vol. 2:4, pp. 77-80, Winter 1983.

12. Paul M. Isaacs and Michael F. Cohen, "Controlling Dynamic Simulation with Kinematic Constraints," *Computer Graphics*, vol. 21, no. 4. Proceedings of SIGGRAPH'87 (Anaheim, CA, July 27-31, 1987)

13. Donald Knuth, *Fundamental Algorithms*, Addison-Wesley Publishing Co., Reading, MA, 1975.

14. Donald Knuth, *Searching and Sorting*, Addison-Wesley Publishing Co., Reading, MA, 1975.

15. Tomas Lozano-Perez and Michael A. Wesley, "An Algorithm for Planning Collision-Free Paths Among Polyhedral Obstacles," *Communications of ACM*, vol. 22, no. 10, pp. 560-570, October, 1979.

16. Richard V. Lundin, "Motion Simulation," *Proceedings of Nicograph 1984*, pp. 2-10, November, 1984.

17. William D. MacMillan, *Dynamics of Rigid Bodies*, Dover Publications, Inc, New York, 1936.

18. W. G. McLean and E. W. Nelson, *Engineering Mechanics: Statics and Dynamics*, Shaum's Outline Series, McGraw-Hill Book Co., New York, 1978.

19. Matthew Moore, "A Flexible Object Animation System," Masters Thesis, University of California, Santa Cruz, Computer & Information Sciences, Santa Cruz, California, March, 1988.

20. Ole Osterby and Zahari Zlatev, *Direct Methods for Sparse Matrices*, Springer-Verlag, Berlin, 1983.

21. Sergio Pissanetsky, *Sparse Matrix Technology*, Academic Press, London, 1984.

22. William H. Press, Brian P. Flannery, Saul A. Teukolsky, and William T. Vetterling, *Numerical Recipes*, Cambridge University Press, Cambridge, England, 1986.

23. Craig W. Reynolds, "Computer Animation with Scripts and Actors," *Computer Graphics*, vol. 16, no. 4, pp. 289-296, Association for Computing Machinery, July, 1982. Proceedings of SIGGRAPH'82

24. Craig W. Reynolds, "Flocks, Herds, and Schools: A Distributed Behavioral Model," *Computer Graphics*, vol. 21, no. 4, pp. 25-34, Association for Computing Machinery. Proceedings of SIGGRAPH'87 (Anaheim, CA, July 27-31, 1987)

25. David F. Rogers, *Procedural Elements for Computer Graphics*, McGraw-Hill Book Company, New York, 1985.

26. Robert Skinner, U Cal. Santa Cruz, CIS Dept. personal communication.

27. Scott N. Steketee and Norman I. Badler, "Parametric Keyframe Interpolation Incorporating Kinetic Adjustment and Phrasing Control," *Proceedings of SIGGRAPH '85*, vol. 19, no. 4, pp. 255-262, July, 1985.

28. David Sturman, *A Discussion on the Development of Motion Control Systems*, Association for Computing Machinery, July 1987. SIGgraph '87 Course 10 Notes: Computer Animation: 3-D Motion Specification and Control.

29. Demetri Terzopoulous, John Platt, Alan H. Barr, and Kurt Fleischer, "Elastically Deformable Models," *Computer Graphics*, vol. 21, no. 4. Proceedings of SIGGRAPH'87 (Anaheim, CA, July 27-31, 1987)

30. Tetsuya Uchiki, Toshiaki Ohashi, and Mario Tokoro, "Collision Detection in Motion Simulation," *Computers & Graphics*, vol. 7:3-4, pp. 285-293, 1983.

31. Jane Wilhelms, "Towards Automatic Motion Control," *IEEE Computer Graphics and Animation April, 1987*, vol. 7, no. 4, pp. 11-22, April, 1987.

32. Jane Wilhelms, "Using Dynamic Analysis for Animation of Articulated Bodies," *IEEE Computer Graphics and Applications*, vol. 7, no. 6, June, 1987.

Example 1: early stage rockpile

Example 2: man sitting
positioned with collision detection

Examples 3-5: falling domino movie

Realistic Animation of Rigid Bodies

James K. Hahn

Ohio Supercomputer Center and Department of Computer and Information Science
The Ohio State University
1224 Kinnear Road, Columbus, OH 43212

Abstract

The theoretical background and implementation for a computer animation system to model a general class of three dimensional dynamic processes for arbitrary rigid bodies is presented. The simulation of the dynamic interaction among rigid bodies takes into account various physical characteristics such as elasticity, friction, mass, and moment of inertia to produce rolling and sliding contacts. If a set of bodies is statically unstable, the system dynamically drives it toward a stable configuration while obeying the geometric constraints of the system including general *non-holonomic* constraints. The system also provides a physical environment with which objects animated using more traditional techniques can interact. The degree of interaction is easily controlled by the animator. A computationally efficient method to merge kinematics and dynamics for articulated rigid bodies to produce realistic motion is presented.

CR Categories and Subject Descriptors: I.3.7 [Three-Dimensional Graphics and Realism]: Animation

Additional Key Words and Phrases: Modeling, Simulation, Rigid bodies, Dynamics

1. Introduction

In traditional computer graphics, objects in a scene are looked upon as geometric shapes devoid of dynamical properties. The result is that the animator is forced to use his intuition about the physical world in planning the motion of objects in the scene. Since we are so sensitive to detecting anomalies in everyday physics and real motions tend to be complex, such techniques have generally proven unsatisfactory. Many animators have relied on specialized software

©1988   ACM-0-89791-275-6/88/008/0299 $00.75

(usually ad hoc) to model specific types of motion. Analogous to the development of physically based illumination models in computer graphics display algorithms, we need to think of objects in a scene as real objects having mass, moment of inertia, elasticity, friction, etc.

We present a simulation system for computer animation capable of realistically modeling the dynamics of a general class of three dimensional motions of arbitrary rigid bodies. The system introduces the following concepts absent in previous dynamics simulation systems:

- Using collision analysis, the interaction among objects can be realistically simulated in a completely general way. This includes continuous contact and complex contact geometry, allowing the solution of general constraint problems including *non-holonomic* constraints. Collision analysis makes it possible to solve the constraint problems using only the absolute minimum quantities needed to describe motion, the first derivatives of position and orientation (velocity and angular velocity).

- The motion of articulated figures, whose limbs are under kinematic control of the animator, can be solved by simple conservation of momentum arguments. The algorithm is linear in the number of links moved and does not involve numerical solutions of differential equations involving joint forces or torques.

- The system provides a physically realistic environment with which objects animated using more traditional techniques, such as key-framing and forward and inverse kinematics, can interact.

2. Other Works in Dynamics Simulations

Recently there has been a rising interest in dynamics simulations in computer animation. Weil [18] has simulated the motion of cloth. Terzapoulos et al. [17] and Haumann [9] have investigated the dynamics of flexible objects in modeling their deformations.

In rigid body motion, the emphasis has been in simulating articulated figures. Armstrong and Green [1] and Wilhelms and Barsky [19] have used dynamics to simulate human figures. Isaacs and Cohen [12] have used similar strategies but have also incorporated kinematic control of some of the joints. Two serious drawbacks of the dynamics approaches are the large computation time and the problem of control. Our method for articulated figure motion solves a slightly different problem of internal kinematic control of the limbs and external dynamic analysis. We feel that this is simpler and more effective in generating realistic motion in many cases.

The dynamics of contact between bodies that result in jointed mechanisms have been solved by researchers in studying articulated figures using simple constraints. This involves formulating a different solution for each configuration of constraints. Recently, Witkin et al. [20] have investigated purely geometric constraints to deal with several classes of constraint problems. Barzel and Barr [2] have used a similar strategy but in the context of dynamics simulations. This works well for animating the process of satisfying the constraints and is more general in the sense that different configurations of constraint do not need different solutions. However it is still specialized in the sense that for each different class of constraint one must be able to define the constraint in the form of an equation relating the coordinates and formulate a different solution. Other systems have modeled contacts between objects directly using repulsive forces [17, 20] and by using imaginary springs and dampers [19]. Our model takes a more rigorous and completely general approach that is able to realistically simulate friction (especially the transition between sliding and sticking contact) and elastic properties (especially the transition between impact and continuous contact) of any contact between arbitrary rigid bodies.

3. Overview of the System

The system was implemented on the Symbolics 3600 family of machines using Common LISP with Flavors. The general flowchart is given in Figure 1.

Each object in the scene to be simulated is given physical characteristics such as shape, density, coefficient of restitution, coefficient of friction, and link hierarchy if any. From these, other properties such as total mass, center of mass, moment of inertia tensor, and *principal axes* are calculated.

The dynamic state of each object include the linear and angular velocities, the position, and the orientation. The current dynamic state is used to solve for the dynamic state at an infinitesimal time increment dt later. Usually no oversampling (more than 30 per second video and 24 per second film) is necessary and dt represents the time increment between frames of the animation. The update is done in two steps. First, the objects are moved using the current dynamic state. This involves solving for the positions and orientations of the objects using self-starting numerical solutions of sets of coupled first order differential equations (such as

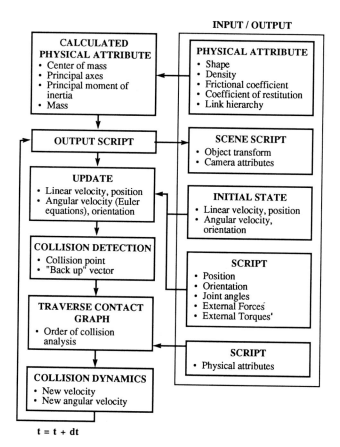

Figure 1. Flowchart of the system

Runge-Kutta [10]). If the motion of the object is "scripted" then the state is read in. Second, the objects are checked for intersections. If contact occurred, the new dynamic state for the objects that were effected are calculated using impact dynamics in an order given by traversing the "contact graph".

4. Motion of Rigid Bodies Under External Forces and Torques

The general motion of a rigid body can be decomposed into a linear motion of a point mass equal to that of the body located at the center of mass of the body under an external force and a rotational motion about the center of mass under an external torque. The linear motion under a force **F** can be calculated by solving the set of coupled differential equations

$$\dot{V} = F / m$$
$$\dot{X} = V \qquad (1)$$

where m is the mass of the object, **X** is the position vector, and **V** is the linear velocity.

4.1 Euler Equations

If we choose to solve the rotational dynamics in a body fixed coordinate system given by a set of axes known as the *principal axes*, a set of simplified coupled first order differential equations for the angular velocity $\mathbf{W}$, known as the *Euler equations*, results (Appendix B). These along with

$$\dot{\mathbf{T}}_x = \mathbf{W}_x$$
$$\dot{\mathbf{T}}_y = \mathbf{W}_y \qquad (2)$$
$$\dot{\mathbf{T}}_z = \mathbf{W}_z$$

where $\mathbf{T}$'s are the orientations in the principal axes coordinate, form a set which can be solved by a numerical technique such as Runge-Kutta [10]. Analytic solutions also exist for the equations in which Jacobian elliptic trigonometric functions are used [11]. These solutions may have an advantage when efficient packages are available for elliptic functions [14]. The analytic solutions could also make motion planning easier.

4.2 Moment of Inertia Tensor and the Principal Axes

The moment of inertia tensor for a rigid body, which is the rotational analogue of mass, is given by [16]

$$\mathbf{I} = \int \rho \, (\mathbf{R}^2 \, \mathbf{U} - \mathbf{R} \, \mathbf{R}) \, dv \qquad (3)$$

where ρ is the density of the object, $\mathbf{R}$ is the location vector of the volume element dv, $\mathbf{U}$ is the unity dyadic, and $\mathbf{R} \, \mathbf{R}$ is a dyad product. This is a *Hermitean* or a symmetric tensor of the second rank. The 3 x 3 matrix form of $\mathbf{I}$ is given in Appendix A. The inertia tensor can be transformed under rotation and translation to any coordinate system (Appendix A). The numerical integrations for the inertia tensor are performed in a coordinate frame where the origin coincides with the center of mass of the object to facilitate the separation of linear and rotational motion.

We can rotationally transform the inertia tensor to a coordinate frame in which the tensor is diagonalized. The existence of such a coordinate frame for any inertia tensor is guaranteed by the fact that it is a Hermitean [7]. This is just the problem of finding the eigenvectors $\mathbf{E}$ and its associated eigenvalues i for the matrix $\mathbf{I}$.

$$\mathbf{I} \cdot \mathbf{E}_j = i_j \cdot \mathbf{E}_j \qquad (1 \le j \le 3) \qquad (4)$$

A numerical solution such as the power method [10] can be used to find the largest and the smallest eigenvalues and the associated eigenvectors. The $\mathbf{E}$'s which are the axes of the coordinate system in which $\mathbf{I}$ is diagonalized are known as the *principal axes* and the i's which are the diagonal elements of the tensor in the principal axes coordinate are known as the *principal moments of inertia*. Intuitively the principal axes correspond to the "axes of symmetry" of an object and the principal moments of inertia corresponds to the associated moments of inertia.

It is important to realize that for any arbitrary shaped object, one can find the principal axes and the principal moments of inertia. They are invariant geometrical descriptions of the object in the body fixed coordinate system and need to be calculated only once for each object.

4.3 Dynamics of Articulated Figures

In most interesting human or animal motion, all the joints are under some autonomous control. Cases where limbs react to other limb motion or external forces and torques with absolutely no internal muscle control are rare. Also, empirical studies have shown that the unrestrained human limb motion are determined by intelligent trajectory planning in purely kinematic terms [4]. Even constrained systems in which all the parts cannot be defined as a mechanical system (e.g. where joints are controlled by feedback systems consisting of muscles and sensors) cannot be modeled using pure dynamics. Therefore the computationally intensive solution for the internal dynamics of articulated figures may be unjustified except for modeling inanimate jointed objects. We use kinematics to control joint trajectories [5] and dynamics to model the effects of limb motion and external forces and torques on the body as a whole.

The articulated body is defined in the form of an arbitrary tree of links. The tree structure makes the kinematic control easier but is not necessary for the dynamics analysis. In fact any system in which quanta of masses are moved within the body by the animator, such as an object changing shape, can use approaches similar to the following.

The dynamics of the figure as a whole proceeds as in the treatment of a single rigid body. The total moment of inertia tensor is calculated by summing the inertia tensors of individual links in the world coordinate and then transforming to the body fixed coordinate system with its origin at the center of mass of the articulated body. The principal axes are calculated from the total inertia tensor.

When the joints are being driven kinematically, there are additional motions of the whole object in the body fixed reference frame due to the conservation of linear and angular momentum of the system. When a joint j is moved with angular velocity $d\mathbf{W}_j$ in the joint fixed coordinate system, (Figure 2) the whole body must rotate by

$$d\mathbf{W}' = -\mathbf{I}_t^T \left[\left(\sum_i \mathbf{I}_i \right) d\mathbf{W}_j + (\mathbf{R}_j \times (d\mathbf{W}_j \times \mathbf{C}_j)) \left(\sum_i m_i \right) \right] \qquad (5)$$

in the body fixed coordinate system to conserve angular momentum. $\mathbf{I}_t^T$ is the transpose of the total inertia tensor of the whole body, the first sum is the moment of inertia tensor associated with the joint (i.e. the inertia tensors of all the descendants of j) in the joint coordinate system, $\mathbf{R}_j$ is the location of the joint with respect to the body fixed coordinate system, $\mathbf{C}_j$ is the location of the center of mass of the descendants of the joint in the body fixed coordinate system, and the last sum is the total mass of the descendants.

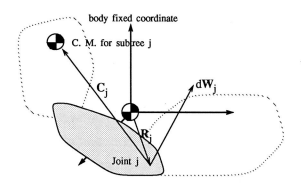

Figure 2. Moving joint j by dW_j in the body fixed coordinate

The linear momentum is conserved by finding the new center of mass of the whole body after the change and moving the body so that the center of mass coincides with the origin of the body fixed frame.

The above analysis is done at each time step for the joints that are being driven. The order in which the joints are treated is given by traversing the tree from the leaves toward the root. Then the inertia tensor of a subtree can be used to calculate the inertia tensor of its ancestor joint.

There is a new angular velocity of the entire body due to the change in the inertia tensor

$$W'_t = I_t^{T'} \cdot L_t \qquad (6)$$

where $I_t^{T'}$ is the matrix transpose of the new total inertia tensor and L_t is the invariant total angular momentum of the body.

5. Interaction Among Objects

Dynamics simulations (and disciplines involved in solving mechanical problems in general) have used the concept of *holonomic constraints* to solve the dynamics of continuous contact between objects. Holonomic constraints are a class of constraints in which one can define the constraints in the form of an equation of coordinates [7, 16]. They are abstractions of a small subset of the general constraint introduced to facilitate an analytic solution. The majority of constraints do not have such simple abstractions. As an example, the constraints of the links in a chain cannot be abstracted as, for example, a 3-degrees of freedom ball and socket joint. In fact each link has 6 degrees of freedom until they are in contact with other links and then the interaction is very complex (Figure 13). The most general constraint should therefore not be expressed in terms of what the objects *must* do (remain on a point, a line, etc.) but in terms of what the objects *must not* do (penetrate each other).

In the system, interactions among objects are simulated using collision detection to model the general constraints and impact analysis to solve the dynamics. Impact analysis

has been extended to include continuous contacts and simultaneous contact of many bodies. This makes it possible to solve the dynamics of arbitrary interactions without solving differential equations involving finite forces and torques. It also makes possible the realistic simulation of the transition between instantaneous and continuous contacts and between sticking and sliding contacts.

5.1 Impact Dynamics

An analysis of the impact process of two rigid bodies was proposed by Routh in the late nineteenth century [15]. Routh included the effect of the *Coulomb* model of friction and partially elastic materials employing graphical solution methods. His work remains essentially unchanged in modern expositions [6]. The following uses analytic and numerical solution techniques involving only the states before and after the collision.

When two bodies collide and the contact area of one of the bodies is locally planar, one can define the normal N to the tangent surface of contact between the two bodies (Figure 3). If a surface of contact cannot be defined for the impact (for example when a point of one object strikes the point of another) the outcome is theoretically indeterminate. In the system, we average the normals of neighboring polygons. In the following, "normal" refers to N and "tangential" refers to the direction along the tangent surface of contact.

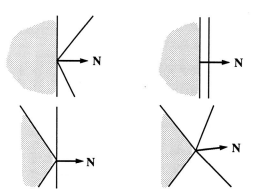

Figure 3. Modes and normals of local contact

In an impact process, the bodies act on each other with *impulse* P

$$P = \int_{\Delta t} F \, dt \qquad (7)$$

where F is the large force between the objects that act through an infinitesimally short time interval Δt. Since the integral is over time as Δt approaches 0, any finite forces such as gravity does not contribute to P. The conservation of linear and angular momenta gives (Figure 4)

$$m_1 (V'_1 - V_1) = - P_1$$
$$m_2 (V'_2 - V_2) = + P_2 \qquad (8a)$$

$$I_1 \cdot (W_1' - W_1) = R_1 \times (- P_1)$$

$$I_2 \cdot (W_2' - W_2) = R_2 \times (+ P_2) \qquad (8b)$$

The subscripts stand for each of the bodies and the primes denote the quantities after the impact. The moment of inertia tensors and the angular velocities are transformed from the body fixed frames to the world coordinate frame before they are used in these equations.

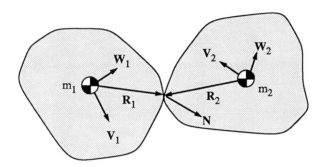

Figure 4. Collision between two objects

Here we introduce an empirical result known as the *generalized Newton's rule* [6].

$$\frac{(V_1' + W_1' \times R_1) \cdot N - (V_2' + W_2' \times R_2) \cdot N}{(V_1 + W_1 \times R_1) \cdot N - (V_2 + W_2 \times R_2) \cdot N} = - \varepsilon \qquad (9)$$

The constant of proportionality, ε, known as the *coefficient of restitution* depends to a large extent on the elasticity of the materials of the two constituent objects. ε has a value ranging from 0, corresponding to a perfectly inelastic collision to a value of 1, corresponding to a perfectly elastic collision where no kinetic energy is lost.

Now we consider friction between the two bodies at the moment of impact. Coulomb's law states [13]

$$| F_t | \leq \mu \, F_n \qquad (10)$$

where t is the tangential component and n is the normal component of the force F between the objects. The positive number μ is the coefficient of friction and depends solely on the materials of the two bodies. When $\mu = 0$ the interaction is frictionless. If the two objects are moving tangentially relative to each other at the point of contact then the equality holds in (10). We first assume that the two bodies do not slip on impact at the point of impact. Then

$$[(V_1' + W_1' \times R_1) - (V_2' + W_2' \times R_2)]_t = 0$$

$$[(V_1' + W_1' \times R_1) - (V_2' + W_2' \times R_2)]_r = 0 \qquad (11)$$

where t and r are the orthogonal components of the velocity vector perpendicular to N. Equations (8), (9), and (11) give us 15 independent equations in 15 unknowns (P and for both

objects V' and W'). If the solution for P satisfies

$$|N \times (P \times N)| \geq \mu \, |P \cdot N| \qquad (12)$$

then by (10) the no slip assumption that leads to (11) is not valid and the two bodies are sliding at the point of contact. In this case

$$P_t = 0$$

$$P_r = \mu \, |P \cdot N| \qquad (13)$$

where t is the direction given by $(P \times N)$ and r is the direction given by $N \times (P \times N)$, can be substituted for (11). The new set of 15 equations can be solved for the unknowns.

V' and W' for both objects constitute the new state after the collision. For the collision of a rigid body with an object of infinite mass (e. g. floor or other objects that effect the environment but are not in turn effected by it) the development is similar except only the conservation of momentum and energy of the one body is considered resulting in 9 equations in 9 unknowns (P, V', and W' for the body).

5.2 Continuous Contact

After a collision analysis is performed between two objects, if the relative velocity of the objects at the collision point in the direction of the normal of local contact is less than a small threshold then the objects can be considered to be in continuous contact. If the objects are applying a force on each other, for example when one of the objects is the floor, the dynamics can still be simulated using the impact equations (8), (9), (11) and (13). Although the forces and torques do not appear explicitly, their contribution is seen as the gain in momenta of the object during dt which are the impulses that the support applies to the object in the impact process. Even though we are approximating continuous contact with a series of instantaneous contacts, oversampling is usually not necessary.

5.3 Collision Detection

In order to minimize the number of polygon to polygon intersection tests, a hierarchical method involving bounding boxes is used. At the bottom of the hierarchy, each edge of object 2 is tested against each polygon of object 1 and vice versa. Since the collision detection is performed at discrete intervals of time, two types of penetrations are possible [3].

In Figure 5, the collision point is given by the "inside" vertices of the edges that intersect polygons. Assuming that object 1 is stationary in world coordinate one can define a ray originating from the collision point in a direction given by the relative velocity of the two objects at the collision point. If we assume that the velocity of the two objects at the collision point remains constant during the time step, the ray represents the path that the collision point of object 2 took when it penetrated object 1. The intersection between the ray and the polygons of object 1 represents the actual pene-

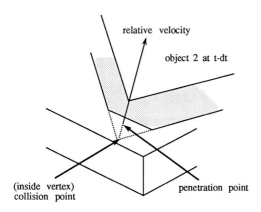

Figure 5. Point collision detection

tration point at which the two objects collided. In order to determine the actual positions and orientations of the objects at time t, both objects must be backed up to the time of the collision and collision dynamics used to generate the new velocities and thus the positions and the orientations at t. In our implementation, assuming sufficiently small dt, object 2 is "backed up" at time t so that the two objects touch but do not penetrate.

Figure 6 represents an edge collision where an edge penetrates more than one polygon. The penetration point is calculated by intersecting the polygon swept by the edge during the time step with the edges of the pierced polygons. The collision point is calculated by finding the intersection between the penetrating edge and a ray originating from the penetration point in a direction given by the negative of the relative velocity.

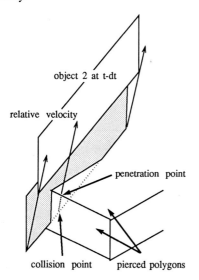

Figure 6. Edge collision detection

The above algorithm assumes that the time step dt and/or the velocity of the polygons of the objects are small enough such that the distance covered during dt is much smaller than the dimensions of the polygons. If this were not

the case then one must consider the volume swept by the bounding boxes and the polygons during dt in the collision detection algorithm not to miss the collision.

5.4 Complex Contact Geometry

For a scene consisting of a number of bodies in simultaneous contact, the impact analysis is applied to each pair of objects. If an object belongs to more than one such pair, then the contributions from each of the impacts are summed. An arbitrary order in handling the contact pairs could result in penetration between objects even after the collision analysis because of the necessity to "back up" after an impact is discovered.

In general, the contact geometry of a scene can be represented as a graph (Figure 7). The nodes represent the

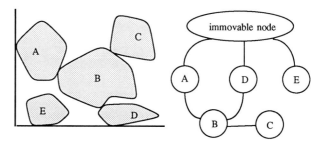

Figure 7. Contact geometry and associated graph

objects and the edges represent contacts. The special immovable node represents the set of all immovable objects in the scene. In order to prevent objects from being "backed up" into immovable objects, the contact pairs are handled in an order given by a breadth first search of the graph starting from the immovable node. If there are no immovable nodes, then the breadth first search can start from any node. In graphs involving cycles the last contact pair to be considered in the cycle must be checked so that the objects are not "backed up" into each other.

6. Control Issues

In any simulation system, there is a trade-off between automation and control by the animator. In our system the animator has a great deal of flexibility in determining how much of a control he has on the motions of objects in the scene. He can take full advantage of automation by specifying the initial state of the system and letting the system generate the subsequent motions. Through a series of experimentation, the desired overall motion can be achieved in a relatively short period of time. Our experiences have shown that most sequences (averaging approximately 10 seconds of animation) can be generated after only a few trials. By controlling the physical characteristics of the object (possibly as a function of time) the animator can manipulate the physics to his liking.

Some of the objects can be under the direct control of the animator allowing the integration of traditional animation techniques with simulation. The trajectories of these objects are usually scripted by specifying the position and orientation of the objects as a function of the frame number. In order to apply impact dynamics, the script is numerically differentiated to get the velocities as a function of time. A weighted average of the scripted velocities and the velocities given by the impact dynamics (if any) can be used to move the object. The amount of effect that the other objects have on the object being moved is controlled by scaling the mass and the moment of inertia of the object being moved. With a high scaling factor, the object effects the environment more and follow closely the scripted trajectory.

Some of the objects can be moved by applying forces and torques directly. Control is harder since the effect on an object is not clear. Inverse dynamics [12] can be used to calculate in advance the forces and torques needed to move an object in a desired trajectory .

7. Examples of Animation

Figures 9-16 illustrates a few of the wide range of realistic animation sequences generated with the system [8].

The collision detection algorithm, which is of order n^2 in the number of polygons when the objects are close enough, takes most of the calculation time in most sequences. Figure 8 gives approximate calculation times per frame with and without collision detection.

Animation	Without collision detection	With collision detection
Figure 9	.05	1.33
Figure 10	.05	6.97
Figure 11	.50	0.54
Figure 12	.60	3.41
Figure 13	.15	6.31
Figure 14	.07	8.60
Figure 15	.15	0.59
Figure 16	.04	1.52

Figure 8. Calculation time per frame in seconds

Figure 9 illustrates how the animator can direct the overall motion (even fairly complex motion). We wanted the car to come off the ramp, bounce off of a second car, and then crash into a third car. The low level details of the motion were generated by the system. Figure 10 (showing procession and nutation of the tops) illustrates how the laws of physics can be manipulated to get a desired effect. We wanted the tops to spin slowly to prevent temporal aliasing. In order to keep the tops from falling over because of a small angular velocity, the moments of inertia were increased artificially. In the articulated figure animation (Figure 11), the joint trajectories were kinematically specified and the system generated the external motion. In Figure 12, the motion of the rocket was scripted by the animator. The plate pieces realistically react to being pushed by the rocket. In the colli-

sion analysis, the mass and the moment of inertia of the rocket were set essentially to infinity compared to those of the plate pieces. In Figure 13, the top link is fixed. The other links in the chain are free to move without artificially imposed constraints. The chain was released from an initial state. The motion reflects the fact that the links are faceted and have some friction. Figures 14, 15, and 16 give examples of continuous and complex configuration of contacts among arbitrary shaped objects.

8. Conclusion

We are currently studying the possibility of using various strategies to search the space spanned by the dynamic state of an object to maximize or minimize certain quantities such as the closeness to a desired trajectory for an object. This type of motion planning would make it possible to precisely control the animation using our system. We are also in the process of implementing a near linear order collision detection algorithms employing neighborhood or spatial information.

In the system, the dynamics simulation proceeds from an initial state by a time series analysis of the linear and rotational motion. The rotational dynamics is simplified by solving the Euler equations in the principal axis reference frame. The external dynamics of kinematically driven articulated figures are solved principally by using conservation of momenta. The complex interactions between objects (including continuous contacts) are modeled in a completely general and novel way using collision detection and impact dynamics. The use of conservation of momenta in the dynamics analysis allows the solution for the motion involving only the velocities and not the accelerations. Scripts can be specified to integrate simulation and traditional animation techniques and to influence the dynamics.

The variety of realistic animations generated with the system show promise in systems based on physical simulations becoming an integral part of animation of rigid bodies.

Acknowledgments

I would like to thank Rick Parent, Brian Guenter, Michael Girard, and everyone in the "Symbolics Group" at ACCAD for many helpful discussions and software support. I would also like to thank Chuck Csuri and Tom Linehan for providing a free and supportive research atmosphere without which this work would not have been possible. This research was supported in part by a National Science Foundation grant DCR-8304185.

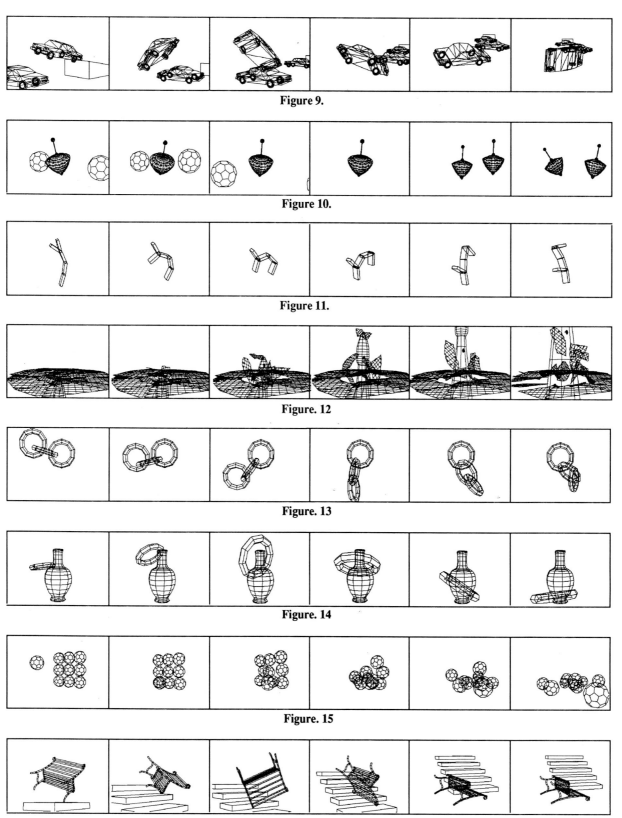

Figure 9.

Figure 10.

Figure 11.

Figure. 12

Figure. 13

Figure. 14

Figure. 15

Figure. 16

Appendix A

In the 3 x 3 matrix form of the moment of inertia tensor of an object, the diagonal elements or the *moment of inertia coefficients* are given by [7, 16]

$$I_{xx} = \int \rho \, (y^2 + z^2) \, dv$$
$$I_{yy} = \int \rho \, (x^2 + z^2) \, dv \qquad (A1)$$
$$I_{zz} = \int \rho \, (x^2 + y^2) \, dv$$

and the off-diagonal elements or the *product of inertia* are given by

$$I_{xy} = \int \rho \, (x \, y) \, dv$$
$$I_{xz} = \int \rho \, (x \, z) \, dv \qquad (A2)$$
$$I_{yz} = \int \rho \, (y \, z) \, dv$$

where the subscripts stand for the matrix indices, ρ is the density of the object, and the integral is over the volume of the object. The inertia tensor can be transformed to any coordinate frame. The matrix of the tensor transforms under a 3 x 3 orthogonal matrix $\mathbf{A}$ as a *similarity transform* [7]

$$\mathbf{I'} = \mathbf{A} \ \mathbf{I} \ \mathbf{A}^T \qquad (A3)$$

where the superscript T stands for the matrix transpose. For our purposes of rotational transform the matrix $\mathbf{A}$ is the direction cosine matrix of the two coordinates. For the translational transform, by the matrix form of the tensor (A1) and (A2)

$$I'_{xx} = I_{xx} + m \, (y^2 + z^2)$$
$$I'_{yy} = I_{yy} + m \, (x^2 + z^2)$$
$$I'_{zz} = I_{zz} + m \, (x^2 + y^2) \qquad (A4)$$
$$I'_{xy} = I_{xy} + m \, (x \, y)$$
$$I'_{xz} = I_{xz} + m \, (x \, z)$$
$$I'_{yz} = I_{yz} + m \, (y \, z)$$

where x, y, and z gives the translation of the coordinate frame and m is the mass of the object.

Appendix B

The rotational dynamics is given by

$$d\mathbf{L}/dt = \mathbf{N} \qquad (B1)$$
$$\mathbf{L} = \mathbf{I} \cdot \mathbf{W} \qquad (B2)$$

where $\mathbf{L}$ is the angular momentum of the body, $\mathbf{N}$ is the external torque being applied to the body, $\mathbf{I}$ is the moment of inertia tensor of the body, and $\mathbf{W}$ is the angular velocity of the body that we want to solve for. The major obstacle for a simple solution is that the rotational equivalent of mass, the moment of inertia tensor, is not constant with respect to an inertial reference frame but changes as the body rotates. This can be avoided by solving the rotational dynamics in a frame that is fixed in the body. Taking the time derivative of (B1) with reference to a coordinate frame fixed in the body

$$d\mathbf{L}/dt + \mathbf{W} \times \mathbf{L} = \mathbf{N} \qquad (B3)$$

Substituting (B2) into (B3)

$$\mathbf{I} \cdot d\mathbf{W}/dt + \mathbf{W} \times (\mathbf{I} \cdot \mathbf{W}) = \mathbf{N} \qquad (B4)$$

If we choose the principal axes as the body fixed axes and transform (B4) to the body fixed coordinate we get a set of simplified differential equations

$$I_x \, \dot{W}_x + (I_z - I_y) \, W_z \, W_y = N_x$$
$$I_y \, \dot{W}_y + (I_x - I_z) \, W_x \, W_z = N_y \qquad (B5)$$
$$I_z \, \dot{W}_z + (I_y - I_x) \, W_y \, W_x = N_z$$

where the products of inertia do not appear. These are known as the *Euler equations* [7]. The x, y, and z are the directions of the principal axes.

References

1. Armstrong, William W. and Green, Mark W.. "The Dynamics of Articulated Rigid Bodies for Purposes of Animation". *Proc. Graphics Interface 85* (1985), pp. 407-415.

2. Barzel, Ronen and Barr, Alan H.. "Modeling With Dynamic Constraints". *ACM SIGGRAPH '87 Course Notes* (1987).

3. Boyse, John W.. "Interference Detection Among Solids and Surfaces". *Communications of the ACM 22*, (January 1979), pp. 3-9.

4. Flash, Tamar and Hogan, Neville. "The Coordination of Arm Movements An Experimentally Confirmed Mathematical Model". *MIT A.I. Memo 786* (November 1984).

5. Girard, Michael and Maciejewski, A. A.. "Computational Modeling for the Computer Animation of Legged Figures". *Computer Graphics 19, 3* (July 1985), pp. 263-270.

6. Goldsmith, Werner. *Impact: The Theory and Physical Behavior of Colliding Solids*. Edward Arnold Pub. Ltd., London, 1960.

7. Goldstein, Herbert. *Classical Mechanics*. Addison-Wesley Publishing Company, Reading, MA, 1950.

8. Hahn, James. "Rigid Body Dynamics Simulations". *ACM SIGGRAPH '87 Film and Video Show* (1987).

9. Haumann, David. "Modeling the Physical Behavior of

Flexible Objects". *ACM SIGGRAPH' 87 Course Notes* (1987).

10. Hornbeck, Robert W.. *Numerical Methods*. Quantum Publishers, Inc., New York, NY, 1975.

11. Hughes, Peter C.. *Spacecraft Attitude Dynamics*. John Wiley & Sons, Inc., 1986.

12. Isaacs, Paul M. and Cohen, Michael F.. "Controlling Dynamic Simulation With Kinematic Constraints, Behavior Functions and Inverse Dynamics". *Computer Graphics 21, 4* (July 1987), pp. 215-224.

13. Kane, Thomas and Levinson, David. *Dynamics: Theory and Applications*. McGraw-Hill, New York, N.Y., 1985.

14. Press, William H.. *Numerical Recipes*. Cambridge University Press, 1986.

15. Routh, E. J.. *Dynamics of a System of Rigid Bodies*. Macmillan and Company, Ltd., London, 1905.

16. Symon, Keith R.. *Mechanics*. Addison-Wesley Publishing Company, Reading, MA, 1971.

17. Terzopoulos, Demetri, Platt, John, Barr, Alan, and Fleischer, Kurt. "Elastically Deformable Models". *Computer Graphics 21, 4* (July 1987), pp. 205-214.

18. Weil, J.. "The Synthesis of Cloth Objects". *Computer Graphics 20, 4* (August 1986), pp. 49-54.

19. Wilhelms, J. and Barsky, B.A.. "Using Dynamic Analysis for the Animation of Articulated Bodies Such as Humans and Robots". *Proc. Graphics Interface 85* (May 1985), pp. 97-104.

20. Witkin, Andrew, Fleischer, Kurt, and Barr, Alan. "Energy Constraints On Parameterized Models". *Computer Graphics 21, 4* (July 1987), pp. 225-229.

MOTION INTERPOLATION
by
OPTIMAL CONTROL

by

Lynne Shapiro Brotman
Arun N. Netravali

AT&T Bell Laboratories
Murray Hill, NJ 07974

ABSTRACT

Motion Interpolation, which arises in many situations such as *Keyframe Animation*, is the synthesis of a sequence of images portraying continuous motion by interpolating between a set of *keyframes*. If the keyframes are specified by parameters of moving objects at several instants of time, (e.g., position, orientation, velocity) then the goal is to find their values at the intermediate instants of time. Previous approaches to this problem have been to construct these intermediate, or *in-between*, frames by interpolating each of the motion parameters independently. This often produces unnatural motion since the physics of the problem is not considered and each parameter is obtained independently. Our approach models the motion of objects and their environment by differential equations obtained from classical mechanics. In order to satisfy the constraints imposed by the keyframes we apply external control. We show how smooth and natural looking interpolations can be obtained by minimizing a combination of the control energy and the roughness of the trajectory of the objects in 3D-space. A general formulation is presented which allows several trade-offs between various parameters that control motion. Although optimal parameter values resulting in the best subjectively looking motion are not yet known, our simulations have produced smooth and natural motion that is subjectively better than that produced by other interpolation methods, such as the cubic splines.

CR Categories and Subject Descriptions: I.3.6 *Computer Graphics*: Methodology and Techniques - Interaction Techniques, I.3.7 *Computer Graphics*: Three Dimensional Graphics and Realism - Animation, I.6.3 *Simulation and Modelling*: Applications

Additional Keywords: Animation, Dynamics, Interpolation and Control Theory.

©1988   ACM-0-89791-275-6/88/008/0309 $00.75

1. Introduction

Specification of motion in computer synthesis of image sequences has been done traditionally by an animator. Ideally, as in other human-machine interactions, the animator would like to minimize the amount and the complexity of information that he specifies and maximize the amount of information that the machine synthesizes. In *keyframe animation*, for example, a frame sequence portraying motion is created by interpolating between a set of keyframes specified by the animator. If the keyframes are specified by parameters of motion (e.g. position, orientation, velocity) then the goal is to find their values at intermediate instances of time.[1] Early keyframe systems used linear interpolation to produce these *in-betweens*. This often resulted in motion that appeared unnatural and jerky. More recently, work aimed at increasing realism has used splines for separately interpolating parameters of motion, resulting in increased smoothness of motion.[2-4] Also, use of quaternions has been suggested for handling rigid-body orientation in order to eliminate the artifacts which occur in systems that use ordinary splines.[5] While such geometric interpolation methods guarantee smoothness of motion and give sufficient control to the animator to tailor it, they do not necessarily produce motion that is *natural*.

Motion in our environment is due to forces and torques acting on bodies with physical properties such as mass, shape, moments of inertia, and is constrained by several factors such as obstacles, joints, etc. Clearly, to achieve authentic motion, laws of dynamics must be adhered to. Unfortunately, incorporation of dynamics requires formulation and numerical integration of a complex set of connected differential equations. Moreover, since motion is completely determined once the differential equations and their initial conditions are known, control that the animator needs to tailor motion is lost. Also, the complexity of these differential equations denies the animator a simple relationship between the parameters that control the dynamics and the resulting motion. Thus we have the familiar dilemma: on one hand, an animator wishes to tailor motion to portray drama, expression, etc., and can do so by specification of keyframes followed by interactive, geometric but not necessarily natural looking interpolation; on the other hand, to make the motion look natural, complexity of simulation of natural processes has to be dealt with along with a simple method of control. Ideally, if the animator specifies only the keyframes and computer minds the physics, we have the best of both worlds. This has been recognized recently by several people.[6-9]

Use of principles of dynamics to simulate motion of physical bodies including linked figures, although new in computer graphics,[6-8] has been practiced in other fields such as mechanics and robotics for a number of years. Unfortunately, such simulation does not allow the animator to shape the motion explicitly. One way to shape the trajectories is to add external forces and torques in the differential equations representing the dynamical model. However, the animator should not be burdened with the determination of the appropriate amount, place and duration of these external forces. This view is similar to the one put forth by Isaccs and Cohen[9] in the context of dynamic simulation of linked figures. They advocate use of *behavior functions* and *inverse dynamics* to compute the desired external forces. Given the keyframes and differential equations that model dynamics, the amount and the duration of these forces is not unique and since improper design of forces can lead to jerky and unnatural motion, (although obeying physics) we propose to find the *best* set of forces. We hypothesize that the smoothest and most natural motion is obtained when the applied external force has the least energy and is continuous. Thus, we construct interpolated motion as a solution of the differential equation obtained by modelling dynamics which is constrained to pass through keyframes by applying the least amount of external force. In addition to the usual keyframe specification, the animator is now required to specify the dynamics, but the computer does the rest.

2. The Approach

We present a new approach for solving the motion interpolation problems in the context of keyframe animation. We model motion of objects and their environment by differential equations obtained from classical mechanics and use external control to force the motion to satisfy constraints imposed by keyframes. Currently, objects are modelled as rigid bodies. The model can be extended to handle articulated and deformed bodies at a cost of increased complexity. In addition to characteristics of objects and the environment traditionally modelled in graphics, such as shape, shading and illumination, our model requires specification of mass and for problems involving rotation, inertial parameters. The model of the environment may require knowledge of factors such as gravity, friction, and wind pressure.

We start with a differential equation which models each object's motion. Since the solution of this differential equation, starting with some initial condition, will not, in general, pass through the keyframes, "external control" is necessary. In many cases, there is a natural place for application of control (or force) and it is included in the model. Otherwise, the place and form of the control (i.e., how it affects the differential equation) is chosen somewhat arbitrarily. The next step is to obtain a trajectory of the object such that it requires the least amount of control and simultaneously maximizes some measure of smoothness of the trajectory while passing through the keyframes. We choose "least amount of control" to mean the least amount of control energy which is defined by the integral of the square of the control value over time. This optimization is performed using algorithms of control theory.[10] Our hypothesis, which is supported by simulations, is that the most natural motion results when the least amount of smooth control is applied to an object. The principal drawback of our approach is a significant increase in the computational burden over that required for other interpolation methods such as cubic splines.

2.1 Mathematical Formulation

Let $\mathbf{r}(t) = \begin{bmatrix} x(t) \\ y(t) \\ z(t) \end{bmatrix}$, be a column vector at time t in 3D-space with respect to a coordinate system fixed in time. The equations of motion for a general rigid body can then be written as:

$$\sum \mathbf{F}_0 = m \frac{d^2\mathbf{r}(t)}{dt^2} \qquad (1)$$

$$\sum \mathbf{M}_0 = \frac{d\mathbf{H}(t)}{dt} \qquad (2)$$

where $\sum \mathbf{F}_0$ is the vector sum of all forces acting on the body (i.e., natural forces such as gravity and friction as well as externally applied control forces), m is the mass, and $\sum \mathbf{M}_0$ and $\mathbf{H}$ represent the moment of the forces and the angular momentum of the body about the center of mass, respectively. In many cases, $\frac{d\mathbf{H}(t)}{dt}$ can be written as $\mathbf{I} \frac{d^2\boldsymbol{\theta}(t)}{dt^2}$, where $\boldsymbol{\theta}(t) = \begin{bmatrix} \theta_x(t) \\ \theta_y(t) \\ \theta_z(t) \end{bmatrix}$ and $\theta_x(t), \theta_y(t), \theta_z(t)$ are the angles of rotation about the x,y,z axes, respectively. $\mathbf{I}$ is the moment of inertia about the same axes. In other cases, depending on the type of rotation, equivalent forms relating angular acceleration to the moment of external forces can be used from classical mechanics.[11] We state the problem as follows:

Given differential equations of motion (1) and (2) over a time interval $[0, t_N]$, and the key-frame constraints*

$$\mathbf{r}(t_i) = \mathbf{r}_i \qquad (3)$$

$$\boldsymbol{\theta}(t_i) = \boldsymbol{\theta}_i \qquad (4)$$

$$\frac{d\mathbf{r}(t_i)}{dt} = \mathbf{v}_i \qquad (5)$$

$$\frac{d\boldsymbol{\theta}(t_i)}{dt} = \boldsymbol{\omega}_i \qquad (6)$$

where t_i, $0 \leqslant i \leqslant N$, are instants of time $(0 = t_0 < t_1 < ... < t_N)$, and $\mathbf{v}_i$ and $\boldsymbol{\omega}_i$ are linear and angular velocities, respectively; *find* the trajectories $\mathbf{r}(t)$ and $\boldsymbol{\theta}(t)$ such that they satisfy equations (1-6), and are natural and smooth.

In general, some external forces and torques are necessary to satisfy the constraints of equations (3-6). In most cases, there are an infinite number of possible forces and torques that can force the trajectory to satisfy the above constraints. Our goal is to minimize the energy expended by these forces and torques since we believe that the most natural motion will occur when the least amount of force is applied. Smoothness of such a trajectory is dependent upon the characteristics of differential equations (1) and (2). In most problems, these differential equations are at least second order and if the forces are not discontinuous, the solution is at least twice differentiable. This suggests that the external forces should be continuous as well.

To formalize our approach, we use *state-space* notation which is convenient for the application of control theory. This is done by converting differential equations (1) and (2) into a first order vector differential equation. As an example, if $\sum \mathbf{F}_0$ and $\sum \mathbf{M}_0$ in equations (1) and (2) do not contain any $\mathbf{r}$- or $\boldsymbol{\theta}$-dependent quantities, then this conversion is achieved by defining the state, $\mathbf{s}(t) = \begin{bmatrix} \mathbf{r}(t) \\ \boldsymbol{\theta}(t) \\ \dfrac{d\mathbf{r}}{dt} \\ \dfrac{d\boldsymbol{\theta}}{dt} \end{bmatrix}$

Equations (1) and (2) can now be expressed as

$$\frac{d\mathbf{s}(t)}{dt} = \begin{bmatrix} \mathbf{0} & \mathbf{0} & \mathbf{1} & \mathbf{0} \\ \mathbf{0} & \mathbf{0} & \mathbf{0} & \mathbf{1} \\ \mathbf{0} & \mathbf{0} & \mathbf{0} & \mathbf{0} \\ \mathbf{0} & \mathbf{0} & \mathbf{0} & \mathbf{0} \end{bmatrix} \mathbf{s}(t) + \begin{bmatrix} \mathbf{0} \\ \mathbf{0} \\ \sum \mathbf{F}_0/m \\ \mathbf{I}^{-1}\sum \mathbf{M}_0 \end{bmatrix}$$

where $\mathbf{0}$ and $\mathbf{1}$ are 3×3 zero and identity matrices, respectively. The quantity $\mathbf{s}(t)$ is called the *state* since it encapsulates all the information necessary for further evolution of the trajectory based on the differential equation. $\sum \mathbf{F}_0$ and $\sum \mathbf{M}_0$ contain control forces and torques, and can be written as $\mathbf{G}(t)\,\mathbf{u}(t)$, where $\mathbf{u}(t)$ is the control vector and $\mathbf{G}(t)$ determines how control is related to the differential equation. Thus the above differential equation can be written in general[†] as:

$$\frac{d\mathbf{s}(t)}{dt} = \mathbf{F}(t)\,\mathbf{s}(t) + \mathbf{G}(t)\,\mathbf{u}(t) \qquad (7)$$

Since constraints of equations (3-6) are linear in $\mathbf{r}(t)$, $\boldsymbol{\theta}(t)$, $\dfrac{d\mathbf{r}}{dt}$ and $\dfrac{d\boldsymbol{\theta}}{dt}$, they can be expressed by proper choice of matrices $\mathbf{M}_i$ and vectors $\boldsymbol{\Psi}_i$ where,

$$\boldsymbol{\Psi}_i = \mathbf{M}_i\mathbf{s}(t_i), \quad i = 1, \ldots, N \qquad (8)$$

---

* $\mathbf{r}(t), \boldsymbol{\theta}(t), \dfrac{d\mathbf{r}(t)}{dt}, \dfrac{d\boldsymbol{\theta}(t)}{dt}$ may be specified at different instants of time and they may be specified partially.

† If $\sum \mathbf{F}_0$ and $\sum \mathbf{M}_0$ contain $\mathbf{r}(t)$ and $\boldsymbol{\theta}(t)$ dependent terms, then $\mathbf{F}(t)$ would have a different form. If this dependency is nonlinear, then equation (7) will be nonlinear. Example of section 2.2 illustrates this conversion to the first order vector differential equation in detail.

We have thus converted a higher order differential equation into a first order vector differential equation and the set of constraints defined by the keyframes into a set of linear constraints on the state vector. We wish to determine the control that minimizes a weighted sum of control energy and a measure of the smoothness of the trajectory $s(t)$. That is, we want to minimize:

$$J = \int_0^{t_N} [(s^T(t) A\, s(t)) + (u^T(t) B\, u(t))]dt \qquad (9)$$

where A and B are appropriately chosen positive semidefinite matrices and the superscript T denotes the transpose. The above expression for J has sufficient generality to incorporate a variety of situations. For example, if we define the "smoothest" to mean the minimum of

$$\int_0^{t_N}[(\frac{dx}{dt})^2 + (\frac{dy}{dt})^2 + (\frac{dz}{dt})^2 + (\frac{d\theta_x}{dt})^2 + (\frac{d\theta_y}{dt})^2 + (\frac{d\theta_z}{dt})^2]dt, \text{ then}$$

$A = \begin{bmatrix} 0 & 0 & 0 & 0 \\ 0 & 0 & 0 & 0 \\ 0 & 0 & 1 & 0 \\ 0 & 0 & 0 & 1 \end{bmatrix}$. On the other hand, to minimize control energy, B

would be set to identity matrix, and A to zero. As shown in the example below, by properly choosing A and B, different combinations of control energy and roughness of the trajectory can be minimized. Thus, the problem is: *Given the differential equation in state variable form (7) and constraints as in equation (8), obtain a control function* $u(t)$ *such that J of equation (9) is minimized.*

2.2 An Example

Consider a truck of mass m moving along the x-axis. The frictional force on the truck is inversely proportional to the speed of the truck (proportionality constant: μ) and control is the force along x-axis applied by either the truck's gas peddle or the brakes. The differential equation is:

$$m\frac{d^2x(t)}{dt^2} = -\mu\frac{dx(t)}{dt} - u(t), \quad 0 < t < t_N \qquad (10)$$

Suppose we want to specify the truck's position and velocity at three instants of time as:

$$x(0) = 0$$

$$x(t_1) = x_1; \quad \frac{dx(t_1)}{dt} = v_1$$

$$x(t_N) = x_N \qquad (11)$$

In accord with the previous discussion, we seek a control function $u(t)$ that minimizes

$$J = \int_0^{t_N}[\left(\frac{dx(t)}{dt}\right)^2 + u^2(t)]dt \qquad (12)$$

Minimization of $\int_0^{t_N}\left(\frac{dx(t)}{dt}\right)^2 dt$ results in the smoothest trajectory $x(t)$, since larger variations in $x(t)$ will result in larger values of $\left(\frac{dx(t)}{dt}\right)^2$. Similarly, minimization of $\int_0^{t_N} u^2(t)dt$ minimizes the magnitude of the total control, which tends to make the trajectory dominated by the solution of the unforced differential equation (10) (i.e., with $u(t) = 0$). We employ a weighted combination of these two. Now, to convert this problem to state-space notation, we define the state $s(t)$ as

$$s_1(t) = x(t)$$

$$s_2(t) = \frac{dx(t)}{dt} \qquad (13)$$

then

$$\frac{ds(t)}{dt} = \begin{bmatrix} 0 & 1 \\ 0 & -\frac{\mu}{m} \end{bmatrix} s(t) + \begin{bmatrix} 0 \\ -\frac{1}{m} \end{bmatrix} u(t) \qquad (14)$$

Thus, in this case,

$$F = \begin{bmatrix} 0 & 1 \\ 0 & -\frac{\mu}{m} \end{bmatrix}, \text{ and } G = \begin{bmatrix} 0 \\ -\frac{1}{m} \end{bmatrix}.$$

The constraints given by (11) are written as:

$$[1\ 0]s(0) = x(0)$$

$$[1\ 0]s(t_1) = x(t_1), \quad [0\ 1]s(t_1) = v_1$$

$$[1\ 0]s(t_N) = x(t_N) \qquad (15)$$

which define M and Ψ. The *performance index J* of Equation (12) can be written in the form of Equation (9) as follows:

$$J = \int_0^{t_N}[(s_2(t))^2 + u^2(t)]dt$$

$$= \int_0^{t_N}[(s^T(t)\begin{bmatrix} 0 & 0 \\ 0 & 1 \end{bmatrix} s(t)) + (u^T(t)u(t))]dt \qquad (16)$$

Thus, in this case, $A = \begin{bmatrix} 0 & 0 \\ 0 & 1 \end{bmatrix}$ and $B = [1]$.

Within this formulation several other meaningful quantities can be minimized by the proper choice of A and B. For example, if we want only a minimum energy control we set $A = \begin{bmatrix} 0 & 0 \\ 0 & 0 \end{bmatrix}$ and $B = [1]$. If we want the trajectory to be very smooth, then we can increase the value of A, e.g., $A = \begin{bmatrix} 0 & 0 \\ 0 & 1000 \end{bmatrix}$ while keeping B the same.

2.3 Solving the Control Problem

While control theory can be applied to nonlinear differential equations, we have chosen for simplicity to solve only the linear problem.[*] For this case, as before, the differential equation is written in state-space notation as:

$$\frac{ds(t)}{dt} = F(t)s(t) + G(t)u(t), \quad 0 \leq t \leq t_N \qquad (17)$$

Solving a control problem with several *interior point constraints* such as those of equation (8) is computationally complex since it leads to a *multi-point boundary value problem*[10]. We can reduce the complexity of the problem by viewing it as a series of *terminal constraint* problems. That is, we solve the problem one interval at a time starting with interval $[0, t_1]$ and ending with interval $[t_{N-1}, t_N]$. For the first interval, we have the following problem:

Given

$$\frac{ds(t)}{dt} = F(t)s(t) + G(t)u(t), \quad 0 \leq t \leq t_1$$

and the key conditions

$$s(0) = s_0$$

$$M_1 s(t_1) = \Psi_1, \qquad (18)$$

find the control $u(t)$, $0 \leq t \leq t_1$ such that it minimizes

$$J_1 = \int_0^{t_1}[(s^T(t)A\,s(t)) + (u^T(t)B\,u(t))]dt \qquad (19)$$

---

[*] The nonlinear problem may be solved by linear expansion of the differential equation about an initial guess of the trajectory and then solving the linear problem. The resulting solution is then taken as the new guess of the trajectory and this iterative process is continued.

The solution to this problem is not optimal in the sense of minimizing J, but since $J = \sum_{i=0}^{N-1} J_i$ the solution is not far from being optimal. Using control theory,[10] it can be written as:

$$\mathbf{u}(t) = -\mathbf{B}^{-1}\mathbf{G}^T[\mathbf{K}(t) - \mathbf{R}(t)\mathbf{Q}^{-1}(t)\mathbf{R}^T(t)]\mathbf{s}(t) - \mathbf{B}^{-1}\mathbf{G}^T\mathbf{R}(t)\mathbf{Q}^{-1}(t)\boldsymbol{\Psi}_1 \quad (20)$$

where

$$\frac{d\mathbf{K}(t)}{dt} = -\mathbf{K}(t)\mathbf{F} - \mathbf{F}^T\mathbf{K}(t) - \mathbf{A} + \mathbf{K}(t)\mathbf{GB}^{-1}\mathbf{G}^T\mathbf{K}(t), \quad \mathbf{K}(t_1) = \mathbf{0} \quad (21)$$

$$\frac{d\mathbf{R}(t)}{dt} = -(\mathbf{F}^T - \mathbf{K}(t)\mathbf{GB}^{-1}\mathbf{G}^T)\mathbf{R}(t), \quad \mathbf{R}(t_1) = \mathbf{M}_1^T \quad (22)$$

$$\frac{d\mathbf{Q}(t)}{dt} = \mathbf{R}(t)^T\mathbf{GB}^{-1}\mathbf{G}^T\mathbf{R}(t), \quad \mathbf{Q}(t_1) = \mathbf{0} \quad (23)$$

Equations (21), (22) and (23) are solved backwards in time (i.e., from t_1 to zero) and their solutions are used to compute the control function function $\mathbf{u}(t)$. Equation (20) indicates that control is obtained as a combination of a time varying matrix multiplying the state $\mathbf{s}(t)$ and another time varying matrix multiplying the keyframe condition at time t, i.e., $\boldsymbol{\Psi}_1$. These matrices are defined in terms of three other time varying matrices $\mathbf{K}(t)$, $\mathbf{R}(t)$ and $\mathbf{Q}(t)$; and their evolution in time is governed by the differential equations (21-23). Thus the principal cost of our approach is the numerical integration of equations (21-23). Although due to the generality of presentation, these equations may appear formidable, in practice matrices $\mathbf{F}, \mathbf{G}, \mathbf{A}$, and $\mathbf{B}$ are sparse and in such cases, a large number of components of matrices $\mathbf{K}(t)$, $\mathbf{R}(t)$ and $\mathbf{Q}(t)$ are identically zero. In the control theory literature, equation (21) is commonly referred to as the *Ricatti* equation and since it is nonlinear, care is required in its numerical integration. Equations (22) and (23) are linear and can be integrated easily. It is worth noting that if we want to minimize only the control energy (i.e., $\mathbf{A} = 0$ and $\mathbf{B} = 1$), then $\mathbf{K}(t)$ is identically zero and considerable simplification results.

After solving first the control $\mathbf{u}(t)$ and then the trajectory $\mathbf{s}(t)$ for subinterval $[0, t_1]$, we solve the identical problem for subinterval $[t_1, t_2]$. The state at t_1, $\mathbf{s}(t_1)$, which is known by solving the problem for the first subinterval, now becomes the initial keypoint for the next subinterval, $[t_1, t_2]$. Thus,

$$\mathbf{s}(t_1) = \mathbf{s}_1$$

$$\mathbf{M}_2\mathbf{s}(t_2) = \boldsymbol{\Psi}_2 \quad (24)$$

We have imposed continuity of state at t_1 and because the state includes the trajectory and its first derivative (for a second order differential equation), we have constrained the trajectory and its first derivative to be continuous across the subintervals $[0, t_1]$ and $[t_1, t_2]$. This process is continued to the last subinterval, $[t_{N-1}, t_N]$.

3. The Truck Example

The truck problem presented in section 2.2 was expanded to include additional keypoints and was then solved using our approach with $\mathbf{A} = \begin{bmatrix} 0 & 0 \\ 0 & 1 \end{bmatrix}$ and $\mathbf{B} = [1]$. The graph in Figure 1 shows the path of the truck computed using the optimal control approach. This path is smoother than that shown in Figure 2 which was computed using an interpolating cubic spline. To bring out the differences in smoothness, both these figures also show the rate of change of $x(t)$, or the velocity. As expected, the spline interpolation shows velocity as a number of quadratic functions pieced together. The amount of variation in the velocity is large compared to that produced by the optimal control method. Although it is difficult to illustrate, difference in the naturalness of motion is quite evident on the screen. This may be due to our approach requiring nearly thirty times less control energy than the spline method. To force the solution of the differential equation to be an interpolating cubic spline, a large control or force is necessary, making the trajectory appear unnatural. Plots of control used by both methods are shown in Figures 3 and 4. These plots also illustrate discontinuity of control at the boundaries of subintervals. Discontinuity is particularly severe for the spline method, which further reduces its naturalness.

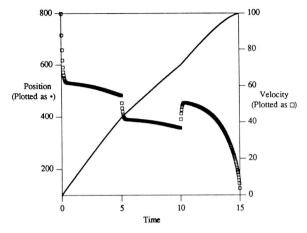

Figure 1: Position and Velocity of Truck Computed Using Optimal Control

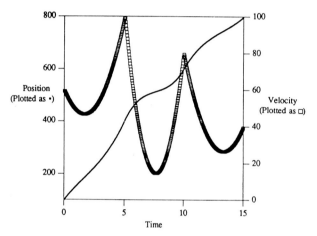

Figure 2: Position and Velocity of Truck Computed Using Cubic Spline

Solution of the control problem as posed in equations (17-19) has some undesirable properties. The continuity constraints we have imposed ensure that the solution is smooth across subintervals (i.e., the position and velocity are continuous) and that the trajectory is smooth within a subinterval. However, most of the control is applied at the beginning of each subinterval.* (See Figure 3). Although the resulting motion is relatively smooth, it can be improved, particularly at the boundary of subintervals. One method of doing this, while still solving one subinterval at a time, is to impose the additional constraint that control be a continuous function of time throughout $[t_0, t_N]$ and then minimize the energy in control as well as its first derivative. This would result in a smoother control function which in turn would increase the smoothness of the trajectory at the boundary of two subintervals. This revised approach is described below.

4. A Continuous Control Approach

First we augment the state by including the control. We define the derivative of control as:

$$\mathbf{w}(t) = \frac{d\mathbf{u}(t)}{dt} \quad (25)$$

---

* Intuitively speaking, this may be due to the fact that early application of control within a subinterval allows the control to have the largest impact in shaping the trajectory. Later application of control may require larger control and therefore larger control energy to satisfy the terminal keyframe constraints.

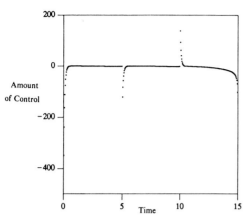

Figure 3: Amount of Control Applied to Truck Using Optimal Control

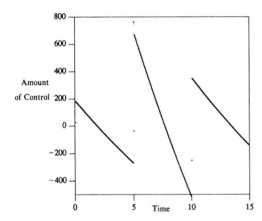

Figure 4: Amount of Control Applied to Truck Using Cubic Spline

and construct a new state equation:

$$\frac{d\overline{s}(t)}{dt} = \begin{bmatrix} F(t) & G(t) \\ 0 & 0 \end{bmatrix} \overline{s}(t) + \begin{bmatrix} 0 \\ w(t) \end{bmatrix} \quad (26)$$

where

$$\overline{s}(t) = \begin{bmatrix} s(t) \\ u(t) \end{bmatrix} \quad (27)$$

As before, we solve the problem one subinterval at a time, starting with the subinterval $[0, t_1]$. The initial value of the control, $u(0)$, is simply set to zero.* For this subinterval, the key conditions become: *

$$\overline{s}(0) = \begin{bmatrix} s(0) \\ u(0) \end{bmatrix} \triangleq \begin{bmatrix} s(0) \\ 0 \end{bmatrix} \quad (28)$$

$M_1 s(t_1) = \Psi_1$ becomes

$$[M_1 0] \begin{bmatrix} s(t_1) \\ u(t_1) \end{bmatrix} = \overline{\Psi}_1 \triangleq \overline{M}_1 \overline{s}(t_1) \quad (29)$$

---

* Any other value can be chosen, but we choose zero in the spirit of keeping control as small as possible. Optimum value can also be found, but this leads to a more complex *two-point boundary value* problem.[10]

The new control, $w(t)$, is derived to minimize:

$$\overline{J}_1 = \int_0^{t_1} [(\overline{s}^T(t)\overline{A}\,\overline{s}(t)) + (w^T(t)\overline{B}w(t))]dt \quad (30)$$

where matrices $\overline{A}$ and $\overline{B}$ are chosen as before. Now the problem is in the same symbolic form as the previous problem with barred quantities replacing unbarred quantities. By ensuring that the new state, $\overline{s}(t)$, remains continuous across the subintervals $[0, t_1]$ and $[t_1, t_2]$, we ensure that the state and the control remain continuous. Because components of $s(t)$ are trajectory, its first derivative, and control, we have ensured their continuity throughout the interval $[t_0, t_N]$. Additionally, our new performance index minimizes the energy in $w(t)$, and therefore control fluctuations are minimized. The overall effect of this is that the resulting motion is smooth and natural. The following example illustrates this revised approach.

4.1 Revised Approach for the Truck Example

To solve the truck example described in section 2.2 by this revised approach, we first augment the state equation (14) to include the derivative of control:

$$\frac{d}{dt}\begin{bmatrix} s_1(t) \\ s_2(t) \\ u(t) \end{bmatrix} = \begin{bmatrix} 0 & 1 & 0 \\ 0 & -\dfrac{\mu}{m} & \dfrac{-1}{m} \\ 0 & 0 & 0 \end{bmatrix} \begin{bmatrix} s_1(t) \\ s_2(t) \\ u(t) \end{bmatrix} + \begin{bmatrix} 0 \\ 0 \\ 1 \end{bmatrix} w(t) \quad (31)$$

At $t = 0$, key conditions are:

$$\begin{bmatrix} s_1(0) \\ s_2(0) \\ u(0) \end{bmatrix} = \begin{bmatrix} s_1(0) \\ s_2(0) \\ 0 \end{bmatrix} \quad (32)$$

At $t = t_1$, only $s_1(t_1)$ is known, therefore:

$$\overline{M}_1 \begin{bmatrix} s_1(t_1) \\ s_2(t_1) \\ u(t_1) \end{bmatrix} = [1 \ 0 \ 0] \begin{bmatrix} s_1(t_1) \\ s_2(t_1) \\ u(t_1) \end{bmatrix} = s_1(t_1) \quad (33)$$

The matrices

$$\overline{A} = \begin{bmatrix} a & 0 & 0 \\ 0 & b & 0 \\ 0 & 0 & c \end{bmatrix} \quad \text{and} \quad \overline{B} = [e] \quad (34)$$

will minimize

$$\overline{J}_1 = \int_0^{t_1} [ax^2(t) + b\left(\frac{dx(t)}{dt}\right)^2 + cu^2(t) + e\left(\frac{du(t)}{dt}\right)^2]dt \quad (35)$$

The new results are shown in Figures 5 and 6. It can be seen that the new path is smoother than that generated by the original approach, and there are no discontinuities in $u(t)$. However, in order to achieve this increased smoothness, the amount of control has increased. For this example, the control energy used by the revised approach is fifteen times that of the original approach, but it is still only half that required by the interpolating cubic spline.

5. The Aircraft Example

To demonstrate the ability of this algorithm to handle more complex problems, we chose to simulate the problem of perturbation of an aircraft from a straight-line flight.[12] Consider an aircraft of mass m moving along its equilibrium flight direction, X, which is in the aircraft's plane of symmetry, Y is out the right wing and Z is down. The velocity of the perturbed motion is not allowed to deviate far from the x-direction so we can describe its orientation by the *sideslip* angle β and the *angle of attack* change $\Delta\alpha$ as shown in Figure 7.

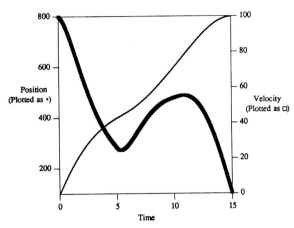

Figure 5: Position and Velocity of Truck Computed Using Revised Optimal Control

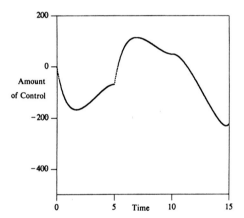

Figure 6: Amount of Control Applied to Truck Using Revised Optimal Control

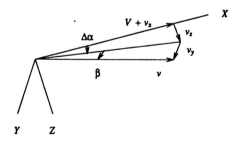

Figure 7: Coordinate System for aircraft example.

With V the equilibrium velocity, the components of instantaneous velocity are given by:

$$v = V + v_x, \quad v_y = V\beta, \quad v_z = V \Delta \alpha \qquad (36)$$

The force and moment equations are:

$$F_x = m\frac{dv_x}{dt}, \qquad M_x = I_x\frac{d\omega_x}{dt} - J_{zx}\frac{d\omega_z}{dt}$$

$$F_y = mV\left(\frac{d\beta}{dt} + \omega_z\right), \qquad M_y = I_y\frac{d\omega_y}{dt}$$

$$F_z = mV\left(\frac{d(\Delta\alpha)}{dt} - \omega_y\right), \qquad M_z = I_z\frac{d\omega_z}{dt} - J_{zx}\frac{d\omega_x}{dt} \qquad (37)$$

where, the components of $\boldsymbol{\omega}$ are the time derivatives of the *Euler angles*.

The matrices for the state equation of this problem using the notation in equation (26) are:

$$F(t) = \begin{bmatrix} 0&0&0&0&0&0&1&0&0&0&0&0 \\ 0&0&0&0&0&0&0&1&0&0&0&0 \\ 0&0&0&0&0&0&0&0&1&0&0&0 \\ 0&0&0&0&0&0&0&0&0&1&0&0 \\ 0&0&0&0&0&0&0&0&0&0&1&0 \\ 0&0&0&0&0&0&0&0&0&0&0&1 \\ 0&0&0&0&0&0&0&0&0&0&0&0 \\ 0&0&0&0&0&0&0&0&0&0&0&-V \\ 0&0&0&0&0&0&0&0&0&0&V&0 \\ 0&0&0&0&0&0&0&0&0&0&0&0 \\ 0&0&0&0&0&0&0&0&0&0&0&0 \\ 0&0&0&0&0&0&0&0&0&0&0&0 \end{bmatrix}, \quad G(t) = \begin{bmatrix} 0&0&0&0&0&0 \\ 0&0&0&0&0&0 \\ 0&0&0&0&0&0 \\ 0&0&0&0&0&0 \\ 0&0&0&0&0&0 \\ 0&0&0&0&0&0 \\ a&0&0&0&0&0 \\ 0&b&0&0&0&0 \\ 0&0&c&0&0&0 \\ 0&0&0&d&0&e \\ 0&0&0&0&f&0 \\ 0&0&0&g&0&h \end{bmatrix}$$

where

$$a = b = c = \frac{1}{m}, \quad d = \frac{I_z}{I_xI_z - (J_{zx})^2}$$

$$e = h = \frac{J_{zx}}{I_xI_z - (J_{zx})^2}, \quad f = \frac{1}{I_y}, \quad g = \frac{I_x}{I_zI_x - (J_{zx})^2}$$

The control used in the spline method is several times higher than that used by our method. Figures (8-9) show, as examples, the control applied in both approaches for translational motion. This example also illustrates one of the major advantages of this approach — the ability to handle dependencies between the parameters of motion. The dynamic equations given in (37) show that linear and angular motion are coupled. For example, the translational motion along the y-axis is affected by the rotational motion about the z-axis. Since our algorithm uses the dynamics, it produces interpolations which incorporate these dependencies. The resulting animation looks more natural than that generated by interpolating cubic spline.

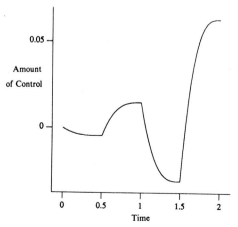

Figure 8: Control Applied to Translational Motion Along X-axis (Revised Optimal Control)

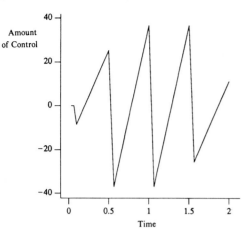

Figure 9: Control Applied to Translational Motion Along X-axis (Spline)

6. Summary

The algorithm presented in this paper provides a systematic method for obtaining smooth natural looking motion from keyframes. It also provides a large amount of flexibility in specifying the keypoints, since any portion of the state can be specified at any time. Thus any combination of position, orientation, translational and angular velocities can be specified at any key point. We have demonstrated that control theory formulation is appropriate and results in desirable characteristics in animation. Although within this formulation various measures of smoothness of the trajectory and control energy are possible, we have found that the appropriate measure is a weighted combination of integrals of the square of the first derivatives of trajectory and control. Weights determine the relative importance given to the trajectory derivative and the control energy and can be used as an additional tool by the animator for the particular application at hand. We have also shown that for additional visual smoothness, control should be a continuous function of time. Since most differential equations resulting from modelling dynamics are at least second order, our animation results in trajectories that are at least twice continuously differentiable. Compared to the traditional approach to animation, our approach requires more computations and additional information such as: models of the dynamic behavior of the objects in the environment and proper choice of the performance index. Much of the computational burden comes from the need to solve several differential equations. Some of these differential equations arise from the dynamic modelling and are therefore common to any other approach that models dynamic behavior. Additional equations due to control-theory formulation depend upon the precise choice of the smoothness criteria used. Although our animation looks natural and smooth, we have not yet performed any subjective tests to correlate quality of motion (e.g., natural, smooth and visually pleasing) with the choice of the performance index or whether computationally cheaper approximations will suffice. Our test models have been restricted to that of simple rigid bodies with three or six degrees of freedom. We also restricted ourselves to linear differential equations and linear constraints. However, the method can be extended to non-rigid bodies and nonlinear situations.

7. Acknowledgements

We thank Dave Hagelbarger, Roger Faulkner, Debasis Mitra and Jerry Weil for help in various phases of this project. In addition, Don Mitchell, Bruce Naylor and David Thomas helped sharpen many of our *wet* ideas.

REFERENCES

1. Magnenat-Thalmann, N. and Thalmann, D., *"Computer Animation: Theory and Practice"*, Springer-Verlag, 1985.

2. Stern, Garland, "Bbob - a System for 3-D Key-Frame Figures Animation", SIGGRAPH'83, Tutorial Notes on Introduction to Computer Animation, pp. 240-243.

3. Sturman, David, "Interactive Keyframe Animation of 3-D Articulated Models", Graphics Interface, '84, pp. 35-40.

4. Kochanek, Doris H. U. and Bartels, Richard H., "Interpolating Splines for Keyframe Animation", Graphics Interface '84, pp. 41-42.

5. Shoemake, Ken., "Animating Rotation with Quaternion Curves", SIGGRAPH'85, Computer Graphics 19 (3), pp. 245-254.

6. Armstrong, W. W. and Green, Mark, "The Dynamics of Articulated Rigid Bodies for the Purposes of Animation", Graphics Interface, '85, Montreal, pp. 407-416.

7. Wilhelms, Jane and Barsky, Brian A., "Using Dynamics for the Animation of Articulated Bodies Such As Humans and Robots", Graphics Interface '85, Montreal, pp. 407-416.

8. Raibert, Marc H., et. al., "Experiments in Balance with a 3-D One-Legged Hopping Machine", The International Journal of Robotics Research, Vol. 3, No. 2, 1984, pp. 75-92.

9. Isaacs Paul M. and Cohen, Michael F., "Controlling Dynamics Simulation with Kinematic Constraints, Behavior Functions and Inverse Dynamics", SIGGRAPH'87, Computer Graphics 21 (4), pp. 215-224.

10. Bryson, A. E. and Ho, Y., "Applied Optimal Control: Optimization, Estimation, and Control", Hemisphere Publishing Corp., 1975.

11. Goldstein, H., "Classical Mechanics", Addison-Wesley, Inc. 1951.

12. Halfman, R. L., "Dynamics", Addison-Wesley, Inc. 1962.

Getting Graphics in Gear:
Graphics and Dynamics in Driving Simulation

Rod Deyo

John A. Briggs

Pete Doenges

Evans & Sutherland
Salt Lake City, UT 84108

Abstract

Man-in-the-loop simulation uses a person in the control loop to provide feedback to the system operations. Proper operator cueing must be provided to ensure a realistic response. Real-time computer graphics and dynamics both play dominant roles in providing these necessary cues. Dynamics simulation of modern vehicles requires a multi-body non-linear approach for acceptable fidelity of motion. A vehicle can be modeled as a set of linked rigid bodies, whose connections are described by a graph. Real-time constraints on the computation of non-linear dynamics equations require the development of naturally parallel recursive algorithms, whose organization closely follows the system graph. Significant speed-up can be accomplished using these parallel algorithms.

CR Categories and Subject Descriptors: J.6 [**Computer-Aided Engineering**]: Computer-aided design; G.1.0 [**Numerical Analysis**]: General - Parallel algorithms; J.7 [**Computers in Other Systems**]: Real time; I.6.3 [**Simulation and Modeling**]: Applications; I.3.7 [**Computer Graphics**]: Three-dimensional Objects and Realism - Animation; Color, shading, shadowing, and texture.

General Terms: Algorithms, Performance, Human Factors

Additional Key Words and Phrases: Vehicle simulation, Real-time dynamics, Parallel algorithms, Real-time graphics, Engineering simulation, Visual systems

Introduction

In the last fifteen or so years, man-in-the-loop simulation using computer-generated, real-time graphics has assumed a major role not only in pilot training, but also in engineering applications for land, sea, air, and space vehicles. Man-in-the-loop simulation uses a person in the control loop of a simulation to provide feedback to the system operations. The operator experiences a synthetic environment, manipulates his controls in response to the situation, and experiences the results of his actions. In a real-time simulator, the dynamics model is continually evaluated to give feedback to the operator. On the basis of this data, the simulator provides realistic environmental cues to allow him to control the simulated vehicle in the same way that he would in the real world.

The goal of human interaction with a design is to tune raw performance, stability, ride quality, and safety margins, to suit human tolerances in control, task loading, and comfort. Through the use of simulation, training or design testing can often be achieved at lower cost, experiments can be conducted under controlled, repeatable circumstances, and — important for engineering — vehicle designs can be evaluated while minimizing the number of prototypes.

An important engineering use of simulation with a person in the loop is to determine vehicle response and to study the man-machine interface before the start of a vehicle test program. For example, a new aircraft can be modeled and test flown even before it leaves the drawing board. The pilots can give valuable feedback to the designers about the plane's characteristics at an early enough stage to permit changes in the airframe. Integration of the avionics systems can be achieved at an earlier time. Workload measurements can be made, and different alternatives can be tested. Computer graphics represents a large portion of the cost of man-in-the-loop simulation. Hence, as the capabilities of computer image generation have improved and the relative cost of simulation has dropped, there are better economic justifications for its use. In some applications, such as the space shuttle simulator, there has never been a good alternative to simulator training. In other areas, however, such as vehicle engineering, cost of man-in-the-loop simulation testing has always been an important consideration, and, as a result, has only recently been low enough to justify simulation on a large scale.

Computer graphics is the critical element in creating a realistic operator environment in a simulator, but the graphics must work in concert with the rest of the system to be believable. In particular, the vehicle motion and the scenes generated must seem realistic in order not to seem like an arcade game. To show how real-time computer graphics and dynamics must work together in vehicle simulation, we have selected a specific application to discuss — driving simulation. We will give a brief history of the use of synthetic imagery in simulation, identify the components of a modern simulator with emphasis on the role of the visual system, present a new approach to computing vehicle dynamics that promises significantly improved vehicle models for realistic motion, and conclude with a view of the future.

Historical Perspective

Department of Defense initiatives through the military and its contractors have done much to advance the state-of-the-art in simulation and computer graphics. For example, seminal work in computer graphics conducted at the University of Utah under the leadership of Dr. David Evans two decades ago was largely sponsored by the Department of Defense's Advanced Research Projects Agency.

The U. S. Air Force supported in part the first use of CRTs in driving simulation at MIT in 1962 [24]. This work by T.B. Sheridan, H.M. Paynter, and S.A. Coons was the earliest use of an artificial display of a vehicle path in dynamic perspective. A refined implementation was developed by W.W. Wierwille, G. A. Gagne, and J. Knight at Cornell Aeronautical Laboratory in 1966 [26].

Use of these same techniques occurred at General Motors in the late 1960's. In the early 1970's, both Volkswagen [23] and the Swedish Road and Traffic Institute (VTI) [21] built driving simulators with visual and motion subsystems. A number of simulators were built over the next decade. For example, simulators at the Virginia Polytechnic Institute and State University [4] and Deere and Company [9] were developed primarily to support human factors research. Another system, complete with motion platform, was constructed at Universitaet der Bundeswehr Muenchen for research into guiding land vehicles with computer vision — a sort of robot-in-the-loop simulation [7]. The graphics associated with these systems were limited. Line segments representing the road were displayed on a single CRT or projected on a flat screen in front of the driver.

In 1984, over twenty years after the MIT project, Daimler-Benz built, in Berlin, the first driving simulator expressly as an aid to designing vehicles [10] [13]. This system marked the first use of a 180-degree-wide image on a dome in a driving simulator. For the first time a driver was able to use his peripheral vision in a natural way. The Daimler-Benz simulator was built to allow test drivers to make subjective judgments about the handling qualities of new automobile designs.

Today's Advanced Simulator

Our advanced man-in-the-loop simulator (Figure 1) is made up of a few, expensive subsystems that combine to create a complete synthetic driving environment for the operator:

- The host computer (Figure 1g) controls all of the real-time operations of the system, including computation of the vehicle and motion platform dynamics. All calculations for the entire system are performed within a 10 ms time frame. An integrated data base contains visual models, geometric data on the simulated environment, data relating to the sounds encountered, and mechanical characteristics of the vehicle.

- The visual system calculates the correct image (Figure 1b) based on position information from the host computer. It removes hidden areas, computes the sun angle, smooth shades, textures, and anti-aliases the result. There is a high degree of parallelism in the foregoing operations, allowing about ten GIPS (Giga Instructions Per Second) operation in a large system.

- Multiple CRT projectors (Figure 1a) display an image on the dome. Special screen material is used for maximum brightness and contrast.

- The motion platform (Figure 1-2,3,d) is a configuration of hydraulic actuators that can move the operator's cab in any direction or angle by combining motions about the x, y, z, yaw, pitch, and roll axes. The control signals to the motion platform are filtered ("washed out") to transform the virtual real-world motion computed by the dynamics software into movements achievable by the system.

- The sound subsystem (Figure 1e) uses multiple speakers to generate appropriate sounds to simulate the engine, gear whine, wind noise, passing traffic, etc.

- Instrumentation (Figure 1h) provides data to the host computer to monitor the the entire system and ensure the driver's safety.

- Control force loaders (Figure 1c) are used to provide appropriate forces back to the operator through the steering wheel, brake pedal, and transmission lever to replicate the feedback forces found in a real car.

- The operations console (Figure 1f) allows a single person to oversee all of the simulation activities, allowing flexible control over vehicle tests.

Relating Graphics and Dynamics Under Real-Time Constraints

Driving simulation for automotive engineering must provide enough accuracy in simulating vehicle motion and in

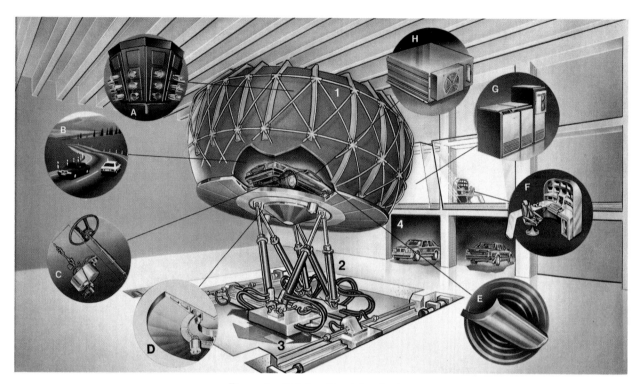

Figure 1 - Driving Simulator System

subsystems cueing (visual, sound, motion, control force feedback, and instruments) to stimulate realistic driver responses that accurately portray flaws or inadequacies in the "paper" design of the target vehicle. The fidelities of graphics and dynamics crucial to driver cueing are measured by different yardsticks than those employed in non-real-time modeling. For example, the graphics realism of ray-tracing or total correlation between dynamics response from instrumented cars and vehicle models needing overnight computer runs are not necessarily pertinent.

Fully interactive real-time simulation demands care in the relative realism of the environmental scene (scene specificity and density) and dynamics accuracy significant to the driver response (chassis accelerations and control forces). Also important is the rate at which new cues are delivered to the driver and the time lag between his control commands and the corresponding cue changes. What is the proper balance between real-time constraints and the cueing rates needed to support a driver's decision process? What is the allowable system time lag before false driver responses are induced?

The subtlety of human perception and response while interacting with a vehicle forces difficult compromises. The dynamics considerations bearing on driver behavior demand an almost open-ended fidelity escalation. A driver's sensitivities to visual and tactile cues tend to peak in the region of a few hertz while steering in response to sudden external stimuli and at tens of hertz for periodic and impulsive road features. Rates of cueing tend to cap the

response bandwidth of simulator vehicle dynamics. Much higher frequencies can arise from mechanical resonances of suspension parts and body torsion/flex, or the dynamic response of an on-board digital control system. How will the dynamics simulation deal with cueing-significant modal energy which is coupled by system non-linearities from these higher frequency ranges down into the ranges of driver sensitivities?

Simulation-aided engineering requires vehicle designers to trust simulation realism when no equivalent physical vehicle system has been prototyped or tested. Computer-aided design and analysis tools can often supply reliable subsystem data. Since the total system can behave differently from the sum of its parts, how can the designer trust a simulator whose response might compromise the otherwise adequate subsystem data?

The answers to all these tough questions can be summarized with a few rules of thumb:

- Provide flexibility in trading system resources to enhance temporarily the specific areas of experimental focus at the expense of others.

- Ensure that the minimum requirements of human perceptual cueing thresholds and of vehicle operations are met by simulator performance and functionality.

- Attempt to drive overall simulator response as close to the step-steering and steady state (in both phase and frequency) responses of the vehicle as practical.

319

- Provide constant interfaces between different forms of the same data distributed within the simulator so that changes afforded by technology advances can be easily incorporated into simulator improvements.

- Develop simulator software architectures that port easily into future computer systems.

- Provide as much reserve capability as economically possible.

CIG Demands of High-Performance Driving Simulation

The use of real-time, man-in-the-loop simulators for the evaluation of designs of high-performance land vehicles has greatly lagged flight simulation. Major advances in dynamics, washout, motion, and graphics have recently set the stage for another leap.

The current state of CIG (Computer Image Generation) evolution is closely approaching photographic realism with update rates, lag, and image quality that suffice for a broad range of operational and perceptual objectives. Recent advances in computing and mechanical dynamics techniques have set the stage to achieve vehicle behavior in a simulator rivaling the quality of CIG real-time graphics, and to afford dynamics quality capable of unmasking subtle CIG shortcomings rarely encountered before now.

CIG improvement is driven by operational maneuvering and perceptual requirements [8]. Driving involves very low eye heights where optical flow density must change very rapidly over the field of vision available in a car. The driver must be able to judge speed and proximity to obstacles very quickly by visualizing textural cues in and around the road as well as passing 3D features. The visual depiction of the road surface must be good enough for the driver to anticipate road hazards like bumps and ice. When appropriate, urban, country, and highway scenes must be possible with contending traffic and pedestrians to saturate the driver's task loading and reaction times.

The basic psychology of vision and kinematics of driver responses at the controls of the car also demand CIG fidelity. The effective resolution of the CIG image determines what the driver can detect and recognize. A driving simulator should ideally match the lag, from control input to visual result, at a few tens of milliseconds typical of responsive cars. The rate of image refresh and update must satisfy eye demands for visual tracking, smooth motion of scenery, flicker-free viewing and discrimination of temporal events that may alter driver response.

The current generation of top-end real-time CIG is represented by such products as the Evans & Sutherland CT-6. This system offers critical improvements in scene performance needed to discriminate the nuances of vehicle behavior possible with the dynamics techniques covered in the following section. Synthetic and photographic texture along with high 3D feature densities now allow sound judgments to be made about speed and distance. Subpixel anti-aliasing allows road signs and road surfaces to be visualized reliably at varied vehicle speeds. Generalized occultation allows complex traffic movement over rolling terrain, around urban clutter, and among other traffic. Multiple eyepoints can support the virtual eyepoints of mirrors and the simultaneous observation of own-vehicle chassis and suspension behavior from external vantage points while driving the car through difficult maneuvers.

Figure 2 shows a typical driving landscape and situation achievable with CT-6 for driving simulation. Figure 3 represents the kind of car-external viewing of critical moments in suspension deformation and chassis excursions. This real-time visual display can complement a designer's study of subtle car subsystem motion over specific road geometries.

Real-Time Vehicle Dynamics

Overview   Non-real-time computer simulation of complicated mechanical linkages has been performed for machines, robots, spacecraft, and ground vehicles. True real-time simulation is more difficult and hitherto done only for relatively simple mechanical systems, complex systems with approximated governing equations, or by using specialized computer hardware. For example, aircraft are usually treated as relatively simple mechanical systems subject to complicated forces calculated from experimental data, while automobile systems are often approximated by eliminating velocity coupling effects. Engineering simulation of modern high performance vehicles demands a multi-body nonlinear approach in order to provide acceptable fidelity of motion; software flexibility is required to deal with the varied nature of vehicle engineering problems. A solution to real-time engineering simulation requires both cost-effective computational capacity and the adaptability of general purpose computers and software. Simulator system integration and introduction into the real-time software of motion-base washout and vehicle subsystem models must be facilitated by the use of standard operating systems and programming languages.

Two significant approaches to real-time vehicle dynamics modeling, albeit at very different levels, are those implemented by the Swedish Road and Traffic Research Institute (VTI) [21] and Daimler-Benz [10] [13]. The VTI model employs a simple, planar three degree-of-freedom car, but carefully considers tire and other forces. Daimler-Benz achieves real-time with a much more sophisticated, but still simplified, vehicle dynamics model. It has successfully been used to perform driver behavior and vehicle design studies. Small velocity coupling terms are neglected in the equations of motion to achieve real-time performance.

We are primarily interested in the accurate prediction of vehicle dynamics, rather than kinematics or inverse dynamics [17]. The approach we use decomposes the system into a set of rigid bodies (a rigid body requires distances between points within the body to be fixed) that are connected by joints that allow relative motion between the bodies, subject to various forces, moments, and additional constraints.

Figure 2 - Advanced Real-Time Display

The resulting linked multi-body system can be described by a directed graph [27] (cf. Figure 5), where the bodies form vertices and the joints, edges connecting the vertices. People and robot arms, usually without closed loops in their connections, form special *tree* graphs contractible to a single base vertex. A tree graph has a natural direction outward from the base vertex. In a tree graph, an outboard body's (a body directed further out along a branch from the base body) Cartesian position and velocities can be expressed in terms of an inboard body and relative joint coordinates and velocities, recursively providing the coordinates needed for determining motion. Here we use the term *recursive* to mean either moving inward or outward along the tree graph, using data from bodies along the branch to determine the position and motion of the next. General graphs, with embedded closed loops, are required for more complicated systems, such as automobile suspensions.

To derive kinematic relations for our system in the presence of closed loops, we first cut the closed loops, so that a recursive relative joint coordinate description can be employed. Next, D'Alembert's virtual work principle [12] is utilized to derive the equations of motion, augmented by the introduction of reaction forces from the closed loop joint constraints via Lagrange multipliers. The relative joint coordinate formulation, implemented in a recursive algorithm (with concurrent execution of each branch), leads to the efficiencies required for real-time simulation, without the need for approximation of the equations of motion. External forces are computed from the tires, drivetrain, gravity, wind resistance, brakes, springs, dampers, stabilizer bars, and suspension stops. Since our vehicle bodies are subject to additional kinematic constraints from cutting the closed loops in the graph, we arrive at a set of coupled differential-algebraic equations (DAE's), in which differential equations of motion and algebraic equations of constraint must be simultaneously solved. At all times, the numerical solution must closely satisfy the imposed kinematic constraints, so some form of constraint stabilization is required. In addition, stability must be preserved, even in the presence of high frequency force inputs.

Figure 3 - Car Dynamics (Frames 80ms apart)

Dynamics Modeling Techniques Computational dynamics is currently a very active area of research [14]. Equations of motion for a complex system can be generally divided into two categories depending on the choice of system coordinates [15]: In the first, no attempt to choose a minimal set of coordinates is made, opting instead for a maximal set of Cartesian coordinates for each body [22]; in the second class, a minimal, or at least small, set of relative coordinates is used recursively to identify a body's position [16]. The first method has the advantages of generality and relatively simple equations and the disadvantage of rarely being optimal for a given mechanism or vehicle. Commercial codes, such as DADS [25] or ADAMS [5], use generalized Cartesian coordinates for each body and apply a maximal set of constraints. This is similar to finite element methods in structural mechanics where a very large, but sparse, equation set is generated. In the second method, a minimal set of relative joint coordinates is used, and fewer constraints must be applied, but the equations are often extremely complex. This minimal coordinate description is very effective in describing spacecraft and robots, since these systems naturally form tree graphs. A complication occurs when closed loops appear in the system graph, since the relative joint coordinates are then subject to additional constraints from the closing of the loop, and so are not independent. Wittenburg [27] considered the idea of cutting the closed loop to form a tree graph, and adding Lagrange multipliers to the equations of motion to satisfy the now missing constraints. Once the system graph is a tree, recursive methods developed by Hooker and Margulies [16] for spacecraft, and Armstrong [1] and Luh, *et. al.* [20], for robotics, can be used to recover body accelerations. Bae [2], using these ideas in his thesis, derived an algorithm combining cut joints with recursion. In addition, he discussed issues relating to the natural parallelization of the resulting algorithm. Essentially, we have implemented Bae's work, adding additional techniques for stable integration and pipeline delay reduction to the parallel recursive algorithm.

Vehicle Graph   A typical modern high-performance sports sedan consists of a chassis, the two MacPherson front

suspension subsystems, the steering rack, and the two rear suspension arms. The MacPherson front suspension subsystem is detailed in Figure 4. This suspension allows both *jounce* (spindle vertical motion) and *steer* (the rotation of the spindle) as independent motions. Steering is done by motion of the tie-rods (which act as distance constraints) connecting the rack and spindle. The corresponding vehicle graph is shown in Figure 5. There are four closed loops

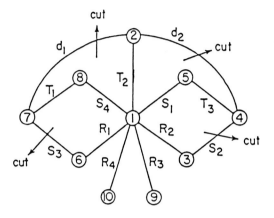

Figure 5 - Vehicle Graph with Closed Loops

from the front suspension and steering linkages. If we cut the links between rack and spindle, and lower control arm and spindle on both sides, we produce the tree graph shown in Figure 6.

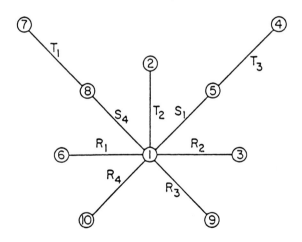

Figure 6 - Graph after Cutting Closed Loops

Vehicle Coordinates   In Figure 6, the chassis is the base body vertex, whose coordinates are the three Cartesian degrees of freedom $\vec{r}_1$ of the center-of-mass in the inertial frame and a vector $\vec{p}_1$ of four Euler parameters [14] [12] describing its orientation. The lower control arm Cartesian position is determined by the chassis position and specification of the revolute joint angle (the rear suspension arms have a similar description). The strut's position is given by the chassis and spherical joint orientation (again using

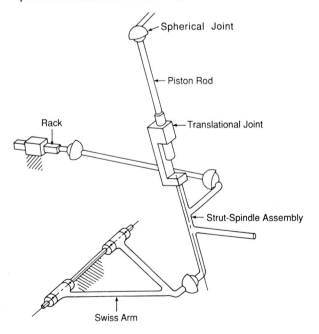

Figure 4 - McPherson Strut Front Suspension

Euler parameters). The spindle's position can be found from the strut's position and the translational joint distance. The position of the rack relative to its translational joint with the chassis is prescribed by the driver's steering input. Notice that we have not yet closed any of the four loops in Figure 6.

The four tires are not treated as individual bodies, but are given only a single rotational degree of freedom and resulting inertia. In our model, there are 10 rigid bodies, 4 tires, and 26 body and relative joint coordinates (not all independent) used in the kinematic description of the vehicle tree graph. The constraints from the closed suspension and steering loops must be added to these 26 coordinates. Neglecting the tire as a full body is reasonable, since tire inertial forces can be separately calculated and added as additional external coupling torques to the equations of motion. Flexibility in any of the bodies is not presently considered, but can be added as additional generalized deformation coordinates.

Holonomic Vehicle Constraints The vehicle coordinates are subject to holonomic constraints [12] $\vec{\Phi}(\vec{r}_i, \vec{p}_i) = 0$ from the closed loops in the graph and are not independent. Constraints of this type reduce the number of independent coordinates by the row-rank of the Jacobian of partial derivatives of each constraint component by the coordinates. When the constraints are independent, the row-rank is the number of constraint equations. The MacPherson front suspension requires the spindle to meet the lower control arm at a spherical joint as shown in Figure 4. Counting both the right and left sides, gives 6 independent constraints. The rack-spindle distances give 2 more independent constraints, while the normalization of the three sets of Euler parameters provides 3 more. The driver steering commands produce 1 more constraint on rack motion. Since each of these constraints is holonomic, and they are all independent, we have $26 - (6 + 2 + 3 + 1) = 14$ independent degrees of freedom in our vehicle (exclusive of the drivetrain and other subsystems).

Non-holonomic constraints [12] (non-integrable relations involving the coordinates) are encountered in our model only in the kinematics of tire roll-without-slip on a surface. The resulting tire constraint forces are treated as external forces on the spindle and tire.

Recovery of Outboard Positions, Velocities, Accelerations The velocity and acceleration formulas involve joint matrices B_1 and B_2 which give the linear relation between outboard body velocity and inboard body and relative joint velocity. We write the Cartesian velocity of outboard body i+1 as $\dot{\vec{Y}}_{i+1} = B_1 \dot{\vec{Y}}_i + B_2 \dot{\vec{q}}_{(i+1)i}$ where for body i, its global translational and angular velocities are combined as $\vec{Y}_i = [\dot{\vec{r}}_i^T \ \vec{\omega}_i^T]^T$. The corresponding acceleration formula is $\ddot{\vec{Y}}_{i+1} = B_1 \ddot{\vec{Y}}_i + B_2 \ddot{\vec{q}}_{(i+1)i} + \vec{D}_{(i+1)i}$, where the velocity coupling terms $\vec{D}_{(i+1)i}$ contain the coordinate velocities and derivatives of the joint matrices B_1 and B_2. The B_i matrices and $\vec{D}$ vector must be individually constructed for each specific joint type.

These kinematic formulas are used to express the global Cartesian position, velocity, and acceleration of an outboard body in terms of an inboard body and relative joint position, velocity, and acceleration. All body global coordinates, velocities, and accelerations are determined recursively moving outward in the graph from the initial base body.

Recovery of Coordinate Accelerations We generate our dynamical equations using D'Alembert's principle of virtual work [12]. By using relative joint coordinates, rather than Cartesian coordinates, the unknown joint constraint forces are automatically eliminated from our equations. Using virtual work instead of alternative variational methods avoids the additional step of forming complicated Lagrangians or Hamiltonians and their Euler-Lagrange equations. Additional difficulties with variational formulations can occur when non-conservative forces, such as friction, are present. By using the virtual work principle, we can treat both conservative and non-conservative forces in a straightforward manner, while the remaining cut joint constraints are easily incorporated into the principle using Lagrange multipliers.

The result of our derivation of the equations of motion, and choice of kinematics, is a parallel algorithm that allows the inward recursive elimination of the relative joint accelerations, and accumulation of generalized mass, velocity, force, and constraint terms into a single matrix equation that is solved for the base body accelerations and Lagrange multipliers. The remaining coordinate accelerations are recursively recovered by moving outward in the graph from the base body. The organization of the algorithm closely follows the system tree graph, and so exhibits the inherent parallelism of each independent branch. The algorithm's recovery of the coordinate accelerations is fully non-linear, in that velocity coupling terms $\vec{D}$ are not assumed negligible. The assumption of slow rates of angular change, so that coupling from the Euler terms $\vec{\omega} \times J\vec{\omega}$ is small, fails during high speed maneuvering of vehicles. The inclusion of these non-linear terms is critical for simulating the effects of anti-lock braking systems (ABS) [18] and four-wheel steering controls.

External Forces We include external forces such as tire forces, gravity, wind resistance, engine and brake torques, springs, dampers, stabilization bars, suspensions stops, and internal reactions in the model. The most difficult and critical forces to model are the ones generated by the tires. Because of the complexity of road-tire interaction, the forces and moments are taken from measured data as a function of normal force, slip angle, and camber angle. Attention must be paid to how the tire forces change during conversion from a no-slip to a slip condition, in order to minimize longitudinal force discontinuities.

Complex drivetrain models for both manual and automatic transmissions have been developed. They are based on combining individual drivetrain components such as engine, clutch, transmission, torque converter, and differential together with proper feedback. Each component is modeled using experimental data generated for that subsystem. Our current drivetrain models have a single degree of rotational freedom, which is independently integrated to find rotational velocity and applied wheel torque.

Integration of Accelerations   We symbolically write the result of the recursive algorithm's recovery of the accelerations as evaluating the right-hand side $\vec{f}(t, Y)$ of the first-order equation $\dot{\vec{Y}} = \vec{f}(t, Y)$ where $\vec{Y}$ is the state vector of 26 chassis and joint coordinates, and their velocities. Included in this recovery of the accelerations was the twice-differentiated acceleration form of the constraints in order to have sufficient equations to determine both the base body accelerations and the Lagrange multipliers. But the constraint equations themselves have not been included. If they are solved as part of the system, the resulting DAE's are stiff and awkward to integrate [11]. Ignoring our constraints for the moment (we return to them in the next paragraph), our equation can be integrated using standard techniques from numerical analysis to advance $\vec{Y}(t)$ to $\vec{Y}(t + \Delta t)$. Because of real-time limitations, methods that require only a single new evaluation of $\vec{f}$ for each time step can currently be used. This limits us to conditionally-stable explicit methods such as Adams-Bashford and Adams-Moulton Predictor-Corrector schemes [19], without a final update. When such explicit methods are used, great care must be taken in how the resulting equations are partitioned to avoid instabilities resulting from high frequency force inputs. To improve total system bandwidth, after the system has been properly partitioned into slow (chassis) and fast (suspension) components, a hybrid integration scheme where the low frequency slow components are integrated with an explicit method and the high frequency fast components with an implicit method is advantageous. The non-linear equations from the implicit integrations can be solved using quasi-Newton methods [6].

Constraint Stabilization   The numerical solution of our differential equation must satisfy all cut joint constraints. These additional algebraic equations force us to solve the differential equations on the curved configuration manifold (the algebraic manifold embedded in parameter space on which the system trajectories are forced by the constraints to move), rather than in the flat parameter space itself. Special techniques are needed to correct the solution produced by our standard "Euclidean" integration methods, in order to retain accuracy and stability. For very short times, since the differential form of the constraints are incorporated into our equation, the solution will approximately satisfy the cut joint constraints. For longer times, either Baumgarte's method [3] of modifying the equations to make the configuration manifold a stable attractor (so that points close to the configuration manifold will move nearer in time along their trajectories), or a coordinate partitioning method [25] of updating the dependent coordinates can be used. Baumgarte's method essentially introduces a primitive feedback loop to control error growth,

while the partitioning method uses Newton-Raphson iteration to force the dependent coordinates to satisfy all constraint conditions. Either of these can ensure that accumulated numerical error will not cause the solution to drift too far off the configuration manifold.

Organization of Recursive Algorithm   At the start of each time step, the global orientation, position, and velocity of each body is calculated from the relative joint positions and velocities by moving outward in the graph from the base body (Figure 7a). All local vectors are converted to global coordinates. The driver steering, brake, accelerator pedal position, and other inputs are obtained

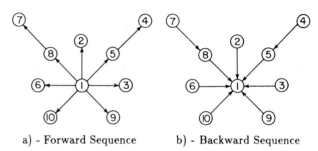

a) - Forward Sequence   b) - Backward Sequence

Figure 7 - Computation Paths

from sensors and used to determine rack position and velocity, brake, and drivetrain parameters. External forces and moments are then calculated; tire, brake, spring, damper, stabilizer bar, aerodynamic, gravitational, and drivetrain forces and torques are independently determined by special subsystem models. The inertia matrices are updated to the global coordinate system. Next, concurrently on each branch, the accelerations are recursively eliminated moving inward along the graph toward the base body (Figure 7b). When the base body is reached, and the base body equation assembled, it is solved for the chassis Cartesian accelerations and Lagrange multipliers using Gaussian elimination. Recovery of the outboard body Cartesian and relative joint accelerations is then begun, concurrently moving outward (Figure 7a) in the graph. When this is completed, all accelerations have been calculated, and the integration scheme advances the solution to the next time step.

Computer Architectures and Software   The requirement of implementing a parallel algorithm with a small number (4-8) of concurrent tasks leads to a single bus architecture with global memory. Care must be taken to avoid bus contention from simultaneous memory accesses or message passing. Modern optimizing FORTRAN and C compilers running under POSIX-type operating systems provide software flexibility. Specialized simulation computers with non-standard languages suffer from insufficient adaptability, limited transportability, and narrow growth potential. Upgrading of a simulator computer system is simplified by writing software in standard languages.

Algorithm Timing   Table 1 shows the results of timings of the recursive algorithm taken on Alliant FX/8 (in parallel and serial mode) and VAX-series computers (in se-

RELATIVE TIME TO FINISH ONE ALGORITHM STEP
(ALLIANT FX/8 WITH 8 CE'S = 1 UNIT)

Alliant FX/8	(8 CE's - parallel code)	1
Alliant FX/8	(4 CE's - parallel code)	1.25
Alliant FX/8	(2 CE's - parallel code)	2.0
Alliant FX/8	(1 CE - serial code)	3.2
VAX 8800	(serial code)	4.5
VAX 780	(serial code)	21.5

Table 1 - Algorithm Timings

rial mode only), using optimized FORTRAN code for each machine. The Alliant FX/8 was run with 1, 4, and 8 compute elements (CE's) available for concurrency to the algorithm. Asymptotic behavior of the algorithm speed-up beyond 4 CE's on the FX/8 is seen. The parallel algorithm provides a considerable improvement in speed over the serial version. The time obtained with 8 CE's allows real-time simulation.

Future Directions in Real-Time Visuals for Driving Simulation

There are some exciting developments, in both CIG technology and advanced vehicle systems for safety and traffic control, that will usher in a wave of simulation opportunities with the driver in the loop. There are related developments in personalized parallel computing and in dynamics methods that will allow real-time simulation to be moved out of the simulator bay and into the office. To boot, the dynamics methods summarized in the previous section along with networking can aid the ready fusion of pre-existing mechanical models with various forms of both real-time and non-real-time mechanical dynamics simulation. This section samples some enticing opportunities now contributing to a small revolution in the way mechanical designers will integrate traditional finite element analysis, design sensitivity/optimization, and life-cycle analysis with mechanical dynamics and vehicle-environment studies.

Future real-time CIG enhancements will boost scene density and specificity. Lag will be further reduced to improve the step response of the simulated vehicle and to meet the demands of eye-tracking displays. Modeling systems now under development will allow complex road systems and environments to be generated from photos with increasing reliance on automated image processing and expert system methods. The occulting generality of next-generation CIG will allow for arbitrary traffic encounters and for complex geometries of roads to be integrated easily with appropriate cuts and fills into surrounding landscapes. Photographic texture and feature densities will become commonplace.

Next-generation dynamics must be capable of modeling high-speed control systems and subtle mechanical res-

onances that affect driver performance. The approach to dynamics summarized in this paper has the flexibility and inherent modeling rigor to grow with these demands.

Interactive dynamics is on the verge of spilling out of the expensive high-performance computers of big simulators into the office. Products will likely emerge that package the robust dynamics methods typified in this paper with specially tailored parallel compute engines affording real-time and enhanced slow-time, mouse-driven, interactive dynamics on workstations. The emergence of high-speed networking will also help support the linkage of very complex parallel dynamics algorithms running on super-minis and super-computers with interactive dynamics visualization at workstations and graphic terminals. If similar dynamics models and processing techniques can be distributed as widely, there may emerge CAD standards that allow design data across the simulation spectrum to be moved easily around the organizational environment. As a result, dynamic study can become a more routine element of integrated mechanical design systems.

Conclusion

This paper has shown how graphics and dynamics must work together in driving simulation to provide realistic operator environmental cueing. A new approach to real-time vehicle dynamics, exploiting natural parallelism in the vehicle system graph, was discussed. We have aspired to present our view of a path to the future in vehicle simulation.

Acknowledgments

This paper would not have been possible without the efforts of the Simulation Technology Group and the continuing support of management at Evans and Sutherland. We want to express our appreciation to the following individuals: D. Anderson, D-S. Bae, J. Drosdol, E. Haug, W. Kaeding, J. Kuhl, W-S. Lee, G. Lerner, E. Pankiewicz, B. Thomson, C. Walther. In addition, we want to thank the engineering and simulation groups at Daimler-Benz AG and Bayerische Motoren Werke AG for their cooperation.

References

[1] Armstrong, W. Recursive Solution to the Equations of Motion of An N-Link Manipulator. In *Proc. 5th World Congress on Theory of Machines and Mechanism*, Vol. 2, (Montreal, 1979), 1343-1346.

[2] Bae, D. and Haug, E. A Recursive Formulation for Constrainted Mechanical System Dynamics. *Technical Report* 86-14, Center for Computer Aided Design, College of Engineering, University of Iowa, 1986.

[3] Baumgarte, J. Stabilization of Constraints and Integrals of Motion in Dynamic Systems. *Computer Methods in Applied Mechanics in Engineering*, 1 (1972), 1-16.

[4] Casali, J. and Wierwille, W. The Effects of Various Design Alternatives on Moving-Base Driving Simulator Discomfort. *Human Factors*, 22, 6 (1980), 741-756.

[5] Chace, M. Methods and Experience in Computer Aided Design of Large-Displacement Mechanical Systems. In *Computer Aided Analysis and Optimization of Mechanical System Dynamics*, E. Haug. (ed.). Springer-Verlag, Heidelberg, 1984.

[6] Dennis, J. and More, J. Quasi-Newton Methods, Motivation and Theory. *SIAM Review* 19, 1 (1977), 46-89. September 1967, pp. 250-253.

[7] Dickmanns, E.D., and Zapp, A. Guiding Land Vehicles Along Roadways by Computer Vision. Presented at AFCET Conference "Automatique 85 - the tools for tomorrow", Toulouse, October 1985.

[8] Doenges, Peter K. *Overview of Computer Image Generation in Visual Simulation*, Presented at ACM Siggraph Technical Courses, July, 1985.

[9] Duncan, J.R., and Wegscheid, E.L. Off-Road Vehicle Simulation for Human Factors Research. *Paper 82-1610*, 1982 Winter Meeting, American Society of Agricultural Engineers (Chicago, Dec. 14-17, 1982.)

[10] Drosdol, J. and Panik, F. The Daimler-Benz Driving Simulator: a Tool for Vehicle Development. *SAE Technical Paper* Series, 850334, (Feb. 1985).

[11] Gear, W. Differential-Algebraic Equations. In *Computer Aided Analysis and Optimization of Mechanical System Dynamics*, E. Haug (ed.) Springer-Verlag, Heidelberg, 1984.

[12] Goldstein, H. *Classical Mechanics*. Addison- Wesley, Reading, Mass., 1980.

[13] Hahn, S., and Kalb, E. The Daimler-Benz Driving Simulator Set-Up and Results of First Experiments. In *Summer Computer Simulation Conference Proceedings* Simulation Councils, Inc., San Diego, 1987, pp. 993 - 998.

[14] Haug, E. (ed.) *Computer Aided Analysis and Optimization of Mechanical System Dynamics*. Springer-Verlag, Heidelberg, 1984.

[15] Haug, E. Elements and Methods of Computational Dynamics. In *Computer Aided Analysis and Optimization of Mechanical System Dynamics*, E. Haug (ed.).

[16] Hooker, W. and Margulies, G. The Dynamical Attitude Equations for an n - Body Satellite. *J. Astronaut. Sci.* 12 (1965), 123-128.

[17] Issacs, P. and Cohen, M. Controlling Dynamic Simulation with Kinematic Constraints, Behavior Functions and Inverse Dynamics. *Computer Graphics* 21, 4 (July 1987), 215-224.

[18] Kempf, D., Bonderson, L., and Slater, L. Real Time Simulation for Application to ABS Development. *SAE Technical Paper* 870336, 1987.

[19] Lambert, J. *Computational Methods in Ordinary Differential Equations*. John Wiley, New York, 1973.

[20] Luh, J., Walker, M., and Paul, R. On-line Computational Scheme for Mechanical Manipulator. *J. Dyn. Syst. Measurement Control* 102 (1980), 69-76.

[21] Nordmark, S. VTI Driving Simulator - Mathematical Model of a Four-wheeled Vehicle for Simulation in Real-Time. *VTI Rapport* Nr 267A 1984. Statens vag- och trafikinstitut, Linköping, Sweden, 1984.

[22] Orlandea, N., Chace, M., and Calahan, D. A Sparsity-Oriented Approach to the Dynamic Analysis and Design of Mechanical Systems- Parts 1 and 2. *J. of Engineering for Industry* (1977), 773-784.

[23] Richter, Bernd. Driving Simulator Studies — the Influence of Vehicle Parameters on Safety in Critical Situations. SAE Technical Paper Series, 741105, (Feb. 1974).

[24] Sheridan, T.B., Paynter, H.M., and Coons, S.A. *Some Novel Display Techniques for Driving Simulation*. In IEEE Transactions on Human Factors in Electronics, Vol. HFE-5, September 1964, pp. 29-32.

[25] Wehage, R. and Haug, E. Generalized Coordinate Partitioning for Dimension Reduction in Analysis of Constrained Mechanical Systems. *J. of Mechanical Design*, 104 (1982), 247-255.

[26] Weirwille, W.W., Gagne, G.A., and Knight, J. R. A Laboratory Display System Suitable for Man-Machine Interface. In *EEE Transactions on Human Factors in Electronics*, Vol. HFE-8, No. 3.

[27] Wittenburg, J. *Dynamics of Systems of Rigid Bodies*. B. G. Teubner, Stuttgart, 1977.

APPLICATIONS OF COMPUTER GRAPHICS TO THE VISUALIZATION OF METEOROLOGICAL DATA

T. V. Papathomas, J. A. Schiavone and B. Julesz

AT&T Bell Laboratories
Murray Hill, New Jersey 07974

ABSTRACT

The need to visualize huge amounts of numerical data is exemplified in the field of meteorology, where measurements of many atmospheric parameters are routinely taken over large geographical areas for the purpose of monitoring and predicting weather. Computer graphics has provided and will continue to offer powerful tools to meet this visualization challenge, principally in three areas: first, efficient graphics algorithms for displaying the data; second, novel special-purpose graphics hardware; and third, interactive techniques for graphically manipulating the data at close to video rates. This paper reviews past and current uses of computer graphics for gaining insight from measured or modelled meteorological data.

CR CATEGORIES AND DESCRIPTORS:

H.1.2 [Models and Principles]: User/Machine Systems — human information processing;

I.3.7 [Computer Graphics]: Three-Dimensional Graphics and Realism;

J-2 [Physical Sciences and Engineering]: Earth and Atmospheric Sciences.

Additional Key Words and Phrases: Stereo, animation, motion, perception, clouds, fog, atmospheric phenomena, weather forecasting, modelling, image processing, interactive workstations, display techniques.

1. Introduction

Meteorology is a relatively young science in spite of the long history of human interest in knowledge about the weather. The weather affects nearly everyone on a daily basis and it occasionally affects smaller subsets of people catastrophically, endangering their lives and property. Nevertheless, significant barriers prevented early technological advancement in meteorology: the difficulty in conducting meteorological experiments on a "remote" atmospheric fluid as well as the difficulty in developing physical models of atmospheric dynamics.

©1988   ACM-0-89791-275-6/88/008/0327 $00.75

The difficulty in performing experiments on the atmosphere has only been alleviated in the last century and a half when technological advances finally permitted humans to effectively observe atmospheric properties. The telegraph spawned the *synoptic* era in the late 1800s, permitting simultaneous low-resolution 2-dimensional measurements of ground level weather features. Radio technology initiated the *radiosonde* era in the 1930s, allowing 3-dimensional measurements to be made through the depth of the atmosphere via balloon-borne sensor packages. Because these data sets were relatively sparse, interpreting observations was hardly a problem. However, with the advent of the computer which promoted numerical weather prediction and the transistor which spurred the development of remote sensing technology, meteorologists were suddenly overwhelmed with high-resolution, 3-dimensional observational data beginning in the 1960s. Computer graphics found an early home in meteorology during this recent *data-rich* era as meteorologists strove to exploit their newfound enrichment of data.

This paper briefly reviews the history of computer graphics adoption by meteorologists and then focuses on some current state-of-the-art applications. Our goal is to first provide a comprehensive yet cursory review of the full arena and then to highlight the work of a few select institutions which have had a long-term commitment to computer graphics applications in meteorology. Regrettably, space limitations prevent us from citing all of the many individuals and institutions who have made outstanding contributions to meteorological visualization. Finally, we provide a short summary of our expectations for the future of computer graphics applications in meteorology.

2. Historical Perspective

2.1 History of Graphics Needs in Meteorology

The types of data prevalent during each of the different observational eras strongly influenced the types of visualization graphics employed by meteorologists. During the *synoptic* era of low-resolution 2-D measurements, meteorologists were satisfied with simple graphic symbols to plot cold and warm fronts, station model symbols to list weather observations for a particular location on a weather map, and contour plots to depict 2-D data fields (Figure 1). The introduction of routine 3-D observations during the *radiosonde* era placed an additional burden on meteorologists to perceive the 3-D structure of the atmosphere. This was accomplished by stacking sets of height-sequenced contour plots of atmospheric data fields on clipboards and flipping through them to develop a mental picture of the 3-D structure of the data fields. The advent of space-borne cameras at the beginning of the *data-rich* era placed 2-D image data into the hands of meteorologists for the first time. The fact that these images were arriving at rates of at least once an hour promoted animation as a tool to aid the meteorologist in mentally extrapolating cloud features into the immediate future. Finally, the current expanded use of supercomputing power for numerical weather prediction and the budding development of high-resolution atmospheric sounders are now requiring meteorologists to work with what are effectively 3-D images of the atmosphere.

2.2 History of Capabilities for Visualizing Meteorological Data

Facsimile technology was introduced about four decades ago for the transmission and display of weather data. Because of its simplicity and robustness, it has been a standard piece of equipment in the meteorologist's office [Peti85]. The *image processing* field found a new area for applications about a quarter century ago in response to the introduction of the meteorological satellite [Huss86]. Soon thereafter techniques were developed for displaying satellite images in *stereo* [Pich73] and *animation* techniques and *interactive* workstations were introduced in meteorology in the early 1970s [Smit75]. Finally, the last decade has seen the application of *computer generated imagery* to the display of weather events [Hibb85], [Grtj84], [Hasl85], [Gelb87].

2.3 History of Graphics Applications in Meteorology

The earliest implementations of automated graphics (a looser interpretation of computer graphics) in meteorology were produced to support the weather forecasting operations of what was then known as the United States Weather Bureau. Teletype transmission of weather maps was introduced in the early 1930s [Bell31] which was upgraded to facsimile transmission of contoured weather maps by the 1940s. During the early years of numerical weather prediction in the 1950s, contoured data fields were depicted with line printers by filling the regions between contours with different types of print.

The earliest actual computer graphics applications to meteorology were done at research institutions. The first dedicated effort to develop computer graphics tools specifically for meteorologists began at the National Center for Atmospheric Research (NCAR) in the late 1960s with the genesis of the NCAR Graphics Package. The first dedicated effort to digitally manipulate meteorological image data began at the University of Wisconsin in the early 1970s with the development of the Man-Computer Interactive Data Access System (McIDAS). Some of the first applications of stereo graphics were conducted in the late 1970s at the National Aeronautics and Space Administration (NASA) Goddard Space Flight Center on their Atmospheric and Oceanographic Information Processing System (AOIPS).

Incorporation of these computer graphics research concepts into operational facilities began at the National Weather Service (NWS) when it initiated procurement for the Automation of Field Operations and Services (AFOS) system in the 1970s. AFOS provided interactive graphics capabilities to the Government's operational forecast offices for the first time in the early 1980s. The National Oceanic and Atmospheric Administration (NOAA), in a continuing forward-looking effort to modernize weather forecast operations in the NWS, established the Program for Regional Observing and Forecasting Services (PROFS) in 1980 which has devoted a significant effort to developing interactive graphics applications. Also, commercial applications of computer graphics in meteorology began to appear in the 1980 time frame with an abundance of vendors targeting the lucrative television weather broadcast market. Research and development for interactive meteorological data handling continues to increase during the 1980s with many different government, academic, and private institutions now participating.

3. Current Applications

3.1 Meteorological Data Visualization Issues

Meteorology can be used as a typical example to illustrate the visualization problem for large-scale scientific data sets. To process and assimilate the huge bodies of measured or numerical model data, the ideal site might include high-speed supercomputers, an efficient interactive environment (possibly aided by a rule-based interface to the data bank), and "real-time" graphics capabilities. However, the fact that storage capacity increases are not keeping up with those of computational speed and semiconductor memory size and speed, have led Upson to conclude that "a researcher can compute more than he can store; he can store more than he can comprehend" [Upso87]. Computer graphics and visual psychophysics are two areas that provide valuable tools for confronting the major challenge of visualization in meteorology.

We shall first examine the role of computer graphics. Recent progress in graphics hardware and software has made it possible to create animation sequences for weather episodes of ever increasing complexity. Although practically all advances in graphics algorithms can be applied to the display of weather phenomena, we mention concisely in this subsection a few recent display techniques that are highly relevant to meteorology. Fournier, Fussell and Carpenter [Four82] devised a recursive subdivision algorithm to apply efficiently Mandelbrot's "fractional Brownian motion" model [Mand68] for natural phenomena. Models for the diffuse reflection of light as it interacts with clouds of small particles are studied in [Blin82]. Reeves developed a method for rendering fuzzy objects, called particle systems [Reev83], while he and Blau implemented algorithms for shading and rendering particle systems [Reev85]. Light scattering models were used by Kajiya and Von Herzen [Kaji84] to develop algorithms for ray tracing volume densities (clouds, fog, dust, etc.). Gardner sought to compromise the conflict between realistic images and computational time by adopting the impressionist painters' approach of "representing the essence of natural scenes as simply as possible." He achieved remarkable results by using textured quadric surfaces bounded by planes to portray clouds and trees [Gard84]. He also developed a highly efficient approach to render realistic cloud scenes (see Figure 2) by modulating the shading and translucence of simple surfaces using a texturing function [Gard85]. Perlin developed highly efficient schemes for rendering a wide variety of natural scenes [Perl85]. In particular, his method of generating "1:f noise" for fractal surfaces offers considerable computational savings over subdivision-based [Four82] or Fourier-space [Voss83] techniques. The clouds in Figure 3, generated by Don Mitchell and composited with other 3D graphical elements by Eric Hoffert on the AT&T Pixel Machine, were obtained by using Perlin's approach. An additional advantage is that Perlin's algorithm can be performed on parallel machines. Miller's method [Mill86] also enjoys this advantage. Yaeger and Upson's paper [Yaeg86] is a prime example of combining numerical physical simulation (fluid dynamics) with visual simulation (particle rendering). There is a definite need and a trend for synergies such as this to benefit both participants, in this instance the fields of the numerical physical sciences and computer graphics. Max approached the problem of light diffusion through clouds [Max86a] and atmospheric illumination [Max86b] by developing scattering models; similar problems are considered in [Rush87] and [Nish87].

Unfortunately, as a rule, there is a long delay in applying the advances in computer graphics, like the ones outlined above, to the physical sciences. An exception, among many, to this rule is the work of Gelberg and Stephenson [Gelb87], who applied state-of-the-art graphics and image processing techniques for presenting and interacting with data in the earth and planetary sciences. One of their meteorology-related products is *SuperSeer*, a cloud prediction and display system [Gelb87]. Figure 4, rendered on a Pixar Image Computer, is an example of their work.

We next turn briefly to a few general remarks on results from experiments in visual psychophysics. Regarding *depth perception* (DP), Julesz was the first to devise random-dot stereograms to show that DP is possible in the absence of any monocular cues, as long as the appropriate binocular horizontal disparity is present [Jule60]. Binocularly viewed stereo pairs have been used extensively to enhance the percept of the third spatial dimension [Pich73], [DesJ80], [Hasl81], [Schi86], [Papa87]. Of course, many other cues can be used to elicit depth perception, with or without stereo pairs. For static images, these include geometrical perspective [Vond86], shadows and shading, texture perspective, distance blurring, and occlusion. For dynamically changing scenes, the kinetic depth effect (KDE, the ability to extract the third dimension from an animated series of projections obtained from rotating an object), closely related to motion parallax, must be added to the list. As far as *motion perception* is concerned, it has been demonstrated that luminance elicits stronger motion perception than color [Rama78], and that shape is a very weak token for "carrying" motion [Burt81]. We cannot go into detail on the relative importance of other attributes (orientation, spatial frequency, depth etc.) in the perception of motion. The interested reader may consult [Hoch78] as a starting point. Motion blur has been employed in computer-generated images [Potm83]. Motion is important for three reasons: First, in the form of time animation, it reveals the atmospheric evolution; second, when generated by the user through real-time interactive techniques, it provides a useful tool for efficient visual data exploration and pattern detection; finally, it is possible for the viewer to "move about in the scenery," providing powerful KDE clues for discerning the 3D structure of the objects. The authors produced realistic stereo animations of complex meteorological phenomena [Schi86] [Papa87] paying special attention to the issues of visual perception.

In the special case of meteorology there are some particular issues and concerns. The small thickness of the atmosphere (relative to its horizontal extent) necessitates a "stretched" z-axis for visualizing weather phenomena. Also, the desire to view the distribution of several variables simultaneously has given rise to a few interesting solutions: one is to portray each variable by a different attribute (color for variable A, height for variable B, iso-valued contours for variable C, etc.); another is to assign different transparency indices to the various surfaces that represent the variables. Both of the above methods result in images that are highly "unrealistic," illustrating that there may be instances in scientific computing in which the visualization technique may have to transcend "realism." Finally, the need to associate the atmospheric phenomena to the underlying map and terrain imposes additional display constraints that must be addressed.

3.2 Current Hardware Capabilities

Most research meteorological institutions today use minicomputer workstations, although most have access to supercomputers. The graphical needs of remote operational weather sites are served by personal computers and minicomputers. The last five years have seen the emergence of powerful dedicated graphics and imaging machines. Typical examples are: the Silicon Graphics IRIS workstation with a special-purpose set of VLSI chips for graphics; the Pixar Image Computer with up to three parallel channel processors, each with four processors and a throughput of 120 MIPS; and the parallel-architecture AT&T Pixel Machines with up to 82 floating-point signal processors and peak throughput of 820 MFLOPS.

3.3 Current State-of-the-Art Systems

3.3.1 NCAR — NCAR Graphics

3.3.1.1 Background. The earliest computer graphics tool tailored for meteorologists was the NCAR Graphics package developed at the National Center for Atmospheric Research in the late 1960s [Wrig73]. NCAR's Warren Washington provided early evidence of the utility of NCAR Graphics through his pioneering work in making 16 mm color movies depicting time varying parameters relevant to global climatology. NCAR Graphics has been a popular 2-D monochrome graphics package for over 15 years and it is currently undergoing a major upgrade (see Section 4.1).

Richard Grotjahn and Robert Chervin [Grtj84], in the early 1980s, pushed NCAR Graphics to its limits in an effort to convey the results of a major global meteorological measurement program enacted in 1979. They used NCAR Graphics to generate individual frames for a number of movies depicting the atmospheric evolution during the field program. They experimented with anaglyphic stereo, mesh representations of surfaces, and drop shadows within the confines of NCAR Graphics to provide visual cues of the 3-D nature of the atmospheric features. They also experimented with various means to show atmospheric air parcels to depict the overall motion of the atmospheric fluid.

NCAR Graphics' current restriction to wire-frame representation of 3-D surfaces inspired a number of other scientific investigators at NCAR to apply the 3-D solid rendering capabilities of MOVIE.BYU to their scientific results, as described below.

3.3.1.2 System. The new release (Version 2.00) of the NCAR Graphics software is not tailored to any specific computer. It consists of the following components: 1) A level 0A Graphical Kernel System (GKS) package. 2) An intermediate-level library, the System Plot Package Simulator (SPPS). 3) A set of high-level graphics utilities. 4) A Computer Graphics Metafile (CGM) translator with drivers for several plotting devices. 5) Test drivers and miscellaneous databases, including map data. This version contains software to color-fill map regions defined by geopolitical and geographical boundaries. The graphics software, however, is essentially vector-based.

Another meteorological graphics package developed at NCAR by J. B. Klemp and his colleagues is PolyPaint, which is also highly portable because it conforms to FORTRAN 77 and GKS standards. The system is interactive, allowing the user to specify transparency indices, shading techniques, view-position, -angle, and -distance, direction of eyesight, and type of light source. In the first stage, PolyPaint transforms 3-D grid data to polygons and, in the second stage, it shades these polygons according to the technique selected. Contour lines, which are very useful for visualizing the spatio-temporal distribution of key variables, are rendered as thin shaded surfaces in 3-D. Film recorders are used to produce animation sequences.

3.3.1.3 Example. The example picture (Figure 5) was produced by Klemp and Rotunno [Klem85] to visualize the results of their numerical cloud model. The model is designed to study the structure of convective clouds, which produce most of the local severe weather events we experience: thunderstorms, hailstorms, and tornadoes. Such storms are difficult to observe directly in detail and the models are used to derive details on the active physical processes that may not be observable otherwise.

Figure 5 shows a set of three horizontal slices through part of a mature, intense thunderstorm in a 3-D perspective view. The slices are at the ground and at 4 and 8 kilometers above the ground. The white arrows depict the horizontal wind flow within each plane and the red and green contours show the updraft and downdraft regions, respectively. The yellow line marks the storm's gust front — the ground-based boundary where the cold storm downdraft meets the warm environmental air. The blue-shaded areas mark the precipitation fields, with the lighter blue indicating heavier precipitation.

3.3.2 University of Wisconsin — McIDAS

3.3.2.1 Background. The University of Wisconsin's McIDAS has been another pioneer for computer graphics applications to meteorology [Smit75]. Its original mission in the early 1970s was to provide convenient interactive viewing of weather satellite imagery. Over the years McIDAS has evolved into a workstation which combines data access and processing with sophisticated display techniques. McIDAS can generate multicolor composites of conventional, model, and satellite weather data in a wide variety of 2-D and 3-D displays as well as animations of these analyses. Systems based on McIDAS are in place at a number of Government forecasting facilities.

Mainly through the efforts of William L. Hibbard and J. T. Young [Hibb85] [Hibb86a], McIDAS has become an impressive platform for animated 3-D stereo depictions of a broad spectrum of meteorological data. A large effort was devoted to providing as many simultaneous visual cues as possible to afford the user a striking impression of the atmosphere in its truest form: that of a 3-D, time-evolving fluid. Cues such as perspective, motion parallax, stereoscopic perception, depth precedence, shading, and drop shadows were all explored and used to enhance the visual perception of depth. Several different types of stereo display techniques were tried, including anaglyphic, polarization, and electronic shutter techniques.

3.3.2.2 System. The McIDAS package runs on IBM 370-architectured computers as well as on IBM-PC/ATs and IBM PS/2s. It supports up to 50 custom-built graphics workstations, each with a resolution of 480 × 640 pixels. Statistical encoding is used to compact the 6-bit/pixel images down to 3 bits/pixel, thus allowing

128 frames for animation with an additional 64 frames of graphics overlay. The package consists of a core of roughly 300,000 lines of FORTRAN code for data acquisition, storage, analysis, management and graphical interaction and another 300,000 lines for miscellaneous tasks. For the 3-D graphics software, an 8-bit z-buffer algorithm is used for hidden-surface removal, with depth scaling to utilize all 256 levels. In addition to true stereo, perspective, shading, and variations in texture, brightness and color, some novel graphics techniques are used to display information at all depths. These include the use of transparent and grid mesh surfaces, and groups of moving small objects to portray wind streamlines. The result is the simultaneous depiction of multiple variables for a given weather episode. Surface rendering is done by Gouraud shading of triangular patches, but a special shading function is used for clouds. Rendering progresses in two stages: first, for the opaque objects, characterized by brightness and depth, and then for the translucent objects, characterized by brightness, depth, and alpha (translucency index). Although no anti-aliasing is employed, the light source is placed in the same direction as the viewer, minimizing the effects of aliasing by causing the edges of shaded objects to be relatively dim. Wind streamlines are rendered as shaded translucent tubes, whose alpha depends on the velocity of the corresponding parcel, giving rise to a motion-blur effect (see Fig. 6).

The system is highly interactive. The user can select options using a variety of input devices (keyboard, joystick, mouse, and graphics tablet). A 2-D cursor is drawn to help the user interact with the displayed information, with future plans for a 3-D cursor. The user has control over the contents, spatial and time extents, perspective point and information density [Hibb86b].

3.3.2.3 Example. The image shown in Figure 6 is derived from Robert Schlesinger's thunderstorm numerical model. It depicts wind trajectories and a transparent 0.5 g/m^3 cloud water concentration surface, the approximate cloud boundary. The horizontal domain of the model is about 50 kilometers square and the heights are labeled in kilometers.

3.3.3 NASA — AOIPS/2

3.3.3.1 Background. Another early leader in meteorology computer graphics technology has been the NASA Goddard Space Flight Center with its AOIPS system [Hasl83]. The initial version of AOIPS was built in 1976 as a high-performance, interactive meteorological processing system. Its software was designed to use state-of-the-art image processing for satellite image analysis functions such as cloud tracking and height determination. The software was later extended to include radar, aircraft, and ground-based meteorological data. The system is principally used by NASA atmospheric scientists in support of their research activities. From 1984 through 1987 AOIPS was upgraded to AOIPS/2 using new hardware: 32 bit computers, a modern operating system, commercially available image terminals, and an upgraded, integrated software system.

A. F. Hasler and his colleagues [Hasl85] have produced some outstanding animations of satellite imagery, using two separate types of images of the same cloud scene, as described below, to depict cloud-top features with striking realism. Interesting animated applications of these techniques are a number of movies depicting a viewpoint that moves over and around different kinds of cloud masses providing the illusion that one is actually flying over them.

3.3.3.2 System. AOIPS/2 resides on a VAX 11/780 host with four MicroVAX II satellites and associated peripherals. The imaging and graphics tasks are performed by dedicated combinations of MicroVAX and International Image System (IIS) Model 75 image terminals with hardware features like zoom, pan, histogram computation, etc. Some of the graphics and image processing software (scaling, noise removal, image enhancement, perspective projection, etc.) is resident on the IIS75; the rest was developed at NASA/GSFC. The IIS75 has 12 frames of image memory (512 × 512 × 8 bits) and two frames of overlay graphics memory. It is equipped with a track ball and a 3 × 5 button board; programs are accessed via a menu tree or by abbreviated commands.

The meteorological data is received from a wide variety of sources (National Weather Service surface and upper-air data, and geostationary satellites). As the data arrives, it is formatted and placed in rotating (FIFO) files. The user can then control the animation parameters to display sequences of frames. One of the noteworthy features in AOIPS/2 is the ability to create true stereo images from two satellites or synthetic stereo pairs. The latter are obtained with a method which uses a visible image containing high resolution information on texture and shadows and an infrared image which contains cloud-top height information. Recently, an automated stereo analysis algorithm has been developed to obtain 3-D contours on the Massive Parallel Processor (MPP) [Hasl88].

3.3.3.3 Example. Figure 7 shows a typical frame from one of the animations of the perspectively rendered visible/infrared satellite imagery combinations described in Section 3.3.3.1 above. The view is of Hurricane Diana as it was centered off the North Carolina coast on September 11, 1984. The satellite images were acquired from a NOAA TIROS-N operational weather satellite which provided 1-kilometer resolution images.

3.3.4 NOAA — PROFS

3.3.4.1 Background. NOAA's forward-looking PROFS effort yielded the PROFS workstation system in the early 1980s and it has been a leader in developing interactive graphics applications. Since the PROFS mission is ultimately to enhance weather forecasting operations of the National Weather Service, PROFS has expended a considerable effort experimenting with and developing a high-quality human-interface to computer graphics workstations. Special field evaluation exercises are enacted at least once each year when a collection of operational weather forecasters are gathered at the PROFS facility and placed in a highly realistic but simulated operational forecasting setting. After several weeks of using the PROFS prototype equipment, the participants are debriefed regarding their reactions and recommendations for the facilities. This drives the improvements that are incorporated into the following year's version of the PROFS prototype.

PROFS graphics applications span the full range of meteorological data, including conventional point observations, satellite imagery, and radar imagery through a network of DEC VAX and PDP computers. Animation is used extensively and detailed, colored, graphical screen menus are used to control the workstation.

3.3.4.2 System. The main objective of PROFS graphics has been to provide the operational weather forecaster an interactive environment for viewing large volumes of measured meteorological data. The emphasis has been on the speed of response and "user-friendliness" rather than on realism of depiction [MacD85]. The latest version of the system is the DAR^{3}E workstation [Denver AWIPS-90 (Advanced Weather Interactive Processing System for the 1990's) Risk Reduction and Requirements Evaluation] which features a mouse-driven menu nesting interface. This interface allows the user to change color tables, to change the color and texture of graphics primitives, to control the loading of specific frames or sequences of frames, and to request the coordinates and numerical value at selected points. A separate custom-built input device with dedicated buttons is also used for faster interactive control.

The resolution is 1024 × 1024 for single-image graphics, and 512 × 512/256 × 256 for animation sequences of up to eight/thirty-two frames (RAMTEK 9400 color display system). The software package supports primarily 2-D graphics with the ability to view any combination of up to 7 related variables simultaneously. This is accomplished by a technique called "family graphics," in which each variable is loaded on a separate bitplane in binary mode and then displayed by loading the proper color table.

3.3.4.3 Example. A recent PROFS effort has focused on using novel display techniques applied to ground-based weather data to enhance the human understanding of atmospheric data fields. A. E. MacDonald and Philip McDonald use 3-D polygon shading graphics (a modified version of NCAR's PolyPaint) to display the spatiotemporal distribution of a parameter (e.g. pressure) through shading (to show its value), equi-pressure contour lines, and pseudo-color (to show its deviation from the mean). An example of this work is shown in Figure 8, one frame from an animation of 10 days of hourly observations. The objective is to enhance the meteorologist's perception of the pressure's geographical variation. Current plans are to extend this by displaying three different parameters simultaneously, e.g. pressure by shaded surfaces, temperature through color, and water vapor through contour lines.

4. Expectations for the Future

4.1 Meteorology

The future holds exciting prospects for computer graphics applications in meteorology. We briefly explore these prospects from the three categories of interest: *research* systems, Government forecasting *operational* support systems, and prospects for the *end-users* of weather information.

We expect that *research* systems will continue to pave the way in applying novel computer graphics techniques to meteorology. NCAR is now in a transition period with its NCAR Graphics package, as it is in the process of incorporating interactive, solid modeling, and color capabilities into its supported software package. A key driver in this effort is a newly established project to address the needs of meteorology data visualization at NCAR. The upgraded version is expected to be complete in 1989. Another major recent NCAR project is UNIDATA [Fulk87], a national program to help universities access, analyze, and display a wide range of atmospheric data. UNIDATA is developing graphics software and specifies standards for target workstation and networking hardware. The University of Wisconsin has two principal directions for the future. One is the interactive 4-D McIDAS workstation [Hibb88] with plans to improve interactive performance, pixel depth, and frame sizes. The other is the low cost, personal computer-based PC-McIDAS workstation which is being used as one type of UNIDATA workstation, giving universities and others access to data broadcast by the University of Wisconsin [Ide88]. NASA's National Space Science Data Center (NSSDC) is developing an interactive discipline-independent tool box, called the NSSDC Graphics System (NGS), to support the visualization of data on the NSSDC Computer Facility [Trei87]. Another recent revolutionary development from this organization is the Common Data Format (CDF) standard, a data-independent abstraction for multidimensional data structures [Trei86]. The concept is evolving into a standard method for storing space and earth science data for a variety of applications. NOAA's PROFS organization is continuing its effort to adapt state-of-the-art technology for operational forecasting, with a near-term focus on solid-model visualizations of sparse meteorological data. Bob Wilhelmson of the University of Illinois and the National Center for Supercomputer Applications (NCSA) and other scientists at NCSA will be monitoring and probing simulations over very high-speed links from the supercomputer to powerful local workstations, looking at how the simulations are progressing, interactively steering the calculation, and selecting data to be saved and studied at later times.

A number of major Government forecasting *operational* support systems are expected to be implemented from now through the mid 1990s. Among these are: NOAA's Automated Weather Interactive Processing System, the Air Force's Automated Weather Distribution System, the Navy's Tactical Environmental Support System, the FAA's Central Weather Service Unit, and the Federal Emergency Management Agency's Integrated Emergency Management Information System. All of these systems will greatly improve the interactive graphics facilities available to support the operations of the Government weather forecasters.

Enhanced computer graphics applications will also directly affect the *end-user* of weather information, the general public, primarily in two areas: television weather broadcasting and in videotex services. The weather information vendors will continue to play a lead role in developing creative new ways to improve the communication of weather forecasts to the general public on television weather segments. We expect to see an increased use of 3-D image rendering and animation. Aviation weather applications are driving the incorporation of more and more weather graphics data into videotex services to provide users with on-demand access to near-real-time radar and satellite data. We expect to see greater use of color graphics and imagery in this arena.

4.2 Computer Graphics

A recent study [Hama83] has shown that the time required by a computer to solve a benchmark problem (set of partial differential equations) has been decreasing geometrically by an annual factor of 2.15 over the past 35 years, due to a combination of hardware and algorithmic improvements; the contributions of the two components (hardware and software) are almost equal. We can safely extrapolate that similar decreases in computational time will also be occurring for graphics for the next several years due to improvements in both graphics hardware and algorithms.

On the hardware front, the recent trend is to employ dedicated high-performance graphics engines and/or powerful multiprocessor parallel-architecture computers. Significant gains have been accomplished by these technologies and there is still ground to break. Although these machines are expensive for the average forecast office, past experience, as cited earlier, indicates that hardware prices will drop sharply from year to year.

On the software front, there is a tendency to incorporate physical laws of motion in graphics algorithms (such as assigning mass and momentum to objects) for achieving higher levels of realism [Pane87] [Fren88]. Indeed, the meteorology arena can contribute realism to the graphics arena through physical meteorological models and measured weather data which can be used for realistically portraying atmospheric phenomena such as clouds, lightning, and haze. Finally, we expect great improvements in the interactive capabilities of today's graphics packages for meteorologists. These range from the use of sophisticated window techniques to the inclusion of expert system front ends, which will enable forecasters to optimize their efficiency in manipulating and visualizing the vast amounts of data at their disposal.

Acknowledgements

We thank William L. Hibbard, A. F. Hasler, Joseph Wakefield, Robert Lackman, Thomas Stephenson, Barbara McGeehan, Philip McDonald, and Joseph B. Klemp for additional insight regarding their systems beyond what is published and for photographs of their work. We appreciate receiving photographs of computer-rendered images from G. Y. Gardner, Eric Hoffert and Don Mitchell. We also are grateful for the critique of our manuscript provided by the reviewers.

References

The references provided herein have been culled, because of space limitations, from a much larger bibliography. The full bibliography is available from the authors.

[Bell31] Bell Telephone Laboratories, Weather Maps Transmitted by Teletypewriter System, *Bell Laboratories Record*, 3-4, September 1931.

[Blin82] Blinn, J. F., Light Reflection Functions for Simulation of Cloud and Dusty Surfaces, *Computer Graphics*, Vol. 16, No. 3, 21-29, 1982.

[Burt81] Burt, P., and Sperling, G., Time, Distance and Feature Trade-offs in Visual Apparent Motion, *Psychol. Review*, Vol. 88, 171-195, 1981.

[DesJ80] DesJardins, M., and Hasler, A. F., Stereographic Displays of Atmospheric Model Data, *Computer Graphics*, Vol. 14, No. 3, 134-139, 1980.

[Four82] Fournier, A., Fussell, D., and Carpenter, L., Computer Rendering of Stochastic Models, *Comm. of the ACM*, Vol. 25, No. 6, 371-384, 1982.

[Fren88] Frenkel, K. A., The Art and Science of Visualizing Data, *Comm. of the ACM*, Vol. 31, No. 2, 111-121, 1988.

[Fulk87] Fulker, D., Director's Report, *UNIDATA Newsletter*, 2, 2-3, Fall 1987.

[Gard84] Gardner, G. Y., Simulation of Natural Scenes Using Textured Quadric Surfaces, *Computer Graphics*, Vol. 18, No. 3, 11-20, 1984

[Gard85] Gardner, G. Y., Visual Simulation of Clouds, *Computer Graphics*, Vol. 19, No. 3, 297-303, 1985.

[Gelb87] Gelberg, L. M., and Stephenson, T. P., Supercomputing and Graphics in the Earth and Planetary Sciences, IEEE *Computer Graphics and Applications*, 26-33, July 1987.

[Grtj84] Grotjahn, R., and Chervin, R. M., Animated Graphics in Meteorological Research and Presentations, *Bulletin of the American Meteorological Society*, 65, 11, 1201-1208, November 1984.

[Hama83] Hamann, D. R., Doing Physics with Computers, *Physics Today*, May 1983.

[Hasl81] Hasler, A. F., DesJardins, M., and Negri, A. J., Artificial Stereo Presentation of Meteorological Data Fields, *Bulletin of the American Meteorological Society*, 66, 970-973, 1981.

[Hasl83] Hasler, A. F., Advances in Systems for Interactive Processing and Display of Meteorological Data, Preprints, *Conference on Aerospace and Aeronautical Meteorology*, Boston, American Meteorological Society, 60-62, June 1983.

[Hasl85] Hasler, A. F., Pierce, H., Morris, K. R., and Dodge, J., Meteorological Data Fields 'In Perspective', *Bulletin of the American Meteorological Society*, 66, 795-801, 1985.

[Hasl88] Hasler, A. F., Strong, J., Morris, R., and Pierce, H., Automatic Analysis of Stereoscopic Image Pairs from GOES Satellites, *Proceedings Third Conference on Satellite Meteorology and Oceanography*, Anaheim, CA, 1988.

[Hibb85] Hibbard, W. L., Krauss, R., and Young, J. T., 3-D Weather Displays Using McIDAS, Preprints, *ICIIPSMOH*, Los Angeles, American Meteorological Society, 153-156, 1985.

[Hibb86a] Hibbard, W. L., Computer-Generated Imagery for 4-D Meteorological Data, *Bulletin of the American Meteorological Society*, 67, 1362-1369, November 1986.

[Hibb86b] Hibbard, W. L., 4-D Display of Meteorological Data, *Proceedings of the 1986 Workshop on Interactive 3D Graphics*, Chapel Hill, N.C., 23-36, 1986.

[Hibb88] Hibbard, W. L., A Next Generation McIDAS Workstation, Reprints, Fourth Int'l Conf. on Interactive Info. and Processing Systems for Meteorology, Oceanography and Hydrology (*ICIIPSMOH*), Anaheim, CA, American Meteorological Society, 56-61, 1988.

[Hoch78] Hochberg, J. E., *Perception* 2nd ed. Prentice-Hall, Englewood Cliffs, NJ, 1978.

[Huss86] Hussey, K. J., Hall, J. R., and Mortensen, R. A., Image Processing Methods in Two and Three Dimensions used to Animate Remotely Sensed Data, *Proceedings of IGARSS Symposium*, Zürich, 771-776, 1986.

[Ide88] Ide, J. R., The UNIDATA PC-McIDAS Workstation: a Technical Discussion, Preprints, *ICIIPSMOH*, Anaheim, CA, American Meteorological Society, 332-335, 1988.

[Jule60] Julesz, B., Binocular Depth Perception of Computer-Generated Patterns, *Bell System Tech. J.*, 1125-1162, 1960.

[Kaji84] Kajiya, J. T., and VonHerzen, B. P., Ray Tracing Volume Densities, *Computer Graphics*, Vol. 18, No. 3, 165-174, 1984.

[Klem85] Klemp, J. B., and Rotunno, R., Taking a Good Look at Data, *NCAR Annual Report for 1984*, Report NCAR/AR-84, 46-49, 1985.

[MacD85] MacDonald, A. E. Design Considerations of Operational Meteorological Systems: A Perspective Based upon the PROFS Experience, *ICIIPSMOH*, Los Angeles, American Meteorological Society, 16-23, 1985.

[Mand68] Mandelbrot, B. B., and VanNess, J. W., Fractal Brownian Motions, Fractional Noises and Applications, *SIAM Review*, Vol. 10, No. 4, 422-437, 1968.

[Max86a] Max, N. L., Atmospheric Illumination and Shadows, *Computer Graphics*, Vol. 20, No. 4, 117-124, 1986.

[Max86b] Max, N. L., Light Diffusion through Clouds and Haze, *Computer Vision, Graphics and Image Processing*, Vol. 33, 280-292, 1986.

[Mill86] Miller, G. S. P., The Definition and Rendering of Terrain Maps, *Computer Graphics*, Vol. 20, No. 4, 39-48, 1986.

[Nish87] Nishita, T., Miyawaki, Y., and Nakamae, E., A Shading Model for Atmospheric Scattering Considering Luminous Intensity Distribution of Light Sources, *Computer Graphics*, Vol. 21, No. 4, 303-310, 1987.

[Pane87] Panel on the Physical Simulation and Visual Representation of Natural Phenomena, *SIGGRAPH '87*, Vol. 21, No. 4, 335-336, 1987.

[Papa87] Papathomas, T. V., Schiavone, J. A., and Julesz, B., Stereo Animation for Very Large Data Bases: Case Study — Meteorology, *IEEE Computer Graphics and Applications*, 7, 18-27, 1987.

[Perl85] Perlin, K., An Image Synthesizer, *Computer Graphics*, Vol. 19, No. 3, 287-296, 1985.

[Peti85] Petit, N. J. and Lyons, W. A., Low-cost Stand-alone Receiving and Video Facsimile Display Systems for GOES-TAP and WEFAX/APT, *ICIIPSMOH*, Los Angeles, American Meteorological Society, 295-299, 1985.

[Pich73] Pichel, W., Bristor, C. L., and Brower, R., Artificial Stereo: A Technique for Combining Multichannel Satellite Image Data, *Bulletin of the American Meteorological Society*, 54, 688-691, 1973.

[Potm83] Potmesil, M. and Chakravarty, I., Modeling Motion Blur in Computer Generated Images, *ACM SIGGRAPH '83 Proceedings*, Vol. 17, No. 3, 389-399, 1983.

[Rama78] Ramachandran, V. S., and Gregory, R. L., Does Colour Provide an Input to Human Motion Perception? *Nature*, Vol. 275, 55-56, 1978.

[Reev83] Reeves, W. T., Particle Systems — A Technique for Modeling a Class of Fuzzy Objects, *ACM Trans. on Graphics*, Vol. 2, No. 2, 91-108, 1983.

[Reev85] Reeves, W. T., and Blau, R., Approximate and Probabilistic Algorithms for Shading and Rendering Structured Particle Systems, *Computer Graphics* 19, 3, 313-322, 1985.

[Rush87] Rushmeier, H. E., and Torrance, K. E., The Zonal Method for Calculating Light Intensities in the Presence of a Participating Medium, *Computer Graphics*, Vol. 21, No. 4, 293-302, 1987.

[Schi86] Schiavone, J. A., Papathomas, T. V., Julesz, B., Kreitzberg, C. W., and Perkey, D. J., Anaglyphic Stereo Animation of Meteorological Fields, Preprints, *Second ICIIPSMOH*, Boston, American Meteorological Society, 64-71, 1986.

[Smit75] Smith, E. A., The McIDAS System, *IEEE Transactions on Geoscience Electronics*, GE-13, 123-134, 1975.

[Trei86] Treinish, L. A., and Gough, M. L., A Software Package for the Data-Independent Management of Multi-Dimensional Data, Submitted to EOS, *Transactions of the American Geophysical Union*, December 1986.

[Trei87] Treinish, L. A., Gough, M. L., and Wildenhain, W. D., Animated Computer Graphics Models of Space and Earth Sciences Data Generated via the Massively Parallel Processor, NASA Frontiers of Massively Parallel Scientific Computation, *Report* NASA/N87-26531, 217-222, July 1987.

[Upso87] Upson, C., Large Scale Computer Animation in the Computational Sciences, Course No. 28 Notes for Computer Graphics and Animation in the Physical Sciences, *ACM SIGGRAPH 1987*, 64-65, 1987.

[Vond86] Vonder Haar, T., Meade, A., Brubaker, T., and Craig, R., Four-Dimensional Digital Imaging for Meteorological Applications, Preprints, *ICIIPSMOH*, Miami, American Meteorological Society, 1986.

[Voss83] Voss, R., Fractal Forgery, Course No. 10 Notes for State-of-the-Art in Image Synthesis, *ACM SIGGRAPH 1983*.

[Wrig73] Wright, T. J., Utility Plotting Programs at NCAR, *Atmospheric Technology*, 51-57, September 1973.

[Yaeg86] Yaeger, L., and Upson, C., Combining Physical and Visual Simulation — Creation of the Planet Jupiter for the Film '2010', *Computer Graphics*, Vol. 20, No. 4, 85-93, 1986.

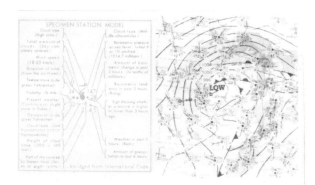

Figure 1. Simple graphic symbols used in the past to plot frontal boundaries, station model symbols to list conventional weather observations for a particular location on a weather map, and contour plots to depict 2-D data fields.

Figure 3. The clouds in this image were generated by the techniques in [Perl85]. The X29 aircraft database was provided courtesy of Evans and Sutherland Computer Corp.

Figure 2. Cloud scenery from [Gard85].

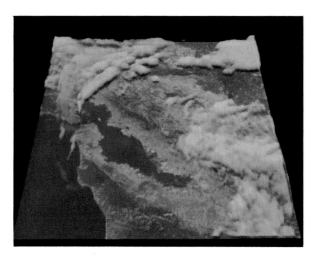

Figure 4. "Clouds over San Francisco" from [Gelb87].

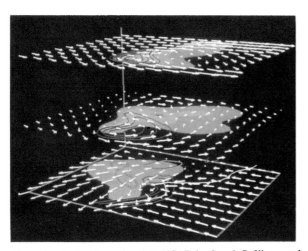

Figure 5. A graphic produced at NCAR by Joseph B. Klemp and Richard Rotunno to visualize the results of their numerical cloud model.

Figure 7. Perspective view of Hurricane Diana produced by A. F. Hasler as it was centered off the North Carolina coast on September 11, 1984.

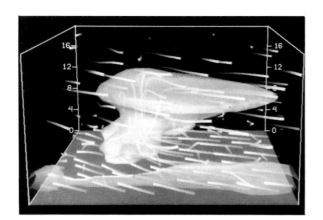

Figure 6. Image produced by William L. Hibbard and David Santek and derived from Robert Schlesinger's thunderstorm numerical model.

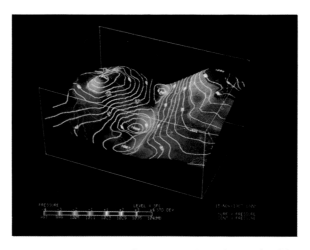

Figure 8. Image from a surface pressure observations produced by Alexander E. MacDonald and Philip McDonald.

A HAND BIOMECHANICS WORKSTATION

David E. Thompson[1], William L. Buford, Jr.[2], Loyd M. Myers[2],
David J. Giurintano[2] and John A. Brewer III[1]
1. Louisiana State University, 2. GWL National Hansen's Disease Center

Abstract

Interactive graphics for hand surgery was used to apply mathematical modeling and describe the kinematics of the hand and its resultant effect on hand function. Dynamic high resolution displays and three-dimensional images were tailored for use with a specific patients' hand and a new and powerful design and analysis tool produced. Methods were developed to portray kinematic information such as muscle excursion and effective moment arm and extended to yield dynamic information such as torque and work. This prototype workstation has been developed in concert with leading orthopedic surgeons and therapists.

CR Categories and Subject Descriptors: I.3.0 (Computer Graphics): General; J.6 (Computer Aided Engineering)- Computer Aided Design (CAD); J.3 (Life and Medical Sciences) - Biology; Health.

General Terms: Computer Aided Design, Computer Graphics, Orthopedic Surgery, Hand Surgery, Hand Therapy, CT and MR Imaging.

1 Introduction

The ascension of computers for modeling in science and engineering is certainly a well acknowledged and accepted trend. What has not been made widely known, however, is the limited application of this same technology to medicine. While an engineer uses computers daily through Computer Aided Design (CAD) to assist him in his endeavor, there are no such tools for the private medical practitioner. At best, a surgeon's secretary uses a word processor or his accountant uses a spreadsheet or accounting package to assist him in the business aspect of his practice. There are *no* interactive computer modeling tools in use today to assist medical specialists such as orthopedic surgeons or physical therapists. This situation is the result of the fact that no conclusive evidence for the value of such modeling in the treatment of patients exists.

Several years ago, Louisiana State University and the Rehabilitation Research Branch at the National Hansen's Disease Center joined efforts to initiate a basic research program on the biomechanics of the human hand. In this work, it became obvious that computers could do many things to assist us in this research. What we also discovered, however, was that the computer could be used as a bridge between mathematics and the clinical world of the orthopedic surgeon. Through interactive graphics, the surgeon could 'see' mathematical phenomena and thereby learn from the knowledge base which the mathematics represented. What made this so valuable was that the surgeon could gain

©1988   ACM-0-89791-275-6/88/008/0335 $00.75

from mathematical models and graphics without becoming an expert in their use. However, as the mathematics became better developed, it was determined that powerful workstations were a prerequisite if the simulations were to remain robust and interactive. Thus, we began to envision a workstation which would be of direct use in the practice of orthopedic surgery, in research and in education.

In the following sections, the initial demonstration prototype for this workstation will be discussed along with suggestions for future enhancements.

Background

In this work, we have designed a workstation environment which involves orthopedic surgery, physical therapy, mathematic modeling, interactive graphics, and kinematics.

1.1 Biomechanics of the Hand

The hand is a marvelous mechanical structure comprised of bones, ligaments which serve to loosely connect structures, muscles which act as tension motors, tendons which serve as cables to connect muscles to bone, and a covering of protective soft tissue and skin. Muscles produce torque and/or movement at joints only through tension, and for every muscle there are one or more muscles which serve to oppose it through counter-torque and/or opposing motion.

The hand and the action of the flexor tendons have been extensively investigated and the literature on the hand has a long heritage. In 1850, Fick [11] initially developed experimental procedures for determining the moment arms of the joints of the hand. Fick was a leader in studying the mechanics of muscles [12]. However, a hundred years lapsed before any other investigators extended his studies. Most studies were principally concerned with anatomy or were anecdotal in nature. In 1961, Landsmeer [18] proposed three models of a tendon crossing a joint, thereby demonstrating that there are important differences in the action of tendons at various joints.

Brand [4] explained how a transfer of a tendon from a lesser functional location could be used to replace a deficiency in the hand's ability to perform the most elementary tasks. Brand proposed that the effects of muscle forces imposed on joints should be balanced. He stated the importance of knowing the proper axes of motion of joints and the necessity of observing the excursions of tendons required to produce joint motion and torque. Transfer operations must use muscles which meet force and excursion requirements or the range of motion of the joint will be reduced, not just at the joint to which the transfer was made, but for all of the joints the transfer crosses.

Flatt [14] and Fischer [13] measured cadaver specimens to ascertain the relationship to forces and torques for the fingers and what factors were important for surgical replacement of joints altered by rheumatoid arthritis.

In Brand [6] and Brand, et al. [5], a muscle model was used to convert cadaver measurements into a table of relative tension and excursion potentials for each muscle of the forearm and hand. Brand discussed the general effects of edema, friction, and scarring on the ability of tendons to effect joint motion or produce torque. Data on the mechanical leverage of tendons, termed their moment arms, was presented along with joint ranges of motion and tendon excursions for most muscles in the hand.

The human hand presents the mathematical modeler with a formidable task: representing the behavior of 44 separate muscle-tendon units, 27 major bones, and at least 18 joint articulations resulting in 27 or more degrees of freedom. The modeler must also encode the behavior of the tissues surrounding the muscles and bones and the ligamentous structures which modify their action. A great deal is known about hands, but little is known about how the mechanisms of the hand work together to achieve their function.

Recently, mathematical models have been developed to describe the internal forces of hands (An et al. [2,3]). Such models are only appropriate for the static hand and have no general solution since most joints have more than a sufficient number of muscles to control the joint. This arrangement presents a mathematical closure problem, and forces the modeler to make additional assumptions about the distribution of forces, torques, or energy expenditure between the muscles. To solve this problem, various optimization methods have been employed and the results, while extremely valuable, are limited in their scope. Most of the methods currently employed in reconstructive surgery of the hand are, however, subjectively based with diverse results and are not based on quantifiable analytical rationale. Surgical procedures on joints and muscle-tendon systems are performed daily without regard for fundamental biomechanical principles.

Much of the work in our lab is directed towards understanding the mechanics of the hand. Results of this research [24,1,6,26], include measurements of required muscle excursions, and determinations of effective muscle-tendon moment arms throughout each joint's angular range of motion. The moment arms for the muscles which cross the carpometacarpal (CMC) joint of the thumb (refer to Figure 11) form the basis for a model of CMC joint kinematics [24,21]. When defined in mathematical terms or even when using cleverly defined graphical plots [26], the analytical results for a simulated tendon transfer go unused in the environment which has the greatest need: the orthopedic clinic. Through the use of a realistic interative graphics description of the musculo-skeletal system, the results of a proposed operation can be appreciated by a technically naive clinician.

Ou [21] developed a single joint model to predict the excursions of all eight tendons which serve as motors for the CMC joint of the thumb. For the model, the tendon's path was assumed to be a straight line from the pulley point to the attachment point. Although quite simple, Ou's model showed good agreement with the experimental data for all eight muscles of a rigid thumb.

Buford [7,9] extended Ou's work by developing a detailed interactive computer graphics simulation of the math model and adding a menu-driven program allowing clinical data to be entered and a tendon transfer operation to be simulated and observed. Buford defined the bones of the thumb by digitizing X-rays of a cadaver specimen used by Ou. The simulation was displayed on an Evans and Sutherland PS330 color graphics system connected to a VAX host computer. A graphics control program allows the user to interactively rotate, flex-extend, or abduct-adduct the thumb at the CMC joint. The metacarpal and distal interphalangeal joints are similarly user-controlled and were modeled as simple flex-extend joints. With real time interaction, one can observe the tendon paths, the moment arms of the tendons at the CMC joint, display the results, and see the resultant excursions of proposed transfer operations.

Three dimensional control coordinates of the CMC joint model determined by Buford et al. [7,8] for the eight muscles of the thumb are used as parameters representing muscle tendon lines of action in this graphical simulation. Giurintano [15] further improved this work by describing the paths of the flexor tendons as combinations of elementary building blocks to represent tendons in sheaths, tendons or muscles which bowstring across joints, or tendons which behave according to Landsmeer's [18] model and traverse the joint space in a circular path. Tension fractions can be used to provide an estimate of the relative moment producing potential of each muscle.

1.2 The Man-Computer Interface

Ideally, the interaction between man and computer is at an intuitive level sufficient to allow non-computer professionals to use advanced computer analysis tools. The need for real user-friendliness has never been so acute as in this application. The intended eventual user of this workstation will be a surgeon or therapist with limited or no computer knowledge or experience who wishes to use the system daily. The time pressures of a real clinical situation cannot be overemphasized and the system must therefore offer services not otherwise attainable and it must be fast and user-friendly. In our laboratory, surgeons and therapists have used the workstation and have commented that they know how they want the simulation to behave, but can not express themselves using simple menus and keyboard commands.

Modern man-computer interactions are shaped more by the inadequacies of the operating system or workstation tools than by what is natural and direct. Surgeons and therapists should not have to be expert typists or fluent in FORTRAN, command languages, or database details. The use of the computer should be obvious, natural, and direct; man should interact on his terms and in his style, not forced to cryptic commands and methods based on what is readily accomplished in assembly language. Our work on man-computer interaction is therefore directed at understanding the use of speech, vision, and gesture and devising new workstation tools to accomplish natural interaction[25].

1.3 Imaging

The field of medical imaging has expanded enormously. Ordinary radiographic (X-ray) imaging is a relatively mature field. Simple X-rays, however, do not provide the information necessary to define three dimensional structures. When computerized tomographic (CT) scans were introduced, the resulting improvement in visualizing three dimensional structures was so great that every major medical center in the world now has a CT scanner. Unfortunately, while the CT scanner proved of enormous benefit in resolving the details of bone structures due to the large density gradients involved, soft tissue information was limited. The development of magnetic resonance imaging (MRI) devices, however, allows a dramatic improvement in the details of soft tissues but poor resolution in bone since the current technology is principally based on hydrogen protons which are notably absent in bone structures.

These developments in imaging have influenced the development of a workstation presented here. Indeed, without the ability to define the three dimensional database for every patient's hand, the concept would have little practical application. Although the initial scientific studies reported in the literature regarding CT and MR imaging were involved in clarifying and improving the visualization of each image slice, there is now an added emphasis on visualization of complete three dimensional structures derived from many serial sections. One of the earliest of these was reported by Vannier et al. [29,30] who discussed the use of the computer in planning facial reconstructive surgery.

Earlier works which used some form of biomechanics modeling or 3-D visualization of tissue structures were reported by Williams and Seireg [27], Dev [10], Hemmy et al. [16], and Herman and Liu [17]. Murphy et al. [20] and Rhodes et al. [22] describe the use of CT imaging, reconstruction algorithms, and CAD techniques to design custom prostheses. White [32] and Vogel [31] describe the application of CAD techniques to provide radiologists and surgeons detailed views and models to assist in radiographic therapy and prosthetic implants. Systems combining advanced interactive three dimensional visualization techniques tailored to specific patients with a fully articulated kinematic model have not been described previously. This has added impetus to our research into the tools and knowledge required to construct the first workstation for orthopedic biomechanics that encompasses the simulation of both the kinematics and dynamics of the human hand.

The most recent work in our laboratory involves a special 3-D graphics editor for segmenting image data containing multiple bones which appear fused following edge detection. Myers et al. [19] use an interactive technique to split bone profiles at joint spaces. Scherrer and Hillberry [23] used mathematical descriptions to accurately represent articular surfaces but assumed that the surface data existed and was not merged with the adjacent bone surface.

2 Methods and Materials

2.1 Image Data

The algorithms we have developed use data taken from a cadaver hand specimen mounted in wax on a positioning fixture. This was attached to a Siemens Somatom DR3 CT scanner. For this work, 172 non-overlapping slices were taken ($KV = 125, Mas = 780$) at one millimeter increments. The specimen was rotated $90°$ and 111 slices at one millimeter spacing were taken to improve joint reconstruction operations. The planar scans were reconstructed as 512x512 voxel images with a mathematically pure convolution kernel to insure the integrity of the data in subsequent enhancement operations. All image data was transferred to magnetic tape for porting to the computing and display systems.

2.2 The Computing and Display Environment

A Digital Equipment Corporation VAX 11/750 was used to store the raw and converted scan data and generate the 2-D edge data and the composite 3-D database. The graphics display system was an Evans and Sutherland PS 390 high performance raster color graphics unit which handles display transformations, data structure interactions, and interactive device I/O in real time. The full hardware environment is depicted in Figure 1.

Software was developed along three major lines:

1. Scan data analysis programs were developed in FORTRAN on the VAX system and a database was written to disk in a format equivalent to a PS 390 vector list.

2. A display data structure language was used to define the hierarchical display data structure. The bottom nodes of this structure are the vector lists for the data derived from the image scans. Named elements of the structure define transformation nodes which are required to position the elements relative to each other and to dynamically alter their positions through rotations about their axes of motion.

3. Input devices are logically connected to the display transformations at the named nodes using a function network. This code allows the user to interact with the image in real time.

The elements of the software are depicted in Figure 2.

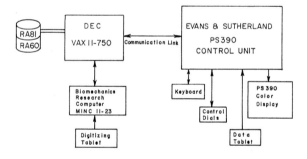

Figure 1: The computing and display systems provide a high speed, multiprocessor, multitasking environment for real time interactive graphic simulation of a kinematic model of the hand.

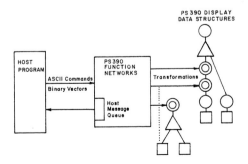

Figure 2: The interrelationships of the three types of software.

2.3 Hand Image Generation

A program to generate a viewable hand structure from multiple serial CT or MR scans has been developed by our group. Although others have developed similar techniques, our goal has been to identify the soft tissues and bones and to segment the bones into individual datasets with as little human intervention as possible. If the workstation is to be used by paramedical personnel, this segmentation must be accomplished as quickly as possible. These algorithms permit a database for each individual patient that is tied to a kinematic model permitting joint angulation. While all current 3-D imaging techniques result in a single large data structure which moves as a single entity, our method derives independent data structures for each object of interest in the hand. This is a major advance and an essential ingredient in coupling the display to an articulated kinematic model.

This procedure requires four steps: (1) A set of serial CT or MR scans is obtained with a scan density determined by the application; (2) The entire bone structure is identified as an entity; (3) This structure is segmented into whatever detail is necessary; and (4) Joint axes are aligned and defined. The last three steps are discussed in further detail in the following sections.

2.3.1 3-D Reconstruction

Edge points are determined by a comparison of the pixel intensity data with a bone threshold value. This is typically 176 CT units [17,30]. The resultant edge points are then closed with a generalized curve-tracing algorithm (Figure 3). Based on the zoom factor, reconstruction center, table position and the slice orientation, the pixel position data for each 2-D slice is converted into 3-D coordinates centered about the physical CT scan aperture center at table position zero. By utilizing such an "absolute" coordinate system, we are able to load and generate images from multiple scans taken at varying zoom factors, reconstruction centers, and orientations, combining them into a single image without using intermediate transformations. This technique establishes a gross orientation, but precise alignment of sagittal and transverse scans is accomplished interactively with the aid of a movable depth clipping plane to correctly align the images. We have found it necessary to use scans taken at various orientations to generate the requisite joint detail. The vectors resulting from the conversion of the scan data are stored in their edited, transformed states upon completion of the edit session to ensure that their precise alignment is retained.

2.3.2 Segmentation

The vectors representing bone outlines (Figure 4, 5) from the transverse and sagittal sets of orthogonal sections were combined into a single 3-D structure and sent to the PS 390 for display, segmentation, and transformation. Segmentation is accomplished by the use of an interactive 3-D graphics editor (Figure 6, 7) which provides the user with the following real-time operations:

o Full rotation, translation, scaling, front and back surface clipping, and manipulation of the relative positions of sagittal and transverse scans to allow for the correction of error in the positioning of the specimen at the time of the scan.

o When in the hand icon block (mid left of display), the graphics tablet allows the user to select icons which represent bone data files into which subsequently picked individual curve vector lists will be stored or removed.

o When in the menu block (lower left of display), the cursor is used to select editing operations which include:

   - storage of the next selected vector list to the current bone file

   - removal of the last selected vector list from the current bone file

   - interactive splitting of a single vector list into two sub-lists

   - restoration of previously split vector list

o When the cursor is within the 3-D viewing window, it is used to specify the individual curve vector to which the current menu selection operation will apply.

Color on the PS 390 is used to great advantage in the editor software. As shown in Figure 6, the currently active bone data file icon is highlighted in red in the menu window. A change of color of the displayed curves denotes they have been picked and appended to the active data file. Red is used within a dialogue box to send error messages to the user when an abnormal condition has occurred.

In curves where the division between bones is ambiguous, the original CT scan is searched for a path of minimum intensity between two user-specified points (Figure 8). The algorithm searches a progressively widening neighborhood composed of the average intensities of the eight adjacent rays of an expanding radius until a minimum is found. The search is restricted to a user definable angle about the line segment connecting the initial points. The search angle, maximum radius of search, and search type may be interactively altered by the user in order to obtain the best possible surface for a given structure. In the case of multiple minima about a certain point, the algorithm minimizes the gradient of the growing curve. Curves generated in this fashion become part of the data structure and can be edited recursively.

2.3.3 Identifying Joint Axes

Following the completion of the segmentation process for each bone, the sagittal and transverse vector lists are combined into a single 3-D structure. The user then interactively defines a position and orientation for the bone and its joint axes of motion which are incorporated into the kinematic hand model.

2.4 Biomechanics Modeling on the Workstation

As an example of the manner in which additional biomechanical models are integrated into the system, a special multi-joint model of the flexor tendons [15] will be discussed.

Our kinematic model of the flexor tendons does not incorporate force analysis, and elastic, viscous, and inertial effects are ignored. The model has been designed, however, so that these features may be added to the simulation. This model has been used because of its realism and its accurate prediction of tendon excursion. The model can describe the paths of the Flexor Pollicis Longus (FPL), the Flexor Digitorum Profundus (FDP), and the Flexor Digitorum Superficialis (FDS) tendons.

It is assumed that the axes of rotations of the joints of the fingers are fixed with respect to the proximal bone segments. In this work, these positions were determined through cadaver dissection and verified by insertion of these data into the display simulation. The CMC joint of the thumb and metacarpophalangeal (MCP) joints of the finger were assumed to be three degree of freedom joints. The proximal interphalangeal (PIP) and distal interphalangeal (DIP) joints of the thumb and fingers were modeled as one degree of freedom joints.

This model uses elemental building blocks to construct the paths of the flexor tendons. These blocks are connected by control points tied to the data structure in a manner that permits them to move with the appropriate bones as the fingers articulate. Homogeneous matrix transformations are used to transform the control points from a reference position to any new position of a finger in space.

The various tendon elements are shown diagramatically in Figure 9. Here tendon model element A is used to simulate a tendon traveling in a straight line. The tendon could be traveling through a tendon sheath, bowstringing across a joint, or exiting from a sheath and inserting onto a bone. Element B is a simulation of a tendon traveling in a circular path as it crosses a joint. Landsmeer's [18] third model is the basis of this simulation. Element C is a tendon dividing and then reconnecting to create a loop. The division and reconnection of the FDS is the basis for this building block. Tendon model element D is used to model a tendon segment dividing and inserting into a bone with dual attachment points. This building block models the most distal path of the FDS.

The FPL crosses the web space of the thumb from the wrist in a straight line, travels through a sheath and inserts into the distal bone. To represent this path, one combines elements A and B in the sequence A-B-A-A from proximal to distal. Figure 10 shows the construction of the FPL model from the building blocks.

In a similar manner, the path of the FDP is also constructed by combining elements A and B. The only difference in the two paths is

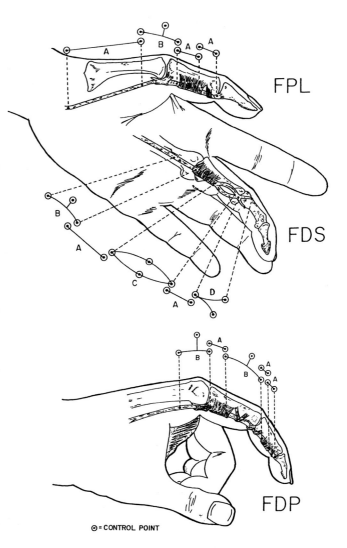

Figure 9: A diagram of the basic tendon building blocks used in the flexor tendon models.

the use of Landsmeer's third model at the MCP joint of the finger as opposed to the tendon bowstringing across the CMC joint of the thumb. This results in the FDP model sequence B-A-B-A-A (reference tendons shown in purple in Figure 10).

The path of the FDS may be anatomically described as following Landsmeer's third model at the metacarpal joint, traveling through a tendon sheath, dividing, reconnecting, and then dividing again before attaching to the middle phalanx. The path of the FDS is represented by the combination of elements B-A-C-A-D (reference tendons shown in gold in Figure 10).

In the workstation, the PS 390 is continually updating the values of the viewing transformations and the functional rotations of the joints of the hand. On demand, these values are passed to the VAX and used to compute the positions of the control points and a set of splines used to represent each tendon. These are returned to the PS 390 for immediate display. The major limitation of the model is the speed of computation in the VAX.

In this manner, any biomechanical model which can be related to the display data structure and its transformations can be added to the simulation. This extensibility is one of the features essential for the continued growth of the workstation and its repertoire of models and functions.

2.5 An Interactive Medical Application

The use of the workstation in a clinical situation is demonstrated through a simulated tendon transfer operation. Additional information about the programming and use of the simulation is presented in greater detail in Buford [7].

The current workstation prototype includes a screen for testing tendon transfer operations to restore function to a hand that has a loss of function of the intrinsic muscles. These are muscles that are contained within the hand as contrasted with the extrinsics which are located in the forearm and transmit their action across the wrist through long tendons. The demonstration includes the users choice of accepted sites for rerouting an extrinsic muscle to replace an intrinsic deficit in the thumb. The actual site for inserting the transfer onto the thumb is left up to the user. Several aids are available to assist in the use of the workstation and, for the transfer task, to inform the user of the viability of the operation. These include:

The Symbolic Muscles Display is an area in the upper right quadrant of the graphics screen where a bar graph of the length of each thumb muscle is displayed. The display (Figure 11) includes markers which depict the resting length of the muscles and are drawn scaled to the fiber lengths of the individual muscles [5]. As the finger is moved by the user, the lengths of the muscles are recalculated and displayed.

A structure has been included in the display to assist the viewer in orienting the view in three dimensions relative to cardinal viewing directions. This is a pylon marked with the directions *dorsal, volar, radial,* and *ulnar.*

The analysis of the balance and functionality of a joint can best be assessed if one is able to visualize the torque or moment potential at each joint. A set of moment arm vectors is included at the base of the joint under study which can be studied by the user to determine if the transfer he has chosen leads to a functionally acceptable joint.

An animation sequencer (Figure 12) is available to provide a preprogrammed set of joint motions. This permits the user to observe the torque or moment balance for a standardized motion sequence. A FORTRAN program on the VAX computes the moment arm vectors for each muscle during this motion. At each increment of motion, the transformed tendon coordinates are acquired from the moment arm display control network. The host program calculates the new vectors and refreshes each moment arm vector in the moment arm display through the control networks.

The menu display provides an area in the lower right quadrant of the screen for selection using the data tablet and the picktext display presents picked coordinates during tendon transfer simulation.

A major impetus for the creation of this simulation is the natural, graphics-based connection it provides between the worlds of mathematical modeling and clinical practice. The hand simulation uses the technique of menu selection via a tablet, and the natural coupling of joint angles to rotating control dials. The large number of interactive features included in the simulation are based on the concept that the use of such a system should be as natural as possible.

Kinematic computations for the simulation are performed by the transformation monitor and the pulley to insertion distance networks. The transformation monitor provides a running calculation of the three dimensional coordinates of tendon insertion points. The network calculates the revised positions of the eight thumb tendon insertion points following all Euclidean transformations. It receives as inputs the real values representing the rotations applied to the joints, and vectors representing the translations applied to the bones of the thumb. The original tendon insertion points are those defined with respect to the lowest level 3-D coordinate space of the thumb data structure (points on the surface of each bone).

Figure 12: A multiple exposure photograph showing the standard thumb positions which are sequenced through to display a moment arm summary.

3 Results and Conclusions

The workstation described has been designed to allow the interaction of a medical professional with an anatomically accurate set of hand bones for each specific patient. The interaction is controlled through the use of a kinematic model with extensibility into the dynamic regime. This will prove invaluable in the future development of computer aided design algorithms for surgical planning, analysis of the biomechanics of the hand, and the planning of physical therapy specifically for each patient.

In addition to the direct research application of the workstation to surgical planning and analysis and to hand model development, the workstation offers potential for improved visualization of other anatomical data. The sequence of motion shown in Figure 13 is indicative of the detail, clarity, and realism of the model and the associated data structure. The increased perceptual cues provided by viewing a 3-D structure in motion cannot be duplicated with a series of still 3-D images produced at multiple viewing angles. The ability of the operator to interactively control this real time motion further facilitates the accurate perception of the object. We therefore consider interactive, real-time motion a minimum requirement in such a workstation.

The combination of mathematical modeling and graphics simulation with the sophisticated imaging techniques now available to the medical community represents a logical next step in the use of radiologic imaging in three dimensions.

The development of a prototype biomechanics workstation is now nearing completion. The initial goals have been met and new ones formulated. Affiliations with national and international caliber surgeons are also now in place to allow continued development of the workstation to make it a clinically viable tool. With the mathematics and the system already developed, additional enhancements to the models and the user interface remain our highest priorities. The kinematic models, the data structure, and the biomechanics models were designed to be extensible, thus providing the framework and system for accomplishing this goal.

The power of small interactive graphics workstations has also reached a critical point where the development of a truly natural and interactive clinical tool is possible. One industry analyst [28] has predicted that a desktop graphics workstation having 23MIPS, 3MFLOPS of processing power, 50Mbytes of RAM, and 200Mbytes of secondary storage would become available for approximately $3,000 in the year 2000. A higher performance system having 300MIPS, 45MFLOPS of processing potential is projected to retail for approximately $12,000. This is the level of processing power and cost which we project as being prerequisite to the adoption of this technology into the clinical world of the medical professional.

The techniques developed and reported here are based on excessive radiation exposures necessary to obtain the detailed CT scans we have used. The expected improvements in imaging technology will, however, allow the immediate application of our methods to clinical use. In this project we have demonstrated not only the technical feasibility of implementing a biomechanics workstation, but also the real necessity for applying the computer as a clinical, research, and educational tool. When combined with the continued development of the hardware and software for workstations and new user friendly environments, the future for this technology is indeed bright and promising.

4 Acknowledgement

The funding for this research was provided by the U.S. Public Health Service, Department of Health and Human Services under research contract 240-83-0060. Additional computing support was provided by the Computer Graphics Research and Applications Laboratory, Department of Mechanical Engineering, Louisiana State University through a joint research program with Digital Equipment Corporation. Evans and Sutherland has provided a PS 390 display system for use in this project.

The images for this research were provided by Digital Diagnostics, Inc. of Baton Rouge, LA (Dr. Charles Grieson, Director). They provided both support and scan time for this project.

References

[1] Agee, John M., Brand, Paul W., Thompson, David E. The Moment Arms of the Carpometacarpal Joint of the Thumb: Their Laboratory Determination and Clinical Application. **Proc. of the 37th Annual Mtg., Am. Soc. for Surgery of the Hand.** *14*, [New Orleans, LA, Jan 1982].

[2] An, K.N., Chao, E.Y., Cooney III, W.P., Linscheid, R.L. Normative Model of Human Hand for Biomechanical Analysis. *J. Biomechanics, 12*,10 [1979], 775-788.

[3] An, K.N., Ueba, Y., Chao, E.Y., Cooney III, W.P., and Linscheid, R.L. Tendon Excursion and Moment Arm of Index Finger Muscles. *J. Biomechanics 16*,6 [1983], 419-425.

[4] Brand, Paul W. Biomechanics of Tendon Transfer. Symposium on Tendon Transfer in the Upper Extremity. *Orthopedic Clinics of North America, 5*,2 [April 1974], 205-230.

[5] Brand, Paul W., Beach, R.B., Thompson, D.E. Relative Tension and Potential Excursion of Muscles in the Forearm and Hand. *J. Hand Surgery, 6*, 3 [May 1981], 209-219.

[6] Brand, Paul W. **Clinical Mechanics of the Hand.** CV Mosby Pub., [St. Louis, 1985].

[7] Buford, Jr., William L. An Interactive Three Dimensional Simulation of the Kinematics of the Human Thumb, Ph.D. Dissertation, Dept of Engineering Science, Louisiana State University, 1984, also University Microfilms International, [Ann Arbor, MI, 1985] 85-15 133.

[8] Buford, William, Myers, L. and Thompson, D. E. A Computer Graphics System for Musculoskeletal Modeling. **Proc. 8th Annual EMBS Conference,** *1*, [Fort Worth, TX 1986], 607-610.

[9] Buford, William L. and Thompson, D. E. A System for 3D Interactive Simulation of Hand Biomechanics. *IEEE Trans. Biomedical Engr., BME 34*,6 [June, 1987] 434-453.

[10] Dev, Parvoti. A Simulator for the Analysis of Wrist Position Control. **Proceedings of the 1982 American Control Conference,** [Arlington, VA., June 14-16, 1982], 1199-1204.

[11] Fick, R. Statische Berachtung der Muskulature des Oberschenkels. *Z Rationelle Med, 9,* [1850], 94-106.

[12] Fick, R. **Handbuch der Anatomie und Mechanik der Gelenke unter Berücksichtigung der Bewegenden Muskein.** 1904-1911, *3,* Specielle Gelenk und Muskelmechanik, Gustav Fischer, [Jena, 1911].

[13] Fischer, C. W. A Treatise on the Topographical Anatomy of the Long Finger and a Biomechanical Investigation of its Interjoint Movement. Ph.D. thesis, Engineering Mechanics, Univ. of Iowa, Univ. Microfilms, Inc. [Ann Arbor, MI 1969].

[14] Flatt, Adrian E., Fischer, G.W. Biomechanical Factors in the Replacement of Rheumatoid Joints. *Ann. Rheum. Dist., 28,* [1969].

[15] Giurintano, David J. and Thompson, D.E. A Kinematic Model for the Flexor Tendons of the Hand. **Proc. IEEE/EMBS,** Paper 40.330.4, [November, 1987].

[16] Hemmy, David C., D.J. David, G.T. Herman. Three-Dimensional Reconstruction of Cranio-Facial Deformity Using Computed Tomography. *Neurosurgery, 13,* 5 [Nov. 1983], 534-541.

[17] Herman, G.T., Liu, H.K. Three - dimensional display of human organs from computed tomograms. *Computer Graphics and Image Processing, 9* [1979] 1-21.

[18] Landsmeer, J.M.F. Studies in the Anatomy of Articulation. *Acta. Morphol. Neerlando-Scandinavia, 3,* [1961] 287-321.

[19] Myers, Loyd M., W.L. Buford, and D.E. Thompson. A Graphics Editor for 3-D CT-Scan Data for Musculo-Skeletal Modeling. **Proc. Computer Assisted Radiology** [Berlin, July 1987], 477-483.

[20] Murphy, S.B., P.K. Kijewski, S.R. Simon, H.P. Chandler, P.P. Griffin, D.T. Reilly, B.L. Penenberg, and M.M. Landy. Computer-Aided Simulation, Analysis, and Design in Orthopedic Surgery. *Orthopedic Clinics of North America, 17*,4 [October 1986] 638-649.

[21] Ou, C. Austin. The Biomechanics of the Carpometacarpal Joint of the Thumb. Ph.D. Dissertation, Department of Mechanical Engineering, Louisiana State University, [Baton Rouge, LA, Dec. 1979].

[22] Rhodes, Michael L., Kuo, Y.M. and Rothman. S.L.G. Systems Integration for the Manufacturing of Custom Prostheses and Anatomical Models. **Proc. Computer Assisted Radiology,** [Berlin, July 1987], 416-423.

[23] Scherrer, P.K., and Hillberry, B.M. Piecewise Mathematical Representation of Articular Surfaces. *J. of Biomechanics, 12,* [1979], 301-311.

[24] Thompson, David E. Biomechanics of the Hand *Perspectives in Computing, 3,* 3 [Oct. 1981], 12-19.

[25] Thompson, David E., Brewer, J.A. and Scott, S.R. Human-Machine Interaction: The Audio Connection. *Computers in Mechanical Engineering, 1,* 2, [1982], 14-18.

[26] Thompson, David E., Buford, W.L., Brewer, J.A. and Myers, L.M. Simulating Hand Surgery: A Work in Progress. *SOMA, 2,* 2 [June, 1987], 6-12.

[27] Williams, R. and Seireg, A.A. Interactive Computer Modeling of the Musculo-skeletal System. *IEEE Transactions on Biomedical Engineering*, *24*, 3, [May 1977], 213-218.

[28] Rubenstein, Richard. Future Trends in Computer Technology: Computer Systems in the Year 2000. Presentation to the VAXstation University Consortium, [November 1987].

[29] Vannier, Michael W., Marsch, J.L. and Warren, J.O. Three Dimensional Computer Graphics for Cranio-facial Surgical Planning and Evaluation. **Proceedings of SIGGRAPH'83**, [Detroit, Michigan, July 25-29, 1983]. In *Computer Graphics*, *17*,3 (July 1983), 263-273.

[30] Vannier, Michael W., Marsh, J.L., Warren, J.O. Three Dimensional CT Reconstruction Images for Craniofacial Surgical Planning and Evaluation. *Radiology, 150*, 1 [January 1984] 179-184.

[31] Vogel, John C. Automated Machining of Custom Anatomical Models Using a Small-Scale Integrated Facility. Paper MS85-1098, Autofact Conference, Society of Automotive Engineers, [Detroit, Michigan, Nov. 1985], 14.37-50.

[32] White, David N. Multidimensional Surgical Imaging: Changing the Link Between Radiologist and Surgeon. *Administrative Radiology*, [October 1986], 51-54.

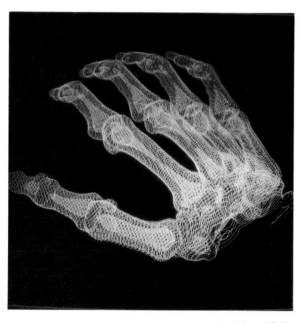

Figure 4: The concatenation of transverse and sagittal plane CT-Scans into a composite image provide the exceptional anatomical detail and clarity essential to the medical community.

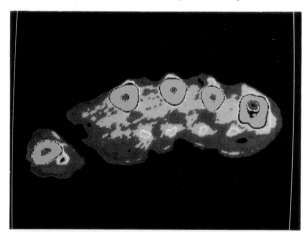

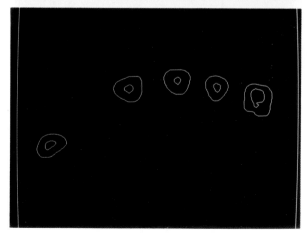

Figure 3: A CT scan (top) and the resulting vector list of bones (bottom) following 2-D curve tracing. The thumb is on the left and the palm is downward.

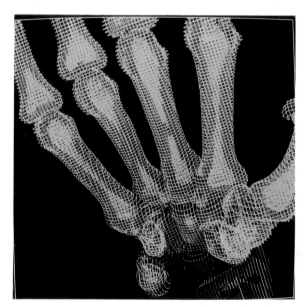

Figure 5: The bones shown here appear to be fused. The surface separating each articular (joint) surface is identified on each CT scan allowing profiles for individual bones to be vacuumed and concatenated into a single data structure to permit relative motion.

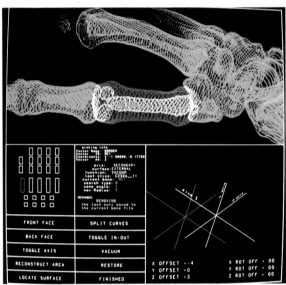

Figure 6: A 3-D graphic editor for segmenting a composite image of multiple scans into individual bones. In the image shown, the contours of the first metacarpal are being identified and stored into the data file associated with the finger icon highlighted at the middle left side of the display.

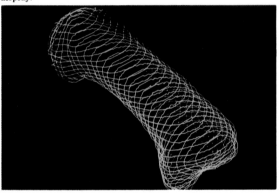

Figure 7: The thumb metacarpal following segmentation. This data structure can be inserted into the kinematic model, thereby personalizing the display for a specific subject.

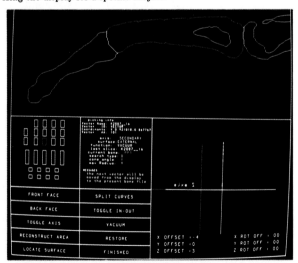

Figure 8: A proximal phalanx showing the process of resolving the interjoint surfaces at the MP (right) and PIP (left) joints.

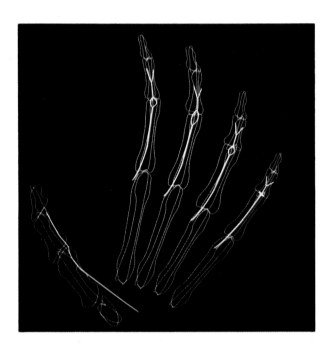

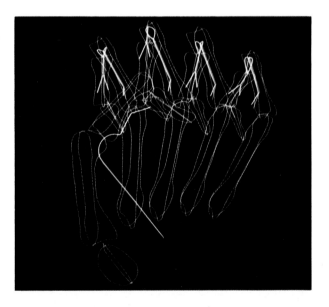

Figure 10: Photographs of the interactive display showing all of the flexor tendons of the hand. The tendons are generated on a continuous basis as the joint angles are changed. The simplified data structure shown here can be replaced by actual hand structures derived from CT scans.

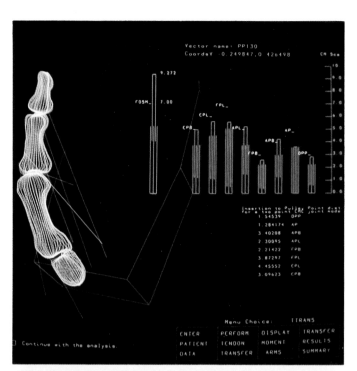

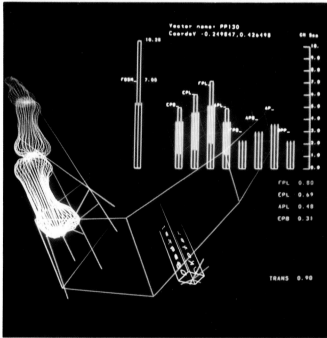

Figure 11: A symbolic display of the muscles at the CMC joint of the hand. Although only the thumb structure is shown here, the lines of action of the muscles and their effective moment arms are continuously displayed. In this display, a simulated tendon transfer is shown in green.

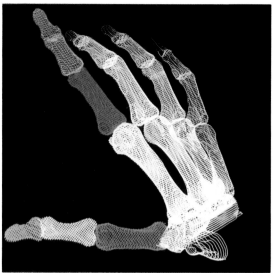

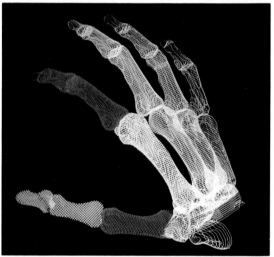

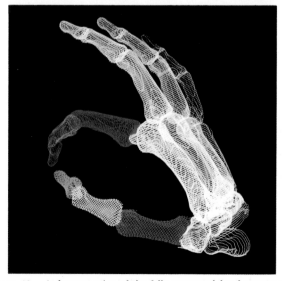

Figure 13: A demonstration of the fully segmented hand structure undergoing dynamic motion from full extension of the thumb and index finger into tip pinch.

Panels

Screen PostScript

Chair:	Charles Geschke (Adobe Systems, Inc.)
Panelists:	Mark Callow (Silicon Graphics)
	James Gosling (Sun Micrsystems, Inc.)
	Leo Hourvitz (NeXT, Inc.)
	Scott McGregor (Digital Equipment Corporation)

One of the most exciting and controversial areas in display graphics today is the use of PostScript for screen display and window systems. PostScript is an interpretive programming language with powerful, resolution-independent graphics capabilities.

PostScript played a key role in bringing about the desktop publishing revolution and is now a de facto standard for laser printers. In the words of Arthur C. Clarke, "PostScript output is the future of words on paper."

Recently several products have brought PostScripts to the screen. These range from basic PostScript output display to an entire window system based on PostScript. Printing and screen display can now be driven from a common format.

This panel brings together pioneers and leading developers of PostScript screen technology from Sun Microsystems, Adobe Systems, Digital Equipment Corporation, Silicon Graphics and NeXT. The panelists contrast their different design approaches, discuss "real-world" applications and speculate on future directions.

User Interface Toolkits; Present and Future

Chair: Brad A. Myers (Carnegie Mellon University)

Panelists: Owen Densmore (Sun Microsystems, Inc.)
                David Goldsmith (Apple Computer, Inc.)
                Andrew Schulert (Apple Computer, Inc.)
                Smokey Wallace (Digital Equipment Corporation)

The days when people implemented user interfaces from scratch are almost over. Implementers now expect to use some kind of users interface toolkit when constructing their systems. These toolkits may contain such things as moused-based menus, buttons and scroll-bars, as well as facilities for handling the keyboard. These low level primitives out of which user interfaces are constructed are often called interaction techniques. This panel discusses what interaction techniques can be found in toolkits today and what will be available in the future. Other topics to be covered included the internal structure of the toolkit (why are they mostly object-oriented?), and tools for helping the programmer use the toolkits (often called user interface management systems).

Parallel Processing for Computer Vision and Display

Chair: Rae A. Earnshaw (University of Leeds, UK)

Panelists: Peter M. Dew (University of Leeds, UK)
                Henry Fuchs (University of North Carolina at Chapel Hill)
                Tosiyasu L. Kunii (University of Tokyo, Japan)
                Micheal J. Wozny (Rensselaer Polytechnic Institute and NSF)

Current developments in parallel processing are of increasing interest to those concerned with the creation, display and analysis of pictures. This panel explores the impact that developments in parallelism are having in the traditional areas of computer graphics and visualization.

State-of-the-art topics include SIMD machines, VLSI and ULSI architectures for vision and image, high performance visualization of 3-D models, parallel algorithms, low-level vision, theoretical aspects, image segmentation, CSP arrays and transputers, real-time 3-D graphics and pattern recognition.

The following are of great significance:
- Computer graphics and computer vision strategies are being brought together via vision and AI techniques.
- Ingenious developments in parallel architectures are producing systems capable of exploitation in novel and revolutionary application areas.
- The sum total of these tools is a range of powerful and innovative systems that will change the face of computer graphics and the traditional man/machine interface.

Four Paths to Computer Animation: Entertainment, Broadcast, Education and Science - Will Their Futures Converge?

Chair:	Nancy St. John (Pacific Data Images)
Panelists:	Robert Abel (Queens Road Film Services, Inc.)
	Jim Blinn (Jet Propulsion Laboratory)
	Carl Rosendahl (Pacific Data Images)
	Craig Upson (Stellar Computer, Inc.)

Scientific graphics gave birth to the computer animation field in the 1960s. In the early 1970s, broadcast and educational computer animation were offshoots from scientific animation, and in the early 1980s, broadcast animation gave birth to entertainment animation. What will the 1990s bring? Already, entertainment companies are providing computers for scientific and educational use while entertainment and broadcast animation are using more and more science. Will these four fields coverge into one field again? Or will there still be science animation as opposed to education animation or entertainment animation rather than broadcast animation.

The panelists attempt to address these questions and present representative work from their respective fields. A lively discussion should ensue with the presentation of different perspectives of where computer animation will and should go.

Computer Graphics and the Changing Methodology for Artists and Designers

Chair:	Alyce Kaprow (The New Studio)
Panelists:	Rob Haimes (Consultant)
	Joel Slayton (San Jose University)
	Paul Souza (WGBH Educational Foundation)

As computer graphics become a standard addition in the artisit's and designer's studio, the notion of the process of visual communication and visual problem solving is changing. Along with this comes a newly defined approach to visual problem solving based on the additional capabilities of the designer/artist. There is also a need to understand the distinct differences between the disciplines of art-making and graphic design, which are often considered one and the same by developers of graphic systems. Because the computer is capable of synthesizing many tasks and operations, the lines often drawn between visual art, music, poetry, sound and environmental design will become faint, allowing us to define a new aesthetic. The state of the art, or more accurately, the state of the market, available to artists and designers has a long way to go to make this technology accessible and affordable to all. However, even with all the present limitations and hesitations, it is still a time to become aware of the inevitable changes and to be a direct participant in the development of this technology. The use of such equipment promises to expand our abilities beyond anything that has been previously investigated. It is essential that those artists and designers who embrace this technology help form it into a meaningful and useful toolbox.

What Can We Learn by Benchmarking Graphics Systems?

Chair: Ricki Blau (University of California, Berkeley)

Panelists: Alan Broder (Mitre Corporation)
Mark A. Charette (Electronic Data Systems Corporation)
Brian Croll (Sun Microsystems, Inc.)
Turner Whitted (Numerical Design, Ltd.)

As a growing user population relies on computer graphics as a tool in everyday work, there is increasing interest in the performance of graphics systems. Recent proposals for standard graphics benchmarks demonstrate this interest. This panel discusses some of these proposals and investigates general issues in measuring the performance of graphics systems. Can a standard set of benchmarks reveal accurate insights to a varied constituency? What are the right and the wrong parameters to measure? How can we obtain the information we want? What comparisons are useful? Panelists consider the structure, contents and interpretation of benchmarks and offer alternative approaches to performance measurement.

The panelists include benchmark designers, system builders and users with wide experience in the performance analysis of software and hardware for graphics. The goal of the panel is to suggest ways to obtain meaningful performance measurements.

The Reality of Computer Graphics in the Motion Picture Industry

Co-Chairs: Richard Hollander (Video Image Associates)
Micheal Wahrman (deGraf/Wahrman, Inc.)

Panelists: Mike Fink (Peak's Island Productions)
Kirk Thatcher (Henson Associates)
Ralph Winter (Paramount Studios)

This panel addresses the state of computer generated imagery in the film industry as it exists today. It is five years since the release of Tron and the use of computer generated effects in the motion picture industry is still quite limited. Many of the people in the field of computer graphics believe that Hollywood is moving inexorably in the direction of computer generated imagery for special effects and animation, but in the indusrty itself there is no such perception. In fact, one occasionally hears computer graphics described as "cold, expensive, over-rated and of no particular interest to the movie-going audience."

This panel presents the attitudes of the Hollywood entertainment creative and decision-making community towards computer graphics, animation and special effects. Questions to be discussed include:
• Who uses computer graphics today?
• Why don't they use more of it?
• Why is the perception that there is no audience demand?
• What can be done to improve the acceptance of this medium in the film industry?

X Window System

Chair:	George Champine (Digital Equipment Corporation)
Panelists:	James Gettys (Digital Equipment Corporation)
	Goerges Grinstein (University of Lowell)
	Bertram Herzog (University of Michigan)
	Robert Scheifler (Massachusetts Institute of Technology)

The X Window System has now been endorsed by every major workstation manufacturer, and is rapidly becoming a de facto industry standard for application interfaces. However, the impact on graphics is far from clear and X is still evolving.

Major issues to be addressed by the panel include: lack of world coordinate output (a la PostScript); relationship to NeWS and MS-Windows; support of images and live video; adequacy of the toolkit; 3-D extensions to X; and role of the X Consortium.

X has generated considerable controversy because it introduces yet another drawing package whose relationship to existing graphics standards is unknown, as is its applicability to graphics applications. This issue is also addessed.

Media Technology

Chair:	Andrew Lippman (MIT Media Laboratory)
Panelists:	Walter Bender (MIT Media Laboratory)
	Marvin Minsky (MIT Media Laboratory)
	David Zeltzer (MIT Media Laboratory)

Media technology is a new research field that is only recently gaining legitimacy and widespread recognition as an intellectual domain. The field can be described as the convergence of the areas of computing, communications and information. Systems that result from research in this field are the synthesis of these into new forms of interaction, learning, creative expression and entertainment. A theme of much work is either the merger of the creative users of media with its developers, or the notion of building direct, intuitive interfaces to information systems, or the more general goal of making computer systems that enhance human creativity. Underlying technologies that form the basis for the field include sound and image processing in human cognitive processing. This panel explores current work in the field.

Hardware Strategies for Scientific Visualization

Chair: Robert Haber (NCSA and University of Illinois at Urbana-Champaign)

Panelists: Jim Clark (Silicon Graphics)
Thomas A. DeFanti (University of Illinois at Chicago)
Lou Doctor (Raster Technologies, Inc.)
Frank Moss (Stellar Computer, Inc.)

This panel explores competing strategies for hardware systems that respond to the needs of scientific visualization in today's world of large-scale numerical simulations. The panelists debate the merits of a variety of system architectures, ranging from systems based on PC's, to workstations, to supercomputers. New technologies for networking and distributed graphics are presented for post-simulation analysis and real-time, interactive monitoring and steering of numerical simulations.

Visualization users and vendors examine how well the computer graphics industry is responding to the needs of the scientific visualization community by asking the following questions:
• Do technologies ported from CAD/CAM and commercial animation adequately serve the needs of scientists?
• Do they deal with the real bottlenecks in the visualization process?
• Is the level of intergration of graphics hardware, software tools and video animation equipment adequate?
• Is the visualization market large enough to support the rate of product development that scientists are demanding?

Software Directions for Scientific Visualization

Chair: Gordon Bancroft (NASA/Ames Research Center)

Panelists: Roy Hall (Wavefront Technologies)
Mike Kaplan (Ardent Computer)
Al Lopez (Apollo Computer, Inc.)
Alvy Ray Smith (Pixar)

This panel focuses on the visualization needs of scientists and engineers. How are they being addressed by current trends in software? What tools are available now? How are they being used? What still needs to be provided?

Key topics to be discussed are: existing and emerging standards for visualization: support for network environments and distributed applications: the role of commercial animation packages; new techniques such as volume visualization; and how one deal with the huge quantities of data involved in scientific visualizations.

Other issues to be addressed are:
• Where will new developments come from?
• What will be required of end-users?
• What can be expected from software providers?
• How can research activities in computer graphics be translated into tools for scientists?
• How can the scientific community share and coordinate ongoing developments?

Designing Effective Pictures: Is Photographic Realism the Only Answer?

Co-Chairs:	Steven Feiner (Columbia University)
	Jock Mackinlay (Xerox PARC)
Panelists:	Jim Blinn (Jet Propulsion Laboratory)
	Donald P. Greenberg (Cornell University)
	Margaret A. Hagen (Boston University)

With each passing year, advacnes in software and hardware have allowed us to generate increasingly more realistic images. Although the quest for photographic realism offers us a compeling touchstone by which to measure our progress, it emphasizes only one of many possible pictorial styles. This panel addresses important questions about the creation of effective computer graphic images such as:
- When is realism needed?
- How can a stylized image more appropriate?
- How can different modeling and rendering styles be combined in the same image?
- How does the cost of attaining realism affect the mixture of realistic and stylized aspects?
- What are the principles for designing effective images?
- Can appropriate designs be selected automatically to fit the particular user and situation?

Extending Graphics Standards to Meet Industry Requirements

Chair:	Albert J. Bunshaft (IBM Corporation)
Panelists:	Salim Abi-Ezzi (Rensselaer Polytechnic Institute)
	Gregory D. Laib (IBM Corporation)
	Richard Puk (Puk Consulting Serivces)

Users are forcing the coexistence of graphics systems with ease of use and performance as their requirments. At the same time, product developers are concerned about upward compatibility as well as exploitation of technology. There are still a number of technical questions remaining as to which path is the best to follow. This panel covers possible extensions to GKS, PHIGS and X Windows by discussing the efforts to understand and improve these standards. The panel members represent implementers, researchers and independent consultants who have participated in the development of these systems.
- The most recent status of efforts in these areas are discussed including the GKS Revision Cycle, PHIGS+, X-PEX and other related activities. This panel updates the technical community on these efforts and exposes them to opposing viewpoints. Theaudience is encouraged to express their opinions. The panel members focus on the following subjects: extending existing graphics standards; PHIGS+ - extensions to PHIGS for curves, surfaces, light source modeling and shading; and extending X Windows Systems for high-performance 3-D graphics.

Index

Credits for Cover and Title Images

Front cover: A Museum of Constructivist Art

Copyright © 1988 by Cornell University, Program of
  Computer Graphics

Modelers/Programmers: Shenchang Eric Chen,
  Stuart I. Feldman, Julie M. O'Brien

Insights: The image of a constructivist museum was
rendered using the radiosity method which accounts for
area light sources, color bleeding, soft shading, shadow
generation and produces a view-independent solution.
Computation times were accelerated using the
progressive refinement approach described in this
issue. The algorithm provides a useful solution almost
immediately and progresses gracefully and
continuously to the complete radiosity image shown.

The model includes more than 20,000 elements and
200 discrete area light sources. The complexity of the
environment as well as the indirect diffuse skylighting
illumination from above would have made it
impractical to render with traditional radiosity
methods and impossible to simulate using standard ray
tracing methods.

Production notes: The experimental modeling and
rendering software was developed by a number of
students and staff at the Program of Computer
Graphics and is part of a long term continuing research
effort sponsored by the National Science Foundation
under a grant entitled "Interactive Computer Graphics
Input and Display Techniques." The computations
were performed on Hewlett Packard 825 SRX
workstations and displayed at a resolution of
1280×1024. The museum model was inspired by the
Menil Collection Museum designed by Renzo Piano and
Richard Fitzgerald. Digital color separations were
prepared by Xerox PARC from the frame buffer data
and calibrated to the chromaticities of the monitors
used in the lab at Cornell.

Reference: *A Progressive Refinement Approach to Fast
Radiosity Image Generation*, p 75.

Title page: A Lilac Twig

Copyright © 1988 by University of Regina, Department
  of Computer Science

Artist: Przemyslaw Prusinkiewicz, James Hanan and
  F. David Fracchia

Insights: The essential characteristics of the
development of lilac inflorescences were inferred from
observations of real inflorescences and expressed using
the formalism of Lindenmayer systems. The input L-
system consists of 27 productions and has only 1691
characters in total. The mathematical model captures
the topology and geometry of the branching structure,
the shapes of leaves, and the positions of individual
leaves and flowers. Each flower consists of five cubic
surfaces.

Production notes: The image was generated on a
Silicon Graphics IRIS 3130 workstation at a resolution
of 2048×1536 pixels. Digital color separations were
prepared by Xerox PARC from the frame buffer data.

Reference: *Developmental Models of Herbaceous
Plants for Computer Imagery Purposes*, p 141.

Colophon

These proceedings are printed in full-color from
camera-ready copy provided on reduction mats by the
authors. Most color images were provided as
photographic prints, although a couple arrived as
transparencies. Front matter and back matter was
prepared and typeset by the production editor at Xerox
PARC. Cover typesetting (front cover, inside front and
back covers, title page, copyright page) was prepared by
Association Press in Chicago. Pages were assembled
into 22 signatures of 16 pages and 1 signature of 4 pages
and printed on a four-color sheet-fed offset press. The
22,000 copies of the proceedings require 37 tons of
coated paper! The cover is printed using a five color
process (cyan, magenta, yellow, black, plus black
overlay) and laminated with film.

Digital color separations were prepared at Xerox
PARC by Maureen C. Stone and Richard J. Beach for
four images: the museum image on the front cover, the
lilac twig on the title page, the steel mill on page 83 and
the weeping willow on the back cover. Funding for this
experiment was provided by SIGGRAPH to explore
preparing commercial-quality color separations from
digital data. The images arrived on magnetic tape in
various formats, including a simple byte stream of
frame buffer data. The color calibrations from Cornell
established the chromaticities of the phosphors and the
white point of the monitor. The production editor
visited Cornell in Ithaca, NY, to see their "normal"
viewing situation in the computer graphics lab (as
expected, it's very dark). Color measurements of the
color separation process and the Dupont Chromalin
color proofing process permitted color transformations
to be computed. The images were rendered using an
experimental Interpress 3.0 implementation running in
Cedar. The color separated data was output to
magnetic tape as 300 dot-per-inch separations using
percentages of cyan, magenta, yellow and black. The
tapes were processed on a Crossfield digital color
system at Kedie/Orent in Sunnyvale, CA, to produce
four film negatives (CMYK) and a Chromalin color
proof. The proceedings' printer used these negatives
directly.

The steel mill image printed here is more faithful to
the monitor image than either of the previous
reproductions in the February, 1988 issues of
Communications of the ACM or *Computer Graphics*.
For instance, the frame buffer data has no blue haze
and the color of the hot steel is yellow, not white.

The front cover image of the museum interior is
reproduced without ever having been photographed!
The image was commissioned by John Dill, the
SIGGRAPH '88 program chair. The composition of the
image and the colors were adjusted by the artists to
ensure that reproduction would be optimum. In
particular, the colors of the carpet and the "red and
blue" chair were made more "natural" to avoid the
extreme fully saturated colors available on a monitor
but not with printing inks.

Credits for Back Cover Images

Top left: Eric the Dynamic Worm
Copyright © 1988 by Alias Research Inc.
Artists: Gavin Miller: rendering and procedural worm modeling; Freddi Gitelman: modeling of the desk, lamp and book; Andrew Pearce: modeling of the floors and walls.
Production notes: The background to this piece was created using the Alias 2 modeling package. The worm was defined procedurally using the Alias Scene Description Language. The dynamic model simulated the elastic properties of the worm including the time-dependent effects of muscle contractions. In the animation, Eric dangles perilously over the edge before falling off. The image was rendered on a Silicon Graphics 4D/70G workstation using the Alias2.3 renderer with the natural phenomona option. A procedural solid texture was used to create the wood on the desk and a cubic environment map was used to make the reflections.
Reference: *The Motion Dynamics of Snakes and Worms*, p 169 .

Top right: Red and White Cars on a Forest Road
Copyright © 1988 by Evans and Sutherland Computer Corporation
Artist: T.C. Brown, Rick Chambers, Chuck Clark, Mike Cosman, Marlin McDaniel, Margo Taylor, Steve Winters, Steve Zimmer
Insights: This image is a visual presentation of real-time dynamics models which have full vehicle response. The details shown in the background and on the cars were achieved largely through the use of photo-derived texture.
Production notes: The image was rendered in real time (20 milliseconds per frame) by an Evans and Sutherland CT6 image generator.
Reference: *Getting Graphics in Gear: Graphics and Dynamics in Driving Simulation*, p 317 .

Middle left: Painting with ConMan
Copyright © 1988 by Silicon Graphics Inc.
Artist: Paul Haeberli
Insights: ConMan is a primitive visual programming language that lets users construct interactive applications by making connections between simple components. This image shows how several components can be connected together to create a paint program. Here a color editor controls the drawing color while the brush shape is provided by a 2-D shape editor. Two additional components, a view editor and a geometry transformer, let us scale or rotate the brush shape. With ConMan it's easy to modify or extend applications by changing the interconnection of the components on the fly.
Production notes: Photographed from the screen of a Silicon Graphics 3130 workstation.
Reference: *ConMan: A Visual Programming Language for Interactive Graphics*, p 103 .

Middle right: Weeping Willow
Copyright © 1988 by AMAP
Artists/Programmer: Philippe de Reffye, Marc Jaeger
Insights: The image is a particular output of a growth simulation program that integrates botanical knowledge of the architecture of trees. The same procedural methods can produce a wide variety of plants. Images of the same tree at different times of its life can be calculated. On the weeping willow image the bending of branches by gravity has been simulated.
Production notes: The image was rendered on a Silicon Graphics Iris 4D workstation at a resolution of 1024×1024 pixels using software developed by AMAP (Atelier de Modelisation et d'Architecture des Plantes). Digital color separations were prepared by Xerox PARC from the frame buffer data.
Reference: *Plant Models Faithful to Botanical Structure and Development*, p 151 .

Lower left: Volume-Rendered Pawl
Copyright © 1988 by Pixar
Artist: Malcolm Blanchard
Insights: The results of a stress analysis on a mechanical part are displayed using volumetric rendering in the top image. This is contrasted with a conventional surface rendering of the same data on the bottom. Notice that in the volumetric version internal stresses can be seen in addition to the surface data.
Production notes: The images were produced on a Pixar Image Computer using Pixar's ChapVolumes package for the volume image and Pixar's ChapReyes package for the surface image. The stress-analysis data was generated by PDA Engineering using their PATRAN P/Stress module.
Reference: *Volume Rendering*, p 65.

Lower right: Skelatal Structure of a Hand
No Copyright
Artist: David E. Thompson, Professor, Louisiana State University; William Bufford Jr., Chief, Rehabilitation Research, National Hansen's Disease Center; Loyd M. Myers, Deputy Chief, Rehabilitation Research, National Hansen's Disease Center; David J. Giurintano, Bioengineering Rehabilitation, National Hansen's Disease Center; John A. Brewer, III, Manager, Geometric Modelling, Mentor Graphics; Charles Grieson, Director, Digital Diagnostics, Inc.
Insights: The hand data shown represents 60,000 surface description vectors derived from 300 computer tomography (CT) images of a human cadaver hand. This data was preprocessed, individual bones defined and axes of motion established to permit the motion of the hand.
Production Notes: The image is a single frame taken from a real-time interactive session on a prototype hand biomechanical workstation. All computations were accomplished on a VAX 11/750 and displayed on an E&S PS 390.
Reference: *A Hand Biomechanics Workstations*, p 335.